Transforming the Rural Nonfarm Economy

**Other Books Published in Cooperation with
the International Food Policy Research Institute**

IFPRI

A World Bank and International Food Policy Research Institute Project

Transforming the Rural Nonfarm Economy

Opportunities and Threats in the Developing World

EDITED BY STEVEN HAGGBLADE, PETER B. R. HAZELL,
AND THOMAS REARDON

Published for the International Food Policy Research Institute

The Johns Hopkins University Press
Baltimore

The Johns Hopkins University Press
2715 North Charles Street
Baltimore, Maryland 21218-4363
www.press.jhu.edu

International Food Policy Research Institute
2033 K Street, NW
Washington, D.C. 20006
(202) 862-5600

The findings, interpretations, and conclusions expressed herein are those of the author(s) and do not necessarily reflect the views of the Executive Directors of The World Bank or the governments they represent.

The World Bank does not guarantee the accuracy of the data included in this work. The boundaries, colors, denominations, and other information shown on any map in this work do not imply any judgment on the part of The World Bank concerning the legal status of any territory or the endorsement or acceptance of such boundaries.

LIBRARY OF CONGRESS CATALOGING-IN-PUBLICATION DATA

Transforming the rural nonfarm economy : opportunities and threats in the developing world / edited by Steven Haggblade, Peter B. R. Hazell, and Thomas Reardon.
   p. cm.
  Includes bibliographical references and index.
  ISBN-13: 978-0-8018-8663-8 (hardcover : alk. paper)
  ISBN-13: 978-0-8018-8664-5 (pbk. : alk. paper)
  ISBN-10: 0-8018-8663-5 (hardcover : alk. paper)
  ISBN-10: 0-8018-8664-3 (pbk. : alk. paper)
  1. Agricultural industries—Developing countries. 2. Agriculture—Economic aspects—Developing countries. 3. Developing countries—Rural conditions. I. Haggblade, Steven.
II. Hazell, P. B. R. III. Reardon, Thomas Anthony.
HD9018.D44T727   2007
338.9009172′4—dc22

                                        2006039552

A catalog record for this book is available from the British Library.

Contents

PART IV Synthesis

Figures

Tables

Boxes

Foreword

The rural nonfarm economy (RNFE) plays an important role in the economic transformation of developing countries. While "nonfarm" describes what this sector is not, it actually is a vibrant, often fast-growing, small-scale service and manufacturing sector that holds much promise for pro-poor rural and agricultural transformation. Though it may start as a relatively minor sector in the early stages of development, the RNFE eventually becomes a key contributor to economic growth. Because of the sector's small scale, its low capital requirements, and its seasonality and amenability to home-based activity, growth in the RNFE has important implications for employment growth and the welfare of women and poor households.

Since the green revolution first sparked rapid rural nonfarm growth across broad swaths of Asia and Latin America, the RNFE has attracted considerable interest and study. IFPRI itself undertook a significant program of research during the 1980s on farm-nonfarm growth linkages—research that contributed to an understanding of how agricultural growth can be used to leverage larger income and employment multipliers within the RNFE. Likewise, the World Bank has commissioned a stream of analytical and synthesis work during the past 25 years on the nonfarm dimensions of rural development.

While agricultural growth still remains a powerful motor of RNFE expansion, trade liberalization and the growing forces of globalization and urbanization are changing the context within which rural firms operate. Today many rural regions can capitalize on new opportunities for outside sources of demand for goods and services. Greater competition from the outside has forced changes in the structure and composition of rural economic activity, and many of these changes have proven inimical to the welfare of the rural poor. Urbanization has also created new opportunities for rural-urban migration, with important flows of remittances back to rural areas. These in turn are contributing to growth in the demand for diverse rural outputs and also to investment in their supply. New actors have also emerged to exert an important influence on rural change, including large private firms operating in more integrated marketing chains and nongovernmental organizations that seek to help the rural poor by promoting nonfarm activity. And the spread of information and communication technology into developing countries' rural areas has been an important driver of change within the RNFE in recent years.

Given this changing rural landscape and the importance of nonfarm earnings for poor households, IFPRI decided to undertake a major review and synthesis of related recent studies in order to explore the policy implications and identify future research priorities. An early step in this process was an IFPRI and World Bank co-sponsored conference in 1998 on the rural nonfarm economy that brought together a distinguished group of scholars. That conference provided the launching pad for the synthesis work undertaken by Haggblade, Hazell, and Reardon, which eventually led to the present book.

Both IFPRI and the World Bank are pleased to have supported this work, which we consider essential to unraveling and understanding the dynamics of poverty-reducing growth in rural regions of the developing world, and for designing effective rural-urban linkages.

Joachim von Braun
Director General, IFPRI

Gershon Feder
Senior Research Manager for
Rural Development, World Bank

Acknowledgments

This volume consolidates what we have learned about the rural nonfarm economy over the past several decades. Given the scale and complexity of the subject, we have incurred a great many debts along the way.

We have benefited enormously over the years from our interaction with literally thousands of nonfarm business owners and employees in enterprises ranging from large multinational buyers and exporters to the smallest household-based one-person firms. They have consistently impressed upon us the complexity, dynamism, scale, and rapidity of structural changes currently under way in the rural nonfarm economy. Much of what we have learned has come from direct interaction with them.

During our first effort to integrate the enormous volume of cross-disciplinary material bearing on the rural nonfarm economy, we convened a distinguished group of scholars at Airlie House in northern Virginia to critique an initial set of papers. Participants at that retreat included Raisuddin Ahmed, Marie Elena Cruz, Martine Dirven, Paul Dorosh, Ruben Echeverria, Eric Hyman, Nurul Islam, Peter Kilby, Peter Lanjouw, Carl Liedholm, Donald Mead, Richard Meyer, Keijiro Otsuka, Michael Painter, Per Pinstrup-Anderson, Fernando Rello, Mitch Renkow, Torben Reopstorff, Sherman Robinson, Terry Roe, Alejandro Schejtman, Kostas Stamoulis, Judith Tendler, Erinc Yeldan, and Antonio Yunez. We have had the good fortune to implicate many of them as co-authors in preparing various chapters of this book. Those who escaped this charge have nonetheless left an invaluable imprint on our thinking, prompting the considerable revisions and restructuring that ensued. We are grateful to all who participated for their constructive input and for helping launch us on this endeavor.

In preparing specific chapters, we have received helpful inputs and material from Marshall Bear, Steven Block, Hugh Evans, Peter Kilby, Blane Lewis, Alexandra Miehlbradt, John Pender, Nick Ritchie, David Satterthwaite, Forhad Shipli, Mona Sur, Judith Tendler, Bill Vorley, Steve Wiggins, and the management of Botswanacraft Exports. Ghada Shields and Honglin Wang have plumbed the depths of a series of libraries in a valiant effort to update empirical citations for a large and rapidly growing body of evidence. Two anonymous referees selected by the IFPRI Publications Review Committee provided detailed and constructive comments on an earlier draft of the structural transformation and strategy chapters, while three additional referees offered thorough reviews of the entire manuscript. We are grateful to all of them for their careful reading and helpful suggestions.

At several junctures, the World Bank has provided key support for our efforts. Together with IFPRI, it helped to finance the Airlie House workshop. At a later stage, it supported efforts to prepare the synthesis chapter. In the course of that work, we received consistently astute and detailed commentary from Jock Anderson, Gershon Feder, Felicity Proctor, and Cornelis Van der Meer as well as from a number of participants at in-house seminars at both IFPRI and the World Bank. Bank staff have likewise authored several key chapters. In recognition of this considerable human and financial support, IFPRI and the World Bank have agreed to jointly sponsor publication of this volume.

Finally we wish to thank Joan Hazell, who has graciously hosted a series of editorial retreats, possibly more numerous than she might wish to remember. We recall, in particular, a memorable snowstorm that stranded us in her able care for three days. On that occasion and many others, her ample provisions and good humor provided essential sustenance, enabling our work to continue productively and uninterrupted.

PART I

Overview

1 Introduction

STEVEN HAGGBLADE, PETER B. R. HAZELL,
AND THOMAS REARDON

*How to best integrate farm &
non-farm
activities?*

The rural nonfarm economy has grown too large to ignore. It accounts for 35 to 50 percent of rural incomes across the developing world (Table 1.1). Though often neglected in policy debates, the rural nonfarm economy (RNFE) can contribute significantly to economic growth, directly because of its size and its responsiveness to growing agricultural, urban, and export markets, and indirectly through provision of financing, processing, and marketing services that stimulate and accelerate agricultural growth. Sitting in overcrowded urban capitals, policymakers view the RNFE as a potential breakwater, valuable for stemming the tide of rural-to-urban migration, curbing urban congestion, and reducing pressure on overstretched urban service delivery systems. Sitting in rural compounds, household heads see nonfarm activities as means of diversifying incomes across the calendar year and reducing seasonal and interannual consumption risks. Amid growing landlessness, poor households increasingly depend on nonfarm earnings for their survival, as do public efforts at poverty reduction.

Beginning in the 1990s, widespread economic liberalization has opened up the RNFE as never before—to new opportunities and to new threats. Liberalization, by reducing direct government involvement in production and marketing, has opened up new market opportunities for the private sector, particularly in agricultural processing, input supply, and trade. Relaxed controls on foreign exchange and foreign investment have unleashed a flood of foreign direct investment into Latin America, Asia, and Africa. As a result, large exporters, agribusiness firms, and supermarket chains increasingly penetrate rural economies of the developing world, altering the scale and structure of rural supply chains as they do. These new investments open up opportunities for some rural suppliers to access new markets. But they expose others to new threats by opening up the RNFE to competition from cheap manufactured imports and by imposing quantity requirements and quality standards that risk excluding undercapitalized rural enterprises on which the rural poor often depend.

This book explores the rapidly changing RNFEs of the developing world. By reviewing available empirical evidence and policy experience, the ensuing chapters aim to increase understanding of how rural nonfarm activity can

3

TABLE 1.1 Nonfarm share of rural income, by continent

Region	Nonfarm share of rural income (percent)
Africa	37
Asia	51
Latin America	47

SOURCE: Table 6.1, studies from the 1990s and 2000s only.

NOTE: Total citations include 23 for Africa, 14 for Asia, and 17 for Latin America.

contribute to overall economic growth in developing countries and how the poor can participate in growing segments of this evolving RNFE.

To launch this review, the present chapter provides an initial overview of the RNFE. It highlights the diversity of nonfarm activities and firm sizes as well as a series of resulting misunderstandings that commonly ensue. A set of key definitions lays a common foundation for the discussions that will follow. The chapter concludes with an overview and explanation of the structure of topics to be addressed in the book.

Overview of the RNFE

Scale

Growing interest in the RNFE arises in large part because of its increasing importance as a source of employment and incomes across the developing world. Primary employment shares, which offer the most widely available indicator of the scale of rural nonfarm activity, suggest that the RNFE accounts for about 30 percent of full-time rural employment in Asia and Latin America, 20 percent in West Asia and North Africa (WANA), and 10 percent in Africa (Table 1.2). Inclusion of rural towns—which frequently depend on the rural hinterlands for both inputs and markets—raises nonfarm employment shares by an additional 10 to 15 percent (Hazell and Haggblade 1993). Because these employment data typically measure only primary occupations, to the exclusion of secondary and seasonal pursuits, they often understate the importance of rural nonfarm activity.

Income data, which include earnings from seasonal and part-time activity, offer a more complete picture of the scale of the RNFE. Available from a wide array of rural household surveys, they suggest that nonfarm income accounts for about 35 percent of rural income in Africa and roughly 50 percent in Asia and Latin America (Table 1.1). Standing roughly 20 percent higher than comparable employment data, these income shares confirm the economic importance of part-time and seasonal nonfarm activities (Figure 1.1), many of these performed by women.

FIGURE 1.1   Seasonality of rural nonfarm employment in Ethiopia, 1993

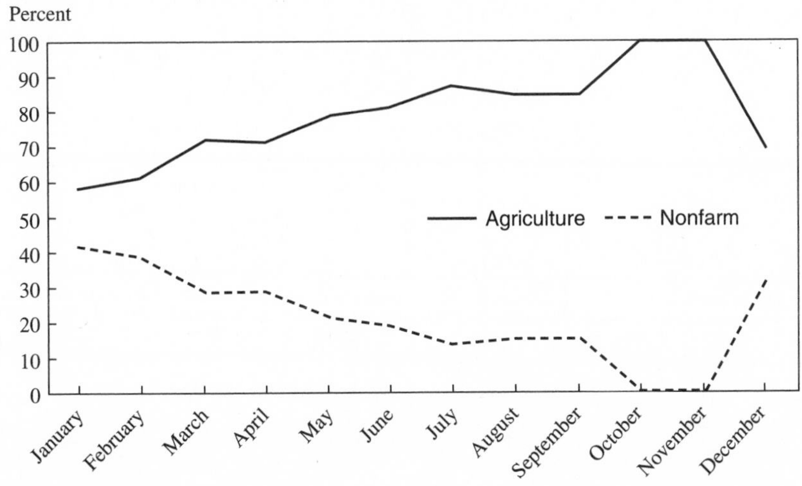

Percent

SOURCE: Habtu (1997).
NOTE: The figure represents the distribution of employment among landless laborers.

Composition

Services and commerce generally account for the bulk of rural nonfarm activity, although shares vary perceptibly among countries and across rural regions. Average employment shares across continents suggest that tertiary activities typically account for between 50 and 75 percent of rural nonfarm activity (Table 1.2). Rural manufacturing, despite the considerable attention it has received, normally accounts for about 20 to 25 percent of total rural nonfarm employment in developing countries.

Below the broad sectoral aggregates, details of specific RNFEs reveal rich differences across countries and even across regions within the same country. Beer brewing raises rural manufacturing shares throughout much of Sub-Saharan Africa. Meanwhile, the production of textiles and straw products, retailing, and health services drive differences between Central El Salvador and other rural regions in the same small country. Significantly greater service sector employment accounts for higher rural nonfarm employment shares in Southeast compared to Northeast Brazil (Table 1.3). These wide variations in the composition of rural nonfarm activity occur for a variety of reasons: because of differences in location, agricultural structure, natural resource endowments, placement of government administrative services, and a rich array of path-dependent historical idiosyncrasies.

can policy be tailored generally?

TABLE 1.2 Composition of rural nonfarm employment, by continent (percent)

	Nonfarm share of rural workforce	Women's share of total RNFL	Share of rural nonfarm employment (RNFL)				
			Manufacturing	Commerce and transport	Personal, financial, and community services	Construction, utilities and mining	Total
Unweighted							
Africa	19	35	21	31	36	12	100
Asia	30	25	22	28	34	15	100
Latin America	30	40	23	22	35	20	100
West Asia and North Africa	24	8	22	24	32	21	100
Weighted by population							
Africa	9	39	19	31	35	15	100
Asia	24	24	27	29	31	14	100
Latin America	31	36	22	23	34	21	100
West Asia and North Africa	21	11	23	22	36	20	100

SOURCES:

Africa—Cameroon: Cameroun (1992), Table 4.41A, pp. 495–497; Ethiopia: Ethiopia (1998), Table 4.15, p. 239; Ivory Coast: United Nations (1996), Table 28, pp. 728–729; Malawi: Malawi (2002), p. 112; Mozambique: United Nations (1986), Table 28, pp. 712–715; Namibia: United Nations (1996), Table 28, pp. 728–729; South Africa: Statistics South Africa (1996), Table 15, pp. 146, 148, 150; Zambia: Zambia (2003), Table 6.15, p. 86.

Asia—Bangladesh: Bangladesh Bureau of Statistics (2003), pp. 181–186; India: United Nations (1996), Table 28, pp. 738–739; Indonesia: Indonesia Bureau of Statistics (1998), Tables 37.1–37.9, pp. 268–276; Iran: Iran (1986), pp. 74–76; Korea: United Nations (1986), Table 28, pp. 728–729; Nepal: United Nations (1986), Table 28, pp. 728–729; Pakistan: Pakistan (2001), Table 2.3, p. 136; Philippines: United Nations (1986), Table 28, pp. 728–729; Sri Lanka: United Nations (1986), Table 28, pp. 728–729; Thailand: Thailand (1996), Table 17, p. 122.

Latin America—Argentina: United Nations (1986), Table 28, pp. 718–719; Bolivia: U.S. Bureau of the Census (2000), Table 095, p. 190; Chile: U.S. Bureau of the Census (2000), Table 095, p. 190; Dominican Republic: U.S. Bureau of the Census (2000), Table 095, p. 190; Ecuador: United Nations (1996), Table 28, pp. 718–719; Guatemala: Guatemala (1981), Table 19, p. 165; Honduras: United Nations (1996), Table 28, pp. 718–719; Uruguay: Uruguay (1989), Table 25, p. 232; Venezuela: Venezuela (1993), Cuadro 58, pp. 393–394.

West Asia and the Near East—Egypt: Egypt (1996), Table 1-25, pp. 38–41; Morocco: Maroc (1995), pp. 64–66; Turkey: Turkey (1995), Table 43, pp. 132–133.

NOTES: Rural nonfarm employment shares are classified according to International Standard Industrial Classification (ISIC) codes: manufacturing (code 2); commerce and transport (codes 6 and 7); personal, financial, and government services (codes 8 and 9); and construction, mining, and utilities (codes 2, 4, and 5). Figures for Africa are based on the following countries (and census years): Cameroon (1987), Ethiopia (1994), Ivory Coast (1986), Malawi (1998), Mozambique (1980), Namibia (1981), South Africa (1996), and Zambia (2000). Figures for Asia are based on the following countries and census years: Bangladesh (2001), India (1991), Indonesia (1995), Iran (1986), Korea (1980), Nepal (1981), Pakistan (1998), Philippines (1981), Sri Lanka (1981), Thailand (1996), and Vietnam (1997). Figures for Latin America are based on the following countries and census years: Argentina (1980), Bolivia (1988), Chile (1984), Dominican Republic (1981), Ecuador (1990), Guatemala (1981), Honduras (1988), Uruguay (1985), and Venezuela (1990). Figures for West Asia and North Africa are based on the following countries and census years: Egypt (1986), Morocco (1994), and Turkey (1990).

TABLE 1.3 Heterogeneity of rural nonfarm activity in Brazil, El Salvador, and Uganda, 1990s (percent)

Primary employment[a]	Rural Brazil, 1996		Rural El Salvador, 1994			Rural Uganda, 1992[a]	
	Northeast	Southeast	West	Central	East	Hoima	Mukono
Mining and natural resources	5.5	1.1	0.0	0.9	0.3	—	—
Manufacturing	3.5	5.6	10.6	13.4	5.6	15.9	13.6
Beverages	0.1	0.2	—	—	—	11.2	3.3
Food processing	1.1	1.3	—	—	—	—	—
Textiles	0.6	0.5	2.0	3.8	1.5	1.2	0.0
Straw	0.6	0.7	2.3	3.1	0.6	2.3	8.6
Wood	0.6	0.5	—	—	—	1.2	0.7
Shoes and leatherware	0.1	0.1	—	—	—	0.0	1.0
Other manufacturing	0.4	2.3	6.3	6.5	3.5	—	—
Construction	2.6	4.0	4.1	6.5	2.8	5.1	5.3
Utilities	0.2	0.5	0.4	0.4	0.0	—	—
Commerce	4.4	4.6	9.3	12.7	9.0	32.1	25.3
Retailing and wholesaling	3.7	3.2	7.1	9.9	7.1	32.1	25.3
Transport	0.7	1.4	2.2	2.8	1.9	—	—

Services	10.8	16.5	9.2	14.6	5.5	7.1	16.8
Restaurant/hotel services	0.8	1.3	0.1	1.3	0.0	2.0	8.8
Finance	0.1	0.2	0.2	0.2	0.2	—	—
Teaching	2.9	2.2	0.8	0.4	0.9	—	—
Health services	—	—	0.5	0.5	0.2	2.3	1.0
Domestic services	—	—	3.0	5.8	2.0	—	—
Personal services	1.0	0.9	—	—	—	—	—
Government services	1.4	1.3	0.5	0.1	0.1	—	—
Other services	4.6	10.6	4.1	6.3	2.1	2.8	7.0
Total nonfarm	27.0	32.3	33.6	48.5	23.2	60.2	61.0
Total agriculture	73.0	67.7	66.4	51.5	76.8	—	—
Total employment[a]	100	100	100	100	100	—	—

SOURCES: Livingstone (1997), Ferreira and Lanjouw (2001), Lanjouw (2001).

NOTES: A dash indicates that data are not available.

[a]Uganda data list percentage of households involved. All other data are percentage of primary employment.

Enterprise Size

Numerically, small-scale rural nonfarm enterprises employing fewer than 5 to 10 workers account for the vast majority of nonfarm establishments. In low-income countries, these small firms likewise account for the majority of non-farm employment (Liedholm and Mead 1999), although this share falls as per capita income levels rise. While purely rural breakdowns are difficult to find, national manufacturing data suggest that, in spite of their small numbers, larger firms typically account for about two-thirds of output and value added in most developing countries (Snodgrass and Biggs 1996). Large firms play particularly important roles in agroprocessing, export, and trading activities. In many situations, large firms occupy strategic positions in local supply chains. Because of this, they often govern prospects for small firm growth (see Chapters 9 and 15).

Equity

Within this highly diverse RNFE, labor productivity varies widely. Alongside highly labor-intensive, often home-based, rural manufacturing activities operate more specialized capital- and skill-using nonfarm activities in commerce, trade, and factory-based manufacturing. Enterprise budgets, such as those from rural Sudan, indicate that labor productivity across nonfarm activities can vary by as much as a factor of 10 or even 20 (Table 1.4).

These disparities, coupled with a paucity of human, financial, and physical assets, often confine low-income households to the low-productivity segments of the RNFE. As a result, the RNFE becomes bifurcated, with richer and more educated households dominating the most lucrative niches, such as formal white-collar employment, while poor households remain relegated to labor-intensive, low-return activities, particularly unskilled wage labor. Income data from rural

TABLE 1.4 Returns to labor in rural nonfarm activities in Darfur, Sudan, 1993

Nonfarm activity	Income per day (Sudanese pounds)	Sector
Tabagmaking	10	Manufacturing
Carpetmaking	21	Manufacturing
Potmaking	23	Manufacturing
Tea selling	60	Commerce
Water peddling	75	Commerce
Food selling	80	Commerce
Shoemaking	150	Manufacturing
Blacksmithing	150	Services
Construction	180	Services

SOURCE: Ibrahim (1997).

TABLE 1.5 Sources of rural income in Sri Lanka by expenditure quintile, 1999–2000 (proportions)

	Source of rural household income, by expenditure quintile				
	Poorest quintile	Second-poorest	Third-poorest	Fourth-poorest	Richest quintile
Agricultural					
Own farm	0.127	0.193	0.225	0.177	0.164
Wage earnings	**0.108**	**0.083**	0.066	0.039	0.019
Other[a]	0.031	0.004	0.034	0.032	0.032
Total agricultural	0.266	0.280	0.325	0.248	0.215
Nonfarm					
Wages	**0.336**	**0.280**	0.206	0.193	0.096
Public salaries	0.108	0.135	0.159	**0.233**	**0.331**
Private salaries	0.136	0.147	0.169	**0.172**	**0.188**
Other	0.008	0.011	0.008	0.009	0.011
Total nonfarm	0.588	0.573	0.542	0.607	0.626
Transfers and remittances	0.146	0.147	0.133	0.145	0.159
Public transfers	0.098	0.076	0.074	0.083	0.114
Private remittances	0.048	0.071	0.059	0.062	0.045
Total income	1.000	1.000	1.000	1.000	1.000

SOURCE: World Bank (2003).

NOTES: Bold type highlights distributional differences in the importance of wage and salary income.
[a]Includes fisheries and estates.

Sri Lanka illustrate this common pattern, with low-income households heavily dependent on wage labor, both farm and nonfarm, while the richest income groups earn a larger share of their income from formal sector salaries (Table 1.5).

Women account for over one-third of the full-time rural nonfarm workforce in most parts of the developing world, with the exception of WANA, where their reported shares fall to around 10 percent (Table 1.2). They also participate extensively in part-time rural nonfarm activity, particularly in home-based manufacturing and services.[1]

Spatial Distribution

Remote locations frequently mandate long and tortuous supply chains linking rural producers with final markets (Figure 1.2). As a result, networks of itinerant

---

1. See, for example, Simmons (1976), Carr (1984), Gabre-Madhin and Reardon (1989), Chen (1996), and Downing and Daniels (1992).

FIGURE 1.2 Cassava marketing and processing channels in Madagascar, 1999

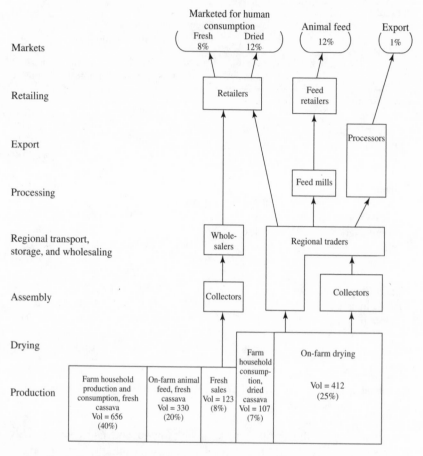

SOURCE: Dostie, Randriamamonjy, and Rabenasolo (1999).
NOTES: Vol, volume in thousands of metric tons; %, percent of total national cassava production.

traders and large-firm intermediaries often form key connective tissue governing the vitality and viability of rural nonfarm supply systems.

Regional clustering and specialization emerge as common features of the RNFE. Silk-weaving factories in Thailand have concentrated in the Northeast, particularly around the town of Pak Ton Chai (World Bank 1983; Haggblade and Ritchie 1992). In Indonesia, producers of rural textiles and of brick and roofing tile exhibit the highest tendency to cluster geographically (Weijland 1999). Some villages in India specialize in production of plastic jewelry (Papola 1987), while others focus on more specialized services, such as snake charming (International Herald Tribune 1989)! Tanning, shoe production, sawmilling, and metal working often congregate in specific locations and in close proximity to one another.[2] These concentrations of rural nonfarm activity emerge for a variety of reasons. Some arise by historical accident, others due to a confluence of unusually favorable natural conditions, some as a result of direct public inoculation.[3]

The composition of nonfarm activity likewise differs significantly among rural towns, urban centers, and rural settings. While home-based cottage industries predominate in rural areas, towns and urban centers witness an increasing share of factory manufacturing, services, and trade (Table 1.6). The composition of services differs as well. Although rural areas house small retail establishments as well as basic farm repair and agricultural input suppliers, service providers such as primary schools, health clinics, barber shops, mills, and transport facilities tend to locate in small towns. Larger settlements attract cinemas, restaurants, wholesale distributors, and higher-level school, health, and communication facilities (Wanmali 1983). Functional economic linkages knit together this hierarchy of settlements with their surrounding rural catchment areas. As a result, rural towns, although formally classified as urban in many national censuses, remain tightly linked to the surrounding rural hinterlands on which they depend for both inputs and markets.

Common Misunderstandings

At the heart of several contentious debates lie two critically important but seemingly innocuous characteristics of the RNFE—its heterogeneity and measurement difficulty. Together, their early recognition will prove instrumental in permitting satisfactory navigation of the highly variegated rural nonfarm terrain.

Heterogeneity

The RNFE includes a highly heterogeneous collection of trading, agro-processing, manufacturing, commercial, and service activities (Tables 1.2 and 1.3). The scale of rural nonfarm activity varies enormously, from part-time self-employment in household-based cottage industries to large-scale agroprocessing and warehousing operations run by large multinational firms. Often highly seasonal, rural nonfarm activity fluctuates with the availability of agricultural raw materials and in rhythm with household labor and financial flows between farm and nonfarm activities (Figure 1.1). Across settings, the composition of nonfarm activity differs considerably as a function of widely variable natural resources, labor supply, location, history, and institutional endowments.

---

2. Freeman and Norcliffe (1985), Kennedy (1999), Schmitz (1999), Burger, Kameo, and Sandee (2001).

3. Schmitz and Nadvi (1999), Ceglie and Dini (2000), Rosenfield (2001a–c), KREI (2005), Sonobe and Otsuka (2006a,b).

TABLE 1.6 Employment shares in Bangladesh, Chile, and Zambia, by activity and size of locality

Country, year	Total labor	Agriculture	Total nonfarm	Manufacturing	Commerce and transport	Personal, financial, and community services	Construction, utilities, and mining
ISIC code		1	2–9	3	6 and 7	8 and 9	2, 4, and 5
Bangladesh, 2000							
Rural	100	58	42	10	17	12	3
Intermediate urban	100	16	84	27	28	23	6
Chittagong and Dhaka	100	8	92	26	29	32	5
Chile, 1984							
Rural	100	65	35	5	9	17	4
Intermediate urban	100	7	93	14	29	41	9
Santiago	100	1	99	20	26	46	7
Zambia, 2000							
Rural	100	90	10	1	2	7	1
Intermediate urban	100	22	78	7	31	30	10
Lusaka	100	0	100	14	22	54	10

SOURCES: Bangladesh Bureau of Statistics (2003), pp. 181–186; Banco Central de Chile (1986), pp. 235–237; Banco Central de Chile (2002), p. 476; Zambia (2003), Table 6.15, p. 86.

NOTE: ISIC, International Standard Industrial Classification.

Measurement Difficulty

Accurate measurement of rural nonfarm activity compounds the difficulty of assembling an accurate portrait of this diverse landscape. The marked seasonality of many rural nonfarm service, manufacturing, and trading activities means that the timing of data collection can easily influence enterprise visibility and measurement. Many itinerant trading and service activities elude enterprise-based survey instruments. Part-time self-employment likewise remains invisible to all but the most detailed household-based inquiries. Because of difficulties in measuring income from seasonal, part-time, small-scale producers who do not normally keep written records, many surveys instead use employment as a proxy for nonfarm activity levels. Differences in definitions of what constitutes a rural area, as well as wide variations in age and gender delineations of workforce participation, complicate comparisons across countries. Social norms governing the economic role of women lead to wild gyrations in officially measured female employment rates, as reported in the standard interviews with male household heads. As a result, employment figures, in particular, offer only a rough indicator of rural nonfarm activity levels.

The combination of extreme heterogeneity together with these practical measurement difficulties leads to several potential sources of confusion. Many studies of rural nonfarm activity focus on rural industry (RI), which includes only manufacturing activity. RI thus comprises a subset of the larger RNFE, which in addition to manufacturing includes commerce and services (Table 1.2). Generalizations based on the subset RI may not prove representative of the broader RNFE. Likewise, rural nonfarm employment (RNFL) often serves as a poor proxy for rural nonfarm income (RNFY), particularly given the low implicit wages in self-employed, highly labor-intensive cottage industries. Summarized in Table 1.7, these and other deceptive dichotomies can lead to serious misunderstandings. Yet their recognition likewise holds the key to unraveling several important apparent contradictions.

Is Nonfarm Growth Good News or Bad?

Depending on the setting and on the measure used, rural nonfarm growth may represent either good news or bad. In stagnant rural economies, measurement of growing RNFL proffers the bad news that landlessness and rising population are pushing households with few assets and opportunities, by default, into low-paying nonfarm activities. In these situations, rural nonfarm self-employment serves as a sponge, absorbing labor force increments into increasingly low-return manual labor. In other settings, including many prosperous rural regions during the Asian green revolution, rapid growth in RNFL and RNFY heralds the good news that broad-based agricultural income gains are propelling in their wake demand-led growth in increasingly high-return nonfarm processing, trading, commercial, and service activities. In general, while growing RNFL may

TABLE 1.7 Deceptive dichotomies related to the rural economy

Dichotomy	Contrasts	Dangers and distinctions
1. RI versus RNFE	Rural industry (RI). Includes manufacturing only. Rural nonfarm economy (RNFE). Includes all sectors: manufacturing, commerce, and services	Many studies focus only on manufacturing. Rural manufactures prove most vulnerable to competition from urban imports. Commerce and services are often the largest and most buoyant sectors of the rural nonfarm economy.
2. RNFL versus RNFY	Rural nonfarm employment (RNFL) Rural nonfarm income (RNFY)	Employment is the most common but most imprecise measure of rural nonfarm activity; seasonality, part-time work, and heterogeneous productivity levels compromise its effectiveness as a measure of welfare. Income growth, unlike employment, signals an unambiguous increase in aggregate welfare.

3. Push versus pull; the sponge versus dynamic growth; bad news versus good news	Economic stagnation "pushes" new labor force entrants into self-employment in increasingly low-return activities.	Buoyant agricultural and rural economies stimulate opportunities for increasingly profitable non-farm activities, "pulling" rural nonfarm activity along in their wake.	Employment growth offers an imprecise measure of welfare because growing RNFL may signal good news or bad. Some measure of returns to labor is required to evaluate the welfare impact of RNFL growth.
4. Off-farm versus nonfarm	"Off-farm" includes all economic activities that take place off the owner's own farm, that is, all activities in ISIC Groups 2–9 plus the household's wage earnings in agriculture.	"Nonfarm" means nonagricultural activities, that is, those with ISIC codes 2–9.	RNFY equals "off-farm income" minus wage earnings in agriculture.

NOTE: ISIC, International Standard Industrial Classification.

represent good news or bad, increasing RNFY and wage rates represent unambiguously good news.

Can the RNFE Serve as an Engine of Growth?

By focusing on rural manufacturing, the segment of the RNFE most vulnerable to competition from outside, some observers have concluded that RI will inevitably decline over time as improved transport opens up rural areas to competition from urban factory-made goods. In the same settings, however, a broader focus on the total RNFE frequently reveals growth in overall RFNY because of offsetting gains in rural services and commerce. Chapters 2 and 4 revisit these issues in detail. For now, readers should simply recognize the differences between the more restrictive RI and the more expansive RNFE, between RNFL and RNFY. Recognition of these distinctions will enable subsequent resolution of several important disagreements and misunderstandings.

Definitions

In an attempt to avoid these common misunderstandings, this book will adopt the definitions summarized in Box 1.1 distinguishing between the RNFE and RI, between RNFL and RNFY, between off-farm and nonfarm activity. Two among these definitions merit special consideration.

RURAL.   Following a long tradition—from Anderson and Leiserson (1978) and Chuta and Liedholm (1979) on down—this book takes a broad view of a rural region as encompassing dispersed rural settlements as well as the functionally linked rural towns where many of the ancillary nonfarm service and commercial activities typically congregate (Figure 1.3). Official definitions of "rural" areas typically refer to settlements below a certain population size, often 5,000 people or fewer. But these cutoffs vary across countries, and some superimpose other attributes such as availability of key infrastructure or administrative services.[4] Given this diversity, it becomes difficult to impose a rigorously uniform definition. Instead, this book adopts a conceptual definition of rural regions as encompassing not only dispersed, primarily agricultural, settlements, but also the regional towns that typically service these predominantly agricultural areas.

NONFARM.   Nonfarm production includes all economic activities other than production of primary agricultural commodities. Nonfarm, or nonagricultural production, thus includes mining, manufacturing, utilities, construction, commerce, transport, financial, and personal services (International Standard Industrial Classification Groups 2–9). Agroprocessing—the transformation of raw agricultural products by milling, packaging, bulking, or transporting—forms

---

4. See De Ferranti et al. (2005) for a good discussion of these definitional differences.

BOX 1.1   Definitions

Rural: Official definitions of "rural areas" include population settlements on farms, in villages and towns below a population threshold that varies across countries. Frequently official cutoffs refer to concentrations of 5,000 people or less. Because of important functional linkages between small towns and surrounding rural farms and settlements, this book adopts a more expansive definition of "rural regions," which include not only rural households but also small settlements and towns closely linked to their surrounding agricultural areas. Where data permit, discussion in this book encompasses nonfarm activity in rural regions of the developing world, including the many nonfarm enterprises operating in small regional towns.

Rural nonfarm economy (RNFE): The "rural nonfarm economy" includes all rural economic activity outside of agriculture. Nonfarm activity may take place at home or in factories or be performed by itinerant traders. It includes small- and large-scale activities of widely varying technological sophistication.

Employment: Including self-employment; wage employment; full-time, part-time, formal, informal, and seasonal employment; and labor used in episodic or intermittent nonfarm production.

Agriculture: Sectoral delineations follow standard national accounting definitions. Agriculture includes the primary production of all unprocessed plant and animal products. It includes crop production, aquaculture, livestock husbandry, woodlot production, hunting, fishing, and forestry—International Standard Industrial Classification (ISIC) Group 1.

Nonfarm production: Nonagricultural, or nonfarm, production includes all other economic activities besides agriculture, including mining and manufacturing as well as utilities, construction, commerce, transport, finance, and personal services (ISIC Groups 2–9).

Rural industry (RI): Including only rural manufacturing (ISIC Group 2), RI constitutes only one component of total rural nonfarm activity, usually about 25 percent of the RNFE.

Off-farm income: Some agriculturally focused studies measure "off-farm" income or employment. By this they usually mean "off the owner's own farm." Consequently, off-farm income includes wage employment in agriculture earned on other people's farms along with nonfarm earnings from the owner's nonfarm enterprises or from nonfarm wage earnings. Rural nonfarm income (RNFY) is thus smaller than total "off-farm income" by the amount of wage earnings in agriculture.

FIGURE 1.3   Alternate definitions of the rural nonfarm economy

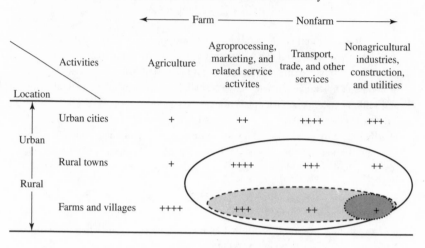

SECTORAL share of economic activity

    ++++ Highest
    +++ Medium
    ++ Low
    + Lowest

Rural nonfarm definitions

    Rural industry
    Rural nonfarm economy, narrow definition
    Rural nonfarm economy, broader definition

SOURCES: Adapted from Anderson and Leiserson (1978) and World Bank (2004).

a key component of the RNFE. In many instances, these nonfarm processing activities take place on the farm, performed by farm household labor. They remain, nonetheless, functionally part of the RNFE.

mills

Organization of This Book

Key Issues

This book addresses a series of complementary issues. Empirically, the ensuing chapters examine the scale, structure, and composition of the RNFE, how these vary across locations, and how they affect the rural poor. Analytically, the book explores structural linkages among rural nonfarm, agricultural, and urban enterprises. It highlights the spatial organization of nonfarm activity as well as key dynamics under way. Finally, discussion turns to a series of key policy issues. In what circumstances is public intervention necessary in the RNFE? How cost-effective have previous intervention strategies proven? What can we learn from prior experience about ways to better help the rural poor participate in rural nonfarm activity and navigate the rapid transition under way? To address these issues, the book structures discussion in four major sections.

Part I: Overview

The remaining chapters in this introductory section build on the brief structural snapshot provided in this chapter. The wide variety of rural nonfarm activity and settings, introduced here, has led to a correspondingly rich disciplinary array of empirical investigations of the RNFE. Chapter 2 chronicles the progress of four major intellectual expeditionary forces that have set out to explore various facets of the RNFE over the past 40 years. Discussion emphasizes how these varied analytical perspectives and tools have contributed, in different ways, to our growing understanding of the many different facets of the RNFE.

Chapter 3 rounds out this introductory section by addressing poverty issues head on, in recognition of the strong equity orientation that has stimulated much of the current policy interest in the RNFE. The frequently small size of rural nonfarm enterprises, their low capital requirements, and their minimal barriers to entry, coupled with increasing concerns about labor absorption in agriculture, have induced strong policy interest in the RNFE as an employer of last resort and a route out of poverty for growing legions of landless rural workers. In response to this growing interest, Chapter 3 introduces key issues and evidence affecting the potential role of the RNFE as a source of livelihood for the rural poor.

Part II: Dynamics and Linkages

Part II examines the dynamics of the RNFE together with the key structural linkages that animate and mediate interaction between the RNFE and other segments of the rural, national, and international economies. Following a broad overview of the role of the RNFE during structural transformation, this section proceeds to examine the dynamics of nonfarm activity from a variety of perspectives. Analytically, this part of the book builds a dynamic portrait of the RNFE, starting with the individual nonfarm enterprise, then moving up to the household, sectoral, regional, and global economies.

Chapter 4 launches this discussion by describing the role of the RNFE in the overall process of structural transformation, during which the share of agriculture in total national output declines and transfers of capital and labor drive a corresponding rise in manufacturing and services. Because many of the resource flows from agriculture to the secondary and tertiary sectors of the economy transit functionally and spatially via the RNFE, the transitions under way in the RNFE become central to understanding the processes that drive overall economic growth. After reviewing a series of common dynamic pathways, the chapter concludes by introducing a typology of regional settings that serves as an aid in categorizing and anticipating rural nonfarm dynamics in an array of common situations.

Chapter 5 focuses on the building blocks of the RNFE by examining the dynamics of individual nonfarm enterprises. It demonstrates how aggregate trends in rural nonfarm activity mask the substantial churning that occurs as individual nonfarm enterprises emerge, some expand, and others die out. Using enterprise-level data collected from household surveys in six different countries, this chapter examines empirical evidence on enterprise birth rates, death rates, and individual firm expansion rates as well as how these vary across locations. The chapter draws on this empirical record to examine the policy implications of this considerable volatility in individual rural nonfarm enterprise dynamics.

Chapter 6 moves to the household level, focusing on how household decisionmaking affects rural nonfarm enterprise dynamics. Given the large and growing share of farm household income derived from nonfarm sources, decisions affecting nonfarm enterprise creation, closure, and growth are commonly made within the confines of a multitasking rural household. Thus nonfarm enterprise dynamics fit into a household decisionmaking environment that helps to shape labor and capital allocations across activities, and thereby outcomes. This chapter helps to develop a fuller understanding of rural nonfarm dynamics and the household decisionmaking environment within which these decisions are frequently made.

Chapter 7 moves to the sectoral level, focusing on interactions between agriculture and the RNFE. It reviews a wealth of evidence accumulated in recent decades on the magnitude of agricultural growth linkages in order to address the following key questions: To what extent does agriculture shape the RNFE? In what instances does agriculture predominate as the engine of rural nonfarm growth? And where do other forces emerge as more prominent?

Chapter 8 explores the spatial dimensions of rural nonfarm growth. Following the presentation of a conceptual framework for understanding the spatial distribution of nonfarm economic activity, the chapter reviews empirical evidence on the location of firms across urban and rural space. Discussion highlights the role of towns and small cities in regional and rural nonfarm development.

Chapter 9 examines how global dynamics increasingly influence the evolution of the RNFE in the developing world. It assesses how the twin forces of globalization and liberalization, in both trade and investment, have touched off a set of rapid changes in agrifood systems across the developing world, particularly since the early 1990s. These changes include increasing concentration, growing multinationalization, and rapidly changing agrifood system organization, institutions, and technologies. This chapter highlights the resulting opportunities and challenges facing rural nonfarm businesses, concluding with a discussion of options as to how the rural poor can navigate this rapidly changing rural nonfarm environment.

Chapter 10 concludes discussion of rural nonfarm dynamics with a case study of trends in the two fast-growing East Asian economies of South Korea and Taiwan. Structural transformation of the rural economy, introduced at the beginning of this section in Chapter 4, has advanced furthest and most rapidly in East Asia. For this reason, a wealth of long-term time-series data permits careful documentation of how that process has unfolded there. This chapter reviews that body of evidence in order to explore the factors affecting trends in the RNFE. It draws on these to anticipate issues and opportunities confronting later-blooming rural economies of the developing world.

Part III: Policies and Programs

Chapter 11 introduces the policy and institutional environment affecting the RNFE. In the public sector, the RNFE typically remains an institutional orphan, cutting across ministerial portfolios without serving as a central focus for any. The private sector, meanwhile, assumes a growing role in influencing the structure and dynamics of the RNFE through a variety of input and output market supply chain relationships between large and small firms. Simultaneously, a welter of private, civil society, and public agencies promote rural nonfarm activity on equity and environmental grounds, mostly on a not-for-profit basis. The chapter explores institutional models that policymakers and equity-oriented private sector participants have erected within this fractured and sometimes conflicting institutional environment to stimulate equity-enhancing growth in the RNFE.

Chapter 12 provides an overview of the broad array of rural nonfarm support programs and policies instituted in the developing world. It traces promotion efforts outside of India and China, highlighting the extent to which efforts elsewhere have drawn inspiration from these two behemoths. The chapter attempts to summarize and categorize the principal approaches adopted to date. Discussion chronicles the broad history of these efforts, identifies key players, contrasts the premises on which they have based their work, and summarizes available evidence on impact and cost.

Chapter 13 examines rural nonfarm policies and programs implemented in India and China, the world's two largest developing countries. Because of the scale of their rural nonfarm economies, the experience of these two giants, in effect, defines the center of gravity for rural nonfarm policy in the developing world. As in other spheres of economic policy, Asia's two dominant economies have followed separate paths, though they started from a similar base. This chapter explores how these differing rural nonfarm development paths can help us better understand differences in overall performance of the two countries and also provides useful indications for other developing countries about options for nurturing a viable rural nonfarm sector in the current global context.

Chapter 14 focuses more narrowly on how new technology has stimulated rapid change in rural nonfarm activity across a broad range of developing country settings. Because of its prospects for raising worker productivity and improving product quality, new technology offers a potentially powerful means of expanding markets as well as worker earnings in nonfarm activities. Yet in spite of its importance, technology has remained underappreciated by many promoters of the RNFE. This chapter aims to redress this past imbalance by focusing specifically on technology and its potential for accelerating income growth and poverty reduction in the RNFE. In doing so, the chapter examines a series of analytical, empirical, and policy questions. The first of these concern sources of innovation: Who and what determine the supply of new rural nonfarm technologies? Second, what determines the adoption of such technologies, particularly by the poor? And finally, where can public intervention play a useful role in pro-poor technology development and diffusion in the RNFE?

Chapter 15 examines policy and promotional interventions from the functional perspective of the supply chain. Because most rural nonfarm enterprises operate in vertical supply chains and because large firms often occupy strategic locations in these supply systems, as input suppliers or marketers of rural firm output, the tracing of alternate, competing supply channels quickly reveals complementarities and conflicts between large and small firms operating in the same vertical supply system. These diagnostics yield important clues as to system dynamics, opportunities for growth, and necessary private sector partnerships required to link rural suppliers with dynamic markets. This chapter explores ways in which analysis of market supply chains has been used in the past by a variety of operational organizations to identify and structure interventions in the RNFE.

Part IV: Synthesis

Building on the evidence and experience reported in earlier sections of the book, Part IV looks forward to assess the implications of past work for future research and policy. Chapter 16 summarizes key research findings and projects how issues and priorities are likely to change in coming years. On the policy side, Chapter 17 draws on past experience to propose a strategy for stimulating equitable rural nonfarm growth in the developing world during the coming decades of the new century.

2 Alternative Perceptions of the Rural Nonfarm Economy

STEVEN HAGGBLADE

Striking diversity pervades the rural nonfarm economy. Activities range from humble home-based cottage industries to private health, education, and transport services to the marketing and processing activities of sophisticated multinational agribusiness firms. This considerable heterogeneity has attracted a wide range of disciplinary and analytical perspectives aiming to explore the promise of rural nonfarm activity as a potential contributor to rural economic growth and poverty alleviation.

Resulting from this diversity of interest, four closely related literatures have emerged examining the rural nonfarm economy (RNFE) from four different perspectives:

1. Agricultural growth linkages—the view from the farm. Inspired initially by the Asian green revolution, this work views rural nonfarm activity primarily as a demand-driven spin-off of agricultural growth. Through a series of important reverse flows—of financing, labor, processing, input supply, and marketing—the RNFE also serves as an accelerator, speeding and enhancing the equity of technologically induced agricultural income growth.

2. Rural nonfarm employment—the view from the firm. In contrast, the rural nonfarm employment literature starts off the farm, often with individual nonfarm enterprises, examining both supply and demand constraints to their expansion. Contributors to this literature worry about entrepreneurship, technical efficiency, rural infrastructure, credit, education, and other factors affecting the supply of nonfarm goods and services. And they see agriculture as the dominant—although not the sole—source of rural demand.

3. Household livelihoods—the view from the hearth. The rural livelihoods literature starts not with sectoral aggregations but rather with the rural household, the key decisionmaking unit in rural economies, allocating labor, land, and capital across activities. Analysts ask why some categories of households specialize while others diversify into different farm and nonfarm enterprises, and often spatially as well. They emphasize risk management, labor allocation, and push and pull factors that induce farm households to diversify into various nonfarm activities.

   4. *Regional development—the spatial perspective.* Geographers, regional planners, and others who contribute to the regional development literature highlight the spatial dispersion of population, production, and settlements. They examine spatial concentration of demand as well as important supply-side determinants of nonfarm activity such as the siting of rural infrastructure and government services. They focus particular attention on the development of rural towns and on the nonfarm traders and service enterprises that set up there to service agricultural growth.

   These four streams of literature overlap to a substantial degree, conceptually in their examination of sectoral linkages between agricultural and nonfarm enterprises and spatially in rural towns where many of the nonfarm businesses emerge. Yet they differ in many fundamental ways as well (Table 2.1). Because of differing units of analysis and widely varying levels of aggregation, each focuses on different decisionmakers and on different structural, environmental, and behavioral parameters. As a result of this broad interest, a multitude of disciplines has contributed to our understanding of the RNFE, including agricultural economics, anthropology, business management, economics, geography, public administration, regional planning, and sociology. Each brings its own prejudices, predispositions, and analytical tools to bear. In doing so, these multiple strands of analysis illuminate different dimensions of the RNFE. The resulting diversity of analytical perspectives weaves a rich tapestry that highlights and contrasts interrelationships, opportunities, and constraints.

   The result is reminiscent of the diversity of disciplinary diagnoses following the fall of Rome. While agriculturalists maintain that declining soil fertility lowered domestic farm output and increased pressure to expand wealth through foreign acquisitions, political scientists attribute the empire's decline to the demise of political accountability after the fall of republican Rome. In contrast, students of economic livelihoods emphasize increasing inequality, heavy taxation, and forced labor requisitions that ultimately drove the peasantry into ruinous opposition, while city planners allege that lead poisoning from water distribution conduits gradually incapacitated imperial decisionmakers. As is always the case, alternative analytical lenses highlight different features of the same central essence.

   This multidisciplinary exploration of the RNFE first flowered in the early 1970s, when widespread concern with rural poverty in the developing world coincided with the excitement surrounding the Asian green revolution. That confluence of opportunity and interest in reducing rural poverty sparked the first major exploration of the RNFE during the 1970s, when three of the four major strands of the rural nonfarm literature first emerged (Table 2.2). A series of severe droughts, most notably in the African Sahel and in Ethiopia during the late 1970s and early 1980s, sparked a fourth strand of inquiry exploring household-

TABLE 2.1 Alternative perceptions of the rural nonfarm economy

Literature	Perspective	Sectoral focus	Unit of analysis	Principal disciplinary contributors	Empirical evidence
1. Agricultural growth linkages	From the farm: RNFE as a demand-driven spin-off from agriculture	Agriculture	Sector	Agricultural economists Anthropologists	Chapter 7
2. Rural nonfarm employment	From the firm: RNFE as a large rural employer	Nonagriculture	Enterprise Supply chain	Economists Management specialists	Chapter 5
3. Livelihoods	From the hearth: household asset allocation between farm and nonfarm activities	All	Household	Agricultural economists Anthropologists Sociologists	Chapter 6
4. Regional development	Spatial: geographic clustering of RNFE, rural-urban links	All	Rural region Supply chain	Anthropologists Geographers Public administration Regional planners	Chapter 8

Can agriculture really act as an engine of growth?

based coping and diversification strategies, many of which relied on rural non-farm activities. These efforts continued as part of the livelihoods literature and increasingly commingled with the other three strands of investigation during a second major surge of interest in the RNFE beginning in the 1990s and continuing into the first decade of the twenty-first century. Once again, poverty concerns have stimulated the renaissance of interest in the RNFE. And again, interest in poverty reduction has coincided with a new economic opportunity. On this occasion, widespread liberalization and globalization have combined to enable supermarket chains and large agribusinesses to penetrate the RNFEs as never before, opening up both new opportunities and new threats for rural entrepreneurs. These renewed multidisciplinary investigations increasingly converge as rural poverty returns to the front burner in policy discussions and a new generation rediscovers the RNFE.

To help promote and accelerate cross-fertilization during this new wave of exploration, this chapter charts the emergence, interaction, and evolution of these four strands of literature. In doing so, it sets the stage on which a series of ensuing chapters will present the detailed empirical evidence assembled by each of these four groups (Table 2.1).

Agricultural Growth Linkages: The View from the Farm

Serious recognition of the importance of the RNFE first emerged during the agricultural growth linkages debates of the early 1970s. That decade began with spreading news of early successes in the green revolution, which overnight transformed agriculture into a credible engine of economic growth. Emboldened, agriculturalists launched the growth linkages literature as a central component of their agrocentric counterattack against two decades of second-class citizenship in development circles.

Antithesis: Industrial Fundamentalism

A stark antiagricultural bias permeated development planning efforts during the 1950s and 1960s. Historical precedent in the West strongly predisposed newly emerging governments to retread the proven industrial path to economic growth. Conventional wisdom held that manufacturing offered the fast track to economic growth because of more rapidly growing market demand, higher productivity, and superior growth-enhancing linkages with other sectors of the economy.

Domestic demand for manufactures was expected to grow more rapidly than for food products as rising income induced households to diversify consumption into nonfoods, in accordance with Engels's Law. In the international arena, emerging evidence on the terms of trade similarly suggested that world demand for agricultural output would prove sluggish compared to the international market for manufactures (Prebish 1950, 1959; Singer 1950).

TABLE 2.2 Literary surges illuminating the rural nonfarm economy

	1950s and 1960s	1970s	1980s	1990s and 2000s
Economic shocks		New agricultural technology	Severe droughts	Globalization
Dominant policy themes affecting the rural nonfarm economy				
Third World and First World donors	Urban industrialization	Rural poverty alleviation	Structural adjustment	Poverty reduction Liberalization
Second World, developing country (China)	Five small industries	CBEs	Internal reforms Rural trade liberalization	Liberalization TVEs
Rural nonfarm literary surges Agricultural growth linkages		Rural employment Production linkages Consumption linkages		
Rural nonfarm enterprise		Magnitude Composition Efficiency		Supermarkets Supply chains Urban deconcentration
Regional development		IRD Decentralization		Decentralization LED
Livelihoods			Coping Diversification	Rural livelihoods

NOTES: CBEs, commune and brigade enterprises; IRD, integrated rural development; LED, local economic development; TVEs, town and village enterprises. A blank space indicates that data are not applicable.

Low productivity of agricultural labor—zero according to some—would permit costless transfer of resources out of agriculture to higher-productivity manufacturing enterprises. The initial free lunch identified in allegedly surplus agricultural labor fueled a lineage of influential two-sector models, from Lewis (1954) to more formalized renderings by Ranis and Fei (1964) and others. Although Lewis (1958) later advocated parallel initial investments in agriculture to enable a productivity boost that would facilitate the release of labor from agriculture,[1] and although Ranis and Fei emphasized the turning point that would potentially choke off industrial growth via rising food prices once supplies of surplus labor from agriculture had been exhausted, most policymakers focused on the initial phase of costless resource transfer out of agriculture. From China to India and throughout the rest of the developing world, policymakers expected agriculture to furnish surplus labor, investment, and foreign exchange to fuel industrial growth.

Likewise, Hirschman's strategy of focusing development resources in lead industries with strong spillovers throughout the economy led him to favor promotion of manufacturing rather than agriculture. His pro-industrial prescription rested on the supposedly feeble production linkages between agriculture and the rest of the economy. In his words, "Agriculture certainly stands convicted on the count of its lack of direct stimulus to the setting up of new activities through linkage effects—the superiority of manufacturing in this respect is crushing" (Hirschman 1958, 110). This confident conclusion has enshrined him as one of the most popular straw men of the linkages literature.

Viewed from the farm gate, the history of development thought traces the rising assertiveness of the agriculturalists. Rather than assigning a purely passive role for agriculture as a pool of underutilized but exploitable resources, they advanced the unobjectionable notion that agriculture also deserved recognition as a producer of food and as a potential market for industrial goods (Johnston and Mellor 1961). This led to renewed proposals for simultaneous investment in agriculture and manufacturing to permit resource transfers out of agriculture without raising food prices and choking off industrial growth.

By the mid-1960s, most practitioners agreed it was possible to launch development by pulling resources from farming. Disagreement centered around how long they could do so with impunity. How long could policymakers extract resources from agriculture without decreasing food production and hence driving up the price of food? The answer, of course, depended on how much surplus labor actually existed on the farm. Thus measurement of rural employment, underemployment, and disguised unemployment became key. For agricultural

---

1. For similar reasons, the neoclassical models of Jorgenson (1961) and Enke (1962) also suggested parallel investment in agriculture and manufacturing. See Johnston (1970) and Timmer (1988) for more detailed reviews of these early debates.

economists, farm management estimates of the marginal productivity of labor in agriculture became a central empirical issue of the 1960s.[2]

From Ugly Sister to Cinderella

In the early 1970s, rising concern about rural poverty coincided with stunning early evidence of agricultural productivity gains from the green revolution technologies in Asia. Together they inspired agriculturalists to advance agriculture's claim from that of a brake on industrial-led growth to the notion that agriculture itself could serve as the locomotive.

The suddenly elevated concern about equity, income distribution, and poverty radically transformed priorities throughout the developing world. Viewed from an equity perspective, industrial growth had proven undependable. Even where growth had been rapid, income distribution and poverty did not necessarily improve. Import substitution had disappointed its proponents. Its focus on large-scale urban manufacturing had precipitated regional polarization, urbanization, and slow growth in employment. The benefits of industrial growth had not spread widely. They had not trickled down. Following Fishlow (1972) and the International Labor Office's (ILO) prominent World Employment Programme[3] came the U.S. Agency for International Development's (USAID) New Directions Mandate of 1973. It stipulated that the majority of U.S. foreign assistance be directed to the Third World's "poor majority," a group subsequently defined to include only the rural poor. The World Bank, led by Robert McNamara, strongly endorsed the new poverty focus (McNamara 1973). In a unanimous about-face, the Western donors dedicated the 1970s to rural development, employment, and equity.

Agriculture took center stage. As the major employer in the developing world and the backbone of its rural economies, agriculture sustained the bulk of the Third World's poor. A wide array of researchers took to the field assembling microdata on rural employment, underemployment, poverty, and income distribution.[4] They were there when the green revolution flooded onto the irrigated rice and wheat fields of Asia from the late 1960s onward.

Like all successful insurgencies, the green revolution arrived at a time when the old regime, that of industrial fundamentalism, was fractured and faltering. As manufacturing output sputtered, agriculture proved able to grow at historically unprecedented rates. And unlike manufacturing, the new agricultural technology proved labor-using. Superimposed on the equity concerns of the day, this potential for rapid, broad-based agricultural growth fundamentally transformed conventional views of agriculture's potential contribution to economic development.

---

2. See Kao, Anschel, and Eicher (1964), Schultz (1964), and Hirschman (1981a).
3. See ILO (1972, 1979, 1982, 1984, 1986).
4. See Mellor and Lele (1971) and Byerlee and Eicher (1974).

Mellor, Lele, Johnston, and Kilby led the charge,[5] arguing that agriculture, instead of remaining a perennial supporting actress, could play a leading role in development efforts. Agriculture could drive economic growth. They founded their case on linkages. Countering Hirschman (1958), Johnston and Kilby (1975) documented the considerable production linkages generated by the new green revolution agricultural technology. The new high-yielding varieties demanded pumps, sprayers, fertilizer, cement, construction labor, and repair facilities from nonagricultural firms. They generated substantial backward linkages. Furthermore, considerable milling, processing, and distribution of agricultural produce took place in rural areas, thus generating important forward production linkages as well. The new agricultural technology fundamentally altered input-output relationships.

Still more important were the consumption linkages that Hirschman had ignored altogether. As Mellor and Lele (1973) originally pointed out, consumption linkages from growing farm income induce sizable second rounds of rural growth via increased consumer demand. Where new technology or investment in agriculture leads to increased income, farm families spend large increments of additional earnings on rurally produced nonfoodgrains. These include nonagricultural goods and services as well as perishable, high-value farm commodities such as milk, meat, and vegetables. Because most are labor intensive, the spending multipliers not only accelerate but also enhance the equity of agriculture-led growth. Thus evidence on consumption linkages contributed in an important way to heated debates over the equity impact of new agricultural technologies.[6] Consumption linkages likewise play a central role in discussions about which farm size to target in research and extension.

Empirical Contributions

A series of empirical issues dominated applied work in agricultural economics during the decade of agricultural empowerment, the 1970s. The first focused on employment, underemployment, and questions of surplus labor. To investigate the surplus labor assumption of the two-sector models, employment and farm management surveys began to assemble data measuring the extent of employment, underemployment, and productivity of farm labor. The early work of the farm management teams first documented the large size of nonfarm labor use, even among agricultural households. Startling many who equate rural economies with agriculture, this work suggested that farm households may devote as much

---

5. Mellor and Lele (1973), Johnston and Kilby (1975), Mellor (1976), Mellor and Johnston (1984).

6. Cleaver (1972), Griffin (1974), Harriss (1977), Ruttan (1977), Grabowski (1979), Pinstrup-Andersen and Hazell (1985), Lipton (1989).

as 30 to 40 percent of their annual household labor to nonfarm pursuits.[7] In doing so, this work inspired a cohort of economists as well as business promotion specialists to explore small-scale and rural nonfarm business activity.[8]

A second set of issues focused on measuring production and consumption linkages. Early empirical work by Mellor and Lele (1973) on the spending patterns of farm households attracted a series of emulators.[9] This growing body of evidence suggests that consumption linkages, which Hirschman had altogether ignored, are roughly four times as important as production linkages.[10] New analytical methods developed by Bell and Hazell (1980) enabled the combination of input-output and consumption parameters to estimate combined linkage effects, inspiring a host of emulators and launching a veritable cottage industry devoted to the measurement of agricultural growth linkages.[11] Empirical work has continued well into the 2000s, as Chapter 7 describes in detail.

In the 1990s and 2000s, evidence of labor market linkages and general equilibrium interactions between agriculture and the RNFE have expanded linkage work beyond its initial concentration on product market consumption and production linkages.[12] Further work on factor market linkages has likewise emerged courtesy of the livelihoods literature, where labor and investment linkages merit particular attention.[13]

Viewed in historical context, Adelman's (1984) classic computable general equilibrium model of growth linkages in the South Korean economy serves as a capstone reference for the agricultural insurgency. Completely reversing the industry-first orthodoxy of the 1950s, her results suggest that agricultural demand-led industrialization can generate superior growth and equity when contrasted with the alternative of export-promoting industrialization strategies. This conclusion ratified a remarkable about-face, badly rattling the old con-

---

7. See Norman (1972), Byerlee and Eicher (1974), Byerlee et al. (1977), Matlon (1979), and the numerous studies cited by Cleave (1974). Chuta and Liedholm (1979) and Anderson and Leiserson (1980) review much of this early evidence, while Lanjouw and Lanjouw (2001), Haggblade, Hazell, and Reardon (2002), and Reardon et al. (1998) summarize more recent findings.

8. Oshima (1971), Liedholm (1973), Chuta and Liedholm (1979), Ho (1979), Kilby (1982).

9. See, for example, King and Byerlee (1978), Hazell and Roell (1983), and Hossain (2004).

10. See Chapter 7 as well as Gibb (1984), Haggblade and Hazell (1989), Ranis, Stewart, and Reyes (1990), and Bagachwa and Stewart (1992).

11. Examples include Bell, Hazell, and Slade (1982), Subramanian and Sadoulet (1990), Lewis and Thorbecke (1992), Delgado et al. (1994), Vogel (1994), de Janvry and Sadoulet (2002), Dorosh and Haggblade (2003), and Dorosh, Naizi, and Nazlil (2003).

12. See Haggblade and Liedholm (1991), Reardon (1997), Barrett, Reardon, and Webb (2001), de Janvry and Sadoulet (2002), Dorosh and Haggblade (2003), Foster and Rosenzweig (2004), and Chapter 7 on the importance of wage and labor market links between agriculture and rural nonfarm activity.

13. See Reardon, Crawford, and Kelly (1994), Ellis (1998, 2000), and Chapter 6.

ventional wisdom of industrial fundamentalism. Thanks to growth linkages, agriculture had become a respectable engine of economic growth.

Rural Nonfarm Employment: The View from the Firm

A sizable rural nonfarm employment literature emerged in the early 1970s, inspired by findings from farm labor surveys that first began documenting the surprisingly large share of rural employment and income contributed by nonfarm activities. The small size, modest capital requirements, and apparent labor intensity of the nonfarm activities spurred keen interest in these potentially equity-enhancing pursuits. In exploring this new terrain, the rural nonfarm employment literature—together with its close relatives examining small-scale enterprise, the informal sector, and microenterprise[14]—has tackled a series of key empirical questions: Does the RNFE really exist? Is it worth promoting? And if so, how, given rapid recent changes in the dynamics of rural economies? By addressing each question in turn, it is possible to sketch a roughly chronological map of the terrain covered by early explorers of the RNFE.

Does It Exist?

In the 1950s and 1960s, rural nonfarm activity did not exist in the minds of policymakers and practitioners. They lived, after all, in a two-sector world. Agriculture was rural and backward. Manufacturing was urban and modern. Commerce and services, largely ignored in this era, promised to blossom later, with economic growth and diversification (Chenery and Syrquin 1975). In the meantime, urban industrialization would chart the pace and path of economic growth.

Rural nonfarm activity remained nearly invisible. It was acknowledged only by proxy through its surrogate, small-scale industry. Policymakers of the day largely ignored small enterprise except in Nigeria (Kilby 1962) and in India, where Gandhian philosophy and Ford Foundation funding supported Staley and Morse's (1965) classic initial efforts at small enterprise promotion. Even the Chinese devoted the 1950s to large-scale industry. After collectivization in 1958, they introduced priority for rural small industry to support agricultural growth, starting in 1962 but with particular emphasis from 1968 onward. Their strategy

---

14. Because most nonfarm employment in developing countries is rural and small-scale, the closely related literatures on "small-scale," "micro," "informal sector," and "rural nonfarm" enterprises overlap to a considerable extent. Reviewing evidence from a broad range of developing countries, Liedholm and Mead (1987) note that rural areas normally account for between 30 and 85 percent of national manufacturing employment, while 40 to 95 percent of manufacturing takes place in small-scale firms, defined as those employing under 50 workers. During the 1970s, and especially the 1980s, considerable empirical and analytical work relevant to rural nonfarm firms appeared under these other labels.

of "walking on two legs" and mandated priority for the "five small industries" attracted international attention, though little emulation.[15]

While pioneering industrial censuses in the mid-1960s offered glimmers of the vast numbers of small-scale (and predominantly rural) nonfarm industrial enterprises,[16] the intellectual respectability of the small enterprise aficionado in this era depended on promoting entrepreneurship. Staley and Morse (1965), McClelland and Winter (1969), and Kilby (1971) all focused on entrepreneurship, on small enterprises as seedbeds of new entrepreneurs, the driving force in economic development. They saw small firms as teeming laboratories from which the future captains of industry would spring.[17]

Two widespread beliefs, permeating the 1950s and 1960s, challenged these early small enterprise efforts and strongly influenced the research agenda for the explosion of data collection that was to follow. First was the conventional wisdom among industrial planners that bigger was better because it was efficient. Hoselitz (1959) and others spoke of the inevitable and desirable demise of rural household-based industry. From diminutive to disparaging, the modifiers applied to nonfarm enterprises included "primitive," "obsolete," "household," "tiny," "cottage," "dwarf,"[18] "artisan," "handicraft," "traditional," "stone age," and "nonfactory." Focusing almost exclusively on manufacturing, most observers viewed small firms as backward, primitive, and inefficient. Thus the first article of faith in this era enshrined a widespread belief in the inefficiency of small firms.

The second belief concerned the inferiority of rural nonfarm goods and services. Most observers presumed that as incomes rose consumers would readily prefer imported manufactures over low-quality rural nonfarm substitutes. Hymer and Resnick (1969) took this position most forcefully. They ended the 1960s with a final shot at two-sector modeling, identifying an ingenious free lunch in the demise of the RNFE. Hymer and Resnick suggested that consumer substitution of rural nonfarm goods (Z-goods) for imported manufactures, rather than Lewis's surplus agricultural labor, could finance economic growth. By freeing up productive resources formerly used in inefficient Z-good production, the opening up of trade would allow a region to increase farm production and import preferred, efficiently produced manufactures, thus increasing consumption possibilities, aggregate production, and welfare.

But this "Z-goods-substituting" growth strategy depended on the inferiority of rural nonfarm goods and services. Although Hymer and Resnick (1969)

---

15. See Ho (1986a), Saith (1987), Tomich, Kilby, and Johnston (1995), and Lin and Yao (1999).

16. See, for example, Kilby (1962), East Pakistan Small Industries Corporation (1964), and India (1968).

17. For an update on these debates, see Grosh and Somolekae (1996) and Kilby (2003).

18. We are grateful to Carl Liedholm (1985) for preserving this unfortunate label in our collective memories.

*rural non-farm goods may be declining w/
globalization, but commerce & services
(non-tradeables) are not.*

presented no empirical evidence, the mathematics of their model demanded inferiority in order to produce unambiguous results. Later they did present evidence of declining rural industries—mostly home-based handicrafts—in Burma, the Philippines, and Thailand between 1870 and 1938 (Resnick 1970), though they largely ignored rural commerce and services. Their assertion of inferiority motivated both the faithful and the doubters to gather empirical evidence on the income elasticity of demand for rural nonfarm output.

Is It Worth Promoting?

In the 1970s, as investigators took the field to explore the RNFE, they enjoyed equity-based backing from the policymakers. But, on efficiency grounds, prior preconceptions placed them clearly on the defensive. Allegedly crippled on both the supply and the demand side—by inefficient technology and flagging demand—the RNFE had to answer serious charges before it could prove worthy of promotion. Thus, in addition to assembling basic descriptive profiles documenting the size, composition, and income distribution consequences of rural nonfarm earnings, empirical work also examined the production efficiency of small rural firms as well as consumption preferences for rural nonfarm output.

In addressing these issues, a pair of major research efforts propelled empirical exploration of the RNFE. The first issued from the ILO, whose World Employment Programme, beginning in 1969, proved instrumental in reorienting attention toward employment and equity. Through their worldwide research program and in-depth country missions—to Kenya, Colombia, Sri Lanka, Iran, and the Philippines—the ILO researchers became forceful advocates for small-scale, labor-intensive nonfarm enterprises. In an important departure from prior convention, they reached beyond manufacturing to include commerce and service activities in their reviews. Suddenly the scale of nonfarm activity ballooned into something truly enormous. They dubbed these nonfarm firms the "informal sector" and ascribed to them the powerful promise of a "sleeping giant" (ILO 1972). Casting their research net wide, they contributed substantially to the assembly of detailed rural income distribution profiles, even though their nonfarm business investigations tended to emphasize urban activity.[19] According to Kilby (1988, 224), "The discovery of the urban informal sector, circa 1972, led in turn to the pursuit of its rural counterpart."

The second major group involved in primary data collection converged on the RNFE from an alternate direction, via spin-offs from agriculture. Much of the early work in this stream is associated with the African investigations of Michigan State University (MSU) and affiliated researchers.[20] In 1971, MSU's USAID-funded African Rural Employment Project became the first to explic-

---

19. See, for example, ILO (1984, 1986).

20. Shortly afterward, a second wave, this time of Asia scholars, continued along this farm–to–rural nonfarm path (Chinn, 1979; Islam 1987a).

itly incorporate a rural nonfarm component.[21] This effort launched Liedholm and associates as major contributors to the emerging body of empirical evidence on rural nonfarm activity. Along with Anderson, Chuta, Ho, Islam, Kilby, Mead, Oshima, and Shand, they have become principal architects of the emerging conventional wisdom concerning the RNFE.

Early on, the efficiency issue attracted widespread debate, as analysts worried about a possible trade-off between equity and efficiency, between employment and growth.[22] Summarizing a decade of furious activity, White's (1978) review established the following new orthodoxy. First, small-scale and intermediate technologies are almost always technically efficient. That is, with the same capital-labor combination, no other technology can produce greater output. Second, when inputs are priced at their opportunity cost, many labor-intensive or intermediate technologies are economically efficient, that is, lowest-cost producers, particularly in consumer goods industries and in low-wage countries. Although Little, Mazumdar, and Page (1987) later expressed iconoclastic second thoughts, the weight of empirical evidence suggests that small-scale enterprises can be economically efficient across a broad range of activities and countries.[23]

The debate over consumption preferences has proven similarly conclusive. Analysis of household survey data consistently rejects Hymer and Resnick's hypothesis of inferior rural nonfarm goods and services.[24] Virtually all empirical studies have reported positive income elasticities, in many cases in excess of one. Cottage manufactures typically attract the lowest income elasticities of demand, while demand elasticities for imported and factory manufactures generally prove higher. Commerce and services such as transport, education, health, and ceremonial services often have the highest income elasticities of all.[25] Consequently, rising agricultural income will lead to higher expenditure on rural nonfarm output, particularly in commerce and services.

At the end of the 1970s, a pair of major reviews summarized the state of understanding about the RNFE in developing countries. The studies, by Anderson and Leiserson (1978) and Chuta and Liedholm (1979), agreed that the sector was larger than most had anticipated at the start of the decade, providing

---

21. Liedholm (1973), Liedholm and Chuta (1976).

22. Although this choice of technique literature is enormous, a perusal of Sen (1968), Pack (1972), Timmer (1972), Bhalla (1975), Steel (1977), Stewart (1977), White (1978), Carr (1982), Liedholm and Mead (1987), and the special issue of World Development (1977) will offer a good introduction.

23. See Bhalla (1975), Stewart (1977), White (1978), Page and Steel (1984), Cortes, Berry, and Ishaq (1987), Liedholm and Mead (1987), Pack (1987), and Mead (1991).

24. See King and Byerlee (1978), Hazell and Roell (1983), Deb and Hossain (1984), Hazell and Ramasamy (1986), Rogers (1986), Amane (1989), Hossain (1988b), Evans (1990), and Lewis and Thorbecke (1992).

25. See, for example, Hossain (2004), King and Byerlee (1978), Hazell and Roell (1983), and Hossain (2004).

primary employment for 20 to 30 percent of the rural labor force and employing another 20 percent part time or seasonally. Given low capital requirements
and low barriers to entry, the RNFE enabled widespread participation by the rural poor. In most places, over 90 percent of rural nonfarm enterprises operated
with fewer than five workers. The studies concluded that the efficiency of small
rural producers was established across a range of products and that preliminary
results strongly suggested that consumer spending on rural nonfarm output rose
with income. Feeding back into the agricultural growth linkages literature, they
agreed that agriculture represented the key source of rural nonfarm demand and
that agricultural policy, therefore, would be the key determinant of growth in
rural nonfarm activity. Anderson and Leiserson likewise presented a prescient
discussion of the spatial implications of rural nonfarm growth. Although often
forgotten in the nonfarm shift to small-scale enterprise in the early 1980s, their
views found a cohort of kindred spirits in the regional planning branch of the
rural linkages literature.

How Can It Be Promoted?

By the beginning of the 1980s, the principal investigators of the RNFE had concluded that rural nonfarm activity was indeed worthy of promotion. Attention
then shifted to how to do so. In addressing this question, many students of the
RNFE came to focus on small-scale enterprises (SSEs), both rural and urban.
In part, the shift to small-scale firms mirrored a widespread deemphasis of
rural development and a growing concern about overly rapid urbanization and
urban poverty. The widely publicized work of Hernando de Soto (1989) on the
"informal sector" proved influential in turning attention toward nonfarm activity in urban areas. Given the common focus on manufacturing and given that
most rural industries proved to be small, at the end of the 1970s many in this
group—Anderson, Chuta, Ho, Kilby, and Liedholm—switched to a focus on
small-scale manufacturing in both rural and urban areas.[26] There they joined
Steel (1977), Schmitz (1982), Harper (1984), Page and Steel (1984), Mead
(1985), Tendler (1989), and Snodgrass and Biggs (1996) as contributors to the
closely allied SSE literature. Part III of this book reviews the ebb and flow of
these promotional experiences in some detail.

The Asian Explosion

During the mid-1980s, a coalition of Asia scholars—Choe, Ho, Hossain, Islam,
Lo, Oshima, Lim, Mukhopodahay, Shand, and colleagues—became concerned
about slowing labor absorption in South Asian agriculture. Four major edited

---

26. Note the change in focus by comparing the following: Anderson and Leiserson (1980)
with Anderson (1982) and Anderson and Khambata (1982), Liedholm and Chuta (1976), and Chuta
and Liedholm (1979) with Chuta and Liedholm (1982) and Liedholm and Mead (1987), Ho (1979)
with Ho (1982), and Johnston and Kilby (1975) with Kilby (1982).

volumes between 1985 and 1987 attest to the widespread concern about sluggish employment growth in Asia and the potential of the RNFE to absorb growing workforce increments.[27]

Historical reviews by the Asia scholars flagged troubling signals emerging from rural nonfarm employment trends in South Asia. Rapid population growth there, coupled with increasing landlessness and an inability of agriculture to absorb labor force increments, was leading to increased rural nonfarm employment. But it had been growth by default in increasingly low-paying nonfarm pursuits. In contrast, agricultural advance in Japan, Taiwan, and other newly industrializing countries in East Asia brought with it rapid expansion of increasingly remunerative rural nonfarm activity. This difference has led many to worry that where agricultural growth lags, rural nonfarm employment may simply serve as a "sponge" or employer of last resort offering menial, low-productivity jobs.

The East Asian studies likewise improved our understanding of rural non-farm activity along several important dimensions. Building on evidence from Taiwan and the Philippines, Ranis and Stewart (1993) reformulated the Hymer-Resnick model by distinguishing between modern and traditional Z-goods. In doing so, they generated completely different growth dynamics. While Hymer and Resnick's gloomy predictions about the demise of many labor-intensive, household-based industries may have been right, later evidence suggests that they were wrong about rural factories, commerce, and services (Fabella 1985). Recent work by Hayami (1998b) and colleagues has examined the importance of relational contracting that links rural-based firms with urban producers and exporters through carefully managed vertical supply chains in a wide variety of subsectors throughout East Asia. In a growing number of instances, urban overcrowding and high labor costs are stimulating the development of urban-to-rural subcontracting as a new source of rural nonfarm growth in high-density regions of Asia.[28]

China has likewise contributed to the recent surge in rural nonfarm literature reemerging from Asia. The early history of rural industrialization in China, from its collectivization in 1958 to the establishment of the five priority small industries in the 1960s,[29] has attracted ongoing academic interest.[30] The subsequent steady growth of collectively owned commune and brigade enterprises from 1968 to 1978 has been variously portrayed as "phenomenal" by the

---

27. Choe and Lo (1985), Mukhopadyay and Lim (1985a,b), Shand (1986a), Islam (1987a). See also the important country case study on Thailand (World Bank 1983).

28. See, for example, Watanabe (1971), Mead (1985), Hayami, Kikuchi, and Marciano (1996), and Liu and Otsuka (1998).

29. The five priority small industries include iron and steel, cement, chemical fertilizer, energy, and farm machinery.

30. See Riskin (1971), Perkins (1977), Sigurdson (1977), Perkins and Yusuf (1985), and Lin and Yao (1999).

favorably disposed (Saith 1987) and as "indiscriminate" by the more skeptical (Ho 1986a). From 1984 through the early 2000s, an extraordinary burst of growth in China's rural town and village enterprises (TVEs) has generated considerable international attention. Widely acclaimed as the most dynamic segment of the Chinese economy, the TVEs' contribution to gross national industrial output increased from 9 percent in the late 1970s to 58 percent in the late 1990s (Lin and Yao 1999). As elsewhere in densely populated Asian settings, although agriculture clearly served as the motor of China's rural nonfarm growth during the 1980s, international export markets and urban subcontracting to rural TVEs have enjoyed increasing prominence during the late 1990s and the early years of the twenty-first century. Chapters 10 and 13 examine these developments in greater detail.

Latin American Revival

In stark contrast to the widespread interest among scholars of Africa and Asia, Latin American scholars largely neglected the RNFE for many decades. If they addressed the subject at all, it was to explain the paucity of rural nonfarm activity (Berry 1976, 1987). Unlike African and Asian society, Latin American society retains a strong urban orientation. Large landholders live in big cities. They educate their children there or abroad. Extreme inequality of income and land distribution, coupled with ethnic tension and social friction between the descendants of European colonizers and indigenous Indians, translates into low status and limited mobility for peasant farmers. The structure of urbanization mirrors this polarized distribution of wealth and political power across much of Latin America, where regional scientists have historically noted a tendency toward overurbanization as well as the dominance of a few very large cities.[31] As a result, much of the agriculturally linked nonfarm activity grew up in large cities or on self-contained haciendas. This leads some specialists to argue that nonfarm activity in Latin America will occur mainly in urban centers rather than in rural areas and that a significant increase in rural nonfarm employment will require a decentralization of urban settlement patterns and industrialization (de Janvry, Sadoulet, and Wilcox 1986).

After many years of neglect, Latin American scholars have joined the rural nonfarm debates in force, beginning in the late 1990s. Renewed concern with rural poverty has coincided with the availability of a large body of detailed rural household data, generating a spate of empirical studies of the RNFE, much of it based on World Bank–funded living standard measurement surveys.[32] Apparently rapid growth in the level of rural nonfarm activity has further fueled regional interest in the RNFE.

---

31. See Bairoch (1988) and the many case studies cited in Blitzer et al. (1988).
32. See, for example, Reardon, Berdegué, and Escobar (2001) and De Ferranti et al. (2005).

Rapid concentration in agribusiness and food retailing has emerged prominently in Latin America since the 1990s as liberalization has facilitated trade, foreign direct investment, and the application of supply chain organizational models from the outside world. As a result, during the 1990s the share of supermarkets in total food retailing grew from 20 percent to over 70 percent in both Brazil and Argentina. In Mexico, Costa Rica, and El Salvador, the supermarkets controlled over half of all food retailing by the end of the twentieth century. Over 1,000 major retail outlets from Royal Ahold to Carrefour and Wal-Mart opened in Latin America during the 1990s (Reardon and Berdegué 2002). Similar concentration has emerged in dairy industries and in agroprocessing more generally.[33] The resulting changes in minimum quantities required, product grades, and standards have meant that small rural nonfarm firms face extraordinary challenges adjusting to this new competitive environment, as discussed in greater detail in Chapter 9.

Recent Latin American studies, like those from East Asia, increasingly document how motive forces outside of agriculture may propel growth of the RNFE. While agricultural growth linkages have received comparatively little attention in Latin America, nonagricultural motors such as tourism and mining play a more prominent role (Da Silva and Del Grossi 2001). Rural subcontracting, the *maquilla* phenomenon, likewise constitutes a growing source of rural nonfarm employment gains in Latin America as urban firms seek to lower labor and factory rental costs by subcontracting production to rural firms. As in the large metropolitan suburbs of Asia, subcontracting appears to offer a significant source of nonfarm employment growth in rural Latin America.

Empirical Contributions

The rural nonfarm employment literature has painted the rich portrait we have today of the size, composition, location, and basic characteristics of the RNFE. Chapter 1, and indeed most later chapters of this book, draw extensively on this large and growing body of evidence. These data have contributed to the efficiency debates, summarized earlier, and to resolving the questions of equity and poverty pursued in Chapter 3. Detailed case studies chronicle the diverse and evolving motors of change in the nonfarm economy, from population growth to agriculture to tourism, mining, and urban-led urban-to-rural subcontracting. They likewise highlight the rapid structural change under way in a variety of rural nonfarm supply chains. More recently, the long-standing interest by this group in the RNFE has begun to translate into an increasing availability of long-term time-series data sets that permit detailed examination of enterprise, household, and sectoral dynamics. An array of these time-series studies—such as

---

33. Jank, Farina, and Galan (1999), Dirven (2001), Gutman (2002).

those by Liedholm (Chapter 5), Foster and Rosenzweig (2004), and Hossain (2004)—are examined in detail in Part II of this book.

Household Livelihoods and Coping: The View from the Hearth

Integrated Farm-Nonfarm Households

Most rural nonfarm activities are undertaken by diversified rural households that operate farm and nonfarm enterprises simultaneously. In such cases, the household constitutes the key decisionmaking unit owning and allocating productive assets—such as land, entrepreneurial and management skills, labor, and capital—across economic activities. Enterprise-level studies of rural nonfarm business offer many insights into the productivity, profitability, and business incentives of specific nonfarm activities. Yet when these take place within a diversified farm-nonfarm household, broader risk-sharing and diversification priorities influence labor and other asset allocations to nonfarm activities. Consequently, a complex set of household decisionmaking criteria determines the dynamics of rural nonfarm labor allocations and output supply. The plentiful literature on household decisionmaking,[34] therefore, contains key elements necessary for understanding the growth and evolution of rural nonfarm activity.

In response to a series of agroclimatic shocks and the dislocations accompanying structural adjustment programs of the 1980s and 1990s, a cohort of poverty-oriented practitioners has built on this early household work in an effort to understand how poor rural households have adapted to their radically altered production environment. Because rural nonfarm activity has loomed large in household adaptation strategies, much of this literature focuses on de-agrarianization, diversification into rural nonfarm activity, and migration.[35]

By pulling together elements of the household economic models and field methods developed for conducting participatory rural assessments, analysts have developed a set of analytical tools for examining rural livelihoods and the environment conditioning the response options available to poor households. The analytical framework places at its core the five key productive assets of poor households—human, physical, financial, natural, and social capital. Analysis focuses on understanding how poor households develop livelihood strategies given the institutional context and asset endowments that shape their opportunities. A considerable body of empirical work on household responses and livelihood strategies has emerged from this literature, pro-

---

34. See Singh, Squire, and Strauss (1986) for a good introduction to this literature.
35. For a good introduction to this literature, see Reardon, Matlon, and Delgado (1988), Bernstein, Crow, and Johnson (1992), Reardon and Taylor (1996), Bryceson and Jamal (1997), de Haan (1999), Ellis (2000), Barrett, Reardon, and Webb (2001), Little et al. (2001), de Haan and Rogaly (2002), and Ellis and Freeman (2004).

Could RNFE be the answer to rising food prices & environmental degradation?

viding valuable insights into the evolution and opportunities of rural nonfarm activity for the rural poor.[36]

Push versus Pull Factors

Determinants of livelihood diversification fall into two broad categories. The "coping" literature examines how farmers in low-potential and risky environments —those subject to drought, flooding, or environmental degradation—often adapt by deploying household resources to a range of farm and nonfarm activities.[37] The closely related discussions of household income "diversification" examine situations in which opportunities in the RNFE permit expansion of the range of household economic activities and thereby increase household welfare.[38]

PUSH FACTORS. The coping literature emerges from risky agricultural zones, mostly arid regions with irregular rainfall such as the West African Sahel and rain-fed areas of India.[39] It examines farm household behavior in physically or environmentally constrained production environments where agricultural output and prices vary wildly across years and where many household face land or labor constraints. In these risky environments, missing insurance and credit markets lead households to self-insure against risk through a variety of coping behaviors (Barrett, Reardon, and Webb 2001). In many cases, social organizations emerge to spread risks across households and regions (Rosenzweig and Stark 1989). At the same time, individual households frequently turn to nonfarm activity as a means of insuring families against crop failure.[40] But given the low-potential environments in which these responses typically emerge, the result often turns out to be distress diversification into low-return nonfarm activities, what Von Braun, Puetz, and Webb (1989) call diversification for "bad" reasons. Seasonal labor migration emerges in these circumstances as an important hedge against covariant rural risks.[41]

Case study evidence confirms that households in high-risk and low-potential agricultural environments routinely respond by turning to nonfarm activities. In Sri Lanka, high population density and acute population pressure drive poor rural households to seek over half their income off the family's own

---

36. See Bryceson (1996, 1999), Bryceson and Jamal (1997), Carney (1998), Ellis (1998, 2000), Barrett, Reardon, and Webb (2001), and Ellis and Freeman (2004).

37. See, for example, Reardon, Matlon, and Delgado (1988), Rosenzweig and Stark (1989), Agarwal (1990), Alderman and Paxson (1992), and Hart (1994).

38. See, for example, Barrett, Reardon, and Webb (2001), Bryceson (2002), and Barrett et al. (2004).

39. See, for example, Reardon, Matlon, and Delgado (1988), Bernstein, Crow, and Johnson (1992), Reardon and Taylor (1996), Bryceson and Jamal (1997), and Little et al. (2001).

40. See Von Braun and Pandya-Lorch (1991), Reardon, Delgado, and Matlon (1992), and Hart (1994).

41. Lucas and Stark (1985), de Haan (1999), de Haan and Rogaly (2002).

farm (Von Braun and Pandya-Lorch 1991). Farmers in the West African Sahel cope with their unpredictable agricultural environment by devoting significant resources to nonfarm commerce and labor migration to Ivory Coast (Reardon, Matlon, and Delgado 1988). Likewise, in northern Ghana women's rural non-farm activities prove important as a household strategy for coping with agricultural production shortfalls (Abdulai and Delgado 1999).

PULL FACTORS.   Many farm households in prosperous agricultural zones pursue opportunities for diversification into attractive nonfarm activities. In the wetter and more stable Sudanian agricultural zone of West Africa, farm households are more likely to diversify into local nonfarm activities. In contrast, the riskier Sahelian zones induce substantially greater dependence on labor migration to other zones (Reardon, Delgado, and Matlon, 1992). Indeed, evidence from a series of sites across Africa suggests that high-income farm households appear to be more able to diversify into high-return nonfarm activities requiring skilled labor, while poorer households depend on unskilled wage labor or low-return, labor-intensive nonfarm activities.[42] Wealthy households, when asked why they diversify, mention profit maximization while lower income households emphasize risk minimization (Bryceson 1997). Similarly, historical evidence from Japan furnishes evidence of wealthy farm households diversifying into subcontract weaving and commerce in textiles (Hayami 1998a). Better-off farmers, with necessary capital and skilled labor, appear generally best able to respond to the pull of profitable nonfarm opportunities in buoyant rural economies.

Assets and the Poor

The livelihood literature's focus on asset endowments and allocation by the poor offers several key insights into the role of rural nonfarm activity. By tracking capital and labor flows across activities, the livelihoods literature has provided considerable new evidence on factor market linkages between agriculture and nonagriculture. This analysis provides important extensions of the agricultural growth linkages discussions, which have focused principally on production and consumption linkages. Across a broad range of settings, studies of livelihood diversification have found substantial intrahousehold capital flows from nonfarm enterprises that households use to finance agricultural investment and input purchases.[43]

Moreover, the focus on assets held by poor households highlights important barriers to entry that often limit poor household participation in fast-growing, high-return nonfarm activity. Education frequently limits poor households' ac-

---

42. Freeman and Norcliffe (1985), Bryceson and Jamal (1997), Barrett et al. (2004).
43. See Lucas and Stark (1985), Evans and Ngau (1991), Von Braun and Pandya-Lorch (1991), Reardon, Delgado, and Matlon (1992), Hart (1994), and Ellis and Freeman (2004).

cess to the most lucrative nonfarm employment opportunities, while a shortage of financial capital prevents them from investing in transport, mechanical milling, and other high-return nonfarm business opportunities. Instead, the poor depend on low-return, unskilled, labor-intensive activities such as basket-making, weaving, and casual labor.[44] These results suggest that access to growing market segments may require improved skills training for the poor, a finding mirrored in some of the rural nonfarm employment literature (Lanjouw 1999; Lanjouw and Feder 2001).

Empirical Contributions

The household-based coping and diversification literature has contributed in several important ways to our understanding of rural nonfarm activities. The detailed micro data on which these studies are founded have helped document the income distribution consequences of rural nonfarm activity. They likewise provide important recent evidence on the dynamics of rural nonfarm activity and changes over time in varying environments and among different household groups. Chapter 6 explores this evidence in detail.

By emphasizing the distinction between favorable and unfavorable agronomic zones and between forces "pushing" and "pulling" farm households to enter nonfarm pursuits, the livelihood literature reinforces findings from the growth linkages and rural nonfarm employment literatures that underline the important dichotomy in the RNFE between promising high-return nonfarm opportunities and growth by default into laborious, low-paying, low-skilled nonfarm pursuits. Chapter 3 reviews this evidence to explore the equity impact of rural household diversification into nonfarm activity.

Regional Development: The Spatial Perspective

An eclectic contingent of social scientists has studied spatial features of rural economic growth in the developing world, in parallel with the other lines of investigation (Table 2.1). Two surges of interest in the geography of rural regions, the first in 1970s and the second beginning in 1990s, have largely mirrored the ebbs and flows of the growth linkages literature. Common inspiration, antecedents, and findings motivate a closely allied set of investigations.

Urban Growth Poles

Urban growth poles dominated spatial thinking in the 1950s and 1960s. The geographic counterpart to import-substituting industrialization, they promised that economic growth concentrated in a given location would spread to surrounding hinterlands through forward and backward production linkages. Most

---

44. Evans and Ngau (1991), Dercon and Krishnan (1996), Barrett, Reardon, and Webb (2001).

development planners invested their hopes in large-scale, urban-based manufacturing as the economic engine most likely to drive these growth poles. Prevailing wisdom held that spread effects would dominate over backwash effects and that the economic pulsations emanating from the growth pole would trickle down, spreading benefits of economic growth to surrounding regions.[45]

After several decades of urban-based industrial promotion, dissatisfaction with the resulting highly localized pockets of modern growth and the vast surrounding seas of rural poverty contributed to the urgency of the equity-focused rural reorientation of the 1970s.[46] The translation of interest from urban to rural areas triggered a wave of analytical and operational work in regional planning, much of it under the auspices of the United Nations Center for Regional Development in Nagoya, Japan.

Regional Development

The spatial reorientation, from urban to rural areas, arose quite naturally in the rural development decade of the 1970s. Because the bulk of the developing world's poor lived in rural areas, geographic dispersion of basic services was seen as central to efforts at promoting equity and alleviating poverty. Many likewise saw regional development itself as a contributor to rapid growth. As agriculture became recognized as a motor powerful enough to drive economic growth, supporting infrastructure, processing, marketing, credit, input supply, and related farm services became recognized as critical inputs necessary for lubricating that agricultural engine. A well-articulated network of rural markets, towns, and nonfarm support services became an important pillar supporting not only regional equity but also accelerated, agriculture-led economic growth.

Drawing on theoretical work in economic geography (see Chapter 8), a series of analytical and operational paradigms has explored these connections, first as part of integrated rural development efforts and subsequently under the banner of urban functions in rural development, rural-urban exchange, rural-urban linkages, and local economic development. While Chapter 12 reviews the operational work emanating from these efforts, the following discussion explores key ideas, analytical perspectives, and empirical contributions.

The first major effort to incorporate spatial dimensions in regional planning emerged during the integrated rural development (IRD) programs of the 1970s, which aimed to stimulate regional economic growth by providing a package of infrastructure and government services designed to simultaneously support agriculture, nonfarm businesses, and the growth of rural markets and towns.[47]

---

45. Perroux (1950, 1955), Myrdal (1957), Hirschmann (1958), Friedmann (1966, 1973), Berry (1967, 1970), Hansen (1981), Stohr and Taylor (1981).

46. For a critique of growth pole strategies, see Hansen (1967), Darwent (1969), Lo and Salih (1978), Richardson (1976, 1978), Meyer (1984), and Tacoli (1998).

47. Ruttan (1975, 1984), Holdcroft (1984), USAID (1987), World Bank (1987).

Now largely discredited,[48] for reasons described in Chapter 11, IRD projects represented the first widespread opportunity to apply regional planning in rural areas of the developing world.

Regional planners began splitting off from IRD efforts in the second half of the 1970s to pursue more focused efforts supporting rural development by targeting key missing infrastructure in rural towns. Led by Rondinelli and colleagues,[49] the urban functions in rural development (UFRD) model held sway for about a decade, until the mid-1980s. Empirically, this work involved cataloging the spatial location of key transport, processing, repair, communication, education, health, and administrative services in a given rural region.[50] Key gaps in the hierarchy of service centers would then signal opportunities for intervention, usually in the form of public investments in rural town infrastructure (Rondinelli 1987a). However, given mistrust of the mathematical scaling techniques used to evaluate settlement and service hierarchies and given a perception of arbitrariness in rankings and selection of missing services to fill, the regional planners encountered difficulty persuading decisionmakers to invest as the models recommended (Belsky and Karaska 1993).

As a result, the successor rural-urban exchange (RUE) model focused regional planning efforts still further.[51] Rather than evaluating all nonfarm services across an entire rural region, the model concentrates on rural-urban linkages (RUL) specific to the two or three most important primary commodities of a regional economy. Strongly influenced by the agricultural economics and growth linkages literatures, the RUE proponents examine spatial flows of a handful of the most important primary commodities in a given regional economy. By tracing the physical flows from farm to final consumer, they attempt to identify bottlenecks or inefficiencies in specific production-distribution systems. As with UFRD, these bottlenecks signal opportunities for intervention. But where the UFRD model evaluated the full cross-section of nonfarm services within a region, the RUL model focuses on services critical to the principal commodity supply chains.[52]

Beginning in the mid-1990s, a new wave of local economic development (LED) efforts has applied similar analytical tools to focus still further on promotional efforts by specific local government authorities. Drawing on business

---

48. See Tendler (1993) for a recent attempt to distill positive lessons from IRD projects in Northeast Brazil.

49. Rondinelli and Ruddle (1978), Rondinelli and Evans (1983), Rondinelli (1985).

50. See, for example, Wanmali (1983, 1988a), Evans (1986), and Rondinelli (1987b).

51. See Bromley (1983), Karaska and Belsky (1987), Bendavid-Val (1987), Antipolo (1989), Evans (1990), Belsky and Karaska (1993), Rondinelli (1993), and Tacoli (1998) for reviews of these shifting analytical frameworks.

52. Bendavid-Val (1987, 1989), Karaska and Belsky (1987), Bendavid-Val, Downing, and Karaska (1988), Evans, Cullen, and Little (1988), Evans (1990, 2001), Belsky and Karaska (1993), Rondinelli (1993).

school methods for evaluating competitive advantage and economic clusters of related firms,[53] they have developed and refined an assortment of closely related analytical tools—including participatory analysis of competitive advantage as well as subsector and cluster analysis—to aid in understanding competitive input supply relationships in key local supply chains.[54] By tracing commodity and service flows between farms, nonfarm service providers, and rural towns, supply chains become a vehicle for organizing spatial relationships. In the early years of the twenty-first century, proponents of RUL and LED are launching a new wave of locally focused efforts at promoting mutually beneficial interactions between rural areas and local towns.[55]

Rural Towns: Parasites or Promoters of Rural Development?

A crucial premise underlies much of the work on rural towns and regional economic development—that agricultural growth and the development of rural towns are mutually beneficial. According to advocates of both UFRD and RUL, agricultural growth stimulates demand for nonfarm goods and services, which are most economically supplied to dispersed farms from centralized locations in rural towns. In turn, the availability of these nonfarm inputs and support services —transport, credit, spare parts, repairs, extension—accelerates the diversification and growth of agriculture. Thus agriculture stimulates the growth of rural towns, and they in turn promote agricultural advance by facilitating information and commodity flows. The interaction is symbiotic and therefore mutually beneficial.[56]

Not everyone agrees. Many, in fact, take the opposite view. They see economic flows between farms and rural towns as one-way plumbing installed primarily to extract resources from rural areas. Thus the commodity, labor, and cash flows between agriculture and rural towns siphon the lifeblood from rural hinterlands, leaving them weakened, anemic, and impoverished.[57] According to this view, the "backwash" (Myrdal 1957) or "polarization" effect (Hirschman 1958) dominates, as towns drain rather than stimulate their surrounding catchment areas. Harriss and Harriss (1984), Hart (1989), and others advance similar arguments contesting the validity of the rosy scenario painted by proponents of the agricultural growth linkages model of rural growth.

Anthropologists who have studied spatial features of rural marketing systems offer a valuable perspective that helps mediate between these two polar-

---

53. See Porter (1985, 1998) and Chapter 15.

54. See Nel (1996), Dowds and Hinojosa (1999), Meyer-Stamer (2002), and Evans (2004).

55. See, for example, ILO, UNOPS, EURADA, Italian Cooperation (2000), Evans (2001, 2004), Helmsing (2001), Tacoli and Satterthwaite (2003), and UN-Habitat (2005).

56. Gibb (1974, 1984), Rondinelli (1983, 1987a,b), Karaska and Belsky (1987), Ranis (1989), Bagachwa and Stewart (1992), Evans (1992), UNDP/UNCHS (1995).

57. Lipton (1977), Schatzberg (1979), Southall (1982), Friedmann (1988).

opposite views.[58] They posit that the structure of rural marketing systems mirrors existing social relations. Thus in egalitarian settings, where land and income are evenly spread across households, markets tend to be evenly distributed over space, with considerable interaction and competition taking place. Because this structure results in competition within and between markets, no unfair bargaining leverage or surplus extraction results. But where great disparities in wealth lead to large plantation owners or traders controlling licenses, transport, and commodity flows to and from a given region, top-heavy marketing systems emerge. Called "primate" or "dendritic" systems, they feature many small rural markets supplied by a single large market that is in turn dominated by a wealthy trader or plantation owner. With limited competition and little interaction among rural markets, these monopsonistic systems facilitate resource transfers from farmers to towns.

Thus the parasitic view may be correct in the presence of great disparities in asset ownership and control. On the other hand, if egalitarian social and economic relations prevail, growth of agriculture and rural towns is likely to prove mutually beneficial.[59] This suggests that cities themselves are not intrinsically parasitic. Rather, the interests that control them may be.[60] Corroborating this view, some evidence suggests that changing social structures may, in fact, alter the relations between city and hinterland.[61] If so, the social signature represented by physical marketing networks may indeed be a useful diagnostic tool for distinguishing settings where rural-urban market relationships are likely to benefit both farmers and nonfarm businesses from regions where unequal exchange relationships might be expected to entrench control of local vested interests (Painter 1987b).

Government Decentralization

When rural development rises periodically to prominence, it invariably raises with it issues of local decisionmaking, financing, and operational control. During

---

58. See Smith (1976, 1977, 1984) and Painter (1987a,b) for a good introduction to this work and Berg (1992) for a discussion of the policy implications. The "real markets" literature, exemplified by writers such as De Alcantara (1993) and Crow (2001), offers a similar perspective. From urban studies, Tacoli (1998) and Tacoli and Satterthwaite (2003) offer a good discussion of evidence and issues affecting rural-urban exchange.

59. See, for example, Southall (1988).

60. A series of regional case studies corroborates the notion that commercial relationships between rural towns and surrounding farms reflect the prior underlying distribution of political and economic power (Hardoy and Satterthwaite 1986; Blitzer et al. 1988; Tacoli 1998; Tacoli and Satterthwaite 2003). While in general, according to Satterthwaite (2000, 3), "Many of the fastest growing cities were those in areas with the most rapid increase in the value of agricultural production," exceptions occurred wherever a few large landholders tightly controlled markets in the region. In this case, parasitic landholders constrained the development of rural towns. In both cases, the underlying structure of economic power affects spatial dynamics and distribution of gains from regional growth.

61. See Spodek (1975, 1986) and Preston (1978).

the 1970s, concern with rural poverty inspired a large concentration of work on various forms of decentralization (see, for example, Cheema and Rondinelli, 1983). Again at the dawn of the twenty-first century, rising concern with rural poverty has resurrected interest in local decisionmaking.[62] While Chapter 12 reviews the operational experience emerging from these efforts, discussion here focuses on a series of important analytical and empirical contributions.

Many of the nonfarm services required to facilitate rural economic growth are public goods such as roads, communications, power, water, education, and public health systems. So, not surprisingly, according to a series of regional case studies, growing government services frequently prove vital to the growth of rural towns (Rondinelli 1983; Hardoy and Satterthwaite 1986). This, in part, explains the large growth of service sector employment in growing rural regions as well as their frequent omission from private sector–focused rural nonfarm enterprises surveys.

Political and economic power relationships, emphasized in the livelihoods literature, resurface in discussions of government decentralization. Because local elites typically capture power in decentralized governments, decentralization often fails to remedy inequities within rural regions (Manor 1999). As a result, local resource mobilization may prove regressive rather than pro-poor (Ellis and Freeman 2004). Similar tension arises between local and central government authorities. While fiscal decentralization often proves necessary to empower local authorities and provide the resources they require to operate effectively, frequently cash-strapped central governments do not readily concede control of scarce fiscal resources.[63] For this reason, new generations of community-based rural development programs frequently rely on social investment funds allocated by community-based organizations (World Bank 2005). Clearly, distribution of control over economic resources and political power influences not only opportunities for local economic growth but also economic prospects for poor households in the region.

Empirical Contributions

Spatially oriented investigators have compiled a considerable volume of empirical evidence bearing on the geographic distribution,[64] nature, and magnitude of the RNFE as well as its relations with agriculture. They have contributed hundreds of case studies as well as statistical analysis of the relationship between

---

62. Litvack, Ahmad, and Bird (1998), Manor (1999), Tacoli and Satterthwaite (2003).

63. See Bahl, Miner, and Schroeder (1984), Bahl and Linn (1992), Bird and Vaillancourt (1998), and Tacoli (1998).

64. See Ancey (1974), Southall (1979), Freeman and Norcliffe (1985), Karaska and Belsky (1987), Evans (1990), Fafchamps and Shilpi (2003), and De Ferranti et al. (2006).

agricultural advance and the growth of surrounding small towns.[65] Important new consumption data have emerged from the rural-urban exchange surveys. These investigations have spatially tagged rural household expenditures and thus offer further evidence on the size of demand linkages from agriculture to nonfarm activities located in rural areas and rural towns.[66] Regional input-output tables and social accounting matrices constructed by the regional planners provide new evidence on the size of production and consumption linkages.[67] Important empirical work on local government finance in developing countries has contributed to our appreciation of local resource constraints as well as practical issues affecting the feasibility and scope of decentralized regional development efforts.[68]

Given their operational orientation, regional planners and colleagues have acquired considerable experience with the siting of rural and rural town infrastructure. Both the agricultural growth linkages and the rural nonfarm employment literatures hold as an article of faith that infrastructure matters, that strategic provision of facilities may be crucial in enabling growth linkages to achieve their full potential. As direct promotion of rural nonfarm activity becomes more widespread, practitioners are increasingly asking practical questions about sequencing, location, and targeting. The regional planners provide a source of experience and expertise to be tapped in those efforts.

Confluence and Feedbacks

Four strands of literature converge on the RNFE, each from a different perspective. Because they all focus on the same central essence, it is not surprising to find overlap, commonalities, and interactions. But differences inevitably arise as well given the diverse disciplinary and analytical perspectives. And both contribute to improved understanding of the RNFE. While consensus provides the building blocks of current conventional wisdom, disagreement motivates further exploration and investigation.

Commonalities

EQUITY MOTIVATION. Concern about equity has stimulated most investigations of the RNFE. The dramatic spotlight of the early 1970s on poverty and

---

65. See Wanmali (1983, 1987, 1988b), Gibb (1984), Mohan (1984), Ndua and Ngethe (1984), Rondinelli (1985, 1987b), Hardoy and Satterthwaite (1986), and Satterthwaite (2000).
66. See Bendavid-Val, Downing, and Karaska (1988), Evans, Cullen, and Little (1988), and Lewis and Thorbecke (1992).
67. Applegate and Badger (1979), Richardson (1985), Lewis (1988), Lewis and Thorbecke (1992), Thorbecke (1994), Parikh and Thorbecke (1996).
68. Bahl, Miner, and Schroeder (1984), Bahl and Linn (1992), Bird and Vaillancourt (1998).

rural development launched three of the four major streams of rural nonfarm investigation. Thirty years later, at the launch of the twenty-first century, resurging equity concerns have renewed broad-based interest in the RNFE. Because most of the developing world's poor continue to live in rural areas, where population pressure leads to growing land fragmentation, the importance of nonfarm opportunities will surely accelerate in coming decades. So the welfare of the rural poor will continue to attract policymakers to the RNFE.

STRAW MEN.   All branches of investigation initially responded to the same conventional wisdom. Hirschman's dismissal of agriculture as a low-linkage, underpowered engine of growth drew heavy fire from agriculturalists after the green revolution. Urban growth poles, the spatial analog of Hirshman's industry first strategy, aroused a similar welter of opposition from regional planners, who found the growth poles wanting as vehicles for stimulating rural growth.

Hymer and Resnick have been singled out for similar scrutiny. By pronouncing rural nonfarm products inferior, they incited a flurry of consternation. Negative consumption linkages would erode agriculture's claim as an engine of rural growth. Declining demand would cripple growth prospects for rural nonfarm employment and household income diversification. And it would largely undermine efforts to facilitate mutually beneficial rural-urban linkages. Because of the fundamental challenge they posed, Hymer and Resnick aroused legions to action. Few straw men have been so regularly and emphatically renounced. Still, their challenge proved valuable in stimulating empirical work on spending patterns and on the dynamics of rural nonfarm activity. Forcing policymakers to distinguish among the many distinct components of the highly heterogeneous RNFE, this empirical work has highlighted the differing trajectories of its various constituent elements. It suggests that while household-based cottage industries frequently face precarious futures, prospects for commercial and service enterprises often prove more buoyant.

MUTUAL BENEFIT CLAIM.   Most writing on the RNFE shares the same fundamental premise: that growth in rural nonfarm businesses, agriculture, and rural towns are mutually reinforcing, within households and across sectors. According to this mainstream view, agricultural income growth stimulates demand for rural nonfarm goods and services, many of which develop in rural towns. These services and their supporting spatial infrastructure, in turn, facilitate information and commodity flows, thereby accelerating both agricultural advance and the rural nonfarm response. Households that earn money in nonfarm pursuits often invest in agriculture and hence stimulate further rounds of rural growth.

Contrasts

NAYSAYERS.   In each branch of investigation, this good news scenario has attracted its doubters. Harriss (1987a,b), Hart (1989), and Ellis (2005) doubt that agriculture can effectively stimulate nonfarm activity in rural regions, Hart on the grounds that investment flows out of the region signal lack of profitable nonfarm investment, Harris on the grounds that demand linkages are more likely to favor imports than locally produced nonfarm manufactures, and Ellis on the grounds that diversification into nonfarm activity frequently signals sluggish rather than stellar agricultural growth. Others doubt the economic desirability of teeming throngs of small-scale, labor-intensive nonfarm businesses. Klein and Tokman (2000) see workers in small household businesses, instead, as a reserve army of underemployed labor enabling larger private firms to circumvent minimum wage laws and social legislation. Little, Mazumdar, and Page (1987) question the economic efficiency of small enterprises, while Snodgrass and Biggs (1996) and Hallberg (2001) contend that large populations of small firms stem primarily from market imperfections rather than from any intrinsic economic efficiency. Lipton (1977) and Southall (1988) doubt that rural towns will necessarily stimulate growth in their hinterlands, particularly in situations where unequal exchange relationships allow urban dwellers to siphon surpluses and impoverish the countryside.

All examine the same empirical evidence. Everyone sees transporters, grain dealers, and barbers operating from rural towns. Yet various camps interpret the available evidence very differently. Where the believers see transporter margins that reflect fuel and vehicle depreciation costs, the doubters see unscrupulous monopolists overcharging rural citizens with no locomotion of their own. Where the believers see grain merchants in town who stabilize seasonal prices, support transport costs, and incur storage losses, the doubters see wealthy sharpsters lowballing farm-gate prices to desperate farmers with no alternative outlet. Where the believers see rural barbers springing up to meet growing demand from prosperous yeoman farmers, the doubters see price-gouging businessmen overcharging powerless peasants, perhaps by announcing prices during the shave!

GEOGRAPHIC DIVERSITY. As these caricatures suggest, each view contains an element of truth. In different settings, one will be closer to the mark than the other. In rural Latin America, where a single hacienda owner may control all transport and distribution in his regional fiefdom, new maize varieties for peasant farmers will disproportionately boost income of the nonfarm monopsonist who markets the produce and supplies imported consumer goods. Yet in rural Taiwan, with its even distribution of land, well-developed rural transportation network, and competitive rural markets, new rice varieties will yield greater returns to farmers and a more equitable distribution of the productivity gains with nonfarm business operators. As the doubters point out and the livelihoods literature emphasizes, the initial distribution of assets and of political power strongly influences prospects for rural nonfarm growth that is beneficial to the poor.

HETEROGENEITY. While regional planners have emphasized the importance of services and commercial activity, many rural nonfarm employment specialists have concentrated primarily on manufacturing. Meanwhile, the livelihoods literature and broad nonfarm surveys have cataloged the enormous heterogeneity of the RNFE. Gradual recognition of this diversity has proven key to resolving debates about prospects for rural nonfarm growth. The uncertain future for labor-intensive, low-return cottage industries contrasts starkly with the buoyancy and high returns of more capital- and skill-using nonfarm pursuits in agroprocessing, transport, and services. The great challenge for equity-motivated policymakers is to find ways that poor households can participate in the buoyant, high-return segments of the RNFE.

Future Interaction

Two millennia ago, all roads led to Rome. Today, a great many analytical roads similarly converge in the RNFE. As a result, policymakers and observers have traversed the rural landscape from many different directions. The resulting diversity of perceptions and experience has contributed to our understanding of different facets of the RNFE and how it functions across a broad range of settings. At the same time, the diversity of analytical perspectives has inspired debate, spurring a welter of empirical investigation. The resulting intersection of interest and evidence has laid the empirical foundations that enable us, in coming chapters of this book, to evaluate the scale, structure, and growth potential of the many different segments of the RNFE. Following a detailed examination of the evidence in Parts I, II, and III of this book, Part IV concludes by summarizing key findings and suggesting areas in which collaboration and investigation will prove most fruitful. As the third millennium begins and interest in the RNFE resurges, continued interaction across disciplines, continents, and analytical perspectives can only improve prospects for enhancing policymakers' recognition of the circumstances in which rural nonfarm activity can contribute to improvements in rural equity and growth.

3 Does the Rural Nonfarm Economy Contribute to Poverty Reduction?

PETER LANJOUW

Equity concerns have motivated much of the current policy interest in the rural nonfarm economy (RNFE). Given its large size, and given growing pressure on farmland in many developing country settings, the RNFE emerges as a potentially significant alternate employer for members of landless households. Moreover, given frequently small firm sizes and the modest capital equipment employed by many, policymakers presume that the RNFE will prove accessible to the rural poor. This chapter reviews a broad range of available evidence in order to assess the potential poverty-reducing impact of the RNFE. Few dispute that the nonfarm sector represents a significant part of the rural economy in most countries of the developing world.[1] And in many countries, it appears to be growing over time.[2] To what extent, then, do the poor benefit from the RNFE and from the changes currently under way?

Simple stories about growth in the nonfarm sector driving down rural poverty typically do not survive close scrutiny. In some countries, such as China, rural poverty has been declining alongside a growing nonfarm sector (see Ravallion and Chen 2004). But this does not necessarily mean that the nonfarm sector was responsible for lifting the poor above the poverty line. The direction of causality could well have been in the opposite direction. It is also possible

I am grateful to Steven Haggblade for helpful advice and guidance in the preparation of this chapter. The views presented here are my own and should not be taken to reflect those of the World Bank or any affiliated institution. I am responsible for all errors.

1. In addition to the general review provided in Chapter 1, see Reardon, Berdegué, and Escobar (2001) for recent evidence on the size of the nonfarm sector in Latin America; Liedholm et al. (1994), Reardon (1997), and Ellis and Freeman (2004) for evidence from Africa; and Visaria and Basant (1993), Rosegrant and Hazell (2000), Foster and Rosenzweig (2004), and Kijima and Lanjouw (2005) for profiles from Asia.

2. Lanjouw and Lanjouw (2001), Reardon, Berdegué, and Escobar (2001), and Hazell, Haggblade, and Reardon (2002) provide recent surveys of the literature and document its rapid expansion in recent years. Lanjouw and Feder (2001) analyze the rationale for public intervention as well as available options.

that both poverty and the nonfarm sector were driven by third forces, such as migration patterns or technological change in agriculture.[3]

In other parts of the world, poverty and the nonfarm sector have not necessarily moved in parallel. In some countries, poverty may have been stagnant or even rising while the nonfarm sector has expanded. Here, too, we cannot draw simple conclusions. While the growing nonfarm sector may not be driving down poverty, it is quite possible that poverty would have risen markedly had the nonfarm economy not expanded. Population growth, leading to declining per capita landholdings and to environmental degradation, could be a powerful force raising poverty if offsetting factors such as an expanding nonfarm sector or growing agricultural productivity were not present. Again, the relationship between poverty and the nonfarm sector may be more subtle than initial impressions would suggest.

This chapter examines recent evidence of the relationship between rural poverty and the nonfarm economy. It starts, in the next section, with a brief review of the patterns of rural poverty in developing countries. The following section considers some categorizations of the types of nonfarm activities observed across the developing world and examines the principal routes through which the nonfarm sector could be expected to influence living standards of the poor. It asks to what extent the poor are able to participate in those activities most likely to raise their living standards. Discussion highlights the specific role played by nonfarm employment generation programs in alleviating poverty, emphasizing the need to consider the indirect effects of the nonfarm sector on rural living standards. The chapter then moves on to examine empirical evidence from a variety of developing countries in an attempt to quantify magnitudes of the transmission mechanisms highlighted in the previous section. In an attempt to provide a measure of coherence to the empirical story, most of the evidence presented refers to the specific case of rural India. However, the discussion attempts to complement this evidence with findings from other countries. The chapter emphasizes that while there is a large and growing literature on the relationship between poverty and the nonfarm economy, studies that are able to rigorously demonstrate the causal impact on poverty of involvement in the nonfarm economy remain rare. The chapter concludes by summarizing the policy implications of these findings.

A Profile of Rural Poverty

During the past two decades, the analysis of poverty has become a mainstream activity in many development and academic institutions. The literature on the

---

3. Indeed, Ravallion and Chen (2004) argue that agriculture growth played a more important role in explaining the decline in rural poverty in China during the past two decades than did expansion of the secondary or tertiary sector.

scale and dimensions of the global poverty challenge has grown rapidly during this time and has periodically been summarized in a variety of academic studies as well as policy reports such as the World Bank's World Development Reports, the United Nations Development Program's Human Development Reports, International Fund for Agricultural Development's Rural Poverty Report, and the Oxfam Poverty Report.[4] From this literature and experience a number of stylized facts about rural poverty have emerged, many of which help us assess the relationship between rural poverty and the nonfarm economy. It is clear, for example, that the dimensions of rural poverty and characteristics of the rural poor vary significantly across countries. And these specific features of rural poverty have a strong bearing on how the nonfarm sector can influence rural poverty. A starting point in any investigation of how the RNFE might help to reduce poverty is to first understand the nature of the rural poverty problem.

POVERTY AND ACCESS TO LAND. Discussions about the impact of the nonfarm sector on poverty often implicitly assume that the poor are those with little or no land. In some parts of the world, notably in parts of Sub-Saharan Africa, this is not necessarily the case. The poor often include cultivating households that face constraints not so much in terms of access to land, but in terms of other important inputs or in terms of access to key infrastructure services or markets. For such households, the best strategy to escape poverty is to raise the productivity and profitability of their land. For them, the extent to which the nonfarm sector can contribute to this is of greatest importance. Even in countries where the poor are in general those with small or no landholdings, it is not necessarily the case that all landless households can be thought of as poor. Indeed, it is precisely because of the expansion of the nonfarm sector in many rural economies that the correlation between landlessness and poverty is often fairly weak. Many studies have documented that poverty rates among the landless in rural areas are often lower than among marginal landowners or other rural population subgroups (de Janvry et al. 2001). For example, in Ecuador, Lanjouw (1999) documents a 69 percent incidence of poverty among the rural landless compared to an overall rural poverty rate of 76 percent. Similarly, in the Indian state of Tamil Nadu during the decade of the 1990s, Jayarman, Kijima, and Lanjouw (2003) document a persistently lower incidence of poverty among the landless than among the rural population as a whole.

POVERTY AND AGRICULTURAL WAGE EMPLOYMENT. A fairly robust stylized fact about rural poverty in many parts of the developing world is that the poor are highly represented among agricultural wage laborers. Unskilled labor is often the only asset the poor can depend on in efforts to raise their living standards. Agricultural wage labor, particularly casual, daily-wage employment,

---

4. Lipton and Ravallion (1995) provide a valuable academic contribution in Volume 3 of their *Handbook of Development Economics*.

is seen in many places as an occupation of last resort. Remuneration is typically low, the work is physically demanding, employment is prone to significant seasonal variation, and it can be associated with a lack of social status. A key question concerning the impact of the nonfarm sector on poverty thus centers on whether, and to what degree, labor is shifting out of the agricultural sector and into the nonfarm sector.

POVERTY AND EDUCATION.   Throughout the developing world, the rural poor are typically highly represented among those with little or no education. Despite steady progress in recent years in raising enrollment rates among children in many parts of the developing world, adult education levels are often still very low. For example, in 1999 illiteracy rates among adult males in South Asia (excluding Sri Lanka) ranged from a high of 48 percent in Bangladesh to a far from negligible 28 percent in India. Among adult women, low education levels are even more widespread. Fully 77 percent of women in Nepal were illiterate in 1999, 71 percent in Bangladesh, 70 percent in Pakistan, and 56 percent in India (Drèze and Sen 2002).[5] Poverty rates among households with poorly educated household heads are commensurately high. In Guatemala, with an overall illiteracy rate of 31 percent, illiteracy rises to 46 percent among the poor and falls to as low as 17 percent among the non-poor (World Bank 2004). Such patterns are widely repeated throughout the developing world.

THE SPATIAL DISTRIBUTION OF RURAL POVERTY.   Demombynes et al. (2004) demonstrate, on the basis of poverty maps produced through the combination of household survey and population census data, that highly disaggregated geographic profiles of poverty typically reveal great heterogeneity in poverty rates across localities. The poorest localities in rural areas are usually found in remote areas. World Bank (2004) documents, on the basis of a poverty map for Guatemala, that communities located along the main road networks are generally less poor than those located some distance away. Similarly, in rural Northeast Brazil, for example, Ferreira and Lanjouw (2001) document a head-count poverty rate of 52 percent in remote rural areas compared to 46 percent in small rural communities and 16 percent in periurban areas.[6] Similarly, Lanjouw (1999) indicates that in rural Ecuador poverty rates in the "dispersed" rural areas are markedly higher than in those areas with a modicum of infrastructure.

POVERTY AND SOCIAL STRATIFICATION.   In many countries, the poor are disproportionately represented among certain population groups, defined in terms

---

5. World Bank data suggest that in 2002 the low-income countries combined had an overall illiteracy rate of 28 percent among adult males and of 47 percent among females (World Development Indicators 2004).

6. Population densities are also typically low in remote areas, so the higher poverty rates do not necessarily translate into larger numbers of poor people.

of ethnicity, nationality, race, caste, or other related characteristics. Such groups may face specific constraints in participating in the nonfarm sector. In India, the high incidence of poverty among scheduled castes (SCs) and scheduled tribes (STs) has long been recognized.[7] Similarly, in Vietnam ethnic minorities tend to be concentrated in remote areas and to have lower living standards than the ethnic majority (Van de Walle and Gunewardena 2001). In South Africa, poverty is highly concentrated among the African population (Hoogeveen and Özler 2004), and similar patterns are observed for the black and indigenous population in Brazil (Ferreira, Lanjouw, and Neri 2003). Similarly, the World Bank (2004) documents dramatically higher levels of poverty among the indigenous population in Guatemala than in the population as a whole.

POVERTY AND GENDER. Conventional methods for analyzing poverty are not always very well suited to the task of comparing poverty levels between men and women. It is common to measure economic well-being in terms of per capita household income or consumption, and this effectively assumes equal sharing of incomes within households. Studies that probe this assumption, however, generally fail to find much evidence in support of equal sharing. Other studies attempt to distinguish between male-headed and female-headed households. For example, Drèze and Srinivasan (1997) study the relative poverty of widow-headed households in rural India and argue that poverty rates among this particular group of households is markedly higher than for the general population. In general, it is accepted that analysis of poverty in rural areas should take note of the particularly vulnerable position of women in many parts of the developing world.

The previous discussion highlights an important point, namely, that the conceptualization and measurement of poverty is far from standardized. Conclusions about the impact of the RNFE on poverty are often directly related to the particular method employed to measure poverty. A classic example concerns the distinction between relative and absolute poverty. If expansion of the nonfarm sector is associated with widening inequality, it could well be that even though the poor saw a rise in their incomes as a result of nonfarm employment, their relative position had fallen vis-à-vis the non-poor. Thus in relative (but not absolute) terms, their poverty had risen. It is important to verify to what extent conclusions are robust to alternative poverty measures.

---

7. In India, the disadvantaged position of SCs and STs has resulted in the institution of a range of policies of affirmative action in terms of public employment or access to certain public services, and it may have helped to secure greater participation of SCs and STs in the nonfarm sector than would otherwise have been the case. Pande (2003) analyzes the impact of reservation in political representation in India and finds that this has increased transfers to minority groups.

Analytical Links between Rural Nonfarm Income and Poverty

The Heterogeneity of Rural Nonfarm Earnings

There is extensive documentation of the great heterogeneity of nonfarm activities in developing countries (see Tables 1.2 and 1.3). It is thus important to refrain from viewing that sector as a uniform, homogenous set of activities and to recognize that the sector is essentially defined only in terms of what it is not: agricultural. From the perspective of understanding the relationship between poverty and nonfarm activities, it is sometimes helpful to classify nonfarm activities into different categories and to focus on the differences between such categories.

HIGH- AND LOW-RETURN ACTIVITIES.   The heterogeneity of nonfarm activities is clearly manifested in the wide divergence of returns across occupations in the nonfarm sector. Because unskilled labor is the one asset most poor households possess, and because many turn to nonfarm activity because of a shortage of land and financial capital, returns to labor in nonfarm activities become a crucial determinant of its potential contribution to poverty reduction.

Returns to labor vary markedly across nonfarm activities. Ibrahim (1997) documents returns to labor in rural nonfarm activities in Darfur, Sudan, that range from a low of 10 to 25 Sudanese pounds per day from a variety of cottage manufacturing activities (potmaking, carpet weaving, tabagmaking) to 150 to 180 pounds per day from shoemaking and service sector employment in blacksmithing and construction (see Table 1.4). Similarly, Hossain (1984) documents a sixfold difference in value added per worker in rural Bangladesh across occupations such as coir rope and mat making on the one hand and activities such as tailoring, dairying, and sugar processing on the other (see Table 6.2).

Employment in different types of nonfarm activities is not uniform across the population. Hossain (1984) documents far higher rates of employment of rural Bangladeshi women in those occupations and cottage industries where value added per worker is low. Lanjouw and Stern (1998) show evidence from a detailed village study in North India that, while the relatively highly paid nonfarm jobs only sometimes require special skills and levels of education, employment in such jobs is concentrated among those villagers with more years of schooling, who come from the high-ranked castes and have significant networks of contacts outside the village.

A FEASIBLE THREE-WAY BREAKDOWN.   Available survey data are rarely able to effectively capture returns to labor from nonfarm activities in rural areas. Most such jobs occur in the informal sector. Many are seasonal and may not be full time. Earnings often accrue via piece-rate contracts rather than fixed wages or derive from self-employment rather than wage employment. It is difficult, therefore, to unambiguously classify specific jobs as high- or low-return occupations. However, available data do usually provide some kind of functional classification that permits an exploration of the poverty-reducing impact of different return segments of the rural nonfarm economy.

One particularly useful way of breaking down nonfarm activity is to partition it into three subgroups: casual nonfarm wage employment, self-employment or home-enterprise activities, and regular, salaried employment. It is generally instructive to consider whether households involved in the nonfarm sector have been "pushed" into such activities due to a lack of alternative options in agriculture or whether they have been "pulled" away from their original occupations into this sector as a result of the higher incomes offered. Remuneration levels in casual, nonfarm wage employment are generally low. It is common for such activities to involve strenuous physical work: in the case of construction, for example, pulling rickshaws or portering. Often the work is associated with significant health risks, such as exposure to pollution or chemicals. Participation in this subsector may thus often be the consequence of push factors, and one would consequently not expect poverty levels in this subsector to be particularly low.

Self-employment and own-account activities represent the second category of participation in the nonfarm sector. Here one is likely to observe residual, last-resort, "push" activities such as small-scale retailing, but also high-return, sophisticated enterprises such as private medical practices or small factories connected via subcontracting links to urban-based, export-oriented firms. The distribution of returns in this sector is thus likely to be widely spread, but once again there should be no presumption that nonfarm self-employment activities are necessarily associated with high incomes.

High and stable incomes are more commonly associated with regular, salaried employment in the nonfarm sector. It is not always fully appreciated that in many developing countries public sector employment in health, education, administration, railways, policing, and so on is quite significant, even in rural areas. Fisher, Mahajan, and Singha (1997) note that almost 20 percent of total nonfarm employment in rural India was generated by public sector services. There are also many larger, formal sector, nonfarm enterprises located in rural areas (e.g., mining, energy, manufacturing) that are able to offer employment on a noncasual, long-term basis. Regular employment of this type is typically widely sought in rural areas. It is attractive not only for the relatively high incomes associated with such employment, but also for the stability of these incomes over time.

Figure 3.1 depicts how incomes from these three categories of nonfarm employment are distributed in the Indian state of Tamil Nadu; it is based on National Council for Applied Economic Research (NCAER) survey data from 1993–94 (Jayaraman, Kijima, and Lanjouw 2003; Lanjouw and Shariff 2004). From this figure it can be readily observed that incomes from casual wage employment are spread narrowly around a relatively low average income level. Nonfarm self-employment earnings are somewhat higher on average than earnings from the other forms of nonfarm employment measured and have a rather fat positive tail, indicating some occurrence of high incomes. This observation

FIGURE 3.1   Probability density function of nonfarm incomes in Tamil Nadu, 2003

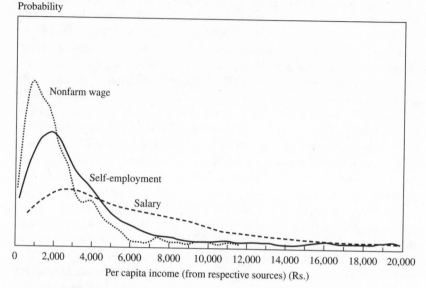

Probability

0   2,000   4,000   6,000   8,000   10,000   12,000   14,000   16,000   18,000   20,000

Per capita income (from respective sources) (Rs.)

SOURCE: Jayaraman, Kijima, and Lanjouw (2003).

is even more pronounced in the case of salaried nonfarm income. Here earnings are higher, on average, than from casual and self-employment activities, the result of a high frequency of households reporting particularly high nonfarm salaried incomes.

Other methods that can assist us in the interpretation of the relationship between poverty and the nonfarm sector include distinguishing between permanent and seasonal nonfarm occupations, between formal and informal sector occupations, between skilled and unskilled occupations, and between broad industrial and occupational classifications. What becomes clear from such exercises is that the poor are highly concentrated in some categories and figure hardly at all in others. We shall look further at how one should interpret such patterns later.

Mechanisms for Transmission from the Nonfarm Sector to Poverty Alleviation

In thinking about the contribution the nonfarm sector can make to reducing poverty, it is useful to consider possible transmission mechanisms. An obvious first step is to ask whether the poor directly participate in the nonfarm sector. Taking into account the heterogeneity of the nonfarm sector, in particular that some activities are considerably more remunerative than others, one can ask whether the poor face any obvious impediments to participation in those subsectors that are the most likely routes to upward mobility. Are the poor excluded because they lack required skills and education? Are nonfarm activities concentrated in locations where the poor are not highly represented? Do the poor lack access to information and important networks of contacts due, perhaps, to their social status or gender? Are they excluded because they lack the wealth necessary to pay bribes or otherwise secure favorable treatment? The essential question is whether those subsectors of the nonfarm economy that can be expected to function as "pull" mechanisms do in fact serve as a source of upward mobility for the poor.

A second line of transmission from the nonfarm sector to poverty alleviation can be gauged through an assessment of how well the nonfarm sector operates as a safety net for the poor segments of the population that are "pushed" out of their traditional occupation. Droughts and other natural calamities are all-too-frequent occurrences in many parts of the developing world and can spell catastrophe for populations in affected areas. Such events are often associated with a widespread collapse of agriculture and related activities, compelling households to look to the nonfarm sector for alternative income sources. Even in less stark circumstances associated with more idiosyncratic events such as illness, injury, or some other household-specific occurrence, individual households may find themselves in need of an alternative to cultivation or agricultural labor as a source of income. When households are pushed out of the agricultural sector in such circumstances, they often run the real risk of falling into poverty or seeing their current poverty level deepen markedly. The availability of nonfarm employment opportunities, even those not associated with high incomes, can thus be very important in preventing incomes from declining further. Such nonfarm opportunities function as a safety net in preventing household incomes from falling rather than contributing in a significant way to raising incomes. Forming an overall assessment of the contribution of the nonfarm sector to poverty alleviation requires that this safety net feature of the sector be given due attention.

A third line of transmission is through indirect channels. Given the profile of poverty briefly described earlier, and the empirical evidence further presented later, it is clear that the poor often have only limited direct involvement in the nonfarm sector. Yet general equilibrium linkages between the nonfarm and the agricultural sectors can still imply that growth in the nonfarm sector translates into rising incomes of the poor in the agricultural sector. For example, rising nonfarm incomes (among the non-poor) could lead to rising demand for agricultural products produced by (poor) farmers. Similarly, nonfarm incomes could finance new investments in agriculture, leading to a rise in demand for agricultural labor. Likewise, expansion of the nonfarm sector could lead to tightening of the agricultural labor market and therefore to rising agricultural wages. Empirical evidence is often difficult to obtain, but in the final analysis it may well be that the greatest contribution of the nonfarm sector to poverty comes via such indirect channels.

Empirical Evidence

Rural Nonfarm Earnings as a Route Out of Poverty

CROSS-SECTION EVIDENCE.   Evidence from cross-sectional data on the overall incidence of nonfarm earnings across the welfare distribution is mixed.[8] Table 3.1 shows that in rural India, for example, nonfarm incomes account for about 30 to 40 percent of total income in all rural income quintiles. In rural Ecuador, however, overall nonfarm income shares rise markedly with consumption quintile. In the poorest quintile, only about 22 percent of income comes from nonfarm sources, while in the top quintile nearly two-thirds of income comes from nonfarm sources. In contrast, in central Kenya nonfarm earnings accrue largely to those in the lowest income groups.

These contrasting patterns arise because of the heterogeneity of rural nonfarm activities. Table 3.2, panels a and b, look within the nonfarm sector in India and Ecuador, respectively, to distinguish which nonfarm activities are associated with the highest incomes. In rural Ecuador, for example, enterprise income is very strongly correlated with consumption quintiles, while labor incomes are more evenly distributed across quintiles. The relatively even distribution of labor income likely arises, at least in part, from the failure to separate casual from regular employment earnings. In India it can be clearly seen that while self-employment and home enterprise activities are fairly evenly distributed over the income distribution, nonfarm casual labor incomes accrue mainly to those in the lowest quintiles, while regular nonfarm incomes accrue mainly to the rich. At the all-India level, the pattern observed is quite similar to that presented in Figure 3.1 for Tamil Nadu.

In many countries, the probability of being poor is appreciably lower among households that partake in certain categories of nonfarm activity, particularly white-collar nonfarm wage employment. In these cases, the inverse association that may arise between poverty and nonfarm incomes sometimes serves as a foundation for the argument that expansion of the nonfarm sector can have an important beneficial impact on poverty. For that position to be justified, however, there must clearly be an expectation that the poor can partici-

---

8. See, for example, reviews by Haggblade, Hazell, and Brown (1989), Bagacha and Stewart (1992), Reardon (1997), the FAO (1998), Barrett, Reardon, and Webb (2001), Lanjouw and Lanjouw (2001), and Reardon et al. (2001), as well as country-specific evidence for Egypt and Jordan in Adams (1999, 2000); for Pakistan in Adams and He (1995); for Vietnam in Van de Walle and Cratty (2003); for periurban Tanzania from Lanjouw, Quizon, and Sparrow (2001); and for four different African countries in Ellis and Freeman (2004).

TABLE 3.1 The equity impact of rural nonfarm income (percent)

| | Rural nonfarm income as a share of total income | | | | | |
| | Equity-enhancing | | Neutral | | Inequitable | |
Quintile[a]	Kenya 1975	Pakistan 1989	India 1999	Ethiopia 1990	Ecuador 1995	Vietnam 1997
Poorest	82	75	32	32	22	40
Q2	80	63	39	—	37	42
Q3	45	36	38	30	37	50
Q4	40	33	39	—	46	60
Highest	—	21	31	31	64	82

SOURCES: FAO (1998), Lanjouw (1999), Lanjouw and Shariff (2004).

NOTE: A dash indicates that data are not available.

[a]Kenya data are provided by quartile, Ethiopian data by tercile.

pate in an expansion of the nonfarm sector, that there are no important factors that serve to prevent their involvement in the RNFE.

TIME-SERIES EVIDENCE. A recent paper on the role of the nonfarm sector in the reduction of poverty in Vietnam analyzes detailed panel data between 1992–93 and 1997–98 to inquire into the ability of the poor to participate in the rapid diversification taking place in rural Vietnam (Van de Walle and Cratty 2003). The study finds that ethnic minority groups in Vietnam are more likely to be poor than the majority population and are also less likely to become employed in the expanding nonfarm sector. Similarly, those with higher education levels are less likely to be poor and more likely to become involved in nonfarm activities. Location also appears to play an important role in determining where nonfarm activities proliferate, and it is far from obvious that this coincides with those areas where poverty is concentrated. The authors argue, on the basis of the evidence they analyze, that the emerging rural nonfarm sector in Vietnam is unlikely to serve as the main route out of poverty for many of Vietnam's poor.

Panel data are a particularly valuable information source on participation of the poor in the nonfarm sector and the contribution of nonfarm employment to poverty reduction. Such data allow one to examine whether, and to what extent, poor persons in an initial period obtain access to nonfarm opportunities and then see their incomes rise as a consequence. Unfortunately, panel data remain relatively scarce, and analyses of the type described earlier are still quite rare.[9]

NONFARM EMPLOYMENT PROBABILITIES. Nationally representative data for a single cross-section of the population, on the other hand, are available in

---

9. See Hossain (2004) for a welcome exception to this rule.

TABLE 3.2a Sources of income in rural India by per capita income quintile, 1993–94 (percent)

| Quintile | Agriculture | | Nonfarm income | | | | | Real per capita income (rupees) |
	Cultivation	Agriculture wage labor	Wage labor	Self-employment	Regular employment	Total nonfarm employment	Other	Total	
Lowest	38.2	28.2	15.8	11.4	4.4	31.6	2.0	100	1,146
Q2	38.0	21.3	14.7	16.8	7.0	38.5	2.3	100	2,113
Q3	45.2	13.4	10.1	16.3	11.7	38.1	3.2	100	3,141
Q4	50.1	7.5	6.1	14.6	18.6	39.3	3.2	100	4,712
Highest	64.5	2.1	2.0	7.9	21.1	30.9	2.5	100	11,226
Total	54.9	8.0	5.9	11.5	17.1	34.4	2.7	100	4,468

SOURCE: Lanjouw and Shariff (2004).

TABLE 3.2b Sources of income in rural Ecuador by expenditure quintile, 1999 (percent)

	Agriculture		Nonfarm				
Quintile	Own farm	Labor	Labor	Enterprise	Total	Other	Total
Poorest	69	6	6	16	22	3	100
Q2	46	13	11	26	37	4	100
Q3	46	14	9	28	37	3	100
Q4	41	8	9	37	46	5	100
Q5	27	6	12	52	64	3	100

SOURCE: Lanjouw (1999).

a growing number of developing countries. Such data provide a valuable "snapshot" of living conditions during a specific period of time and can be used also to examine the size of and participation in the nonfarm sector at that time. A number of studies have analyzed cross-sectional data to assess the probability of employment in the nonfarm sector for different segments of the population. They have often employed multivariate regression techniques to determine the contribution of various household and individual characteristics to the probability of nonfarm employment, controlling for other characteristics. Such studies have, for example, allowed researchers to discover whether a person of a given ethnic group is more or less likely to be employed in the nonfarm sector, holding constant education levels, landholdings, and other characteristics.

An example of such cross-sectional analysis is presented for the case of rural India in Table 3.3. The relationship between occupational choice of adult males and household characteristics is explored for rural India using a multinomial logit model of occupational choice.[10] The analysis considers seven broad occupations in rural areas: agricultural casual wage employment, regular farm employment, cultivation, nonfarm regular employment, nonfarm casual wage (daily-wage) employment, nonfarm own-enterprise activities, and other (plus nonworking) activities.[11] "Explanatory" variables include a selection of individual and household characteristics. At the individual level we consider the age, educational status, and caste or religious status of each person. At the household level, we have information on the size of the household to which each person belongs and the household's per capita landholding. On the one hand, landholding might capture the extent to which a household is committed

---

10. See Greene (1993) for an exposition of this model.

11. In this analysis we concentrate on the reported *principal* occupation of males and, as a result, are unable to consider the set of issues associated with combining farm activities with nonfarm activities during the course of, say, an agricultural year (with its associated peak and slack seasons).

TABLE 3.3 Occupational choice in rural India, 1999

	Not working	Cultivator	Nonfarm regular worker	Nonfarm casual worker	Nonfarm self-employed worker	Farm regular worker
Age	-0.706	0.008	0.086	0.044	0.070	0.040
	(-95.46)	(1.60)	(9.90)	(6.10)	(11.40)	(2.40)
Age squared	0.009	0.000	0.000	-0.001	-0.001	0.000
	(91.10)	(3.70)	(-3.95)	(-7.91)	(-8.06)	(-2.03)
Literate but below primary school level	0.444	0.322	1.096	0.493	0.646	0.181
	(8.3)	(10.7)	(16.1)	(12.1)	(17.4)	(1.8)
Primary school completed	1.164	0.615	1.815	0.794	0.992	0.385
	(25.2)	(19.7)	(28.6)	(19.4)	(26.1)	(3.8)
Middle school completed	2.094	0.911	2.649	0.932	1.353	0.114
	(50.2)	(30.0)	(46.1)	(23.0)	(37.0)	(1.0)
Secondary school completed	3.429	1.331	3.846	0.950	1.916	0.710
	(72.7)	(35.8)	(65.8)	(18.2)	(45.2)	(6.1)

University completed	4.665	1.556	5.346	0.630	2.629	1.130
	(44.2)	(15.7)	(51.0)	(3.8)	(25.8)	(4.3)
SC or ST	−0.372	−0.770	−0.459	−0.107	−0.825	−0.482
	(−12.38)	(−35.46)	(−12.47)	(−3.63)	(−29.21)	(−6.70)
Muslim	0.292	−0.308	0.236	0.374	0.655	−0.636
	(6.60)	(−8.75)	(4.20)	(8.50)	(18.40)	(−4.52)
Number of household members	0.092	0.143	0.028	0.012	0.084	0.420
	(23.4)	(45.6)	(5.6)	(2.6)	(22.5)	(3.9)
Per capita amount of land owned (ha)	4.360	5.930	2.873	−1.781	0.691	1.496
	(47.6)	(71.1)	(25.0)	(10.9)	(6.0)	(5.3)
Constant	7.974	−2.154	−5.907	−1.962	−3.324	−4.202
	(70.20)	(−24.08)	(−35.72)	(−15.66)	(−29.44)	(−13.56)

Number of observations	95,553
Log likelihood	−124,882
Pseudo-R^2	0.216

SOURCE: Kijima and Lanjouw (2005).

NOTE: A multinomial logit model is used. The numbers in parentheses are z-values.

to agriculture and cultivation, and in this sense one might expect a negative relationship between nonfarm employment and landholdings. On the other hand, per capita landholdings might proxy wealth and contacts, thereby providing some indication of the extent to which individuals are better placed to take advantage of *opportunities* in the nonfarm sector.[12]

Those engaged in agricultural wage labor are taken as the comparison group in the model presented in Table 3.3. This implies that parameter estimates for the categories that are included should be interpreted not as correlates of employment in a given occupational category, but as indicators of the strength of association of a particular explanatory variable with the respective occupational category *relative* to the strength of association of the same explanatory variable with agricultural labor.

The multinomial logit models confirm that, relative to agricultural wage labor, the probability of employment in any of the three nonfarm subsectors is consistently lower for those who belong to the SCs or STs and for those with no education than for those in other groups. Drawing on these parameter estimates, Kijima and Lanjouw (2005) indicate that the predicted probability of employment in agricultural labor would be about 33.7 percent if all individuals were members of SCs or STs (with education levels and other characteristics corresponding to the overall average in the population) and that this probability would fall to 23.6 percent if their caste status were switched to non-SC or -ST. They also note that the predicted probabilities of regular nonfarm employment increase markedly with education levels (at mean values of other characteristics), while they fall sharply in the case of agricultural labor and more moderately in the case of casual nonfarm employment. There is little evidence that education plays a strong role in self-employment activities. Once again, this is possibly the consequence of the heterogeneity in the kind of self-employment activities in which people engage.

Interestingly, the multinomial model in Table 3.3 also suggests that in rural India the probability of employment in regular nonfarm activities and in nonfarm self-employment (relative to agricultural labor) is significantly higher for those with more per capita landholdings. As mentioned earlier, it is possible that per capita landholdings are proxying the ability to access information and networks. It is not clear how general this result is for developing countries as a whole. Unconditional correlations between landholdings and nonfarm income shares are usually strongly negative in most developing countries (see Table 3.4). Moreover, multivariate models for El Salvador, Ecuador, and periurban Tanzania,

---

12. See Lanjouw and Stern (1998). It is often noted that the market for the purchase and sale of land is rather thin in rural India as opposed to the market for land tenancy (see Jayaraman and Lanjouw, 1999). Landholdings may therefore be reasonably exogenous in the kinds of models estimated here.

similar to the one presented here, find no evidence of a positive relationship between landholdings and nonfarm employment probabilities (Lanjouw 1999, 2001; Lanjouw, Quizon, and Sparrow 2001).

Analyses such as that presented earlier for the case of India have been carried out in a number of developing countries.[13] Often these analyses are undertaken on the basis of probit or logit models that study the simple dichotomous question of involvement or noninvolvement in the nonfarm sector. These studies tend to find consistent evidence that important segments of the population in poverty are significantly less likely than others to participate in the nonfarm sector, particularly in those activities that would appear to be able to lift them out of poverty.

The relationship between gender and the probability of nonfarm employment is one taken up in a number of studies. A broad picture that emerges, but that is not necessarily repeated with statistical significance in all studies, is that the involvement of women in the nonfarm sector is generally low and that, where women are involved in the nonfarm sector, they are generally concentrated in the less remunerative activities (see Table 3.2). Lanjouw and Shariff (2004) document a significantly lower probability of nonfarm employment by women from region-level multinomial logit models used for rural India. Canagarajah, Newman, and Bhattamishra (2001), in a study of Uganda and Ghana, found that women participate actively in the nonfarm sector. On average, however, females were observed to earn less than men from nonfarm activities. An interesting observation from this study was that female heads of households were more likely than men to participate in nonfarm self-employment activities, and these activities tended to be among the most remunerative. Lanjouw (1999) documents that in Ecuador the probability of nonfarm employment was markedly higher for women than men, holding other characteristics constant, but that such employment occurred overwhelmingly in low-productivity, last-resort activities. A similar pattern of women clustering in the low-return activities was observed by Ferreira and Lanjouw (2001) in Northeastern Brazil, while in El Salvador, Lanjouw (2001) documents a significantly lower probability of nonfarm employment for women altogether.

Regardless of the specific methodology, a robust stylized fact that emerges from most of these studies concerns the strong association between nonfarm employment and relatively high education levels. Similarly, nonfarm participation is also generally observed to be higher in those locations that are less remote and in those where infrastructure service provision is higher and population density is greater. In some cases, such as in India and Vietnam, as discussed earlier, an individual's social position (including race and ethnicity) contributes

---

13. A special issue of *World Development* guest edited by Reardon, Berdegué, and Escobar (2001) presents a set of studies employing such techniques for Latin America.

TABLE 3.4 Correlates of poverty reduction and agricultural wage growth in rural India, 1987–99

	Percent change in regional head counts (1987–93 and 1993–99)	(Probability value)	Percent change in regional agricultural wages (1987–93 and 1993–99)	(Probability value)
Percent change in				
Agricultural wages	−0.391***	(<0.0001)	—	—
Agricultural wage labor	0.159***	(<0.0001)	—	—
Regular nonfarm (NF) employment	0.023	−0.6110	−0.005	−0.934
Casual NF employment	0.048	−0.5270	0.204**	−0.028
NF self-employment	−0.067	−0.3190	0.0320	−0.699
Proportion of land irrigated	−0.086**	−0.0200	−0.020	−0.670
Proportion of landless households	−0.014	−0.8480	−0.093	−0.300
Region-level base-year controls				
Agricultural wages	−0.045 ***	(<0.0001)	−0.059***	(<0.0001)
Agricultural wage employment	0.002	−0.7930	−0.014**	−0.033
Regular NF employment	0.011	−0.1110	0.014*	−0.057
Casual NF employment	−0.004	−0.7430	−0.008	−0.589
NF self-employment	−0.015**	−0.0370	0.008	−0.354
Proportion of land irrigated	−0.439**	−0.0270	0.014	−0.954
Proportion of landless households	0.745	−0.1600	0.378	−0.364
Head-count rate	−0.017***	(<0.0001)	—	—
1987–93 dummy	−0.112	−0.1080	−0.250***	−0.003

State dummies (Bihar omitted)

Andhra Pradesh	-0.619 ***	-0.0010	-0.205	-0.295
Assam	0.022	-0.9190	0.014	-0.956
Gujarat	-0.684***	(<0.0001)	-0.181	-0.358
Haryana	-0.077	-0.7440	0.510*	-0.083
Himachal Pradesh	-0.165	-0.5010	0.404	-0.195
Karnataka	-0.726***	(<0.0001)	-0.023	-0.899
Kerala	-0.467*	-0.0850	0.112	-0.733
Madhya Pradesh	-0.443***	-0.0030	-0.202	-0.266
Maharashtra	-0.621***	-0.0002	-0.183	-0.352
Orissa	-0.110	-0.4980	-0.135	-0.501
Punjab	0.260	-0.2810	0.920***	-0.002
Rajasthan	-0.376**	-0.0210	-0.167	-0.398
Tamil Nadu	-0.479***	-0.0070	-0.063	-0.766
Uttar Pradesh	0.001	-0.9950	0.073	-0.713
West Bengal	0.030	-0.8480	0.043	-0.820
Intercept	1.930***	(<0.0001)	1.640***	(<0.0001)
Number of observations	117		117	
Adjusted R^2	0.493		0.742	

SOURCE: Kijima and Lanjouw (2005).

NOTES: The specifications reported here include two additional dummies representing the Inland South region of Andhra Pradesh and the Western region of Haryana, respectively. These two dummies are interacted with the percentage change in regular nonfarm employment and the percentage change in agricultural wages, respectively. In the former region, regular nonfarm employment was observed to increase sevenfold between 1993 and 1999 (while the head-count rate for this region was estimated to have fallen by 68 percent over the same period). In the latter case, real agricultural wages were calculated to have risen fivefold between 1987–88 and 1993–94 (while poverty was estimated to have doubled during this period). Failure to control for these two extreme outliers would have left most parameter estimates in the above models unchanged, but would have pointed to a highly nonrobust positive relationship between expansion of regular nonfarm employment and growth in poverty. *** indicates significance at the 1 percent level, ** indicates significance at the 5 percent level, and * indicates significance at the 10 percent level.

separately to the probability of nonfarm participation. But this is less clearly a general rule.

The evidence thus suggests that the likelihood of involvement in the nonfarm sector, particularly in the more attractive jobs, is not uniform across individuals. It seems reasonable to suppose that in many rural areas there is excess demand for nonfarm employment. This raises the question of how nonfarm jobs, be they regular or casual, are allocated. One possibility is that characteristics such as education serve an important screening function in terms of influencing who has access to nonfarm employment. Caste, ethnicity, gender, and wealth might also play roles. We have noted that these factors do not appear to favor the poor, who generally have low education levels, are highly represented among the marginalized social groups, and lack the wealth to pay bribes, access networks of contacts, and so on.

The Rural Nonfarm Economy as a Safety Net

The nonfarm sector serves an important safety net function in rural areas by providing employment—even if poorly remunerated—that helps to prevent vulnerable sections of society from sliding further into poverty. There has long been a practice in many developing countries of providing workfare programs in rural areas to mitigate the adverse distributional consequences of macroeconomic or agroclimatic shocks.[14] Drèze (1990) attributes much of postindependence India's general success in avoiding widespread famine in the face of numerous droughts and crises to the introduction of such programs. While the general focus of such projects is to provide rapid transfers of income to those populations most affected by the specific crisis, it turns out that in most cases participants are required to work to obtain benefits, and the work is usually on some large-scale construction project. Thus an important feature of these workfare programs is that they generate nonfarm employment.

The nonfarm employment generation associated with workfare programs is clearly of a rather special type. It is worthwhile examining such programs closely, however, because the elements of design that account for their success are also present in the more general expansion of low-productivity nonfarm wage employment opportunities in developing countries. Public works projects owe their general success to the requirement that participants work in order to obtain benefits in the project. In addition, it is well recognized that a critical feature of their design is that the wage offered in such projects is kept low relative to alternative earnings opportunities in the surrounding areas. This combined work requirement and low wage ensure that public works projects can rely on

---

14. Ravallion (1991, 1999) analyzes such workfare projects and offers guidelines for an appraisal of their effectiveness. Subbarao et al. (1997) draw lessons from cross-country experience. Datt and Ravallion (1994) estimate the net income gains to participants from such projects.

self-targeting by the poor. Only those without an obvious alternative source of income will be willing to undertake physical labor in return for a relatively low income. Thus well-designed workfare programs can be extremely well targeted, providing governments with an efficient means of transferring resources to the most needy during times of crisis.

In earlier sections we have seen that at least some segments of the RNFE are associated with low returns. Casual, daily-wage earnings opportunities are often associated with strenuous physical effort and sometimes with health hazards as well. It is clear that those rural households with other, more attractive, income-earning options tend to opt for those instead. As with public work projects, there is an element of self-targeting associated with these low-return nonfarm employment opportunities. Thus the important point to take away is that while there are many nonfarm jobs in rural areas that can be seen as residual activities that are of limited productivity and yield low incomes, these jobs can be serving the same kind of function that employment in a public works project does during times of crisis. At any moment in time, households might be exposed to idiosyncratic shocks and crises and may find themselves unable to fall back on insurance, credit, or other means of offsetting income shortfalls. Their ability to secure some earnings, however limited, through nonfarm employment opportunities can be of great assistance in preventing them from sliding into poverty or, if they are already poor, from falling into deeper poverty.

Indirect Effects of Rural Nonfarm Activity on Poverty

The indirect impact that nonfarm employment can exert on rural poverty is likewise potentially important. The general equilibrium of the rural economy ensures that there are myriad ways in which incomes of households can be influenced by factors that occur outside their immediate sector of employment. An important recent paper by Foster and Rosenzweig (2004) provides a theoretical exposition of how the nonfarm economy interacts with the farm economy, building on the great heterogeneity of nonfarm activities in rural areas and highlighting the importance of general-equilibrium relationships. The authors argue that a key distinction has to be made between traded and nontraded goods and services, and they emphasize the significance of wage and salary employment in nonfarm activities as opposed to the self-employment activities that have traditionally been the focus of attention. Foster and Rosenzweig (2004) analyze NCAER data from rural India covering roughly 250 villages over the period 1971, 1982, and 1999 to study the evolution of the nonfarm economy in rural India. They suggest that a growing rural-based export-oriented manufacturing sector can be expected to have an important pro-poor impact in rural India, possibly more significant than that expected from agriculture-led growth. This follows from analysis of their data indicating that rural diversification of employment in rural India has tended to be more rapid and extensive in places where agricultural wages are lower and where agricultural productivity growth has been less marked.

Kijima and Lanjouw (2005) attempt to trace the interrelationships among poverty, agricultural labor, and nonfarm employment in rural India. Table 3.4 presents estimates from two models using a National Sample Survey (NSS) region-level panel data set where, for each of about 60 NSS regions, data on changes in poverty, agricultural employment and wage rates, and nonfarm employment are available for two periods: 1987–88 to 1993–94 and 1993–94 to 1999–2000.

The first model looks at the factors that explain changes in poverty over time. Extensive research along these lines has been undertaken in recent years by Datt and Ravallion (1997, 2002) and Ravallion and Datt (1996, 1999) using a state-level panel data set spanning about 40 years and starting in the late 1950s. A consistent message from this literature is that poverty in India falls with higher farm yields, development spending, and nonagricultural output and that poverty rises with higher inflation. A further observation is that initial conditions also matter: states with higher initial levels of education and infrastructure were observed to achieve more rapid poverty reduction. Although Ravallion and Datt pay close attention to the important role played by nonagricultural output growth on poverty (and note that the elasticity of poverty with respect to nonagricultural output varies considerably by state), the data they analyze do not allow them to focus specifically on the *rural* nonfarm sector. The region-level data set constructed by Kijima and Lanjouw (2005) is not as rich as that constructed at the state level, but it does offer an opportunity to inquire specifically into the relationship between rural poverty and rural nonfarm employment (as well as to study the relationship between poverty and agricultural employment and wage rates).

In the first model reported in Table 3.4, the percentage change in poverty is regressed on percentage changes in agricultural wage rates, agricultural wage employment share, regular nonfarm employment share, casual nonfarm employment share, nonfarm self-employment share, the proportion of land under irrigation, and the proportion of landless households. In addition to these indicators of change over time, Kijima and Lanjouw include as control variables the base-year values of the same variables for their respective spells, as well as the base-year head-count poverty rate, a dummy representing the 1987–88 to 1993–94 spell, and dummies for each of the major Indian states. The data do not control very well for important determinants of poverty reduction, such as agricultural productivity growth and development spending. (It is unlikely that the proxy variable, proportion of land irrigated, can fully capture these effects.) As a result, the results in this model must be viewed as suggestive at best.

From the first model in Table 3.4 it can be seen that, all else equal, poverty falls significantly with increases in agricultural daily wage rates and rises with growth in agricultural wage employment shares. An increase in agricultural wage rates of 10 percent is associated with a 4 percent fall in poverty, while a 10 percent increase in the percentage of the population employed as agricultural laborers is associated with a 1.6 percent increase in the poverty head-count rate. Controlling for changes in agricultural wage and employment rates, poverty does not appear to vary with changes in nonfarm employment, irrespective of subsector. As agriculture intensifies (proxied by an expansion in land under irrigation), poverty also falls. Growth in landlessness does not appear to independently correlate with changes in poverty. Controlling for changes over time, higher initial agricultural wage rates are also associated with larger reductions in poverty, and the larger the initial share of nonfarm self-employment and of land under irrigation, the larger the reduction in poverty. In this model of poverty reduction there is only very limited evidence that the nonfarm sector plays a direct role. This is consistent with the idea that few of the poor appear to gain access to nonfarm jobs.[15]

The second model in Table 3.4 regresses the percentage change in agricultural wage rates on changes and base-year employment levels in subsectors of nonfarm employment, proportion of land irrigated, and percentage of landlessness. Again a dummy for the 1987–98 to 1993–94 spell and state dummies are added as controls. This specification is much in the spirit of Bhalla (1993), based on state-level time-series data covering the period 1971–72 to 1983–84, in which it was found that nonfarm employment exerted a more discernable impact on agricultural wages than did agricultural productivity.

Expansion of casual nonfarm employment is strongly correlated with growth in agricultural wage rates. This is consistent with a process of labor market tightening. While the poor may not always find it easy to gain access to even casual nonfarm employment, the siphoning off of the non-poor out of agricultural labor and into casual nonfarm employment puts pressure on agricultural wages.[16] This rise in agricultural wage rates then helps to reduce overall poverty levels. Further, agricultural wage rates tend to rise less rapidly in those regions with high initial wage levels and with high initial shares of agricultural employment. There is also some evidence that, all else equal, a higher initial share of regular nonfarm employment is associated with a more rapid rise in agricultural wages.

Thus the Kijima and Lanjouw study points to a picture of poverty reduction in rural India driven to a large extent by changes in agricultural wage rates

---

15. In addition, these findings do not necessarily contradict the previously cited studies by Ravallion and Datt that point to an important role for nonagricultural output in reducing poverty. The difference is that this study includes agricultural wages as a control. The impact of nonfarm employment on agricultural wages is considered in the next regression.

16. Sharma (2001) also observes a positive impact of nonfarm employment shares on agricultural wages from cross-sectional regressions of agricultural wages for 1983 and 1993–94 on productivity per worker, landlessness, and nonfarm employment shares. Lanjouw and Shariff (2004) obtain similar results from a model based on NCAER data for 1993. They distinguish between types of nonfarm employment and observe the most significant relationship between (male) agricultural wages and employment in construction activities.

and employment shares in agricultural labor. There is little evidence that an expansion of nonfarm employment has an important *direct* effect on poverty. This does not mean, however, that the nonfarm sector is unimportant for poverty reduction. Rather, expansion of nonfarm employment, particularly the unskilled casual employment opportunities that appear to present the poor with fewer barriers to entry, may play an important role in putting pressure on the agricultural labor market and in raising agricultural wage rates. Thus the *indirect* effect of rural nonfarm employment on rural wage rates may prove quite important.

The patterns presented here for rural India cannot be expected to necessarily fit well in other settings. Panel data from Bangladesh do suggest a similar labor market tightening, with expansion in high-productivity rural nonfarm employment pulling labor away from low-return manual labor both on farms and off (Hossain 2004). But in Vietnam, Van de Walle and Cratty (2003) indicate that nonfarm wage and salaried employment represents a relatively unimportant segment of the nonfarm economy relative to nonfarm self-employment. Such observations have also frequently been made in the African setting. In such settings, general equilibrium effects might not be felt very strongly through labor market linkages, although they could well still be present in other forms. It is unlikely that a general story can be told about whether, and how, the nonfarm sector exerts an indirect effect on rural poverty. But as can be seen in the Indian case, these indirect effects can be important—to the extent that they might even dwarf direct effects. Arriving at an overall assessment of the impact of the nonfarm sector on poverty requires that some attention be paid to such indirect effects. Unfortunately the panel data that are best suited to such analyses are still relatively uncommon.

Conclusions

Current interest in the rural nonfarm economy arises in large measure because policymakers see the potential for high-paying nonfarm employment to directly raise incomes of the rural poor. Unfortunately, available empirical evidence suggests that this direct route out of poverty proves muted in practice, constrained by a variety of forces. Because the poor are often poorly educated, with limited land and financial capital, and because they have low social rank and are often women, both economic and social barriers prevent them from accessing the most lucrative nonfarm activities. Instead they most commonly remain confined to the low-return segment of the rural nonfarm economy. Thus policymakers should not presume that an expanding RNFE will necessarily translate into declining poverty. To strengthen the direct impact of rural nonfarm growth on poverty reduction, policymakers will need to expand education for the rural poor and work to remove various social and economic barriers that currently limit their entry into more lucrative nonfarm professions.

However, low-return, residual nonfarm activities do perform an important distributional function. While these activities do not lift the poor out of poverty, they play a critical role in protecting the poor from further declines in income. The mechanism at work is epitomized by public works schemes that are set up in many developing countries in response to macroeconomic or agroclimatic shocks: a work requirement by beneficiaries combined with low wages paid ensures that only the most desperate and the poorest are targeted. Policymakers are often concerned with the question of whether public works programs can be scaled up and regularized to the point that they can offer a guarantee of employment even in noncrisis periods. Clearly the extent of public resource mobilization that would be necessary for this to happen will depend directly on the size of the nonfarm sector (particularly the low-return segment) and the extent to which employment in that sector is rationed to the poor. Nevertheless, the introduction of nonfarm employment-guarantee schemes, such as the self-targeting labor-intensive construction works introduced in rural India, offers one possible way in which policymakers could expand the scope of the nonfarm economy to serve this safety net function.

Rural nonfarm earnings may likewise contribute significantly to poverty reduction even in cases in which the poor are not directly employed in the RNFE. In rural India, general equilibrium linkages between the nonfarm economy and the agricultural labor markets appear to be strong. Growth of the nonfarm sector, particularly the casual wage subsector, appears to be strongly associated with rising agricultural wages. The mechanism at work is likely to be a simple one of the agricultural labor market tightening as the nonfarm sector siphons labor out of the agricultural sector. In other countries, these labor market linkages may not play such an important role. However, in those cases, too, there are possible linkages between the farm and nonfarm sectors—in output markets, input markets, and capital flows between nonfarm and farm enterprises—that would enable the poor who remain primarily engaged in the agricultural sector to benefit indirectly from expansion of the nonfarm sector. These indirect linkages are possibly very significant. Although product market linkages have received considerable attention (see Chapter 7), the capital flows have not, probably because of a paucity of data well suited to such analysis. From available evidence, however, it appears that public investments in rural infrastructure—including roads and communication and credit systems, which facilitate the flow of people, goods, financing, and price information across space—can only improve the functioning of rural labor, capital, and output markets and thereby enhance these indirect contributions of rural nonfarm activity to rural poverty reduction.

PART II

Dynamics and Linkages

4 Structural Transformation of the Rural Nonfarm Economy

PETER B. R. HAZELL, STEVEN HAGGBLADE,
AND THOMAS REARDON

Functionally, the rural nonfarm economy (RNFE) plays a pivotal role in the process of structural transformation, during which the agricultural share of total national output declines and transfers of capital and labor drive a corresponding rise in manufacturing and services. Because many of the resource flows from agriculture to the secondary and tertiary sectors of the economy transit functionally and spatially via the RNFE, an understanding of the forces that drive change in the RNFE becomes central to understanding the processes that drive overall economic growth.

This chapter examines the broad dynamics that take place within the RNFE during structural transformation. In doing so, it sets the stage for a sequence of more in-depth discussions of the various dimensions of rural nonfarm dynamics in the remaining chapters of Part II. Although changes in the RNFE unfold across a wide variety of settings, several common patterns and signature characteristics typically emerge. Because these prove useful in understanding common trends, identifying opportunities, and designing appropriate policy interventions, this chapter concludes by proposing a typology of different situations that will prove useful in both the analytical and the policy discussions that ensue in coming chapters of this book.

Dynamics of Structural Transformation

Agriculture and Structural Transformation

At an aggregate level, structural transformation is a widely observed process by which broad-based productivity growth accompanies a shifting sectoral composition of economic activity. Widespread agreement exists that the share of agriculture will fall during this transformation and that transfers of capital and labor from agriculture will facilitate growth in the expanding industrial and service sectors of developing economies (Chenery and Syrquin 1975; Timmer 1988; Table 4.1). Disagreements emerge, however, about whether policymakers can siphon resources from agriculture with impunity or whether prior

TABLE 4.1 Growth in rural nonfarm income (percent)

	Rural nonfarm income shares		
	Of farm household income	Of rural income	Of national income
China			
1978–80	17	—	4
1985	25	—	7
1990	26	—	10
1995	37	—	26
1997	39	—	28
India			
1968	—	26	—
1980	—	36	—
2000	—	46	—
Japan			
1950	22	—	—
1960	42	—	—
1970	63	—	—
1981	80	—	—
1987	84	—	—
South Korea			
1971	18	—	—
1981	33	—	—
1991	46	—	—
Taiwan			
1970	45	—	—
1975	47	—	—
1980	65	—	—
1987	78	—	—
Thailand			
1976	35	—	—
1986	46	—	—

SOURCES: Oshima (1984), Hazell and Haggblade (1991), Poapongsakorn (1994), Hayami (1998a), Fan, Hazell, and Thorat (1999), Huang (1999), Chadha (2003).

NOTE: A dash indicates that data are not available.

investments in agricultural productivity are necessary to enable these resource transfers to take place without raising food prices or urban wage rates and choking off industrial development (see Chapter 2). However, there is little doubt that in its early stages, developments in the RNFE remain inextricably intertwined with those in agriculture.

Initial settlement of rural areas almost always depends on agriculture. Unique among economic pursuits, agriculture requires physically dispersed production. In some instances, other activities—such as mining, tourism, entrepôt trade, or administration—may also motivate initial human settlement in rural areas. Without these intrinsically rurally based economic activities, human settlement will not normally occur in rural areas. In most developing country settings, agriculture forms the backbone of the rural economic base. As the largest employer in rural areas, the largest income generator, and the largest purveyor of raw materials, agriculture clearly plays a predominant early role in influencing the size and structure of the RNFE.

Thus the process of rural development normally begins with a countryside populated by self-sufficient, primarily agricultural households producing for themselves most of the farm and nonfarm goods and services they require (Figure 4.1). Trade and commerce remain marginal given the subsistence orientation of agriculture, the prevailing low-input farm technologies, and the limited transport and communications infrastructure in rural areas.

In zones of rapidly growing agricultural productivity, the composition and patterns of growth observed in the RNFE differ markedly from those in stagnant rural settings. For this reason, the following discussion distinguishes between processes and outcomes operating in these two very different environments.

Productive Agricultural Zones: The Pull Scenario

Where new technologies, modern farm inputs, and market access increase, they lead to increased agricultural surpluses and increased opportunities for trade. In these settings, rising agricultural productivity stimulates growth of the RNFE through a number of key linkages. Rising labor productivity on the farm increases per capita food supplies and releases farm family workers to undertake nonfarm activities. For this reason, green revolution India saw agricultural labor fall from 75 to 65 percent of the rural labor force in the first 25 years following the release of green revolution rice and wheat varieties (Hazell and Haggblade 1991). Equally important, increases in farm incomes, together with high rural savings rates, make capital available for investment in nonfarm activities. These savings rates have reached up to 25 to 35 percent in many areas of green revolution Asia (Bell, Hazell, and Slade 1982; Hazell and Ramasamy 1991). Increasingly productive modern agriculture requires inputs and services such as the provision of seeds, fertilizer, credit, pumps, farm machinery, marketing, and processing, all of which create a growing demand for nonfarm firms that can provide these inputs and services. As their incomes increase, farm

FIGURE 4.1   Emergence and evolution of rural nonfarm activity

Phase 1: Integrated farm-nonfarm households

Phase 2: Market exchange

Phase 3: Specialization

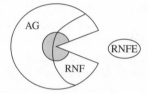

Phase 4: Spatial concentration in towns

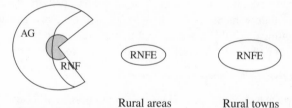

Rural areas   Rural towns

NOTE: AG, agriculture; RNF, rural nonfarm; RNFE, rural nonfarm economy. Shaded areas represent subsistence production; clear shapes represent market exchanges.

households increase the share of their expenditures devoted to nonfood items, in accordance with Engels's Law. Rural services, such as improvements in housing, schooling, health, prepared foods, entertainment, and rural transport services, commonly attract the fastest-growing shares of rural spending. Typical results, such as those reported from rural Bangladesh, highlight the robust spending on rural services, where expenditure elasticities are double those for rural manufacturing and foods (Table 4.2).

To meet this growing demand, rural households increasingly diversify into production of rural nonfarm goods and services (Table 4.1). As they do, they begin to specialize, taking greater advantage of their individual skills, resource endowments, and market opportunities. Some nonfarm activities, initially under-

TABLE 4.2 Consumer spending patterns in rural Bangladesh, 2000

Item	Average income share (%)	Marginal income share (%)	Income elasticity of demand
Food	52.0	33.6	0.6
Cereals	24.8	7.4	0.3
Noncereal crops	14.6	10.5	0.7
Fruits	1.5	1.7	1.1
Fish	6.3	6.8	1.1
Livestock products	4.8	7.2	1.5
Manufactures	19.8	16.6	0.8
Clothing	5.7	5.3	0.9
Other industrial	14.1	11.3	0.8
Services	17.2	26.1	1.5
Housing	6.2	7.3	1.2
Education	4.1	8.3	2.0
Health care	2.3	2.6	1.1
Transport	2.5	4.3	1.7
Recreation	0.7	1.6	2.3
Other	1.4	2.0	1.4
Savings	11.2	23.8	2.1

SOURCE: Hossain (2004).

taken by farm households for home consumption, spin off as separate full-time commercial activities (Figure 4.1).

As a consequence of this specialization, greater trade develops between rural households, small market centers, and rural towns. These burgeoning rural towns frequently grow quite rapidly, particularly in prosperous agricultural zones.[1] Rural towns not only stimulate rural nonfarm activity through the provision of key productive infrastructure and concentrated markets; they likewise create new markets for neighboring agriculture. Recent decades have seen an explosion in urban demand for higher-value agricultural products—including milk, meat, vegetables, flowers, and fruits—across Asia, Latin America, and Africa. Rural towns similarly stimulate additional agricultural production by improving the range, quality, and availability of farm inputs, financial services, agricultural markets, and processing services (Hardoy and Satterthwaite 1986; Tacoli 1998).

---

1. Hardoy and Satterthwaite (1986), Rondinelli (1987a,b), Satterthwaite (2000).

As towns grow, they attract more workers from the rural hinterland. The share of agriculture in the total workforce begins to decline, even though absolute levels of agricultural output and employment may continue to grow for some time. Over time, agriculture becomes progressively less important as the economic motor for the regional economy. Eventually it becomes a relatively minor economic activity in some rural regions as well as in many national economies.

The composition of rural nonfarm activity changes perceptibly in these buoyant agricultural settings. Increases in real wages raise the opportunity cost of labor, thereby making low-return nonfarm activities uneconomic. This leads to the demise of many low-productivity craft and household manufacturing activities and to the growth of higher-return nonfarm activities such as mechanical milling, transport, commerce, and personal, health, and educational services. Time-series data from rural Bangladesh during a period of rapid agricultural diversification and growth in high-value agriculture demonstrate this common tendency for productive agricultural zones to pull labor into increasingly high-return nonfarm activities, particularly in commerce and services (Table 4.3). Though both rich and poor households benefit from growing rural labor productivity, better-off households prove best able to take advantage of the opportunities in high-return business and service activities.

Low-productivity household manufacturing frequently declines as a result of wage pressure on the supply side and competition from urban imports on the demand side. The demise of these rural nonfarm goods explains, in part, why employment in services and commerce frequently grows faster than in manufacturing. Consumption spending likewise favors rapid growth in rural services (Table 4.2). As a result, time-series data from a wide array of countries suggest that rural commerce and services typically achieve annual growth rates 2 to 4 percentage points higher than those of rural manufacturing (Table 4.4).[2]

Stagnant Rural Zones: The Push Scenario

In regions without a dynamic economic base, patterns of growth in the RNFE unfold very differently. Where population growth continues unabated for many generations, land availability diminishes, and ultimately, in the absence of careful land management, so does soil fertility. Without technological advance in agriculture, labor productivity and per capita farm production fall.

In these settings, growing landlessness pushes labor force increments into nonfarm activity by default. Falling agricultural labor productivity, a low opportunity cost of labor, and declining household purchasing power induce

---

2. Bryceson (1996) and Bryceson and Jamal (1997) provide additional evidence on the importance of service sector growth in Africa, while Chapter 13 provides similar evidence for China and India.

TABLE 4.3 Transition to high-return nonfarm activities in Bangladesh, 1987–2000

Activity	Labor productivity (taka/day)			Employment and income changes, 1987–2000 (%)			
				Primary employment		Total employment hours	Income
	1987	2000	% change	Land-poor	Land-rich		
Agricultural labor	0.9	1.0	12	–22	–5	–13	–5
Road construction	1.0	1.2	24	—	—	–14	
Cottage industry	1.2	1.1	–8	—	—	–1	1
Shopkeeping	1.2	1.6	27	—	0	17	
Rickshaw transport	1.4	1.4	–3	6	–1	19	
House construction	1.5	1.7	9	1		29	
Services	1.7	2.3	36	0	12	–4	3
Business	2.3	3.4	54	2	8	13	7
All activities	1.4	2.3	59	—	—	3	2

SOURCE: Hossain (2004).

NOTE: A dash indicates that data are not available.

TABLE 4.4 Annual growth in rural nonfarm employment, by sector (percent)

Country (years)	Total rural labor	Agriculture	Total RNFL	Mining	Manufacturing
ISIC code		1		2	3
Bangladesh (1991–2001)	0.2	0.1	0.7	0.0	−0.2
Cameroon (1976–87)	0.5	0.5	0.8	1.7	−1.5
Chile (1970–84)	0.5	0.1	1.4	1.6	−7.6
Dominican Republic (1970–81)	−0.4	−1.4	2.2	5.5	1.1
Ecuador (1974–90)	0.7	0.2	1.9	3.4	0.6
Egypt (1960–86)	0.4	0.0	1.4	1.9	1.4
Guatemala (1973–81)	0.6	0.2	2.2	0.7	0.1
Honduras (1974–86)	1.0	0.8	2.1	1.9	1.0
India (1971–91)	0.9	0.8	1.3	1.2	1.0
Indonesia (1971–95)	0.7	0.4	1.5	3.5	1.1
Iran (1976–86)	0.2	0.1	0.3	−2.8	−2.1
Korea (1970–80)	−0.1	−0.3	0.6	−0.4	1.1
Malawi (1977–81)	1.4	1.4	1.7	−0.2	0.5
Morocco (1971–94)	0.6	0.5	1.0	−1.0	0.6
Pakistan (1981–98)	−0.2	−0.8	0.9	−1.2	−1.6
Philippines (1970–80)	0.2	0.4	−0.1	2.0	−2.0
Turkey (1970–90)	0.4	0.4	0.9	0.6	0.7
Venezuela (1981–90)	1.5	1.5	1.7	3.4	1.2
South Africa (1985–96)	−0.5	−1.7	0.2	−2.4	0.2
Average (unweighted)	0.5	0.2	1.2	1.0	−0.2

SOURCES: Bangladesh Bureau of Statistics (1994, 2003), Cameroun (1976, 1992), Egypt (1996), Guatemala (1981), Honduras (1976), India (1971, 1991), Indonesia (1974, 1998), Iran (1976, 1986), Korea (1972), Malawi (1980, 2002), Maroc (1995), Pakistan (2001), Statistics South Africa (1996), Turkey (1972, 1995), United Nations (1986, 1990, 1996), U.S. Bureau of the Census (2000), Venezuela (1985, 1993).

NOTE: A dash indicates that data are not available.

diversification into low-return, labor-intensive nonfarm activities such as basket-making, gathering, potterymaking, weaving, embroidery, or matmaking. Specialized nonfarm enterprises and households emerge not to exploit potential productivity gains, but because of an absence of opportunities in agriculture and a shortage of investable capital. Declining economic conditions likewise motivate households to seek farm and nonfarm employment opportunities in more distant regions. Thus migration serves as a regional safety valve.

Rural residents seek out exchange opportunities in these settings, too, but mainly by trying to identify market outlets for labor-intensive cottage industry goods. Rural towns, rather than accelerating agricultural advance, become evac-

Utilities	Construction	Commerce	Transport	Financial services	Personal and social services
4	5	6	7	8	9
0.6	1.4	0.0	2.2	0.0	0.0
5.9	2.2	2.4	2.9	2.0	0.5
5.4	3.3	−0.7	−4.9	18.6	0.0
8.4	5.4	2.4	−1.9	−3.5	3.9
0.1	2.1	1.9	2.1	5.0	3.0
2.4	3.0	−0.1	2.1	—	1.4
−10.8	23.2	2.8	3.8	0.0	4.5
12.7	−4.6	2.0	1.0	6.4	3.2
—	1.6	1.7	1.8	9.0	—
3.0	2.4	1.4	2.3	4.1	1.3
3.4	−1.0	0.1	2.2	2.1	5.4
2.1	0.1	0.9	1.1	3.9	−0.2
0.3	0.2	2.4	−0.7	1.9	2.9
0.9	1.7	1.4	1.6	9.2	−0.4
1.1	4.4	−0.2	−0.1	0.7	0.0
2.9	0.4	−0.5	1.0	—	0.4
3.0	1.5	1.0	0.9	1.7	0.7
0.3	0.1	1.4	1.8	3.6	2.5
−1.9	−0.3	1.3	1.8	5.0	1.2
2.2	2.5	1.1	1.1	4.1	1.7

uation points for labor-intensive rural nonfarm exports. A stagnant, low-input agriculture generates little demand for inputs or high-value repair, processing, and personal services.

Many describe this bleak downward spiral as a process of "agricultural involution."[3] As one review comparing stagnant and rapidly growing agricultural regions in India concludes, "The difference between the faster growing agricultural areas and others is primarily in terms of the productivity and income levels in rural industries. . . . Slowly growing agriculture not only fails to introduce any structural changes in rural industries . . . but also tends to keep those engaged in rural industries at a subsistence level of productivity and income" (Papola 1987, 104).

---

3. See Bryceson and Jamal (1997) for a good collection of case studies describing these dynamics.

Urbanization and Globalization

Improved rural infrastructure, increasing urbanization, and trade liberalization open the RNFE to outside incentives and competition. In doing so, they delink growth of the RNFE from agriculture to varying degrees. In some instances, these outside markets provide a stimulus to rural business activity. Rural subcontracting has grown rapidly in recent decades, particularly in densely populated and highly congested urban areas of Asia and Latin America. Export markets have opened up opportunities for a variety of rural enterprises—from rural rattan furnituremakers in Indonesia to rural weavers in Thailand to rural basketmakers in Botswana.[4] Improved communications grids have stimulated rapid growth in rural cell phone businesses as well as scratch card sales and servicing.[5]

While urbanization and globalization open up new opportunities for rural nonfarm enterprise growth, they introduce new risks as well. The forces of international trade and globalization often bring new competition to local markets—sometimes with breathtaking speed. South African supermarket chains have aggressively expanded northward following the advent of majority rule in 1994 and the demise of economic sanctions that had previously prevented their expansion. Major supermarket chains, such as Shoprite and Pick 'n Pay, have opened outlets in cities and rural towns in Zambia, Malawi, Mozambique, Botswana, and Uganda and are considering forays into West Africa. In each locality, their entry has significantly altered product selection and market share in favor of imported South African brands at the expense of local farmers, processors, food suppliers, and retailers (Weatherspoon and Reardon 2003). Globalization has produced a similar consolidation of rural supply chains throughout much of Latin America and Asia (see Chapter 9).

In the past, some categories of rural nonfarm activity have thrived because of protection from outside competition by high transport costs, restrictive production and trade policies, subsidized inputs and credit, and preferential access to key markets.[6] But the combined forces of globalization and market liberalization have removed many of these barriers, effectively "deprotecting" the RNFE. The transition may prove brutally abrupt for many traditional small-scale manufacturing activities whose products cannot compete with higher-quality, mass-produced goods. For this reason, the initial stages of deprotection can lead to massive job losses in the RNFE, even though many of these jobs may later be recovered as new types of rural nonfarm activity sprout up, as in India during the 1990s (Bhalla 1997).[7] Because poor households and female-

---

4. See Haggblade and Ritchie (1992) and Kapila and Mead (2002).
5. See, for example, Chowdhury (2000) and World Bank (2004).
6. See Chapter 13 for detailed examples from India and China.
7. Saith (1992) and Start (2001) describe this overall transition as consisting of four phases. First is a subsistence rural economy, followed by a second period of rural productivity growth. In

dominated activities predominate among the low-investment, low-productivity rural nonfarm activities, they tend to face the most difficult adjustment during this transition.

Determinants of Alternative Rural Nonfarm Trajectories

Engines of Growth

Humans settle in rural areas where core economic activities enable them to earn a satisfactory living. For example, the establishment of a mine in a previously unpopulated rural area generates jobs and income that, in turn, create local demand for ancillary goods and services, many of them nonfarm services such as education, health, transport, and entertainment. As the region's economic base (the mine) expands, so too does demand for these ancillary goods and services. If the economic base (the mine) shuts down, people move away and the rural community disappears. The economic base of a rural region encompasses those core productive activities that remain competitive in external markets. As a result, the tradable goods resulting from these activities face highly elastic demands, so their prices remain unaffected by levels of local output. The total economic activity in the region depends on the size of the economic base and the demand it generates for local providers of goods and services.

In most developing country settings, agriculture forms the core of the rural economic base. Consequently, the dispersion of fertile soils, water, grazing land, and infrastructure largely governs the spatial distribution of population across rural regions of the developing world. Though less important in the aggregate, many rural regions also have natural resources—minerals, timber, or exotic natural settings—that sustain the production of exportable raw materials, processed goods, and tourism services. Administrative or entrepôt trading centers can also serve as economic bases along transport corridors that transit remote rural locations. Economists refer to these core activities as "tradables" because they are competitive with imported goods by virtue of their rural location, while regional scientists refer to them as the region's "economic base."[8] In the case of a rural region, these goods may be domestically tradable even if not exported internationally.

Demand-Led Spin-Offs

Activities comprising a region's economic base generate local demand for ancillary production and consumption activities. In the same way that agriculture

a third phase, the opening up of rural areas to competition from urban products places pressure on rural manufactures. In a final, fourth phase, the RNFE must face up to global competition but at the same time benefits from new opportunities for urban-led subcontracting and export growth.

8. See Richardson (1985) for a good introduction to the regional science literature.

generates production and consumption linkages with the surrounding region (see Chapter 7), a region's core natural resource or administrative businesses generate local demand for schools, health clinics, restaurants, and commercial services in the region. Regional scientists refer to these ancillary activities as "nonbase" activities, while economists typically refer to them as "non-tradables." Both disciplines consider them freight cars rather than locomotives; their numbers and speed derive directly from the power of the engines propelling them.

Not surprisingly, different engines generate different patterns of rural nonfarm growth. Even within agriculture, linkages differ across crops and even across technologies within the same crop. Growth in irrigated paddy production by large farmers generates different input and consumption linkages than does rain-fed smallholder production. Small-scale sapphire mining by legions of pick-and-shovel wildcat miners generates different patterns of demand and input linkages than large-scale mechanized open pit mining. Ultimately, the economic base sustains economic activity in the rural region, with overall income levels depending on the magnitude of the resulting production, consumption, and productivity linkages.[9]

Engineers and Lubricants

Human skills, inventiveness, and investable resources determine which engines of growth spark to life in a given rural region. Consequently entrepreneurship, education, experience, and incentives all influence outcomes in any particular setting.

A series of key lubricants can influence incentives and facilitate the development of regional economic engines as well as their second-round linkages. Policy variables that facilitate regional growth dynamics include physical infrastructure, market institutions, education, credit, and a series of macro, trade, and industry-specific policies. These are discussed in greater detail in Part III of this book.

Distribution and Equity

Agriculture employs a majority of the poor in the developing world (Sanchez and Swaminathan 2005). Because small farmers' access to new agricultural technologies hinges on the divisibility and accessibility of these technologies, government policies can influence the equity impact of initial rounds of agricultural growth.[10] Public research on divisible or low-input farm technologies, such as open-pollenating maize rather than hybrids or crops like cassava that produce high yields without purchased inputs, generate equitable first rounds

---

9. See Chapter 7 for a formal discussion of these linkages and multipliers.
10. See, for example, Ruttan (1975), Mellor and Johnston (1984), and Lipton and Longhurst (1989).

of growth in the rural agricultural base.[11] The income distribution of initial growth in the rural economic base, in turn, governs consumption linkages and hence the local as opposed to the import content of second rounds of demand-led growth.

As opportunities emerge in the RNFE, household endowments of financial and human capital determine which nonagricultural opportunities are available to low-income groups. Many congregate in low-capital, low-skill, and hence low-return nonfarm activities such as weaving, gathering, matmaking, and unskilled wage labor (see Table 6.2). The members of many farm and land-less households are too poorly educated or skilled to access salaried employment in technical or administrative posts. Meanwhile, more highly educated rural dwellers enjoy access to formal sector salaried employment in rural towns. In the presence of significant disparities in asset endowments, powerful self-selection processes operate in the marketplace, and the less able often are left behind.

A Typology of Settings

To categorize the wide variety of regional settings prevailing in the developing world, the following typology considers two key dimensions (Table 4.5). First, a region's economic base and its potential govern inherent prospects for regional economic growth. Second, the distribution of assets across household groups influence prospects for poor households to access growing market opportunities.

ECONOMIC BASE.   Not all rural regions are blessed with intrinsically high economic potential. Many remain resource-poor, isolated, and backward. Others enjoy vast tracts of fertile soil, minerals, timber, or other types of exploitable natural wealth. For prescriptive purposes, it is useful to consider three simple groupings based on the state of a region's economic base.

First are resource-poor areas, endowed with marginal land that low and erratic rainfall or steep slopes render ill suited to agricultural production. An absence of exploitable minerals, forests, or exotic natural settings makes resource-based economic activity questionable. In such situations—for instance, in the northern part of the West African Sahel, the Indian state of Bihar, and the Andean zones of Ecuador and Peru—very poor populations eke out a living from nomadic herding, seasonal migration, or risky, low-productivity agriculture.

A second situation arises in regions where the economic base remains weak, yet unexploited potential does exist. This may happen, for example, where fertile soils, minerals, a strategic location, or great natural beauty is found, but exploitation of this economic potential requires investment in infrastructure (irrigation or roads, perhaps), technology, human capital, or marketing

---

11. See, for example, Byerlee and Eicher (1997), Lipton and Longhurst (1989), and Nweke, Spencer, and Lynam (2002).

TABLE 4.5 A typology of rural regions

Asset distribution	Rural economic base		
	Sluggish		Dynamic
	1. Resource-poor	2. Unexploited potential	3. High-potential, fast-growing
a. Unequal	1a. Poor-unequal Andean zones of Ecuador and Peru Bihar, India Northern Mexico Northeast Brazil Southern Madagascar	2a. Unexploited-unequal Bangladesh, 1960–85 Southern Brazil, 1950–70 Cerrado, Brazil, before 1980 Honduran hillsides Cancun, before 1967	3a. Dynamic-unequal Bangladesh, 1985–95 Southern Brazil, 1970–90 Cerrado, Brazil, from 1980 Central plains of Chile, 1990s South Africa Cancun, after 1967
b. Equal	1b. Poor-equal West African Sahel Northeast Thailand Ethiopian highlands	2b. Unexploited-equal Punjab, 1950s Ethiopian lowlands Southern Sudan Northern Mozambique Central and Eastern Zambia Botswana, before 1980	3b. Dynamic-equal Punjab, 1970s Taiwan, 1950–70 Uganda, 1990s Vietnam, 1980 on Southern coastal China, 1990 on Botswana, after 1980

arrangements. This was the case in Bangladesh from the 1950s through about 1985, in the Indian Punjab during the 1950s, and in Cancun, Mexico, before 1967. In such cases, some sort of investment or collective action proved able to ignite impressive growth—led by agriculture in the Punjab and in Bangladesh and by tourism development in Cancun.

A third case occurs when a dynamic economic base already exists, as in the agricultural boom of the central Chilean plain during the 1980s and 1990s, in the commodity boom of the 1960s and 1970s in the Zambian copper belt, and in Uganda's agricultural recovery during the 1990s. In these settings, rapid growth in agriculture and mining stimulated not only significant income gains for local households but also widespread growth in ancillary nonfarm activities. In these types of regions, growing markets for the RNFE provide a multitude of investment opportunities, though not all are easily accessible by the poor.

ASSET DISTRIBUTION.   Within any given rural region, regardless of its economic base, the current distribution of assets, income, power, and wealth may vary substantially. In highly egalitarian settings, widespread access to land, education, credit, and information enables broad economic mobility and widespread participation in overall economic growth.

In unequal settings, however, growth of the tradables sector may accelerate inequality, as differential access to education, technology, capital, commercial position, and political power translates into first mover advantages for the elite. The often extreme heterogeneity of nonfarm firm sizes and technology accentuates this disparity. Rural nonfarm economies throughout much of the developing world house large numbers of labor-intensive, home-based nonfarm activities—such as basketmaking, embroidery, and weaving. Though significant to the poor households that undertake them, these activities prove vulnerable to the changing circumstances that emerge during economic growth or liberalization. Small-scale producers of processed foods, for example, do not easily integrate into modern retailing systems because of low volumes, inconsistent quality, and lack of standards and packaging for their products. Hence they risk losing out as supermarkets and large suppliers begin to dominate market supply channels.

THE RESULTING TYPOLOGY.   Together, these two dimensions result in a six-cell categorization of the many diverse regional landscapes of the developing world. Table 4.5 provides an illustrative classification of rural regions using this typology. In doing so, it illustrates the frequency with which regions can change categories over time, typically as a result of key investments that enable regions to tap into unexploited economic potential.

Conclusions

Both the composition and the dynamics of the RNFE differ across settings, as varied initial endowments and human responses propel the RNFE along a wide array of potential growth paths. The typology proposed in this chapter classifies these many varied potential situations along two key dimensions, the first affecting prospects for aggregate growth and the second affecting access by the poor to growing market segments. Because of its utility in clarifying analytical and policy discussions, this typology will recur in coming chapters of this book.

The typology, and the broad discussion it encapsulates, suggests that policymakers searching for ways to ensure equitable rural nonfarm growth will need to consider two key dimensions of rural development. First, they will need to identify economic engines that can sustain broad-based rural economic growth. Second, they must foster processes that enable asset- and income-poor households to benefit from the rural nonfarm opportunities that ensue.

5   Enterprise Dynamics in the Rural Nonfarm Economy

CARL LIEDHOLM

The broad structural dynamics under way in the rural nonfarm economy have been examined in Chapter 4. Yet beneath the aggregate trends lies considerable subsurface activity among the individual enterprises that form the basic building blocks of the rural nonfarm economy (RNFE). Even when aggregate census data suggest static overall nonfarm activity levels, they mask what is often considerable movement in and out of the nonfarm business world as individual firms emerge, some expand, and others die out. Aggregate growth in the RNFE stems from a combination of net new firm creation and expansion of existing enterprises. These two alternative sources of rural nonfarm growth typically signal very different underlying economic dynamics within the rural economy.

To better understand key dynamics affecting the RNFE, this chapter explores the causes and magnitude of enterprise start-up, closure, and expansion. Using firm-level data collected from household surveys in six different countries, it examines evidence on birth, death, and individual firm expansion rates as well as how these vary across locations. After reviewing empirical methods and findings, the chapter explores policy implications of the considerable volatility among individual rural nonfarm enterprises. The remaining chapters in Part II of this book examine the behavior of higher orders of nonfarm enterprise aggregation—in households, sectors, regions, and the national economy.

Methods

Alternate Survey Methods

Information required for the analysis of firm dynamics in developing countries is rarely available. Standard census data offer static portraits of existing enterprises. Many fail to capture data on the smallest enterprises; consequently, these remain particularly scarce. Even when special surveys of microenterprises are conducted, they tend to focus on the current status of the firms and rarely shed light on their evolution over time.

Given weaknesses in the existing data sources and in the conventional survey procedures used to generate them, new approaches must be used when undertaking studies of the dynamics of rural nonfarm enterprises in developing countries. New survey methods as well as new analytical procedures are required. Candidates considered by empirical researchers include modified baseline surveys, closed enterprise surveys, tracer surveys, retrospective surveys, and panel surveys. The strengths and weaknesses of each of these survey methods will now be examined briefly.

MODIFIED BASELINE SURVEYS.   Rural nonfarm enterprise baseline surveys involve door-to-door enumeration of nonagricultural income-earning activities chosen from a stratified random sample of enumeration areas. They have traditionally provided a one-shot picture of the numbers, types, and locations of these enterprises along with the numbers and categories of workers. These surveys differ from the traditional industrial censuses in that they canvas not just the obvious "business" doors of larger firms but also the "household" doors, enabling them to find the smaller, "invisible" enterprises that are hidden within the confines of the household. The random selection of locations to be surveyed makes it possible to generalize these findings to generate countrywide estimates. By adding to the surveys two questions relating to the year of start-up and the number of workers at start-up, important dynamic information can also be gleaned to provide insights on the birth and growth of these enterprises. Details of the conduct of such modified enterprise baseline surveys are provided in McPherson and Parker (1993).

CLOSED ENTERPRISE SURVEYS.   By extending the baseline survey exercise it is possible to generate information on those elusive enterprises that have closed. This has been done by undertaking a "closed enterprise" survey in the same areas covered by the modified baseline survey. In such surveys, the door-to-door enumeration also collects information on businesses previously operated by people in the area but now no longer in operation.[1] Statistics are collected on the size of the business at start-up and at closure, the age of the business at closure, and the reasons for closure. While such surveys can generate comprehensive information on the reasons for and the timing of closures, they are less useful in determining annual closure rates. This is because, in addition to the recall errors of the respondents (respondents may forget or may choose not to tell about enterprises that have ceased operation), closed enterprises that operated outside the entrepreneur's home will tend to be systematically missed in these types of surveys because the questionnaire asks only about enterprises that operated at that location.

TRACER SURVEYS.   Tracer surveys provide another mechanism for generating information on the dynamics of nonfarm enterprises. These surveys seek

---

1. This procedure was pioneered by Joan Parker and C. Aleke Dondo in their Kenyan survey of micro and small enterprises (Parker and Aleke Dondo 1991).

to determine what has happened over time to a limited number of enterprises (or entrepreneurs) that had been enumerated in some earlier period, typically more than five years previously. Such surveys can generate useful information not only about the time path of enterprise growth but also about closed enterprises. The principal limitation of these surveys is that they usually cover only a few firms initially. Many of these cannot be found, leading to possibly large selectivity biases. Early attempts to trace such firms have met with mixed results; 75 percent of the "disappeared" firms were successfully traced in Ecuador (Middleton 1989), but that percentage declined to one-third in Sierra Leone (Chuta and Liedholm 1985) and Nigeria (Frischman 1988).

RETROSPECTIVE BORE HOLE SURVEYS. Another survey approach is "bore hole" interviews—retrospective histories—of selected entrepreneurs and their firms, often focusing on particular sectors. These surveys can be undertaken even in those countries where no previous baseline surveys have been conducted. Such in-depth retrospective histories of entrepreneurs and their firms can provide important insights into the pattern of change in existing firms and the constraints, both internal and external, they have faced at different stages in their life cycle. The detailed information can also generate a path analysis of the critical junctures in the development of the firm and entrepreneur. The weaknesses of such surveys are that coverage is limited, as in tracer surveys, and no information is generated on start-up or closure rates.

PANEL OR PROSPECTIVE SURVEYS. A final survey approach involves conducting longitudinal surveys of existing firms on a repeat basis over a period of time. The traditional method of conducting such panel surveys is to repeatedly sample the same group of respondents quarterly or at least once a year, thereby generating a time-series as well as a cross-section data set. Ideally, however, if all the firms in selected areas are included in the panel and the same areas are enumerated each period, all births and closures in these areas will also be detected. Thus, in addition to annual enterprise growth rates, these area-based panel surveys make it possible to generate annual enterprise start-up and closure rates. The more frequently these surveys are conducted, the less likely it will be that the births and deaths of the short-duration firms will be missed. If flow variables such as wages and output are included in the questionnaire, panel surveys can generate annual enterprise growth estimates based on measures other than employment. The disadvantage of panel surveys is that they provide information on only a limited period of a firm's life cycle; moreover, they are relatively expensive to administer and analyze.

Analytical Perspectives

The information generated by such surveys can be analyzed in a variety of ways to illuminate firm-level dynamics in developing countries. For classification purposes, it may be useful to group these studies by their degree of aggregation (Liedholm and Mead 1991), as follows:

- Studies of the dynamics of the individual entrepreneur (micro-micro level)
- Studies of the dynamics of the firm or enterprise, focusing on its birth, death, and expansion (micro level)
- Subsector studies focusing on patterns of development among groups of firms within a particular network of functionally linked rural nonfarm firms (meso level)
- Intersectoral linkages and macroeconomic analysis focusing on the relationships between sectors or subsectors within an economy and changes in the overall structure of the economy (macro level)

Studies of the relationship between entrepreneurship and firm dynamics (micro-micro level studies) date back to the early 1960s. These studies, which have been usefully reviewed and summarized by Kilby (1971, 1988, 2001) and Anderson (1982), typically seek to identify empirically the determinants of the evolution of entrepreneurial capacities and their effects on firm performance. A separate literature has emerged in subsequent years focusing on the differences in experience between male and female entrepreneurs (Grown and Sebstad 1989; Downing and Daniels 1992). Many of these studies extend to the household, examining the interrelationship between the entrepreneur and the other activities of the household.

The dynamics literature at the enterprise or firm (micro) level has been limited in the past. Economic theory in this area is quite sparse. Jovanovic's (1982) "learning" model posits that both the initial size and the age of the enterprise should be inversely related to its growth. An intriguing hypothesis about another entrepreneurial characteristic, gender, has been formulated by Downing and Daniels (1992), who hypothesize that female entrepreneurs are more risk averse than their male counterparts and thus their enterprises are less likely to grow. Moreover, as one moves beyond the "homogeneous product" assumptions, variables that reflect the underlying demand and supply conditions, such as sector, location, and even country, could be expected to affect enterprise growth (Liedholm and Mead 1999). This theoretical and empirical literature has been summarized by Mead and Liedholm (1998). Among the key empirical issues that have been addressed are the following: What is the magnitude of firm birth rates, and what are the major determinants of new firm creation? What are the central factors of firm survival? How rapidly are firms expanding, and what are the key determinants of firm growth? Such enterprise studies, however, do not typically incorporate the potentially important household interactions (see Chapter 6).

At a meso or subsectoral level, interest in business dynamics has increasingly focused on systemic changes occurring within aggregations of functionally related enterprises. Analysts adopting this perspective refer to these functionally linked enterprise supply systems variously as subsectors, clusters, supply chains, or value chains.[2] In these systems approaches, the universe of firms examined includes firms of all types and sizes engaged in the production and distribution of a particular group of commodities. Key issues examined include the dynamics of final market demand and of individual channels that supply them, the changing role of different types of firms and mechanisms coordinating key supply channels, the determinants of these changes, and the changing competitive position of different actors and supply channels within the subsector (see Chapter 15 for some examples).

At the macro level, a complex interaction of forces operating on both the demand and the supply side of the market drives evolution of the RNFE. The demand side forces have received the primary attention, with agriculture, the principal source of rural income, typically accorded the central role (see Chapter 7). Subsequently, the supply side forces have also begun to receive attention. Haggblade and Liedholm (1992), for example, have added labor market interactions to the standard demand linkage model of rural nonfarm growth. Recent empirical work by Foster and Rosenzweig (2004) and Hossain (2004) has also emphasized the important labor market interactions between farm and rural nonfarm enterprises.

Data Sources

This chapter assembles evidence primarily from a series of six surveys explicitly designed to explore nonfarm enterprise dynamics. Given the sample size limitations of the tracer and bore hole surveys and the virtual absence of panel surveys, this empirical analysis must, to a large extent, rely on a set of modified baseline surveys with retrospective information as well as closed enterprise surveys developed to explore nonfarm enterprise dynamics among micro and small enterprises (MSEs) in the developing world. Mead and Liedholm (1998) review the overall framework and findings of this body of MSE research. This chapter analyzes data from the subset of these MSE surveys that enables locational breakdowns between rural and urban enterprises. The eligible set includes surveys from five core African countries—Botswana, Kenya, Malawi, Swaziland, and Zimbabwe—along with a survey of the Dominican Republic. These six unique surveys generated comparable, nationally representative data on approximately 30,000 firms. They were based on a complete enumeration of all MSEs in a random sample of locations geographically stratified by degree of urbanization and other key characteristics.[3]

---

2. For an introduction to this literature, see Boomgard et al. (1992), Porter (1998), Kaplinksy and Morris (2000), and Jaffee et al. (2003) as well as the more detailed description in Chapter 15.

3. Data for the six core countries come from Botswana (1,362 enterprises, surveyed in 1992), Kenya (5,353 enterprises, 1993), Malawi (9,672 enterprises, 1992), Swaziland (2,759 enterprises, 1992), Zimbabwe (5,575 enterprises, 1991), and the Dominican Republic (4,568 enterprises, 1992).

One limitation of these surveys, for our present purposes, is that they exclude large-scale enterprises, defined as those employing more than 50 workers. Thus they cannot be generalized to the entire RNFE. Nevertheless, they do offer extensive detail and a unique opportunity to examine enterprise dynamics among the MSEs on which the rural poor most frequently depend.

A quick profile of these data suggest that start-up rates among MSEs are quite high, typically exceeding 20 percent per year (see Mead and Liedholm 1998). They likewise indicate that most MSEs operating in rural areas are extremely small. The majority of such firms in most countries, in fact, are one-person firms (Table 5.1). As a result, self-employment dominates this segment of the RNFE, while relatively few of the rural MSE firms employ more than 10 persons. These findings provide some support for the phenomenon of the "missing middle" in countrywide enterprise size distributions that has been described in the literature (see, for example, Kilby 1988).

Enterprise Dynamics: Micro Determinants

What dynamic patterns can be seen in the growth of micro and small rural nonfarm enterprises, and how do they differ from those of their urban counterparts? Locational differences in firm births and closures will be examined first, followed by a review of differences in net firm expansion.

Start-ups

How do the start-up rates of rural firms compare with those of their urban counterparts? Disaggregated by locality size, the findings from the six countries studied present a mixed picture. Rural enterprise start-up rates are substantially (at least 4 percentage points) higher than those of firms in urban areas in Botswana and are somewhat higher in Swaziland (Table 5.2). A similar locational firm birth rate pattern has also been reported for the Dominican Republic, where the firm birth rate in rural areas (22.2 percent) exceeded that in urban areas (16 percent) during 1992–93 (Cabal 1995).

In two other African countries, however, the opposite pattern is found, with urban start-up rates somewhat higher than for their rural counterparts.[4] These differential patterns may be explained by such factors as the performance of the agricultural sector as well as the level and rate of growth of overall economic activity in these countries. Additional start-up rate observations are needed, however, before the relationship between these variables and firm birth rates can be rigorously analyzed.

---

4. The results from these two countries, Zimbabwe and Malawi, are similar to the earlier birth rate findings reported for Sierra Leone (Chuta and Liedholm 1985), where the annual rural birth rate in urban areas was 14.9 percent and that in the rural enumeration areas was only 10 percent.

TABLE 5.1 Characteristics of micro and small enterprises, 1998 (percent)

	Botswana	Kenya	Malawi	Swaziland	Zimbabwe	Dominican Republic	Lesotho	Jamaica
Share of all rural nonfarm enterprises that are one-person enterprises	65	47	61	69	69	22	79	62
Share of all rural nonfarm enterprises with 10–50 workers	3	2	1	2	2	18	1	2
Locational breakdown of rural nonfarm employment								
Urban areas	24	15	12	25	30	46	18	26
Rural towns	28	7	4	10	6	18	10	13
Rural areas	48	78	84	65	64	36	72	61
Sectoral breakdown of enterprises, rural areas only								
Manufacturing	34	27	36	70	75	15	62	35
Commerce	64	66	60	24	16	75	27	52
Share of rural enterprises owned by females	75	46	46	84	60	46	73	62

SOURCE: Survey data reported in Mead and Liedholm (1998).

NOTE: In the sectoral breakdown, the remainder of the enterprises are in services.

TABLE 5.2 Annual firm birth rates by size of locality

Country	Year	Annual firm birth rate (percent per year)			
		Urban	Rural towns	Rural areas	Overall
Botswana	1991	23	24	27	25
Dominican Republic	1992	16	24	22	21
Kenya	1992	22	20	21	21
Malawi	1991	23	21	22	22
Swaziland	1990	20	21	22	22
Zimbabwe	1990	21	19	19	19
Average		21	22	22	22

SOURCE: Computed from individual country survey data.

Closures

Figures on enterprise closure rates disaggregated by size of locality are particularly scarce. In the Dominican Republic, the only country for which the requisite figures exist, the annual enterprise closure (death) rate in rural areas (33.8 percent) was substantially higher than that in urban areas (24.5 percent) for 1992–93 (Cabal 1995). In that country, firm birth and death rates followed the same locational pattern, with both higher in rural areas.

It is possible to construct a profile of the closed rural enterprise from the findings of the "closed enterprise surveys" conducted in the Dominican Republic and the five African core countries. Three principal conclusions emerge from this analysis. First, only about half of the closures of rural enterprises in these countries occurred due to business failures, that is, because the enterprise was not financially or economically viable. Approximately a quarter of the rural enterprises closed for personal reasons, such as bad health or retirement, while others closed because better options became available or because the government forced them to close. A comparable study in rural Bangladesh in 2003 found similar results (World Bank 2004).

Second, most of the closures due to business failure occur in the initial years of operation. Indeed, over 50 percent of the rural enterprise closures in Zimbabwe, Swaziland, and Kenya had taken place before the end of the third year of operation.

Third, the findings derived from a "hazard analysis" of the closed enterprises in Swaziland and Zimbabwe provide a picture of the characteristics of enterprises that are most likely to close (McPherson 1995). The results indicate that a rural firm is more likely to close during any given year, holding all other variables constant, if it does not grow; starts large, not small; operates in the trading sector; operates out of the entrepreneur's home; and is owned and operated by a female entrepreneur. Clearly, with high rates of entry and exit, the rural enterprise scene in Africa is a rapidly changing one. To this churning must be added the expansion and contraction of the existing enterprises.

Firm Expansion

The overall expansion of existing enterprises varies significantly by location. As indicated in Table 5.3, a striking finding was that in all countries except Kenya, enterprises located in urban areas grew much faster than those in rural areas. Indeed, the worldwide average growth rate for urban enterprises was over

TABLE 5.3 Annual employment growth rates of existing micro and small enterprises

| | Growth rate (percent) | | |
Country	Urban	Rural[a]	Entire country
Botswana*	12	7	8
Kenya*	25	30	29
Malawi*	16	10	11
Swaziland*	12	6	7
Zimbabwe*	9	7	7
Dominican Republic*	16	13	15
Colombia[b]	15	—	—
Ghana[c]	12	—	—
India[c]	16	—	—
Lesotho*	12	4	6
Niger*	9	8	9
Nigeria[c]	16	—	—
South Africa*	24	—	—
Worldwide	15	11	11

SOURCES: South Africa—Liedholm and McPherson (1991); Swaziland—Fisseha and McPherson (1991); Lesotho—Fisseha (1991); Zimbabwe—McPherson (1991); Kenya—Parker and Aleke Dondo (1991); Nigeria—Chuta (1989); Ghana—Steel and Webster (1990); Colombia—Cortes, Berry, and Ishaq (1987); Dominican Republic—Cabal (1995); India—Little, Mazumdar, and Page (1987); Botswana—calculated from data generated by Daniels and Fisseha (1992); Niger—Joumard, Liedholm, and Mead (1992); Malawi—calculated from data generated by Daniels and Ngwira (1993).

NOTES: Growth rates are average annual growth rates in terms of employment. Average annual growth rates are defined as follows: (A–B/B)/C, where A = number of workers now, B = number of workers when enterprise started, and C = number of years firm has been in existence. A dash indicates that data are not available.

* indicates countries for which data are from our surveys.

[a]Includes rural areas (enumeration areas) plus secondary towns.

[b]Metal firms only.

[c]Manufacturing enterprises only.

4 percentage points higher than that for rural enterprises. In several countries, the urban rate was more than double the rural rate. One of the reasons for the relatively slower rural growth rates is that typically fewer rural enterprises were expanding. A regression analysis of the determinants of enterprise growth applied to the survey data in Botswana, Kenya, Lesotho, Swaziland, and Zimbabwe also revealed that rural enterprises were likely to grow less rapidly than their urban counterparts (Liedholm and Mead 1999). In a separate regression with only rural nonfarm enterprises included, it was found that a rural firm is more likely to expand, holding all other variables constant, if it starts smaller, is younger, operates in manufacturing or services, and is owned and operated by a male entrepreneur (Liedholm, McPherson, and Chuta 1994).

As indicated in Table 5.4, the percentage of very small enterprises (with one to four workers) that grew was lower in rural than in urban areas in four of the five countries surveyed. The highest percentage of growing rural firms was found in Kenya, where over a third of the very small enterprises had expanded.

How many of these small rural enterprises "graduated" to a much larger size category? A small minority of the rural firms that started very small did manage a more sizable expansion and employed over 10 workers at the time of the African surveys. Although overall only 0.9 percent of the very small enterprises "graduated" to this larger size class, these firms contributed over 20 percent of the new jobs created (Mead 1994a). In two countries, Kenya and Botswana, the graduation rate was higher in rural than in urban areas (Table 5.4). It is also noteworthy that over 50 percent of the existing rural enterprises with 10 to 50 workers had started with fewer than 4 workers (Mead 1994a). Unfortunately, comparable graduation rates for rural firms in other areas of the world are not available. There is some limited evidence, however, that the overall graduation rates in Latin America and Asia are at least as high as those in Africa (Liedholm 1992).

To what extent have government policies inhibited the graduation of firms and thus contributed to the "missing middle" in the enterprise size distribution? It is frequently argued (Snodgrass and Biggs 1996) that most governmental regulations fail to reach the micro firms. As they increase in size, however, they become more visible and are subject to government policies and thus have a disincentive to expand beyond a certain size. Timberg (1978) has noted the large number of firms just below the size required for registration as a factory in India, and de Soto (1989) has described the high transaction cost associated with registration. Evidence from Africa (McPherson and Liedholm 1996), however, suggests that registration and other government regulations and taxes did not inhibit the growth of enterprises in the countries studied. The owners of fewer than 10 percent of the rural firms said they were directly affected by any rules or regulations, while the tax structure, both on the books and as enforced, was regressive by size of enterprise and did not present a barrier to expansion.

TABLE 5.4 Employment growth patterns by locality size

	Botswana	Kenya	Malawi	Swaziland	Zimbabwe
Percent of all rural nonfarm jobs coming from enterprise expansion					
Urban	26	27	24	37	20
Rural towns	25	27	18	28	18
Rural enumeration areas	28	28	20	22	19
Percent of all rural nonfarm enterprises that had grown					
Urban	24	36	28	31	18
Rural towns	21	35	26	28	23
Rural enumeration areas	19	35	23	17	20
Of those that started very small (with 1–4 workers at start): Percent of those that started very small that had grown at all					
Urban	23	36	27	30	17
Rural towns	21	35	26	27	21
Rural enumeration areas	18	35	23	17	18
Percent of those that started very small that had graduated to 10+ workers					
Urban	1	1	1	2	1
Rural towns	1	0	0	1	0
Rural EA	2	2	0	0	1

SOURCE: Computed from survey data.

In Africa, some have argued that a "managerial bottleneck" rather than a policy constraint impedes graduation. Kilby (1988) contends that there is a deficiency not in innovation or risk taking, but rather in the "mere management—coordination and control—functions of the entrepreneur." More testing is required to verify the importance of this particular bottleneck.

Decomposing Sources of Total Nonfarm Employment Growth

What percentage of the new rural nonfarm jobs in rural areas came from the expansion of existing firms, and what percentage came from new business creation? The distinction between the two is important, because in many cases the forces leading to the growth of employment are different. A higher percentage of the new jobs arising from new start-ups typically reflects survival activities by individuals with few options. Although it is not always true, a significant proportion of new enterprise starts are driven by the necessity of finding any source of income, particularly in cases in which agriculture is languishing and/or population growth is high. A substantial share of new rural nonfarm starts are one-person enterprises, the least efficient and lowest-return size category, and these tend to be concentrated in activities with the lowest barriers to entry and the largest degree of overcrowding (Liedholm and Mead 1999).

New rural nonfarm jobs arising from an expansion of existing enterprises are more likely to reflect a response to an identified business opportunity and should be particularly strong when agriculture is prospering. Indeed, there is accumulating evidence that economic efficiency and returns resulting from an expansion of existing enterprises are generally higher than can be accounted for by new business start-ups (Liedholm and Mead 1987; Daniels, Mead, and Musinga 1995). To oversimplify a complex set of relationships, jobs arising from net expansion of existing firms are more likely to reflect demand-pull forces, while new start-ups are more likely to reflect supply-push forces.

A glance at Table 5.4 reveals that only 23 percent of the new rural jobs created in the five African core countries came from a net expansion of existing firms. The remainder came from start-up firms. This finding indicates the relative importance of supply-push rather than demand-pull forces and the marginal nature of most of the new jobs. This is not just a rural phenomenon, however. For example, in two countries, Kenya and Botswana, the percentage of jobs created through net enterprise expansion was higher in rural than in urban areas. The reverse pattern was found in the other three surveyed countries (Table 5.4). It is also important to note that the highest expansion rate among existing enterprises in rural areas was found in Kenya and Botswana, perhaps reflecting the relative importance of the demand-pull forces in the rural areas of these two countries.

Enterprise Dynamics: Macro Determinants

Although the growth of rural nonfarm enterprises depends on a complex interaction of forces operating on both the demand and the supply side of the market, the demand-side forces have typically received primary attention at the macro level. Of all the macro demand-pull forces, agriculture has typically been accorded the central role, while others, such as large-scale industry and macro policy, have been considered of lesser importance.

As the major source of rural income, agriculture generates the principal source of demand for rurally produced consumer and intermediate goods. The well-known debates on agricultural growth linkages revolved around how powerful these demand linkages are. A review of this literature suggests that growth multipliers generally lie in the range of 1.3–1.8, which means that every dollar of technology-induced agricultural income generates an additional 30 to 80 cents in rural nonfarm income (see Chapter 7). About two-thirds of the total of agricultural growth linkages stem from consumption linkages, with production linkages providing the remainder.

These more aggregate sectoral and macro studies, however, have not been able to examine how agricultural growth has affected the composition of rural nonfarm enterprise growth in terms of start-up enterprises and the expansion of existing enterprises. Although a paucity of both time-series and cross-section data precludes rigorous statistical analysis, some insights into this issue may be gleaned from an analysis of the data from the six core countries.

An examination of the dynamic data from our sample reveals that the overall performance of rural nonfarm enterprises stands out in two countries, Botswana and Kenya. For example, the percentage of job growth resulting from firm expansion in these countries was significantly higher than in the others. Moreover, a greater percentage of the expanding rural enterprises in these two countries "graduated" into the 10-plus workers size category. Finally, in a statistical analysis of the determinants of existing firm growth, controlling for the effects of the other independent variables, only the country dummies for Kenya and Botswana differed statistically (positively) from Zimbabwe (Liedholm, McPherson, and Chuta 1994). Which of the macro determinants enumerated earlier might account for these differences in enterprise dynamics?

The Macroeconomic Policy Environment

Overall macroeconomic conditions, in terms of both level and growth of per capita income during the 1980s, might explain the relatively successful rural enterprise performance in Botswana, whose per capita income level (US$2,790 in 1992) and gross national product (GNP) growth rate per capita (6.1 percent per year from 1980 to 1992) were exceptional within Africa. They do not explain, however, what happened in Kenya, whose overall macro indicators (1992 GNP per capita of $310 and annual GNP per capita growth of +0.2 percent) more closely resembled those of Malawi (1992 GNP per capita of $210 and annual GNP per capita growth of –0.1 percent).

Agriculture

One must therefore turn to a consideration of the overall performance of the agricultural sectors in these countries. A review of the published figures on the annual growth of food production per capita from 1980 to 1991 reveals that Kenya was the only country among the five to experience positive growth (World Bank 1993). There food production per capita increased at an annual rate of 0.5 percent, and the demand-driven spin-off from it no doubt served to propel Kenya's rural enterprise sector. During the same period, changes in food production per capita was negative in Malawi (–2.7 percent), Swaziland

(–0.9 percent), Zimbabwe (–1.0 percent), and even Botswana (–3.7 percent). Although agriculture was clearly not central in explaining rural enterprise performance in Botswana, where agriculture was less than 5 percent of GNP and other sources of demand predominated, its role was important in the other countries. This appears to be particularly true in Swaziland and is important for understanding the desultory performance of rural enterprises there. The percentage of new enterprises that had grown or graduated was low, and the percentage of the jobs from new starts was high. Likewise, the differential performance gap between rural enterprises and their urban counterparts was very great (Table 5.4). The poor agricultural performance in that country was apparently sufficient to outweigh a buoyant overall economic performance (1992 per capita GNP of $1,090 and annual GNP per capita growth from 1980–92 of +1.61 percent).

The character and composition of agricultural growth also appear to affect the performance of rural enterprises. An illuminating example comes from a study analyzing how Malawi's decision in 1990 to permit smallholders to grow the major export crop, burley tobacco, might have affected rural enterprises (McPherson and Henry 1994). The study compared areas that now have large amounts of smallholder tobacco with closely paired control areas that had little or no smallholder production, but rather large estates producing tobacco. Existing enterprises in the smallholder burley-growing areas grew at an average annual rate of 8.8 percent from start-up, a rate that was significantly (statistically) higher than the 5.9 percent rate experienced in the control areas. Furthermore, the percentage of rural enterprise employment growth that came from enterprise expansion rather than from new start-ups was higher in the smallholder burley areas. Finally, the study found evidence in the smallholder burley area of a more rapid sectoral shift toward nonfarm activities with higher productivity and profits, such as food and beverage retailing. These results are consistent with a demand-driven pattern of enterprise growth coupled with labor market tightening described in Chapter 3.

Large-Scale Firms

Beyond agriculture, however, it would also be instructive to examine how large-scale industries affect rural nonfarm enterprise dynamics. Large-scale industry's role can be positive, enhancing the demand for products from smaller firms and providing improved technology or cheaper inputs (see Chapters 14 and 15). Large firms can also have a negative effect on smaller firms, particularly when they directly compete with them in the same markets (see Table 15.1). Sorghum beer production in Southern Africa provides an example of this direct competition between small and large producers (Boomgard et al. 1992). The empirical evidence on the demand linkages between small- and large-scale enterprises, however, is quite sparse, particularly among those located in rural areas (Liedholm and Mead 1987).

The forward linkages from rural nonfarm enterprises to larger firms are typically rather small. The vast majority of the output of small-scale rural nonfarm enterprises is sold directly to the final consumers.[5] Empirical evidence from Africa indicates that small firms that sell directly to final consumers are less likely to grow than those that sell to traders and manufacturing firms (Liedholm and Mead 1999). This corroborates findings from a number of subsector case studies that found that traditional, vertically integrated household producers typically wither under pressure from technically superior competing supply channels. As a result, growth opportunities for small firms often require that enterprises shift to growing market channels that access improved inputs or growing markets via larger firms (see Chapter 15).

The institutional arrangements by which rural nonfarm enterprises have moved beyond direct sale to final consumers include subcontracting, franchising, flexible specialization, and a consortium approach. Subcontracting has been the most prevalent of these arrangements and has been particularly widespread in Asia. Studies in Bangladesh, Thailand, and Indonesia have revealed that these subcontracting arrangements have reached into remote rural areas of these countries (Mead 1992a, 1985; Hayami 1998a). Most of this activity, however, has been concentrated in three industries: garments, wood, and fabricated metal products. Such subcontracting arrangements appear to be much rarer in Africa, although extensive subcontracting was revealed in studies conducted in rural Egypt. Indeed, a rural blacksmith supplied bolts to one of the large-scale automobile plants in Cairo (Davies, Mead, and Seale 1992). Subsector studies have proven to be useful vehicles for identifying these various linkages between large enterprises and small rural nonfarm activities and the degree to which they complement and compete against one another in particular areas (see Chapter 15).

Conclusions and Policy Implications

Rural nonfarm enterprises are a particularly dynamic component of rural economies. New firms are being created at a high rate; over 20 percent are new entrants each year in the countries examined here. But large numbers of them, over 50 percent in many cases, disappear within the first three years. The annual growth rate of surviving rural nonfarm enterprises is high, but a minority of enterprises fuels the bulk of this expansion. Jobs created through the expansion of existing enterprises are more likely to reflect increasing efficiency and demand-pull forces in the economy. These expanding firms are more likely to

---

5. The final consumers represented 89 percent of the total buyers of MSE products in rural Honduras and 81 percent in Egypt (Liedholm and Mead 1987).

be younger, to have started smaller, and to be operated out of the entrepreneurs' homes by males in the manufacturing or service sector. In the six core countries examined, the majority of new jobs came not from demand-pulled expansion, but rather from start-up firms. Given the desultory overall performance of the agricultural sector in African countries, it is not surprising that the majority of new enterprise jobs in rural areas have come from start-up firms, which typically signals that a sluggish rural economy with limited alternatives is pushing households into rural nonfarm enterprise creation.

Several policy and project implications emerge from the present findings. At the most general level, it is important to recognize that policies aimed at creating a more dynamic agricultural sector also provide the fuel for a demand-pulled expansion of existing rural nonfarm enterprises, the type of employment growth that reflects increased prosperity.

At the project level, the findings provide a reminder that the "clients" of assistance efforts, the rural enterprises, are a heterogeneous group with different opportunities and needs that vary over the life cycle of the enterprise. The constraints and opportunities faced by rural enterprises at start-up, for example, are quite different from those faced by existing enterprises seeking to expand (Liedholm and Mead 1999). Indeed, given the large numbers of new starts every year, the high attrition rates in the early years of a new rural nonfarm enterprise's life, and the multiple needs of new entrants, one might ask how many resources should be devoted to helping new establishments get started. In contrast, existing enterprises seeking to expand can often make a substantial contribution to growth. Yet the typical intervention of providing small amounts of working capital may be inadequate, for many of the firms seeking more vigorous growth paths report that the most serious problems they face are in the area of markets. This suggests that unblocking market constraints further up the supply chain will be key to expanding opportunities for these growing firms.

6 Household Income Diversification into Rural Nonfarm Activities

.THOMAS REARDON, JULIO BERDEGUÉ,
CHRISTOPHER B. BARRETT,
AND KOSTAS STAMOULIS

The traditional vision of rural economies as purely agricultural is clearly obsolete. Farm households across the developing world earn an increasing share of their income from nonfarm sources (see Table 4.1). The specialized nonfarm households that emerge often diversify into multiple business activities. Decisions affecting nonfarm enterprise creation, closure, and growth are thus commonly made within the confines of a multiactivity rural household. Thus nonfarm enterprise dynamics, discussed in Chapter 5, fit into a household decision-making environment that helps to shape outcomes as well as labor and capital allocation across activities. Consequently, a fuller understanding of nonfarm enterprise dynamics requires an assessment of the household decisionmaking environment within which these decisions are frequently made.

Households' motives for diversification, as well as the opportunities available to them, differ significantly across settings and income groups, suggesting an important distinction between diversification undertaken for accumulation objectives, driven mainly by "pull" factors, and diversification undertaken to manage risk, cope with shock, or escape from agriculture in stagnation or in secular decline, hence driven by "push" factors. Discussions of these push and pull factors are found in many household and regional case studies examining patterns of household income diversification in the developing world.[1] While diversification driven by pull factors is usually associated with an upward spiral of incomes and assets for the households thus engaged, diversification driven by push factors sometimes extracts a household from poverty. In other instances, the push into rural nonfarm activity may represent a holding pattern or a process of immiseration (even "growth with immiseration," as Barrett 1998 puts it) as the household adds the equivalent of subsistence-level nonfarm activity to a risky and poor agricultural income base. It thus becomes important for policymakers to understand the nature and patterns of household income diversification

---

1. See Evans and Ngau (1991), Davies (1993), Francis and Hoddinot (1993), Reardon, Crawford, and Kelly (1994), Webb and Von Braun (1994), Bryceson and Jamal (1997), Reardon (1997), Reardon et al. (1998), Ellis (2000), Barrett et al. (2004), and Ellis and Freeman (2004).

and distinguish the factors that drive households into nonfarm activity so they can use this knowledge to inform programs and policies in the rural nonfarm economy (RNFE).

This chapter addresses these issues by focusing on four key questions: First, how should one conceptualize a farm household's decision to diversify its income sources into rural nonfarm activities? Second, what is the empirical evidence concerning the extent and nature of that diversification? Third, what is the empirical evidence concerning the determinants of that diversification? Fourth, what are the program and policy implications? To address these questions, this chapter reviews findings from several hundred rural household surveys in developing countries.[2]

Conceptual Framework: Why Rural Households Diversify into Rural Nonfarm Activities

The rural household or individual's decision to supply labor to the rural nonfarm sector can be conceptualized as a specific application of the class of behavioral models of factor supply in general and of labor in particular.[3] Economists model the labor supply as well as the capital investment function (for own-enterprise start-up or upgrading of, say, household i to activity j) as a function of incentives and capacity variables. The household is assumed to want to maximize its earnings subject to constraints imposed by its limited resources and in trade-off with its desire to minimize risk.

The "determined variable" for our present purposes is "diversification" into nonfarm activity through labor supply and capital investment decisions. The diversification choice can be broken down into five interdependent and simultaneous choices regarding the following:

- Nonfarm participation: choice of farm sector activity versus nonfarm activity
- Level of nonfarm activity
- Sectoral choice within the RNFE: manufacturing versus services
- Location: whether to undertake the activity locally or elsewhere via migration
- Form: whether to undertake self-employment or wage employment (the functional choice)

---

2. The review draws from earlier reviews of mainly African and Latin American evidence— Reardon (1997), Reardon et al. (1998, 2000), Reardon, Berdegué, and Escobar (2001), and Barrett, Reardon, and Webb (2001)—and also updates those reviews and adds Asian evidence.

3. See, for example, Sadoulet and de Janvry (1995) for the economic theory of general factor demand and supply models and Rosensweig (1988) for labor market models.

On the other hand, there are three "determinants" of these five choices:

- The set of incentive "levels" facing the household, including relative prices of outputs from and inputs to activity *j* versus activities *k, l,* and *m*
- The instability of incentives: the set of incentive "variations" facing the household, including the relative risks (climatic, market, and other risks) of activity *j* versus activities *k, l,* and *m*
- The set of capacity variables (capital assets including human, social, financial, organizational, and physical assets that enable the undertaking of activities)

The following discussion considers the categories of this conceptual framework, focusing first on empirical evidence concerning the choices that households in various regions make as revealed by patterns of diversification into rural nonfarm activity and then on the perspectives and findings of the literature on the determinants of diversification into nonfarm activity.

Patterns of Household Diversification into the RNFE

Participation in Nonfarm Activity

Contrary to the traditional image, diversification into rural nonfarm employment is extremely widespread and important. Table 6.1 reviews survey evidence concerning the shares of rural nonfarm income (RNFY) in total income. Because of differences in timing, degrees of coverage, survey methods, and definitions used, these results should be taken as broadly indicative. The table shows that RNFY constitutes roughly 35 percent of rural household income in Africa and about 50 percent in Asia and Latin America. Suffice it to say that most of the studies reported showed from moderate to fast growth in the share of RNFY in total income over the past two decades. In China, for instance, in 1981 only 15 percent of rural households worked off farm, compared to 32 percent in 1995 (De Brauw et al. 2002). In Bangladesh 42 percent of rural income came from RNFY in 1987, but by 2000 the share was 54 percent (Hossain 2004). Clearly integrated farm-nonfarm households are a common sight across the developing world, and the upward trend is steep.

The average composition of income, of course, hides the distribution over households within the RNFE. The range of households undertaking both farming and rural nonfarm activities is generally around 30 to 50 percent,[4] but a number of studies are showing even higher participation, such as in Kenya, where

---

4. Berdegué et al. (2001), Corral and Reardon (2001), Deininger and Olinto (2001), Ruben and Van Den Berg (2001), Smith et al. (2001), Barrett et al. (2004).

TABLE 6.1 Rural nonfarm income: Case study evidence from the 1990s and 2000s

| | | Composition of nonfarm earnings (% of total income) | | | | |
| | | Nonfarm share of total income (%) (a) | Local (%) (b) | Transfers and remittances[a] (%) (c) | Ratio of local to external nonfarm income (b/c) | |
Country	Year					Source
Africa						
Ethiopia	1989–90	36	—	—	—	Webb and Von Braun (1994)
	1999	20	—	—	—	Deininger et al. (2003)
Ghana	1992	31	31	0.3	102.7	Winters et al. (2006)
	1998	42	42	0.1	417.0	Winters et al. (2006)
Ivory Coast	1993–95	7	—	—	—	Barrett et al. (2005)
Kenya	1994–96	29	—	—	—	Barrett et al. (2005)
Kenya, western	1993	80	53	27	2.0	Francis and Hoddinott (1993)
Malawi	1990–91	34	26	9	3.0	Peters (1992)
	2004	64	59	5	13.2	Winters et al. (2005)
Mali, southern	1994–96	6	5	1	5.0	Abdulai and Crole-Rees (2001)
Mozambique	1991	15	14	1	25.0	Tschirley and Weber (1994)
Namibia, unfavorable zones	1992–93	93	16	78	0.2	Keyler (1996)
Namibia, favorable zones	1992–93	56	37	19	2.0	Keyler (1996)
Niger, unfavorable zones	1989–90	52	33	19	1.7	Hopkins and Reardon (1993)
Niger, favorable zones	1989–90	43	38	5	7.8	Hopkins and Reardon (1993)
Rwanda	1991	15	—	—	—	Barrett et al. (2005)
	1999–2001	20	20	-7	—	Dabalen, Paternostro, and Pierre (2004)
Tanzania	1991	11	10	1	10.0	Ellis (1999)
	2000	46	46	—	—	Ellis and Freeman (2004)

						Source
Uganda	1996	34	25	9	3.0	Canagarajah, Newman, and Bhattamishra (2001)
	1999–2000	54	—	—	—	Balihuta and Sen (2001)
Zimbabwe, overall	1990–91	38	26	12	2.2	World Bank (1996)
Zimbabwe, poor	1990–91	31	17	14	1.3	World Bank (1996)
Africa, average		37	26	11	2.5	
Africa, excluding Namibia		34	28	6	4.7	
Asia						
Bangladesh	2000	65	56	9	6.4	World Bank (2004)
	2000	54	—	—	—	Hossain (2004)
China	1993	30	—	—	—	Kung and Lee (2001)
	1997	36	—	—	—	Fan, Zhang, and Zhang (2002)
India	1993–94	37	35	2	17.0	Lanjouw and Shariff (2002)
Korea, Republic of[b]	2003	54	38	16	—	KREI (2005)
Nepal	1996	39	28	11	2.6	Winters et al. (2006)
Pakistan	1990–1991	54	37	17	2.2	Adams (1998)
	1999	67	—	—	—	Kurosaki and Khan (2006)
Philippines	1994	51	—	—	—	Estudillo and Otsuka (1999)
	1998	77	61	16	3.8	Estudillo, Quisumbing, and Otsuka (2001)
Sri Lanka	1999–2000	71	56	15	3.8	World Bank (2003)
Vietnam	1998	40	35	5	6.5	Winters et al. (2006)
Vietnam, Northern Uplands	2002	40	28	12	2.3	Minot et al. (2006)
Asia, average		51	40	11	3.7	

(continued)

TABLE 6.1 *Continued*

Country	Year	Composition of nonfarm earnings (% of total income)				Source
		Nonfarm share of total income (%) (a)	Local (%) (b)	Transfers and remittances[a] (%) (c)	Ratio of local to external nonfarm income (b/c)	
Latin America						
Brazil	1997	39	37	2	20.0	Da Silva and Del Grossi (2001)
Chile	1996	41	39	2	20.0	Berdegué et al. (2001)
Colombia	1997	50	48	2	20.0	Echeverri (1999)
Ecuador	1994	35	33	2	22.3	Winters et al. (2006)
El Salvador	1995	41	39	2	20.0	Elbers and Lanjouw (2001)
	1995	38	—	—	—	Lanjouw (2001)
Guatemala	2001	72	55	19	3.0	Tannuri-Pianto et al. (2004)
Haiti	2000	51	44	7	6.5	Winters et al. (2006)
	1996	68	—	—	—	Wiens and Sobrado (1998)
Honduras	1997	22	—	—	—	Ruben and Van Den Berg (2001)
	1998	31	—	—	—	Isgut (2004)
Mexico	1997	43	36	7	5.5	de Janvry and Sadoulet (2001)
Nicaragua	2003	67	50	17	2.9	Yúnez-Naude and Taylor (2001)
	1998	42	37	5	7.0	Corral and Reardon (2001)
Panama	2001	30	28	2	12.8	Winters et al. (2006)
Peru	1997	79	70	9	8.2	Winters et al. (2006)
	1997	44	—	—	—	Escobal (2001)
Latin America, average		47	41	6	6.8	

NOTES: A dash indicates that data are not available.

[a]Includes public transfers as well as private remittances. In the case of Sri Lanka, public transfers account for the majority of external nonfarm income transferred to rural areas.

[b]Farm households only.

the share is 90 percent (Barrett et al. 2004). Engaging in multiple activities is termed "pluriactivity" in the literature, and this can be contrasted with specialization. Comparisons of individual versus household pluriactivity have been rare in the literature, but the results for China, for example, as reported by Knight and Song (2003), are probably indicative: 65 percent of households operate in both the farm and nonfarm sectors, while only one-third of individuals do. This relative specialization by individuals makes economic sense, and the diversification by households makes risk management sense.

One would expect the frequency of pluriactivity to be inversely related to the average income level of the zone.[5] In poor areas, where households typically participate in both farm and nonfarm activities, they may not engage in either very efficiently, but they are able to manage risk, compensate for a poor asset base, and survive. In contrast, in richer zones the specialization rate is higher. More households specialize in purely farm or purely nonfarm pursuits. Given the efficiency gains from specialization, this positive correlation between income and specialization makes economic sense. Comparing individual households, however, we see the opposite relationship. Increasing household income is typically associated with higher rates of pluriactivity.[6] However, closer inspection reveals that this more extensive diversification at the household level actually involves specialization among individuals. Richer households commonly have individual members who specialize in nonfarm work, often highly paid wage employment, or work as managers of specialized nonfarm trading, transport, and processing businesses.

These zonal and household strata patterns of pluriactivity versus specialization are mirrored on average over countries and regions. African households in general exhibit higher rates of pluriactivity, whereas in the wealthier Latin American countries household specialization is more common. In part, the sharp seasonality of rain-fed African agriculture generates a long dry season during which most households need to undertake some form of remunerative activity. For this reason, the agricultural and nonfarm calendars are typically countercyclical (Figure 1.1).

The picture just drawn is of course a static one, but the reality is that households and communities follow paths of development that include alternative income-earning strategies. Examples of work examining these activity portfolio formation paths include that of Barrett et al. (2005) at the household level in Africa (Ivory Coast, Kenya, and Rwanda) and that undertaken at the community level in Honduras. This work on "dynamics" is important for RNFE development programs designed to target household groups and communities.

---

5. Reardon (1997), Reardon et al. (2000), Barrett, Reardon, and Webb (2001), Deininger and Olinto (2001), Reardon, Berdegué, and Escobar (2001).
6. Berdegué et al. (2001), Ruben and Van Den Berg (2001), Corral and Reardon (2001), Barrett et al. (2004), Smith et al. (2001).

RNFY versus Farm Wage Labor Income

Contrary to conventional wisdom, RNFY typically far exceeds farm wage labor incomes. In spite of a common tendency in the literature and in policy discussions about farmers' income diversification to emphasize the importance of off-farm agricultural wage labor, available empirical evidence suggests that RNFY typically greatly exceeds the value of farm wage earnings. A series of several dozen household case studies indicates that RNFY exceeds agricultural wage earnings by a factor of 5 to 1 in Latin America and by 20 to 1 in Africa (Reardon 1997; Reardon et al. 1998; Reardon, Berdegué, and Escobar 2001), and in India by 4.5 to 1 (Lanjouw and Shariff 2002), to cite but a few examples of a general pattern.

Exceptions occur in two situations. The first is among the landless poor and in zones with substantial commercial farming, such as the ranching areas of Argentina, the fruit zones of Chile, and the sugar zones of Honduras. The second is found, but only in a relative sense, among the poorest stratum everywhere. For example, in India, while the ratio of nonfarm to agricultural wage income is 4.5 to 1 for the average household, for the poor that ratio is only 0.75 to 1 (Lanjouw and Shariff 2002). Farm wage labor has the lowest entry barriers —and the lowest returns—of all activities.

Local RNFY versus Migration

Available evidence contradicts the traditional assumption that earnings from labor migration exceed those from local nonfarm activities. Contrary to conventional wisdom, RNFY far exceeds migration incomes. These incomes can be earned in either the farm sector (by a Oaxacan peasant, say, working on a tomato farm in Northern Mexico) or the nonfarm sector (by a Honduran rural girl, say, working in a *maquiladora* in a secondary town); the only qualification is that they are not earned locally.

In Latin America, even in areas of heavy emigration, such as Mexico and Central America, local nonfarm earnings normally exceed those of migrant remittances. A study of *ejidal* households in Mexico, for example, finds that only 7 percent of incomes come from migration compared to 36 percent from local nonfarm earnings (de Janvry and Sadoulet 2001). A dozen studies from Latin America suggest that local nonfarm earnings exceed those earned by migrant family members by a ratio of 7 to 1 (Table 6.1). This finding belies the view commonly held in Latin America that migration income is much greater than local RNFY. In fact, available evidence suggests quite the opposite. Corral and Reardon (2001) find that, even in Nicaragua, with its reputation for heavy reliance on remittances to rural families, only 10 percent of households have migrant members, and of those, four out of five work in domestic urban locations, while only one migrates to international destinations.

Similarly, in Africa a set of over 25 case studies suggests that local non-farm earnings exceeded the value of migrant income by a factor of over 2 (Table 6.1). In resource-poor rural zones, however, remittances become more important than in dynamic rural regions. Comparison of favorable and unfavorable rural zones in Burkina, Namibia, and Niger suggests that the share of migrant earnings in total income roughly triples in importance in poor regions (Table 6.1). In areas of extreme rural poverty, such as the former South African home-lands and the desert areas of Namibia and Botswana, migratory labor becomes very important, accounting for half of rural incomes (Table 6.1; Nattrass and Nattrass 1990). These areas appear exceptional, however. Even in northern Burkina Faso during the serious drought of 1984, average migration remittances totaled only a tenth the value of local nonfarm incomes (Reardon, Matlon, and Delgado 1988).

The importance of migration varies significantly over time. In the Sahel after the 1984 drought, the share of migration income in total rural income was about three times higher than the average share over the first half of the 1980s (Reardon, Matlon, and Delgado 1988; Reardon, Delgado, and Matlon 1992). Though clearly important for some rural households, migrant earnings are highly variable (de Haan 1999; de Haan and Rogaly 2002). On average, they appear to be significantly less important than local rural nonfarm earnings.

In Asia, too, local nonfarm income is typically much more important than migrant remittances, except in the few countries where international migration has become extremely important (such as the Philippines) and rural-urban migration has grown very rapidly. For example, De Brauw et al. (2002) show that while a Chinese farmer working in the nonfarm sector in 1981 was three times as likely to work locally as to work as a migrant worker, by 2000 the ratio was 1 to 1. However, Lohmar et al. (2001) show that most of this migration was actually rural to rural, reflecting the immensely fast rural industrialization in China, a relatively rare situation in developing countries.

It is also the case that in many of the countries in transition, with notable exceptions, local sources of nonfarm income far exceed overall transfers to households, including private transfers such as remittances and public transfers such as pensions. Winters et al. (2006) found that the share of income from transfers in overall household income ranged from 11 percent in Nepal to 0.3 percent in Ghana. However, the share of households with some income from transfers ranged from 54.7 in Panama to 23.7 in Equador.

Rural Nonfarm Wage Income versus Self-Employment Income

Contrary to conventional wisdom, rural nonfarm wage income is often more important than rural nonfarm self-employment earnings. Despite widespread self-employment, particularly among family-based one- and two-person enter-prises, nonfarm wage employment appears to be at least as large a contributor to RNFY. Over regions, the importance of wage income (versus self-employment income) tends to be correlated with higher incomes and denser infrastructure. This spatial perspective is explored further in the section of this chapter on determinants.

In Latin America, nonfarm wage earnings (as a level, not a rate) commonly exceed the value of self-employment earnings. In Brazil, Chile, and Colombia, in Mexican *ejidos,* and in Nicaragua, the share of nonfarm income from wage employment is on average much higher than that from self-employment. In contrast, in Ecuador, Honduras, and Peru, self-employment is more important than nonfarm wage employment, particularly in poorer zones. These differences can also be observed over different zones within a given country. For example, Berdegué et al. (2001) show that in Chile the wage employment share in the RNFE is much higher in the more favorable zones compared to the less favorable areas. Ruben and Van Den Berg (2001) and Isgut (2004) show that nonfarm wage income is much higher than self-employment income in the northern region of Honduras near towns that are linked to better infrastructure and in zones with a higher density of rural towns. Yet in the southern zone, where infrastructure and town density are lower, self-employment is much more important.

Out of seven African household studies that permit this comparison, four (in Botswana, Kenya, Malawi, and Zimbabwe) show that nonfarm wage income is nearly twice as important as self-employment, while the other three (in Rwanda, Ethiopia, and Sudan) suggest the reverse (Reardon 1997). In all regions, the wage share of nonfarm earnings increases near towns, while part-time self-employment looms largest in remote rural areas.

In India, Lanjouw and Shariff (2002) found that rural nonfarm wage income was twice as important as self-employment income in a national sample, both for the average household and for the poorest quartile. However, the average household earned only a quarter of its nonfarm wage income from casual nonfarm labor versus three quarters for the poor quartile, indicating that uneducated poor households relied on low-skill, low–entry barrier labor.

Services versus Manufacturing

Contrary to conventional wisdom, as reflected in a long history of government and donor programs focused on rural manufactures rather than services, service sector income is often more important than income from rural manufacturing. In spite of the common emphasis on rural industries, manufacturing typically accounts for a minority of RNFY, except in hinterland areas.[7] For example, in rural El Salvador, service sector jobs are twice as prevalent as small-scale man-

---

7. Reardon (1997), Reardon et al. (1998), Barrett, Reardon, and Webb (2001), Reardon, Berdegué, and Escobar (2001).

TABLE 6.2 Capital intensity and returns to labor in rural nonfarm activities in Bangladesh, 1980

Industry	Capital per worker (Tk)	Value added per worker (Tk/day)	Share of female workers (%)
Tailoring	4,982	27.5	20
Producing dairy products	3,076	23.4	10
Gur (sugar) making	711	20.0	0
Carpentry	3,009	19.9	4
Jewelrymaking	1,283	18.7	2
Blacksmithy	760	15.8	2
Handloom weaving	1,594	15.1	38
Oil pressing	1,006	12.6	43
Potterymaking	799	11.8	47
Paddy husking	303	7.4	56
Making bamboo products	313	5.2	49
Matmaking	465	5.2	63
Making fishing nets	265	4.8	63
Making coir rope	145	4.1	64

SOURCE: Hossain (1984), cited in Lanjouw and Lanjouw (2001).

NOTE: Tk, taka.

ufacturing jobs. In poorer zones and among poorer households, however, labor-intensive household-based manufacturing may predominate, as does beer brewing in much of Africa, the production of straw products in Andean zones, and weaving in Northeast Thailand.[8]

Within any given sector, specific activities and technologies differ considerably according to household investment capacity, education, and labor mobility. Because returns to rural nonfarm labor vary positively with investment per worker and because poor households have the least to invest, self-employment among low-income households often affords the lowest returns within the RNFE. Women, because of the severe restrictions on their mobility, frequently remain overrepresented in low-paying, household-based, labor-intensive activities (Table 6.2).

Determinants of Household Diversification into the RNFE

The determinants discussed in the previously elaborated conceptual framework inform our discussion in this section, first on incentives, then on capacity for rural households to diversify.

---

8. World Bank (1983), Fisseha (1985), Lanjouw (1999).

Incentives to Diversify

The "incentives" variables in the conceptual framework include the set of incentive "levels" facing a household, including relative prices of outputs from and inputs to both nonfarm and farm activities as well as among nonfarm activities, and the set of relative risks of the activities. These two sets of incentives variables have been the main focus of the determinants discussed in the development literature on diversification, with less emphasis on the capacity variables. To simplify the discussion in the literature, we can say that the livelihood and other diversification analyses tend to distinguish between incentives that "pull" and those that "push" households to diversify.

PULL VARIABLES.   The pull factors include higher payoffs from or lower risk to rural nonfarm activities than those related to farm activities. Higher returns allow farm households, inter alia, to accumulate capital that in turn can be reinvested in farm technology, upgrading and ratcheting up farm incomes as well. There is some evidence of a Markovian process whereby farm or migration income is invested in nonfarm activity that in turn finances farm technology upgrading, cash cropping, education, and further rounds of nonfarm income diversification. See, for example, evidence from the Philippines (Estudillo and Otsuka 1999), Mali (Dione 1989), and China (Mohapatra et al. 2005).

Many studies at a national or regional level show returns to nonfarm activities well above returns to farming. The returns to nonfarm activity are highest near towns and in more favorable agricultural zones where effective demand is high.

High returns to local nonfarm activities tend to occur in regions where there is some growth motor, such as agriculture, mining, or tourism. These create consumption and production linkages with the nonfarm sector and drive up demand for nonfarm goods and services. Chapter 7 explores these growth linkages in considerable detail. Here we summarize by noting that growing agricultural zones, for example, generate rising demand for nonfarm goods and services and provide raw materials to support processing and trade. Increased economic activity results in higher demand for labor and rising wage rates. All these factors stimulate the emergence of high-return rural nonfarm activities. The cotton zones of the southern Sahel, the green revolution in Punjab, the fruit-producing zone of Central Chile, and the coffee zones of Southern Brazil have all witnessed periods of agriculture-led growth in their rural nonfarm economies (Reardon 2000; Reardon, Berdegué, and Escobar 2001). Though returns to labor vary substantially across activities (Table 6.2), rising wage rates encourage diversification out of the most labor-intensive, low-return nonfarm activities and into more remunerative nonfarm pursuits (Table 7.1). One often sees a sequence of diversification, first into self-employment manufactures (for example, food processing and preparation), then into wage employment in manufactures, then into self-employment in services (such as petty commerce, bicycle repair, and so on), and then into wage employment in services such as transport, teaching, and truck or farm equipment repair. As a result, at the start of a long growth process one often sees manufacturing self-employment dominant, and at the end sees services wage employment dominant, as in Latin America (Reardon et al. 2001). The mechanisms driving growth of the nonfarm share in areas with some initial motor (such as a farming, mining, or tourism boom) may be more complex, however. Such growth may involve a dynamic interactive process between the sectors and locations. For example, the initial surplus from an agricultural boom may be invested in education and migration, which in turn may be reinvested in upgrading farming and investment in more capital-intensive local nonfarm activities, as shown in a recent study from Luzon in the Philippines (Estudillo and Otsuka 1999).

PUSH VARIABLES.   The incentives tending to push households into the RNFE are more complex. Households are pushed into nonfarm activities by factors that can be "idiosyncratic" (related to a single household or group of households) or "common" (related to all households in a zone or region), using Dercon's (2002) distinction. Moreover, as Alderman and Paxson (1994) note, there is a fundamental bifurcation of strategies to deal with risk and shocks in income. On the one hand, households pursue "risk management strategies" that involve choosing income diversification strategies that permit income smoothing over time, with the poor choosing to diversify ex ante into activities that have a low positive covariance with the returns to agriculture, and "income skewing," which is a choice of activities with low risk (even if they have low returns). On the other hand, households pursue "risk coping strategies" that involve precautionary savings and asset management, involvement in informal and formal insurance arrangements, and diversifying income post facto, after a shock such as a drought. These concepts aid us in analyzing the push factor incentives driving income diversification.

A first push factor is the drop of seasonal income from farming to levels not sufficient for survival in the off season, which pushes households into nonfarm activities to smooth their income and consumption interseasonally. This interseasonal smoothing of income is not actually a means of coping with a shock, because the shock is not unexpected, but is regular, and thus is a long-term factor in the climate for which farmers compensate with long-term ex ante off-season income diversification.

A second push factor is a transitory drop in income in a given year, say from a drought, that forces farmers to cope ex post facto.

A third push factor is a permanent (interyear) drop in or chronic insufficiency of farming income, say for physical reasons such as environmental degradation, chronic rainfall, deficit, disease, or market or policy reasons.[9] Meso

---

9. Since the early 1970s, in Brazil's central plains rapid farm mechanization has displaced thousands of smallholder cotton producers, who have subsequently sought refuge in rural nonfarm employment (Chase 1997; Tacoli and Satterthwaite 2003).

Across much of Sub-Saharan Africa the post–structural adjustment period witnessed rapid subsidy withdrawal from agriculture, input supply constraints, and uneven private sector responses

variables such as average landholding, land distribution, and population pressure clearly condition household diversification decisions. Over generations, as inherited landholdings fall below the minimum required to support a farm family, smallholders face little choice but to diversify into nonfarm activity. For this reason, growing landlessness in South Asia has triggered strong interest in rural industries as a means of absorbing new increments to the labor force in the presence of declining agricultural land availability.[10] Evidence from a series of Latin American case studies suggests that as household landholdings decline, the share of nonfarm income in total household income rises (Reardon, Berdegué, and Escobar 2001).

At the micro level, household landholdings clearly affect diversification decisions. The share of rural nonfarm earnings in total household income is usually highest for the smallest farm sizes in Latin America, for example (Reardon, Berdegué, and Escobar 2001), or in Bangladesh (Hossain 2004). As agricultural land becomes scarce, households must seek compensating earnings in the nonfarm economy. For this reason, landless households typically depend most heavily on nonfarm earnings (Table 6.3).

Note that the assessment of "relative return" is not only between farming and local nonfarm activity, but also between migration and local nonfarm activity. Matshe and Young (2004) analyzed this choice in rural Zimbabwe and found that those able to migrate tend not to undertake local nonfarm activity due to its low relative returns.

A fourth push factor is strong variation (risk) in farm incomes, say due to rainfall instability, driving households to engage in nonfarm activities with lower risk (even if they have low returns) or with returns that do not vary with farming outcomes. Degradation of fragile soils or rangeland, particularly in drought-prone regions, leads to irregular but sharp downturns in farm and livestock production. Well-documented responses to the severe, recurring droughts in the Sahel and the horn of Africa epitomize this common response.[11]

The third and fourth push factors tend to occur together. In areas with poor agroclimates and risky, less dynamic agriculture, nonfarm activity enables households to moderate risk and cope with periodic severe downturns in agricultural productivity (Box 6.1). However, in regions where agriculture is the driving force of rural economies, nonfarm income can be covariant with that from agriculture: in bad years opportunities for earning nonfarm income are

---

to the exit of marketing parastatals, all of which has placed smallholder farmers under pressure, leading many to seek supplementary earnings in nonfarm pursuits (Bryceson and Jamal 1997; Bah et al. 2003).

10. Mukhopadhyay and Lim (1985b), Shand (1986b), Islam (1987a).

11. See Reardon, Delgado, and Matlon (1992), Habtu (1997), and Reardon, Matlon, and Delgado (1998), Box 8.1.

TABLE 6.3 Rural nonfarm income by size of landholding

Country	Landholdings (ha)	Nonfarm share	
		Employment (%)	Income (%)
India, 1988	Landless	46	—
	0.01–0.40	29	—
	0.41–1.00	19	—
	1.01–2.00	14	—
	2.01–4.00	12	—
	4.01+	09	—
Korea, 1996	0.0–0.49	—	80
	0.5–0.99	—	64
	1.0–1.49	—	49
	1.5–1.99	—	42
	2.0+	—	37
Thailand, 1981	0.0–4.1	—	88
	4.2–10.2	—	72
	10.3–41.0	—	56
	41.0+	—	45

Country	Landholdings (ha)	Nonfarm income share (%)
Northeast Brazil, 1996	Landless	54
	0.01–0.49	34
	0.50–0.99	28
	1.00–2.99	31
	3.00–4.99	03
	5.00+	25
Nicaragua, 1998 (mz)	Landless	74
	0.01–1.99	37
	2.00–4.99	31
	5.00–19.99	27
	20.00–50.00	38
	50.00+	17
Northern Nigeria, 1992	0–1.9	67
	2–3.9	57
	4+	47

SOURCES: Meagher and Mustapha (1997), Rosegrant and Hazell (2000), Corral and Reardon (2001), Ferreira and Lanjouw (2001).

NOTES: A dash indicates that data are not available. Mz, manzana (0.7 ha).

BOX 6.1   Distress diversification

The Darfur region of Western Sudan has suffered from recurrent drought and fighting for most of the twentieth century. Eleven famines have visited the region over the past 90 years, four of them since the country's independence in the 1960s. In this primarily agrarian society, recurrent drought and environmental degradation have fueled steady decline in agricultural productivity and steady increase in annual food deficits. Case history interviews with 60 households in this region suggest a sequence of coping behavior in response to these pressures. In the aftermath of the 1983–84 drought, distress sales of livestock coupled with drought-related deaths reduced cattle holdings by 80 percent and holdings of camels, sheep, and goats by 31 percent and 47 percent, respectively. Many families likewise resorted to selling household furnishings, land, and even trees. By 1990, some 20 percent of the population had become landless.

As options in agriculture contracted, households turned to the nonfarm economy for survival. Some family members migrated to towns and even internationally, to Libya, in search of paid employment. Households living in proximity to small urban centers collected grass and wood to sell to petty traders in outlying assembly markets. Exports of handicraft items such as styled leatherwork, pottery, metalwork, mats, baskets, and carpets increased. As a coping strategy, many resorted to petty trade—so many that markets rapidly became saturated. According to Ibrahim, "There are too many sellers dealing in the same commodity— a classic case of perfect competition under free entry conditions." In this situation, rural nonfarm diversification represents not a route out of poverty, but rather an attempt to cope with growing destitution. (Ibrahim 1997)

---

reduced. As a result, nonfarm income in these regions tends to depend more on income from migration or from towns, income sources not subject to risks that are covariant with those of the local agricultural economy (see Table 6.4). The millet zone of the northern Sahel and rain-fed areas of South Asia typically confront this situation. In these settings, local nonfarm activities with low entry costs and low capital requirements become highly congested and generate low returns (see Table 6.2). A study comparing slow- and fast-growing agricultural regions of Thailand concludes, "If agricultural growth is weak, the result is not only a slowdown in the growth of high-value-added nonfarm activities but also a push for poorer farmers to seek employment in low-productivity nonfarm jobs" (Poapongsakorn 1994). Box 6.2 explores these diverging regional diversification patterns in greater detail. Comparisons of diversification strategies across agroecological regions find risk-induced diversification highest in riskier dryland areas. As a recent African study notes, "Households are considerably

TABLE 6.4 Household income diversification in sluggish versus dynamic rural regions

	Type of regional economic base		
	Sluggish or deteriorating		Dynamic
	1. Resource-poor (low-potential, ecologically fragile, drought-prone)	2. Unexploited potential	3. High-potential, fast-growing
Motivation for diversification	Seek refuge from eroding returns in agriculture Cope with past disasters Reduce future risks		Seeking higher-return opportunities in growing nonfarm markets Improving factor returns by deploying labor and capital in slack agricultural seasons Smoothing seasonal income and consumption Accumulating investment funds across enterprises to replace missing credit markets
Opportunities for diversification			
Asset-poor households	Labor emigration Unskilled nonfarm employment Labor-intensive exports Z-goods		Local wage labor Labor-intensive services, commerce, or manufacturing for local markets
Asset-rich households	Skilled wage employment (government or private sector) Transport or commercial enterprises		Skilled wage employment (government or private sector) Skill- or capital-intensive rural nonfarm enterprises

BOX 6.2   Diverging regional patterns of household diversification

From the 1960s, steady growth in rice production coupled with cassava and sugar export booms boosted agricultural earnings in Central Thailand. Meanwhile, the low-potential, rain-fed Northeast remained far behind. These diverging trends in the agricultural base of each region resulted in widely different patterns of household income diversification. In the more agriculturally prosperous central region, rising labor demand in agriculture raised wage rates. Growing paddy, sugar, and cassava surpluses led to the emergence of thousands of rice mills as well as sugar refineries, cassava brokers, producers of tapioca pellets, construction operations, metal workshops, and agricultural equipment manufacturers, as well as livestock feed and village retail shops. Meanwhile, in the sluggish Northeast households also diversified, not because of expanding opportunities but rather because of the inability of agriculture to keep pace with the growing population. In this resource-poor region, rural nonfarm diversification centered around labor-intensive export activities such as gemstone cutting, silk weaving, and production of artificial flowers, all for export. (Poapongsakorn 1994)

more diversified in the higher risk, drier environment of agropastoral areas of Kenya than they are in the more humid, higher agricultural potential setting of Ivorien rice systems" (Barrett et al. 2004).

A fifth push factor is idiosyncratic credit or insurance market failure, which drives households to self-insure and self-fund input purchases. This outcome is signaled in rural nonfarm studies,[12] as well as in migration remittance-use studies.[13] Weaknesses in rural factor markets likewise tend to encourage household diversification. Where credit and insurance markets are missing, rural nonfarm activity becomes a vehicle for self-insurance and for financing agricultural inputs and assets. Weak land and labor markets may also encourage diversification. A skilled tradesman, for example, a metal worker or mason, who inherits farmland but cannot rent it out or hire labor in the absence of well-functioning factor markets, may diversify into farm production rather than specializing in his skilled trade full time lest his landholdings yield him zero returns. Therefore, while we emphasize diversification into nonfarm activity, we acknowledge that in some circumstances the diversification can be for the same motives but in the opposite direction (Barrett, Reardon, and Webb 2001).

---

12. See, for example, Evans and Ngau (1991), Loveridge (1992), Hopkins and Reardon (1993), Reardon, Crawford, and Kelly (1994), and Savadogo, Reardon, and Pietola (1995) .

13. Dione (1989), Collier et al. (1990), Van Zyl et al. (1991), Francis and Hoddinot (1993), Schultz (1996), Estudillo and Otsuka (1999).

Capacity to Diversify into RNF Activities

STATIC AND DYNAMIC CAPITAL HOLDINGS.   Recall that the "capacity variables" enabling households to undertake rural nonfarm activities, given the incentive levels, include capital assets such as human, social, financial, organizational, and physical capital. The capital can be public or private goods and can be at the meso or regional level, "common" to an area of households, or "idiosyncratic," related to a household or a group of households.

To conceptualize the role of capital as a determinant of rural nonfarm activity, one can see RNFY as based on activities that have a production function, one of the variables of the function being capital assets. Note that rural nonfarm activities differ widely in the types and levels of capital they require. Teaching rural school requires education, repairing farm vehicles requires tools, long-distance commerce requires a truck, but being a porter in a rural market requires only the worker's back. Of course there is a strong correlation between the income from an activity and its capital requirement (Barrett, Reardon, and Webb 2001).

Based on this correlation, one can think of each rural nonfarm activity as having a vector of capital requirements, K^* (i.e., investments in various capital assets), that constitute the minima required by the production technology and transaction requirements to enter and sustain the activity. These K^* are functions of the technology as well as the "target market" with its specific demands of volume, quality, and other transactional requirements.[14] Hence, for example, rural producers of cheese for the town or city market will face very different requirements in terms of product quality, safety, and packaging than will producers of cheese for the rural market, and these requirements translate into minimum capital investments, such as cooling tanks for the milk, packaging machines, and so on, relative to more artisan-level cheese manufacture.

Research on the dynamics of rural nonfarm capital investment shows that investments can be intertemporarily reinforcing. An initial investment in nonfarm activity, via migration or local nonfarm earnings, can over time set in train rural nonfarm activity differentiation over households. For example, Francis and Hoddinott (1993) show that migrants returning to the cities of Western Kenya bought land and made key investments in rural nonfarm activities requiring higher capital (e.g., construction), which in turn were translated into further investments in land and agriculture. A similar analysis was done in the cotton zones of Mali by Dione (1989).[15] High initial stocks of human, financial, and physical capital enable rich households to obtain skilled employment and purchase

---

14. See Reardon (2003), extending the "investment poverty" concept of Reardon and Vosti (1995), which in turn extended the "threshold investment" concept of David (1975).

15. Dione (1989), Collier (1990), Hien (1991), Van Zyl et al. (1991), Francis and Hoddinot (1993), Schultz (1996), Estudillo and Otsuka (1999).

BOX 6.3   How poor households diversify differently

Following a boom in rice production in the Muda River region of Malaysia during the 1970s, agricultural employment and wage rates rose sharply, by over 50 percent in real terms. This induced a subsequent phase of widespread agricultural mechanization. By the 1980s, virtually all farms in the region harvested paddy by combine, either owned or rented. The resulting labor displacement in agriculture led local household members, particularly married men, to diversify into nonfarm activities. As a result, a study in one village of this region found that the share of married men engaged primarily in nonfarm activities increased from 5 percent in 1977 to 30 percent in 1987.

Yet the character of that employment differed significantly between the poor and the rich. Members of poorer households, slightly under half of the nonfarm workers, found employment in low-wage nonfarm jobs such as construction labor, quarry work, lorry driving, and rice mill labor. The remainder, from better-off households, found nonfarm work in more lucrative pursuits such as transport and trade enterprises, government jobs, and brokering and contracting services. On average, this better-off group earned incomes triple those of the low-wage group. Better education, larger landholdings (which enabled rental income or sales), and strong political contacts enabled this group to finance and access the more lucrative segments of the rural nonfarm economy. As in most places, the rich and the poor diversify differently because of differential access to human, financial, physical, and political capital. (Hart 1994)

---

the vehicles and equipment necessary for exploiting high-return opportunities in trade, processing, and services. Skill-based and financial barriers to entry do not deter wealthy households, whose members systematically cream off the most lucrative opportunities in the RNFE (Box 6.3). As a result, these households earn returns many times greater than do poor households (Table 6.5). Conversely, asset-poor households remain confined to the low-return segment of the RNFE.

Note that the diversification of household income into nonfarm sources can in turn, in a second round, alter agricultural assets, technology, and activity composition, thus influencing further rounds of income diversification as well as welfare. For a discussion of the effects of nonfarm employment on agriculture, see Reardon (2000).[16] An interesting new strand of work is emerging on the effects of nonfarm employment on land assets via effects on environ-

---

16. See also, for example, Evans and Ngau (1991), Loveridge (1992), Hopkins and Reardon (1993), Reardon, Crawford, and Kelly (1994), and Savadogo, Reardon, and Pietola (1995) .

TABLE 6.5 Returns to rural nonfarm activity by
household income level in Coast Province, Kenya, 1984

Household income category	Average nonfarm earnings (Ksh/worker)
Low	1,887
Medium	4,480
High	8,133

SOURCE: Foeken (1997).

NOTE: Ksh, Kenya shillings.

mental practices. See, for example, Holden et al. (2004). These effects will serve to condition (as an incentive and capacity variable) the ensuing rounds of decisions concerning livelihoods strategies, including RNFE participation.

MESO-LEVEL ASSETS.   The first capacity variable can be thought of as a set of meso-level assets, typically (but not always) public goods, classed as hard and soft infrastructure. Note that, as in the case of other capacity variables, there is a side to each that also involves incentives. For example, where infrastructure is good, transport costs are low, so effective output prices of nonfarm products are higher. However, this is a two-edged sword, for the road can make it cheaper to ship raw products to a town or city for processing. Most descriptive studies, such as that of Anderson and Leiserson (1980) and household econometric studies of rural nonfarm activity, include several infrastructure variables. Nearly all the studies find that infrastructure is an important determinant of the RNFE.

Proximity to towns and access to infrastructure such as roads, electricity, and water are crucial capacity determinants of rural nonfarm employment and income levels. A number of Latin American studies showing this are reviewed in Reardon, Berdegué, and Escobar (2001), African studies in Barrett, Reardon, and Webb (2001), and South Asian studies in Hossain (2004) and Lanjouw and Shariff (2002).[17] Winters, Davis, and Corral (2002) employed factorial analysis and found these public goods crucial in households' RNFE participation choices in Mexico. Livelihood studies likewise document the importance of links between rural and urban livelihoods (Kamete 1998).

There have been relatively few studies that disaggregate rural nonfarm activities and analyze them in terms of spatiality using household data. Fafchamps and Shilpi (2003) present a fascinating (and useful for program design and targeting) mapping of self-employment RNFE versus wage-employment RNFE versus farming and farm wage labor at various distances from Nepalese cities, towns, and local markets. They show that rural nonfarm wage employment falls

---

17. Barrett, Reardon and Webb (2001), Block and Webb (2001), Canagarajah, Newman, and Bhattamishra (2001), Smith et al. (2001).

away quickly as one leaves periurban areas for the hinterland, but that there is a U-shaped pattern for self-employment, because some rural nonfarm activity in the hinterland serves local needs not met by supply from urban areas.

Sometimes such access compensates for lack of private assets such as education, although education and roads are themselves often correlated. In Thailand, for example, villagers living near the silk garment center of Pakton Chai are able to work as household contract weavers, earning wages at rates eight times those of workers from more remote rural households who are confined to working as raisers of silkworms and producers of cocoons and yarn (Figure 15.2). Similarly, educated landless workers living in the densely populated rural zones of the Pacific region of Nicaragua, well served by roads and near major cities and ports, were top earners of RNFY in Nicaragua (Reardon, Berdegué, and Escobar 2001). In contrast, those in the hinterland were relegated to small-scale manufactures, local stagnant markets, and low returns to their labor.

Analyses using gross measures of infrastructure can often be misleading, however, disguising intrazone differences that in turn disguise significant pockets of deprived households that must then rely only on subsistence agriculture. Given general infrastructure access in a particular region, different households can still face very different transaction costs in undertaking rural nonfarm activity. Households located in the hinterland of the central mountain area of Peru have significantly lower RNFY than to those well served by infrastructure near towns (Escobal 2005). They face different marketing costs for their products and different input costs, and they have different catchment areas for their markets and thus face different effective demands.

MESO-MICRO-LEVEL ASSETS.   The second set of capacity variables is at a meso-micro level, typically private goods. A good example is the set of organizational and social capital assets. These have been relatively underexplored in the rural nonfarm literature, but should be studied much more given that such social linkages can be critical to reducing transaction costs and risks for those engaging in rural nonfarm activity. Some studies have addressed this link, such as Winters et al. (2002) for Mexico and Zhang and Li (2003) for China, finding that social capital, such as membership in organizations and "connections," generally had important effects on participation in the RNFE. Lanjouw and Shariff (2002) studied the impact of caste on the RNFE in India, where membership in a scheduled caste increases the probability of nonfarm activity.

MICRO-LEVEL CAPACITY.   The third set of capacity variables is at the micro level, typically private goods. A good example is human capital in general, for which most studies show a strong effect on participation in and returns to the RNFE.

A major thrust of this analysis related to the quality of human capital; hence the effect of education on the RNFE (Evans and Ngau 1991; Reardon 2001). A first example is education, a key source of human capital, which offers a potentially important route to higher-return nonfarm opportunities (see

---

BOX 6.4   Education-led diversification

Madzu village in Western Kenya enjoys fertile soils, a good climate, and 1,500 to 1,800 millimeters of rainfall per year. Remote location coupled with rudimentary infrastructure leaves the village isolated. Given a high population density of over 1,100 per square kilometer, land availability is low and the poverty rate surpasses 50 percent. In this unfavorable setting, two successful Madzu farmers found a route out of poverty via the rural nonfarm economy, both thanks to early investments in education.

One farmer, a retired primary school teacher, managed to educate his eight sons on his teacher's salary at a time when school fees were low. With remittances they sent, the father purchased a dairy cow and 800 tea bushes. He now enjoys a steady income from milk sales and the sale of tea to the Kenya Tea Development Agency.

A second village resident channeled savings from his civil service job into the purchase of three dairy cows and fertilizer for his maize plot. This chemical fertilizer, together with the manure from his cows, enables him to achieve higher than average yield on his maize. In both cases, early investments in education led to a flow of nonfarm wage earnings that in turn financed investments in agriculture and resulted in a diversified and growing household asset and income trajectory over time. (Marenya et al. 2003)

Box 6.4). Less educated households rely instead on low-paying farm wage employment or very low-productivity nonfarm pursuits (see Corral and Reardon 2001 for Nicaragua; Lanjouw and Shariff 2002 for India; and Hossain 2004 for Bangladesh). In contrast, the more educated, particularly those living near roads and towns, earn higher nonfarm incomes in skilled activities such as teaching. Abdulai and Delgado (1999) confirm these findings and also disaggregate them by gender and show that the effect of education on nonfarm earnings and participation is even higher for women than for men in Ghana. A few studies, such as that of Taylor and Yúnez-Naude (2000) for Mexico, disaggregate schooling effects on returns to nonfarm activities of different types relative to cash and subsistence farming and farm-wage labor. They find that education's payoff is highest in rural nonfarm wage labor, but less so in cash cropping and rural nonfarm self-employment, indicating that there are significant interactivity differences in skills. Some studies pay close attention to the gradations of schooling and relate those to nonfarm wage employment versus self-employment. For example, in the study of Ecuador by Elbers and Lanjouw (2001), the least educated were found to do low-paying nonfarm work in manufactures or services, those with basic education to manage small enterprises mainly in manufactures, and those with more education to work in the higher-paying wage jobs such as teaching or to have larger local enterprises.

On the other hand, many studies also focus on the simple availability of household labor, for example, to allow some members of the household to attend to farming and the production of Z-goods (rural nonfarm goods) and the rest to work off farm (e.g., Reardon et al. 1992 for the case of Burkina Faso), in particular where farming is labor intensive, such as in the rice areas of the Philippines (Estudillo and Otsuka 1999). Into this strand of literature fits work on gender time allocation and nonfarm activity. Moreover, a new strand of work emerging from the new economics of labor migration is focused on the effects of the household decision to send out migrants on household labor allocation to the RNFE and farming (for instance, see the work done in China by Taylor, Rozelle, and De Brauw 2003). This strand shows that migration reduces labor allocation to farming but not to local self-employment, which is seen as a high return activity. This work then adds to the strand of work on migration remittance investment in nonfarm activity, such as the study in Western Kenya (Francis and Hoddinott 1993) and the Luzon region of the Philippines (Estudillo and Otsuka 1999).

A second example of a micro-level private goods asset is household landholdings. We included those in our discuss of incentives as well, for they are the example par excellence of a variable that potentially affects both incentives and capacity to undertake nonfarm activity. The effect of landholdings on participation in and earnings from rural nonfarm activity is complex: land can serve as collateral where credit markets function and thus can increase access to credit, which in turn can be used to invest in physical capital needed for more remunerative nonfarm work; landholding (compared with landlessness) can be the key that allows individuals to enter organizations and groups and thus accumulate social capital that aids them in rural nonfarm activity; and land can simply be the determinant of farm investment and access to working capital and income, for most nonfarm activity investments are based on one's own liquidity. In studies that separate (in two-staged regressions) the decision to participate in the RNFE from earnings from the RNFE, such as that done by Abdulai and Delgado (1999), in the second stage one finds that once one controls for assets such as education, the land effect is not significant. The findings in the literature regarding landholding effects on nonfarm activity are thus often mixed, for the farm household might be more able to undertake nonfarm activity (due to the above three factors) but have less incentive (because it has more farm income). This leads us directly to a key finding of this review regarding the "meso and micro paradoxes" of the RNFE.

Meso and Micro Paradoxes

Because of differences in initial asset endowments, rich and poor households diversify differently. The rich typically engage in more capital- (including human capital) intensive and more remunerative activities, leaving the poor confined to labor-intensive, highly contested niches with low barriers to entry and low returns. A series of African household diversification studies underlines this tendency, noting that wealthier households often mention "profit maximization" as their motive for entering into rural nonfarm activities, whereas lower-income households emphasize "risk minimization" and "income stabilization" (Bryceson and Jamal 1997). A comparison of alternative livelihood strategies suggests that poor households are more likely to get caught in short-run recovery strategies, while rich households profit from diversification to initiate structural improvement strategies. According to one major review, "Diversification can be described as a survival strategy for vulnerable households and individuals who are pushed out of their traditional occupations and who must resort to different activities to minimize risks and make ends meet. Conversely, wealthier groups with better education and skills can be pulled by new opportunities" (Tacoli 2003). These results echo the findings on enterprise birth and death rates from Chapter 5. The rapid churning initiated by large numbers of new one-person startup enterprises typically emerges as a result of survival strategies by poor households pushed into low-return rural nonfarm activity for lack of better alternatives.

Thus arise two important paradoxes. The first, a "meso paradox," arises in resource-poor areas where households have a high incentive but a low capacity to diversify. That is, they face a greater need to diversify into the RNFE to compensate for their poor agricultural base (Reardon et al. 1998; Reardon, Berdegué, and Escobar 2001). Yet these poor regions have a lower capacity than well-endowed areas to generate rural nonfarm activity, especially of the nonrefuge variety.

The second, or "micro paradox," emerges at the household level. Poorer households have a high incentive but a low capacity to diversify successfully, even if in some cases they rely more on nonfarm activity in percentage terms. The poorer households typically remain relegated to low-paying, low-productivity, risky jobs in the rural nonfarm sector—the equivalent of subsistence farming, which offers no path out of poverty, just a means of bare survival. The poor face significantly higher incentives to earn RNFY, but they have lower capacity to succeed. In order to confront these two dilemmas, the empirical evidence reviewed here suggests several key directions for policy intervention.

Strategic and Policy Implications

Policymakers in the twenty-first century are attracted to the RNFE because they hope diversification into rural nonfarm activity will offer poor households a route out of poverty. But before decisionmakers can realize this dream, they will need to resolve both the micro- and meso-level paradoxes.

First and foremost, to counter the meso paradox it will be necessary to create a favorable environment for dynamic diversification of the rural economy.

This will require dynamic engines of regional growth and a buoyant economic base in agriculture, tourism, or mining. Sparking these engines to life will generate opportunities in the RNFE for rich and poor alike, particularly when initial income increments are distributed broadly enough to yield wide increases in spending on local goods and services. As regional wage rates rise, the composition of the RNFE will change and returns to labor will increase, enabling the poor as well as the rich to benefit from regional growth via nonfarm diversification.

For the long run, resolution of the micro paradox will require increased investment in rural education and health. Ultimately, if the poor are to access the most lucrative nonfarm jobs, they must upgrade their human and physical capital. The policy challenge is to equip poor households to move from "refuge" nonfarm jobs to more remunerative ones. For that they need a variety of private assets such as education, health, and capital and public assets such as roads, electricity, information, and market institutions that enable them to access dynamic markets.

Fortunately, resolution of the meso paradox will contribute directly to solving the micro paradox, because poor households rapidly translate higher earnings into growing expenditures on health and education. For this reason, health and education services are among the most buoyant segments of the RNFE in prosperous rural regions.

7 Sectoral Growth Linkages between Agriculture and the Rural Nonfarm Economy

STEVEN HAGGBLADE, PETER B. R. HAZELL,
AND PAUL A. DOROSH

The density, composition, and evolution of rural nonfarm activity vary considerably across geographic settings and over time. Chapter 4 has examined broad trends in that evolution, highlighting an array of causal forces driving change in the rural nonfarm economy (RNFE).

In many settings, agriculture plays a predominant role, governing the scale, structure, and evolution of rural nonfarm activity. As the green revolution unfurled across Bangladesh during the 1980s and 1990s, soaring paddy production, the sinking of 750,000 shallow tube wells, and sale of over a million treadle pumps launched an explosion in the RNFE as 50,000 paddy mills, 80,000 small traders, and 160,000 rural mechanics launched operation, generating a highly visible agriculturally driven surge in rural nonfarm activity (Figure 7.1).[1]

Yet agriculture does not unilaterally govern the size, composition, and evolution of the RNFE. In the early 1990s, rural manufacturing grew substantially in villages surrounding metropolitan Manila, not because of growth in agriculture, which had peaked in the prior decades, but because urban firms faced increasing incentives to move production to suburban locations in search of lower rents and lower wages (Hayami, Kikuchi, and Marciano 1996).

To what extent does agriculture shape the RNFE? In what instances does agriculture predominate as the engine of rural nonfarm growth? And where do other forces emerge as more prominent? The ensuing discussion explores these questions in detail in an effort to summarize the considerable body of evidence accumulated in recent decades on the magnitude of agricultural growth linkages.

The views presented in this chapter represent those of the authors and should not be taken to reflect those of the World Bank or its affiliated institutions.

1. Ahmed (2000), Chowdhury and Haggblade (2000), Shah et al. (2000), Mandal and Asaduzzam (2002), World Bank (2004).

FIGURE 7.1 Rice marketing in Bangladesh, 1990

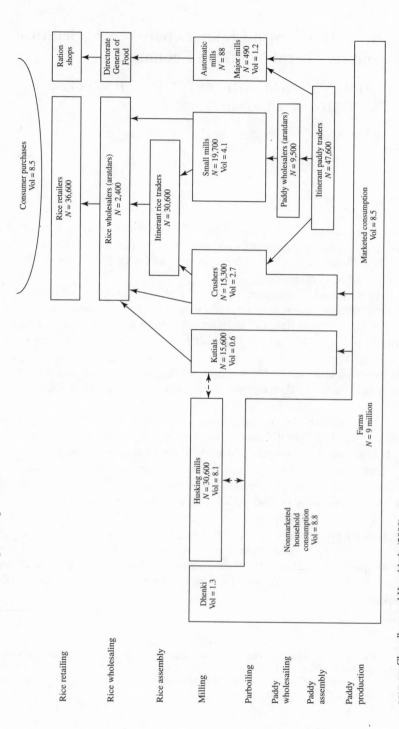

SOURCE: Chowdhury and Haggblade (2000).

NOTES: N, number of enterprises; Vol, volume in million metric tons (MMT) of rice equivalents; ←-→ indicates contract milling.

A Typology of Linkages

Agriculture to Rural Nonfarm Activity

Analytically, and in roughly chronological order, students of the rural economy have classified agricultural growth linkages into four main categories. *Production linkages* include forward linkages from agriculture to nonfarm processors of agricultural raw materials as well as backward linkages to input suppliers of farm equipment, pumps, fuel, fertilizer, and repair services. These input-output relationships generate distinctive patterns of rural nonfarm activity across different agricultural regions. In western Colombia, the rapid growth of smallholder coffee farming in the early 1900s stimulated a collateral rise in rural transport services, coffee processing, and local production of jute bags and pulping machinery (Berry 1995). The spurt in Vietnam's rice production during the 1990s generated growth in rural nonfarm activity concentrated mainly in favorable agricultural zones and dominated by farm input supply, milling, and commerce (Trung 2000).

Consumption linkages include spending by farm families on locally produced consumer goods and services. A classic early study in green revolution India determined that higher-income small farmers spent about half of their incremental farm income on nonfarm goods and services and another third on perishable agricultural commodities such as milk, fruit, and vegetables, thus generating strong demand linkages for locally supplied consumer goods and services (Mellor and Lele 1973).

Factor market linkages between agriculture and the RNFE have received growing attention in the linkages literature in recent years. In rural labor markets, the strong seasonality of demand in agriculture generates corresponding surges in rural nonfarm activity typically tied to troughs in agricultural labor demand.[2] And, as Chapter 3 emphasizes, links between labor demand and rising rural wage rates may offer important connective tissue by which poor households in one sector can benefit from growth in the other (Figure 7.2). Similarly, cash surpluses from agricultural sales frequently finance nonfarm investments, while reciprocal reverse flows from rural nonfarm activities finance the purchase of agricultural inputs.[3]

Productivity linkages between agriculture and the nonfarm economy have emerged most recently in the growth linkage discussions.[4] More nebulous and difficult to measure, these interactions include an array of beneficial macro

---

2. In addition to Figure 1.1, see Norman (1973), Romjin (1987), and Itoh and Tanimoto (1998) for evidence from Nigeria, Thailand, and Japan, respectively.

3. See Lucas and Stark (1985), Collier and Lal (1986), Evans and Ngau (1991), Reardon, Crawford, and Kelly (1994), Carter and Wiebe (1990), Marenya et al. (2003), and Ellis and Freeman (2004).

4. See Block and Timmer (1994) and Tomich, Kilby, and Johnston (1995).

FIGURE 7.2   Trends in real rural wage rates for casual labor in India, 1983–93

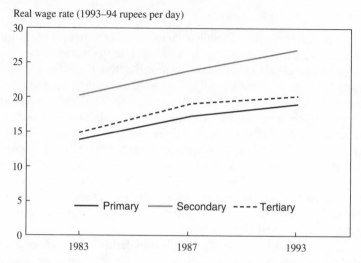

SOURCE: Dev (2002).

linkages transmitted from agriculture to the nonfarm economy. In particular, lower food prices may increase the productivity of poor manual laborers, a linkage of considerable potential importance given growing awareness of the beneficial impact of food prices on nutrition and workforce productivity (Behrman and Deolalikar 1988; Strauss and Thomas 2000). Some proponents have suggested that rising agricultural productivity also improves food security and political stability, leading to higher productivity of capital and learning by doing on the part of both government and firms (Block and Timmer 1994). Others emphasize knowledge flows that accelerate productivity growth in both agriculture and nonfarm production (Tomich, Kilby, and Johnston 1995). These effects correspond analytically to the productivity-enhancing technical change induced by international trade (Grossman and Helpman 1992).

Reverse Linkages

Early linkage discussions focused primarily on agriculture as the engine of rural economic growth. More recently, with growing recognition of the surprisingly large scale of rural nonfarm activity in many rural areas, the prospect for a reversal of this causality, from nonfarm to farm, has received growing recognition.[5] Certainly production linkages cut both ways. The establishment of rural

---

5. Ranis, Stewart, and Angeles-Reyes (1990), Reardon, Crawford, and Kelly (1994), Marenya et al. (2003), Ellis and Freeman (2004).

canneries can stimulate on-farm production of tomatoes, fruits, and other perishables (Reardon, Crawford, and Kelly 1994). Likewise, in the consumption arena, nonfarm income—perhaps from mining or rural administrative centers—generates demand for local agricultural products. Hence the commonly observed truck farming that grows up around rural and urban towns.

Factor markets inherently involve ebbs and flows between agriculture and nonfarm activities. Productivity linkages similarly run in both directions, as nonfarm firms introduce benefits to farmers in the form of timely repair services, improved input supply, output marketing, and enhanced farmer incentives.[6] In many instances, liquidity provided by nonfarm earnings provides funds for the purchase of the modern hybrid seeds and fertilizer necessary for increasing farm productivity.

Empirical Evidence

Cross-Section Evidence of Agricultural Growth Linkages

A broad array of empirical work has explored the relationship between changes in agriculture and changes in the RNFE. A cross-country comparison from 43 different countries charts the increasing importance of rural nonfarm activity as agricultural income per capita increases (Haggblade and Hazell 1989). It documents the close connection between nonfarm activity and the development of rural towns. From 0.37 in rural areas alone, the simple correlation coefficient between agricultural income per capita and nonfarm share in rural employment doubles, to 0.77, in rural areas plus rural towns. The jump in rural towns confirms what Chapter 8 and many observers have emphasized—that measurement of the nonfarm spin-offs from agricultural growth requires inclusion of the many agriculturally related nonfarm activities that take root in rural towns.[7]

Based on cross-section comparisons across regions in a given country, many authors have identified clear links between the level of agricultural development and that of the RNFE. In an array of Asian and African countries, empirical studies have found high levels of agricultural income and productivity correlated with high levels of rural nonfarm income.[8] A two-edged sword, agriculture when enfeebled will likewise prove a drag on the RNFE. Reardon's (1997)

---

6. See, for example, Ranis, Stewart, and Angeles-Reyes (1990), Evans and Ngau (1991), and Tomich, Kilby, and Johnston (1995).

7. Gibb (1974), Anderson and Leiserson (1978), Rondinelli (1987b,c), Haggblade, Hazell, and Brown (1989), Evans (1990), Satterthwaite (2000), Tacoli and Satterthwaite (2003).

8. See Reardon (1997) for evidence from 27 case studies in West Africa, Haggblade, Hazell, and Brown (1987) for evidence from Togo and Sierra Leone; Vaidyanathan (1986), Papola (1987), Radhakrishna, Sudhakar, and Mitra (1988), and Chadha (1993) for state and district-level comparisons across India; Evans and Ngau (1991) for data from Kenya; McPherson and Henry (1994) for evidence from Malawi; and Trung (2000) for a recent study from Vietnam.

review of several dozen African case studies explicitly notes that a productive agriculture increases nonfarm activity in rural areas, while sluggish agriculture instead induces emigration.

A cross-section econometric study across 85 different districts in India estimates agriculture to rural nonfarm income multipliers averaging 1.37 (Hazell and Haggblade 1991). That is, a 1 rupee increase in agricultural income produces roughly an additional 37 rupees in rural nonfarm earnings. About half of the increase in rural income occurs in rural areas and half in rural towns. But the strength of the agricultural growth linkages varies considerably across zones. Because of higher agricultural incomes and better infrastructure, agricultural growth linkages in the green revolution states of Punjab and Haryana achieve agriculture to rural nonfarm income multipliers roughly triple those in less favorable agricultural zones.

Agriculture influences not only the quantity but also the composition of rural nonfarm activity. Comparisons between low- and high-productivity agricultural regions suggest that labor market linkages play a key role in the shifting composition of rural nonfarm activity. Where agriculture increases the demand for labor, as it does initially in most green revolution settings, agricultural growth raises rural wage rates and the opportunity cost of labor, thereby rendering low-return nonfarm activities uneconomic.[9] As a result, agriculturally advanced Bangladeshi villages, where farmers plant a majority of their land in high-yielding rice varieties, experience higher agricultural incomes, agricultural wages, and nonfarm income per capita than do villages still dependent on traditional varieties (Hossain 1988b). The higher nonfarm income in prosperous villages reflects a greater concentration of high-return transport and service activities and less low-wage cottage industry, construction, and earth hauling (Table 7.1). Similarly, cross-regional studies from rural India, Togo, and Sierra Leone show a positive correlation between earnings per worker in agriculture and in rural nonfarm activities.[10]

Yet some cross-section studies of agriculture's impact on the RNFE produce ambiguous results, as Vyas and Mathai (1978), Unni (1990), and Leones and Feldman (1998) have noted. An understanding of labor market linkages provides a likely explanation for this reported noncorrelation, because in most cases the ambiguity appears to stem from use of rural nonfarm employment rather than income as the measure of nonfarm activity.[11] Even if perfectly mea-

---

9. Rising farm wages also lead, over time, to growing incentives for farm mechanization and other labor-saving on-farm technologies. See, for example, Duff (1987) and Estudillo and Otsuka (1999).

10. See Chadha (1986), Haggblade, Hazell, and Brown (1987), Papola (1987), Radhakrishna, Sudhakar, and Mitra (1988), and Jayaraman and Lanjouw (1999).

11. To complicate matters further, these correlation studies apply an array of proxies for agricultural advance, including agricultural employment, incomes, wage rates, productivity, and level of commercialization.

TABLE 7.1 Labor market influences on the size and composition of rural nonfarm activities in Bangladesh, 1982

	Income per hour in agriculturally underdeveloped regions (Tk/hour)	Percent by which agriculturally developed regions exceed underdeveloped areas[a]		
		Income per hour[b]	Employment (hours/week)	Income per household
Agriculture	5.1	29	8	40
Nonagriculture				
Services	11.4	4	30	35
Cottage industry	4.4	90	−81	−63
Wage labor[c]	2.8	6	−41	−38
Trade	2.3	195	−28	113
Total nonagriculture	4.4	59	−29	12

SOURCE: Hossain (1988a, 95, 120).

[a]Hossain distinguishes agriculturally "developed" and "underdeveloped" regions by a number of criteria: access to irrigation, use of modern rice varieties, and fertilizer consumption, among others. In the agriculturally developed regions, modern varieties cover 60 percent of cropped area compared with only 5 percent in the underdeveloped areas.

[b]Calculated from Hossain (1988a), Tables 48 and 64.

[c]Nonfarm wage labor includes earth hauling, construction, transport, and "other" employment.

sured, employment offers an imprecise measure of nonfarm activity because high nonfarm employment may emerge in two very different environments. Table 7.2 illustrates this problem by contrasting two very different settings that generate identical gains in rural nonfarm employment. The first represents a typical green revolution Asian setting where growing farm incomes and labor demand induce rising wage rates, growth in high-wage rural nonfarm activity, and growing per capita income (as in Tables 7.1 and 4.3). In the second setting, high population growth in the presence of a sluggish agriculture dampens consumer purchasing power and rural wage rates, by default giving rise to employment growth in low-productivity, tedious nonfarm activities. Though rural nonfarm employment rises, wage rates and per capita income fall. Thus equivalent gains in rural nonfarm employment may signal good news or bad. Even where the impact of agricultural income growth on nonfarm income is clearly positive, because of favorable consumption and input demand linkages, its impact on total nonfarm employment remains ambiguous (see Tables 7.1 and 7.2).

Although cross-section comparisons of agricultural and rural nonfarm *income* typically yield positive correlations, one cannot necessarily infer causality from these associations. Favorably endowed zones may simultaneously attract high-productivity agriculture, infrastructure investments, improved agricultural

TABLE 7.2 Contrasting sources of rural nonfarm employment growth in an Asian rice-growing economy (percent)

	The green revolution (pull)	The sponge (push)
Initial shock	Improved agricultural technology,[a] labor-using	Population growth[b]
Resulting changes		
Rural nonfarm employment	1.9	1.9
Total rural employment	6.6	2.1
Rural wage rate	6.6	−3.9
Nonfarm income	1.1	−4.7
Total real per capita incomes	7.4	−4.4

SOURCE: Haggblade and Liedholm (1991).

NOTES: Using a price-endogenous model, with stylized data drawn from the Muda River region of Malaysia, these results simulate the following impacts:

[a]Labor-using technical change in agriculture that increases foodgrain output by 80 percent and is adopted by 50 percent of farmers.

[b]A population growth rate of 6 percent over three years, which is just sufficient to generate an equivalent increase in rural nonfarm employment.

extension and technology adoption, public investment in schools, roads and government offices, as well as external nonfarm investment.[12] So further evidence is required to establish the nature of the common association between high agricultural and high rural nonfarm incomes.

Time-Series Evidence of Agricultural Growth Linkages

EAST ASIA.   Time-series evidence from countries with fast-growing agriculture suggests that agriculture may generate powerful growth linkages with the RNFE.[13] East Asia, in particular, has sparked keen interest; many observers have asked why rural nonfarm activity flourished in Japan and Taiwan in the post–World War II period, while in South Korea it did not. In 1980, farm households in Japan and Taiwan earned 80 percent and 65 percent of their income, respectively, from off-farm sources, three-fourths of it in high-paying wage employment in rural towns and nearby urban areas. Yet Korean farmers earned only 33 percent of their total household income from nonfarm sources (only 15

---

12. Hazell and Haggblade (1991) explicitly correct for endogeneity of agriculture, infrastructure, and nonfarm activity through the use of agroclimatic instrumental variables in fitting agricultural incomes. After doing so, statistically significant links remain between a growing agriculture and agriculturally induced growth in the RNFE. Foster and Rosenzweig (2004) use 28 years of panel data from India to correct for these fixed effects.

13. See Mellor (1995) for an interesting set of case studies exploring the relationship between agricultural and nonagricultural growth.

percent if remittances are excluded), less than half of it in wage employment.[14] Moreover, the structure of employment in Korea's rural economy had not changed significantly in the prior decade (Park 1986). Japan and Taiwan, on the other hand, witnessed rapid increases in rural nonfarm employment and income shares (Ho 1982; Shih 1983).

In explaining this disparity, most analysts point first to differences in agricultural performance.[15] They identify lower initial agricultural productivity in Korea, a relative neglect of agriculture, and its consequently lower growth rate. Weaker agricultural growth diminished rural consumption linkages in Korea and at a later stage restricted the prospects for labor release from agriculture to high-paying, full-time, off-farm employment.

In addition to having more rapidly growing agricultural incomes, Japan and Taiwan invested more heavily in rural roads, railroads, and electricity and adopted a policy environment supportive of dispersed manufacturing, commercial, and service activity. By the early 1960s, Japan and Taiwan boasted a paved road and rural electrical network with densities over five times those in Korea (Saith 1987). Rather than following suit, South Korea concentrated its industrial infrastructure in its two major cities, Seoul and Pusan.

Comparison of the historical records in Taiwan and the Philippines leads to similar conclusions. In the Philippines, although agricultural growth linkages emerged, they proved weaker than in Taiwan because of policy biases in favor of urban and large-scale nonfarm firms, less attention to rural infrastructure, and a less conducive agricultural policy environment (Ranis and Stewart 1993). Unfavorable macro policies—including tight controls of foreign exchange and credit, highly subsidized credit to large firms, and heavy protection of large-scale, urban-based import substituting industries—likewise stifled rural nonfarm growth even in the presence of significant agricultural growth (Bautista 1995).

East Asian evidence suggests two distinct phases in rural nonfarm growth, at least in rural manufacturing: an initial agriculturally induced phase of rural industrialization followed by an urban-led dispersion of subcontract manufacturing to rural areas (Chapter 10). Amsden (1991) suggests that in Taiwan a classic case of agriculture-led rural nonfarm growth launched the first phase of that country's rapid growth of rural manufacturing. Demand linkages from agriculture—for locally specific mechanical equipment produced by rural blacksmiths, for repair services and farm inputs plus the consumer demand generated by a multitude of small family farms—indeed combined to stimulate demand for rurally produced goods and services. Likewise, forward linkages from agriculture to early export industries such as those producing canned fresh fruits and vegetables were instrumental in the rapid rise of rural nonfarm activity in

---

14. Ho (1986b), Oshima (1986a), Park (1986).
15. See Ho (1979, 1982, 1986b), Kada (1986), Oshima (1986a,b), Park (1986), and Saith (1987).

the 1950s and 1960s (Ho 1979; Ranis and Stewart 1993). After about 1966, however, Amsden contends that Taiwan entered a second phase of urban- rather than agriculture-led rural industrial growth. Focusing on nonagricultural raw materials, this second phase of export-led industrial growth was stimulated by progressive deconcentration of manufacturing activities from urban centers to suburban and surrounding rural areas in order to avoid urban congestion, higher wages, and rental rates.

A much smaller study of rural manufacturing on a major highway loop near metropolitan Manila likewise identifies a second phase of urban-led rural industrialization beginning during the 1990s. Monitoring in these villages over several decades recorded a spurt in rural metalworking when seven new establishments began manufacturing simple tin Christmas ornaments for export under subcontract to firms in Manila, presumably in order to benefit from lower wage and factory rental costs in rural areas.[16] Similar suburban-led rural industrialization has also emerged via rural subcontracting from China's export-oriented town and village enterprises (Liu and Otsuka 1998).[17]

Rather than generalizing to the entire RNFE, it is important to note that all three of these studies focus exclusively on rural manufacturing. Given the greater locational insulation of commerce and services from urban competition, it seems probable that the shifting engines of rural nonfarm growth may apply more to manufacturing than to tertiary sectors.

FAST-GROWING AGRICULTURAL ZONES ELSEWHERE.   In other regions of the world, many observers fear that prospects for East Asia–style growth in high-return nonfarm activity will prove less favorable.[18] Given greater landlessness in South Asia, Southeast Asia, and Latin America, they fear that employment in agriculture may not keep pace with population growth. Consequently, the RNFE will become an employer of last resort, a sponge by default absorbing labor force increments unemployed in agriculture into progressively lower-return nonfarm activities (see Table 7.2).

In spite of these reservations, the limited evidence emerging from Latin America and South and Southeast Asia suggests that, even where landlessness and tenancy exist, agricultural growth can stimulate not only increasing rural nonfarm employment, but also growing nonfarm incomes as a result of diversification into higher-return nonfarm activity. Time-series studies from prosperous agricultural regions in Bangladesh, Colombia, the Indian Punjab, Indonesia, Malaysia, Malawi, the Philippines, Thailand, and West Bengal describe changes in the rural economy that suggest that rising agricultural income, wage rates,

---

16. Hayami, Kikuchu, and Marciano (1996), Kikuchi et al. (1997), Kikuchi (1998).

17. Da Silva and Del Grossi (2001) notes a similar change in Brazil from agriculture-led rural nonfarm growth to urban-powered rural settlement and economic activity powered by demand for housing, tourism, and leisure services.

18. Islam (1984, 1987c), Deshpande and Deshpande (1985), Mukhopadhyay (1985), Ho (1986a), Shand (1986b).

and consumption demand from farm households have stimulated increases in rural nonfarm employment and incomes as well as a shift to more lucrative non-farm activity.[19] In fast-growing agricultural zones of Malawi, where the spread of burley tobacco production by smallholders triggered rapid growth in farm incomes during the 1980s, McPherson and Henry (1994) discovered significantly faster growth of rural nonfarm enterprises and wage rates than in nonburley zones. They likewise found the most rapid growth in higher-return nonfarm activities such as food and beverage retailing. In Haryana, India's fastest-growing agricultural state during the 1960s, the miracle decade of agriculture-led growth produced a dramatic fall in low-return rural cottage industries together with a big jump in factory employment, commerce, and services (Bhalla 1981). Elsewhere in India, an array of village studies has documented how a growing agriculture leads to the tightening of rural labor markets and increased wage rates in rural nonfarm activities (see Chapter 3). Similarly, significant income gains registered in Ugandan export agriculture during the early 1990s stimulated a perceptible demand-led surge in rural nonfarm activity (Reinikka and Collier 2001). As one review concludes, "Historical and current experience suggest that employment generation and industrial and commercial development in rural areas are highly correlated with the rate of growth of agricultural output. This evidence . . . comes mainly from areas that have experienced high agricultural growth rates over long periods, such as the Indian and Pakistan Punjabs, Kaira District in the Gujarat State of India, Malaysia, Taiwan (China), Japan, and some European countries, including Italy and France" (Bhatt 1998, 289).

AREAS OF SLUGGISH AGRICULTURAL GROWTH.   Slow-growing agricultural regions have enjoyed less careful scrutiny in the past, though rising concern about rural poverty has elevated policymakers' interest in these areas in recent years. Where available, study results suggest that a sluggish agriculture gives rise to anemic nonfarm incomes and wage rates. Though rural nonfarm employment may actually increase in lackluster agricultural zones (Table 7.2), it normally emerges in low-wage, last-resort activities such as basket weaving, embroidery, and gathering activities. Bhalla's (1994) study of agricultural involution in low-growth agricultural districts in Bihar and Madhya Pradesh, India, and Balisacan's (1993) discussion of slow-growing agricultural zones in the Philippines both document the resulting prevalence of low-productivity rural nonfarm activity.

Even from one year to the next, downward fluctuations in agriculture can generate perceptible downturns in rural nonfarm activity. Between 1978 and 1983, abnormal weather precipitated a 42 percent fall in agricultural income in

---

19. See Gibb (1974), Anderson and Khambata (1982), Bose (1983), Sander (1983), World Bank (1983), Chadha (1985, 1986), Kasryno (1986a), Shand and Chew (1986), Reinhart (1987), McPherson and Henry (1994), Poapongsakorn (1994), Hossain (2004), World Bank (2004), and Table 4.3.

the Bicol region of the Philippines and an associated 49 percent fall in rural non-farm business incomes (Ranis, Stewart, and Angeles-Reyes 1990). Similarly, a devastating drought during the 1983–84 crop season in the North Arcot region of India triggered a 34 percent fall in agricultural income, dragging in its wake a 24 percent fall in nonfarm earnings (Hazell and Ramasamy 1991). A series of West African case studies indicates that rainfall-induced reductions in year-to-year agricultural output lead to a simultaneous falloff in rural nonfarm income during the affected year (Reardon 1997).

PANEL DATA.   These year-to-year fluctuations complicate time-series comparisons and point to an important weakness in the time-series evidence. Because temporal comparisons measure outcomes at two points in time, they normally trace the impact of many changes at once. Even in the presence of major structural changes in agriculture (before and after the introduction of green revolution varieties or before and after a major land reform), factors other than agriculture will certainly have changed. At a minimum, population and labor supply will have changed, often substantially, as the result of agriculturally induced migration into the zones with increased labor demand. Weather, the state of infrastructure, and government policies all may vary over time, commingling their contribution with the impact of the growth (or reduction) in agriculture.[20]

To avoid this problem, Foster and Rosenzweig (2004) have applied a panel data set spanning nearly three decades (1971 to 1999) from 240 villages across India to explore the relationship between agricultural productivity growth, agricultural income, and rural nonfarm employment. This work highlights the importance of labor market linkages between agricultural and rural nonfarm activity, particularly in the presence of mobile nonfarm capital and good rural infrastructure, which permit footloose rural manufacturing to relocate in pursuit of low rural wages. Their cross-section econometric results document a significant correlation between higher agricultural yields, higher farm income, higher wage rates in both agricultural and rural nonfarm activities, and higher local nonfarm incomes. However, when village-level fixed effects are accounted for, the link between agricultural productivity and rural nonfarm activity becomes statistically negligible. The authors conclude that because agricultural productivity drives up both farm and nonfarm wage rates, footloose rural factories relocate from high-wage to low-wage rural villages. Thus, over time, growth in agricultural income leads to an offsetting decrease in rural manufacturing. These countervailing effects neutralize the initial productivity-led income gains in agriculture, thereby offsetting demand-driven spending increments on local rural nonfarm goods and services. These results suggest that over long periods, wage rate movements in agriculture and in rural nonfarm labor

---

20. A broad array of analysts has noted the difficulties of conducting time-series comparisons of agricultural growth linkages. See, for example, Bell, Hazell, and Slade (1982), Ranis, Stewart, and Angeles-Reyes (1990), and Hazell and Ramasamy (1991).

markets may significantly alter both the scale and the composition of the RNFE, a finding echoed by a similar panel study in rural Bangladesh (Hossain 2004).

In most settings, however, time-series data on rural nonfarm activity remain in short supply. Therefore, in order to isolate the impact of agricultural growth on rural nonfarm activity, a large component of the linkages literature has drawn on micro field data to construct counterfactual modeling estimates of the impact of agricultural growth on the nonfarm economy.

Modeling Agricultural Growth Linkages

Pros and Cons of Modeling

Apart from a handful of econometric estimates, most attempts at quantifying agricultural growth linkages have focused on counterfactual modeling (Table 7.3). Drawing on a generation of detailed microeconomic evidence from farm budget studies and from nonfarm enterprise surveys, analysts compute input-output relationships that measure the strength of backward and forward production linkages. Similarly, household expenditure surveys, if sufficiently detailed, permit assessment of the locational implications of consumer spending patterns.[21] Following early applications by Bell and Hazell (1980), Adelman (1984), and Thorbecke (1985), an expanding legion of social accounting matrix (SAM) builders has contributed to a growing array of empirical detail on economic interactions across national and regional economies. The subsequent integration of these SAMs into computable general equilibrium models with endogenous prices and factor mobility has enabled incorporation of labor and capital flows between agriculture and nonfarm businesses into the linkages models. The strength of the modeling approach lies in its ability to isolate the probable impact of agricultural growth from other forces affecting the RNFE, forces such as population growth, migration, government policy, major price shocks, and the vagaries of local meteorology.

The counterfactual modeling approach, however, presents several inconveniences that must also be recognized. One difficulty with this approach is that when data or behavioral parameters are unavailable or imperfectly understood, modelers resort to assumptions. In product markets, in particular, supply elasticities of farm and nonfarm goods have been the subject of considerable debate. Most linkages studies—the input-output (IO), the semi-input-output (SIO), and all SAM-based multipliers—assume a perfectly elastic supply of rural nonfarm goods and services. Some analytical models, such as the unconstrained IO and SAM multiplier estimates, assume a perfectly elastic supply of all products, including crop agriculture. Yet this remains a contentious assumption in many

---

21. See, for example, Mellor and Lele (1973), King and Byerlee (1978), Hazell and Roell (1983), Lewis (1988), Bendavid-Val (1989), Hazell and Ramasamy (1991), and Delgado, Hopkins, and Kelly (1998).

TABLE 7.3 Summary of empirical estimates of agricultural growth multipliers

	Agricultural growth multiplier[a] (number of cases)		Differences in indirect income gains		
				Compared to endogenous price multipliers	
Estimation method	National	Rural region[b]	National – rural	National	Rural
I. Econometric	1.97 (6)	1.39 (3)	0.58	0.22	−0.07
II. Modeling					
A. Fixed price					
1. Input-output	2.78 (5)	1.90 (2)	0.88	1.03	0.44
2. Semi-input-output	2.10 (14)	1.69 (14)	0.41	0.35	0.23
B. Endogenous price	1.75 (11)	1.46 (2)	0.29	0.00	0.00

SOURCE: Table 7A.1.

NOTES:

[a]Change in total gross domestic product divided by initial shock in agricultural income. The numbers in parentheses represent the number of studies summarized.

[b]Includes rural regions or villages.

settings, particularly given the wealth of supply response studies documenting generally inelastic aggregate output supply response in agriculture (Binswanger et al. 1987; Binswanger 1989).

Projection of consumption linkages likewise hinges on values of marginal budget shares, though many times SAM builders have only average budget shares (ABSs) at their disposal. Because these normally understate incremental expenditures on nonfarm goods and services, use of the ABSs will normally underestimate marginal spending on nonfoods.

Factor market linkages likewise pose thorny analytical and empirical questions for the modelers. Rural labor markets, though highly variable and only imperfectly understood (Reardon 1997), exhibit a wide range of institutional particularities and rigidities—including long-term contracts, constraints imposed by caste systems, and the frequent immobility of women's labor—with which modelers must come to grips (Bhallah 1994; Jayaraman and Lanjouw 1999). Capital flows and savings allocation become even more difficult. Given the fungibility of funds, the invisibility of many of these flows, and respondents' reluctance to discuss indebtedness, modeling of these capital flows is more frequently based on intuition and assumption than on detailed understanding of these admittedly difficult-to-track flows. The sectoral allocation of investment becomes important in evaluating the dynamic effects of agricultural growth. Yet frequently the magnitude and even the direction of these flows remain subject to large margins of imprecision. Possibly for this reason, the bulk of linkage modeling assessments have ignored dynamic investment-led growth paths. Instead they have focused on comparative-static changes in output and income resulting from exogenous growth in key sectors of the economy. In doing so, modeling assessments have focused on consumption and production linkages, for which detailed empirical evidence has been painstakingly accumulated over the past several decades (see Chapter 2).

Methods

UNCONSTRAINED LINEAR FIXED-PRICE MODELS.   Studies of growth linkages most commonly apply some variant of the linear IO model. In its most basic form, the IO model uses fixed IO coefficients and assumes fixed prices and perfectly elastic supply in all sectors. With perfectly elastic supply, any increase in demand leads only to higher output, with no change in price. Total supply in each sector (Z) is modeled as the sum of interindustry input demand (AZ) and final demand (F), where final demand includes consumption by households (βY) and exogenous sources of demand such as exports (E). Income (Y) is related to production through a fixed value-added share (v) in gross commodity output (Z).

$$
\begin{aligned}
Z &= AZ + F \\
&= AZ + \beta Y + E \\
&= AZ + \beta v Z + E.
\end{aligned}
\tag{1}
$$

Because supply is assumed to be perfectly elastic in all sectors,[22] total output and incomes are determined by the level of exogenous demand (E), the identity matrix (I), and a matrix of multipliers (C):

$$
Z = (I - C)^{-1} E.
\tag{2}
$$

Perfectly elastic supply in all sectors is, of course, an unrealistic assumption in many developing countries, particularly for some sectors. Given high rates of seasonal labor underemployment, typically low capital requirements, and substantial rates of reported excess capacity in many rural nonfarm businesses, a highly elastic supply of rural nonfarm goods and services is frequently an appropriate assumption.[23] In contrast, shortages of skilled labor, foreign exchange,

---

22. As Haggblade, Hammer, and Hazell (1991) and Bigsten and Collier (1995) note, the existence of a real multiplier hinges on the existence of slack resources that can be pulled into productive activity.

23. Liedholm and Chuta (1976), Steel (1977), and Bagachawa and Stewart (1992) report rates of excess capacity of between 33 percent and 60 percent for the countries of Sierra Leone, Ghana, and Tanzania, respectively.

and fixed capital frequently constrain output in the formal industrial sector. Likewise, in agriculture, seasonal labor bottlenecks, land availability, soil fertility, input supply, marketing infrastructure, and moisture constraints frequently limit supply responses.

Even so, some analysts suggest that agricultural supply elasticities may be high, at least over a certain range (Thorbecke 1994; Delgado et al. 1998). Anecdotal reports of piles of rotting fruit unable to find their way to market and excess bags of grain unevacuated from specific remote regions bolster these claims in some limited circumstances. Yet, apart from these episodic special cases, the overwhelming bulk of empirical evidence points to a low aggregate supply response in agriculture (Binswanger 1989). If farmers in the developing world could, in fact, increase crop output in unlimited amounts, agriculture would indeed represent a powerful engine of economic growth, for both malnutrition and poverty would vanish overnight as hungry farmers availed themselves of this perfectly elastic cornucopia.

By ignoring supply constraints altogether, unconstrained IO and SAM multiplier models exaggerate the magnitude of intersectoral linkages. Given that over half of the reported indirect effects in these unconstrained models come from demand-induced growth in foodgrains and other allegedly elastically supplied agricultural commodities, this questionable assumption biases anticipated indirect income gains substantially upward. Side-by-side comparisons with alternative formulations suggest that the unconstrained IO models overstate agricultural growth multipliers by a factor of 2 to 10 (Haggblade, Hammer, and Hazell 1991).

CONSTRAINED LINEAR FIXED-PRICE MODELS.   To better simulate real-world supply rigidities, SIO models classify sectors into two groups, those that are supply constrained (Z_1) and others that are perfectly elastic in supply (Z_2).[24] As described in equations 3 and 4, the SIO model permits output responses only in the supply-responsive sectors (Z_2). Perfectly elastic supply ensures fixed prices for these (Z_2) goods. In the other group, that of supply-constrained products (Z_1), perfect substitutability between domestic goods and imports guarantees that border prices will ensure fixed prices for these goods as well. For these models to produce a reasonable approximation of reality, the supply-constrained sectors must correspond to tradable goods whose domestic supply remains fixed at the prevailing output price. In these supply-constrained sectors (Z_1), increases in domestic demand merely reduce net exports (E_1), which then become endogenous to the system and are determined by the matrix of SIO multipliers (C^*):

$$Z_1 = A_1 Z + \beta_1 v_1 Z + E_1. \tag{3a}$$
$$Z_2 = A_2 Z + \beta_2 v_2 Z + E_2. \tag{3b}$$

---

24. See Tinbergen (1966), Kuyvenhoven (1978), and Bell and Hazell (1980) for further discussion of the SIO method. In cases in which equations are specified for all accounts of a complete social accounting matrix, SIO models are also termed "constrained SAM multiplier models."

$$E_1 = (I - C^*)^{-1} Z_1. \tag{4a}$$
$$Z_2 = (I - C^*)^{-1} E_2. \tag{4b}$$

As social accounting matrices have grown in popularity, SAM-based multiplier estimates have emerged to complement and extend the early linkages work. In spite of sometimes different labels, the SAM-based multipliers are formally identical to the IO and SIO models. All require an IO table to calculate the production linkages. All adopt fixed prices, fixed IO coefficients, and fixed marginal budget shares. All come in unconstrained and constrained versions. The SAMs themselves become convenient tools for summarizing the raw data and results. They also provide a basis for incorporating capital, trade, and government accounts. Frequently, given their origin in poverty and income distribution analyses, the SAMs offer great detail on factor allocation and distribution of income across household groups. What many in the literature call "unconstrained SAM-based multipliers" are formally identical to the unconstrained IO models. Similarly, the "constrained SAM-based multipliers" are formally identical to the SIO models (Haggblade, Hammer, and Hazell 1991; Lewis and Thorbecke 1992).

One interesting methodological innovation emerging from the SAM-based stream of linkages work is the "mixed multiplier" model proposed by Parikh and Thorbecke (1996). This variant considers some sectors perfectly inelastic in supply, some perfectly elastic, and some elastic but only over a specified, finite range. This formulation clearly requires detailed knowledge of a local economy and of the extent of excess capacity in all sectors. Where available, this information allows a more refined assessment of the indirect spin-offs of agricultural growth.

ENDOGENOUS PRICE MODELS. A further step toward realism in modeling linkages involves endogenizing prices and relaxing the assumptions of a fixed output of tradable goods and a perfectly elastic supply of nontradable goods. Haggblade, Hammer, and Hazell (1991) relax the assumption of a perfectly elastic supply of nontradable goods by introducing an upward-sloping supply of nontradables. However, their very simple model ignores the possibility of price responsiveness in the supply of tradable goods, and it assumes perfect substitutability between domestically produced and imported tradable goods.

To capture these effects as well as macroeconomic effects of changes in the real exchange rate requires a model with full price endogeneity, such as a computable general equilibrium model. Modeling endogenous prices greatly increases the data requirements, including behavioral parameters, many of which are difficult to obtain. Moreover, rural labor and capital markets—with their wide range of institutional particularities and rigidities—are especially difficult to model. Nonetheless, the importance of food and other agricultural price changes, particularly for low-income households, suggests that even a rudimentary inclusion of these effects on product, factor, and capital markets is desirable. De Janvry and Sadoulet (2002) illustrate this by measuring the potentially powerful poverty-reducing effects of agricultural growth resulting from indirect effects on food prices and wage rates.

Results

PRODUCTION AND CONSUMPTION LINKAGES.   Given that linkage studies have been undertaken in a large variety of settings, at different points in time, using a range of analytical methods and varying units of analysis, it is perhaps not surprising that they have produced a wide range of results (Tables 7.3 and 7A.1). Consider the results from the Muda River region of Malaysia, a bell-wether benchmark that has served as a rallying point for both linkage loyalists and doubters. Using a regional SAM disaggregated with 35 production accounts and 6 household groups together with a SIO model, the widely reported Muda study estimates a regional agricultural growth multiplier of 1.83. That is, every dollar in direct agricultural income generated by the Muda River project's investment in irrigation infrastructure and agricultural support triggered an additional 83 cents in second-round income gains elsewhere in the regional economy, 79 cents in nonfarm activity, and 4 cents in other agriculture. Of this incremental income gain, about 80 percent stems from consumption linkages and the remaining 20 percent from production links with agriculture.

Depending on the economy, the magnitude of the agricultural growth linkages varies considerably. Different agricultural technologies, income distributions, business and technical skills, spatial patterns of population, networks of infrastructure, and political, ethnic, and institutional environments all contribute to widely variable nonfarm responses to agricultural growth. Available estimates of agricultural growth linkages generally prove highest in Asia, where high-input agriculture generates strong backward linkages,[25] and where consumption diversification into nonfoods stimulates consumer demand for nonfarm goods and services. They become lower in Africa because of lower-input agriculture, which generates fewer backward linkages, and because lower incomes generate less consumption diversification into nonfoods. In Latin America, rural linkages appear to be low because of the extreme inequality in land and income distribution, absentee ownership of large landholdings, and the consequently feeble rural consumption and input linkages emanating from the often urban-based and urban-supplied hacienda owners.[26] However, given the high input intensity in agriculture and established supply networks from large cities, urban and aggregate national growth linkages prove substantial (de Janvry and Sadoulet 2002).

The unit of analysis also affects the results in a systematic way. While spending linkages to urban-produced goods constitute a leakage to the region,

---

25. See Bagachwa and Stewart (1992), Table 5.15, for quantification of the considerably lower input intensity of African agriculture.

26. Haggblade and Hazell (1989), de Janvry and Sadoulet (1993), Berry (1995).

they represent a gain to the national economy. By including urban as well as rural sources of demand-induced income growth, national multipliers necessarily exceed those limited to a rural region. On average, the 50-plus multiplier estimates summarized in Table 7.3 suggest that indirect income gains at the national level exceed those for rural regions by 50 to 150 percent, increasing indirect income gains by 30 to 90 cents for each initial dollar of agricultural income growth.[27] Inclusion or exclusion of government accounts likewise affects the results. In the Muda case, 6 of the 83 cents in incremental earnings accrued to government. In a comparable North Arcott study, government agencies earned 14 of the 87 cents in indirect income gains emanating from the green revolution varieties in the region (Hazell and Ramasamy 1991). Given that indirect taxes account for the majority of tax revenues in many developing countries, inclusion of indirect taxes in value added can significantly enhance projected results.

The choice of analytical method also affects projected linkages considerably. For this reason, the analyst must be careful to select the method embodying assumptions most appropriate to the economy under investigation. The unconstrained, fixed-price multiplier methods (the IO and unconstrained SAM-based multipliers) necessarily project indirect income gains higher than those obtained from the other methods. In the studies summarized by Table 7.3, the unconstrained IO multipliers generate indirect income gains that exceed those of the price endogenous models by 50 to 100 percent, increasing projected indirect income gains by 44 to 109 cents. Though in isolated instances and over very short ranges agricultural output of individual crops may prove elastic, the weight of available empirical evidence suggests that the bulk of agricultural production remains supply constrained in most of the developing world (Binswanger 1989). Consequently the unconstrained IO estimates, based as they are on the presumption of a perfectly elastic supply in all sectors of the economy, project generally overly optimistic growth multipliers.

Models that incorporate price endogeneity tend to reduce measured agricultural growth multipliers. Most analytical studies have nonetheless adopted fixed-price methods because of their simplicity and their tractability. For a village or a small rural region, this may well be reasonable. But as analysis moves closer to the national level, the fixed-price assumption becomes more difficult

---

27. The detailed African studies reported by Delgado, Hopkins, and Kelly (1998) suggest even greater increases, with indirect income gains increasing by 125 percent to as much as 600 percent when moving from a rural region to the national level (Table 7A.1). These large increases arise not only because the catchment area expands to include demand linkages from urban areas, but also because the classification of coarse cereals as nontradable within an SIO framework implies a perfectly elastic supply of sorghum, millet, and maize. Given technology, water, and peak season labor constraints, however, the output supply of these crops is normally considered inelastic. Under these conditions, as de Janvry (1994) points out, supply-constrained nontradables are best modeled using a price-endogenous model, which will reduce the projected multipliers.

to defend, particularly if the anticipated shock is large relative to the overall economy. Moreover, in the case of a large shock to a major agricultural sub-sector, macroeconomic effects on foreign savings or the real exchange can be-come important, as well.[28] Efforts to compare the effect of upward-sloping sup-ply curves—as opposed to perfectly elastic ones—suggest that, in the presence of upward-sloping supply curves, fixed-price SIO income multipliers in devel-oping countries may overstate indirect income gains by 20 to 25 percent (9 to 17 cents), depending on the region (Table 7A.1). Full computable general equi-librium (CGE) estimates produce variable results, in part because of the op-posing effects of modeling a positively sloped supply curve both for tradables (which tends to increase the multipliers) and for nontradables (which tends to decrease the multipliers). In a recent comparison of SIO and CGE results for four African countries (Dorosh and Haggblade 2003), CGE multipliers were lower than SIO multipliers by 35 to 65 percent (42 to 104 cents) in two coun-tries, but higher than SIO multipliers by about 45 percent (19 to 25 cents) in the other two countries (Table 7A.1).

MODELING FACTOR MARKET LINKAGES.   In rural labor markets, available modeling estimates generally confirm strong links between agricultural growth and labor demand in growing segments of the RNFE.[29] Early estimates of the employment gains generated by agricultural growth suggest strong employ-ment increases in related nonfarm activities, particularly those supplying con-sumption goods and services to farm households.[30] In some instances, the non-farm employment gains exceed the direct gains in agriculture.[31] Subsequently, full general equilibrium models in the tradition of Adelman (1984), de Janvry and Sadoulet (2002), and others offer the important benefit of tracking changes in both labor demand and wages in response to agricultural growth. One such study from Bolivia uses a CGE model to compare alternative agricultural growth strategies, projecting the highest growth in wage rates (5.5 percent) and gross domestic product (5.6 percent) from potato-led growth (De Franco and Godoy 1993).

Investment dynamics emanating from agricultural growth have remained confined to national-level simulations and econometric work.[32] Given diffi-culties in determining the spatial flows of savings and investments, few studies

---

28. Note that most fixed-price multiplier analyses do not formally specify a macroeconomic closure for the foreign trade account. It is important to realize, though, that in a standard SIO model the level of foreign savings (equal to the current account deficit) is endogenous. That is, capital is implicitly allowed to flow into the region or country so as to finance any increase in the current ac-count deficit. See Dorosh and Haggblade (2003).

29. Mellor and Lele (1971), Mellor and Mudahar (1974), Krishna (1975), Ahmed and Herdt (1984), Haggblade and Liedholm (1991).

30. Mellor and Mudahar (1974), Krishna (1975), Ahmed and Herdt (1984).

31. See, for example, Ahmed and Herdt (1984) and de Janvry and Sadoulet (2002).

32. Adelman (1984), De Franco and Godoy (1993), Block and Timmer (1994), Block (1999).

have ventured to extrapolate the consequences of investment-led growth between rural and urban areas.

PRODUCTIVITY LINKAGES. Empirical investigations of productivity linkages from agriculture to the rest of the economy rely on a single analysis by Block and Timmer (1994), an evocative analysis that, by the researchers' own admission, blurs together consumption, production, and productivity effects. Hence their work, while important in highlighting this potentially important set of linkages, should be considered illustrative and evocative rather than definitive. The growing body of microeconomic evidence documenting the important impact of adequate nutrition on learning and on worker productivity (Strauss and Thomas 2000) does, however, offer indirect support for their thesis.

REVERSE LINKAGES. In general, demand linkages (production and consumption) from nonfarm to farm activities are much smaller than those from agriculture to rural nonfarm activities, both because of more inelastic supply in much of crop agriculture and because of the smaller nonfarm base. Indeed, when computed these reverse demand linkages from nonfarm activities to agriculture emerge as smaller or statistically insignificant.[33] Studies such as that by Parikh and Thorbecke (1996), which aim to measure these nonfarm-to-farm linkages at a village level, generate large results by virtue of their assumption of a perfectly elastic supply of agricultural goods over an initial range.

Factor market flows clearly move in both directions. They represent probably the most important of the reverse linkages (Table 7.4). Though these flows remain an integral part of neoclassical CGE models, structural rigidities prevailing in some locations imply that ground-truthing of the kind commonly available from the household case studies described in Chapter 6 will enhance understanding of the actual fluidity of labor flows across sectors and space.

Linkage Debates

Asian Doubters

The linkages literature originated in Asia with the advent of the green revolution. So it is perhaps natural that the richest literature and the loudest debates have emanated from that region. Prominent skeptics of the basic tenets of agricultural growth linkages have included Vyas and Mathai (1978), Harriss and Harriss (1984), Harriss (1987a,b), Hart (1987, 1989), and Leones and Feldman (1998). Their critiques and qualifiers have proven useful in highlighting the nature of agricultural growth linkages and the circumstances under which agriculture will or will not generate rapid growth in the RNFE.

---

33. Block and Timmer (1994), Delgado, Hopkins, and Kelly (1998), Block (1999), and Bravo-Ortega and Lederman (2005) find smaller reverse linkages, while Hazell and Haggblade (1991) find them statistically insignificant.

TABLE 7.4 Sources of start-up capital in rural nonfarm enterprises (percent of enterprises obtaining capital from each source)

Country	Own savings		Other sources of capital				Total
	Total	Share from agriculture	Friends and relatives	Moneylenders	Banks	Other	
Bangladesh							
Rural areas, 1980	72	33	2	6	0	22	100
Rural areas, 2000	77	—	6	4	11	2	100
El Salvador, 1996	70	—	11	12	7	0	100
Ghana							
Rural towns, 1984	0	—	87	3	7	3	100
Rural areas, 1992	—	71	—	—	—	29	100
India, agricultural trading firms							
Coimbatore district, 1980	92	13	8	0	0	0	100
Tanzania							
Arusha region, 1981	80	—	15	4	1	0	100

SOURCES: Liedholm and Chuta (1976), Ahmed (1984), Thomi and Yankson (1985), Harriss (1987b), Bagachwa and Stewart (1992), Abdulai (1994), Lanjouw (2001), Hossain (2004).

NOTE: A dash indicates that data are not available.

Doubts about the power of agricultural growth linkages revolve around three principal observations. First, the skeptics note that forces other than agriculture may strongly influence the growth of the RNFE. In a rural town in North Arcot, India, the local silk industry expanded rapidly following the green revolution, apparently unrelated to developments in local agriculture, because silk production there was based on imported rather than local inputs and on export rather than local markets (Harriss and Harriss 1984; Harriss 1987a,b). Other observers point to cases in which rural nonfarm employment has grown at rates higher or lower than agriculture, or even ones in which negative agricultural growth has occurred in the presence of nonfarm employment growth. Yet most of these studies track rural nonfarm activity via total nonfarm employment, an imprecise and undiscriminating indicator at best.[34] Even so, the doubters raise an important basic point: that agriculture is not the only force governing the growth of the RNFE. Nor is it always a sufficient condition for rural nonfarm growth, as the discussion of conditioners later in this chapter suggests.

Second, the doubters note that agricultural income growth may stimulate demand for urban rather than rural products. They observe that following the green revolution in North Arcot, farmers increased their use of sophisticated manufactured inputs such as tractors and petrochemical fertilizers, while consumers increased their purchases of imported goods such as cosmetics, ready-made clothes, plastics, and bottled cold drinks. These goods were normally produced in Madras or other large urban areas, not in the rural region (Harriss and Harriss 1984). Similarly, in the Muda River region of Malaysia, growing farm income resulted in increased consumption of television sets and other consumer electronics imported from urban areas and even from Thailand (Hart 1987, 1989). As these examples suggest, agricultural growth may well stimulate demand for urban or imported goods. Yet in these and other well-known instances, rural firms have been able to compete in supplying rural pump sets, farm tools, basic agricultural machinery, tailored clothing, and local beverages.[35] Moreover, rural businesses earn commercial margins selling imported goods, suggesting that rural services and marketing can coexist with imported manufactures. The relative shares of imported and local nonfarm goods and services will, of course, vary across settings. In the case of both Muda and North Arcott, rural nonfarm multipliers remained large—over 75 cents in rural nonfarm earnings for each dollar increase in agricultural income—even after accounting for rural purchases of these imported goods (Bell, Hazell, and Slade 1982; Hazell and Slade 1987; Hazell and Ramasamy 1991). Elsewhere this may not be the case given that basic conditions affecting both the composition of demand and the rural nonfarm supply response differ among regions in important ways.

---

34. See Vyas and Mathai (1978), Leones and Feldman (1998), and Chapter 1.
35. See Child and Kaneda (1975), Chuta and Liedholm (1979), Tomich, Kilby, and Johnston (1995), Hayami (1998c), and Shah et al. (2000).

Likewise, in evaluating the prospects for urban as opposed to rural demand linkages, it is important to distinguish between rural manufacturing on the one hand and rural commerce and services on the other. Because of the easy transport of urban manufactures as infrastructure improves, rural manufacturing remains the most vulnerable segment of the RNFE.[36] At the same time, rural commerce and services remain more insulated from urban-based competition.

In rural commerce and services, even the most prominent doubters acknowledge that agricultural growth will stimulate rural nonfarm activity. Comparing time-series data between 1973 and 1983 in a market town of North Arcot, India, the Harrisses noted a large increase in rice milling and trading following the introduction of green revolution rice varieties in the region (Harriss and Harriss 1984; Harriss 1987a,b). Moreover, the number of welding and general engineering firms more than doubled over the same period, focusing principally on agricultural input supply and repairs for products such as pump sets, electric and diesel motors, irrigation pipes, agricultural trailers, and bullock carts. The Harrisses also recorded a substantial increase in local consumption linkages, primarily involving service providers such as pawnbrokers, lawyers, doctors, transporters, cycle hire and repair shops, barber shops, and laundries. Similarly, Sander's early study of green revolution Philippines in the region around Cabantuan city found that farmers' spending stimulated nonfarm employment, primarily in commerce (grocery stores, restaurants, cafes, and transport) and in services (most notably in private secondary education) following the introduction of new varieties of "miracle" rice (Sander 1983). In the Muda River region of Malaysia, Hart noted moderate diversification of the nonfarm economy, primarily through the expansion of commerce and services, in this case primarily government services (Hart 1989). In all of these Asian cases, the agriculturally induced linkages consisted most prominently of services and commerce.

Third, the doubters suggest that investment linkages emanating from agricultural growth may result in a transfer of savings and investment out of the rural region. In Malaysia, Hart (1989) notes that historic partitioning of economic roles induces the ethnic Chinese who run many rural nonfarm businesses to channel their profits to urban areas, where opportunities for Chinese are greater. Even among ethnic Malays living in rural areas, large-scale government inducements to improve investment opportunities may have encouraged an outflow of savings to unit trusts and other investment schemes established in urban areas. Indeed, in their efforts to quantify regional economic flows, Bell, Hazell, and Slade (1982) note a large outflow of savings from the Muda region. Similarly, in North Arcot, India, attempts to track the flows of savings and investment emanating from agricultural growth suggest that nonfarm business owners evacuated a substantial share of profits from rural areas into urban in-

---

36. See, for example, recent evidence from Bangladesh in Table 16.2.

vestment (Harriss 1987a,b), a finding corroborated during the construction of a social accounting matrix for that region (Hazell and Ramasamy 1991). While first-round rural growth multipliers remained large, even after accounting for these outflows, the transfer of capital outside the rural region foreshadows a lower investment-led growth trajectory in future years.

These observations raise the important distinction between first-round income gains from an initial agricultural spurt and the subsequent rounds of investment-led growth. Modelers distinguish between these "level effects," jumps to a new income level, and "rate effects," changes in the rate of income growth over time. Indeed, empirical measurement of growth linkages has focused almost exclusively on the comparative-static estimates of income gains, that is, the level effects resulting from agricultural growth. In large part because of the empirical difficulties associated with measuring and tracing the geographic deployment of savings and investment, few quantitative studies have ventured into dynamic modeling of the impact of investment linkages and the rate effects in and outside the rural regions.[37] Here the doubters point to an important but difficult empirical issue that indeed deserves more careful scrutiny in future empirical work.

African Believers

In general, the growth linkages discussions emerging in Asia in the early 1970s were exported to Africa in the 1980s and have taken root in Latin America only since the mid-1990s. In that transition, Africanist scholars appear generally optimistic that agricultural growth linkages exist in rural Africa, albeit at levels lower than those found in Asia. Both agricultural specialists and students of the RNFE routinely express confidence in the importance of agricultural stimulus to rural nonfarm activity.[38] A study from Burkina Faso highlights the striking importance of agriculturally related rural processing and input supply business, noting that these account for over three-fourths of rural nonfarm employment (Wilcock 1981). Perhaps because of the prevalence of local beer brewing from millet, sorghum, and maize,[39] many observers readily acknowledge that the bulk of rural nonfarm activity is, in fact, agriculturally based. For Africanists, growth linkages clearly exist. The hard question is how to trigger agricultural growth in the first place (de Janvry 1994).[40]

---

37. Adelman (1984), De Franco and Godoy (1993), Block and Timmer (1994), and Block (1999) do incorporate dynamic investment linkages from agriculture, though at a national level.

38. See, for example, Chuta and Liedholm (1979), Freeman and Norcliffe (1985), Haggblade, Hazell, and Brown (1989), Bagachwa and Stewart (1992), Reardon et al. (1993), Delgado et al. (1994), and Reardon (1997).

39. See Freeman and Norcliffe (1985), Milimo and Fisseha (1986), Chuta and Liedholm (1989), and Haggblade (1992).

40. Indeed, some scholars have raised doubts about the prospects for broad-based agriculture-led growth in Africa (Maxwell 2003; Ellis 2005). A related body of research has focused on African

Latin American Skeptics

In contrast, Latin American specialists have only tepidly participated in the agricultural growth linkages debates. From the nonfarm perspective, Latin Americanists have explored reasons for the paucity of both rural towns and rural nonfarm activity, an absence they ascribe to the highly urbanized concentration of population and to the highly stratified society and economic control that pervades much of the continent (Berry 1976, 1995). These factors result in minimal farm-nonfarm linkages in Latin American's rural towns, particularly compared with those in Asia and Africa (Table 7.5), although commercial links with large cities prove more substantial. Given the highly skewed distribution of land and because of the urban-focused consumption patterns of an often absentee landlord class, rural nonfarm consumption linkages remain less significant as well (Haggblade and Hazell 1989; de Janvry and Sadoulet 1993). Although evidence of agricultural growth linkages does exist, particularly at the urban and national levels, many Latin American scholars believe that stimulus to rural nonfarm activity will depend disproportionately on nonagricultural motors such as tourism and urban-to-rural subcontracting for export markets.[41]

Overall, the Latin American discussions underline two important conditioners of agriculture-led growth in the RNFE. Income and asset distribution clearly influence the distribution of income emanating from agricultural growth, and hence the nature of consumption linkages. Likewise, the existing structure of urban settlements, markets, and economic power also powerfully shapes prospects for an effective rural nonfarm supply response.[42]

Is Generalization Possible?

Given the extreme heterogeneity of rural nonfarm activity, agricultural growth, like other stimuli, will affect various components of the RNFE differently. Like-

---

"deagrarianization." This work notes that agricultural income has fallen in many places following liberalization and the consequent withdrawal of agricultural support programs, forcing many rural households to supplement their livelihoods through rural-to-urban migration or diversification, often into unskilled rural nonfarm activities (Bryceson and Jamal 1997; Bryceson 2002). Explanations advanced for this increasing reliance on urban and rural nonfarm income include languishing opportunities in agriculture, growing population pressure, land shortages, environmental degradation, declining formal urban employment, and rising Western consumerism, which renders agriculture a low-prestige occupation. Most of these explanations are consistent with the growth linkages literature, which likewise notes that stagnating agriculture will propel rural labor into migration or low-productivity rural nonfarm activities.

41. Reinhart (1987), De Franco and Godoy (1993), de Janvry and Sadoulet (1993, 2002), Reardon, Berdegué, and Escobar (2001).

42. Differences in definitions of what is considered rural may also explain the apparently lower rural nonfarm growth linkages in Latin America. If Latin American countries generally define settlements over 2,000 as urban while Asian countries use a population size cutoff of 10,000 or larger, at least some of the reported differences in rural nonfarm activity may stem from simple definitional differences of what is considered rural (Tacoli 1998; De Ferranti et al. 2005). We are grateful to Steve Wiggins for pointing this out.

TABLE 7.5 Locational distribution of agriculturally induced nonfarm income growth

	Change in agricultural income	Resulting nonfarm income gains	Nonfarm income increments per $ of farm income gain		
			Rural	Towns	Total
North Arcot, India, 1982 (millions of rupees)					
Rural	408	111	0.27		
Urban villages	13	18			
Regional towns	8	200			
Total	428	329	0.26	0.51	0.77
Kutus region, Kenya, 1987 (millions of shillings)					
Rural	61	17	0.28		
Regional towns	3	8			
Total	64	25	0.26	0.13	0.40
Michoacan region, Mexico, 1984 (thousands of pesos)					
Rural	129	43	0.33		
Regional towns	90	5			
Total	219	48	0.19	0.02	0.22

SOURCES: Figures computed based on Hazell and Ramasamy (1991), Lewis and Thorbecke (1992), Yúnez-Naude, Taylor, and Dyer (1998), and Rosegrant and Hazell (2000).

NOTE: A blank cell indicates that data are not applicable.

wise, because of varying economic structures across continents and regions, the impact of agriculture will differ across locations. Yet even within this overall diversity, several general conclusions do emerge.

GENERALIZATION 1: GROWTH LINKAGES FREQUENTLY PROVE SUBSTANTIAL.   On balance, available evidence suggests strong linkages between agriculture and the RNFE—strongest in Asia; weaker in Africa, though with the potential to increase with changes in the input structure of agriculture and with rising incomes; and least strong in Latin America for structural reasons. Differences in available estimates of growth linkages emerge because of differing types of agriculture, economic and social settings, units of analysis, and modeling assumptions. In the end, a plausible range for national agricultural growth multipliers stands between the SIO and price-endogenous estimates. Best-guess generalizations probably lie in the range of 1.6 to 1.8 in Asia and 1.3 to 1.5 in Africa and Latin America.

GENERALIZATION 2: CONSUMPTION LINKAGES DOMINATE.   A predominance of empirical studies in the developing world suggests that consumer spending accounts for about 80 percent of agricultural demand linkages, while production linkages account for the remainder.[43] Consumption linkages appear weakest in Latin America and in estate-led agricultural growth in general (Haggblade and Hazell 1989; de Janvry and Sadoulet 1993). Comparisons across a broad group of developed and developing countries indicate that consumption linkages fall from 80 percent of demand linkages in poor countries to about 60 percent in the developed world because of the rising input intensity of agriculture and the growing importance of backward linkages (Vogel 1994). In the developing world, however, particularly in Asia and Africa, consumption linkages from agriculture to the nonfarm economy remain of principal importance, as Mellor and Lele (1973) first suggested.

GENERALIZATION 3: RURAL SERVICES AND COMMERCE ACCOUNT FOR THE MAJORITY OF RURAL NONFARM LINKAGES.   Within the RNFE, manufacturing appears most vulnerable to competition from urban goods. Because growing agriculture often brings with it improvements in marketing infrastructure, it facilitates the penetration of urban manufactures in rural areas. So rural manufacturing typically undergoes a substantial transformation in buoyant agricultural regions as low-quality, low-productivity manufacturing in cottage and home-based industries is displaced by the twin pressures of rising rural wages and growing competition from imports. Meanwhile, rural services such as housing, education, transport, health, and personal services grow briskly, largely insulated from outside competition.

GENERALIZATION 4: LABOR MARKET LINKAGES STRONGLY INFLUENCE THE GROWTH AND COMPOSITION OF THE RNFE.   Via labor demand and rural wage rates, agricultural growth influences the composition of rural nonfarm activity (Table 7.1). Because agricultural growth induces a decline in low-wage non-farm activities such as basket weaving and potterymaking while at the same time encouraging growth in higher-return services and factory manufacturing, the net impact on total nonfarm employment remains ambiguous.

GENERALIZATION 5: CAPITAL FLOWS ARE IMPORTANT, THOUGH IMPER-FECTLY UNDERSTOOD.   Capital flows between agriculture and the RNFE appear very important in both directions, though most evidence remains more anecdotal than empirical. Where available, data on sources of investment and working capital in both agriculture and nonfarm businesses suggest a regular flow of funds in both directions. While tracing these flows within a given firm or household remains relatively straightforward, flows across households become difficult to quantify given an absence of institutional intermediation and the reticence of traders and households to reveal their indebtedness to probing

---

43. See Bell, Hazell, and Slade (1982), Ahmed and Herdt (1984), Chadha (1986), Haggblade and Hazell (1989), Ranis, Stewart, and Angeles-Reyes (1990), Bagachwa and Stewart (1992), and Delgado, Hopkins, and Kelly (1998).

outsiders. Consequently, our understanding of these capital flows remains only partial and imperfect.

GENERALIZATION 6: PRODUCTIVITY LINKAGES ARE PROBABLE BUT LARGELY UNMEASURED. Productivity linkages from agriculture to the nonfarm economy emerge as likely, though direct evidence remains tentative. The large body of microeconomic literature linking food prices, nutrition, human learning, and productivity provides the strongest available evidence of these productivity linkages. Given growing concern about poverty, this feature of agricultural growth linkages will require further work.

Conditioners of Agricultural Growth Multipliers

WHO RECEIVES THE INITIAL INCOME SHOCK? Available empirical evidence suggests that the power of agricultural growth linkages depends on a variety of conditioning factors. Most important are the consumption preferences of the farmers receiving the initial income shock. Because consumption linkages account for about 80 percent of indirect income gains, the propensity of farm households to consume local products as opposed to imports becomes crucial to the spatial distribution of the indirect income gains. For this reason, much of the linkages literature has attempted to identify the farmer groups that offer the most powerful local consumption linkages (Table 7.6).

Many prominent proponents have advocated a "unimodal" agricultural growth strategy, which is shorthand for a small-farm focus in agriculture-led growth (Mellor and Johnston 1984). Yet some confusion surrounds this conventional orthodoxy because the unimodal blanket shrouds a remarkably supple tent into which advocates have swept "small farms," "peasant farmers," "larger, more commercialized farms," "larger farms that are really medium-sized farms by most standards," "middle-sized farms," and "dominant cultivating classes."[44] Confusion arises because of widely differing farm sizes in Asia compared to Africa and Latin America and because of consumption data that are frequently collected by expenditure class rather than by farm size, coupled with the well-known lack of correspondence between the two. In the end, the important generalization emerging from this debate is that resident farmers who consume and send their children to school in rural areas generate the largest rural nonfarm consumption linkages. If their hearts and their spending remain focused in rural areas, they will generate growth in rural nonfarm activity, particularly in commerce and services such as transport, prepared foods, education, and medicine.

FACILITATING THE RESPONSE OF RURAL NONFARM PRODUCERS. In response to an initial demand stimulus from agriculture, the supply responsiveness

---

44. See Mellor and Lele (1973), Hazell and Roell (1983), Mellor and Johnston (1984), Harriss (1987a,b), Ranis and Stewart (1987), and Tomich, Kilby, and Johnston (1995).

TABLE 7.6 Characteristics of farmers who generate maximum rural nonfarm growth linkages

Setting	Reference	Evidence	What farm size generates the maximum rural nonfarm growth linkages?
India	Mellor and Lele (1972)	Marginal budget shares by rural expenditure decile	Higher-income rural people (6th to 8th rural expenditure deciles), members of the dominant cultivator class
Malaysia and Nigeria	Hazell and Roell (1983)	Marginal budget shares by farm size	Larger farmers (but "large farms in our sample are really medium-sized farms by most standards"), medium-sized farms
Taiwan	Ranis and Stewart (1985)	Marginal budget shares by labor intensity of farm production	Small farmers, tenants, wage earners
Global	Tomich, Kilby, and Johnston (1995)	Review of literature on consumption and production linkages	Small farmers, suggesting a broad-based, "unimodal" strategy "involving the majority of farms (which are inevitably small)"

of rural nonfarm producers will depend on a variety of structural features of the rural economy:

- The distribution of necessary entrepreneurial and technical skills varies across locations and will strongly influence supply response. Ethnicity, caste, historical specialization, and features of the local educational system all influence the availability of human skills necessary to enable local nonfarm producers to respond. The distribution of political power and social capital and the degree of trust across ethnic groups likewise play key roles in determining the location of nonfarm activity emanating from agricultural growth.
- The quality of rural infrastructure and the degree of integration and openness of the rural economy also matter a great deal. Virtually all case studies of agricultural growth linkages and the RNFE emphasize the importance of rural infrastructure in facilitating communication, transport, and credit flows and improving the responsiveness of the nonfarm economy to increases in demand from agriculture.[45]
- Population density and distribution govern the cost, profitability, and minimum efficient scale of rural production. In general, increasing population density favors local production by reducing the catchment area necessary to achieve minimum efficient scales of production and reduce transport costs, thereby improving the prospects for rural firm response.
- The general policy environment likewise plays an important role in facilitating (or depressing) rural nonfarm enterprise growth. Tax rates on imports and on local production, interest rates, and labor market regulation can all influence the size and spatial distribution of nonfarm activity.[46]
- The average per capita income affects the marginal propensity to purchase nonfoods. Richer regions typically have higher demand for nonfoods and for high-value and processed foods.[47]

Because these conditioners vary across settings, reported agricultural growth multipliers vary substantially. A study incorporating three of these effects (income levels, infrastructure quality, and population density) estimates that agricultural growth multipliers range from 1.9 in the high-income, high-density, high-infrastructure Indian states of Punjab and Haryana to as low as 1.3 in low-income states such as Bihar (Haggblade and Hazell 1990). The indirect effects triple in favorable settings, suggesting that these conditioners will be

---

45. Barnes and Binswanger (1986), Evans (1990), Hazell and Haggblade (1991), Ahmed and Donovan (1992), Fan, Hazell, and Thorat (1999).
46. Anderson and Leiserson (1978), Chuta and Liedholm (1979), Haggblade, Liedholm, and Mead (1986), Ranis, Stewart, and Angeles-Reyes (1990), Bautista (1995).
47. Hazell and Roell (1983).

crucial in determining the settings in which growth linkages achieve their full potential.

Looking Forward

Changing Motors of Rural Nonfarm Growth

Agriculture, because of its economic importance in rural areas, plays a predominant role in influencing the size and structure of the RNFE early on. At later stages of economic growth, as population density increases, per capita incomes (and hence consumption patterns) change, and as transport improves, rural settlement may be encouraged by forces other than agricultural potential. In crowded settings such as the urban centers of East and South Asia, urban decongestion becomes an important stimulus motivating voluntary movement of people and factories from urban to rural areas.

Today China and the East Asian tigers have moved into a phase in which urban-led rural manufacturing growth probably predominates. In South Asia, extremely high population densities and rising incomes have made possible the beginnings of a shift to urban-led rural industrial growth in small zones clustered around major metropolitan centers and transport arteries. Yet agriculture remains the dominant player in rural areas there and will probably remain so for another generation. Likewise, in Africa, rural population densities remain low and agriculture remains the dominant economic force in rural areas. So there, too, agriculture will remain a primary governor of overall rural nonfarm activity. Meanwhile, in Latin America—where high concentrations of economic power, dendritic markets, and social and ethnic cleavages have shackled economic development in rural areas for generations—modern nonfarm activity, like population, infrastructure, and wealth, has remained concentrated in towns. For the foreseeable future, despite ongoing patterns of globalization, agriculture will remain the key driver of rural nonfarm activity in South Asia and rural Africa. Elsewhere, agriculture will remain a force to be reckoned with, though no longer necessarily the dominant factor influencing rural nonfarm activity.

Policy Prescriptions

Wherever agricultural growth occurs, it holds the potential to stimulate second rounds of growth in the RNFE. To maximize the domestic and rural nonfarm spin-offs from agricultural growth, several key prescriptions appear to have maintained their currency over time and across geographic settings.

First, put very simply, agricultural growth should target farmers who shop in rural areas. Because consumption linkages dominate as a stimulus of rural nonfarm activity, the single most important determinant of linkages is the consumption preferences of farmers who enjoy the initial gains in agricultural income. Evidence suggests that targeting different categories of farmers remains an important policy variable largely under the control of government agricultural research and extension services. Comparisons of maize breeding in Africa contrast Zimbabwe and South Africa, where government researchers focused on hybrids appropriate for large commercial farmers, while recent breakthroughs in West Africa have focused instead on open-pollinating varieties more easily adopted and maintained by small farmers (Byerlee and Eicher 1997). Agricultural research and extension programs can target different categories of farmers, and the choices they make will have fundamentally important implications for the size and nature of nonfarm spin-offs emanating from agricultural growth.

Second, rural infrastructure, such as roads, electricity, telecommunications, and the basic public services necessary to sustain rural towns, seems generally to enhance agricultural growth linkages. Other key conditioners of agricultural growth linkages, such as population density, ethnicity, caste, and the availability of local entrepreneurship, are less amenable to policy manipulation. Chapters 11–13 explore in greater depth how both infrastructure and programs of direct support to rural nonfarm firms might improve their responsiveness and hence accentuate the potential spin-offs emanating from agricultural growth.

Ultimately, ministers of finance must join with ministers of agriculture in recognizing that agricultural growth generates not only direct consequences for income distribution and poverty alleviation but also important indirect consequences via agriculture's growth linkages to the RNFE. Yet agricultural growth does not simply appear, like manna from heaven. It requires discipline, focus, and sustained investment by government, farmers, researchers, extension personnel, processors, and farm input suppliers. Most agricultural research is a public good, with strong externalities and a compelling need for substantial, sustained public investment (Anderson, Pardey, and Roseboom 1994). In general, it has proven highly profitable (Evenson and Gollin 2003). Sustained public investment in agricultural research requires political will and, in many cases, elevated priority for agricultural spending. Growth linkages can occur on the heels of agricultural growth. But, as de Janvry (1994) and others have emphasized, the operative constraint in many cases is how to trigger that agricultural growth in the first place. Chapter 17 returns to this theme, suggesting alternative development strategies for various regional settings.

Appendix 7A: Supplementary Table, Agricultural Growth Multipliers

See table on pages 174–182.

TABLE 7A.1 Empirical estimates of agricultural growth multipliers

	Study			Initial increase in agricultural income[a]
(Source) and method	Country	Year	Unit of analysis	
I. Econometric estimates				
(1)	Ghana	1966–91	Nation	1
(4)	Philippines	1961–84	Nation	1
(7)	Ethiopia	1975–82	Nation	1
(8)	Kenya	1972–92	Nation	1
(8)	Zimbabwe		Nation	1
(9)	Less developed countries	1960–2000	International	1%
(9)	Latin America		Country cross-section	1%
(18)	India	1971, 1981	85 districts	
(18)	India average	1971, 1981	Region	1
(18)	Punjab	1971, 1981	Region	1
(18)	Bihar	1971, 1981	Region	1
(27)	Thailand	1971–88	Nation	1

Additional income generated[a]				Total income multiplier[b]	Comments
By sector		By location			
Nonfarm	Other agriculture	Rural	Urban		
1.15	—	—	—	2.15[c]	Two-stage least squares results; with ordinary least squares, multiplier falls to 1.73
1.32	—	—	—	2.32[c]	
0.45	0.09[d]	—	—	1.54	Investment linkages positive but not statistically significant
					Reverse linkages, nonfarm to agriculture, are smaller (0.42 for services, 0.04 for manufacturing)
0.93	0.34[d]	—	—	2.27	Investment linkages positive and statistically significant
					Reverse linkages from nonfarm to agriculture are smaller, one-third the size
0.63	0.30[d]	—	—	1.93	
0.15%	—	—	—	—	Pooled time-series, cross-section data
0.12%	—	—	—	—	Pooled time-series, cross-section data
0.37	—	0.21	0.16	1.37	"Urban" includes rural towns only
0.58	—	0.34	0.24	1.58	Higher multiplier due to higher infrastructure, population density, and agricultural income
0.22	—	0.12	0.11	1.22	Reverse linkages from nonfarm to agriculture not statistically significant
0.61	—	—	—	1.61[c]	

(*continued*)

TABLE 7A.1 *Continued*

(Source) and method	Study Country	Year	Unit of analysis	Initial increase in agricultural income[a]
II. Modeling estimates				
A. Fixed-price models				
1. IO and SAM multipliers (unconstrained supply response assumed in all sectors)				
(3)	Mexico	1986	Nation	1 GO
(21)	Zaire	1987	Nation	1
(23)	Kenya	1987	1 village	1
(32)	27 countries	Various years		
(32)	Low-income countries		Nation	1 GO
(32)	Low-income countries		Nation	1
(32)	Mid-income countries		Nation	1 GO
(32)	Mid-income countries		Nation	1
(30)	Mexico	1994	Rural region	1
(31)	Indonesia	1980	Nation	1
(31)	Gambia	1990	Nation	1
2. SIO and mixed SAM models (constrained supply response in some sectors)				
(5)	Muda	1967–74	Rural region	1
(12)	Burkina	1985	Rural region	1
(12)			Nation	1
			Sahel region	1
(12)	Niger	1990	Rural region	1
(12)			Nation	1
			Sahel region	1
(12)	Senegal	1990	Groundnut basin	1
(12)			Nation	1
			Sahel region	1
(13)	Madagascar	1984	Nation	1

| Additional income generated[a] | | | | | |
| By sector | | By location | | Total income multiplier[b] | Comments |
Nonfarm	Other agriculture	Rural	Urban		
—	—	1.30	1.74	—[c]	GO multipliers
—	—			3.13[c]	Traditional agriculture
—	—	—	—	1.86	Foodcrops 1.86; coffee multiplier 1.83
2.75 GO	—	—	—	—	GO mulipliers
1.72	—	—	—	2.72[c]	Computed from GO assuming $va/x = 0.8$ in agriculture and 0.5 in nonagriculture
3.5 GO	—	—	—	—	GO mulipliers
1.50	—	—		2.50[c]	Computed from GO assuming $va/x = 0.7$ in agriculture and 0.3 in nonagriculture
—	—	0.94	0.03	1.94[c]	
—	—	1.33	0.98	3.31[c]	Foodcrops
—	—	0.79	0.45	2.24[c]	Rice
0.79	0.04	—	—	1.83	Agricultural tradables
—	—	—	—	1.31	Sorghum and millet tradable
0.61	1.27	—	—	2.88	Sorghum and millet nontradable
—	—	—	—	4.33	Sorghum and millet nontradable
0.56	0.21	—	—	1.77	Sorghum and millet tradable
0.67	0.29	—	—	1.96	Sorghum and millet tradable
1.44	0.90	—	—	3.34	Sorghum and millet nontradable
0.26	0.77	—	—	2.03	Sorghum and millet tradable
0.43	1.05	—	—	2.48	Sorghum and millet nontradable
0.65	1.46	—	—	2.73	Sorghum and millet nontradable
1.12	1.54	1.80	0.86	3.66	Irrigated rice (organic fertilizer modeled as nontradable input)

(continued)

	Study			Initial increase in agricultural income[a]
(Source) and method	Country	Year	Unit of analysis	
(13)	Madagascar	1984	Nation	1
(13)	Madagascar	1984	Nation	1
(14)	Cameroon	1985	Nation	1
(14)	Gambia	1990	Nation	1
(14)	Lesotho	1987	Nation	1
(14)	Madagascar	1984	Nation	1
(14)	Niger	1987	Nation	1
(14)	Nigeria	1987	Nation	1
(14)	Tanzania	1976	Nation	1
(14)	Zaire	1987	Nation	1
(15)	Pakistan	2001	Nation	1
(15)	Pakistan	2001	Nation	1
(15)	Pakistan	2001	Nation	1
(16)	Sierra Leone	1975	Rural region	1
(17)	Asia	1989	Rural region	1
(17)	Africa	1989	Rural region	1
(17)	Latin America	1989	Rural region	1
(19)	Zambia		Rural region	1
(20)	North Arcott, India		Rural region	1
(21)	Zaire	1987	Nation	1
(22)	India	1974	Nation	1
(23)	Kenya	1987	1 village	1

| Additional income generated[a] | | | | Total income multiplier[b] | Comments |
| By sector | | By location | | | |
Nonfarm	Other agriculture	Rural	Urban		
—	—	—	—	2.41	Irrigated rice (organic fertilizer modeled as tradable input)
1.66	0.46	0.66	1.46	3.12	Coffee; large export taxes account for one-third of multiplier
—	—	—	—	3.02	Export crop growth; large taxation increases government income
—	—	—	—	1.43	Rice
—	—	—	—	1.14	Foodgrains
—	—	—	—	2.61	Irrigated rice (organic fertilizer modeled as nontradable input)
—	—	—	—	1.55	Foodgrains
—	—	—	—	2.15	Foodgrains
—	—	—	—	1.53	Foodgrains
—	—	—	—	2.30	Modern plantation agriculture
—	—	—	—	2.51	Irrigated wheat
—	—	—	—	2.30	Irrigated paddy
—	—	—	—	2.71	Growth in livestock
—	—	—	—	1.35	Unconstrained IO multiplier is 4.01
0.58	0.06	—	—	1.64	
0.18	0.10	—	—	1.28	Ox cultivation technology raises multiplier to 1.47
0.21	0.05	—	—	1.26	
0.11	0.30	—	—	1.41	
0.87	—	—	—	1.87	
—	—	—	—	1.74[c]	Constraining agricultural activities reduces indirect effects by 65%
1.15	0.00	—	—	2.15	
—	—	—	—	1.43[c]	Foodcrops and coffee give same result
					Constraining agricultural activities reduce indirect effects by 50%

(*continued*)

(Source) and method	Study Country	Year	Unit of analysis	Initial increase in agricultural income[a]
(24)[e]	India	1990	2 villages	1
(26)	Mauritania	1985	Region	1
(28)	Malawi	1990	Nation	1
(29)	India	1985	1 village	1
B. Endogenous (variable) prices				
(2) CGE	South Korea	1963–78	Nation	1
(6) CGE	Kenya		Nation	1
(10) Simulation	Nigeria		Nation	1
(11) CGE	Africa	Circa 1990	Nation	10% agricultural TFP
(11) CGE	Asia	Circa 1990	Nation	10% land productivity
(11) CGE	Latin America	Circa 1990	Nation	10% land productivity
(14) CGE	Gambia	1990	Nation	1
(14) CGE	Madagascar	1984	Nation	1
(14) CGE	Niger	1987	Nation	1
(14) CGE	Nigeria	1987	Nation	1
(16) Simulation	Sierra Leone	1975	Rural region	1
(16) Simulation	Muda River, Malaysia	1972	Rural region	1
(25) Simulation	India	1960s	Nation	1

| Additional income generated[a] | | | | Total income multiplier[b] | Comments |
| By sector | | By location | | | |
Nonfarm	Other agriculture	Rural	Urban		
—	—	—	—	3.87[c]	Irrigated crop agriculture; mixed multiplier assuming 10% supply response in agriculture
0.41	0.00	—	—	1.41[c]	
—	—	—	—	1.66	
—	—	—	—	1.18[c]	Negative shock in agriculture triggers fall in rural nonfarm income
—	—	—	—	1.64[c]	Agricultural demand-led industrialization fastest and most equitable
—	—	—	—	1.20	
—	—	—	—	2.23[c]	Balanced food and export promotion strategy
—	—	—	—	1.43	Converted to value-added multiplier using SAM shares
—	—	—	—	1.92	Converted to value-added multiplier using SAM shares
—	—	—	—	2.35	Converted to value-added multiplier using SAM shares
—	—	—	—	1.62	CGE increases indirect effects by 44% compared with SIO
—	—	—	—	1.57	CGE decreases indirect effects by 65% compared with SIO
—	—	—	—	1.80	CGE increases indirect effects by 45% compared with SIO
—	—	—	—	1.73	CGE decreases indirect effects by 36% compared with SIO
—	—	—	—	1.26	Upward-sloping supply of nontradables reduces multiplier 25% below SIO
—	—	—	—	1.66	Upward-sloping supply of nontradables reduces multiplier by 10% compared with SIO
—	—	—	—	1.70	

(*continued*)

TABLE 7A.1 *Continued*

SOURCES:

1 Abdulai (1994)
2 Adelman (1984)
3 Adelman and Taylor (1990)
4 Bautista (1990)
5 Bell, Hazell, and Slade (1982)
6 Bigsten and Collier (1995)
7 Block (1999)
8 Block and Timmer (1997)
9 Bravo-Ortega and Lederman (2005)
10 Byerlee (1973)
11 De Janvry and Sadoulet (2002)
12 Delgado et al. (1994)
13 Dorosh and Haggblade (1993)
14 Dorosh and Haggblade (2003)
15 Dorosh, Niazi, and Nazli (2003)
16 Haggblade, Hammer, and Hazell (1991)

17 Haggblade and Hazell (1989)
18 Hazell and Haggblade (1991)
19 Hazell and Hojati (1994)
20 Hazell, Ramasamy, and Rajagopalan (1991)
21 Koné and Thorbecke (1992)
22 Krishna (1975)
23 Lewis and Thorbecke (1992)
24 Parikh and Thorbecke (1996)
25 Rangarajan (1982)
26 Rogers (1986)
27 Siamwalla (1995)
28 Simler (1994a)
29 Subramanian and Sadoulet (1990)
30 Yúnez-Naude, Taylor, and Dyer (1998)
31 Thorbecke (1994)
32 Vogel (1994)

NOTES: A dash indicates that data are not available. A blank cell indicates that data are not applicable. CGE, computable general equilibrium model; GO, gross output; IO, input-output model; SAM, social accounting matrix; SIO, semi-input-output model; TFP, total factor productivity; *va,* value added.

[a]The standard measure is 1 unit of local currency. In some instances, however, authors list results as percentage changes rather than in absolute values.

[b]Initial shock in agricultural income plus indirect gains in nonfarm and additional agricultural income.

[c]Converted from gross output or percentages to value-added multipliers.

[d]Includes dynamic feedbacks from savings in one period to investment and output in the next.

[e]Allows for user-specified capacity constraints in the elastically supplied sectors.

8 Cities, Towns, and the Rural Nonfarm Economy

MITCH RENKOW

This chapter provides a conceptual framework for understanding the spatial distribution of nonfarm economic activity in rural areas of developing countries. Such a framework is essential for understanding the potential scope as well as the limitations of nonagricultural production in rural economic development. It is particularly useful in assessing what kinds of productive activities are more likely to be carried out in concentrated settlements vis-à-vis less densely populated areas within the rural space.[1] It also serves to inform analysis of linkages between urban and rural populations and the spatial distribution of different-sized urban centers. While other chapters in Part II of this volume deal specifically with the functional nature of these linkages, the discussion in this chapter focuses on spatial issues and how these interactions influence the location of nonfarm firms and nonfarm production across the rural space.

The main theme of the conceptual framework proposed here is that an observed spatial pattern of firm location and settlement size fundamentally depends on the tension between the benefits of spatial concentration and the costs of "economic distance." This theme echoes the analytical insights into the spatial organization of production that have emerged from a number of diverse fields that have recently been formalized in a body of work dubbed the "new economic geography." Thinking about the rural nonfarm economy in this way requires careful consideration of the interaction between factors that tend to disperse productive activities throughout rural areas with factors that tend to promote agglomeration economies typically associated with urban production of goods and services.

The chapter begins by providing an overview of key concepts and models that geographers, economists, and others have developed in analyses of the spatial organization of economic activity. It distinguishes between models that are

---

1. As in the rest of this book, the term *rural* is defined as outside of large metropolitan areas. Thus the rural space encompasses intermediate-sized cities (sometimes termed "secondary cities"), smaller towns (also termed "market towns" or "rural service centers"), and the rural countryside.

largely descriptive (in the sense of ignoring underlying microfoundations) and more recent work in which agglomeration economies related to market size are endogenously determined. The ensuing discussion reviews empirical evidence on the location of firms in urban and rural spaces of less developed countries (LDCs), paying special attention to the variety of forward and backward linkages that connect rural and urban firms and households and how well existing data on the size of rural nonfarm firms, the density of rural nonfarm employment, and the evolution of the rural nonfarm economy support theoretical predictions. The chapter concludes by considering the role of towns and small cities in regional development. In doing so, it assesses various planning approaches that have been employed to promote towns and small cities in LDCs in light of the conceptual framework developed here.

Spatial Models of Economic Activity

Research on the spatial distribution of production spans a wide variety of disciplines, including urban and regional economics, geography, urban planning, and regional science. While a comprehensive survey of this vast literature is well beyond the scope of this chapter, it is nonetheless useful to draw out a few of the more important conceptual threads that are interwoven in that body of research. In part, this is a way of compiling key concepts and defining terminology to be employed throughout the rest of the chapter. But, more important, understanding a bit about the evolution of thought concerning how and why nonfarm firms locate where they do will prove useful in thinking about the design, implementation, and efficacy of development policies targeting rural towns and small cities.

The von Thünen Model

The oldest, and perhaps best-known, spatial economic model was developed by J. H. von Thünen in the early 1800s. Von Thünen's model focuses on the endogenous formation of agricultural land rents in the area surrounding a fixed urban location. The model considers the case of a town located in the center of a uniformly populated, homogeneous agricultural region. The town is assumed to be spaceless and hence can be treated as a single point. Three assumptions characterizing the local agricultural economy guarantee that perfect competition prevails: that profit-maximizing landlords have complete information about prices, transport costs, and production methods; that landowners employ constant returns to scale (CRS) agricultural technology; and that all prices and transport costs are fixed (Richardson 1978, 16). The spatial land market equilibrium derived by von Thünen features a land rent gradient that declines monotonically with distance from the town. Given this rent gradient, it follows that production will be organized spatially so that crops are produced within concentric rings: crops with the highest value per unit of land (net of transport costs) will be grown closest to the town, with ever-lower-valued crops produced farther from the town.[2]

The von Thünen model has had a profound influence on the way economists think about the spatial location of productive activities, which extends well beyond agriculture. Beginning with the work of Alonso (1964) and Mills (1967), modern urban economists have relied on the von Thünen model as a basis for analyzing firm location in cities. These authors adapted von Thünen's model to a monocentric urban setting, substituting a central business district for von Thünen's town within an agricultural plain and firms for farms. Monocentric urban models have been used in a variety of contexts to explain the location of firms producing different types of goods, as well as the location of households. It is important to note that this class of urban location models maintains the same assumptions regarding CRS technology and perfect competition and derives similar results regarding the location of production based on the balance between distance from the center and value of output.

While the von Thünen model and its urban analog elegantly explain how and why productive activities would be arranged around a given urban "center of gravity," they in no way explain the location of that center of gravity—or the forces giving rise to it. Or, as Krugman (1995, 53) puts it, these models "simply assume the thing you want to understand: the existence of a central urban market. Indeed, the whole thrust of the model is to understand the forces that spread economic activity *away* from that center, the 'centrifugal' forces if you will. About the 'centripetal' forces that *create* centers, that pull economic activity together, it can and does say nothing." We turn now to models that deal directly with forces concentrating economic activity.

Scale Economies and Central Place Hierarchies

Central place theory has been quite influential in the thinking of geographers, regional scientists, and urban planners. Developed by German economists August Lösch and Walter Christaller in the early part of the twentieth century, central place models remained virtually unknown in the Anglocentric world of neoclassical economics until the 1950s.

Central place theory analyzes the location of urban centers where manufacturing and marketing activities typically concentrate. Like the von Thünen model, central place models assume the existence of cities surrounded by a featureless, uniformly populated agricultural plain. However, central place theory abandons the von Thünen assumption of constant returns to scale; instead, it explicitly recognizes the existence of firm-level scale economies in the production of nonagricultural goods (typically due to indivisibilities in production

---

2. Thiele (1984) provides an empirical validation of the von Thünen model for the case of grain and charcoal production in central Tanzania.

technologies). These scale economies combined with transportation costs lead producers to cluster together in urbanized central places out of which are satisfied the product demands of consumers dwelling within both the urbanized area itself and the surrounding agricultural hinterland. Absent scale economies, production would be equally efficient at any scale, so the existence of transport costs would lead to a uniform spatial distribution of (small-scale) producers. Likewise, scale economies absent transport costs would concentrate all production at one point (Mills 1972).

Interindustry differences in the magnitudes of scale economies and transport costs give rise to hierarchies of central places possessing market areas that are nested within one another. The resulting spatial organization of economic activity is summarized by Johnson (1970, 18–19):

> Small local assembly and distribution activities will be found in villages and hamlets, and these markets will cater to the needs of people living in a relatively small encircling area. The perimeters of such local market areas will depend on the nature of the topography and on the road, rail, and water transport facilities. But these small markets, which for convenience may be called village markets, are interrelated with larger markets located in towns and cities. Surplus products from the village markets move to the town markets, while goods too specialized for villages to produce move from the towns to the villages. As an economy becomes more urbanized, still larger markets will develop in certain cities, particularly in urban centers strategically located for trade (at ports, river junctions, and railway centers) or for specialized production (near deposits of natural resources, near water power, or favored by other important locational factors). To these city markets both town markets and village markets will be delicately attuned, so that the entire hierarchy of exchange facilities will operate as an economic organism influencing the growth and development of an entire region. Moreover, some parts of the market system, usually (but certainly not always) the city components, will be inter-related to varying degrees with foreign markets.

This conceptualization of linkages among urban centers and between urban and rural areas has dominated much of the thinking of planners and geographers analyzing the spatial organization of production in LDCs. Moreover, the core element of central place theory—agglomeration resulting from firm-level scale economies—features prominently in economists' attempts to model the equilibrium size distribution of cities (Henderson 1974), as well as the spatial models of the new economic geography (discussed later). However, central place theory is vulnerable to criticism on the grounds that it is not grounded in market fundamentals. For example, Eaton and Lipsey (1976, 53) note that "many of the classic propositions of [central place theory] are suitable for analyzing optimal rules for collective decisions of a central-planning type, but are quite unsuitable for analyzing the outcome of decentralized decision making . . .

that acts through the market mechanism." Perhaps for this reason, central place theory generally has been a more popular analytical tool among geographers and planners than among economists.

Agglomeration Economies, Growth Poles, and Market Potential Functions

Ubiquitous in much of modern urban and regional economics is the notion that increasing returns to scale exogenous to firms give rise to agglomeration economies that explain the concentration of economic activity in cities. Positive external economies have been attributed to a variety of sources, including complementarities in labor supply and production across firms both within and across industries; smoothing of seasonal fluctuations in demand and input supply; and technological spillovers that reinforce the creation and diffusion of innovations among entrepreneurs (Mills 1972).[3] Like central place hierarchies, agglomeration economies are typically maintained hypotheses in spatial economic models—that is, they are assumed rather than derived.

Two related analytical traditions in spatial economics follow directly from consideration of agglomeration economies. The first is the concept of urban centers as growth poles, or nodes of productive activity that essentially generate their own economic gravitational fields. The traditional view is that urban growth poles cause a spread of benefits of agglomeration economies from more productive (i.e., efficient) urban economies to rural areas. However, history is littered with examples in which these spread effects failed to occur—or occurred more slowly than was desired—after the implementation of policies designed to stimulate regional development in cities designated as growth poles (Unwin 1989). Rather, backwash effects have dominated. By attracting capital, labor, and entrepreneurial talent from the surrounding areas, these backwash effects drain rural areas of their key resources and lead to rising rural-urban inequality. This has led some authors to draw a distinction between generative cities and parasitic cities, depending on the relative strength of spread and backwash effects of their growth (Hoselitz 1957).

The second important concept related to agglomeration economies is the market potential function. The market potential function indexes demand for goods produced in a location as the sum of purchasing power in all other locations, weighted by the distance (i.e., transport costs) to those markets. For example, a typical market potential function for location i is

$$P_i = \Sigma_j \, kY_j D_{ij}^{-b},$$

where Y_j is aggregate income in market j, D_{ij} is the distance between locations i and j, and k and b are parameters. The idea here is that firms tend to locate

---

3. On the other hand, congestion and pollution are oft-cited negative externalities that serve as centrifugal forces opposing agglomerative impulses.

nearest to the maximum number of potential customers. Since the potential customer base includes urban households and firms (in addition to those lying in the hinterland), the possibility for self-reinforcing urban or regional growth is a logical follow-on to this conceptualization of firm location decisions.[4]

The market potential function has proven to be a useful empirical tool for regional economists, geographers, and planners. Market potential indexes have been used to "explain" industrial location across a broad range of economies and countries (e.g., Harris 1954; Keeble, Owens, and Thompson 1982). Until recently, however, there has been little in the way of formal modeling of this approach, because the pecuniary external economies implicit in this line of reasoning could not be accommodated by standard optimization models based on perfect competition.[5] Only with the emergence of models of imperfect competition could these sources of agglomeration economies be reconciled within the context of formal economic modeling. It is to these models that we now turn.

The New Economic Geography

Without a doubt, the largest positive shock to the spatial economics literature in the past several decades is represented by a series of innovative papers by Paul Krugman.[6] Krugman has introduced a spatial component to the intellectual technology underlying the "new trade theory"—the celebrated monopolistic competition model of Dixit and Stiglitz (1977)—to produce what has been dubbed the "new economic geography."

In Krugman's models, as in central place theory, the degree to which economic activity is concentrated within an urban space follows from the interaction between transport costs, firm-level economies of scale in the production of manufactured goods, and factor mobility. Both costly transportation and firm-level economies of scale tend to concentrate production in a limited number of (urban) locations offering greater access to consumers and input suppliers. On the other hand, the limited mobility of some factors (notably laborers cum consumers) provides a countervailing tendency for production to be dispersed.

What differentiates the new economic geography from its predecessors is its ability to formalize the intuitively appealing concepts central to earlier work in this area—central place theory, cumulative causation, and location theory—

---

4. Krugman (1995) points out the links between this line of thinking and some of the key concepts from influential early writings on development economics—Myrdal's (1957) notion of "cumulative causation" and the Big Push theory of Rosenstein-Rodan (1943).

5. "Pecuniary external economies" refers to the situation in which factor prices (such as the wage rate) fall as industry output increases due to the structure of demand for industry output (Layard and Walters 1978). Pecuniary economies are foreclosed by models that assume perfect competition, because the rents associated with those economies would be dissipated through entry of new firms (Scitovsky 1954).

6. While Krugman's work (1991, 1993a,b, 1995, 1996) has been the most influential, Masahisa Fujita has also been an important contributor to this literature. See Fujita (1988, 1993), Fujita and Krugman (1995), and Fujita and Mori (1998).

into a unified framework. Its linchpin is the use of the Dixit-Stiglitz model, which accommodates (albeit in a stylized way) the existence of pecuniary economies.[7] By explicitly addressing the interaction between market size and firm-level economies, agglomeration economies emerge as the endogenous outcome of the interaction of a small number of economically meaningful parameters:

SCALE ECONOMIES.   In monopolistic competition models, the concentration of workers in specific locations underpins scale economies in production (e.g., by facilitating firms' finding adequate labor resources). This in turn affects wages and reinforces the tendency for workers to gravitate to central locations. The larger the scale economies for a particular commodity, the stronger will be the tendency for production of that commodity to be spatially concentrated.

THE SPATIAL EXTENT OF THE MARKET.   In these models, the budget share for (nonagricultural) manufactured goods signifies the extent of demand for those goods and hence the magnitude of external economies related to the size of the market. In other words, the budget share measures the strength of forward linkages circumscribed by consumption demands. The larger the size of the market within a given geographical area, the larger and more varied the amounts of different commodities that will be produced at a central (urban) location servicing those demands.

THE COST OF DISTANCE.   Transport costs define the centrifugal forces that disperse production through space. Ceteris paribus, the more costly the transport of a given commodity or set of commodities, the less concentrated will be the production of that commodity. More generally, production will be more dispersed the greater the transactions costs associated with distance.

The new economic geography produces a more rigorous conceptual basis for many of the stylized concepts that permeate traditional analyses in economic geography. To be sure, these models are quite simple, abstracting mightily from many important real-world features of production and consumption relationships (Hanson 1998). Nonetheless, the insights from this body of work on the linkages between urban and rural populations are useful for assessing the kinds of productive activities most likely to be carried out in concentrated settlements vis-à-vis less densely populated areas within the rural space. These issues are taken up later.

The Location of Nonfarm Production in Rural Space

A unifying aspect of the different approaches reviewed earlier is that they all attempt to explain the linkages between differently sized concentrations of

---

7. The Dixit-Stiglitz model features monopolistically competitive nonagricultural firms producing an array of goods that are close (but not perfect) substitutes in consumption. Scale economies and transport costs provide the incentive for firms to locate near a large consumer market, and sectoral expansion involves a combination of increases in the number of firms (i.e., more product variety) and increases in firm size (Dixit 1993).

consumers and producers. Other chapters in this volume deal specifically with the nature of these linkages. The discussion in this chapter will be confined to exploring how these linkages condition the location of nonfarm firms and nonfarm production in the rural space.

Markets and Rural-Urban Linkages

It is useful to begin by noting the primary spatial markets influencing the location of production in the rural space. In effect, these markets circumscribe the "playing field" on which rural-urban linkages are established.

LABOR MARKETS.   Labor is a mobile factor of production; consequently, labor markets are a prime interface between rural and urban populations. Nonfarm employment represents an important income diversification mechanism for agricultural households in most LDCs (see Chapter 6). Even in highly productive agricultural areas, it is not uncommon for one or more members of a farm household to hold a "town job," especially in Latin America and Asia (Reardon et al. 1998). Both commuting and migration—usually, but not always, from less urban to more urban locations—are means by which spatial labor markets clear.[8] In general, the greater the spatial integration of labor markets, the greater the convergence of wages across locations (Dickie and Gerking 1987). For this reason, rural areas well integrated with urban centers attract a higher density of high-wage rural nonfarm activity (Table 8.1).

CAPITAL MARKETS.   Capital flows in two directions. Profits from agriculture have long been regarded as a prime source of capital for industrial investment (Johnston and Mellor 1961). Evidence from Kenya and Sierra Leone suggests that agricultural surpluses account for between 15 and 40 percent of nonfarm investment (Haggblade, Hazell, and Brown 1989). Typically these investments flow into towns and cities. However, capital flows also move in the opposite direction, from urban to rural locations. Detailed microeconomic evidence from Kenya concludes that farmers' investments in agricultural assets (especially land) hinge critically on nonfarm earnings (Evans and Ngau 1991). Capital flows into rural nonfarm enterprises take a variety of forms, including loans from urban-based financial institutions, external investment in "transplant" industries (discussed later), or migration remittances.

PRODUCT MARKETS.   The prototypical exchange relationship between rural and urban areas involves rural producers trading agricultural products for consumption goods produced in urban areas. Data presented in Chapter 7 indicate that rural-urban consumption linkages are more prominent in Asia than in Africa, partly because food budget shares tend to be higher in rural areas of Africa than in rural Asia and partly because rural-urban transportation networks

---

8. In this context, housing markets are partners with labor markets in facilitating rural-urban linkages.

TABLE 8.1 Predicted probability of participation in rural nonfarm activities in Bangladesh, 2000

Distance from an urban center	Nonfarm wage employment		Nonfarm self-employment
	Low-return	High-return	
Isolated rural region	8	17	16
Integrated rural region	6	27	23

SOURCE: World Bank (2004).

tend to be better developed in Asia. Also, rural-urban trade linkages tend to be weaker in less productive agricultural regions (Rondinelli 1988). However, strong trade linkages may still exist if significant nonagricultural production occurs in these rural areas.

INPUT MARKETS. Agricultural producers generally purchase inputs such as fertilizers from suppliers located in towns and small urban centers. Rural nonfarm industries often procure inputs from urban suppliers as well. On the other hand, rural nonfarm enterprises frequently produce intermediate inputs used in urban-based production processes, most notably agroprocessing and distribution enterprises (Chuta and Liedholm 1982; Freeman and Norcliffe 1985; Milimo and Fisseha 1986).

If labor, capital, and product and input markets circumscribe the playing field on which rural-urban linkages are established, the "rules of the game" driving firm location are the essential economic forces identified in our review of spatial models—economies of scale in production, the structure of demand (and pecuniary external economies associated with it), and the cost of distance. Understanding the location of specific firms in the rural space, then, is a matter of associating the nature of those firms' productive activities with the characteristics of the markets in which they participate.

This conceptualization of the interaction of markets, linkages, and firm location nicely accommodates important empirical regularities that surface in case studies of the rural nonfarm economy in LDCs. These revolve around the size of nonfarm firms, the density of nonfarm employment, and the evolution of the rural nonfarm economy with respect to the economic distance from urban centers of gravity. Note that the term *economic distance* is meant to convey something broader than just physical distance (although physical distance is clearly one important component). Rather, it encompasses the range of transactions costs mediated through the markets noted earlier. We now turn to consideration of how both the types of rural nonfarm firms and the size of those firms will depend on their access (or lack thereof) to urban labor, capital, product, and input markets.

TABLE 8.2 Location of sales and sources of physical inputs for rural nonfarm firms in Kenya, 1977

Source area	Percentage of sales	Percentage of inputs
Same sublocation	76.3	29.8
Within five miles	13.8	8.1
More than five miles	8.2	34.1
Nairobi	1.7	28.0

SOURCE: Freeman and Norcliffe (1985).

Location and Size of Nonfarm Firms

The cost of distance tends to limit the size of the potential customer base in more remote areas. Typically, this results in rural nonfarm enterprises' serving a very localized clientele. In Kenya, for example, fewer than 10 percent of the sales of rural nonfarm firms are made more than five miles from where the goods are produced (Table 8.2). Thus one would expect firm sizes to be smaller the further into the rural hinterland one looks—a supposition that is generally borne out by empirical research. Available empirical research suggests that more than 95 percent of rural nonfarm enterprises employ five people or fewer (Haggblade, Hazell, and Brown 1989; Liedholm and Mead 1999).

Larger-scale, relatively capital-intensive firms in developing countries tend to locate in more highly populated areas where greater opportunities exist to exploit pecuniary external economies. In contrast, rural firms tend to be less capital intensive the greater the distance from sources of financial and physical capital (Rondinelli 1988). Evidence from the Ivory Coast indicates that employment in relatively labor-intensive manufacturing industries such as basketmaking, weaving, and potterymaking increases with distance from an urban center, whereas employment densities in construction industries rise with proximity to towns (Ancey 1974). Typically, this shifting composition of rural nonfarm activity involves a growing prevalence of high-return nonfarm activities as proximity to urban centers increases, as recent data from Bangladesh illustrate (Table 8.1).

There are some exceptions to the general tendency for firm size to be inversely related to distance from an urban center. Large-scale firms may choose to operate in relatively remote areas where key raw materials are located when the costs of transport of those raw materials are high relative to the transport costs of processed materials. In such cases, the costs of distance will dominate the benefits of proximity to the sources of final demand. Milling lumber and processing sugar are examples of activities that greatly reduce transport costs as a proportion of product value. Not surprisingly, it is these sorts of weight-reducing activities that are most commonly engaged in by large-scale rural nonfarm firms.

Transplant industries that locate in a rural area to take advantage of lower wages represent another important exception to the tendency for nonfarm firms to be smaller in more remote locations (Hayami 1998a; Otsuka 1998; Lin and Yao 1999). Transplant firms tend to import many of the financial and physical inputs used in production from outside the region in which production occurs (Jacobs 1984). Therefore, transplant industries may be expected to flourish in rural areas in which labor is relatively less mobile than goods. That is, the viability of transplant firms depends on rural-urban labor market linkages being weaker than linkages in other markets.

Nonfarm Employment and Income Shares

Nonfarm employment shares vary spatially across the spectrum from rural to increasingly large urban localities. Cross-sectional evidence from population censuses suggests that nonfarm employment shares in rural towns are roughly triple those in rural areas (Table 8.3). Evidence from India suggests even greater disparities, with nonfarm employment shares rising from 15 percent in rural areas to 76 percent in rural towns and 95 percent in large urban areas (Hazell and Haggblade 1991).

When these employment data are broken down by type of nonfarm activity, it becomes apparent that certain nonagricultural sectors appear to be "town based" to a much greater degree than other sectors. Specifically, service and commercial employment shares in towns tend to be much greater than in the countryside, whereas manufacturing employment shares in towns normally do not rise as rapidly (Table 1.6). In some instances, particularly in Asia, small and medium-sized rural manufacturing enterprises may cluster together in remote rural locations. However, what empirical evidence there is on manufacturing clusters indicates that these are far more likely to occur in rural towns than in the rural hinterland (Humphrey and Schmitz 1996).

Given our earlier discussion of the expected inverse relationship between rural nonfarm activity and economic distance, we would expect the proportion of nonfarm employment in rural areas to be lowest farthest from urban centers. A recent study from Nepal provides empirical support for this proposition. Measuring distance in time required to reach the nearest town center, it finds

TABLE 8.3 Share of rural labor primarily employed in nonfarm activity, 1960s–1980s (percent)

	Rural	Rural towns	Rural plus rural towns
Africa	14	59	19
Asia	26	81	36
Latin America	28	85	47

SOURCE: Haggblade and Hazell (1989), using census data from 14 African, 14 Asian, and 15 Latin American countries.

rural nonfarm employment shares roughly 10 percent higher in rural areas within a one-hour commute of the nearest urban center than in more isolated rural settlements (Fafchamps and Shilpi 2003).

Spatial Dynamics

Time-series data on spatial dynamics, though sparse, are available for various types of enterprises in differently sized localities in Sierra Leone (Table 8.4). These data indicate that employment in repair services and food processing industries exhibited significant growth in small and medium-sized settlements, while employment in manufacturing industries generally declined in the smallest settlements. A plausible interpretation of these findings is that as economies become more integrated, rural manufacturing firms in particular face greater competition from imports (originating both in large urban centers and nearby rural towns) than do rural firms in the service sector. For this reason, rural manufacturing employment typically grows more slowly than does employment in services and commerce. Indeed, in many situations rural manufacturing employment falls over time (see Table 4.4).

Again, the empirical evidence meshes well with the conceptualization of the interaction of markets and firm location that has been sketched out here. The existence of a continuum of settlement sizes characterized by varying densities of nonfarm activity is essentially a reflection of gradients of firm-specific spatial comparative advantage. Note, however, that these gradients are multidimensional: firms participate in multiple markets, and differing demand structures and production relationships in these markets may well give rise to differing spatial equilibria—that is, to a differing balance of centrifugal and centripetal forces—across industries.

This is largely a restatement of the stylization of higher- and lower-order central places from central place theory. However, the underlying micro-

TABLE 8.4 Growth in nonfarm employment in Sierra Leone by locality size, 1974–80 (compound annual growth rate, percent)

	Locality population size		
Activity	2,000–20,000	20,000–250,000	250,000+
Repairs	15.0	5.2	15.0
Food processing	14.0	33.0	21.0
Woodworking	0.5	8.8	7.6
Clothing manufacture	−0.7	1.8	5.0
Metalworking	−5.8	9.4	10.0
Total small manufacture and repair	−2.4	6.0	5.7

SOURCE: Chuta and Liedholm (1982).

NOTE: Includes only establishments employing fewer than 50 workers.

economic story that has been elaborated here allows us to predict the impact of infrastructure investment and other actions designed to reduce the cost of economic distance. Such interventions will attenuate the centrifugal forces that tend to disperse production. As a result, they ought to provide an impulse toward greater concentration of production in urban agglomerations of varying sizes, and correspondingly less—and less diverse—nonfarm production in the rural hinterland. Indeed, while it is not usually stated in this way, much of the emphasis on regional development planning over the past couple of decades has been oriented toward precisely that end. This topic is taken up next.

The Role of Towns and Small Cities in Regional Development

Much has been written in the planning and geography literature about the desirability of promoting the growth and diversification of small cities and towns in LDCs (Rondinelli 1983; Hardoy and Satterthwaite 1986; Blitzer et al. 1988; Tacoli and Satterthwaite 2003). The traditional rationale is that broad-based economic development is facilitated by the emergence of an integrated settlement system of differently sized towns and cities serving both their own residents and the residents of surrounding rural areas (Rondinelli 1983).[9] This amounts to an application of the basic principles of central place theory to development planning.

The term *urban functions* is widely used to describe the range of services and production relationships that are confined to urban pockets within the rural space. The urban functions possessed by urban centers within the rural space fall into three categories.

MARKETING FUNCTIONS.   Small cities and towns serve as collection, processing, assembly, and distribution points for various commodities. Goods produced in the surrounding rural hinterland (both agricultural and nonagricultural) typically are transported into nearby urban centers for sale. Likewise, rural producers typically purchase their inputs in urban centers (or from urban-based merchants). In Kenya, for example, roughly two-thirds of the inputs used by rural nonfarm enterprises (in terms of value) are procured from town- or city-based sources (Table 8.2).[10]

PRODUCTION FUNCTIONS.   Small cities and towns concentrate productive activities in many types of industries—agricultural processing, manufacturing,

---

9. Much of the underlying motivation for policies promoting towns and small cities stems from the belief that lack of balance in city-size distribution—that is, the concentration of a huge fraction of a country's urban population in one or two "primate cities"—is an important cause of underdevelopment in LDCs (Chen and Parish 1996).

10. In addition, when the data are disaggregated by type of nonfarm firm, it is clear that local sources generally provide raw materials for resource-based enterprises (e.g., agroprocessing), while nonlocal suppliers are far more important as sources of manufactured inputs such as retail goods and machinery (Freeman and Norcliffe 1985).

service, and commercial. Firms located in small and medium-sized towns are typically an important source of certain consumption goods, particularly durables. This is illustrated for the case of Kenya in Table 8.2, which shows that own production and "market centers"—rural locations where vendors congregate on special market days—are the main sources of everyday consumption items (e.g., food), while towns are the most important source for larger-ticket items (e.g., home furnishings). Other town-based firms produce inputs used by rural dwellers in their productive activities—especially, but not exclusively, agricultural production. Finally, urban firms often serve as an important source of employment for rural dwellers.

SERVICE FUNCTIONS.   Small cities and towns offer a range of services and facilities unavailable in the rural hinterland. These include health services (hospitals, clinics), postal services, governmental administrative services, and some types of vocational and higher education, as well as schools (particularly secondary schools), banks, and communications facilities. Two contrasting approaches feature prominently in the geography literature on development planning (see Belsky and Karaska 1990; Hansen 1992; Rietveld 1993; Rondinelli 1993; and Rushton 1993). The location-allocation approach applies operations research methods to the problem of locating "essential" facilities and services to serve a given geographical region (Tewari 1992). This approach centers around programming models that minimize the cost of providing some service (or set of services) to different populations, taking as given an existing spatial distribution of demands for those services. Location-allocation methods have been widely employed in India, Latin America, and Africa (Rushton 1988).

The other important model of development planning is termed functional integration. This approach advocates the use of targeted investments in facilities and infrastructure to *create* a spatial settlement pattern that emulates the hierarchical ideal of central place theory (Rondinelli 1985). Originally developed for the U.S. Agency for International Development in the design of integrated rural development projects in the 1970s, functional integration methods arose in large part as a reaction to the shortcomings of import substitution schemes of the 1950s and 1960s. In particular, it was observed that the benefits from those investments often failed to extend outside of cities in which the import-substituting industries were located (or, even worse, drained surrounding areas of labor, capital, and entrepreneurial talent). Implementation of the functional integration methodology involves using an array of ad hoc spatial measures (e.g., location quotients, concentration ratios, centrality indexes) to inform the "appropriate" targeting of external investment.

Both the location-allocation and the functional integration approaches to development planning seek to determine the optimal provision of public goods in the form of government-funded (or subsidized) facilities or infrastructure. This is hardly surprising given the scale economies involved in—and the likely positive externalities created by—those kinds of investments. Of note, however,

TABLE 8.5 Marginal effect on input demand and output supply of a 1-kilometer decrease in the distance to key input sources and output markets in South India and Zambia

Country	Marginal impact on demand for			Marginal impact on output supply
	Seeds	Fertilizer	Credit	
India (rupees/km)	16.44	24.70*	0.01	124.53*
Zambia (kwacha/km)[a]	—	31.36*	3.21*	52.39*

SOURCES: Wanmali and He (1991), Wanmali (1992).

NOTE: * indicates significance at the 5 percent level.

[a]For Zambia, impacts are for all physical inputs combined, including both fertilizer and seeds.

is the fact that these planning approaches generally ignore the "production functions" of urban areas, except insofar as those production functions are complemented by "service" and "marketing" functions. In many circumstances this is an important oversight, given the critical impact of publicly provided infrastructure on the spatial distribution of nonfarm productive activities.

Consider, for example, the effects of improving a road connecting the countryside to a nearby town—effectively reducing economic distances in the rural hinterland. In the agricultural sector, empirical studies conducted by Wanmali and He (1991) in Zambia and by Wanmali (1992) in India clearly indicate positive marginal benefits to both input demand and output supply from a decrease in distance to input sources and output markets (Table 8.5). However, the degree to which improved transport infrastructure alters the spatial distribution of various types of rural nonfarm productive activities will to a great extent depend on whether that infrastructure better facilitates the flow of people or goods.

On the one hand, improved roads have the potential to facilitate the development and/or expansion of industries located in the countryside by lowering the cost of bringing in inputs and moving goods to final markets. This was certainly the outcome of the development of the canal transportation system in the northeastern United States in the early nineteenth century, for example (Sellers 1991, 43). On the other hand, road improvement facilitates the movement of rural workers and rural consumers to and from towns. Lower transport costs tend to reduce any rural-urban wage differentials, thereby reducing the competitiveness of rural firms vis-à-vis urban firms. Lower transport costs additionally lower the effective cost (inclusive of transport costs) of urban goods to rural consumers, thereby potentially reducing locational rents for certain types of rural firms. As a result, increased spatial integration often exposes rural manufacturers to greater competition from urban producers.

In the specific case of the rural nonfarm economy, then, infrastructure is a double-edged sword. On the one hand, adequate roads, communication facilities, and other public goods are necessary fixed inputs into production, and hence would be expected to facilitate the development and expansion of rural industries. On the other hand, connecting rural places to urban places via infrastructure expansion and improvement may well lead to inadvertent "crowding out" of more remote rural firms and industries by virtue of lowering the cost of distance and their competitiveness with urban firms.

Conclusions

The observed spatial pattern of firm location and settlement size fundamentally depends on the tension between the benefits of spatial concentration and the costs of "economic distance." The interplay of three variables—economies of scale in production, the structure of demand (and related pecuniary external economies), and transport costs—largely governs linkages between differently sized concentrations of consumers and producers, and thereby the location of nonfarm firms and nonfarm production, in the rural space.

Existing empirical evidence is generally consistent with theoretical predictions that distance from urban centers will tend to be negatively correlated with both the density of rural nonfarm economic activity and the size of rural nonfarm firms. However, there does not appear to be an overabundance of readily available data from rural areas of LDCs for testing these theories in a comprehensive way—for example, along the lines of recent work by Hanson (1998) on the geographical concentration of economic activity in the United States. Looking forward, this situation seems likely to change. Recent advances in geographical positioning systems have made spatial analysis of this sort increasingly feasible, even in remote rural areas of the developing world. For this reason, the trickle of recent spatial analyses of the rural nonfarm economy seems likely to accelerate rapidly in coming years.[11]

Operationally, planning approaches to regional development tend to either promote agglomeration economies (via the provision of public goods) or reduce the cost of economic distance (via investments in infrastructure). Both of these outcomes may be expected to strengthen centripetal forces concentrating production in more urbanized agglomerations of varying sizes. These investments, therefore, tend to pressure rural operators while at the same time enhancing the role of rural towns as centers of nonfarm activity.

---

11. See, for example, the discussions in Fafchamps and Shilpi (2003), World Bank (2004), and De Ferranti et al. (2005).

9 Global Food Industry Consolidation and Rural Agroindustrialization in Developing Economies

THOMAS REARDON

Globalization and its close companions, trade and investment liberalization, have touched off rapid changes in agrifood systems across the developing world, particularly since the early 1990s. These changes include increasing concentration, growing multinationalization, and rapidly changing agrifood system organization, institutions, and technologies. The unprecedented speed and depth of these developments (Table 9.1) have astonished not only longtime observers of the rural nonfarm economy, but also the rural firms that struggle to compete in these rapidly evolving supply systems.

This chapter explores the causes of these dramatic changes as well as their consequences for the rural nonfarm economy (RNFE).[1] While a growing number of empirical studies have examined the impact of these changes on farmers, no one has systematically assessed the impact of food industry consolidation on the RNFE. This chapter begins by summarizing available evidence on the profile and pace of current food industry consolidation. It then proceeds to review the resulting changes in procurement systems and how these are shaping opportunities for rural nonfarm retailers, traders, and food processors.

Concentration Downstream in the Agrifood System

Two fundamental changes in agrifood systems have emerged over the past decade and a half—the rapid diffusion of supermarkets and of large-scale food manufacturing / second-stage processing firms in the developing world. Of course these changes have occurred at widely different rates across countries, but they now affect nearly all developing countries. This diffusion implies a concentration in both of these "downstream" segments of the agrifood system—retailing and processing. These changes are important in themselves. They have also set up a cascade of changes upstream in the rest of the agrifood system and

---

1. This chapter draws heavily on several previous publications, in particular Reardon and Barrett (2000), Reardon et al. (2001), Reardon et al. (2003), and Reardon and Timmer (2007), along with other region- or country-specific pieces that are cited.

TABLE 9.1 Growth in supermarket retailing shares, 1990–2005

Country, years	Percent of total retailing	
	1990	2005
Argentina	20	60
China	0	15
Guatemala	10	40
Kenya	0	10
South America	10–20	50–60

SOURCE: Reardon and Timmer (2007).

thus in the rural economy's farm and nonfarm sectors, as if the "tail is wagging the dog." These changes will now be briefly recounted.

Retailing

THREE WAVES OF CONSOLIDATION.   In the first decade of the twenty-first century, supermarkets are retailing roughly 40 to 60 percent of all food marketed in "first-wave supermarketization countries" in much of South America, East Asia, Central Europe, Turkey, and South Africa (Table 9.2). Following 5 to 10 years behind are the "second-wave" countries in Central America, Mexico, Southeast Asia, and Southern Africa, where supermarkets have achieved penetration rates on the order of 20 to 40 percent. Elsewhere, in the "third-wave" countries of South Asia and Africa, the level of supermarket activity remains generally low, at less than 20 percent of food retailing. However, even in these third-wave areas, supermarkets are rapidly emerging in urban markets. While supermarkets account for only 5 percent of India's food retailing and 10 to 15 percent of Russia's and China's, the overall growth rates are spectacular in China. By 2003, supermarket sales there accounted for 30 percent of urban food retailing, up from nearly nothing a decade earlier, and sales were growing at 30 to 40 percent per year (see Dries, Reardon, and Swinnen 2004; Dries, Reardon, and Van Kerckhove 2004; Hu et al. 2004).

DIFFERENCES BY PRODUCT CATEGORY.   The takeover of food retailing in these regions has occurred much more rapidly in processed, dry, and packaged foods such as noodles, milk products, and grains, for which supermarkets have an advantage over small retail stores due to economies of scale. Because the processing and packaging of foods constitute an important share of rural nonfarm activity, the impact of supermarkets on the rural food processors is likely to be substantial, particularly where processing targets sales to nearby towns and cities. In contrast, the supermarkets' progress in gaining control of fresh

TABLE 9.2 Supermarket retailing shares across countries, circa 2005

Country	Supermarket share of food retailing (percent)		
	Total foods	Processed foods	Fresh fruits and vegetables
Developed countries	70–80	—	—
United States	80	—	—
France	70	—	50
Latin America	50–60	—	—
Brazil	75	—	50
Argentina	60	—	—
Chile	50	—	—
Mexico	55	—	25
Costa Rica	50	—	—
El Salvador	50	—	—
Colombia	45	—	—
Guatemala	35	—	—
Nicaragua	20	—	—
Asia	—	—	—
East Asia	—	63	30
Taiwan	60	—	—
South Korea	50	—	—
China	15	—	—
Southeast Asia	—	33	15
Malaysia	45	—	—
Thailand	50	—	—
Indonesia	30	—	10
South Asia	—	—	—
India	5	—	—
Africa	—	—	—
South Africa	55	—	—
Urban Kenya	21	—	4
Nigeria	5	—	—
Ghana	—	—	—

SOURCE: Reardon and Timmer (2007).

NOTE: A dash indicates that data are not available.

food markets has been slower, and there is greater variation across countries because of local habits and responses by wet markets and local shops. Usually the first fresh food categories in which supermarkets gain a majority share include less perishable "commodities" such as potatoes as well as sectors experiencing consolidation in first-stage processing and production: often dairy products, chicken, beef and pork, and fish. In Mexico, where supermarkets hold a 55 percent share of the overall food retail market, their share in the retailing of fresh fruits and vegetables is only 25 percent. Similarly in Indonesia, supermarkets' shares are 30 percent in total foods and 10 percent for fresh fruits and vegetables. This rough ratio of "2 or 3 to 1" appears to be typical in developing regions (Table 9.2). With fresh produce, the convenience and low prices of small shops and fairs, with their varied produce for daily shopping, continue to pose a competitive challenge to the supermarkets. As a result, traditional marketing systems remain competitive in perishable products longer than in nonperishables. Progress for supermarkets, usually steady but much slower in fresh produce, requires investments in procurement efficiency.

Despite the slower growth in the supermarkets' share of the domestic produce market, it is staggering to calculate the absolute market that supermarkets now represent, even in fresh produce, and thus how much more in other products where supermarkets have penetrated faster and deeper. Reardon and Berdegué (2002) calculate that supermarkets in Latin America buy 2.5 times more fruits and vegetables from local producers than Latin America exports to the rest of the world. That figure is 2.0 in China (Hu et al. 2004).

SPATIAL AND SOCIOECONOMIC PATTERNS OF EXPANSION.   Empirical evidence shows that there tends to be a generalized pattern of supermarket diffusion over space and socioeconomic strata within a given developing country, regardless of region. In large urban areas, supermarkets typically start out occupying only a small niche in capital cities, serving the rich and middle class. They then spread well beyond the middle class to penetrate deeply into the food markets of the poor. In some places, such as Brazil and South Africa, this process is well advanced. In other places, such as Kenya, the process of going beyond the initial retail market niche of the upper middle class and the middle class into the food markets of the lower middle class and the working poor is just beginning. Neven (2004) and Neven and Reardon (2004), based on 2003 survey data from urban Kenyan, show that 20 percent of urban food retailing is composed of supermarket sales, and this share is increasing at 18 percent a year. Their household consumption survey data show that for food in general, 80 percent of Nairobi's households shop for part of their food at supermarkets on a regular basis (at least once a month). That figure is 60 percent for the lowest income group. Whites and Asians account for only 15 percent of food sales in Kenyan supermarkets. Some 36 percent of supermarket food sales in Nairobi are to the poor and the lower-income segment of society. That share rises to 56 percent if the lower middle class is included. It is clear that supermarket retailing has moved well beyond the better-off consumers, even in "early stage" supermarket diffusion situations. The survey shows that this is because of the lower prices for staples and processed foods charged by supermarkets compared to traditional retailers. The corresponding figures for purchase of fresh produce in supermarkets are far lower, but with the same intergroup pattern.

At a later stage, supermarkets have also spread from large cities to intermediate towns, and in some countries already to small towns in rural areas. For example, 60 percent of Chilean supermarket sales are made outside the capital city, and about 40 percent of Chile's smaller towns now have supermarkets (Faiguenbaum et al. 2002), as do many medium-sized towns even in low-income countries like Kenya. Some 50 percent of Kenyan supermarket sales are made outside Nairobi. And supermarkets are now spreading rapidly beyond the top 60 cities of China in the coastal, moving to smaller cities and to the poorer and more remote Northwest and Southwest and to the interior (Hu et al. 2004).

GLOBALIZATION. The global multinational supermarket chains, which drive much of this retailing consolidation, have entered Latin America and Asia by a variety of means, including acquisitions, mergers, joint ventures, and direct implantation. As a result, U.S. Wal-Mart is now the largest food retailer in Mexico, while South Africa's Shoprite holds a dominant share in Namibia, Zambia, and Malawi (Reardon and Berdegué 2002; Weatherspoon and Reardon 2003). In some cases, such as in Chile and Kenya, domestic food retailers have led the growing concentration in food retailing.[2] In other instances, such as in Peru and Ecuador and throughout many smaller Latin American countries, major multinationals such as Royal Ahold and Carrefour have played dominant roles (Reardon and Berdegué 2002).

Regional multinationals such as D&S (Chile), Disco (Argentina), Shoprite (South Africa), and Dairy Farm International (Hong Kong) have emerged among food retailers and, to a lesser extent, among processors. These regional multinationals tend to behave like the global multinationals. They acquire and merge with smaller national firms. They also form partnerships and joint ventures with global multinationals to penetrate national markets. For example, two regional multinationals (CSU and La Fragua, based in Costa Rica and Guatemala, respectively), formed a joint venture with Ahold (of the Netherlands) in 2002, and they now operate in six countries of the Central American region (Berdegué et al. 2004).

In any given subregion, the penetration of supermarkets tends to start with the largest and richest national markets and then progressively expands to the other countries from there. Often national or subregional chains move first into the less saturated and, at least initially, less contested markets as they push out of the richest, most competitive markets in search of larger margins.

This rapid consolidation mirrors trends in the United States and Europe. In Latin America, the top five chains in each country account for 65 percent of supermarket sales, compared to 40 percent in the United States and 72 percent in France. The results are striking. Mexican consumers now spend 20 percent of their food budget in Wal-Mart (Reardon et al. 2003).

---

2. Reardon and Berdegué (2002), Neven and Reardon (2004).

Processing

Agricultural processing, too, has witnessed increased concentration and spread of large-scale firms. The large multinational or national processors accumulate dominant market positions nationally and sometimes regionally or globally, as in the case of processed horticultural products in Chile (IANSAFRUT); milk products in Brazil (Nestlé), Argentina (SANCOR), and Russia (Wimm-Bill-Dann and Danone); baked goods and snacks in Mexico (Bimbo) and Argentina (Arcor); and meat products in Brazil (SADIA) and Thailand (CP). Large South African agribusiness firms—commodity traders, farm input suppliers, cotton ginners, and exporters—have likewise expanded north into surrounding Southern African countries, where they now hold significant market shares.

A series of interesting case studies has examined the trajectory of concentration in food processing industries. This trajectory has tended to have a "U shape" over time, with a high degree of concentration initially in food processing, in particular staples processing, before a structural adjustment phase when parastatal firms have a significant presence. After liberalization, there is a proliferation of smaller firms that take advantage of the market space left by the large public sector players (Rubey 1995). Reconcentration then often occurs as large-scale, often multinational, processors buy up the emergent firms. Case studies have examined the markets for processed wheat in Brazil (Farina 1997) and for dairy products in Argentina (Gutman 1999), Chile (Dirven 2001), and Russia (Dries and Reardon 2005). In Chile, for example, in 1999 some 98 percent of all new investment in dairy operations was made by two multinationals and one large domestic firm (Dirven 2001). In general, the surge in concentration during the second half of the 1990s was mainly at the expense of small processing firms, including rural nonfarm firms, an issue to which we shall return shortly.

Causes of Change

Socioeconomic Factors: Necessary but Not Sufficient

Rapid urbanization and growing female workforce participation increase the opportunity cost of women's time as well as their incentives to seek convenience and buy processed foods in order to cut at-home food preparation time. Rising purchasing power, at least among the urban non-poor; the rising opportunity cost of time; and the liberalization of consumer imports have expanded ownership of refrigerators and even automobiles, both of which reinforce the inclination of the emerging middle class and even the working poor to purchase less frequently and in bulk, especially in the case of processed foods, at emerging supermarket chains.

As urban incomes rise, consumers diversify their consumption, according to Bennett's Law, into nonstaple foods such as fruits and vegetables, dairy products, meat, oils, and processed foods. Improving urban infrastructure has facilitated the supply response necessary to accommodate growing demands for these products. For this reason, supermarket penetration typically advances most rapidly in large urban centers and only later spreads into secondary towns. In 2003, for example, Nairobi shoppers enjoyed 460 square feet of supermarket retailing space per 1,000 inhabitants, while settlements of fewer than 25,000 attracted less than 3 square feet per 1,000 persons (Neven and Reardon 2004).

The Changing Policy Environment

Structural adjustment programs, widely instituted across the developing world from the mid-1980s onward, liberalized foreign trade, foreign direct investment (FDI), and domestic markets. By the early 1990s, governments had largely dismantled parastatals, input, and food subsidies and had reduced tariffs and export taxes. They relaxed investment regulations and scrapped floor and ceiling prices. The exit of government marketing agencies created space for private agribusiness operators, while deregulation dramatically enhanced private sector incentives.

In the early 1990s, a cascade of multilateral efforts to liberalize trade and investment magnified and accelerated these trends. The emergence and strengthening of MERCOSUR, NAFTA, COMESA, and ASEAN[3] facilitated flows of both FDI and regional trade.

Domestic and international agribusiness firms responded with a flood of investment, acquisition, and expansion in agricultural processing as well as food retailing. Large-scale domestic and multinational supermarkets, exporters, dairies, and poultry and food processing operations consolidated their market power in formerly fragmented agribusiness markets. Changes in consumer demand and in supply chain technologies accentuated these trends.

The liberalization of FDI regulation (via bilateral or multilateral policy changes) led to a dramatic increase in FDI in the retail and processing sectors. This avalanche of foreign investment downstream in the food system—as compared to the preglobalization emphasis on upstream investments such as in tropical fruit plantations—was in fact the main distinguishing characteristic of the globalization era.

The FDI was driven by push factors (saturated retail and processing sector markets in North America and Western Europe) and pull factors. The French giant Carrefour, for example, earned margins three times higher in Argentina

---

3. Abbreviations for Mercado Comun del Cono Sur (the Southern Cone Common Market), the North American Free Trade Agreement, the Common Market for Eastern and Southern Africa, and the Association of Southeast Asian Nations.

than on its French operations (Gutman 2002). Competition in the receiving regions was generally weak from fragmented traditional retailers.

In Latin America, FDI propelled rapid expansion and consolidation in a range of food processing activities for the domestic market, typically in second-stage processing such as that of dairy products, fruit juices, bread, noodles, and other wheat products (Farina 1997; Gutman 1999; Dirven 2001). In 1995, foreign-owned affiliates of U.S. firms operating in foreign countries sold about five times as much processed food as U.S.-based firms exported to foreign countries (Regmi and Gehlar 2005). Food retailing experienced similar trends. During the 1990s, FDI fueled expansion of multinational supermarket chains such as Dutch Ahold, French Carrefour, U.S. Wal-Mart, and British Tesco into Latin America and East and Southeast Asia (Reardon et al. 2003).

In Africa, political developments in South Africa played a major role in jump-starting supermarket expansion throughout East and Southern Africa. The advent of majority rule in 1994 ended a generation of economic sanctions and enabled South African firms to export goods and capital throughout the continent. After that their major supermarket chains, Shoprite and Pick 'n Pay, expanded quickly into thirteen other African countries and later into India, Australia, and the Philippines (Weatherspoon and Reardon 2003).

As in the United States and Western Europe during much of the twentieth century, the rise of supermarkets drove out the small neighborhood retailers and the open-air markets that characterized food retailing all over the world before 1920. In developing regions over the past decade, small retail firms have faced growing pressure from the ongoing consolidation in agrifood supply chains. Available evidence suggests that rapid concentration triggered the bankruptcy of thousands of small firms over the past decade. Across Asia, Africa, and Latin America, the growth of supermarkets has driven tens of thousands of small retailers into bankruptcy. Over 60,000 small food retailers closed their doors in Argentina from 1984 to 1993 (Gutman 1999), while over 5,000 small food retailers ceased operations in Chile between 1991 and 1995 (Faiguenbaum, Berdegué, and Reardon 2002).

Competition as the Driver of Technology Change

Supply chain logistics developed by global retailers and processors, combined with new models of information-intensive procurement and inventory management, have enabled large firms to radically reduce distribution costs—in their words, to relentlessly "drive costs out of the system." The resulting efficiency gains from scale economies and the modern inventory management involved in shifting to a centralized distribution center procurement system have, for example, enabled a large Chinese supermarket chain to reduce distribution costs by 40 percent (China Resource Enterprises 2002). These efficiency gains fuel profits and enable more rapid expansion, an advantage in newly consolidating markets given distinct first mover advantages in occupying key retailing locations.

Similar centralized distribution occurs in processing firms such as the giant Danone in Russia (Dries and Reardon 2005). These cost reductions through the adoption of retail procurement technology have allowed large retailers and processors to be price-competitive with smaller-scale traditional firms. The specific consequences of this competition for the organization of the procurement system of supermarkets and large-scale processors are discussed in the next section as the key vectors of change facing the food system upstream.

Procurement System Changes Affecting the RNFE

Reardon et al. (2003) lay out the components of the evolution of supermarkets' systems of procuring products from farmers and processors—and thus the "vector of effects" on the agrifood system upstream. Large processing firms tend to make parallel changes in their procurement and distribution systems in order to gain efficiency advantages and to interface more easily with supermarket chains. These changes can be distilled into the "four pillars of supermarket procurement system change" noted in the following four subsections.

Centralization of Procurement

Chains are shifting from local, decentralized procurement (buying products store by store) to the centralization and regionalization of procurement. The growing size of supermarket chains, in terms of both store numbers and volume of sales, typically leads to the centralization of procurement. Supermarket chains set up distribution centers to serve entire regions, which may cover several countries. Thus in 2001 Carrefour established a distribution center in São Paulo to serve three Brazilian states, a total of 50 million consumers (Boselie 2002). China Resource Enterprises of Hong Kong, the tenth largest retailer in China, is currently shifting from store-by-store to centralized procurement for each province. Similarly, Ahold has moved to centralize distribution in Central America via a specialized wholesaler, Hortifruti (Reardon et al. 2003). As a chain spreads over a given region, the logical extension is that there is a shift to the use of distribution centers and sourcing over a region, such as Ahold Central Europe (see Dries, Reardon, and Swinnen 2004).

To defray some of the added costs that accompany procurement consolidation, supermarket chains require that their suppliers adopt best-practice logistics technology. This requires suppliers to invest in equipment and processes that allow frictionless logistical interface with the chain's warehouses. The "Code of Good Commercial Practices" signed by supermarket chains and suppliers in Argentina illustrates the use of best-practice logistics by retail suppliers (Brom 2002). In some instances, these efforts lead to the outsourcing of logistics and wholesaling. Wumart of China intends to build a large distribution center and operate it jointly with Tibbett and Britten Logistics, a British multinational (Reardon et al. 2003). Ahold has partnered with TNT Logistics of the Netherlands

TABLE 9.3 Changing procurement sources in Kenya's Uchumi Supermarket, 1997–2008 (percent of total supply)

	Vegetables			Fresh fruits		
Supplier	1997	2003	2008	1997	2003	2008
Small farms	13	10	15	5	10	10
Medium-sized farms	10	25	30	10	10	10
Large farms	5	15	35	0	15	35
Traditional brokers/wholesalers	70	45	10	70	40	10
Imports	2	5	10	15	25	35
Total	100	100	100	100	100	100

SOURCE: Neven and Reardon (2004).

NOTE: 2008 projections are from Uchumi's procurement manager.

to jointly run its fruit and vegetable distribution operation in Thailand (Boselie 2002).

Specialized Wholesalers

Increasingly, supermarket chains are shifting from traditional wholesalers to specialized or dedicated wholesalers as procurement agents. Supermarkets sometimes buy directly from farmers or other food producers, and sometimes buy via wholesalers (Table 9.3). Where large and efficient wholesale markets exist, supermarkets are inclined to work with them to source commodities, at least in the early stages of market penetration.[4] Where fragmented, poorly coordinated traditional markets exist, many supermarkets establish their own wholesale procurement offices early on to work directly with suppliers, such as Hortifruti in Nicaragua, which is working in the CSU chain.

Often specialized (in a product category) cum dedicated (to supermarkets and export channels) wholesalers then emerge within the wholesale market and grow to focus on the supermarket channel and sometimes are subsequently acquired by supermarket chains to make them in-house profit centers. An example is Freshmark, which started as a separate company and was then acquired by the Shoprite chain (Weatherspoon and Reardon 2003).

The specialized or dedicated wholesalers serve as the chains' agents, meeting their volume and quality requirements. These specialized wholesalers reduce transaction costs and enforce private standards (discussed later) on behalf of the supermarkets. They often expand to serve domestic and export markets, leading to a convergence of the two marketing chains.

---

4. See Berdegué et al. (2004) for documentation of the Central American case.

Contracts

For several decades, in developing regions food wholesalers and exporters have shifted away from spot markets in favor of contracts (implicit or explicit) with farmers that specify volumes, quality, timing, and price (Schejtman 1998; Key and Runsten 1999). More recently, since the turn of the twenty-first century, supermarkets and their specialized wholesalers have introduced contracts with farmers and processors. They enter into de facto, often implicit, contracts via the establishment of "preferred supplier lists." Contracts enable supermarkets and agroprocessors to lower both risks and transaction costs, though they generally favor medium and larger players who can meet the contract requirements. The emergence of contracts also creates favorable conditions for farmers upgrading their investments.

Private Standards

Chains are increasingly shifting away from informal standards—or going beyond existing public standards—to establish private standards, first on quality and eventually on food safety, frequently in response to the inadequacy or even absence of public standards. They impose standards on suppliers via the preferred supplier relationships, gradually phasing in terms of coverage, stringency, and monitoring. These serve as competitive tools in the retail sector as well as ways to coordinate the consistency produced in the supply chains (Reardon et al. 2001). Contracts typically stipulate grades and standards and sometimes also specify labor and environmental standards. Private standards for food safety and quality have proliferated for a variety of reasons. Firms and associations face strong incentives to create and enforce standards and to communicate them to consumers via labels and certification in order to capture rents from quality and product differentiation. In many places and for many products, the need for standards (to define and regulate markets) has outpaced the development of public standards (Farina and Reardon 2000).

In some cases, public grades and standards existed, but in form or degree they failed to meet the needs of the private agrifood system actors. For example, during the 1960s, 1970s, and 1980s the Brazilian government strictly regulated the market in wheat products, though it specified only two grades of wheat flour. With market liberalization around 1990, domestic wheat-milling firms, such as Moinho Pacifico and Pena Branca, were able to offer a wide variety of grades of flours geared to the needs of the bakeries. The millers created their own grading and standards system to supplant the public system and create the incentives for product differentiation. The strategy has turned out to benefit imports as well, because wheat flour is an international commodity that has an adequate and well-known grading system that allows Brazilian milling companies or the food industry (the segment making pasta, bread, and biscuits) to source globally (Farina 1997).

Similarly for coffee, in the second half of the 1990s the Coffee Roasters Association of Brazil, as well as foreign firms such as the relatively small Italian firm Illycaffee, promoted differentiation strategies based on blends of different types and grades of coffee and used these to establish price differentials to create an incentive for coffee growers to make the necessary investments in quality control. Again, the new private standards were much better adapted to the needs for quality and variety differentiation than were the public grades and standards (Zylbersztajn and Farina 1999). As these cases illustrate, standards are not merely public goods used to resolve market failures; they become strategic instruments that food companies use to differentiate their products and protect their market share (Reardon et al. 2001).

Pressures on the RNFE

Technological Change

In general, the new organization of procurement, together with the institution of contracts and private standards, require changes in technology or management for the supplying firms and farms. These changes can prove large and costly, as an example from the Brazilian dairy industry illustrates. During the 1950s, the Brazilian government formulated public milk quality standards (with grades A, B, and C), though they were not implemented until the 1970s, when milk processors and retailers began using them for market segmentation based on quality to take advantage of rapidly expanding urban milk consumption and rising incomes. In the 1990s, the liberalization of FDI led to an influx of FDI and the entrance of global dairy firms such as Parmalat, Royal Numico, and MD Foods, along with new investments by Nestlé. Through the adoption of cost-saving technology, dairy product price competition became intense, resulting in a 40 percent drop in real retail prices for milk between 1994 and 1997, while farm gate prices did not fall. As incomes rose, the dairy products market burgeoned.

Stiff price competition in dairy markets led to the adoption of new strategies of supply chain management. Leading processors such as Itambéé (the largest Brazilian dairy co-op and second-largest dairy processor), Nestlé, and Parmalat imposed new private standards for milk producers to ensure quality and safety and to reduce losses in industrial processing. Among other specifications, these grades and standards require on-farm milk refrigeration together with volume and microbiological requirements (Jank et al. 1999). Better raw material quality reduces losses in industrial processing, allowing large-scale transport and more efficient logistic strategies. A secondary but growing objective is to communicate milk safety procedures to the public and avoid food safety problems (Farina and Reardon 2000).

For the milk producer and first-stage handler (or collector) of milk, the private standards requirement that milk be refrigerated at the farm and collection co-op level implied obligatory large-scale investments in refrigeration equipment. In less than five years, the leading firms completed their "bulking" program, imposing these standards systemwide. Unable to finance these large refrigeration investments quickly enough, thousands of small dairies, located mainly in rural areas, closed their operations in Brazil, Argentina, and Chile.[5]

Consolidation

Over time, growing concentration in food retailing has triggered parallel consolidation in wholesaling, processing, and distribution. In processing, the expansion of supermarkets has tended to favor the expansion of correspondingly large food processors. Supermarket chains prefer, all else equal, to work with large processing companies—in a symbiosis that varies between friendly and contentious—for a variety of reasons. First, chains like to sell recognized brands, which only the large processors produce. Second, they incur lower transaction costs in dealing with a handful of large processors than with many small ones. Third, some supermarkets charge high shelf-space fees, which largely exclude small suppliers. Evidence from Chile, for example, suggests that this practice strongly favors large-scale processors. Likewise, long payment periods favor larger firms with deeper pockets and ready commercial financing. Finally, large processors can consistently supply homogeneous product to a whole national or subregional chain, thus reducing inventory and logistics costs for the supermarket chains.

As a result, the rapid rise of supermarkets favors larger-scale intermediaries and processors. Evidence, though limited, points generally to a relatively rapid exclusion of small processing and food manufacturing firms in the supermarket procurement systems of developing countries. Hu et al. (2004) note that while supermarket chains in Beijing tend to increase processed product diversity, there is a strong tendency toward selection of a small number of medium to large firms capable of delivering product of consistent quality in large volumes and ensuring "one-stop shopping" for the chains. The Xiaobaiyang chain (a local Beijing chain) went from 1,000 to 300 suppliers of processed products (we are not told their locations, so we cannot say whether they are urban or rural) when it went from decentralized to centralized procurement in 2003 (Hu et al. 2004). In addition to lowering their transaction costs, the chains reap economies of scale from the large volumes of processed products moving through their distribution centers, and they save costs by working with larger firms that can ship to their centers or have their own distribution centers. As a result of these pressures, small suppliers must either grow and adapt or exit the supermarket supply chains in favor of those serving the shrinking traditional market channels.

---

5. Jank, Farina, and Galan (1999), Dirven (2001), Gutman (2002).

Impact on the RNFE: Emerging Evidence

Evidence is just now beginning to emerge of how the profound changes in urban food and nonfood markets are affecting the RNFE. Are rural nonfarm firms being displaced or forced to get bigger or better by hiring more labor, investing more capital, or both? Are they changing their product composition and technology? Are they hiring more or less labor? Early glimmers of evidence suggest that there will be effects, many of which will serve as challenges to the RNFE.

Rural Traders

Emerging evidence suggests that small rural traders and the wholesale markets they serve risk being displaced by larger, specialized wholesalers. The leading supermarket chains in Guatemala and Nicaragua, for example, have shifted away from rural small-scale brokers for procuring lettuce and tomatoes. Instead they now procure through several large, specialized wholesalers (Balsevich, Schuetz, and Perez 2006; Flores and Reardon 2006; Hernández, Reardon, and Berdegué 2006). The same has occurred in the beef sector in Nicaragua and Costa Rica (Balsevich, Berdegué, and Reardon 2006).

Projections from Kenya point to similar trends. While traditional wholesale markets and brokers supplied 70 percent of the vegetables and fresh fruits sold by the Uchumi supermarket chain in 1997, that share had fallen to 45 percent by 2003. Uchumi's procurement manager projects that their share will fall to 10 percent by 2008 (Table 9.3).

If one extrapolates from these cases, as supermarkets spread and modernize their procurement systems one would expect significant displacement of small produce traders, a key part of the RNFE at present. This change would parallel what occurred in the United States in the mid–twentieth century.

Rural Processing

For pressures on rural food processing from consolidation "downstream" in the agrifood system, the only evidence of which I am aware relates to the dairy sector. Earlier, in the section on technological change, I related an illustration from Latin America that is also relevant to this subsection; it draws on an analysis of the milk industry in Argentina and Brazil in Farina et al. (2005) as well as Jank, Farina, and Galan (1999), Dirven (2001), and Gutman (2002), case studies that find a close parallel in the analysis of the dairy industry in Russia in Dries and Reardon (2005). These studies show that the pressures of consolidation downstream cause technological change in the upstream dairy segments such as first-stage processing and dairy farming, but also drive restructuring of the upstream segments by pushing out actors unable to make the requisite threshold investments. Of course this does not always happen, for example, where there are only small dairy farms and collection points and the dairy sector is forced to accommodate technology requirements to that scale, as in Poland (Dries and Swinnen, 2005).

Moreover, the restructuring provides opportunities for market access and expansion for upstream processing firms positioned (through, for example, their ability to make threshold investments) to supply the restructured downstream segments. Faiguenbaum et al. (2002) provide a poignant example from Chile, where a dairy processing cooperative, CAFRA, successfully made the big leap. Before the nationwide supermarket chain D&S selected CAFRA as one of its preferred suppliers, CAFRA was relegated to serving the local market in the low-income south of Chile. D&S's national coverage immediately put the CAFRA name in front of consumers all over Chile. The volume, branding, consistency, and quality demanded of it turned it into a national supplier. Meanwhile, other local competitors lost out and were eliminated. As in the global market, the local manifestations of globalization create a "knife's edge," offering bigger wins, and bigger losses, than before.

Illustrations from the cheese sector in Honduras and Chile further illustrate my points concerning consolidation pressures on the dairy sector from downstream food industry segments' transformation. Food retail chains supply mainly urban-manufactured food products to their units in rural towns.[6] Typically, those products come from companies that are highly competitive at a national level, and thus they are cheaper, of higher quality, or supplied to the retail chain at a lower transaction cost than local products. For this reason, packaged cheese from large urban processors has become omnipresent in the small shops in rural Lempira, the poorest area in Honduras. The urban food processors have, apparently, successfully outcompeted small-scale local cheese producers (Reardon 1999).

Similarly, in Chile, we once asked a dairy products procurement officer for a major supermarket chain whether he would be willing to consider adding to his line of cheeses the cheese of a small farmer cooperative we knew. He did two things in answer to our question. He first pulled open his desk drawer to reveal a stack of cheeses and said, "I get about a dozen requests a month from cooperatives asking me that question, and here is the latest stack of samples from the rejected suppliers." He then said, "Follow me. Let's think about your question by looking at the dairy section of the supermarket, the section that I procure for and manage." He showed us that dairy section, which, although vastly more diverse in terms of different products than a traditional shop, is dominated by products from the four or five main dairy product firms in the country; the "niche items" include some local traditional cheeses made by small cooperatives, members of the RNFE. He said, "The group's cheese that you are

---

6. Empirically, they seldom supply imported products except in the early stages of food industry transformation, in very small countries, or both.

suggesting we 'add' to our dairy section would have to displace the three co-op cheeses we already have here. I cannot add space to my section. Can you prove that this cheese is either fundamentally better in quality (but the same price) or a lower price? If not, I will reject it out of hand."

Emerging evidence suggests that these anecdotes do not represent isolated cases. The rapid rise of supermarkets favors larger-scale intermediaries and processors, placing corresponding pressure on small rural nonfarm firms, many of which exit the industry.

Retailing in Rural Towns

While most retail transformation research in developing countries in the 1990s and 2000s has focused on urban areas, I expect a gradual diffusion of that retail transformation to rural towns (but probably not down to the level of small villages), for several reasons. First, urban retail chains and large processors have made strong efforts to expand into secondary cities and then into rural towns—through direct presence in the case of retailers and through distribution systems in the case of processors. Supermarket chains, for example, have a tendency to start in large cities and then, with competition, to spill into secondary cities and smaller towns (Reardon et al. 2003). For example, China's leading retail chain, Lianhua, is investing heavily to expand its presence in rural townships (Hu et al. 2004). Similarly, the Austrian retailer Billa is investing heavily in rural towns in Bulgaria.[7] The Vietnamese convenience store chain G7 Mart announced on March 2, 2006, that it is building 10,000 stores throughout Vietnam, even in remote areas.[8] The list of similar expansion plans is long and recent.

As larger chains move into secondary cities, they commonly push local and regional chains into tertiary cities and small towns, thereby pushing small local chains or independents into large villages. For example, Faiguenbaum, Berdegué, and Reardon (2002) have observed this progression in Chile. The resulting domino effect brings supermarkets into the "market-shed" of RNF producers.

Little empirical work has been done yet on the specific nature and degree of local competition with rural enterprises that this situation creates, but some new studies have addressed this question. An example is the South African study by D'Haese and Van Huylenbroeck (2005) showing that rural residents around towns with supermarkets tend to make their processed food purchases in those towns. That evidence confirms what we hear from qualitative interviews with supermarket managers in many countries: they are seeking to capture rural purchasing power, at least for processed food products that are easily

---

7. "BILLA to expand in smaller towns in Bulgaria," *PlanetRetail,* March 2, 2006.
8. "New retail network to debut in Vietnam," *PlanetRetail,* March 2, 2006.

transported back to rural areas and can be bought infrequently. Currently these products are a key output of the RNF sector. These inroads by the large urban chains increase competitive pressure on existing retailers in rural towns.

Conclusions

The key lesson emerging from this review is that the rural nonfarm enterprises of today produce and sell products in a setting vastly different from that of just 15 years ago. The agrifood economy of the developing world has been transformed by structural adjustment, trade and investment liberalization, consumer demand shifts, and deep changes in agrifood market institutions, organization, and technology. A decade ago, a scattered handful of supermarkets and multinational second-stage processors operated in the developing world. Now they are emerging as a dominant force in the food system and as actors with which small and rural suppliers must increasingly deal. Thousands of small firms and farms have suffered a knockout blow from the new market structures, coordinating mechanisms, and volume and technology requirements. Under current conditions, it appears that only a minority has unambiguously prospered from the rapid changes under way.

A forward-looking rural nonfarm promotion strategy must recognize this ongoing transformation. In specific instances, policymakers will need to determine if and how the poor can compete in rapidly consolidating supply chains. Efforts by private and public partners will need to explore ways in which aggregations of small firms and farms can work in commercially viable supply chains with large firms. They will require situation-specific diagnostics and a willingness to make systemic interventions—in policies, public investment, and/or organizational methods. In instances in which small firms and the rural poor simply cannot compete, public investments in education, agricultural research, credit, or rural infrastructure may assist the poor to shift their livelihood strategies. Above all, policymakers must appreciate that the genie is now out of the bottle and that conditions will continue to change rapidly in the agrifood segment of the RNFE. Small players will be forced to adapt to these rapidly changing supply chains or seek alternative livelihoods.

10 The Rural Industrial Transition in East Asia: Influences and Implications

KEIJIRO OTSUKA

The structural transformation of the rural nonfarm economy, described in general in Chapter 4, has advanced furthest and most rapidly in East Asia. So have the dynamic linkages examined in the subsequent chapters of Part II of this book. Moreover, a wealth of long-term time-series data permits careful documentation of the processes there. Thus a review of that evidence offers the opportunity to anticipate issues confronting later-blooming rural economies of the developing world.

The successful transformation of rural industries in East Asia over the past several decades has been led by small and medium-sized enterprises (SMEs) using labor-intensive technologies (Sonobe and Otsuka 2006a). This transition has attracted renewed interest across the developing world given the surging interest in reducing rural poverty and underemployment through rural nonfarm employment (see Chapter 2). This renewed interest is driven by three realizations: that urban-based industrialization has serious limitations in addressing underemployment in rural areas because urban formal sector firms tend to be large in scale and capital intensive (Evenson and Westphal 1995); that urban congestion and pollution create a strong incentive for policymakers to prefer decentralization of manufacturing to suburban and rural areas (Hayami 1998a); and that the employment effects of the green revolution in Asia have been modest (David and Otsuka 1994), which suggests that, although agricultural development is important, it alone will not solve the rural employment problem. Moreover, there is evidence that in green revolution areas the share of nonfarm employment in overall employment grew more quickly after the green revolution. For example, in central Luzon in the Philippines, the share of nonfarm income in total income increased from 27 percent in 1966–67 to 38 percent in 1986–87 during the green revolution period, and it increased still more, to 51 percent, in 1994–95, when the nonfarm sector began to develop external export markets (Estudillo and Otsuka 1999).

The purpose of this chapter is to identify the basic nature of the rural industrial transformation in East Asia, to explore the factors affecting its success and failure, and to examine its relevance to other areas. This distillation of les-

216

sons focuses on Taiwan and South Korea. A comparative study of the two countries is highly relevant because Taiwan's economic development has been based on the development of SMEs located in rural and suburban areas,[1] whereas South Korea's development has been led by urban-based, large enterprises (Amsden 1989; Hattori 1997). Like most explicit policy pronouncements and survey data, this chapter focuses exclusively on rural manufacturing, a subset of rural nonfarm activity that excludes rural commerce and services.

Two Stages of Rural Industrialization

The evolution of East Asian rural industrialization involved a shift over the past 50 years from relatively undynamic rural activities using traditional technologies targeted to the local rural market to more dynamic activities geared to the demands of the urban and export markets, often linked in subcontracts with urban firms. This shift is mirrored in the economic development literature, which posits a shift from Stage 1 to Stage 2 rural industrialization.

Stage 1 is characterized by Hymer and Resnick (1969) as a stage in which rural industry consists of activities based in households and small workshops that produce a wide range of locally consumed, low-quality commodities, which they called Z-goods. These include products such as spun yarn, processed foods, beverages, and wood products made using traditional production methods. These products are typically agriculture based, relying on raw materials supplied by agriculture. As discussed more generally in Chapter 2, Hymer and Resnick posited that rural industrialization would decline after Stage 1, overwhelmed by an inflow of imported commodities produced by modern technologies in Western nations or by large-scale urban industries. There is indeed evidence that such a fate met Stage 1 rural industrialization in a number of countries in the past century. Resnick (1970) demonstrated that rural industry experienced a remarkable decline from the late nineteenth century to the early twentieth century in Burma, Thailand, and the Philippines. Otsuka, Saxonhouse, and Ranis (1988) observed the abrupt demise of traditional cotton spinning industries in rural areas of Japan during the late nineteenth century immediately after her open door policy began. It has also been reported that the importance of nonfactory production units declined in the course of economic development in Taiwan (Ho 1978, 1982).

Rather than experiencing the permanent demise of rural industry predicted by Hymer and Resnick, however, the majority of East Asia instead underwent a shift from Stage 1 to Stage 2 rural industrialization, in which decentralized, small-scale industries have played a major role in the development of the

---

1. Ho (1978, 1979), Wade (1990), Amsden (1991), Sonobe, Kawakami, and Otsuka (2003), Sonobe and Otsuka (2006b).

overall economy for many decades. To explain this transition, Ranis and Stewart (1993) have introduced the concept of modern Z-goods that are distinct from the traditional Z-goods envisaged by Hymer and Resnick. According to Ranis and Stewart, modern Z-goods are produced by modern production methods and characterized by high demand from urban and overseas markets. The production efficiency of modern Z-goods is supposed to improve with the progress of modern technologies, and demand for them is supposed to increase with income growth, indicating that rural industry engaged in the production of modern Z-goods may have high growth potential. The implicit assumption of this argument is that rural industries introduce new technologies, ideas, and information from urban and foreign enterprises that have better access to modern, advanced technologies and global information networks.[2] Using data from Taiwan and South Korea, this chapter explores the rural industrial transition in East Asia, examining the forces underlying that transformation that made it possible there and potentially elsewhere.

Contrasting Rural and Industrial Transitions

Data

Available data permit examination of the changing structure of rural industrialization in Taiwan and South Korea in selected years from 1930 to the present. In distinguishing between rural and urban areas, analysis follows the methodology developed by Ho (1982), which classifies total geographical areas into urban areas, consisting mainly of major cities, and the remaining rural areas (see the notes to Table 10.1 for definitions). Evidence for the early years comes from data supplied by Ho (1982) for 1930 and 1956/60, whereas reported analysis provides new estimates of the rural employment structure for more recent years.

Note that the earlier data, for 1930 and 1956/60, are not directly comparable with the more recent data, first because the former are based on the population census, whereas the latter are obtained from the industrial census and surveys, and second because only major cities and towns were included among urban areas in the former, whereas major cities and major urbanized provinces were included among urban areas in the latter. A critical shortcoming of this methodology is that the urbanization of rural areas associated with industrialization is regarded as rural industrialization rather than as a change from rural to urban areas. Thus, because of the constraints imposed by available data sources, the restrictive definition of rural areas in this chapter differs from the broader one discussed in Chapter 1, which covers rural villages and small towns.

---

2. See, for example, evidence from Grossman and Helpman (1992), Coe et al. (1997), and Edwards (1998).

As will be seen later, this results in an anomalous phenomenon in South Korea, where industrialization accompanied the development of such large cities as Pohang and Taegu in Kyongsangpuk Do, which are categorized as "rural" in Ho's classification scheme. It must be also pointed out that in this methodology no distinction is made between remote rural areas and suburban areas of large metropolitan areas. Another important caveat is that while the Taiwanese data cover all establishments, the Korean data since the 1970s pertain to establishments employing more than four workers. Although small establishments employing four or fewer workers were relatively few in South Korea, it must be admitted that the Korean data overestimate the size of enterprises and underestimate the importance of rural industries, insofar as very small enterprises were concentrated in rural areas. In spite of these imperfections, the striking nature of the general trends suggests that the data offer satisfactory indicators of the broad tendencies under way.

Key Transitions

Table 10.1 shows changes in the total number of workers in the rural manufacturing industry and their sectoral distribution in rural areas. The periods since the 1970s largely correspond to the period of "miraculous" development, to use the term coined by the World Bank (1993a). The average annual growth rates of gross national product per capita between 1965 and 1990 happened to be the same, 7.1 percent, in both Taiwan and South Korea. Moreover, the structural composition of the manufacturing sectors in both economies was similar (Hattori and Sato 1997).

The period since the mid-1960s can be appropriately characterized as a phase of rapid rural industrialization in Taiwan, compared to a phase of relative stagnation in rural areas of South Korea. This does not imply that rural industries did not grow in South Korea; the number of workers in rural manufacturing industry more than tripled from 1971 to 2002 (Table 10.1). But due to the rapid development of the urban manufacturing sectors, the overall employment share of rural manufacturing industry remained in the vicinity of 30 to 40 percent (Table 10.2). Furthermore, if rapidly industrialized Kyongsangpuk Do was included among urban areas, the rural employment share decreased to about 16 percent in 1995. In contrast, the rural employment share increased from 41 percent in 1976 to 50 percent in 1996 in Taiwan.

Thus there is no denying that significant differences emerged in the pace and extent of rural industrialization between Taiwan and South Korea over the past few decades. Differences in both cultural and political factors help to explain the different paths of development in these two countries.[3] Taiwan's

---

3. Ho (1982), Kuznets (1988), Hattori and Sato (1997), Sato (1997).

TABLE 10.1 Changes in employment structure in the rural manufacturing industry in Taiwan and South Korea, 1930–2002

	1930	1956/60[a]	1976/71[a]	1981	1991/95[a]	1996/2002[a]
Taiwan[b]						
Rural employment (thousands)	78	121	778	938	1,338	1,260
Distribution (%)						
Food, beverages, and tobacco	22	27	10	5	5	5
Wood, bamboo, and furniture	28	14	8	8	7	5
Textiles and apparel	22	23	23	22	16	12
Chemicals, paper, and printing	8	3	22	22	19	18
Nonmetallic mineral products	5	7	6	6	5	4
Metals and machinery	12	12	27	27	44	52
South Korea[c]						
Rural employment (thousands)	286	193	271	543	911	974
Distribution (%)						
Food, beverages, and tobacco	8	31	22	14	7	10
Wood, bamboo, and furniture	25	13	5	2	1	1
Textiles and apparel	54	31	34	41	21	13
Chemicals, paper, and printing	3	6	12	11	16	18
Nonmetallic mineral products	4	7	7	7	8	5
Metals and machinery	5	11	15	23	40	46

SOURCES: For 1930 and 1956–60, the data are from the population censuses summarized by Ho (1982). For other periods, the data on Taiwan are from the Industry and Commercial Census of Taiwan and Fukien Area, and those for South Korea are from the Report on Mining and Manufacturing Survey. Note that for the last three periods, the Taiwan data cover establishments of all sizes, whereas the Korean data pertain to establishments with more than four workers.

[a]The data pertain to 1930, 1956, 1976, 1981, 1991, and 1996 for Taiwan and to 1930, 1960, 1971, 1981, 1995, and 2002 for South Korea.

[b]Rural Taiwan is defined as Taiwan minus five major cities (Taipei, Keelung, Taichung, Tainan, and Kaohsiung) and the Taipei prefecture for the last three periods. The definition of rural areas applied for 1930 and 1956 is slightly different.

[c]Rural South Korea is defined as South Korea minus Seoul, Pusan, and the two most industrialized provinces (Kyonggi Do and Kyongsangnam Do) for the last three periods. The definition of rural areas applied for 1930 and 1960 is slightly different.

TABLE 10.2 Changes in rural employment as a share of total employment in Taiwan and South Korea, 1930–2002 (percent)

	1930	1956/60[a]	1976/71[a]	1981	1991/95[a]	1996/2002[a]
Taiwan						
Total manufacturing	63	37	41	43	50	50
Food, beverages, and tobacco	68	59	48	47	48	45
Wood, bamboo, and furniture	74	53	55	64	76	73
Textiles and apparel	60	38	38	42	60	53
Chemicals, paper, and printing	47	23	46	45	45	45
Nonmetallic mineral products	72	48	56	57	61	55
Metals and machinery	52	50	35	32	48	50
South Korea						
Total manufacturing	84	41	32	27	31	36
Food, beverages, and tobacco	76	63	51	43	48	51
Wood, bamboo, and furniture	90	50	33	21	27	26
Textiles and apparel	89	34	33	34	34	31
Chemicals, paper, and printing	49	22	21	16	31	37
Nonmetallic mineral products	88	62	37	39	54	57
Metals and machinery	67	31	23	20	28	35

SOURCES: For 1930 and 1956–60, the data are from the population censuses summarized by Ho (1982). For other periods, the data on Taiwan are from the Industry and Commercial Census of Taiwan and Fukien Area, and those for South Korea are from the Report on Mining and Manufacturing Survey. Note that for the last three periods, the Taiwan data cover establishments of all sizes, whereas the Korean data pertain to establishments with more than four workers.

[a]The data pertain to 1930, 1956, 1976, 1981, 1991, and 1996 for Taiwan and to 1930, 1960, 1971, 1981, 1995, and 2002 for South Korea.

experience is valuable given the well-documented improvements in income distribution during the rapid growth of the Taiwanese economy owing to the importance of rural industrialization (Fields and Leary 1998; Schultz 1998). It is therefore of great interest to identify the major characteristics of rural industries in Taiwan in comparison with those in South Korea.

AGRICULTURE-LED RURAL INDUSTRIALIZATION.   The rural industrialization of both Taiwan and South Korea was agriculturally based in its early stages, before the 1960s, as was the case in Japan during the early phase of its economic development. In terms of the absolute number of rural workers engaged in rural manufacturing, the pace of rural industrialization was slow in Taiwan and even negative in South Korea for the period from 1930 to 1956/60. In these periods in both countries, the major industrial activities in rural areas were in the subsectors of food, beverages, and tobacco; wood products; and textiles and apparel, which were largely agriculture based. Among these three industrial subsectors, only the employment share of food, beverages, and tobacco increased in both Taiwan and South Korea (Table 10.1). Important commodities included refined sugar and canned fruits (such as pineapples) in Taiwan and vegetable oils in Korea.

The importance of rural food processing industries has declined, however, since the 1970s. Thus it appears that agriculture-led rural industrialization was manifested primarily in the development of food processing industries in the early stage of economic development in both Taiwan and South Korea. Ranis (1995) argues that the development of commercialized agriculture in Taiwan contributed to the commencement of rapid overall development by stimulating the development of rural industries. This argument is consistent with the experience of Japan during the Meiji period, when the development of silk and tea industries in rural areas made significant contributions to the overall economic development and export earnings (Hayami et al. 1991). In contrast, the development of other industries in rural areas, including those making wood products, textiles, and apparel, not to mention the heavy industries (those making metals and machinery) and the chemical industries, was quite limited in both Taiwan and South Korea.

As is shown in Table 10.2, the average share of rural areas in total manufacturing employment declined appreciably in both economies from 1930 to 1956/60, from 63 to 37 percent in Taiwan and from 84 to 41 percent in South Korea. Furthermore, no rural industry recorded an increased employment share in this period. It seems clear that in the earlier periods rural industries produced mostly Z-goods, as defined by Hymer and Resnick (1969). In fact, the rural employment share of even the food, beverages, and tobacco industries declined during the decades after 1930.

STAGE 2 RURAL INDUSTRIALIZATION. Both Taiwan and South Korea experienced the shift from traditional to modern Z-goods production during the "miracle" period, from 1970 forward, with a shift from food processing to the production of metals and machinery. Specifically, the weight of the food processing (cum beverages and tobacco) industry rapidly declined in rural areas, even though its employment share in the economy did not change appreciably. Similar tendencies are also seen in other light industries. Such changes likely resulted from the declining comparative advantage of these formerly key rural industries. Meanwhile, the importance of the heavy industries and the chemical industries in rural areas increased appreciably in both countries. Particularly important in the 1990s were the metal and machinery industries, whose employment has accounted for about half of rural employment in Taiwan and South Korea in recent years (Table 10.1). The rural employment share in these industries has amounted to nearly 50 percent in Taiwan and 36 percent in Korea in the same periods (Table 10.2). Because these are new industries that are known to grow based on the import and assimilation of foreign technologies,[4] it is clear that their products fall into the category of modern Z-goods. Many of these new rural industries were small enterprises producing parts and intermediate products for urban and foreign enterprises under subcontracting arrangements (Levy and Kuo 1991; Abe and Kawakami 1997). Subcontracting arrangements played a key role in stimulating light industries such as textiles, apparel, and footwear in South Korea (Levy 1991; Lee and Suh 1998). The issue of subcontracting is further explored later.

Although we do not discount the significance of growth linkage analysis, which is designed to analyze the impact of agricultural growth on rural nonfarm commerce, services, and manufacturing activity, it appears that forward and backward growth linkage effects on rural manufacturing worked most effectively through the development of the food processing industry in the early stage of economic development. Unlike rural commerce and services, whose growth remains driven by rural consumption patterns, rural manufacturing requires cooperation and coordination between rural and urban enterprises in the heavy industries, such as those making machinery. Consequently, they have become more important in the later stages of industrial development.

DIVERGING PATHS. In the 1960s, both Taiwan and South Korea began to pursue export-led growth based on production by SMEs. The export share in the gross domestic product increased from 14 percent in 1961 to 57 percent in 1986 in Taiwan, whereas it increased from 5 percent in 1961 to 42 percent in 1987 in South Korea.

Taiwan's and South Korea's rural industrialization parted ways in the 1970s, with Taiwan taking the road toward an SME- and countryside-oriented industrialization, while South Korea opted for an increasing orientation toward large and intermediate cities, with medium-sized and large firms located in

---

4. See Grossman and Helpman (1992), World Bank (1993a), Coe et al. (1997), and Edwards (1998).

industrial parks. In the 1970s, the government of South Korea adopted heavy industry promotion polices in which the entry of new enterprises, direct foreign investments, imports of competing products, and even long-term investments were strictly regulated in order to support the selected conglomerates called *chaebol* (Amsden 1989; Hattori and Sato 1997). Industry promotion polices were applied to six selected industries (the integrated circuit, chemical, petroleum, synthetic fiber, iron and steel, and automobile industries), which are subject to scale economies. In contrast, the government of Taiwan did not generally promote specific industries, nor did it support large enterprises (Sato 1997). To some extent, South Korea has reverted to the Taiwanese path since the early 1980s with the abolishment of its heavy industry promotion policies.

Technology Biases

TAIWAN.   Technology and scale biases highlight more visibly than sectoral composition the fork in the road between the Taiwanese and the South Korean rural industrialization strategies. Taiwanese rural industry adapted to lower rural wages with labor-intensive technology and small-scale firms. Entry barriers were low because capital requirements were low. The literature is unanimous with respect to the availability of cheap labor as a major advantage of rural industrialization (e.g., Mead 1984; Lanjouw and Lanjouw 1995). Wages for unskilled labor are significantly lower in rural areas than in urban areas because of the substantial costs of migration from rural to urban areas, labor market and minimum wage regulations in urban areas, and the lower cost of living in rural areas. The seasonality of agricultural production also creates a supply of cheap labor in rural areas during the slack seasons. Given the meager endowment of agricultural land in East Asia, the development of labor-using industries by means of labor-using production methods was the key to the reduction of rural poverty in this region (Oshima 1993).

A comparison of wage and factor use between the urban and rural industries reveals important differences in the rural industrialization of Taiwan and that of South Korea. Table 10.3 displays the ratio of labor productivity, in terms of value added per worker, between rural and urban areas, as well as the factor shares of labor in the aggregate manufacturing sector for recent periods. In Taiwan the ratio of rural to urban wage rates has been stable at around 0.8. Such a wage gap is reasonable considering the cost of rural to urban migration and the difference in the cost of living between rural and urban areas. More detailed examination suggests that suburban areas of large cities, such as Taipei, Taichung, and Kaohsiung, tended to develop more rapidly than remote rural areas (Sonobe and Otsuka 2006b). It seems that "rural" and urban labor markets have been well integrated in Taiwan.

Corresponding to the rural-urban wage gap, labor productivity was significantly and consistently lower in rural areas, even though the gap has narrowed over time. The average factor share of labor was higher in rural areas by 10 to

TABLE 10.3 Ratios of average wage and labor productivity in rural areas to urban areas of Taiwan and South Korea, 1976–2002

	1976/71[a]	1981	1991/95[a]	2001/2[a]
Taiwan				
Ratio of rural to urban wage	0.8	0.8	0.8	0.8
Ratio of labor productivity	0.5	0.6	0.6	0.8
Factor share of labor (%):				
Rural areas	68.1	53.5	53.0	44.4
Urban areas	44.4	38.9	42.7	41.7
South Korea				
Ratio of rural to urban wage	0.7	0.9	1.0	1.1
Ratio of labor productivity	0.8	1.2	1.1	1.9
Factor share of labor (%):				
Rural areas	20.6	22.5	22.3	16.8
Urban areas	24.3	29.5	24.7	29.0

SOURCES: The data on Taiwan are from the Industry and Commercial Census of Taiwan and Fukien Area, and those for South Korea are from the Report on Mining and Manufacturing Survey.

[a]Available census data permit these computations for 1976, 1981, 1991, and 2001 for Taiwan and for 1971, 1981, 1995, and 2002 for South Korea.

25 percentage points until 1991. If the elasticity of substitution in each industrial sector is less than unity, as is likely the case, the higher factor share of labor in rural areas cannot be explained by factor substitution along the given isoquant in response to the regional wage difference. Large differences in labor share and labor productivity will be explained only by the adoption of more labor-using technologies in rural areas to make use of the cheap labor force. Although unreported here, disaggregation into the industrial sectors generally provides results consistent with this explanation.

SOUTH KOREA.   The situation in South Korea was markedly different. While a wage gap similar to that in Taiwan existed in 1971, the gap almost disappeared in 1981 and 1995, and it was reversed in 2002. Moreover, although rural labor productivity was lower than urban in 1971, the former surpassed the latter by a wide margin in 1981 and 2002, and to some extent in 1995. Finally, the factor share of labor in urban areas always exceeded that in rural areas, which is inconsistent with the near equality of rural and urban wages observed in 1981 and 1995. All these tendencies hold true even if newly industrializing Kyongsangpuk Do is reclassified with the urban areas. These results imply that rural industrialization in South Korea depended on the employment of high-wage workers and the adoption of labor-saving production methods. This results in low levels of nonfarm labor absorption, as reflected in the much lower labor share of rural manufacturing income (Table 10.3). This can be explained by the fact that rural industrialization took place primarily in newly established large urban centers with clusters of enterprises producing similar and related products in formerly rural and less urbanized areas (Henderson, Lee, and Lee 2001). Such a development pattern is incompatible with the common perception of rural industrialization.

The urban bias occurred in South Korea because large-scale urban enterprises received subsidized loans and tax breaks for capital formation and agglomeration, which led to the adoption of capital-intensive technology. These preferential incentives, however, were rescinded for Korea's urban firms in the 1980s because of the failure of such policies to develop the economy (World Bank 1993a). Subsequently there was a reversal of technology/scale biases that sent them down the Taiwanese road.

Enterprise Size

The contrasting pattern of rural-urban wage rates, labor productivity, and factor shares between Taiwan and South Korea is reflected in the difference in the size of enterprises between rural and urban areas. Table 10.4 compares the average size of establishments, in terms of the number of workers, in rural and urban areas between the two countries over time. In Taiwan, the average size of establishments has been very small, ranging from 20 to 37 workers in urban areas and from 14 to 20 workers in rural areas. Furthermore, the size of establishments has declined over time in Taiwan. The observations that rural enterprises operated small-scale factories and used less mechanized, labor-using production methods are consistent with the lower wage and labor productivity in rural areas. The number of manufacturing establishments in both urban and rural areas of Taiwan approximately doubled from 1976 to 1991. Because the majority of enterprises in Taiwan operate one factory, the number of enterprises would have almost doubled, indicating that there had been active entry of new enterprises. Entry was easy, partly because capital requirements were very small owing to the small size of enterprises and the adoption of labor-using technologies. The proportion of tiny enterprises with fewer than 10 and fewer than 5 workers accounted for 67 percent and 44 percent or enterprises, respectively, in 1991.

The size of enterprises in South Korea differed substantially. While the average size in rural areas was less than half that of their urban counterparts and similar to that in Taiwan in 1971, the former surpassed the latter in 1995 and 2002. This is consistent with the observation that in South Korea industrialization accompanied the establishment of modern industrialized centers in formerly rural and less urbanized areas. Thus the establishment of new industries outside of traditional urban areas did not aim at using the cheap labor force available in rural areas, which may explain why rural industrialization in South Korea was less successful than in Taiwan.

It is also important to point out that in South Korea the average size of establishments significantly increased from 1971 to 1981 but declined signifi-

TABLE 10.4 Changes in average size of establishments in rural and urban areas of Taiwan and South Korea, 1976–2002

	1976/71[a]	1981	1991/95[a]	1996/2002[a]
Taiwan				
Average in urban areas	36.6	31.8	22.1	19.3
Rural areas				
Average	20.1	18.1	16.6	14.1
Food and related products	8.3	9.5	12.6	13.3
Wood and related products	12.7	10.8	12.8	10.2
Textiles	55.7	37.2	23.8	20.8
Apparel	53.9	48.6	45.0	20.1
Paper	15.0	12.3	9.0	9.1
Chemicals	32.4	28.1	19.8	16.1
Nonmetals	18.3	22.1	22.0	17.3
Basic metals	11.4	8.9	10.0	9.1
Machinery	29.3	19.2	21.4	19.3
South Korea				
Average in urban areas	50.9	67.8	28.8	21.5
Rural areas				
Average	22.5	51.5	34.2	32.3
Food and related products	16.5	27.3	28.0	22.0
Wood and related products	12.0	29.9	18.1	10.6
Textiles and apparel	30.3	72.5	33.9	24.0
Paper	18.0	26.6	—	23.3
Chemicals	27.3	52.5	42.3	39.1
Nonmetals	14.8	30.5	30.5	24.6
Basic metals	47.3	131.3	78.8	76.0
Machinery	24.9	71.6	36.3	37.5

SOURCES: The data on Taiwan are from the Industry and Commercial Census of Taiwan and Fukien Area, and those for South Korea are from the Report on Mining and Manufacturing Survey.

NOTE: A dash indicates that data are not available.

[a]Available census data permit these computations for 1976, 1981, 1991, and 2001 for Taiwan and for 1971, 1981, 1995, and 2002 for South Korea.

cantly from 1981 to 1995. The former period corresponds to the period of heavy industrialization pursued by the Korean government by means of supporting large conglomerates, whereas the latter period includes the period of adjustment of the industrial structure in favor of SMEs.[5] Levy (1991) points out that the increased incidence of subcontracting associated with the active participation of

---

5. Abe and Kawakami (1997), Hattori and Sato (1997), Okuda (1997).

traders contributed to the reduction in the size of enterprises in South Korea. Nugent (1996) observes that the declining production share of large enterprises in South Korea was attributable, among other things, to the increased access of SMEs to financial markets and to the relative decline in the activities of the large general trading companies that had been created to assist large conglomerates (Nugent and Nabli 1992).

Because conglomerates dominated the South Korean economy, changes in the number of establishments may not correspond to the number of enterprises. Nonetheless, it is instructive to learn that the number of establishments in rural areas increased from 12,000 in 1971 to 26,000 in 1991. As in Taiwan, the entry barriers would not have been very high in South Korea in recent years. In fact, after the economic crisis began in late 1997, small-scale business ventures mushroomed in South Korea, favored by the government's attempt to demolish or restructure the large conglomerates.

The direct comparison of establishment sizes between Taiwan and South Korea is fraught with difficulty because the Taiwanese data cover the universe of industrial establishments, whereas the Korean data cover only those establishments employing more than four workers. According to Otsuka (1998), if we exclude small enterprises employing fewer than five workers, the average number of workers in the rural manufacturing industry in Taiwan in 1991, for which data by size class are available, changes from 16.6 to 27.6. The size of 27.6 workers was still smaller than the 34.2 workers employed in rural South Korea in 1995 (and the 43.8 in 1991). This difference will help explain the much smaller factor share of labor in South Korea than in Taiwan (Table 10.3).

Key Influences

Policy Differences

Policy played a role in shaping the results we have reported in both Taiwan and South Korea. On the one hand, it is clear that the size of enterprises is significantly influenced by industrial policies. According to the World Bank studies summarized by Meyanathan (1995), large manufacturing enterprises also dominate in Malaysia, Thailand, and Indonesia, primarily because of the active governmental support for large enterprises. Such a policy bias seems to increase the advantage of vertically integrated large-scale operations and at the same time increase the entry barriers for rural enterprises. Financial policies in favor of large enterprises were often important for urban-based industrialization. On the other hand, whether the export promotion policies (common to both countries) led to relocation of industries toward outer regions, as predicted by Krugman and Elizondo (1996), is difficult to confirm.

Both countries adopted export-led growth, even though the export share has been higher in Taiwan than in South Korea (World Bank 1993a). According to Abe and Kawakami (1997), the export share of SMEs in Taiwan, which tended to be located in rural areas, was consistently higher than the share of large enterprises, which tended to be located in urban areas. This is consistent with the Krugman-Elizondo hypothesis. But in South Korea, urban-based large enterprises have been major exporters.

It is not clear to what extent the export orientation of Taiwanese and South Korean industrialization has affected the nature of rural industrialization per se. Krugman and Elizondo (1996) argue that enterprises supplying their products to domestic markets tend to be located in urban areas because the proximity to markets confers informational and marketing cost advantages. Thus urban-based industrialization tends to occur under an import substitution policy. In contrast, the locational advantages of major cities diminish if products are exported to foreign markets, which tends to facilitate rural industrialization. To what extent such tendencies are observed in Taiwan and South Korea is an important unresolved question.

Rural Infrastructure

The amount and configuration of rural infrastructure abetted the structural trends previously noted in Taiwan and South Korea. In Taiwan, urban centers are dispersed and infrastructure such as roads is evenly distributed, allowing industry to develop in the smaller towns (Ho 1986b). By contrast, in South Korea, industrial activity is in general concentrated in Seoul and Pusan and in large intermediate cities in the areas surrounding those two poles, while infrastructure is concentrated around urban centers and rural roads are inadequate. In the 1960s and the 1970s, the Taiwanese government established industrial estates primarily in rural areas away from major cities by investing in basic infrastructure such as roads, electricity, and telecommunication systems, whereas the Korean government allocated major public funds for the development of industries in large cities (Ho 1982).

Relational Subcontracting

Not only social infrastructure but also "social capital" made significant contributions to rural industrialization in East Asia. The majority of rural entrepreneurs in East Asia, who are enterprise managers and local traders, have been born and grown up in the locality where they operate their businesses, and they generally have work experience either in urban enterprises, with which subcontracting arrangements are made, or in other rural enterprises with which other layers of subcontracts are often made (Otsuka 1998). They have enduring personal relations with locally recruited workers and have established reputations as reliable partners among urban-based entrepreneurs and traders, who offer subcontracts to them.

Hayami (1998a) argues that the system of "relational contracting," which denotes the long-term, continuous contract relations that are enforced and maintained by personal ties, mutual trust, and community obligations, can be a dominant production organization over the vertically integrated large enterprise systems. This relational contracting embraces the operation of small rural enterprises connected by a web of interenterprise cooperation and coordination. Traders and trading houses also assisted the operation of small-scale rural enterprises not only historically in Japan (Hayami et al. 1991), but also contemporaneously in Taiwan (Levy 1991; Sonobe, Kawakami, and Otsuka 2003). If firm size is determined at the point at which the marginal cost of expanding intraenterprise transaction is equated with the marginal cost of increasing market transactions, as argued by Coase (1937), the system of rural-based SMEs is viable only if the transaction costs of interenterprise cooperation are comparatively small. Recent empirical work by Sonobe and Otsuka (2006a) strongly supports this contention. It indicates that industrial clusters of SMEs producing related products, which are common in Taiwan and emerging in China, are formed to reduce transaction costs associated with the division and specialization of labor. The East Asian model of rural industrialization thus attests to the importance of low costs of interenterprise transactions in stimulating the development of small-scale enterprises in rural areas (Sonobe and Otsuka 2006a).

In both Taiwan and South Korea, rural industrialization has shifted rapidly toward subcontracting arrangements between urban large-scale firms and rural SMEs, mainly in metal and textile products. Well-reported examples include putting-out contracts in the garment and textile industries in Japan, the Philippines, Taiwan, and Thailand,[6] as well as the subcontracting of parts and intermediate products in Japan, South Korea, and Taiwan.[7] In all likelihood, the venture businesses currently being developed in South Korea will establish new networks of interenterprise transactions.

These arrangements appear to have been a boon to SMEs in these countries because of the difficulties they would otherwise face in accessing modern technology and production methods; the lack of access to markets and market information, such as designs most demanded by markets; and the lack of capital. Many authors therefore advocate the subcontracting of rural enterprises with urban enterprises and trading houses that possess better knowledge of marketing and modern technology and have better access to financial markets (e.g., Schmitz 1982; Lanjouw and Lanjouw 1995). Furthermore, as was suggested in a classic article by Stigler (1951), subcontracting may promote the division of labor or the specialization of production processes among enterprises so as to reduce the overall production costs (Watanabe 1971; Mead 1984; Sonobe and Otsuka 1999). Specialization makes it possible to operate small-scale factories

---

6. Levy (1991), Itoh and Tanimoto (1998), Kikuchi (1998), Lee and Suh (1998), Ohno and Jirapatpimol (1998), Yamamura, Sonobe and Otsuka (2003).

7. Watanabe (1971), Asanuma (1985), Levy and Kuo (1991).

in rural areas, which reduces the initial capital requirements and, hence, the entry barriers (Watanabe 1970; Mead 1984; Levy 1991). Moreover, if parent companies provide materials under putting-out contracts, working capital for subcontracting enterprises can be saved. Further, materials provided by the urban principal under a putting-out contract usually embody designs demanded by markets, and the contract itself ensures the procurement of materials and the sale of final products. Thus subcontracting can potentially overcome constraints imposed on the development of rural industries. It is essential to undertake a rigorous quantitative assessment of how important subcontracting is for rural industrialization and how the moral hazards and adverse selection that potentially arise under subcontracts can be overcome.

In the case of Taiwan, SMEs acquired new technology and marketing information from abroad through joint ventures and purchase orders from Japanese and American enterprises (Hattori and Sato 1997). In the 1960s, the government promoted direct investment, which attracted those foreign enterprises engaged in labor-using production. Yet the purchase order played a far more important role than direct investment in the development of SME sectors, where the capacity to flexibly and quickly produce a variety of products in small quantities attracted foreign buyers (Sato 1997). A good example is the development of the shoe industry, which depended on the network of subcontracting among SMEs (Levy 1991). There are also cases in which the reverse engineering helped develop industry without much direct contact with foreign enterprises, such as in the machine tool industry (Amsden 1977; Sonobe, Kawakami, and Otsuka 2003). In the case of Taiwan, imports were not severely restricted to protect domestic production, and the joint ventures gradually withdrew in the 1970s and 1980s with the rise in real wages. In contrast, direct investments were strictly controlled in South Korea, and licensing with enterprises in advanced countries has been the major means to introduce modern technologies since the 1970s. Imports were restricted to protect the "infant" industries, and it took a decade or longer for those enterprises among the heavy industries that were established in the 1970s, such as Dynamic Random Access Memory, to export their products to foreign markets (Hattori and Sato 1997). It seems that by taking advantage of large-scale operations, the conglomerates in South Korea have established comparative advantages in those industries subject to scale economies, including high-tech industries that require large investments in research and development.

Indeed rural industries are unlikely to grow rapidly without cooperation with urban enterprises because of their lack of technological knowledge and market information. They can grow faster if they adopt a subcontracting system, because the required materials, which embody designs for highly demanded products, are often provided on credit. In addition, in order to promote industrialization, training managers not only in improved technology but also in marketing and the management of enterprises is essential, for technological, marketing, and managerial knowledge and information are scanty in less developed regions (Sonobe and Otsuka 2006a). Because of information spillovers, investment in new knowledge by individual enterprise managers typically falls short of the social optimum. Therefore, government support for rural industrialization can play a significant role.

Implications

Because of the huge differences in the stages of economic development between East Asia and other less developed regions, such as South Asia and Sub-Saharan Africa, there are enormous differences in the extent and the nature of rural industrialization across major regions (Chapter 1). Nonetheless, there are similarities as well. Rapid entry of small rural enterprises seems to characterize many locations. The study of small enterprises in Southern and Eastern Africa, described in Chapter 5, points out that more than three-quarters of small enterprises that employed 50 or fewer workers were located in rural areas and that these enterprises did not grow in size but grew in number through new entry (see also Mead 1994a). These features are also seen in East Asia, particularly Taiwan, where the number of new small entrants increased with progress in rural industrialization.

The importance of agroprocessing and the early demise of household-based Z-goods are likewise recurring themes. While basketmaking, matmaking, spinning, weaving, potterymaking, and woodcarving are declining industries across much of rural Africa, food processing has grown most rapidly of all manufacturing industries there (Haggblade et al. 1989). Because of the lack of rural industries supplying agricultural inputs in rural areas of Africa, "backward linkage appears far smaller than the forward processing linkages from agriculture" (Haggblade et al. 1989). A similar declining trend in Z-good production, together with increases in food processing in rural areas, has also been observed in East Asia in its early stage of development.

The first major lesson to be learned from the experience of East Asia is that rural industrialization in Stage 1 development is characterized by the development of food processing industries through the forward linkage effects from agriculture. The development of commercial agriculture seems essential at this stage. In order to sustain and boost the development of rural industries, however, modern technologies, market information, and organizational capacity must be transferred from urban to rural areas, judging from the experience of East Asia.

The second lesson, therefore, is that cooperation between rural and urban enterprises is instrumental in moving rural industrialization to Stage 2. In East Asia, vertical subcontracting systems have developed through which modern urban and export industries support rural manufacturers by supplying inputs, technical know-how, and links to external markets. High population density and long-established personal and communal relations play critical roles in the development of these contractual relations between manufacturing enterprises, as well as in other contractual settings such as land tenancy and marketing contracts in East Asia (Hayami and Kawagoe 1993; Hayami and Otsuka 1993). Personal and community ties for the enforcement of contracts seem to be common organizational features in East Asia, reducing the transactions costs needed to link layers of rural and urban enterprises together and permitting significant growth of modern rural industries (Sonobe and Otsuka 2006b).

In other regions of the developing world, vertical supply chains and coordinating mechanisms will likewise assume increasing importance for the survival and growth of rural nonfarm activities. This will be particularly true in the rapidly changing agroindustrial supply chains described in Chapter 9.

PART III

Policies and Programs for Promoting the Rural Nonfarm Economy

11 The Policy and Institutional Environment Affecting the Rural Nonfarm Economy

RAISUDDIN AHMED, STEVEN HAGGBLADE,
PETER B. R. HAZELL, RICHARD L. MEYER,
AND THOMAS REARDON

Prevailing policies and institutions condition development of the rural nonfarm economy (RNFE) in a variety of important ways. In most instances, growth of the RNFE is largely self-directed, driven primarily by competitive forces and growth in demand for its outputs rather than by any deliberate public actions. In other cases, tight controls and protection have coddled favored rural enterprise groups, notably certain categories of rural manufacturing, during the early stages of industrial development (see Chapter 13).

This chapter reviews key elements of the policy and institutional environment and how they have affected development of the RNFE. Subsequent discussion, in this and later chapters, examines the kinds of policies and institutional models that are most effective in stimulating poverty-alleviating growth in the RNFE.

Who Shapes the Environment, and How?

Alongside the multitude of small and medium-sized firms that operate in the rural nonfarm economy, a group of key larger actors makes decisions and takes actions that largely shape the environment and opportunities available in the RNFE. Three particularly influential groups converge in the RNFE, each playing a different but crucial role affecting the structure and dynamics of opportunity for smaller players operating there.

Large Private Firms

Large modern corporations make decisions and take actions that powerfully shape opportunities in the RNFE throughout much of the developing world. More frequently than governments, in many instances, these private firms initiate sweeping changes in the RNFE. In the wake of worldwide trends toward economic liberalization from the 1990s onward, these agents of change have swept ever more powerfully across the RNFEs of the developing world.

Rural areas have attracted several main categories of large firms. Agribusiness firms locate processing plants and collection facilities in rural areas to reduce spoilage and transport costs in weight-reducing processing activities and to take advantage of lower wage rates. Tourism promoters export rural services by developing facilities in unsettled regions, along pristine beaches, in interesting ecological niches, or in favorable climates. Resource extraction —of timber or minerals—likewise requires location in rural areas where raw materials are found. More recently, the food retailers (supermarkets, fast food chains, and minimarket chains) that have grown rapidly in large cities of the developing world, starting in the early to mid-1990s, have begun spreading to intermediate cities and larger rural towns across East Asia, Latin America, Southeast Asia, and, more recently, Africa (see Chapter 9). As they spread, many of these retailers develop local contracting arrangements for the supply of perishable and processed agricultural products. Together, these activities— agriculture and the agroprocessing it supports, tourism, extractive industries, and food retailing—provide the economic scaffolding on which much of the supporting RNFE is built. Decisions by large players on where to establish operations largely govern market prospects for ancillary rural service and commercial activities.

In some situations and supply chains, large firms assume what have traditionally been considered public roles. They provide marketing infrastructure and credit and set industry grades and standards (see Chapter 9). Under export subcontracting systems, they may even implicitly set the exchange rate facing rural nonfarm suppliers.

In some instances, the actions of large firms benefit specific categories of smaller rural nonfarm enterprises. They supply key inputs, improved technology, or market outputs for smaller producers (Table 15.1). Urban ceramics plants supply high-quality ceramic liners to village stove producers in rural Kenya (Jeans, Hyman, and O'Donnell 1991). A network of yarn traders in Northeast Thailand links newly specialized household yarn producers with large mills that serve the large and growing export market (Figure 15.2). The tourism industry, from Cancun to Goa and throughout the developing world, generates service sector jobs as well as markets for agricultural products and the marketing services necessary to deliver them to rural hotels.

In addition to marketing both inputs and outputs, some large firms even offer direct assistance to their smaller client firms. For many years Unilever South Africa ran management assistance courses for the many small retailers who distributed its products (Rodolo 1972). It recognized that well-managed, prosperous small vendors would prove more valuable business partners, so it invested in extension support for small firms.

Yet in other cases, large firms threaten to obliterate entire armies of smaller-scale competitors. The recent entry of large dairies and modern chain retailers has decimated smallholder dairying in parts of Chile, Argentina, and Brazil, where thousands of small dairy operations have closed down over the past decade.[1] Aggressive expansion of factory-brewed sorghum beer during the 1970s and early 1980s threatened the livelihood of over 50,000 home brewers in Botswana (Haggblade 1992). The introduction of mechanized rice mills in Indonesia during the 1980s likewise threatened to put tens of thousands of village women out of business as hand pounders of rice (Timmer 1972).

Changes in market structure induced by large firms frequently require adjustment by small firms if they are to survive in rapidly changing rural nonfarm marketing chains, where some supply channels submerge as newly dominant channels surge. Change arrives swiftly, and small firms must be nimble to effect necessary adjustments. When large food retailers enter regional markets, for example, smallholder farmers and rural processors frequently face difficulties in meeting required volume, consistency, and food safety standards (see Chapter 9). The astonishing power and speed of these moves raise equity concerns and make it increasingly necessary for both small firms and intervention agencies to understand, anticipate, and accommodate changes introduced by these dominant large firms. Recent evidence from the field suggests that today rapidly changing market institutions dominated by large agribusinesses, supermarkets, and export firms represent one of the most powerful forces shaping the business environment and opportunities for that segment of the rural poor with the capacity and resources to respond (see Chapters 9 and 15). For this reason, both equity and growth increasingly demand tools for understanding the structure and dynamics of these rapidly changing supply chains. A growing number of agencies has begun to specialize in working with small firms and small farms on finding ways to facilitate commercial linkages that will enable small rural enterprises to partner with large, often multinational, firms so that the poor may participate more broadly in growing segments of the RNFE.[2]

Governments

Governments powerfully condition opportunities and constraints in the RNFE, though they often do so unintentionally and by default.[3] Many times, national economic policies intended to influence the national economy as a whole generate unintended impacts on individual segments of the RNFE. Less frequently, governments enunciate policies explicitly aimed at influencing the RNFE.

UNINTENDED POLICY CONSEQUENCES. Policies such as exchange rate regulations, tariffs, and licensing and fiscal statutes typically emerge from a set of complex and ongoing negotiations between government, large domestic urban businesses, and foreign interests. The small and the rural nonfarm enterprises

---

1. Gutman (1999), Jank, Farina, and Galan (1999), Dirven (2001).
2. Mead (1994b), LaFleur (2000), ACDI/VOCA (2001), ECI (2001a,b), Hatch (2001), Magistro et al. (2004), Vorley (2004).
3. See Snodgrass and Biggs (1996) for a good discussion of unintentional policy effects.

have little voice in these discussions, most of which proceed with little, if any, thought about their impacts on the RNFE (Liedholm and Mead 1986; Snodgrass and Biggs 1996). In rural areas, agricultural issues rather than the largely invisible RNFE dominate policy discussions. Agricultural research, extension, and infrastructure investment programs, which influence the rate of change in agriculture, simultaneously influence opportunities for agriculturally linked rural nonfarm enterprises (see Chapter 7). Thus, in most situations, the policy environment in which rural nonfarm firms operate emerges by default, out of concerns about other segments of the national economy. As a result, these policies generate unintended impacts on the RNFE, sometimes opening up opportunities and in other instances destroying whole industries.

Macro policies, instituted for a variety of reasons that typically have little to do with the RNFE, affect these firms indirectly via the prices of inputs and outputs that they use. In practice, two common distortions have historically prevailed in many market economies of the developing world. First was a long wave of policies aimed at taxing agriculture in order to transfer resources into industrial investments (see Chapter 2). By penalizing farmers, these policies likewise depressed the markets for rural nonfarm goods and services. For this reason, virtually every major review of rural nonfarm activity has pointed first to the importance of a pro-agricultural policy environment as a fundamental prerequisite for rural nonfarm growth.[4]

Second, a common tendency to subsidize capital and tax labor in large urban firms has tended to discourage labor use in urban areas and conversely to favor labor intensity and limited equipment use among smaller and often rural firms. Interest rate subsidies, foreign exchange rationing, and strong biases in credit allocation in favor of large urban firms have permeated much of the developing world, including South Korea, the Philippines, Brazil, and elsewhere.[5] Similarly, labor laws and minimum wage regulations faced by large urban firms, but largely unenforced in rural areas, induce an economically excessive capital intensity in large and urban firms. Efforts to measure the impact of these distortions suggest that capital costs range from 30 to 65 percent lower in large urban enterprises, while labor costs rise by 20 to 25 percent (Haggblade, Liedholm, and Mead 1986; Snodgrass and Biggs 1996). These disparities suggest that policy environments typically favor labor use and discourage productivity-enhancing investment in machinery and equipment.

A wave of liberalization programs emerging from the structural adjustment efforts of the 1980s and 1990s has also had powerful impacts on the RNFE. Studies suggest that liberalized trade and exchange rate policies generally hurt

---

4. See Anderson and Leiserson (1978), Chuta and Liedholm (1979), Liedholm and Mead (1986), Chadha (1993), Tomich, Kilby, and Johnston (1995), Bhatt (1998), and Lanjouw and Lanjouw (2001).

5. See Haggblade, Liedholm, and Mead (1986), Ho (1986a), and Snodgrass and Biggs (1996).

rural firms that compete with imported goods while helping enterprises that serve export markets or use imported equipment and inputs. Sri Lanka's trade liberalization of the late 1970s seriously dampened activity in rural hand-looming and potterymaking, while rice milling and construction, which use imported equipment and materials, flourished (Osmani 1987). Similarly, liberalization of imported and synthetic fibers in El Salvador placed serious pressure on rural processors of henequen fibers for the manufacture of burlap sacks (Dichter 1986). Because of their low cost and sweeping impact, policies—intentionally or not—often prove to be the most powerful levers by which governments influence incentives in the RNFE.

EXPLICIT POLICY INTERVENTION. In some situations, governments explicitly aim to influence opportunities in the RNFE. They provide roads, power, water, and telecommunications in rural areas and rural towns, some targeted specifically to rural nonfarm firms through the creation of rural industrial estates. Some support small business assistance programs providing credit, input subsidies, and training programs (see Chapter 12). Others intervene in labor and product markets, thereby powerfully shaping opportunities in the RNFE.

In India, the liberalized industrial policy of 1991 ended four decades of heavy protection for specific village industries, exposing them to keen competition and triggering a massive restructuring of rural manufacturing. Similarly, post-war China's collectivized rural nonfarm activity has given way to explicit encouragement of individual private firms and a perceptible spurt in primarily privately owned town and village enterprises. The striking policy reorientation in both China and India clearly demonstrates the potentially overwhelming influence of government policy on rural nonfarm activity (see Chapter 13). Elsewhere in East Asia—in Japan, Taiwan, and South Korea—strong government controls on credit allocation clearly influenced the structure of activity in urban and rural areas (Amsden 1991). The high priority given to public investment in rural infrastructure in both Japan and Taiwan likewise proved a strong stimulus to rural nonfarm activities. In several industries, notably in textiles, direct government investment in model factories played an important role (Saith 1987).

In less directive policy environments elsewhere, governments have concentrated primarily on the creation of physical and social infrastructure and on providing overall economic incentives to nonfarm firms. During the 1950s and 1960s, these incentives favored primarily urban industrialization in Latin America, Asia, and Africa (see Chapter 2). Then in the early 1970s, often with encouragement and financing from Western donors, governments shifted a larger share of their expenditures to the support of rural development. The resulting construction of roads and development of rural health and education facilities laid a foundation for the expansion and modernization of the RNFE.

PUBLIC INVESTMENT IN PHYSICAL INFRASTRUCTURE. The voluminous literature on the effect of infrastructure investment suggests that its most significant impact on the RNFE may come indirectly via its influence on agriculture.

A range of cross-country studies has explored these relationships. Antle's (1983) early cross-section study of 47 developing and 19 developed countries measured the impact of an aggregated infrastructural composite (the gross domestic product of transportation and communications per square kilometer of land area) on agricultural output, finding that a 10 percent increase in infrastructural expenditures resulted in a 4 percent increase in agricultural production. A later study by Binswanger, Khandker, and Rosenzweig (1989), which pooled cross-section and time-series data for 58 countries over 10 years (1969–78), found that a 10 percent increase in road density increased agricultural production by 4 percent, while a 10 percent increase in irrigation facilities generated a 9 percent boost in farm output. Project evaluations from a multitude of specific infrastructural investment projects support these findings. A summary of the impact of World Bank–financed infrastructure investments during the 1980s found returns of 29 percent from highways, 19 percent from telecommunications, 13 percent from irrigation and drainage, and 11 percent from electrification (World Bank 1994).

A series of country case studies offers additional evidence on the impact of physical infrastructure on rural economies. Several have considered the implications for agriculture,[6] while some have directly examined the impact on rural nonfarm activity as well.[7] As a group, the agricultural studies document significant increases in both input use and farm output as a result of increases in access to rural infrastructure. They find that a 10 percent increase in rural road density increases agricultural output by 1 to 7 percent depending on the country, region, and time period.[8] Primary education matters as well, with a 10 percent increase leading to a corresponding 5 to 8 percent boost in agricultural output.[9] One study from India has found that a 10 percent increase in the density of rural banks and electrification contributes 3 percent and 2 percent, respectively, to agricultural growth (Binswanger, Khandker, and Rosenzweig 1989).

Infrastructural impact on rural nonfarm activity also emerges as significant. Telecommunications, credit, and electricity all contribute to increased rural nonfarm activity, as measured by either employment or income.[10] Intriguingly,

---

6. Barnes and Binswanger (1986), Evenson (1986), Binswanger et al. (1987), Binswanger, Khandker, and Rosenzweig (1989), Ahmed and Donovan (1997), Fan, Hazell, and Thorat (1999), Fan, Zhang, and Zhang (2002).

7. Kamal (1983), Wanmali (1985), Fabella (1987), Haggblade and Hazell (1989), Khandker and Binswanger (1989), Ahmed and Hossain (1990), Hossain (1997), Fan, Hazell, and Thorat (1999), Fan, Zhang, and Zhang (2002).

8. Barnes and Binswanger (1986), Evenson (1986), Binswanger, Khandker, and Rosenzweig (1989), Fan, Hazell, and Thorat (1999), Fan, Zhang, and Zhang (2002).

9. Binswanger, Khandker, and Rosenzweig (1989), Fan, Hazell, and Thorat (1999), Fan, Zhang, and Zhang (2002).

10. See Kamal (1983), Barnes and Binswanger (1986), Khandker and Binswanger (1989), and Lanjouw (2001).

for the often-neglected rural service sector, Kamal (1983) finds that rural services enjoyed over half of the nonfarm benefits from telephone expansion in rural Egypt. Two recent studies from China and India suggest that a 10 percent increase in rural education and literacy rates will increase nonfarm output and employment shares by 5 to 6 percent, while a 10 percent increase in rural road density boosts nonfarm output and employment shares by about 2 percent (Fan, Hazell, and Thorat 1999; Fan, Zhang, and Zhang 2002). An array of regression studies confirms that road improvements and decreased distance to markets increase rural nonfarm participation and earnings.[11] Using a composite index of infrastructural development for rural Bangladesh, Ahmed and Hossain (1990) find a 21 percent increase in rural nonfarm income in infrastructurally more advanced villages. Moreover, wage rates rise by 12 percent as labor demand increases, particularly in nonfarm activity.

The importance of rural roads, electricity, and telecommunications in fostering rural nonfarm growth consistently emerges from anecdotal evidence as well. East Asian comparisons among Japan, Taiwan, and South Korea inevitably highlight the importance of rural infrastructure in the rapid growth of rural industries in Japan and Taiwan.[12] Studies done elsewhere highlight the importance of roads (Fabella 1987; Ranis 1989) and of electricity and telecommunications (Oshima 1986b; Lanjouw 1999) in the growth of specific rural industries. Other studies underscore the importance of roads in shifting the composition of rural nonfarm activity. While activities that depend on export markets or imported inputs benefit from rural road construction, those that compete with urban manufactures often suffer. Thus the frequently observed demise of the village tortilla, basket, and pot makers in the face of improved rural road access (Ancey 1974; Rello 1996).

PUBLIC INVESTMENT IN EDUCATION. The weight of available evidence suggests that basic education generally increases the productivity and wages of rural nonfarm workers.[13] Higher education likewise proves helpful in the start-up of modern subcontracting businesses as well as in adjusting to the new technologies and contracting arrangements required in modern agroindustrial supply chains.[14] Prospects for growth appear to expand significantly for entrepreneurs with secondary education and beyond, and education seems to help

---

11. Barrett et al. (2001), Block and Webb (2001), Canagarajah et al. (2001), Smith et al. (2001).

12. Saith (1987), Ranis and Stewart (1993), Kawagoe (1998), Lane (1998), Lee and Suh (1998).

13. Bigsten (1984), Collier and Lal (1986), Ho (1986b), Vijverberg (1988), Moock, Musgrove, and Stelcner (1990), Islam (1997), Abdulai and Delgado (1998), Joliffe (1998), Estudillo and Otsuka (1999), Lanjouw (1999), Trung (2000), Ruben and Van Den Berg (2001), Fan, Zhang, and Zhang (2002), Lanjouw and Shariff (2004).

14. See Bigsten (1984), Collier and Lal (1986), Fabella (1987), Steel and Webster (1991), Francis and Hoddinott (1993), Birks et al. (1994), Simler (1994b), Parker, Riopelle, and Steel (1995), Jollife (1998), and Ohno and Kikuchi (1998).

small firms adjust to new opportunities and new dangers.[15] Yet the impact almost certainly varies by activity and operating environment.[16] It is generally larger in urban areas and among larger firms. A major review of studies estimating the returns to education suggests social rates of return of about 25 percent for primary schooling and about 15 percent for secondary schooling, with some regional variations across the developing world (Psacharopoulos 1985). Like investments in basic physical infrastructure, public investments in rural education appear to increase the productivity and incomes of the rural poor who work in nonfarm activities.

Private Nonprofits

A plethora of private, civil society, and public agencies promote rural nonfarm activity on equity and environmental grounds, mostly on a not-for-profit basis. These agencies see large numbers of poor households engaged in small businesses that provide an important supplement to their meager household earnings. They see the need for increased rural nonfarm earnings in areas where widespread landlessness and diminishing farm sizes limit farming for large segments of the rural population. They note that low capital requirements for labor-intensive rural nonfarm activities ensure easy access to these activities by poor households.[17]

Equity-oriented groups—such as nongovernmental organizations, religious groups, donors, and selected government departments—implement an array of direct interventions on behalf of the poor (see Chapter 12). In recent decades, these efforts have been dominated by the provision of financial services.[18]

INVESTING IN RURAL FINANCIAL INSTITUTIONS. A variety of institutional structures has emerged to deliver savings and credit services to the rural and urban poor.[19] Some, like the Unit Desa, or Village Bank, of Bank Rakyat in Indonesia (BRI-UD), offer market-oriented savings and lending services to individuals through their dense network of rural commercial bank branches. Others, such as several rural credit programs in Bangladesh, have grown to serve millions of poor people by offering loans through joint liability groups. In contrast to the branch banking model, some organizations focus on the establishment of small independent member-owned village banks or credit unions.

Outreach has proven impressive, particularly in rural Asia, where high population densities permit large-scale, low-cost administrative systems serving vast populations. In the year 2000, Indonesia's BRI-UD had $800 million

---

15. Parker (1995), Parker, Riopelle, and Steel (1995), McPherson (1996), Daniels and Mead (1998).

16. Fabella (1987), Vijverberg (1988), Moock, Musgrove, and Stelcner (1990).

17. The voluminous record on credit impact at the household level is examined in Chapter 12. In general, evaluations report some increase in income for the majority of assisted households and firms, with the greatest impact on those who are less poor. See Chapter 12 for details.

18. See, for example, Otero and Rhyne (1994), Morduch (1999a), and Daley-Harris (2005).

19. Lapenu and Zeller (2001), Meyer (2002), Hirschland (2005), Nagarajan and Meyer (2005).

in loans outstanding to 2.7 million rural borrowers, and it reported over 25 million savers. Bangladesh's multitude of large-scale rural credit programs serves about 40 percent of the households in the country, with $390 million in loans outstanding. Thailand's Bank for Agriculture and Agricultural Cooperatives reaches over 4 million clients, lending to about three-fourths of farm households each year (Meyer 2002). In Latin America and Africa, however, rural outreach has proven far more difficult because of lower population densities and higher contact and administrative costs. Consequently, credit programs in those regions have remained concentrated in high-density urban settings, while rural outreach has proven more modest.

Increasingly, major players in poverty lending have focused on attaining financial sustainability as well. The largest of these, Indonesia's BRI-UD, became financially self-sufficient in 1989 after five years of government and donor subsidies and remains highly profitable today (Robinson 2002). Yet other star credit programs, such as that of Bangladesh's Grameen Bank, remained dependent on regular subsidy inflows for over 20 years.[20] Over 100 of the largest microfinance institutions (MFIs) now voluntarily provide their accounts for analysis, though numbers reporting vary from year to year. In 2001, 60 percent of the 148 reporting institutions required ongoing subsidies of about 10 percent of their full operating and financial costs (Meyer 2002). As of 2003, slightly under 50 percent of the 124 reporting MFIs required subsidies, although that proportion rose to over 60 percent among the 49 institutions that focused on poorer clients (Barres 2005). Of the many thousands that fail to report—including several hundred in Bangladesh alone—most continue to rely on ongoing subsidizes.

In spite of accounting and reporting improvements, performance data on microfinance institutions remain spotty. Worldwide, some microfinance specialists believe that only 1 percent of all microenterprise lending programs are financially self-sufficient and that only 5 percent ever will be (Morduch 1999a; Development Finance Forum 2004). Despite widespread ambitions to attain financial self-sustainability, most microfinance institutions continue to rely on regular inflows of government subsidies (Schreiner and Yaron 2001; Armendariz de Aghion and Morduch 2005). Like roads, education, infrastructure, and business development service programs, the credit programs rely on regular infusions of public funds.

Given that the inevitable start-up subsidies necessary to launch these financial institutions compete with other worthwhile public investments—in rural infrastructure, education, and agricultural research—efficient allocation of public resources requires a comparison of the benefits and costs of these alternative investments. Yet the cost of building rural credit institutions remains unknown, or at least unreported in most of the latest generation of impact

---

20. Boomgard and Angell (1994), Yaron, McDonald, and Piprek (1997), Morduch (1999b), Schreiner (2003).

studies.[21] A recent review of the economics of microfinance found "just two serious cost-benefit analyses of microfinance programs" (Armendariz de Aghion and Morduch 2005, 233). Indeed some proponents argue that because credit programs aim to create self-sustaining financial institutions, they should be exempted from the rigors of cost-benefit comparisons. If microfinance interventions succeed in building self-sustaining savings and credit institutions, they argue, there is no public cost, only public gain. The difficulty with this argument is that currently most microcredit institutions are not yet fully cost-covering, and many probably never will be. A recent study from Latin America summarizes the available evidence as follows: "Is public support for microcredit wasted or worthwhile? No one knows. . . . The question is whether microfinance is better than some other development project for the poor" (Navajas et al. 2000, 334). Given the paucity of evidence comparing benefits and costs of microfinance institutions (Schreiner and Yaron 2001; Armendariz de Aghion and Morduch 2005), the bottom line today is that we simply do not know how investment in rural financial institutions stacks up against other alternative uses of public funds.

The Case for Intervention

In an ideal world, government interventions would be justified on the basis of sound economic or social concerns. On efficiency grounds, governments play a potentially key role in ensuring an enabling business environment, supplying necessary public goods and correcting for market failures. On equity grounds, they often intervene to assist the poor in navigating difficult economic circumstances and transitions. Correcting for market failures, pollution, and other externalities may lead to intervention on environmental grounds.

Creating an Enabling Business Environment

POLICY.   The overall business environment in which nonfarm firms operate proves central to their competitive health and to their prospects for growth. Trade, tariff, and exchange rate policies all affect the prices of imported inputs used by rural nonfarm traders, services, and producers—inputs such as fuel, specialized machinery, and cloth. They likewise govern the prices of competitive imports from abroad. Rules on access to foreign exchange, repatriation of profits, and foreign direct investment influence incentives facing foreign investors. For this reason, the wave of economic liberalization washing over the developing world since the 1990s has unleashed a flood of foreign direct investment in agribusinesses, leading to an unprecedented concentration of export

---

21. See Townsend and Yaron (2001), Khandker (2003), and Schreiner (2003) for welcome exceptions to this rule.

and domestic food processing and marketing (see Chapter 9). The prices of factor inputs, credit, and labor govern the profitability of alternative production technologies, while transport and communication costs influence the spatial distribution of rural nonfarm activity (Chapter 8). The stability of prices and of the policy environment itself affects investment incentives and risk premiums. Agricultural policies likewise feature prominently in most discussions of policy incentives affecting rural nonfarm growth.[22]

Policy discussions have likewise focused on the legal and regulatory environment. Zoning and licensing laws, enforcement of fiscal legislation, and labor and social welfare regulations all influence business incentives. Many complain of zoning restrictions that hamper small and rural nonfarm enterprises.[23] Licensing and zoning laws often limit or regulate the operating locations available for specific activities.

INFRASTRUCTURE. Public infrastructure provides lubrication essential for the smooth functioning of the RNFE. Transport infrastructure, electricity, telecommunications, and banks enable the information, commodity, and financial flows essential for rural nonfarm activity.[24] Investments in rural education, health, and skills development likewise provide essential building blocks for prosperous, high-productivity rural jobs.

As nonfarm development becomes increasingly dependent on external markets, newer types of infrastructure and institutions become critical: port facilities, container shipping facilities, air shipment facilities, quality-certifying institutions, and testing laboratories. Growth in the RNFE requires a set of public goods that the private sector, left to itself, will typically not provide in sufficient quantity.

MARKET INSTITUTIONS. An evolving collection of rules, practices, and norms governs transactions among the large and small enterprises that populate the RNFE. Spot markets often prevail in open-air or communal marketplaces. Ongoing relationships build social capital among networks of rural nonfarm traders, assemblers, and processors, often cemented by reciprocal financial and product flows. Large firms serve as clients and customers of smaller entities. They develop systems of exchange involving implicit contracts, formal subcontracts, and supplier credits.

Grades and standards help regulate and moderate exchanges among large and small firms. Historically, public agencies have established grades and

---

22. Johnston and Kilby (1975), Anderson and Leiserson (1978), Chuta and Liedholm (1979), Chadha (1993), Tomich, Kilby, and Johnston (1995), Bhatt (1998), Lanjouw and Lanjouw (2001).

23. De Soto (1989), Mead (1994a), Morrisson et al. (1994), Mead and Morrisson (1996).

24. Fluitman (1983), Saunders, Warford, and Wellenius (1983), Binswanger, Khandker, and Rosenzweig (1989), Ahmed and Hossain (1990), Ahmed and Donovan (1992, 1997), World Bank (1994), ESCAP (2004).

standards as well as the certification systems that enforce them. In recent decades, however, the large supermarkets and exporters that increasingly dominate food and agribusiness marketing chains in the developing world have introduced private grading systems and procedures that have become de facto standards to which smaller players must adjust (see Chapter 9).

Equity Concerns

Because the RNFE plays a key role in the livelihood strategies of the rural poor, changes that adversely affect small rural nonfarm firms and employment require special vigilance by government. Market and trade liberalization, which unleash new forces of competition in rural economies, heighten these concerns. As large firms increasingly penetrate rural areas of the developing world, the legions of small firms exposed as a result to new competition and market concentration may face serious dislocation without some sort of temporary assistance in making the transition to newly ascendant market niches or alternative occupations. Governments across the developing world encounter opportunities and pressures to assist rural producers in navigating these rapid transitions.

Equity considerations also motivate most of the nonprofit agencies that currently intervene in the RNFE. They aim explicitly to open up opportunities for the rural poor to participate more fully in globalizing markets and to diversify their income earnings through nonfarm pursuits.

Environmental Concerns

Some types of rural nonfarm activity pose significant environmental problems in rural areas and rural towns. Tanneries, small-scale chemical plants, textile mills, and even food processing firms pollute waterways in many Asian countries. Some types of large manufacturing firms emit significant volumes of airborne pollutants.[25] For example, in China during the mid-1980s, township and village enterprises produced one-sixth of the water pollution and solid wastes in the country (Kirkby, Bradbury, and Shen 2000). In instances such as these, government has an important regulatory role to play, sometimes by simply imposing in rural settings the same environmental standards and enforcement already practiced in larger urban centers.

Over the past five decades, many governments have intervened inadvertently in the RNFE as policies and decisions made for other reasons have spilled over into the RNFE. Others have elected to intervene explicitly in the RNFE for both economic and political reasons. These interventions have taken a variety of institutional forms.

---

25. See Kirkby, Bradbury, and Shen (2000), Thanh (2002), and Tacoli and Satterthwaite (2003).

Alternative Institutional Models

Institutional Gaps

In spite of its size and economic importance, the RNFE frequently falls through gaping holes in the fabric of existing promotional and support institutions (Gordon and Craig 2001). Ministries of agriculture, which dominate the rural landscape, typically find themselves preoccupied with issues of farm production, research, and extension. Only rarely do they establish marketing divisions to monitor and support rural nonfarm assembly, marketing, and agroprocessing activities (Abbott 1986).

Ministries of commerce and industry concentrate most frequently on large urban centers and on international trade rather than on dispersed, itinerant rural firms. Even notable exceptions such as India's Village and Khadi Industries Commission and China's priority rural industries program concentrated exclusively on rural manufacturing to the exclusion of the often larger and faster-growing rural services and commerce (SGRNFS 1995). Consequently, large segments of the RNFE fall through the cracks.

Private services, even though they predominate in many rural nonfarm economies, find little support from their respective ministries of health, education, and transport. Instead these line ministries typically focus on the delivery of public rather than private services. Yet private schools, private clinics, private transport, and private media and entertainment frequently grow quickly in buoyant rural economies. Similarly, responsibility for siting, financing, and maintaining rural infrastructure remains splintered across line ministries of post, telecommunications, energy, and roads. Meanwhile, secondary roads and maintenance typically fall within the purview of local government authorities. The result is a highly fragmented institutional network from which to deliver public support for rural nonfarm activities.

Integrated Responses

To bridge the sectoral divide that fractures most institutional support networks, governments have responded in a variety of ways. Considerable institutional experimentation took place in the 1970s, during the first great wave of public interest in broad-based rural development.[26] In the course of that and subsequent experimentation, at least seven different institutional models emerged. Four are integrated models that recognize the mutual interdependence between agriculture, nonfarm activity, infrastructure, education, and social services, then try to find institutional models that can coordinate the delivery of these

---

26. See Ruttan (1975, 1984), Rondinelli and Evans (1983), Holdcroft (1984), and Donaldson (1993).

interconnected ingredients. The remaining three models take a sectoral approach to rural nonfarm promotion.

MINISTRIES OF RURAL DEVELOPMENT.   A common response during the 1970s, new ministries of rural development typically assumed a broad cross-sectoral mandate for the provision of agricultural support, social services, non-farm business assistance, and infrastructure. Yet these new omnibus ministries quickly encountered stiff resistance from the old line ministries of agriculture, commerce, roads, post, and telecommunications, which vigorously resisted the erosion of their prerogatives and the resources they controlled. In most settings, the resulting institutional skirmishes and infighting quickly dissipated the influence of the new ministries of rural development. So most governments have abandoned this model as unworkable. The short-lived ministries of rural development have mostly disappeared, their functions subsumed within the line ministries whose mandates they usurped (Holdcroft 1984).

HIGH-LEVEL, SUPRAMINISTERIAL COORDINATING UNITS.   An alternate model called for the establishment of a rural development czar or council, often located in the president's or prime minister's office, to coordinate the rural activities of the line ministries. One example of this approach comes from Botswana, where a rural development coordinator sat in the Ministry of Finance and Development Planning but reported directly to the vice president, who chaired a newly established Rural Development Council (RDC). Because of the high-level political commitment of the Botswana government, the effectiveness of the RDC, and the tight link between RDC priorities, rural development planning, and central government financial budgeting, this system ensured synchronized priorities and activities across central government ministries and their rural counterparts in the local and district governments. Consequently, the system yielded generally impressive results. The small size of the country, its highly professional and effective civil service, and its strong political commitment all contributed to the smooth functioning of this model. However, in other settings these ingredients are not always present.

SPECIAL REGIONAL OR PROJECT AUTHORITIES.   The rural development fervor of the 1970s gave rise to a generation of integrated rural development projects. Funding agencies persuaded host governments to sanction the creation of special regional or project authorities to manage these complex, multisectoral interventions. Heavily subsidized and largely reliant on donor funding, these special project authorities naturally withered as donor enthusiasm faded and the great tide of rural development funding ebbed, leaving the remains of rusted institutional carcasses littered across the rural landscape. Domestic financial stringencies imposed by structural adjustment programs in the late 1980s amplified the contraction in funding available for rural development efforts. Some rural development programs continued to function, nonetheless, notably the large regional development programs of Northeast Brazil (Tendler 1993). The vast majority, however, remain defunct and largely discredited as overly ambitious, excessively expensive, and too difficult to manage (Ruttan 1975, 1984; Holdcroft 1984).

DECENTRALIZATION AND DELEGATION TO LOCAL GOVERNMENTS.   Early in the twenty-first century, as during the 1970s, decentralization and local economic development have emerged as popular strategies for spurring rural development.[27] Some groups refer to these new-generation efforts as territorial development.[28] Given the frequent necessity of local collective action as well as infrastructure and public service provision, efforts to strengthen local decisionmaking and resource mobilization remain central to effective local area development efforts. Recent examples from China of highly dynamic RNFE growth spurred by local government initiative have fueled institutional emulation in India and elsewhere (see Chapter 12). In other settings, however, local governments remain bereft of fiscal resources and decisionmaking authority, both of which financially beleaguered central governments prove reluctant to devolve.[29] Ultimately, for decentralization to work well, central governments must retain a high level of commitment and willingness to concede financial and political control. Yet this commitment requires a level of selflessness that many central government political leaders find difficult to muster. A review from Latin America notes that "Latin America has experienced numerous waves of decentralization since the countries of the region first gained their independence. Each has finally ended with a recentralizing of authority at the national level" (Peterson 1997, 31). While many countries have made progress in decentralizing control, in others the transfer of real authority and resources to local-level decisionmakers remains an ongoing challenge.[30]

Sectoral Institutions

EXPANSION OF RESPONSIBILITIES IN MINISTRIES OF AGRICULTURE.   Because of their extensive presence, ministries of agriculture typically staff the most effective extension network functioning in rural areas. Therefore, they become natural candidates for extending central government mandates in rural areas. In practice, this all too often involves nothing more than the addition of a marketing division or agroprocessing unit within the ministry (Abbott 1986). Historically, these units have fared poorly in ministerial resource allocation decisions because their marketing mandate is viewed as peripheral to the core ministry functions of boosting farm production. In response to greater competition in domestic agricultural markets, as a result of trade liberalization, this

---

27. Rondinelli (1981), Cheema and Rondinelli (1983), Nel (1996), Peterson (1997), Keyfors (1998), Manor (1999), Helmsing (2001), World Bank (2001), Tacoli and Satterthwaite (2003).

28. Farrell and Thirion (2001), Stohr (2001).

29. Bahl, Miner, and Schroeder (1984), Bahl and Linn (1992), Tacoli (1998).

30. Chapter 13 describes the striking contrast between decentralization efforts in China and those in India.

view is now changing in some settings, particularly as countries face greater opportunities to capture more value added from agriculture through agroprocessing and the production of higher-value products. Chile and Brazil, for example, have invested heavily in the past decade to modernize small-scale farming and accelerate agricultural growth by promoting agroprocessing and improved marketing, including stronger links with urban markets (Berdegué 2001).

RURAL INDUSTRY PROGRAMS.   Eschewing the cross-sectoral approach embodied in the integrated models, some countries have instead focused on one portion of the RNFE—rural manufacturing. Both China and India adopted this strategy early on, India with its village and *khadi* industries programs and China with its five small industries policy. Though the industries selected for assistance differed, both countries translated high-level policy commitment for rural industry promotion into a complex system of subsidized inputs, policy protection, quotas, and promotional institutions. Both favored rural manufacturing and largely neglected rural commerce and services. During the 1990s, both governments abandoned these heavily subsidized systems, deprotected the previously favored rural manufacturers, and liberalized incentives to a considerable extent (see Chapter 13). In doing so, they have both ushered in an era of major transition—the large-scale disappearance of many highly protected but uncompetitive rural industries and the rapid growth of other activities, such as export subcontracting and local services.

DEVOLUTION TO THE PRIVATE SECTOR.   Sector- and commodity-specific promotional efforts increasingly rely on private sector service delivery to promote nonfarm business growth. Drawing on early private sector experience (Rodolo 1972), a wave of projects and agencies have experimented with developing business linkages between large and small firms in order to facilitate the commercial provision of marketing and other business development services.[31] In these efforts, promotional agencies play a facilitating role in developing business linkages, branding, grades and standards, and contracting procedures necessary for large numbers of small firms to effectively supply the quality and volume required by large agribusiness firms.[32]

Institutional Tendencies

In spite of increasing concern about rural poverty and the potentially important role the RNFE can play in redynamizing rural economies, large gaps remain in public policies and promotion programs. Though decentralization to local governments and devolution to the private sector have gained momentum in recent years, no clear institutional delivery system currently dominates rural nonfarm

---

31. Barton (1997), Grierson, Mead, and Moyo (1997), Lusby and Panliburton (2002).
32. Edesess and Polak (1993), ACDI/VOCA (2001), Vorley (2001, 2004), Bear, Gibson and Hitchins (2003), Magistro et al. (2004).

promotion efforts. Thus institutional diversity and gaping holes promise to characterize the promotional landscape for the foreseeable future.

From Platitudes to Prescriptions

Platitudes prove difficult to dislodge. And so we are forced to conclude, like a long parade of past observers, that growth in the RNFE will require favorable public policies, adequate infrastructure, human skills, and well-functioning market and credit institutions. Unlike past observers, however, we note that dominant private sector firms increasingly rival public institutions in shaping the policy and institutional environment in which small rural nonfarm firms of the developing world operate.

Moving beyond the standard platitudes will require diagnostic tools that enable interveners to determine which elements of the policy and institutional environment will prove most crucial to rural nonfarm growth in specific instances. Which policies constrain opportunities in a given situation? Which roads will generate the greatest impact? Where can improved marketing, credit, or educational institutions enhance growth prospects for small rural nonfarm firms?

Generic assessment tools will prove appropriate in some circumstances. General overviews of the policy environment may prove useful, particularly in transition economies of Eastern Europe and other similar settings where egregious shortcomings in systems for securing property rights, land tenure, contract enforcement, foreign exchange, and access to credit constrain business activity across all segments of the nonfarm economy (Davis and Pearce 2000).

Frequently, however, growth-enhancing policy, infrastructural, and institutional investments prove commodity- and site-specific. So in many practical cases, situation-specific assessments will prove more illuminating than the generic. After review of a broad spectrum of specific rural nonfarm programs, policies, and settings, in the remaining chapters of Part III, Chapter 17 will propose an operational strategy for building institutional and policy environments that aims to facilitate equitable growth of the RNFE across the many diverse landscapes of the developing world.

12 An Overview of Programs for Promoting the Rural Nonfarm Economy

STEVEN HAGGBLADE, DONALD C. MEAD,
AND RICHARD L. MEYER

Over the past five decades, the world has unleashed enormous energy and creativity into improving the lot of the rural poor. Outside India and China, efforts have often drawn inspiration from these two leaders, initially from India and more recently from China. Following the early India model, much of this effort has targeted small rural nonfarm enterprises, on which the landless poor of the developing world often depend. Featuring a cast of literally thousands, these efforts have involved a wide array of professionals—including civil servants, agronomists, economists, geographers, regional planners, engineers, managers, bankers, businessmen, farmers, and craftsmen—experimenting with virtually every imaginable combination of technical, financial, and policy support for rural nonfarm enterprises.

Indeed, because opportunities and constraints vary widely across countries and settings, this considerable programming diversity is highly appropriate. Would-be promoters of the rural nonfarm economy (RNFE) must navigate a highly variegated landscape populated by a spectrum of nonfarm activities ranging from painfully poor, labor-intensive "survivalist" activities to highly sophisticated, large-scale agribusinesses. Agronomic potential, policy environments, human endowments, and even weather all vary across locations—and frequently over time—generating rapid turnover and mutation of firms (Chapter 5). The resulting heterogeneity of enterprise sizes, activities, and economic environments leads to widely varying prospects for growth, further complicating the task of those who wish to stimulate rural nonfarm activity.

Not surprisingly, the diversity of situations and opportunities leads to a potentially bewildering array of programming options and experiences. This chapter attempts to summarize and categorize the principal approaches adopted to date in developing countries outside of India and China. Because of their scale and contrasting experiences, these two goliaths are treated separately, in Chapter 13. The discussion here traces the broad history of promotional efforts elsewhere, identifying key players, contrasting the premises on which they have based their work, and summarizing available evidence on impact and cost.

The Historical Evolution of Intervention Strategies for RNFE Promotion

Four Strategic Perspectives

Four major strategic thrusts have dominated efforts to stimulate the growth of the RNFE (Table 12.1). The first has focused on small enterprise promotion. Initially led by management specialists focusing on "modern small industry," these efforts gave way to a second wave of poverty-induced interest in the informal sector and microenterprise promotion. Popular among market-oriented governments in the developing world and Western donors who support them, the small enterprise promotion camp houses a heterogeneous amalgam of civil servants, business groups, and volunteer agencies that provide credit, management assistance, technology development, entrepreneurship training, and marketing support to rural nonfarm firms.

A second strategic thrust has focused on promotion of agricultural marketing and agribusiness opportunities in specific commodity subsectors. Unlike the enterprise promotion specialists, who focus on individual small firms, this group examines a network of related large and small enterprises linked together in competing supply chains that assemble, process, and deliver a specific commodity to final consumers. Led by international agribusiness and supported by management consulting firms, agricultural marketing experts, groups in ministries of agriculture and commerce, and market-oriented nongovernmental organizations (NGOs), this group concentrates on constraints and opportunities in specific agricultural commodity subsectors. It focuses attention on large wholesalers, supermarkets, assemblers, and exporters as well as their links to small-scale rural suppliers and retailers. Following diagnostic exercises, interventions typically revolve around the supply of commodity-specific public goods such as marketing infrastructure, grades and standards, and rules of conduct.

The third strategic effort operating in this vast rural intersection has concentrated on regional development, on local governments, and on spatial dimensions linking economic activities across specific rural regions. Seen from this strategic perspective, the unit of analysis becomes the rural region, not an individual enterprise or commodity subsector. Initiated by the creation of central government ministries of rural development, by the empowerment of regional governments, or by the establishment of regional project authorities (see Chapter 11), these efforts have received technical support from an array of regional planners, public administration specialists, geographers, public finance experts, and technicians from line ministries of agriculture, education, and health. These various technical specialists study the spatial dispersion of agricultural potential, rural markets, and human settlement, as well as the hierarchies of towns and the infrastructure they provide in support of agricultural-nonfarm linkages. Interventions by this group have typically focused on programs to improve agricultural production, rural markets, and secondary towns. Many likewise emphasize

TABLE 12.1 Strategies for intervention in support of rural nonfarm enterprises

Strategy	Target	Intervener	Content	Additional relevant chapters, subjects treated
1. Small enterprise development	Enterprises	Ministries of industry and commerce Donor projects NGOs	Mostly supply-side promotion (credit, entrepreneurship, management, technology) Some market development	Chapter 13, India and China Chapter 14, technology Chapter 11, rural credit institutions
2. Agribusiness and agricultural marketing	Supply chains in specific commodity subsectors	International agribusiness Management consultants Ministries of agriculture and commerce Local government market authorities Commercially oriented NGOs	Provision of public goods (infrastructure, grades and standards, rules of conduct) Links between large firms and small	Chapter 9, agro-industries Chapter 15, subsector supply chains

3. Regional development	Rural regions	Central government ministries of rural development Regional and local governments Special project authorities	Multisectoral (agriculture, nonfarm, health, education) efforts Technical inputs Social services Infrastructure	Chapter 8, cities and towns Chapter 11, alternative institutional models
4. Public policy and investment	Macro economy Sectors Subsectors	Central government Local governments	Focus on general enabling environment (policies governing trade, exchange rates and controls, interest rates, taxation, pricing, public investments, enterprise regulation)	Chapter 11, policy and institutional environment Chapter 13, India and China

local governance and decisionmaking. They explore opportunities for siting the rural infrastructure and basic public education and health services necessary to facilitate regional and local economic development.

A fourth strategic perspective explores primarily the broader issues of public sector investments and macroeconomic policy. In the past, many governments, particularly in Asia, have operated highly directive policy environments, channeling investment flows into (and in some cases out of) rural areas and enunciating policies that encouraged or even stipulated by fiat which industries should operate in rural areas. Subsequent liberalization of protective measures and controls on rural nonfarm activity reflected a widespread view that policies had often acted as a significant brake on rural nonfarm development. Policymakers everywhere have seen periods when public support was seen as crucial for financing productivity-enhancing investments in education, financial institutions, and physical infrastructure and for establishing a favorable policy environment for rural business development, reflecting an evolving view of the development process and of government's facilitating role. This perspective reflected the optimistic view that, once released from the fetters of inappropriate policies, the "magic of the market" would unleash a surge of economic activity among nonfarm enterprises in both urban and rural areas (Chapter 11).

Over time, the dominant paradigms within each strategic group have shifted considerably. Many efforts began in urban areas and shifted their attention only gradually and partially to rural areas. Frequently these efforts have moved in parallel, as the following chronology reveals.

Small Enterprise Promotion

Modern-day efforts at business promotion in the developing world began with the classic small enterprise promotion model developed by a team of advisers working in India in the 1950s and 1960s.[1] With Ford Foundation funding, these advisers developed a program of integrated support that focused on stimulating growth in "modern small enterprise," which they defined as those enterprises employing fewer than 100 people.[2] This approach, as summarized in a seminal book by two key participants (Staley and Morse 1965), viewed household and artisanal activities as backward and likely to atrophy with economic growth.[3]

---

1. This section draws on reviews by Stepanek (1960), Staley and Morse (1965), Kilby (1988), Boomgard (1989), Otero and Rhyne (1994), Haggblade (1995), Snodgrass and Biggs (1996), Levitsky (2000), and Snodgrass and Packard Winkler (2004).

2. Though many classifications are possible, this chapter will refer to micro and small enterprises as those employing 10 workers or fewer, medium-scale enterprises as those employing 11 to 100, and large enterprises as employing more than 100 workers. In this classification system Staley and Morse's client group, "modern small industry," falls into the medium-scale category.

3. See Anderson (1982) for empirical evidence of the decline of household industries.

Because of the geographic origins of this approach and because the Indians became its most prominent exporters to the rest of the developing world, it has become known as the India model.

Using an analogy from agricultural research, where a combination of fertilizer, water, and new seeds was seen to produce greater productivity gains than any single element in isolation, Staley and Morse founded their fledgling industrial promotion credo on this same principle of "combinations and interactions." In their words, "Any single-factor approach to small industry development in a newly industrializing country is likely to be ineffective and wasteful. An integrated program that works on a carefully selected combination of factors simultaneously—the exact combination depending on local conditions—is much more likely to prove worthwhile" (Staley and Morse 1965, 353). Hence the comprehensive and highly integrated package of support embodied in the India model. From initial feasibility studies to entrepreneurship and management training, technical research and extension, marketing assistance, and the provision of common workshop facilities, power, road infrastructure, and finance, the India model offered cradle-to-grave support for assisted firms. Generally subsidized, these services and programs typically revolved around a network of industrial estates with contiguous classrooms and office facilities for extension and technical support staff.

Major donors such as the United Nations Industrial Development Organization (UNIDO), the International Labor Office (ILO), and the Swedish International Development Agency enthusiastically exported this model throughout the developing world from the early 1960s on. In 1966 an Indian advisory mission to Kenya led to the establishment of the Kenya Industrial Estates program, which subsequently expanded to operate the Rural Industrial Development Programme. Originally designed with modern urban and medium-scale industry in mind, the India model constituted the state of the art in business promotion practice during the 1960s and 1970s. As attention turned increasingly to rural areas, business promotion specialists transplanted these same tools into rural settings and outside of Asia, where smaller firms and less dense business activity prevailed. With large initial programs in India and Kenya, the India model of nursery industrial estates and complete packages of assistance spread with the creation of large programs in Bangladesh, Botswana, Burkina Faso, Indonesia, Lesotho, Malaysia, Nigeria, Pakistan, Swaziland, and Tanzania.

Beginning in the late 1970s, a wide array of implementing agencies began to take liberties with the basic India model. During the broad rural and poverty-focused reorientation of the 1970s (see Chapter 2), interventions increasingly focused on poor people, smaller-scale informal enterprises, and rural areas. In this climate, a great deal of experimentation took place as old line business promotion agencies endeavored to focus their attention on the plight of the rural poor. In the process, a new cohort of poverty-focused interveners (governments, NGOs, and donors) entered the fray alongside the business management set.

In many cases, these experiments tended to single out one or a few business promotion tools for special attention.[4] A stream of engineering work focusing on low-capital "appropriate technology" began in the early 1970s, following publication of the influential book *Small Is Beautiful* by E. F. Schumacher (1976). Focusing on inexpensive but high-productivity technology, this work led to the development and dissemination of a stream of technical innovations: rice dehullers, silk reelers, maize grinders, oil presses, windmills, hand pumps, and the ubiquitous improved stoves. Key practitioners of engineering research and development for rural nonfarm enterprises currently reside in institutions such as the Intermediate Technology Development Group, begun by Schumacher; Appropriate Technology International, recently reorganized as EnterpriseWorks Worldwide; and the Swiss Center for Appropriate Technology.[5] The private sector, of course, also continues to innovate and disseminate new technology, as the many examples in Chapter 14 attest.

Management extension branched off the industrial estates and moved into rural areas and trading establishments, with pioneers such as the barefoot consultants of Malcolm Harper's Partnership for Productivity (PfP) in Kenya in the mid-1970s (Harper 1977). PfP and others based their efforts on the premise that simple, improved management tools could result in immediate cost savings and increased earnings for even the smallest business. In parallel, organizations focusing on medium-scale businesses, such as the ILO and UNIDO, transferred their management consulting and advising to rural areas through programs such as the ILO's Improve Your Business program (Samuelson 1997).

Large private enterprises likewise offer many of these same support services to small rural nonfarm firms in certain circumstances. Long before management extension became fashionable among governments and donors, Unilever South Africa operated an in-house management support service for retailers of its products (Rodolo 1972). The company recognized that a prosperous, growing network of retailers could sell more of its products and prove more reliable and credit-worthy partners in the future. Similarly, urban-based garment subcontractors and tinmaking firms in the Philippines routinely supply technical advice and quality control to their rural subcontractors (Hayami, Kikuchi, and Marciano 1996). Yet large firms sometimes squash smaller rivals as well (see the many examples in Chapters 9 and 15). Recognizing these important relationships, recent efforts have attempted to foster commercial business linkages between large and small firms in supply chains where their

---

4. In an early evaluation of technical assistance programs for rural industry, Kilby and Bangasser (1978) and Kilby (1979) first voiced the then-heretical view that the most cost-effective interventions were those that focused on a "single missing ingredient" rather than on a full complement of support services.

5. Darrow and Saxenian (1993) provide a detailed roster of 27 agencies specializing in appropriate technology development and diffusion.

interests converge.[6] Related work on enterprise clusters recognizes the important flows—of technology, know-how, and credit—among private firms (Porter 1998; Schmitz and Nadvi 1999). By working through large firms, these efforts aim to leverage intervention efforts and make them commercially sustainable.

Entrepreneurship development, an element of the original India model, retains a devoted following in the more specialized twenty-first century. Based on the notion that entrepreneurs prove to be key motors of business growth and that distinguishing personality traits can be identified and nurtured, several institutions—most notably the Entrepreneurship Development Institute of India; the Creation of Entrepreneurs, Formation of Enterprises (CEFE)[7] program of GTZ (Gesellschaft für Technische Zusammenarbeit); Management Systems International; and the Emprendedores e Tecnologia (Entrepreneurship and Technology) program of the United Nations Conference on Trade and Development—continue to prepare diagnostic instruments and run active entrepreneurship training and promotional programs.[8] Over 100 institutions offer entrepreneurship development training in India alone (Awasthi, Murali, and Bharat 1990; Harper and Finnegan 1998).

Credit schemes proliferated at an astounding rate from the late 1970s through the first decade of the twenty-first century, particularly in urban and high-density rural areas. Because institutional finance from development banks had consistently failed to reach the lowest income groups and because these directed credit models proved costly and unsustainable, attention focused increasingly on new ways of expanding access to credit for the rural poor.[9] The well-documented failures of many directed agricultural and small business credit programs contributed to the emergence of a "new view" of rural finance prescribing a markedly different institutional design involving high interest rates and reduced cost of administration.[10] Following highly regarded poverty lending schemes such as those of the Grameen Bank, the Bangladesh Rural Advancement Committee (BRAC), and the Association for Social Advancement in

---

6. Grierson, Mead, and Moyo (1997), Steel, Tanburn, and Hallberg (2000), Donor Committee (2001), Lusby and Panliburton (2002), Bear, Gibson, and Hitchins (2003), Hitchins, Elliot, and Gibson (2004), Miehlbradt, McVay, and Tanburn (2005).

7. CEFE is also referred to as Competency-based Economics through Formation of Enterprises.

8. McClelland (1961), McClelland and Winter (1969), Kilby (1971, 1988), Awasthi, Murali, and Bharat (1990), ILO (1992), Kolshorn and Tomecko (1995), MSI (1997), Kolshorn and Weihert (2000).

9. Trends in World Bank lending, for example, reveal a clear shift out of lending for small and medium-scale enterprises and into microenterprise credit (Webster, Riopelle, and Chidzero 1996).

10. Adams and Graham (1981), Adams, Graham, and Von Pischke (1984), Von Pischke (1991), Otero and Rhyne (1994), Christen et al. (1995), Meyer and Larson (1997), Vogel and Adams (1997), Yaron et al. (1997), Robinson (2002).

Bangladesh; the government-run Bank Rakyat Indonesia's Unit Desa (BRI-UD, or Village Bank) in Indonesia; and Promotion and Development of Microenterprises and Bancosol in Bolivia, a vast army of imitators has experimented with, expanded, and replicated microenterprise credit schemes. Though most microcredit programs have concentrated on urban areas, several densely populated Asian countries launched pioneering rural credit schemes, including the BRI-UD in Indonesia and Grameen Bank and BRAC in Bangladesh. Typically these programs offer small, short-maturity loans at high, unsubsidized interest rates. They motivate repayment through group lending or through repeat lending in escalating loan sizes. In an effort to become cost-covering, self-sustaining financial institutions, the most efficient slash administrative costs to the bone. They offer stripped-down, no-frills, "minimalist" credit to the poor.[11]

Credit unions offer services to millions more. Some organizations employ a village banking model to build small, member-owned financial institutions. In other locations, commercial banks have opened loan windows to serve poor clients. New start-up banks in several Eastern European countries offer still another model for small enterprise credit, especially in urban areas.

A growing proportion of these credit institutions also offer savings facilities, recognizing that poor people often value a secure place to lodge their hard-won surplus cash as much as the opportunity to obtain credit. A leader in this effort, Indonesia's state bank, BRI, held over $2.1 billion in deposits in 2000, attracting six times as many deposit as loan accounts and with deposits covering lending from 1990 onward (Boomgard and Angell 1994; Robinson 2002). By acting as intermediaries between rural savers and borrowers, these institutions ultimately aim to become financially self-sustaining and move beyond their heavy initial reliance on infusions of government and donor funding (Otero and Rhyne 1994; Development Finance Forum 2004). The goal of these broader institutions has moved beyond microenterprise credit to microenterprise finance, providing self-sustaining savings, lending, and remittance transfer services to the rural poor (see Chapter 11).

In the early years of the twenty-first century, the major focus of direct enterprise promotion remains financial assistance (Figure 12.1). Key players in this effort include credit unions, village banks, NGO microenterprise projects, specialized banks for the poor, and rural branches of national banks, all actively and enthusiastically financed by virtually all donors, from multilateral banks to major bilateral donors and foundations.[12] Even some commercial banks have begun to offer microfinance loans in an effort to expand their lending markets

---

11. Tendler (1989) appears to have been the first to apply the term "minimalist" to these stripped-down, no-frills credit schemes.

12. Otero and Rhyne (1994), CGAP (1995), Hulme and Mosely (1996), Morduch (1999a), Daley-Harris (2005).

FIGURE 12.1   Historical evolution of efforts to promote small and microenterprises, 1950s–2000s

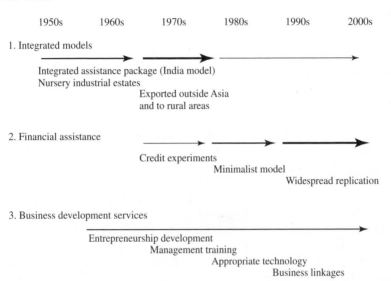

NOTE: The thickness of the arrows indicates the relative scale of each wave of activity.

(Baydas, Graham, and Valenzuela 1997; Valenzuela 2002). Socially oriented commercial investors are likewise becoming increasingly active in funding the most promising microfinance institutions. In spite of questioning by prominent doubters,[13] practitioners' enthusiasm for minimalist credit continues largely unabated.

Over the past five decades, small enterprise promotion has undergone a radical transformation. The dominant promotional model—the comprehensive, high-subsidy, high-input India model of hothouse nursery estates and cradle-to-grave services—has been supplanted by new, polar opposite, paradigms emphasizing a single input, a drive for full cost recovery, and persistent, pragmatic cost cutting intended to strip away all unneeded extra services in the pursuit of focus and financial sustainability. Today the enterprise promotion school encompasses two broad groups: the minimalist credit advocates and a heterogeneous collection of practitioners regrouping and refining methods for cost-effective delivery of business development services "beyond credit."[14]

---

13. Osmani (1989), Adams and Von Pischke (1992), Abugre (1994), Rogaly (1996), Buckley (1997), Dawson and Jeans (1997), Dichter (2006).

14. Chen (1996), Dawson and Jeans (1997), Nelson (1997), Fisher and Sriram (2002).

Agricultural Marketing and Agribusiness

Agricultural marketing and processing often constitute the largest components of the RNFE. In the low-income developing world, agribusiness accounts for roughly half of manufacturing value added (Austin 1992) and 20 to 30 percent of gross domestic product (Jaffee et al. 2003). Its importance has increased rapidly in recent decades. Growing urbanization in the developing world, declining transport costs, and the economic integration accompanying globalization have all contributed to substantial increases in the scale of domestic and international agricultural marketing and agribusiness activity. Spurred by these opportunities, agricultural marketing and agribusiness specialists have invested considerable efforts in developing diagnostic tools aimed at improving the efficiency of agricultural marketing institutions.[15] From this strategic perspective, the unit of analysis and intervention becomes not the enterprise but rather an entire commodity subsector, or value chain—that is, a network of firms interlinked in competing supply channels that assemble, transform, and deliver a particular category of consumption good to the final consumers.

The first big wave of interest in agricultural marketing and agribusiness promotion in the developing world emerged on the heels of the green revolution. Following the widespread release of improved hybrid varieties of rice, wheat, and maize throughout much of Asia and Latin America during the late 1960s and 1970s, marketed volumes increased far faster than rapidly growing farm production. As a result, these growing agricultural surpluses rapidly gave rise to second generation problems of marketing, processing, and distribution (Falcon 1970).

During these early decades, many governments in developing countries intervened directly in agricultural markets through parastatal marketing companies to protect consumers from volatile prices and what they presumed to be predatory private traders.[16] In addition to making traditional public investments in roads and communications infrastructure, many governments invested in more focused types of marketing infrastructure such as wholesale markets, warehouses, ports, and rural market facilities. Common government coordinating tools include zoning regulations, the introduction of grades and standards, inspection of weights and measures, and the establishment of market information systems.[17] A series of diagnostic subsector studies in Latin America

---

15. Goldberg (1968, 1974), Shaffer (1968, 1980), Riley and Weber (1983), Shaffer et al. (1985), Abbott (1986), Holtzman (1986), Mittendorf (1986), Holtzman, Abbott, and Martin (1989), Maxwell and Holtzman (1995), Bourgeois and Herrera (2000), Miles (2001), Magistro et al. (2004).

16. See Tyagi (1990), Jayne and Jones (1997), Timmer (1997), and Kherallah et al. (2002).

17. See Schubert (1983), Abbott (1986), Mittendorf (1986), and Escobar, Reardon, and Berdegué (2001).

during the 1970s led to a variety of supply chain interventions involving zoning, provision of physical infrastructure, introduction of grades and standards, and improved market organization, often with mixed public and private cooperation. Well-known examples include the CORABASTOS (Corporacion de Absticimientos de Bogota), a state-sponsored marketing agency in Bogotá, Colombia, and Brazil's COBAL (Companhia Brasileira de Alimentos), a program for the initiation of a series of rural assembly markets for fruits and vegetables during the 1970s (Harrison et al. 1975; Mittendorf 1986).

Key monitors and interveners in these growing agricultural marketing systems include ministries of agriculture and sometimes commerce, as well as large agribusiness firms, both domestic and international. International management consulting firms and business schools with international and agribusiness specializations, such as Harvard and Thunderbird, offer analytical support to large firms in specific agribusiness topics.[18] In the public sector, agricultural marketing specialists at major U.S. universities—Cornell, Kansas State, Michigan State, and Stanford—have invested in training and in several generations of important diagnostic assessments of agricultural marketing systems in the developing world.[19] Operationally, the Food and Agriculture Organization's marketing group has provided marketing advisers and technical support for marketing reforms that have been supported in later years by the agribusiness group at the World Bank.[20] A handful of NGOs, such as ACDI/VOCA (Agricultural Cooperative Development International / Volunteers in Overseas Cooperative Assistance), the Cooperative League of the USA, EnterpriseWorks /VITA (Volunteers in Technical Assistance), International Development Enterprises (IDE), the Intermediate Technology Development Group, Mennonite Economic Development Associates, and Technoserve, has likewise specialized in agribusiness promotion, focusing on improved processing technologies and marketing arrangements that link small players with large firms in growing market channels.[21]

A second wave of interest in agricultural marketing and agribusiness emerged in the 1990s, launched by the simultaneous liberalization of agricultural markets and trade regimes throughout much of the developing world.[22] Unlike the first era, in which public institutions played a predominant role in agricultural markets, the second phase of agribusiness growth has been

---

18. Goldberg (1968, 1974), Austin (1992), Brown (1994), Murphy (2001).

19. Mellor (1966), Shaffer (1968), Jones (1970), Phillips (1973), Harrison et al. (1975), Lele (1975), Anthony et al. (1979), Riley and Weber (1983), Timmer (1987), Reardon et al. (2003).

20. Abbott (1986), Mittendorf (1986), Jaffee et al. (2003).

21. Bowman and Reiling (1990), Hyman (1993a), EnterpriseWorks Worldwide (1997), Kapila and Mead (2002), Magistro et al. (2004), Neven and Reardon (2004), IDE (2005).

22. This discussion draws on work by Fernandes et al. (2000) and Jaffee et al. (2003) and a stream of studies by Reardon, Bergedué, and colleagues, summarized by Reardon and Berdegué (2002) and in Chapter 9.

dominated by large private firms. A flood of supermarkets and large agribusiness processors across Latin America, Asia, and Africa has led to rapid change in the structure of agricultural marketing systems (Chapter 9). In their drive to remain competitive, the newly ascendant supermarkets and large-scale agribusiness firms have rapidly taken steps to rein in costs and improve the quality, consistency, and diversity of their offerings. Increasingly stringent food safety regulations reinforce incentives for meticulous supply chain management. To reduce costs and improve market coordination, they establish large regional distribution centers and logistics platforms, and many times they contract directly with wholesalers or even large-scale producers. Private branding and quality control lead to the introduction of private grades and standards specifying the quality, safety, volume, and packaging of products. Because competition requires rapid adjustment and execution, the large private food retailers now frequently establish the prevailing grades and standards governing product quality, safety, and packaging.

Traditional interveners are currently scrambling to find ways they can help small agribusiness firms adjust to compete in these rapidly changing food supply chains.[23] A series of innovative government programs in Brazil, Chile, and Mexico aim to equip groups of rural producers to compete in increasingly concentrated agribusiness supply chains (Berdegué 2001; Del Grossi and Da Silva 2001; Reardon and Flores 2006). Publicly funded central facilities for assembly and grading of produce make it possible for small suppliers to supply supermarkets in Chile and Thailand.[24] Amendments to contract law, such as the prompt payment clause introduced on behalf of fruit and vegetable growers in Argentina, can help create a level playing field in which smaller players can more effectively participate (Brom 2002). Extension of food safety certification to smallholders has enabled Guatemalan small farmers to supply supermarket chains there (Berdegué et al., 2005). Credit lines for upgrading machinery and equipment may be necessary to permit the scaling up required by new, more sophisticated buyers. Agribusiness-oriented NGOs assist rural businesses, farmers, or cooperative associations to access lucrative urban and export markets by facilitating input supply, certification of standards, and market contacts with large firms.[25] Similarly, through the Fabrica do Agricultor program in Parana, Brazil, the state government and the World Bank have provided marketing, packaging, and contracting assistance that enables small-scale food processors to supply regional supermarkets (Del Grossi and Da Silva 2001).

---

23. See Vorley (2001, 2004), Jaffee et al. (2003), Neven and Reardon (2004), Reardon (2004), Technoserve (2004), Weatherspoon and Mumbreño (2004), and Goletti (2005).

24. Reardon and Berdegué (2002), Van Roekel et al. (2002).

25. Mead (1994b), De Crombrugghe and Montes (2000), Grierson, Mead, and Kakore (2000), ACDI/VOCA (2001), Rawlinson and Fehr (2002), Stosch and Hyman (2002), Magistro et al. (2004).

In some instances, private firms have assisted small enterprises to participate in these newly ascendant market channels. Hortifruti in Costa Rica and former fresh vegetable exporter Agriflora in Zambia offered technical assistance and financial assistance, through either input credit or help in accessing bank loans, to help smallholders participate in growing export markets (Reardon and Berdegué 2002; Gonzalez-Vega et al. 2006). The Horticultural Export Growers Association in Zambia, a joint government-industry initiative, has introduced a special two-year degree program in horticultural production, grading, and handling that graduated its first class in 2002. The Dutch multinational retailer Royal Ahold offers a supply improvement program for vegetable suppliers in Thailand, specifying the postharvest and production practices required to meet the company's supply standards (Boselie 2002).

Suppliers of business development services have likewise begun to explore ways of facilitating these commercial business linkages between large and small private firms. Rather than becoming direct suppliers of services, those employing this new market development approach aim to facilitate commercially viable business relationships between large and small firms.[26] In many cases, private exporters or brokers provide embedded services such as input credit or technical support to small producers in return for guaranteed sales of their output.[27]

More traditional business development services (BDS) continue to operate through general business development programs, sometimes consolidated in multipurpose agribusiness development centers (ADCs). Offering technical, marketing, and sometimes financial assistance, the ADCs offer the standard enterprise promotion services to the agribusiness community (Lamb and Brower 2001).

Regional Development

Regional and local area development efforts in the developing world have a long though uneven history.[28] They are founded on several key premises. The first holds that an economic catchment area, a geographic unit of intervention, offers many practical opportunities for coordinating and stimulating necessary linkages between agricultural input supply, local infrastructure, nonfarm processing and marketing, human settlement, and social services. Second, many

---

26. Barton (1997), Grierson, Mead, and Moyo (1997), Steel, Tanburn, and Hallberg (2000), Lusby and Panliburton (2002), Bear, Gibson, and Hitchins (2003), Hitchins, Elliot, and Gibson (2004).

27. Escobal, Agreda, and Reardon (2000), LaFleur (2000), Mwanamwambwa-Wright (2000), ECI (2001a,b).

28. See Friedman (1975), Gilbert (1992), Rondinelli (1993), Tacoli (1998), and Tacoli and Satterthwaite (2003).

believe that local participation in decisionmaking, because it is based on a more detailed understanding of local opportunities and priorities, will often prove most effective in mobilizing, allocating, and monitoring the deployment of scarce regional investment resources. Over time, governments have applied these principles in varying scales of complexity.

During the rural renaissance of the 1970s, a wave of large-scale regional development efforts emerged in the form of integrated rural development (IRD) programs. Recognizing the links between agriculture and rural industries, between health and worker productivity, between governance and infrastructure maintenance, these ambitious efforts aimed to integrate provision of social services, productivity growth in agriculture, nonfarm activity, government finance, and rural infrastructure. Though prepared in many flavors, most contained an agricultural production component together with public infrastructure and provision of social services such as education and health services.[29] Key actors in these efforts included central government ministries, local governments, and foreign donors. In some cases, central governments created new ministries of rural development or charged their ministries of agriculture with overall regional development coordination. In other cases, local governments or independent project authorities retained control. These institutional options are described in some detail in Chapter 11.

Following widely touted pilot projects in the early 1960s in Comilla, Bangladesh, and during the late 1960s in Puebla, Mexico, IRD efforts spread like wildfire across the noncommunist developing world. At their peak, hundreds of programs operated in over 50 countries.[30] The World Bank alone supported over 400 IRD activities and spent $6.3 billion on IRD efforts during this period. The U.S. Agency for International Development (USAID) supported IRD projects in over 100 locations. The best known of these efforts include the Bicol River Basin project in the Philippines, the CADU Project in Ethiopia, the Lilongwe Project in Malawi, and the Puebla Project in Mexico.

Breathtaking in their ambition and scope, the IRD efforts in most parts of the world collapsed under the weight of their organizational complexity, administrative infighting, and high cost.[31] A few, such as the Aga Khan–funded efforts in Pakistan, continue to receive kudos (World Bank 1990). In other areas, some programs likewise continue to operate, particularly in South America, though at very low levels and without the major infusion of donor funding that fueled many of the programs worldwide (Tendler 1993).

A set of more focused efforts at regional and local economic development have attracted renewed interest in the 1990s and into the twenty-first century.

---

29. Ruttan (1975, 1984), de Janvry (1981), World Bank (1987).
30. Ruttan (1984), USAID (1987), World Bank (1987), Donaldson (1993).
31. ILO (1974), Holdcroft (1978, 1984), Rondinelli (1986), USAID (1987), World Bank (1987, 1994).

Resurgent interest in decentralization has taken a more overtly political tone this time around; efforts now aim to promote local decisionmaking and thereby stimulate local area development.[32] The economic component of this new wave of political decentralization flies under the banner of local economic development or territorial development.[33] Like the previous approaches, this strategy is based on the premise that a combination of ingredients—agricultural technology, rural roads, and communications facilities—is necessary to stimulate rural growth. In many instances, these territorially based efforts center around the development of social investment funds under which local leaders identify key investments for stimulating local economic and social development. Unlike many of the earlier integrated administrative models, the current approach relies on local administrative bodies instead of special project authorities or central government agencies (see Chapter 11). In this respect, it follows the Chinese model of local government–led rural nonfarm enterprise promotion (see Chapter 13).

The local economic development practitioners have borrowed analytical and implementation tools from the other schools and have made some advances of their own. Frequently they draw on the work on competitive advantage and economic clusters of related firms, a concept closely allied with value chains, supply chains, and subsectors that has come out of agricultural marketing and small enterprise development.[34] They have developed and refined an assortment of assessment tools, including participatory analysis of competitive advantage and subsector analysis, as aids in assessing promising key activities, mapping and understanding competitive and input supply relationships in the supply chains, and developing concrete interventions that can stimulate economic growth among economic clusters of enterprises linked together in what are commonly termed supply chains, value chains, or subsectors.[35] Like the first generation of regional development specialists, the new wave of local economic development has both borrowed from and contributed to the development of analytical and implementation tools used by the small enterprise, agribusiness, and policy wings of the rural nonfarm promotion coalition.

Macroeconomic Policies and Government Investments

Government policies and investments have long played a central role in promoting—and sometimes in hindering—the RNFE. Some governments have intervened explicitly and in highly directive ways, as in India, China, Japan, and elsewhere in East Asia (Chapters 10 and 13). Others have adopted indirect incentive policies, in many cases by default (Chapter 11).

---

32. Rondinelli (1981), Nel (1996), Peterson (1997), Manor (1999), World Bank (2001), Tacoli and Satterthwaite (2003).

33. Nel (1996), Farrell and Thirion (2001), Stohr (2001), Meyer-Stamer (2002), Evans (2004).

34. Boomgard et al. (1992), Porter (1998), Schmitz and Nadvi (1999).

35. Gaile (1992), Dowds and Hinojosa (1999), Evans (2001, 2004), Meyer-Stamer (2002).

Obviously a favorable policy environment leading to broad-based economic growth creates an environment conducive to the growth of productive employment among RNFEs. Conversely, when the economy as a whole stagnates, whether because of poor policies, bad weather, or for any other reason, rural nonfarm enterprises suffer as well, in ways that even the best of projects are unlikely to offset.

Consequently, members of the small enterprise, agribusiness, and local economic development camps evince an increasing awareness of the important opportunities for RNFE promotion via policy reform. The Inter-American Development Bank (IDB), for example, has made policy dialogue one of two key planks in its five-year microenterprise support program (IDB 1997). Likewise, a number of small enterprise promotion groups now explicitly advocate policy dialogue as a necessary component of rural and small enterprise promotion.[36] And the agribusiness literature detailing the dramatic impact of trade and investment liberalization on agribusiness supply chains in the developing world underscores the importance of policy as a powerful instrument for initiating change in the RNFE (Chapter 9). Governments from Vietnam to Latin America increasingly consult with the private sector on policy issues through roundtables and *mesas de concertación*. This convergence of interest suggests that policy-level reviews and interventions may become increasingly common as a tool for stimulating growth in the RNFE.[37]

Few practitioners doubt the power of policies to influence large numbers of rural firms at a single stroke—for good or for ill. Differences emerge, however, when discussing what else governments ought or ought not to do to promote the RNFE. Many counsel that government should confine itself to providing a level playing field, a stable policy environment, secure property rights, basic infrastructure, education, and credit systems, then leave the business of business to private entrepreneurs (Donor Committee 2001). Others suggest that equity, environmental concerns, and even maintenance of competitive advantage mandate a more interventionist stance in order to stimulate local nonfarm growth in which the poor may participate (Porter 1998; Meyer-Stamer 2002).

Governments have adopted highly variable policy stances, and many have changed course substantially over time. The rapid rural nonfarm growth in Taiwan and recently in mainland China have resulted from highly directed government involvement in credit allocation and regulation. The impressive growth in Chilean agribusiness in recent decades has involved a close private-public partnership to make the nation globally competitive in export agriculture. The

---

36. See, for example, Dichter (1986), Women's World Banking (1994), and Snodgrass and Packard Winkler (2004).

37. Dichter (1986), Islam (1987b), Dawson (1990), Grant (1992a), Women's World Banking (1994), Chen (1996), Tacoli (1998), Reardon and Berdegué (2002), Snodgrass and Packard Winkler (2004).

enormous equity implications of globalization, coupled with the experience of agribusiness, small enterprise, and local economic development efforts, suggest that equitable growth in the RNFE will, at the very least, require some sort of public role in facilitating access, grades and standards, and contract laws that will enable small rural producers to link up commercially with the large firms that increasingly dominate agroprocessing and marketing in the developing world. Indeed, many of the most interesting tools from the three nonpolicy schools involve experiments with ways of facilitating commercial supply chain linkages. Even members of the laissez-faire policy school see a role for temporary public subsidies to facilitate these commercial business linkages (Donor Committee 2001).

Intersections

In general, thinking and practice among these diverse strategic groups have evolved in sweeping parallel movements. At an operational level, several converging tendencies have emerged, particularly since the early 1990s.

- *Scaling back.* Small enterprise promotion witnessed a paradigm shift, migrating from the provision of comprehensive, highly integrated support packages to minimalist programs aimed at supplying only one or a few missing ingredients (Figure 12.1). Regional development efforts have similarly scaled back their integrated approaches to focus on smaller, local government–based efforts. Pervasive policy controls and protections in India and East Asia have given way to more laissez-faire policy regimes. Declining government and donor resources have forced a new minimalism among interveners.
- *Promoting private sector involvement.* From direct provision by government or project entities, the small enterprise promoters have increasingly moved toward facilitating commercial business linkages to promote private sector supply of key marketing and technical support. In the agribusiness camp, large private firms have seized the initiative as key shapers of rural nonfarm opportunity. Liberalization has meant that government authorities have ceded terrain to the private sector as well.
- *Working with systems rather than individual firms.* From strategies dealing with individual firms one on one, efforts have turned to system-level interventions, such as policies or intervention via large firms, that can affect multitudes of rural enterprises at a single stroke. Interest in value chains, supply chains, subsectors, and clusters cuts across all four strategic groups.
- *Renewing focus on the policy environment.* In concert with increased liberalization, all groups have come to recognize the importance of the broader policy environment as a key determinant of the success of their efforts.

TABLE 12.2 Classification of interventions for promoting rural nonfarm activity

Decisions and interventions	Demand stimulus for rural nonfarm goods and services	Supply-side interventions
System-level interventions (multiple-firm impact)		
1. Policies (macro, sectoral, and commodity-specific)	Trade policies affecting competitive imports Pro-agricultural policies Government procurement	Macro policies affecting input costs and output prices (interest rates, labor laws, tariffs, taxes) Business regulations affecting competition, registration, and contract enforcement Subsector-specific policies (on licensing, taxation, subsidies, zoning, building codes, health codes, product grades and standards)
2. Public investments		Rural infrastructure (roads, electricity, communications) Rural markets Rural town infrastructure Industrial parks and estates Credit institutions Education
3. Large-firm intermediaries (subsector-, cluster-, supply chain–specific)	Export promotion Marketing linkages (spot markets, subcontracting)	Supplier credits Business linkages supplying technical and management assistance
Direct assistance to individual firms (firm-specific)		
4. Credit		Capital Credit Subsidies Facilities rental

(*continued*)

TABLE 12.2 *Continued*

Decisions and interventions	Demand stimulus for rural nonfarm goods and services	Supply-side interventions

5. Business development services	Marketing assistance
	Business linkages
		Technology research and extension
		Management
		  Entrepreneurship screening and training
		  Management training and advice
		Labor
		  Technical training
		Raw materials
		  Bulk purchasing

The wide variety of economic circumstances prevailing in rural areas has led to a correspondingly broad range of interventions and assortment of tools (Table 12.2). Given the considerable volume of funds expended on rural and rural nonfarm promotion efforts over the past several decades, governments wish to know which combinations of tools have proven most effective and in what circumstances.

Measuring Impact and Cost-Effectiveness

The Availability of Evaluations

Evaluation is not a glamorous business. It frequently proves hot, painstaking, technically difficult, and thankless—a good way to make enemies. The beleaguered evaluator attracts criticism from all sides. And indeed it is easy to find fault. Control groups often refuse to cooperate. Limited budgets prevent large samples or extensive site visits. Project managers who pour their hearts and souls into project start-up and successfully pilot their institutions through inevitably treacherous waters find glib outsiders with designer sunglasses reviewing their efforts an unwelcome intrusion. Certainly no agency wants its star project plucked from the firmament by an unflattering evaluation.

Laboring on in spite of these difficulties, a cadre of heroic evaluators has persisted in the daunting but necessary effort of scrutinizing impacts and costs. In the small enterprise literature,[38] many have labored to improve evaluation

---

38. Harper (1979, 1988), Kilby (1979), Goldmark and Rosengard (1985), Kilby and D'Zmura (1985), Hossain (1988a), Webster (1989), Bolnick and Nelson (1990), Grant (1993), Gaile and Foster (1996), Hulme and Mosely (1996), Hyman and Dearden (1996), Pitt and Khandker (1996,

methods and to gain a better understanding of what interventions work and why. In the agricultural marketing and agribusiness world, impact evaluations prove more elusive, in part because of the high cost and in part because much of this work remains outside the public domain, in the hands of the large agribusiness firms that undertake the investigations and subsequent interventions. A series of recent and ongoing efforts aims to fill the gap in this increasingly important arena.[39] IRD efforts have received considerable scrutiny, most often well after the fact.[40] The newer generation of decentralization, territorial development, and local economic development, however, has yet to produce quantitative measures of impact and cost. Policy impact and assessment of the returns to investment in public infrastructure remain fundamentally important issues that have been addressed earlier, in Chapter 11. Therefore, the discussion here focuses on findings in the other three branches of rural nonfarm promotion.

How Representative Is the Existing Body of Evaluations?

No government or agency offers up its calamities for public scrutiny. So the roster from which evaluators draw is almost certainly biased in favor of the better performers.[41] Once completed, evaluations that prove flattering find their way into multiple copies and fancy fonts, while the less dithyrambic remain buried in single mimeographed copies far from the scrutiny of the outside world. Compounding this natural bias, many reviewers readily acknowledge that they have explicitly sought out better performers in order to learn from their success.[42]

An Asian bias also permeates much of the evaluation literature. A preponderance of infrastructure evaluations has focused on the two large South Asian countries of Bangladesh and India. Similarly, Sebstad and Chen's (1996) review of 32 small enterprise credit evaluations finds that over half of the country-specific cases came from Asia. In fact, Bangladesh alone has hosted six major impact studies since 1992. Though Bangladesh remains an inviting target for evaluators because of its massive programming variety and scale, its disproportionate representation in the evaluation literature leads one to wonder just how generalizable the results may be. Indeed the very particularities that make it a popular hunting ground for interveners and evaluators may make transfer to other settings problematic (Webster and Fidler 1996).

1998), Sebstad and Chen (1996), Webster and Fidler (1996), Webster, Riopelle, and Chidzero (1996), Harper and Finnegan (1998), McVay (1999), Morduch (1999a), Townsend and Yaron (2001), Dunn (2002), Kapila and Mead (2002), Khandker (2005), Armendáriz de Aghion and Morduch (2005).

39. See Berdegué (2001), Kapila and Mead (2002), and Weatherspoon and Reardon (2003).

40. See Ruttan (1975, 1984), de Janvry (1981), Holdcroft (1984), USAID (1987), World Bank (1987), Donaldson (1993), and Tendler (1993).

41. Several reviewers, including Snodgrass and Biggs (1996), underscore this point.

42. See, for example, Grant (1993), Tendler (1993), Gurund et al. (1994), Gaile and Foster (1996), and Webster and Fidler (1996).

Methodological Difficulties in Measuring Impact

A thicket of difficulties confronts evaluators as they seek to assess the impact of various interventions.[43] First are the considerable practical and logistic difficulties in obtaining accurate data on rural nonfarm activity. Enterprise censuses rarely exist to facilitate statistical sampling (see Chapter 5). The businesses themselves often operate seasonally. Many are dispersed, mobile, and small-scale, effectively invisible to all but the most relentless and resourceful interviewers. Most fail to maintain accurate accounts, so interviewers must depend on the goodwill and recall of the respondents.

Fungibility of enterprise assets has proven a problem, particularly in small enterprise credit evaluations. Beneficiaries use borrowed funds for a wide variety of purposes other than financing their nonfarm enterprise (see, for example, Gurand et al. 1994 and Gaile and Foster 1996). Therefore, evaluations that focus on the assisted enterprise as the unit of analysis fail to capture the full benefits (or the full costs) accruing to the assisted household. In response to this problem, many evaluators now look at program impact in the context of the overall household. This increases both data requirements and analytical complexity as analysts seek to sort out the diverse interactions and causations in this broader household setting.

A related challenge concerns the difficulty of providing a satisfactory definition of the "project" under review. Often a particular intervention builds on earlier work by the same organization. Sometimes a new undertaking involves substantial early experimentation as a variety of new and different approaches are tried, rejected, or modified. Particularly in more complex undertakings, the required interventions often evolve over time as particular blockages are identified and dealt with, sometimes through the establishment of private, for-profit enterprises supplying particular services facilitated by the project. In these instances, there is no clear agreement as to appropriate ways of drawing a line around a particular project to be evaluated (Kapila and Mead 2002). Nor do standards exist for projecting the future time path of benefits and costs, though these assumptions often determine the final outcomes in benefit-cost evaluations.

Once these practical difficulties are resolved, the evaluator must grapple with the thorny analytical problem of the counterfactual, determining the state of the world "without" the project intervention. Selection bias among locations and participants, program dropouts, and potential displacement of unassisted firms by those that receive project support all complicate determination of how the affected household would have fared without assistance. Armendáriz de

---

43. For more detailed discussion of these and a range further methodological difficulties, see David and Meyer (1980), Kilby and D'Zmura (1985), Barnes (1996), Sebstad and Chen (1996), Khandker (1998), Coleman (1999), Hulme (2000), Woller (2000), Karlan (2001), Dunn (2002), Meyer (2002), and Armendáriz de Aghion and Morduch (2005).

Aghion and Morduch (2005) provide a useful general review of evaluation strategies for overcoming these difficulties.

Measuring Costs

Impact measurement has attracted the most attention, given the many difficulties it poses. Consequently, some analysts in recent years have tended to ignore cost issues. As a result, they are unable to compare benefits to costs. Evaluators of BDS and financial service programs used to measure benefits and costs. The BDS evaluations often still do (Kapila and Mead 2002). However, with several notable exceptions, most credit evaluations nowadays fail to compare benefits to costs.[44] Instead, many argue that because microfinance interventions aim to create self-sustaining financial institutions, measurement of program costs is not necessary. As a result, for the most common financial interventions we know more about impact than cost-effectiveness (Armendáriz de Aghion and Morduch 2005).

The Record on Impact and Costs

In the face of much variation, a gentle sifting of the evaluation literature does suggest some general conclusions. For greater detail, the reader will benefit from several reviews cited below.

Small Enterprise Promotion

INTEGRATED ESTATES.   The integrated hothouse industrial estates are widely viewed as colossal failures—at the very least in their rural incarnations. A virtual absence of careful benefit-cost evaluations offers the surest sign that the heavy cost of these programs has overwhelmed any income gains to the economy.[45] Most field practitioners doubt that the model was ever cost-effective, even in the urban settings for which it was originally designed.[46] In rural areas, costs have proven higher and benefits slimmer. Conceived in an era of heavy subsidies to medium-scale and large industries, this lavish all-in-one combination package has proven a particularly costly and ineffective model when transplanted to smaller enterprises and to rural zones.

MINIMALIST CREDIT.   Most voluminous by far, the growing evaluation literature on minimalist credit programs bespeaks a confidence on the part of the legion of devoted practitioners that promote these programs. Outreach has

---

44. Exceptions to this rule include Townsend and Yaron (2001), Schreiner (2003), and Khandker (2005).

45. In one memorable speech, in 1984, an African head of state referred to the operators of that country's all-purpose industrial estate as "undertakers."

46. Sanghvi (1975), Somasekhara (1975), Livingstone (1977), UNIDO (1978), Sandesara (1980), Kilby (1982), Kashyap (1988), Chadha (1993), Lee and Suh (1998).

proven impressive, with thousands of microfinance institutions worldwide lending to over 20 million households, many of the largest of these in rural areas of Asia (Meyer and Nagarajan 2000; Lapenu and Zeller 2001). Financial sustainability, however, has proven more elusive. In spite of serious efforts at covering costs, the majority of microfinance institutions still depend on government and donor subsidies for their existence (Meyer 2002; Armendáriz de Aghion and Morduch 2005). Chapter 11 discusses these two dimensions of microfinance performance in greater detail, while the ensuing discussion focuses on client impact, the third dimension of credit program impact (Zeller and Meyer 2002).

At the client level, among the 60-plus credit projects reviewed by Kilby and D'Zmura (1985), Grant (1993), Hulme and Mosely (1996), Sebstad and Chen (1996), Webster and Fidler (1996), Johnson and Rogaly (1997), Wright (2000), Morduch and Haley (2002), and Goldberg (2005), most documented some increase in income for the majority of assisted firms. At the household level, following an injection of no-frills credit, most studies document income increases as well, though the impact varies by gender of entrepreneur, location, and activity. Empowerment of women, measured by evaluators in various ways, typically improves in tandem with income measures, while measures of infant nutrition and educational access prove mixed.

Though generally flattering,[47] these results likely overstate the impact of credit programs because of chronic difficulties in finding suitable control groups and evaluation methods that satisfactorily address persistent problems of displacement, dropouts, and selection bias in favor of higher-productivity locations and more dynamic assisted enterprises.[48] Consider the calculation indicating that among borrowers from the BRI-UD microcredit program in Indonesia, employment doubled, while income grew at an annual rate of 21 percent per year compared to only 4 percent in the general rural population. As the authors of this study note, absence of a well-matched control group cautions restraint in interpreting these results. The comparison group used in this calculation included not a matched set of comparable enterprises, but all rural households, including farmers, nonfarmers, and the landless (Hulme and Mosely 1996, Table 11.7). Even sophisticated econometric analyses with large sample sizes and careful attention to these issues are not immune to selection bias problems,

---

47. Note that traditional small and medium-scale enterprise lending through development banks has not fared so well. For this reason, agencies such as the World Bank have explicitly moved away from small and medium-scale enterprise lending in favor of increased minimalist, microenterprise credit schemes (Webster, Riopelle, and Chidzero 1996).

48. On the displacement problem, see Hossain (1988a), Osmani (1989), and Dawson and Jeans (1997). On selection bias, see discussions by Sebstad and Chen (1996), Pitt and Khandker (1998), and Morduch (1999a). On the dropout issue, see Nagarajan (2001), Armendáriz de Aghion and Morduch (2005), and Alexander-Tedeschi and Karlan (2006).

as debates over the impact of Bangladesh's Grameen Bank underscore (Pitt and Khandker 1998; Morduch 1999a,b). As one recent review has concluded, "Relatively few rigorous studies of impacts have been completed, and the evidence on statistical impacts has been mixed so far" (Armendáriz de Aghion and Morduch 2005).

Emerging evidence on dropout rates suggests that desertions from microfinance institutions (MFIs) may be quite large. Nagarajan's (2001) review of 33 MFIs indicates that annual dropout rates among Asian institutions average over 25 percent of borrowers. If so, this phenomenon bears serious investigation. Why are so many leaving if microfinance is producing generally positive benefits for clients? And if impact studies fail to account for these dropouts, are they not in danger of overstating benefits (Meyer 2002)?

In spite of these measurement difficulties, important regional differences seem to emerge consistently from these results. In general, the more numerous Asian studies of microfinance project a greater impact on the income and empowerment of women than do the African studies.[49] Despite roughly comparable portfolio risks (Barres 2002), loan repayment in Africa averages only 60 percent, far lower than the rate of over 90 percent cited in most Asian studies (Webster, Riopelle, and Chidzero 1997). Given Africa's less rigid and hierarchical social structure, as well as its more even access to land, widespread availability of informal rotating credit societies,[50] and more widespread economic activity of women to begin with, it is not surprising that empowerment gains there turn out to be far less than in Asia. Likewise, many of the operational rules for client selection and close control of repayments have emerged in the densely populated zones where pioneer programs emerged, in urban Latin America and in rural Asia. In Africa, where population density is far lower and client contact costs are consequently higher, these standard operating systems have proven less effective.

Across income groups, distributional analyses suggest that microcredit proves most adept at improving incomes for the better-off poor, those just below the poverty line, rather than for the very poorest. Though the average profits of assisted enterprises typically increase, a small proportion of larger enterprises accounts for the bulk of this growth, while the majority grow only a little (Sebsted and Chen 1996). While loans targeted at the very poor yield limited benefits, those that target the better off achieve a greater impact (Hulme and Mosely 1996). Some evidence even suggests that the very poorest, who lack basic skills and investment opportunities, may emerge more indebted but little better off.[51]

---

49. Abugre (1994), Sebstad and Chen (1996), Webster, Riopelle, and Chidzero (1996), Buckley (1997).

50. In contrast, Africa appears to enjoy less informal trade credit, perhaps because of less landlessness, lower credit demand, and lower input intensity in agriculture.

51. Buckley (1997), Coleman (1999), Meyer (2002).

Several gaps remain. Microfinance has not taught us very much about how to successfully lend to small and medium-scale businesses whose sole source of income for loan repayment is derived from the business rather than from the household. Microfinance has demonstrated how lending organizations can be created to serve the demand for working capital by microfirms, especially in trading. But it has learned little about how to make longer-term loans to finance the fixed capital investments of larger-scale enterprises. Most crucially for those interested in the RNFE, microcredit has not significantly advanced our understanding of how to lend successfully to farm and nonfarm enterprises in rural areas where population densities are lower and where the seasonality in cash flows, lending costs, and risks typically prove greater.

From this vast body of reviews, a series of best practice rules of thumb has emerged for streamlining and honing effective interventions.[52] These have proven valuable in transferring lessons of successful programs and enabling widespread replication throughout the world.

- *Charge interest rates high enough to cover costs.* The poor consistently demonstrate their willingness to pay market interest rates for convenient lending services. These prove necessary to improve prospects for institutional sustainability.
- *Slash costs.* Viable rural financial institutions typically reduce administrative overhead to an absolute minimum. This often involves cutting out technical or management advice that adds few benefits but raises program costs considerably.
- *Motivate repayments.* Though some microenterprise institutions (such as BRI) require collateral, most motivate repayment through a variety of other techniques: group guarantees, escalating repeat loans, short-term loans, and repayment schedules that call for frequent (often weekly) payments.
- *Include savings and other services.* Savings services often attract more clients than credit services, particularly among the poor. They also provide the own-source funds necessary for the creation of self-sustaining financial institutions independent of the current large government subsidies. Some microfinance institutions offer remittance transfer services in an effort to tap into a market valued in billions of dollars annually.
- *Tailor programs to each locale.* Given a wide diversity of existing informal credit systems and a diversity of options for microcredit lending programs, many practitioners counsel against blind replication of models imported from elsewhere.[53]

---

52. See Otero and Rhyne (1994), CDASED (1995), Christen et al. (1995), Webster and Fidler (1996), Yaron et al. (1997), Donor Committee (2001), Von Pischke (2002), CGAP / World Bank (2004), and Armendáriz de Aghion and Morduch (2005).

53. Harper (1988), Hulme and Mosely (1996), Wakefield and Duval (1996), Johnson and Rogaly (1997), Morduch (2000).

While many of the latest generation of evaluations seek to improve the measurement of program benefits, few proceed to compare these benefits with program costs. Unlike the early generation of studies, current credit evaluations rarely compare benefits with costs.[54] As is the case with many other categories of intervention, the lack of cost comparisons in the face of large continuing subsidies has seriously compromised efforts to determine the cost-effectiveness of these investments. Across the board, future evaluations need not only to improve their measurement of program benefits but also to compare these benefits to the costs of public subsidies incurred.

BUSINESS DEVELOPMENT SERVICES.   Efforts at delivering nonfinancial services to rural nonfarm enterprises have proven more heterogeneous and problematic and have produced decidedly less flattering results than programs delivering financial services.[55] Reviews of 34 technical, management, and policy assistance projects indicate that slightly over half generated more income benefits than costs, while the remaining half of benefit/cost ratios hovered around 1 or below.[56] Many hundreds of other project assessments failed to report both benefits and costs, suggesting a probable reporting bias in favor of the better performers.

Like microfinance studies, many of these studies confront serious methodological problems. In addition to the imponderables involved in projecting future benefit streams, analysts frequently depend on "before and after" comparisons rather than control groups. Even studies with control groups frequently remain vulnerable to problems of selection bias. Difficulties in projecting future production flows among beneficiary firms give rise to subjective judgments on the part of evaluators and render these projections susceptible to possible upward bias if forecasted earnings prove overly optimistic.

Efforts at fostering commercially sustainable private sector delivery of business services remain in their infancy. As several prominent BDS practitioners have noted, reliance on purely private sector commercial service delivery will likely never fully address the needs of the poor, particularly in underserved rural markets (Kapila and Mead 2002). A review of 16 different BDS projects reports some effort at cost recovery in two-thirds of the projects. A quarter recover over 60 percent of all costs, while 13 percent achieve 100 percent cost recovery (Goldmark, Berte, and Campos 1997). In settings where large and small firms share common commercial interests, a series of interest-

---

54. As an example of the early generation of credit studies, see Kilby and D'Zmura (1985). For an assessment of the more recent literature, see Armendáriz de Aghion and Morduch (2005).

55. For reviews of a broad range of enterprise promotion efforts, see Snodgrass and Biggs (1996), Harper and Finnegan (1998), Levitsky (2000), Escobar, Reardon, and Berdegué (2001), Kapila and Mead (2002), and Snodgrass and Packard Winkler (2004).

56. Kilby and Bangasser (1978), Haggblade (1982), Davies (1988), Malhotra and Santer (1994), Dawson and Jeans (1997), Nelson (1997), Harper and Finnegan (1998), Kapila and Mead (2002).

ing experiments with vouchers and promotion of commercial business linkages is under way.[57] Where feasible, development of these commercial linkages can generate financially sustainable business relationships, sometimes on a very large scale. Efforts with treadle pump manufacturers in Bangladesh, for example, have resulted in a commercially viable network of 84 pump manufacturers and nearly 1,000 distributors that together have profitably supplied over 1.3 million treadle pumps to rural Bangladeshi households since 1985 (Shah et al. 2000).

As in the case of the credit programs, a series of summaries and best practice reviews has consolidated results of the large body of evaluations of business development efforts.[58] Taken together, this evidence suggests the following broad generalizations about current best practices:

- *Focus on clusters of like enterprises rather than on individual firms.* Because rural enterprises are often small, interventions must affect many firms simultaneously to generate sufficient income growth to defray the costs of the intervention. In general, focusing on a functionally related network of firms—referred to variously as value chains, supply chains, clusters, or subsectors—helps to identify systemic opportunities for assisting many like firms at once.[59] For this reason, the strongest performers among the projects reviewed—such as the 20 to 25 percent internal rate of return to rattan export promotion in Indonesia, the 3.6 benefit-cost ratio for improved poultry stock and veterinary services in Bangladesh, and the 5.6 benefit-cost ratio for ornamental fish marketing in Sri Lanka—all focused on systemic interventions in specific commodity subsectors.[60] Tendler's (1989, 1034) review of six well-performing microenterprise promotion projects likewise concludes: "All the better-performing organizations started out with a narrow focus. They concentrated on a particular task . . . or on workers in a particular trade, sector or income-earning activity." A decade and a half later, Snodgrass and Packard Winkler (2004, 60) reached a similar conclusion after reviewing 42 donor-funded enterprise development projects, finding that "the cluster approach creates greater leverage and systemic reform in the business environment and market institutions than direct firm-level assistance."

---

57. Mead (1994b), Goldmark, Berte, and Campos (1997), Riley and Steel (2000).

58. This section draws heavily on reviews by Boomgard (1989), Grant (1993), Webster and Fidler (1996), Donor Committee (1997, 2001), IDB (1997), Levitsky (2000), Escobar, Reardon, and Berdegué (2001), Kapila and Mead (2002), and Snodgrass and Packard Winkler (2004).

59. See Boomgard et al. (1992), Grant (1993), Malhotra and Santer (1994), Chen (1996), Humphrey and Schmitz (1996), Nelson (1997), Porter (1998), Schmitz and Nadvi (1999), Dawson et al. (2000), Lusby and Panliburton (2002), and Snodgrass and Packard Winkler (2004).

60. Davies (1988), Malhotra and Santer (1994), Kapila and Mead (2002).

- *Focus on a few key missing ingredients.* Cost containment remains a central challenge in moving from high-density urban settings to rural areas. In pursuit of streamlined, low-fat budgets, both credit and business development services have increasingly specialized, focusing on one or a few missing elements that prove key to unblocking opportunities for aggregate nonfarm enterprise growth in a specific setting. In their purest form, these efforts focus on what Kilby (1979) has dubbed the "single missing ingredient." Increasingly, business development efforts have started with a narrow focus, though many have found it necessary to modify their point of intervention as systems evolve and new constraints become binding (Kapila and Mead 2002). As an early review of 32 microenterprise support projects concludes, "The evidence in the sample neither rejects nor supports the 'single missing ingredient' hypothesis about technical assistance. The successful technical assistance programs, however, point to the need to accurately identify the *essential missing ingredients* and to deal with them in an effective and efficient manner" (Boomgard 1989, 75).
- *Reinforce growing markets and market access.* In spite of past suspicions of unregulated markets, most governments today recognize that sustainable development must take account of market forces and that growing markets constitute a prerequisite for growth of the RNFE. Some promotional activities have focused on helping such enterprises participate more actively in dynamic market segments both in rural areas and in urban and export markets (Millard 1996; McVay 1999). Similar opportunities exist for helping small enterprises to supply goods and services to the government (Tendler and Amorim 1996). A number of projects have facilitated the emergence of for-profit enterprises to undertake particular production, trading, or brokering functions in expanding subsectors (Kapila and Mead 2002).
- *Treat firms as clients.* Increasingly, organizations promoting rural enterprise development identify valued BDS and charge fees for these services.[61] In this spirit, Zimbabwe's Improve Your Business program charged full cost for its training services (Harper and Finnegan 1998). A handful of studies has begun to systematically investigate existing privately met demand for BDS (Lusby and Panliburton 2002). In the same way that moneylenders and informal financial markets inspired microcredit practice, reviews of existing business services demanded and supplied (apprenticeship training, management assistance, and the provision of product quality and pricing information) aim to spark similar innovation in nonfinancial service delivery (Barton 1997). Recent work with training vouchers and

---

61. Barton (1997), Steel, Tanburn, and Hallberg (2000).

business linkages between firms of different sizes offers examples of efforts at facilitating private sector service delivery.[62]

Agricultural Marketing and Agribusiness Promotion

Large private agribusiness firms govern many of the opportunities facing smaller, functionally related rural nonfarm businesses. They commission diagnostic assessments and implement many of the most important interventions affecting agricultural markets and agroprocessing in rural areas of the developing world. Yet because these analyses are proprietary, they remain outside the public domain. Even so, available anecdotal evidence suggests that their impact on smaller rural nonfarm firms is often considerable. Over the past several decades, the market dynamics triggered by large agribusiness firms have many times benefited smaller rural nonfarm firms. During the 1990s, export horticulture firms in Kenya and Costa Rica assisted tens of thousands of small growers to access these markets through the provision of inputs as well as technical and marketing assistance (Reardon and Berdegué 2002; Minot and Ngigi 2003). Yet in other instances, large agribusiness firms stifle opportunities for small rural firms, either through outright competition or via the imposition of quantity and consistency standards that small firms find difficult to attain. Across Latin America, the growth of supermarkets has driven tens of thousands of small retailers into bankruptcy (see Chapter 9). Similarly, the growth of supermarket chains in Brazil, Argentina, and Chile has imposed quantity and standardization requirements that rural dairies have found difficult to meet, leading to thousands of bankruptcies among smaller dairies over the past decade.[63] Sometimes small players can respond successfully, as in the spirited rejoinder by a local trader in Mazabuka, Zambia, who effectively countered the arrival of South African Shoprite by consolidating his small shops into a sleek, modern supermarket. Similarly, the Parranque cooperative in Chile enables small farmers to band together to meet the quantity and quality standards required by large supermarkets (Berdegué 2001). While legions of small players submerge, some do successfully adjust and adapt. Survival requires rapid and significant adjustment to new market conditions.

With public sector interventions to improve agricultural markets, rigorous benefit-cost comparisons remain elusive. While costs are easy to measure, benefits prove more difficult. The introduction of grades and standards frequently improves market system performance and growth, but in ways that are difficult to quantify. New wholesale markets may relieve urban congestion, reduce

---

62. Goldmark, Berte, and Campos (1997), Grierson, Mead, and Moyo (1997), McVay (1999), Riley and Steel (2000), Lusby and Panlibuton (2002), Bear, Gibson, and Hitchins (2003), Hitchins, Elliot, and Gibson (2004).

63. Gutman (1999), Jank, Farina, and Galan (1999), Dirven (2001).

pollution, and improve public health; but again, to our knowledge, these benefits have rarely been quantified. A welter of market-oriented interventions by
governments and NGOs has yielded only a trickle of careful empirical impact
analyses.

In spite of a dearth of rigorous benefit-cost analyses,[64] a number of reviews
have attempted to summarize lessons learned from public sector experience in
diagnosing and improving agricultural marketing systems in the developing
world.[65] Drawing on this body of work, several general conclusions emerge for
guiding future work:

- *Develop a new role for government.* Large private firms have partially
  usurped many classic public roles, including the provision of market
  infrastructure and the establishment of key market institutions such as
  food safety standards, grades, and regulations. However, public intervention remains essential in reviewing, endorsing, and standardizing food
  safety laws and making them widely available to potential food industry
  participants. Likewise, it remains necessary for public intervention to fill
  in gaps in market infrastructure that will enable access by key groups of
  local suppliers.
- *Help small players adjust.* To survive in rapidly changing rural nonfarm
  supply chains, small players must adapt, often quickly, or find alternate
  livelihoods. New organizational and logistic arrangements imposed by
  large exporters and retailers require adjustments in production methods,
  quantity requirements, grading, and contracting that weaker members
  find difficult to fathom, finance, and execute. Sometimes public or collective action can remedy asymmetries in power and information. Collective organization and negotiation, punctual training, or bulk facilities may
  be necessary to enable them to respond rapidly and flexibly to these new
  opportunities.[66]
- *Focus on supply chains in specific commodity subsectors.* This leads to opportunities for interventions that assist many like firms simultaneously.
  Whether in the form of policy change, provision of key infrastructure,

---

64. Welcome exceptions include Berdegué (2001) and Kapila and Mead (2002).

65. Harrison et al. (1975), Riley and Weber (1983), Shaffer et al. (1985), Abbott (1986), Mittendorf (1986), Maxwell and Holtzman (1995), Meyer and Larson (1997), Mooney, Stathacos, and
Adoum (1998), Giovannucci (2001), Giovannucci and Reardon (2001), Lamb and Brower (2001),
Kapila and Mead (2002), Reardon and Berdegué (2002), Van Roekel et al. (2002), Jaffee et al.
(2003).

66. These efforts involve thorny political economy issues, which are addressed most directly
in the growing literature on global value chains. See, for example, Kaplinksy (2000), Gereffi and
Kaplinsky (2001), Vorley (2001), Humphrey and Schmitz (2002), Kaplinsky and Morris (2003),
and Giuliani, Pietrobelli, and Rabellotti (2005).

organizational improvements, or introduction of grades and standards, supply chain interventions typically benefit many similar firms at one stroke. As a recent agribusiness review concludes, "AMIS II [the Agribusiness and Marketing Improvement Strategies Project] achieved the most success when its activities had a narrower, as opposed to broader, commodity or industry and geographic focus" (Mooney, Stathacos, and Adoum 1998, 36). Many practitioners agree that focusing promotional efforts on clusters of related firms offers the greatest prospects for successfully assisting many firms at once.

- *Promote collective action, private and public.* Market improvement often requires provision of public goods (roads and physical facilities) as well as behavioral changes requiring adoption and enforcement of new rules, standards, and systems of collective action. Often a mix of public action and collective private intervention is required. Marketing associations, cooperatives, or even influential private firms operating as channel leaders can serve as catalysts of change. In instances in which oligopsony emerges, public or collective action may be necessary to improve the bargaining power of weaker elements in the system, a particularly important consideration in the current poverty-oriented wave of interest in rural nonfarm business development.

- *Minimize the costs of physical infrastructure.* In many cases, physical infrastructure has been overbuilt and underused, particularly when governments and donors are involved. Rigorous comparison of alternatives will often reveal less costly options. In some cases, strategic upgrading of bottlenecks (often bridges or culverts) in rural road systems may obviate the need for more costly cold storage facilities. Incremental investments often prove most prudent. The association of private with public financing proves therapeutic in keeping facilities costs within reason.

- *Separate technical from financial assistance.* Business promotion via agribusiness development centers (ADCs) has produced mixed results (Lamb and Brower 2001; Jaffee et al. 2003). Though some report benefit-cost ratios as high as 5 to 1, detailed descriptions of methods, data, and "without project" baselines remain sketchy. Some operate like miniature India model "one-stop shops" with full business promotion services including technical, marketing, managerial, and financial services. Others offer more streamlined services and aim to play catalytic and facilitating roles. In general, the more costly variants have proven least cost-effective. ADCs have sometimes effectively contributed to market development, particularly by helping domestic firms to identify and land export contracts that expand market opportunities at home. The ADC experience, like much of the small enterprise literature, suggests that promoters should separate technical from financial assistance in order to avoid institutional conflicts of interest and to enable an independent financial appraisal as a check on the feasibility of each proposed commercial activity.[67]

Regional Development.

For a decade and a half, beginning in the early 1970s, integrated rural development (IRD) projects held the limelight in development circles. Governments and donors spent billions of dollars on these ambitious, multisectoral regional development efforts. All major donors, including the Scandinavians, Europeans, and major development foundations boarded the bandwagon. Then, after 15 years of intense IRD activity, governments and donors largely abandoned this favored child. Some regional development authorities continue to operate, though at very low levels compared to the heyday of the 1970s. Most no longer exist or have been folded into line ministries or local government authorities. In the end, governments and donors alike largely voted with their feet to exit these ambitious IRD efforts. Given the scale of the investments poured into these activities, IRD has attracted a series of major reviews on which the following summary is largely based.[68]

Why did the IRD efforts generally fail to generate sustainable regional development? Participants, financial supporters, and reviewers point to a series of common problems. First, these efforts proved far too complex to manage. Myriad new administrative relationships led to conflict, infighting, and coordination difficulties across ministries and other executing agencies. Second, spending on social services and infrastructure often swamped local resources. In the widely touted Aga Khan IRD program in rural Pakistan, project expenditures stood at $500 per household (World Bank 1990). Without commensurate increases in new sources of local revenue, rural authorities could sustain the mandated social expenditures only with steady infusions of outside funding. Third, and closely related, was the importance of a core agricultural production package. The programs that performed best offered a strong agricultural technology package appropriate to farmers that effectively stimulated broad agricultural growth. The Puebla Project, an exclusively agricultural project with strong technical support from CIMMYT (Centro Internacional de Mejoramiento de Maíz y Trigo), generated an internal rate of return of 14 percent (de Janvry 1981). Yet many of the other programs lacked a viable agricultural technology. This resulted in part from a fourth common problem, the pressure to scale up rapidly from successful pilot regions to other locations where circumstances differed, often substantially. Many pilot activities functioned well because they benefited from intensive investment in location-specific diagnostics, data, and manpower

---

67. See, for example, Webster and Fidler (1996), Goldmark, Berte, and Campos (1997), and Donor Committee (2001).

68. Ruttan (1975, 1984), Holdcroft (1978, 1984), USAID (1987), World Bank (1987), Tendler (1993).

recruitment. Subsequent replication in new and different regions proved difficult given the differing circumstances into which the systems were transplanted. Without the time and resources necessary for tailoring schemes to new locations, the rapid expansion of IRD became little more than the imposition of an imported blueprint rather than the initiation of a process for mobilizing local resources and capitalizing on opportunities unique to each locale. Finally, central governments frequently proved reluctant to devolve political or financial control to local governments. The imposition of new obligations without corresponding political authority or fiscal resources led to inherently unsustainable systems that rapidly collapsed following the withdrawal of outside funding.

Against this general backdrop, consistent differences emerge across geographic regions. A review of 400 World Bank IRD projects found the highest share of satisfactory programs in Asia, with much lower success rates in Africa and Latin America (Donaldson 1993). A similar finding, echoed in USAID's in-house review, found the lowest success rates in Africa, a finding attributed to the general difficulties in finding improved agricultural technologies in rainfed agriculture (USAID 1987).

In an effort to identify positive lessons from this experience, the World Bank commissioned a review of 22 rural development projects in Northeast Brazil (Tendler 1993). While these projects had generally failed to meet overall performance targets, many enjoyed moments of glory, episodes or particular activities in which they became noticeably effective contributors to rural development. Such successful episodes generally involved a flexible response by project managers to very specific problems or opportunities with built-in incentives and outside pressures, often from local actors or organizations that were keenly interested in the performance of the project. In several cases, these involved effective responses to agricultural diseases, widely perceived threats to rural welfare that readily mobilized local attention. Often these efforts involved streamlining and simplifying program activities to concentrate on one or two signature activities that served as the "'locomotive' driving the rest of the project" (Tendler 1993, 14).

At least three positive prescriptions emerge from the early IRD experience. In general, they parallel findings in the small enterprise and agricultural marketing literature.

- *Ensure sound macro policy.* A favorable macro policy environment is essential, particularly one that provides adequate incentives for agriculture and rural businesses.
- *Center income-generating efforts around an improved agricultural technology.* An improved agricultural technology proves a necessary motor for rural and rural nonfarm growth. The absence or malfunction of this motor frequently causes the rural economy to stall.
- *Focus on a few key interventions.* The programs that work best seem to be those that do a few things well. In spite of the intellectual attraction of the

systems perspective, in practice it proves difficult to juggle too many moving parts at once. Hence, streamlining and focusing on key opportunities or constraints seem to work best in rural nonfarm promotion and in rural development in general.

The new wave of local area and territorial development programs has not yet, to our knowledge, generated the track record necessary for quantitative evaluation of impact and cost. Nor has the more general literature on political, administrative, and fiscal decentralization empirically assessed the impact of local governance on rural nonfarm activity. Broad studies of the impact of decentralization on economic growth underscore the complexity of these relationships (Von Braun and Grote 2002; Enikolopov and Zhuravskaya 2003). Smatterings of indirect evidence suggest a possible link via local government's influence on rural infrastructure and agriculture, as in the Chinese example discussed in Chapter 13. One cross-country econometric study has found a strong relationship between fiscal decentralization and spending on infrastructure (Estache and Sinha 1995). Rural infrastructure, in turn, strongly affects agricultural growth,[69] which in turn stimulates rural nonfarm activity through a variety of growth linkages (Chapter 7). Though tentative and indirect, this evidence supports the notion that strengthening local governments could indeed contribute to building prosperous rural economies.

A new generation of practitioners has returned to local governments in the developing world with fresh optimism, new analytical tools, and a renewed conviction that improvements in local decisionmaking, administrative capacity, and financial authority can contribute to accelerated rural economic growth. Many of the more recent efforts have revolved around local allocation of social development funds, through which local leaders gain a greater say in identifying key interventions. Evidence to date suggests three principal requirements for effective decentralization in support of local economic development (Tacoli and Satterthwaite 2003):

- Clear devolution of decisionmaking authority from central to local governments
- Control of adequate financial resources at the local level
- Adequate local government staff capacity

Policies and Public Investments

Chapter 11 reviews available evidence on the impact of the policy and institutional environment on rural nonfarm activity As that discussion emphasizes,

---

69. See, for example Barnes and Binswanger (1986), Binswanger, Khandker, and Rosenzweig (1989), Fan, Hazell, and Thorat (1999), Fan, Zhang, and Zhang (2002).

policies provide powerful levers for influencing the welfare of rural nonfarm enterprises. Wielded prudently, they can stimulate opportunities for many like firms at a single stroke. Wielded inadvertently, as they often are, they can stifle rural nonfarm activity instead. Getting the policy environment right enables rural households to apply their ingenuity to solve many rural development problems themselves. Yet getting it wrong can cripple them instead.

The Bottom Line

Opportunities and constraints in the RNFE vary enormously across locations and over time. The resulting diversity of situations has led to an extraordinary array of efforts on behalf of the RNFE. From this broad range of experience, several general principles emerge.

- *Policy interventions are most powerful.* Policy interventions typically offer the most powerful levers, for good or for ill. They affect a multitude of similar firms simultaneously. When carefully designed, they can benefit large numbers of firms at once. Experience suggests that both macro policies and highly tailored subsector-specific rules on grades, contracting, competition, and industry regulation can greatly improve prospects for equitable growth in specific rural nonfarm supply chains.
- *Minimize cost per beneficiary.* The experience of the past 50 years suggests a need to resist overbuilding. Multipurpose rural industrial estates, IRD projects, and overbuilt roads, banks, and marketing infrastructure have frequently led to inefficient public resource use. The most cost-effective inventions typically focus on specific activities and on the minimum elements necessary to effect change among large numbers of rural firms. Though interventions can be large in absolute scale, to be effective they must reduce per-firm costs to a bare minimum. Recent systematic efforts to partner with private firms and facilitate private sector delivery of key marketing, input supply, and credit functions stem from a desire to improve sustainability and reduce costs.
- *Leveraged interventions in specific supply chains yield greatest benefits.* Leverage vastly improves prospects for cost-effective intervention. To generate benefits in excess of program costs, efforts at rural nonfarm promotion need to focus on strategic interventions that will open up growth opportunities for large numbers of rural enterprises at once. Leveraged interventions—via policies, strategic injections of new technology, linkage to large firms, market development, improved supplier credit, or other system-level interventions—simultaneously reduce per-firm costs and increase aggregate impact. For this reason, system-level interventions, those that open up growth prospects for large numbers of firms at a single stroke, prove most cost-effective (Table 12.3).

TABLE 12.3 Cost-effectiveness of alternative interventions for promoting rural nonfarm activity

	Impact	Cost	Cost-effectiveness
System-level interventions (multiple-firm impact)			
1. Policies	High	Low	Very high
2. Public investments			
a. Physical infrastructure	High when appropriately sited	Variable	High when not overbuilt
b. Education	High	Moderate	High
c. Credit institutions	High	Often unmeasured	Rarely measured but potentially high
3. Large firm intermediaries	High	Low	High, but appropriate only when large and small firm interests coincide
Direct assistance to individual firms			
4. Credit	Moderate	Low, though often unmeasured	Rarely measured, though available indicators are moderately optimistic
5. Business development services			
a. To individual firms	Low	High	Low
b. Affecting many firms simultaneously	High	Variable, but low if focused on critical minimum constraints	Variable but potentially high

Future Directions

Key Interventions

Evidence overwhelmingly suggests that a favorable policy and institutional environment provides a necessary foundation for widespread rural nonfarm prosperity and growth. Yet alone, a favorable policy and institutional environment will generally prove insufficient to ensure equitable growth in RNFEs of the developing world during the first half of the twenty-first century. Rapid globalization and penetration of rural areas by large firms will require rapid adjustment by rural firms. Successful transition in the new RNFE will require development of marketing and input supply links with large firms. It will require grades, standards, and contracting enforcement as well as the assembly infrastructure necessary to connect dominant large firms with a multitude of smaller rural players. Huge disparities in asset distribution and access to public services risk trapping the poor in perennial backwaters of the rural economy. Sitting back contentedly in a neutral policy environment will most assuredly risk leaving the poor far behind in the rapid rural transformation now under way. To enable access by the poor, interveners will increasingly need to work with the private sector, particularly the large firms driving change in key commodity subsectors.

In the future, continued reliance on large-scale infusions of credit will prove inadequate in responding to new opportunities and constraints. Currently massive minimalist credit programs are perceived as the silver bullet in many host country and donor arsenals. Most major donors have jumped aboard this bandwagon, responding to the call from the 1997 Microcredit Summit for over $20 billion in microenterprise lending to reach 100 million poor households over the ensuing 10 years (Microcredit Summit 1996). The United Nations has actively encouraged these efforts, declaring 2005 the U.N. Year of Microcredit. And in 2006, the Grameen Bank and its founder, Muhammad Yunus, received the Nobel Peace Price for their efforts in launching the microcredit movement. The scale and enthusiasm of this wave of efforts have inspired a whole new cast of players, bringing new talent and energy to bear on behalf of the rural poor. As a result, many valuable lessons—on cost reduction, on emulating private sector firms offering similar services, and on the general principle of adopting systemic, institution-level interventions affecting many small firms at once— have come out of the minimalist credit model. This enthusiastic surge of activity has undoubtedly energized field workers and improved efforts at delivering nonfinancial services as well.

Even so, looking to the future we see clear limits to the purely finance-led growth strategy embedded in the minimalist credit model.[70] In increasingly

---

70. See Osmani (1989) for an early statement of this position.

saturated informal sector markets, the launching of thousands of additional entrants into labor-intensive, low-productivity activities seems more likely to result in income redistribution among the poor rather than in aggregate economic
growth. Indeed, had the agricultural establishment depended solely on a massive
infusion of rural credit in the 1960s, without improved agricultural technology,
the world would never have seen a green revolution. As one major review of
microcredit programs concludes, "The best evidence to date suggests that making a dent in poverty rates will require increasing overall levels of economic
growth and employment generation. Micro finance may be able to help some
households take advantage of those processes, but nothing so far suggests it will
ever drive them" (Morduch 1999a, 1610). Undoubtedly, savings, insurance,
and other financial products will help rural businesses manage risk and finance
rural investments. Credit, like roads, telephones, and schools, provides an important lubricant enabling commodities and factors of production to flow smoothly
in search of opportunities across rural space. But quantum improvements in rural welfare will require new engines of economic growth, new technologies,
and new ways of doing business. While smoothly functioning financial markets
will be essential in facilitating that transition, history suggests that other forces
will drive and accelerate change.

Key Actors

Major governments and donors have once again called for a renewed commitment to expanding economic opportunities for the rural poor. Yet, given the
post–Cold War climate of declining aggregate aid flows, the future of rural nonfarm enterprise promotion will look very different from its past. The major
external funding injections available for widespread and costly experimentation
during the 1970s will simply not be available in the future. Instead, developing
country governments' own resources will dominate rural nonfarm enterprise
support as never before.

The private sector will likewise play a larger role in the future than in the
past. The liberalization of trade, investment, and markets in the early 1990s has
radically altered dynamics in many rural nonfarm subsectors. While growing
markets open up new opportunities for some rural nonfarm suppliers, rapidly
mutating supply chain management imposes change that many find difficult to
accommodate. Because large private firms increasingly drive market growth
and opportunities, interveners will need to understand how supply chains are
structured and how rural suppliers can benefit from these new opportunities.
Increasingly this will involve working with large firms, or at least understanding how they interact with small players in the RNFE.

13 Contrasting Rural Nonfarm Policies and Performance in China and India: Lessons for the Future

ANIT MUKHERJEE AND XIAOBO ZHANG

China and India together constitute more than one-third of the total world population. They operate the largest economies in the developing world, both overall and in the rural nonfarm economy (RNFE). They dominate in scale, diversity, technological sophistication, and dynamism. Because of the scale of their RNFEs, in a real sense, the experience of these two giants defines the center of gravity of rural nonfarm policy in the developing world.

In the RNFE, as in other spheres of economic policy, these two Asian giants have followed distinctive paths, though they started from a similar base. At the beginning of the 1950s, both China and India were predominantly rural, low-income economies, with agriculture the predominant sector contributing more than three-quarters of the total gross domestic product (GDP).

Over the past five decades, China and India have made rapid improvements in their standard of living, in the structural transformation of their economies, and in the development of their secondary and tertiary sectors (Figure 13.1). Agricultural growth has made both countries self-sufficient in food, providing a surplus for export and capital for other sectors. The rural sector, as a result, has undergone substantial change in composition. Industries and services now form an integral part of the output and employment of the rural sector. The share of agriculture in total GDP has declined to less than one-third in India and less than one-fifth in China. This transition is remarkable considering the initial situation of the two countries half a century ago.

The rural nonfarm sector has played a key role in the economic transition of both countries over the past two decades. A look behind the macroeconomic aggregates reveals more rapid growth of rural nonfarm employment in China than in India, especially over the decade of the 1990s. Since the initiation of the open door policy in China, the dynamic rural nonfarm sector has contributed in a large measure to its remarkable export growth in recent years. Rural township and village enterprises and, more recently, private enterprises, have

The authors are grateful for the financial support of IFPRI and for extremely helpful comments and editing by Steven Haggblade, Peter Hazell, and Kiran Gajwani.

293

FIGURE 13.1   Per capita GDP growth, 1980–2004

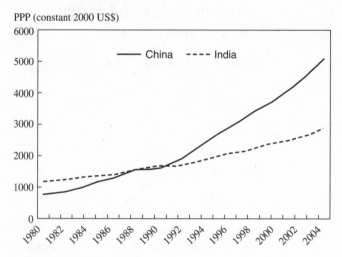

SOURCE: World Bank (2005b).

generated employment for the rural labor force and absorbed labor released from agriculture.

In India, too, the small-scale sector, including traditional village industries, contributes nearly two-thirds of organized sector employment. After a period of sustained expansion in the 1980s, however, growth in output and employment has fallen significantly. During the 1990s, when China's rural manufacturing sector was thriving, India witnessed a decline in the share of rural nonfarm manufacturing in national GDP. Compared to the situation in China, rural nonfarm employment in India has increased only moderately (Figures 13.2 and 13.3).[1]

---

1. As in any comparative exercise, data comparability poses a challenge. Definitions of "rural" and coverage of "nonfarm" activities both merit attention. India defines rural areas as all localities with a population below 5,000, a population density below 400 persons per square kilometer, and at least 75 percent of the male working population engaged in agriculture. In China, the household registration system known as *hukou* has generally been used to demarcate rural and urban areas. Although many rural localities in China have grown into small towns over the past half century, they remain classified as rural. Thus the less rapid growth in "rural" nonfarm employment in India may stem, in part, from the automatic reclassification of rural areas as urban as the nonfarm economy grows. For rural enterprises in India, the Annual Survey of Industries provides data for manufacturing units only, but National Sample Surveys on employment and National Accounts Statistics include all types of rural establishments, both in industry and in commerce and services. Statistics on rural enterprises in China include all enterprises at or below the township level. Apart from manufacturing, the data include enterprises engaged in transportation, commerce, construction, and food services. These caveats have to be kept in mind while analyzing the rural nonfarm sectors in the two countries.

FIGURE 13.2   Rural nonfarm employment, 1978–2000

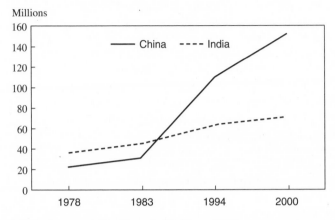

SOURCES: India (various years); Fan, Zhang, and Robinson (2003).

FIGURE 13.3   Rural nonfarm share in total employment, 1978–2000

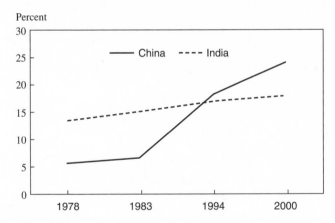

SOURCES: India (various years); Fan, Zhang, and Robinson (2003).

This chapter examines why the development of the rural nonfarm sector has followed different paths in China and India over the past two decades and whether their experience can help us better understand differences in overall performance of the two countries. Can the differences be explained by the evolution of policymaking directed at the rural nonfarm sector over the period leading up to the late 1970s? How much of the current growth and stagnation is the result of institutional differences between the two countries, especially in their political systems, ownership structures, credit institutions, and macroeconomic policies? What lessons can be learned from the relative strengths and weaknesses of the rural nonfarm sector in the two countries?

These questions hold implications for smaller developing countries as well. Ongoing globalization and structural adjustment policies have played a key role in driving recent changes in rural nonfarm economies across the developing world (see Chapters 9 and 10). Now that China and India are both members of the World Trade Organization (WTO), these two large and growing economies exert an increasing impact on world markets for goods as well as services. China has proven able to reap dividends from the open trade regime more effectively than India, particularly in the RNFE. An examination of the causes of this, as well as the potentials, strengths, and weaknesses in China and India, should therefore provide useful indications for other developing countries in the process of nurturing a viable rural nonfarm sector in the current global context.

The Policy Framework for Nonfarm Development

To understand the context of rural nonfarm sector development, it is necessary to look at the path of policymaking since independence in India and China. In this section we focus on those aspects of policy decisions that have had the most significant impact on the rural nonfarm sector.

Common Threads

AGRICULTURE.   Rural development policy in both India and China has focused on agriculture in policy formulation, allocation of public investments, and recurrent budgets. Beginning earlier in India, the considerable investments in research, infrastructure, rural credit, and price support programs led to the launching of green revolution rice and wheat varieties from the second half of the 1960s onward (Fan, Hazell, and Thorat 1999). Though in China policy during the 1950s and 1960s explicitly penalized agriculture, the Chinese reversed course and from the 1980s onward invested heavily in agricultural technology, infrastructure, and input supply to produce a string of technical breakthroughs that have propelled rapid agricultural growth (Fan, Zhang, and Zhang 2004). In both instances, agricultural prosperity has fueled rural economic growth, enabling transfers of labor and capital from agriculture to manufacturing and services while ensuring moderation in urban food prices. In many ways, agricultural policy has formed the cornerstone of rural nonfarm policy in both countries.

COMMERCE AND SERVICES.   In the RNFE specifically, both India and China have concentrated policy and support programs almost exclusively on manufacturing. Both have largely ignored rural commerce and services. Instead, the bulk of policy attention has focused on rural industry and on related macroeconomic policies. In spite of this policy deemphasis, rural commerce and services have flourished, proving the most buoyant segments of the RNFE in both

TABLE 13.1 Distribution of total employment in India, 1978–2000 (percent)

Sector	Rural					Urban				
	1977–78	1983	1987–88	1993–94	1999–2000	1977–78	1983	1987–88	1993–94	1999–2000
Agriculture and allied activities	83.4	81.2	78.3	78.4	76.3	15.3	14.6	13.4	12.3	8.6
Mining and quarrying	0.4	0.5	0.6	0.6	0.5	0.8	1.0	1.2	1.2	0.8
Manufacturing	6.2	6.7	7.2	7.0	7.3	28	26.7	26.0	23.6	22.7
Utilities	0.1	0.1	0.2	0.2	0.2	0.8	0.9	1.0	1.0	0.7
Construction	1.3	1.7	3.3	2.4	3.3	3.8	4.7	5.4	6.3	8.0
Wholesale and retail trade, restaurants and hotels	3.3	3.5	4.0	4.3	5.1	18.8	18.4	19.0	19.4	26.9
Transport, storage, and communication	0.8	1.1	1.3	1.4	2.1	7.9	8.1	7.8	8.0	8.7
Service	4.4	4.9	5.0	5.7	5.2	24.6	25.0	25.7	28.2	23.6
Total (percentage)	100.0	100.0	100.0	100.0	100.0	100.0	100.0	100.0	100.0	100.0
Total employment (millions)	221.3	243.1	252.5	290.3	300.8	49.2	59.6	69.5	81.8	96.0

SOURCE: India, *NSS* for the years covered.

TABLE 13.2 Distribution of rural net domestic product (NDP) in India, farm and nonfarm (percent)

	Share in rural NDP		Share of rural areas in total NDP	
Sectoral divisions	1980–81	1999–2000	1980–81	1999–2000
Agriculture and allied activities	64.4	54.4	94.9	94.0
Manufacturing	9.2	8.1	31.8	29.6
a. Registered	3.2	5.1	20.4	30.1
b. Unregistered	6.0	3.0	45.2	28.8
Utilities	0.6	1.3	40.0	40.4
Construction	4.1	5.0	45.6	39.1
Trade, restaurants, and hotels	6.7	6.9	30.3	22.8
Transport, storage, and communication	1.3	4.2	23.0	34.4
Real estate and business services	4.6	3.2	49.9	29.3
Community social and personal services	7.3	12.5	39.1	41.7
Total rural nonfarm sector	35.6	45.6	35.0	31.6
Total net domestic product (%)	100.0	100.0	58.9	49.5

SOURCE: Chadha (2003).

India and China over the past two decades (Tables 13.1, 13.2, and 13.3). In India, rural commerce and services are now roughly twice the size of the manufacturing sector in terms of employment (Table 13.1).

RATIONALE. The rationale in both countries for developing the rural nonfarm sector has been essentially the same: to provide employment to a growing rural population, to produce goods and services for local consumption, to reap the comparative advantage in terms of labor-intensive modes of production, and to forge links with large-scale, capital-intensive urban industry. Both countries have had some success in meeting these objectives.

While both countries have maintained a common focus on rural industry, policy specifics have differed in India and China, as the following discussion will reveal.

India's Industrial Policy

THE EARLY INDEPENDENCE YEARS. In the decades following World War II in India, the newly independent central government gave primary investment priority to urban-based heavy manufacturing. The emphasis after independence was on replacing imported consumer goods with local import-substituting manufactures. It is interesting to note that in 1948 postindependence India's very first Industrial Policy Resolution mentioned China as a model to be followed in order to organize India's cottage and small-scale industries

TABLE 13.3 Employment in China's town and village enterprises (TVEs), 1978–97

Years	Employment in TVEs		Sectoral share within TVEs (%)				
	Millions	Share of rural labor (%)	Agriculture	Industry	Construction	Transportation	Commerce and services
1978	28	9	22	61	8	4	5
1980	30	9	15	65	11	4	5
1983	32	9	10	67	15	3	5
1984	52	15	5	70	13	2	9
1990	93	22	3	60	15	8	15
1995	129	29	2	59	15	7	16
1997	131	28	2	47	10	3	38

SOURCE: Huang (1999), taken from *Statistical Yearbook of China* and *Township and Village Enterprise Yearbook of China*, various issues.

NOTE: Data before and after 1984 are not comparable because of changes in statistical coverage.

into effective institutions for providing employment opportunities.[2] Under Jawaharal Nehru's leadership, the emphasis of the Industrial Policy Resolution of 1956 turned to large-scale capital-intensive industries such as steel, petrochemicals, engineering, machinery, and so on, under the public sector umbrella. The second five-year plan of 1956 (which came to be known as the Mahalonobis model) set the stage for the development of India's heavy industry.

At the same time, policies reserved special concessions for household and small industries, the village and *khadi* (hand loom) industries championed by Mahatma Gandhi and his followers. The "small-scale" industries were supposed to supply the consumer goods needed by workers in the large-scale sector. The model, therefore, merged Gandhi's and Nehru's divergent visions of industrial development in postindependence India (Little, Mazumdar, and Page 1987). The Small Scale Industries Board and the Central Small Industries Organization were set up following a recommendation of the Ford Foundation team in 1954. These institutions helped in laying the groundwork for the development of the small-scale manufacturing sector for the next two decades. Through a system of direct licensing, production controls in large manufacturers, differential taxation, and direct subsidies, they reserved over 800 items—including hand-loomed items, pottery, matches, and the products of sericulture—for rural and small-scale producers (Kashyap 1988). Direct and indirect subsidy rates reached as high as 70 percent of factory prices (Sandesara 1980).

With the advent of the green revolution in agriculture, farm output and productivity increased in most parts of rural India. Throughout the 1970s, there was a growing demand for goods and services produced locally. Because there was no barrier to entry, small household enterprises catering to the needs of the farm sector flourished in all segments of the nonfarm sector, especially in manufacturing, transport, and services. The positive farm-nonfarm linkage theory, corroborated by several empirical studies (Hazell and Haggblade 1991), was reflected in the government's policy pronouncements, especially the Industrial Policy Resolution of 1980.

The decade of the 1980s was actually the best to date in terms of employment growth. A policy of protection, domestically through the licensing of small-scale units and externally through the imposition of quantitative quotas on imports, coupled with cheap credit, investment subsidy, and infrastructure provision, was instrumental in the substantial increase in both employment and

---

2. The Policy Resolution reads: "Cottage and small-scale industries have a very important role in the national economy. Offering as they do scope for individual, village or co-operative enterprise, and means for the rehabilitation of displaced persons. . . . One of the main objectives will be to give a distinctly co-operative bias to this field of industry. During and before the last war, even a predominantly agricultural country like China showed what could be done in this respect and her mobile industrial co-operative units were of outstanding assistance in her struggle against Japan" (India 1948).

output share of the rural nonfarm sector. Rural employment, especially rural nonfarm employment, grew rapidly. Backward linkages from nonfarm employment to agriculture may have sustained the productivity increase in the farm sector during this period (Fan, Hazell, and Thorat 1999; Mukherjee and Kuroda 2001). More than 45 million jobs were created in the rural areas during the 10 years from 1983 to 1993, most of them in the nonfarm sector (Table 13.1). However, unlike in China, there was no large-scale shift in labor shares between farm and nonfarm sectors.

REFORM. A balance of payments crisis at the beginning of the 1990s produced a macroeconomic crisis for the Indian economy. In response, in 1991 the government adopted a policy of economic reform in both the domestic and external sectors. The most significant aspect of the domestic reform agenda was the liberalization of the industrial sector. The Industrial Policy Statement of July 1991 abolished the licensing regime (known as the "license-permit raj") that had given rise to rents and corruption in the industrial sector. Although the sectors of industry reserved for the small-scale sector remained intact, there was a shift from nontariff barriers to tariff rates that decreased over the whole decade of the 1990s. The Monopolies and Restrictive Trade Practices Act was amended to remove the limit for capital investment. This eliminated the requirement of obtaining the prior approval of the central government for establishment of new undertakings and expansion of undertakings, as well as mergers, amalgamations, and takeovers within the industrial sector. Policy emphasized exports to earn foreign exchange. All industrial units with export potential were allowed to import capital equipment freely.

The economic reform process adversely affected the small-scale sector, especially rural manufacturing. Growth in small-scale units was down by more than half, from over 9 percent in the period between 1981 and 1986 to 4.3 percent from 1996 to 2001. Except in exports, similar decreases in growth rates were recorded for output and employment in small-scale manufacturing during the two periods (Bala Subrahmanya 2004). The share of the rural nonfarm sector in total nonfarm net domestic product (NDP) actually decreased, from nearly 35 percent in 1981 to 31.6 percent in 2001. This indicates a widening gap between secondary and tertiary activity and between rural and urban areas, with serious consequences for both regional and rural-urban income distribution (Table 13.2).

Industrial Policy in China

PREREFORM. Interest in the development of the rural nonfarm sector in China is of a more recent vintage than such interest in India. During the 1950s, China's leaders and policymakers were preoccupied with "catching up" with the developed world, primarily Japan. They placed overwhelming emphasis on heavy industries, and the relative price of agricultural commodities was kept artificially low to transfer resources from rural to urban areas (Lin and Yao 1999).

TABLE 13.4 Composition of rural nonfarm employment in China, 1981

Nonfarm activities	Employment share
Manufacturing	0.45
Construction	0.09
Commerce and commercial services	0.12
Transport and communication	0.05
Services (including government)	0.28
Total	1.00

SOURCE: Ho (1986b).

Promotion of rural industry began during Mao Tse-tung's Great Leap Forward in 1958 with the establishment of large numbers of rural iron and steel foundries aimed at serving agriculture and helping rural areas to "walk on two legs" (Ho 1986a). During the 1960s and 1970s, government promotion efforts focused on five small industries—those producing iron and steel, fertilizer, cement, coal and hydroelectric power, and machinery—with the aim of providing modern inputs for agriculture (Perkins 1977; Sigurdson 1977). This rapid, mandated expansion resulted in the overdevelopment of heavy rural manufacturing activity (Table 13.4). Many plants proved technically inefficient and economically unviable (Ho 1986b).

Rural nonfarm activity was collectivized during the period covered by the first five-year plan (1953–57). Then, in 1958, the Communist Party leadership transformed the rural nonfarm activities into commune and brigade enterprises (CBEs). In China's command economy, these rural enterprises faced severe discrimination in material and equipment allocations because urban manufacturing enterprises received priority. Forced to adapt to these shortages, the rural CBEs endured the sting of periodic criticism as "the tails of capitalism" (Ho 1986). Major reforms from the late 1970s enhanced priority for CBEs by providing tax concessions to qualified enterprises as well as instructions that urban industries farm out production to CBEs wherever possible. The dismantling of the commune system in 1984 led to the development of township and village enterprises and private enterprises as described later.

POSTREFORM.   After a decade of social and economic turmoil between 1966 and 1976, China's economic reforms started in earnest under Deng Xiaoping from 1978 onward. The commune system was abolished, and the household responsibility system came into force. The CBEs that had operated under the old system of rural collective enterprises were renamed township and village enterprises, or TVEs. Agricultural productivity increased dramatically between 1978 and 1985, and the TVE sector flourished concurrently (Fan, Zhang, and Robinson 2003).

From the early 1980s, therefore, there has been evidence of structural change in the Chinese economy (Fan, Zhang, and Robinson 2003). The most significant aspect of this transformation has undoubtedly been the development of the rural nonfarm sector. Inconsequential in the late 1970s, the rural nonfarm sector, especially rural industries, has matured over the past three decades. Considering its growing importance in employment, output, and export, China's rural nonfarm sector has been the main source of the high rates of economic growth in the recent past.[3]

After the start of reforms in the late 1970s, rural industrialization in China can be divided into four distinct periods (Lin and Yao 1999). In the first phase, from 1978 to 1984, rural industrial growth was overshadowed by the unparalleled performance of agriculture, which largely benefited from the rural reform. By 1984 the TVEs produced nearly 16 percent of total industrial output, compared to 9 percent in 1978. Agriculture's share in gross total rural output increased from 24 percent to 33 percent over the period, and its share in rural labor increased significantly, from 9 percent to 14.5 percent.

The second period of rural industrialization in China, from 1984 to 1988, was marked by an acceleration in the rate of growth of output and employment in the rural nonfarm sector. The success of rural reforms in the late 1970s and the early 1980s greatly increased agricultural productivity, permitted the release of labor to the nonfarm sector, and created demand for industrial goods (Fan, Zhang, and Zhang 2004). This period also coincided with more stable institutional arrangements in ownership and with the use of revenue generated in the TVEs. Local governments took the lead in using the capital accumulated during the previous phase of agricultural growth to set up rural industrial units catering to increased local demand. There was a threefold increase in the number of rural enterprises during the period, from 6 million in 1984 to more than 18 million in 1988. The nonfarm share in total rural labor increased from 14.5 percent to nearly 24 percent, while the share in gross rural output increased by more than 20 percent from the 1984 level (Zhang and Tan 2004). The stage was set for the structural transformation in the Chinese economy led by the rural nonfarm sector.

The third period, from 1989 to 1991, was marked by government backlash against the rural TVEs. It is the only phase in the history of China's nonfarm growth when the number of enterprises, the numbers employed, and the share of output of the sector all declined. However, this phase did not last long, and under Deng Xiaoping the political leadership came out in full support of the policy of continuing reform and openness in a famous 1992 visit to Shanghai. The opening up of the economy provided the TVE sector a broader space in which to compete both domestically and internationally.

---

3. The rural sector is mainly defined by the household registration system.

This clearing up of ideological and political confusion has contributed to the current phase of expansion of the TVE sector. By 1997 the rural TVE sector was employing nearly 30 percent of the rural labor force and producing nearly 80 percent of the gross rural output and nearly two-thirds of the total industrial output. Coupled with increased growth of rural private enterprises and the tertiary sector is a higher rate of participation of private capital in the development of the rural nonfarm sector. By the end of the 1990s, China had privatized most of its TVEs.

Macroeconomic Policy and Foreign Direct Investment:
Varying Degrees of Openness

A major difference in macroeconomic policy over the past two decades in China and India was the degree of openness in the two economies. Both countries were relatively closed economies, but India's share of the external sector (exports and imports) in GDP was higher than China's in 1978. By 2000, China's foreign trade share in GDP was nearly 50 percent, while India's was less than 30 percent. As a result of its increasing exports, China maintains a current account surplus, while India is in deficit (Table 13.5).

After the reaffirmation of the open door policy by Deng Xiaoping in 1992, China has seen an explosion of foreign direct investment (FDI) inflows throughout the 1990s and until now (Figure 13.4). The evolution of this policy is no different from the gradual progression of property rights we analyzed earlier. Starting in the early 1980s with the introduction of experimental special economic zones in Guangdong and Fujian, bordering Hong Kong and Taiwan, the policy of establishing preferential tax and tariff structures to attract FDI was extended to Hainan and then to 14 coastal cities, mostly in the southern and eastern part of the country, by the early 1990s. Therefore, the recognition of the open

TABLE 13.5 Foreign trade and foreign direct investment (FDI) in China and India, 1978 and 2000

	China		India	
	1978	2000	1978	2000
External trade and investment (% of GDP)				
Exports of goods	4.6	19.1	5.1	9.2
Imports of goods	5.2	23.1	6.8	12.4
Current account balance	0.3	1.9	0.1	−0.7
Net inward FDI flows	0.1	3.6	0.0	0.6
Share in world trade flows	—	3.7	—	0.7
Share of tariff in government revenue	—	6.3	—	20.1

SOURCE: Tseng and Zebregs (2002), taken from International Financial Statistics.

NOTE: A dash indicates that data are not available.

FIGURE 13.4   Foreign direct investment inflows, 1981–2003

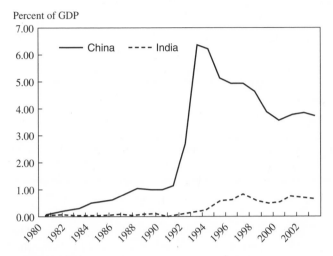

SOURCE: World Bank (2005b).

door policy cleared up any ideological confusion in the minds of the investors, as is reflected in the phenomenal growth of FDI in the past decade.

Linkages between nonfarm employment growth in China and the levels of FDI are difficult to establish due to a lack of data on actual investment in rural enterprises. However, the sectoral data show that nearly 60 percent of the investment was in manufacturing enterprises, and half of that was in labor-intensive manufacturing for export (OECD 2003). As we have already seen, one of the major contributors to China's export growth, especially in consumer goods, has been TVEs, which have been using the comparative advantage of abundant labor in the rural areas. This would indicate that the rural TVEs benefited to a large extent from the inflow of FDI, especially in the past decade.

In contrast, in India FDI is still limited in scale and restricted in scope. Compared to the situation in China, where manufacturing receives the overwhelming majority of FDI, in India nearly 60 percent of FDI approvals between 1991 and 2002 were in five infrastructure industries—energy, telecommunications, electrical equipment, transportation, and chemicals (Reserve Bank of India, various years). Moreover, due to well-developed capital markets, the level of portfolio investment by foreign institutional investors is nearly three times that of FDI. This reflects the priorities of the Indian government after economic reforms started in the early 1990s. There has been a gradual process of privatization of state-owned enterprises and an opening up of infrastructure sectors such as energy and telecommunications in which the government previously enjoyed a monopoly. Emerging sectors such as computer services and software have also attracted higher levels of FDI than medium- and small-scale manufacturing.

The Role of Institutions

Institutional developments and relationships translate government intentions, explicit or implicit, into action. Institutional relationships and governance have evolved significantly in both China and India over the past few decades, and in so doing they have influenced the current levels of dynamism in the rural nonfarm sectors of those countries.

The impact of institutions and governance needs to be analyzed from several vantage points. First, the differences in political economy have to be explained in order to appreciate the process of policy formulation, especially with regard to the rural nonfarm sector. These differences translate into specific policies regarding the role of the state and private actors vis-à-vis the ownership structure, the creation of an enabling environment for the nonfarm sector (including such elements as markets, infrastructure, and other public goods), and the incentives for promoting the rural nonfarm sector, as well as sustaining and expanding it. The outcome of a particular set of policies can be seen both from the rates of growth of the sector as a whole and from the spatial differences in growth patterns. Flexible institutions and responsive governance can correct for structural imbalances and can also eliminate differences between sectors and regions. Therefore, the strengths and weaknesses of the rural nonfarm sectors in China and India may also be thought of as outcomes of institutional development in the two countries, reflecting economic priorities and political environments.

Initial Endowments: Diverging Political and Economic Systems

Comparisons of economic development between China and India dwell for the most part on the differences in political institutions and organization of the economies. It is true that this serves as a good first step toward analyzing the different paths that the two economies have taken over the past 50 years. Our present mandate is to extend this analysis to assess the impact of economic development on the overall progress of the rural nonfarm sector. This would be our contribution to a better understanding of the similarities and contrasts between the rural nonfarm sectors in the two countries.

Policymaking in China is generally regarded as top-down, with the party hierarchy carrying out the orders of the top leadership. If used correctly, the resulting strong organizational capital can be an asset in overcoming common problems caused by coordination failure. In addition, China is a rather homogenous society, lowering the social cost of dealing with conflict. In contrast, the formation of policy in India is thought to be a generally slower process because of the democratic structure and the need to bring various interest groups on board before there can be any radical shift in policy direction.

Most studies on the differences in development between India and China have concentrated on democracy versus dictatorship, or private initiative versus state-led development paradigms. As we shall show later, in the case of the rural nonfarm sector, there is a tendency toward convergence in policy between the two countries. There are several points of similarity, as well as points of contrast. From the point of view of the initial political and economic endowment, however, the differences can be summarized in terms of the ability of the two countries to take collective action and to manage conflicts, both economic and political (Bardhan 2003).

A democratic structure is thought to restrict the opportunity for collective action. Voting in elections is a conduit for expressing opinions about policies and acts of the government, and in a democracy mass mobilization in support of or opposition to particular institutions is largely absent. Moreover, a democratic polity provides enough checks and balances to keep all interest groups within the ambit of the political structure, and economic decisions are therefore more consensual and less radical. This, in turn, gives flexibility to the system to manage political, economic, and social tensions. In a word, in a highly heterogeneous society like that of India, the democratic process is very important for conflict resolution.

On the other hand, a one-party state such as China co-opts all interest groups within the party structure. Policies and programs, once decided upon, are implemented with collective zeal. This explains to a large extent how radical shifts in policy have taken place in China over the past 50 years, starting from the Great Leap Forward and proceeding through the Cultural Revolution, the radical restructuring and reform of the late 1970s, and the reversal in the late 1980s to the initiation of even more radical market orientation in the mid-1990s (Bardhan 2003).

In China, the involvement of local leaders and common party cadres in initiating change in economic policy meant that many of the reforms that occurred in the nonfarm sector were given an official stamp of approval long after they had been tested on the ground. In contrast, in India local governance was restricted to the state level until recently, and many policy decisions, such as those related to land reforms, could not be completed in most parts of the country due to lack of political will.

When China started its major economic reform program in 1978, both land and human capital were much more evenly distributed than in India. The success of the rural reforms benefited almost all the farmers. With limited land, many rural households could tend their land on a part-time basis. Therefore, they had to look for opportunities outside farming. However, due to attachment to their land and restrictions on migration as a result of the *hukou*, or household registration system, it was hard to seek employment opportunities in cities. As a result, many entrepreneurs stayed on their land and created local nonfarm opportunities, in particular in the coastal areas. Moreover, because the majority in the labor force was well educated, a large proportion of the population could share the fruits of economic reform by working in the nonfarm sector, especially in rural manufacturing. In contrast, due to the skewed land and human capital distribution in India, the members of the less educated rural workforce seem to have lost out to the urban-based service industry, which has benefited most from India's gradual liberalization beginning in the early 1990s.

The initial endowment in the two countries, therefore, goes deeper than simplistic notions of democracy and state control. Differences in their political, social, and economic institutions have shaped their policies toward the rural nonfarm sector to a considerable extent.

Ownership Structure: Private Initiative versus Local Government Activism

The historical evolution of the Indian nonagricultural economy has seen a dualism between public ownership of heavy industry and infrastructure (e.g., roads, electricity, water supply, telecommunication, banks) and private initiative in almost every other sector of the economy. In India there has never been any restriction of private enterprise and private property.

On the other hand, for nearly three decades after independence, China followed a policy of collectivization in agriculture and national ownership of heavy industries. Private property was illegal, and the state had the liberty to fix prices. As we saw in the previous section, the "price scissors" were used effectively against agriculture to transfer resources to the urban areas. Moreover, the *hukou,* or household registration system, was used to regulate labor movement between the towns and the countryside. Despite its tremendous distortion of the labor market, it has had a positive side effect of promoting local industrialization. No such restriction has ever been imposed on labor migration in India.

This preamble is important for understanding the ownership structure of rural nonfarm enterprises in China and India. As noted earlier, nonfarm growth in India was organic, encompassing not only rural industry but also service sectors such as trade, transport, and community and social services (Table 13.1). There was no institutional barrier to the setting up of rural nonfarm enterprises by private individuals.

What the Indian state did, however, was to regulate the scale of the enterprises, especially in manufacturing. Rural nonfarm enterprises were broadly classified into the traditional and modern sectors. The traditional sector produces mainly home-spun cloth (*khadi*) and handicrafts (e.g., pottery, baskets). The modern sector is divided into power loomers, which supply raw materials to the textile industry, and providers of all the other types of manufactured goods and services that are present in the rural nonfarm sector. Over time, many manufacturing units have moved to the urban periphery or have located themselves in rural towns to take advantage of market linkages and infrastructure, but they are still classified as rural enterprises. Both the traditional and the modern sectors of rural enterprises fall under the umbrella of small-scale enterprises, which includes those units below a threshold limit of capital investment, which is revised periodically.[4]

Therefore, in India the rural nonfarm enterprise sector is characterized by a clear ownership structure (private ownership of means of production), but not very clear demarcation vis-à-vis location of the enterprises. However, there is considerable government intervention in the form of imposing investment ceilings and implicit subsidies in capital and marketing, and, until recently, protection of small-scale industry through licensing and import barriers. In other words, the regulatory burdens have translated into high transaction costs of setting up and running a business despite clear property rights.

China's rural nonfarm development, on the other hand, has largely been driven by the growth of the TVEs. Unlike the situation in India, it was the local, not the central, government that took the lead in actively promoting the TVEs. Consequently, there is no evidence of ceilings on capital investment limiting the scale of the enterprises, but considerable debate about the ownership and incentive structure of rural firms.

What is not in dispute is that the development of rural enterprises in China started in 1978 with the reform process. Most new-entry Chinese firms were neither private nor state (i.e., national government) firms, but were owned and managed by the local governments (TVEs). In China, local governments played an active role in managing the agricultural collectives and the CBEs under the old system. The management of local government bodies forms both the political and the administrative bureaucracy at the micro level.[5] Moreover, severe interjurisdictional competition forces local governments to create a business-friendly environment. This leads to a convergence in incentives for better performance in mobilizing resources for development. TVEs were rather secure due to protection from the local government at a time when private property rights were not clearly defined on paper.

However, from the mid-1980s there was a large and growing presence of private enterprises (PEs). It is in the analysis of the relative contribution of TVEs and PEs to growth of the rural nonfarm sector that the issue of ownership has assumed significance. One theory (Qian 2003) is that local government ownership is a halfway house between national and private ownership of the means of production. In the absence of the rule of law to protect private property rights until recently, this innovation in ownership structure has been more

---

4. The current investment ceiling is Rs 10 million (nearly $200,000), Rs 50 million (nearly $1 million) for technology-intensive industries.

5. This is different from the situation in India, where the political and the administrative bureaucracies are completely different entities.

secure than those of private enterprises due to the protection of community governments. From 1978 to 1993, the share of state-owned enterprises (owned by national or supralocal county governments) in total industrial output fell from 78 to 43 percent, while that of nonstate firms increased from 22 to 57 percent. Disaggregating the data further, we see that within the nonstate firms the share of firms collectively owned by townships and villages went up from 22 to 42 percent, while that of private firms was around 15 percent in 1993 after being nonexistent at the beginning of the reform period (Qian 2003).

Because the rural nonfarm sector was not protected prior to reform, China's rural enterprises have been able to capture the market niche left by state-owned enterprises and reap the benefits of scale. China does not impose any capital ceiling on private enterprise. In contrast, in India there were heavy regulations on both small-scale and large-scale industries in the private sector in the years prior to the start of economic reform. Therefore, the private enterprises in China have more flexibility in terms of capital investment to adjust to increasing demand.

Since liberalization, large-scale firms in India have reaped the benefits, while the village industry sector has suffered from low levels of labor productivity. The comparison shows that nominally defined secure property rights alone cannot guarantee the attraction of investment. Removing the distortions inherent in the economic system and introducing competition may have a more important role to play in the development of a vibrant rural nonfarm sector.

Provision of Local Public Goods

Differences in policy regarding ownership and promotion of the rural nonfarm sector are manifested in the provision of local public goods, especially infrastructure, in China and India. It is well recognized that the rural nonfarm sector needs supporting infrastructure, both physical and social, for sustained growth. In keeping with differences between the development paths followed by the rural nonfarm sectors in China and India, there are distinct differences between the two countries in the way public goods have been provided.

In India it is now widely recognized in official and academic circles that availability of local public goods in the rural areas has become a major bottleneck in the past decade and a half (Planning Commission 2001). In accord with the Industrial Policy Statement of 1977, industrial clusters were encouraged to take advantage of horizontal and vertical linkages. To promote rural small-scale industries, district industrial centers were formed and entrepreneurs were encouraged to set up units with subsidized loans and reduced taxes. Nationalized banks had stipulated lending norms for loan disbursement in the "priority sector."

On the whole, central schemes and administrative guidelines to create an enabling environment for the rural nonfarm sector have not paid dividends. This is borne out by Table 13.2, where we find that the share of the nonfarm sector decreased in total NDP between 1980 and 2000. Although the share of registered rural manufacturing (essentially the modern small industrial sector) has increased, there has been a substantial decline in the share of unregistered manufacturing, which provides the bulk of employment in the rural areas.

In contrast, local public goods provision has been one of the critical inputs in the continuing growth of the rural nonfarm sector in China. Unlike the situation in India, rural community governments focus on providing local public goods—building roads, providing water and irrigation systems, maintaining law and order, and so on. In this sense, the economic and social part of the administrative structure is more decentralized in China than in India.

In the context of the rural nonfarm development in China, provision of local public goods is the crucial link between the economic and political objectives of TVE promotion by local governments (Qian 2003). Under the guidelines of the national government, in 1992 nearly 59 percent of the after-tax profits of TVEs were reinvested and the rest used for local public expenditure. This created positive linkages between the performance of TVEs, with higher profits leading to greater ability to maintain and improve capital stock, and benefits to the local community in terms of infrastructure, which in turn encouraged diversification of the rural nonfarm sector.

Thus decentralized provision of local public goods has been cited in the literature as one of the major factors sustaining the high growth of rural TVEs as well as PEs in China. The sharing of profit by the local and the national governments creates a win-win situation in which higher rates of reinvestment and better infrastructure lead to a cycle of growth in the nonfarm sector. However, questions have recently been raised about whether this creates path dependency in terms of the levels of development of the TVE sector between different regions of the country.

Financing the Nonfarm Sector: Institutional Lending versus Unconventional Finance

In the area of finance for the rural nonfarm sector, India and China have followed two very distinct paths. The development of the rural sector in India, including both agriculture and industry, has been mirrored by government initiatives in the provision of organized credit by banks and other financial institutions. In 1973, when the green revolution was well under way in most parts of India, the government nationalized all domestic private banks and brought them nominally under the control of the central bank. The demand for credit in the rural sector increased, primarily due to the necessity of purchasing modern inputs such as fertilizer and machinery to augment agricultural production. Although the demand for credit from the rural nonfarm sector lagged behind the demand from agriculture, it also increased in the late 1970s. If both sectors were to grow in a reasonably balanced way, clearly some specific government interventions were required.

The Indian government instituted a policy of "directed credit" through the banking system in rural areas. Lending norms were instituted for the priority sector, which in the nonfood component of total bank lending included mainly small-scale industries. Location of such industries in semiurban or rural areas was one factor that qualified them to access the priority sector credit system. The ratio of priority sector lending in the nonfarm sector has been remarkably stable, at around 36 percent over the past two decades. Moreover, the share of the small-scale sector in total gross nonfood credit has also not shown any fluctuation. This is in spite of the fact that between 1980 and 2000 there were six changes of government, as well as economic reforms from 1991 onward (Reserve Bank of India, various years).

The stability of the priority sector lending indicates that there was a general consensus in government regarding the promotion of the nonfarm sector. This may have been due to the fact that credit delivery has always been an instrument of patronage during elections, with declaration of loan waivers and loan holidays. There is a growing critique about the role of directed credit in government policy from the efficiency angle, in terms of targeting as well as delivery mechanisms (*Economic and Political Weekly* 2004). Although a comprehensive review of government policy in this regard is outside the scope of the present study, a comparison can be drawn between the incentive compatibility of directed credit and the decentralized system of financing that prevailed in China over the past two decades.

Unlike the situation in India, access to formal credit institutions for the rural nonfarm enterprises in China has been limited, at least in the initial phases. Institutional innovations have also been far more diverse. In the absence of a formal banking system, private credit, rural credit cooperatives, and local government support were the only means by which the TVEs could access capital. However, the cooperatives lend mostly to the state-owned enterprises, leading to a transfer of rural household savings to the urban sector (Lin and Yao 1999). Therefore, in explaining the productivity and efficiency of TVEs in rural China, the "hard budget constraint" theory has received widespread attention (Bardhan 2003).

Under the innovative ownership structure of the TVEs, local governments had complete control over their finances, which provided incentives for promotion of the sector. Higher profits meant higher revenues for investing in local public goods, which had both economic and political payoffs. Economically, regions with better infrastructure attracted more investment in the rural manufacturing sector, leading to higher employment and revenues.

The compatibility of economic and political incentives, together with limited access to institutional lending, translated into pressure on the management of TVEs to increase profitability. Higher revenues were divided between local public goods and reinvestment in plants and equipment. As noted earlier, by

1993 nearly 60 percent of TVE profits were being reinvested. The coastal areas of China emerged as the manufacturing powerhouse both in the domestic and in the export markets. The benefits of organic linkages between local government initiative, local public goods, and rural manufacturing, however, have been unevenly distributed across the country.

China's pattern of phenomenal nonfarm enterprise growth through unconventional financing provides a stark contrast to the stability of the directed credit policy in India. At first glance, the policy prescription for other countries may well be that decentralized finance works better in the promotion of rural nonfarm enterprises. Recent experience with rural cooperatives in the agro-processing and dairy sectors of India may also lead one to conclude that hard budget constraints and local initiatives work better in the rural nonfarm sector.

However, it must be kept in mind that China's local government structure is a product of its political system. The incentive compatibility, therefore, has a historical path dependency. In most developing countries, the lowest tier of government does not exist or, even if it does, is not empowered in the same way as in China.

As its market economy matures, China is also setting up conventional institutions; an organized capital market and banking sector are two major institutional changes in that direction. Because almost all the TVEs are privatized, credit constraints can force private enterprises to cut back on investment, leading to a slowing of rural nonfarm growth. The specter of a stagnant rural enterprise sector may lead China to follow India's path of providing directed credit through commercial banks; early signs point in that direction (Lin and Yao 1999, 9).

Assessing Performance

The various policy initiatives and institutional arrangements that have been implemented in India and China in recent decades have influenced performance of the RNFE in a variety of ways. The resulting outcomes reflect comparative strengths and weaknesses of the sector in the two countries and will have a significant bearing on how the sector is able to respond to future challenges and opportunities. We discuss these issues in this section.

Strengths and Weaknesses of the Rural Nonfarm Sector in India

PERFORMANCE.   In India, the rural nonfarm sector existed in a primitive form at the time of independence in 1947. Over 100 years of colonial rule had led to the systematic deindustrialization of key sectors of the economy, notably the hand loom industry. In response, the Gandhian nationalist reaction included a strong populist call for the promotion of village and *khadi* industries. This led to significant protection for specific labor-intensive village and *khadi* industries during the four decades following independence.

The initiation of economic reforms in the early 1990s, however, has effectively removed protections for these village and *khadi* industries. Less efficient than modern small industries (Chadha 1993, 1996) and unable to compete on economic terms, many have closed down, leading to a halving of the rural income share earned by unregistered manufacturing establishments (Table 13.2). Over the same period, from 1980 to 2000, the share of registered manufacturing units increased from 3 to 5 percent of rural income, helping to stabilize rural manufacturing employment and even increase it slightly (Table 13.1). The rural manufacturing sector thus appears to be undergoing a process of readjustment in which unviable units are being weeded out while others grow and maintain their competitiveness. With enabling policies along the lines of those adopted in China, rural manufactures can come out stronger in the process.

Rural services and commerce, however, have continued to grow rapidly. The green revolution, beginning in the mid-1960s in India, saw a rapid increase in agricultural output and productivity. The nonfarm sector, especially rural services, grew to keep up with the local demand. Though more spontaneous than planned, this growth in rural commerce and services accounted for over 90 percent of gains in the rural nonfarm income and employment share over the past two decades (Tables 13.1 and 13.2). In general, India's growth story in the decade of the 1990s has been one of rapid expansion of the service sector, which now has the largest share in GDP. In some ways, India has bypassed the traditional progression from being an agricultural economy to an industrial one (Roach 2004). With nearly 60 percent of the population still engaged in agriculture, there is an opportunity to redeploy labor to the rural service and commercial sector. One major strength of the Indian rural sector is the potential for structural transformation of the rural economy in the coming years, a process already achieved by China.

Recent trends in rural unemployment, however, alert us to challenges ahead. The latest available figures show a sharp increase in rural unemployment, for both males and females, between 1994 and 2000. This is in contrast to the previous declining trend in the rates of unemployment in both the rural and the urban sectors between the late 1970s and the early 1990s. Given the context of extensive rural underemployment, especially in agriculture, there is a danger that this unemployment might lead to social tensions in the near future. To mitigate the crisis, successive governments have resorted to the generation of wage employment through rural public works projects. Although these projects were supposed to be temporary, political considerations have prevented them from being discontinued.

STRENGTHS.   The strengths of the rural nonfarm sector in India are as follows:

- *The institutional basis of the rural nonfarm sector.* In India, the institutions underlying the development of the rural nonfarm sector are very strong.

These include secure property rights; a well-developed financial system, with preferential access to credit for the sector; supporting institutions such as the Small Industries Development Bank of India and state industrial corporations; policies and programs promoting linkage with agriculture, especially agroindustries; domestic marketing channels for rural nonfarm production; and government support for export promotion. The institutional mechanisms for rapid growth of the rural nonfarm sector are already in place.

- *The ongoing decentralization process.* In a curious juxtaposition of political and economic considerations, over the past two decades the state governments in India have been able to exercise far more independence in decisionmaking than before the 1980 period. Regional parties are an integral part of coalition governments at the center. In turn, they have negotiated economic autonomy in the formation of state-specific policies for development. Moreover, with the opening up of the economy in 1991, FDI came to play an important role in the overall policy environment. State governments are in competition with one another to attract higher FDI levels in both manufacturing and infrastructure. In some ways, India's path mirrors that followed by China, although the volume of FDI coming to India is less than 10 percent of that coming to China. On the positive side, however, this situation creates an opportunity for higher levels of investment in the future.

WEAKNESSES. The weaknesses of the rural nonfarm sector in India are as follows:

- *Inadequate infrastructure.* The most significant bottleneck in generating higher levels of rural nonfarm activity in India results from the quantity, quality, and reliability of infrastructure. For example, the recent World Bank Investment Climate Survey for India indicates that power outages were one of the most serious obstacles to the development of the nonfarm sector (World Bank 2005a). Although corrective steps have been taken recently, increased infrastructure remains the most important priority for the future. For the nonfarm sector to achieve a sustained growth rate of between 8 and 9 percent, the investment rate has to be stepped up from the current level of 24 percent to nearly 35 percent over the next decade, with investment directed at the rural sector (Planning Commission 2000, 57). China's success in attracting high levels of FDI for infrastructure investment in both the urban and the rural sectors can be a pointer toward greater policy initiatives, keeping in mind the resources needed for infrastructure in rural India.
- *Regulatory restrictions on the small-scale sector.* Regulation of the small-scale sector constitutes an important aspect of nonfarm development policy

in India. In the initial stages, capital investment restrictions were imposed to protect small-scale industries, especially the rural ones, from predation by large industries. Reservation of products for the sector was initiated to create a domestic market, and quantitative restrictions were imposed to protect the sector from competition from imports.

By the end of the 1990s, however, these very policies had become detrimental to the dynamism of the small-scale sector, especially in the rural areas. Capital investment limits have discouraged economies of scale, and concessions offered to small industry have created adverse incentives against reinvestment. Several official reports have recommended a substantial increase in the capital investment limit (from the present level of around $200,000) to make better use of technology and improve productivity (Planning Commission 2000).

Reservation of products for the small-scale sector has gradually reduced in significance, although this has created rents within the system.[6] The decision of the government to put all the reserved items in the open general license category after April 2005 will mean free import of such items at the prevailing tariff rate. With the latter slated to come down over time to around 20 percent in accord with the WTO norms, this decision will effectively signal the end of protection for the small-scale industry. Examples of sectors that will be affected, such as shoes and textiles, indicate that India's nonfarm sector can survive the competition both domestically and in the export market.

• *Manpower quality deficiencies.* High levels of illiteracy in rural India have hampered the growth of the rural nonfarm sector. As is recognized today, education has both intrinsic and instrumental value (Sen 1999). Apart from having a positive correlation with wages, a minimum basic standard of education is necessary to apply for credit, to be aware of one's rights and responsibilities, and to deal with instances of corruption and malpractice. Often a lack of education is intrinsic to poverty, which seems to have been the case in India until recently.

In the rural areas, lack of education causes labor to be stagnant in agriculture or to move to casual work occupations in the nonfarm sector rather than to salaried employment with higher wages and benefits (Planning Commission 2000). Lack of education, together with lack of technical skills, provides little incentive for rural firms to invest in technology, leading to low levels of labor productivity in the rural manufacturing sector compared to urban manufacturing (Chadha 2003). The same is true in the service sec-

---

6. There are instances of only one firm's producing a reserved product (Bala Subrahmanya 2004).

tor as well, which has the potential for expansion given the already strong base in the urban economy. A higher level of investment to improve both the quality of and access to education—primary, secondary, and higher—needs to be a priority for policymakers.

Strengths and Weaknesses of Rural Nonfarm Development in China

PERFORMANCE.   As a principal driver of China's economic expansion, the rural nonfarm sector is vibrant in many respects. While manufacturing continued to dominate rural nonfarm employment in China during the early reform years, evidence suggests that commercial and service activities have been growing more rapidly in recent years. Over the period from 1984 to 1997, employment gains in commercial and service TVEs increased by 45 million jobs, roughly double the 26 million jobs gained in manufacturing TVEs (Table 13.3).

This strong evidence of structural transformation is in large part due to the absorption of labor from agriculture into rural enterprises, as well as the high rate of technical change (Fan, Zhang, and Robinson 2003). This indicates that China's rural enterprise sector has broadened in scope and increased in scale, with a positive effect on capital and labor productivity. Compared to India, China has been able to reap the benefits of scale economies, which has been noted even in official documents in India (Planning Commission 2000). More ominously, signs of increasing regional inequality are emerging as well, driven by the very development of the rural nonfarm sector and public investments (Zhang and Fan 2004). Moreover, financial sector rigidities may hinder the deployment of capital in the rural sector (Zhang and Tan 2004).

STRENGTHS.   The strengths of rural nonfarm development in China are as follows:

- *FDI inflows and resulting technical change.* Empirical analysis of China's economic transformation points to an important contribution of technical change. Fan, Zhang, and Robinson (2003) show that, for the economy as a whole, 42 percent of total GDP growth was from technical change, while in the rural nonfarm sector the contribution was even higher, 53 percent. FDI has accounted for part of these gains, bringing with it new technologies and ways of doing business. Scope still remains for increasing returns to capital by investing more in agriculture and rural industry. This offers the prospects for continuing productivity-enhanced expansion of the rural nonfarm sector (Fan, Zhang, and Robinson 2003).

  The resulting productivity gains have benefited not only manufacturing but also service and commercial activity. China's tenfold higher levels of FDI emerge significantly in the commercial sphere, where large regional and international retailers and supermarket chains have moved in large numbers (Reardon et al. 2003). In the year 2000, in food retailing supermarkets held a 20 percent market share in China (nearly 50 percent in urban areas) compared to only 5 percent in India (Reardon et al. 2003). The introduction of modern supply chain logistics and just-in-time inventory management by large regional and international retailers has reduced marketing costs in China by as much as 40 percent (Reardon et al. 2003).

• *Private property rights.* From the mid-1990s the TVEs have been completely privatized through the creation of joint stock companies in which the local governments are shareholders. This marks a significant step toward recognition of private property rights that have been accepted as reality by the political leadership. The change in ownership from local governments to private hands gives managers greater autonomy in running the firms and can increase productivity and profit even further.

• *Strong regional competition.* Regional policies in promoting rural non-farm enterprises played an important role in the expansion of the sector. Different regions compete with each other in attracting investments and opening up export markets. Regional competition in China created examples for catch-up within the country, leading to greater investment and output in the rural nonfarm sector.[7]

WEAKNESSES. The weaknesses of rural nonfarm development in China are as follows:

• *Domestic financing of rural nonfarm activity.* China's formal lending institutions are still in the initial stages of maturity. The growth of TVEs and PEs until now has largely been through reinvestment of their own resources. However, with increased competition, profit margins get smaller and the quantum of investable resources consequently becomes less. In this context, a formal banking network with clearly defined lending policies is necessary for the rural enterprises to access capital, especially because formal financial markets (e.g., stock, bond, and insurance markets) are restricted. Sustained growth in the rural nonfarm sector therefore critically depends on devising transparent and targeted financial institutions such as those currently operating in India.

• *Inadequate protection of workers' welfare.* In complete contrast to the rigidity of labor markets in India, the rural nonfarm labor force in China has few safeguards. Labor markets in rural China are demand driven, and managers of firms are under few restrictions to protect workers' welfare. Although this arrangement can be beneficial for a massive absorption of labor from agriculture, as happened in the decade of the 1980s, by the late 1990s the labor market had become integrated in very large measure. Al-

---

7. A comparison can be drawn with the development of software and computer services in India, where states are competing to attract high-tech companies.

though mobilization for labor rights is still rare in China, the pressure of public opinion from export markets regarding poor working conditions has already become an international issue. Moreover, a more balanced relationship between workers and capitalists will help reduce social unrest and ensure more sustainable future growth of the nonfarm sector in China.

• *Regional inequality.* Although increasing regional inequality is a matter of concern for both China and India, the problem is more acute in China. Before economic reforms were initiated in the late 1970s, the emphasis had been on eliminating differences between regions through investment in social and physical capital. From the early 1980s, different regions started growing at different rates (Kanbur and Zhang 2005). As noted earlier, nonfarm sector growth has been one of the main contributors to this divergence in regional development trajectories.

From the emerging intraregional inequality studies, the limits to privatization are becoming evident as well. One factor is the withdrawal of the government from education and health spending. Indicators of health and education in poorer regions of the country are actually showing signs of retrogression (Zhang and Kanbur 2005). This has long-term implications for the quality of the labor force in rural areas, as we have seen in the case of India. The warning signs for China should be India's neglect of social capital investments over the past five decades.

Conclusions: Toward Greater Nonfarm Policy Convergence

In spite of diametrically opposite political philosophies in post–World War II China and India, many of their policies governing rural nonfarm activity proved remarkably similar. After an early period of neglect, agricultural productivity growth became the cornerstone of rural development strategies in both countries, leading to generally prosperous farm sectors. This prosperity formed the basis of the demand for nonfarm goods and services in the rural areas, though more so in the case of India than in China.

In official policy pronouncements and programs, both countries ignored commerce and services, focusing instead on rural manufacturing. In spite of this policy and institutional neglect, commerce and services have proven to be the most dynamic elements of both rural nonfarm economies.

Both countries provided protection for rural industries—low-capital, labor-intensive weaving and village industries in India and capital-intensive activities such as steel and fertilizer manufacture in China. Both countries liberalized after a period of heavy protection for rural manufacturing. But they did so in different ways, in differing institutional environments, and with different consequences.

In India, the policy of protection and promotion of the nonfarm sector in the 1980s was followed by the sudden opening up of the sector to competition in the early 1990s. In the new competitive environment, most small firms, especially those run by households with primitive technology, lost out badly in the period of competition and market integration that followed. The shakeout in the rural nonfarm sector continues even now.

Because of fewer price and quota protections for the rural nonfarm sector, China's TVEs have become internationally competitive more quickly than did India's rural nonfarm manufacturing enterprises when its economy was liberalized. In China, in the planned era, protection was provided mainly for the state-owned enterprises. With the success of rural and agricultural reform in the early 1980s, agricultural productivity increased dramatically, releasing surplus capital and labor for the development of local rural enterprises. Since the 1980s, China has adopted a fiscal decentralization policy, providing a strong incentive for local governments to develop the TVE sector because they can keep most revenues from TVEs. Facing hard budget and interjurisdictional competition, TVEs must be productive to survive in the marketplace. As a result, the viable TVE sector has gradually gained market share from the relatively inefficient state-owned enterprises. Benefiting from an open door policy and export promotion, TVEs reaped the benefit of both internal and external market linkages. Except between 1989 and 1991, there has been comparatively greater policy consistency vis-à-vis the rural nonfarm sector in China than in India.

However, the issue of providing credit and financial services to the rural nonfarm sector concerns policymakers in both countries. Although India has a better-established network of rural credit, it suffers from inadequate delivery systems, which lead to bottlenecks in technological upgrading and output expansion. China, on the other hand, is in the process of setting up systems of credit delivery through normal banking channels and is setting up institutions to monitor the same.

Until now, China's high rates of FDI inflow have been contrasted with the low levels for India as a reflection of the future potential of the two countries. This conventional interpretation has been challenged recently, and the focus has shifted more toward the underlying institutional differences. It has been argued that the opening-up process is more stable in India, where there is already a strong domestic manufacturing base, along with the support of a well-developed financial system and corporate governance (Huang and Khanna 2003). Given more flexible labor market policies and a lifting of restrictions on the scale of enterprises, India is poised to attract significantly higher levels of FDI in the manufacturing sector in the coming years. Judging from China's experience, the RNFE holds the potential for contributing to future economic growth in India.

Pessimism about China stems largely from the slow pace of creating transparency in capital markets and in the judicial system, weaknesses that lead to rent seeking and corruption (Tseng and Zebregs 2002; Zhang and Tan 2004). Moreover, with nearly 90 percent of FDI going to coastal provinces in the south and east, regional inequality is growing much more rapidly than in India. The major challenge facing China in the coming years is to realign its policies for more equitable growth both within and between regions.

A review of the strengths and weaknesses of the RNFE in China and India reveal interesting points of contrast. Financial institutions catering to rural industries are one of India's strengths, but they are still in the process of development in China. Physical and social infrastructure is a bottleneck for India but is one of the factors driving rural nonfarm growth in China. Decentralization and interregional competition has so far worked well in China, whereas centralized decisionmaking and redistributive allocations have stymied competition in India. However, as China's recent experience shows, there needs to be a balance between decentralization and withdrawal of government's role, especially in the social sectors. There are lessons to be learned from both countries in this regard.

India can learn from China how to create a business-friendly investment environment by continuing to remove the regulatory burdens on small rural nonfarm enterprises along with the resulting high transaction costs. China can learn from India how to better protect the rights of both investors and workers as conflicts increase across the rural nonfarm sector.

Increasing inter- and intraregional inequality in nonfarm development is probably the most pressing issue facing policymakers in both countries. Both face pressures of migration from regions of low rural nonfarm development to regions of high growth. Given that India and China face similar challenges in the future, we anticipate greater convergence in the two countries' rural nonfarm policy directions in coming years.

14 Technology as a Motor of Change in the Rural Nonfarm Economy

STEVEN HAGGBLADE, THOMAS REARDON, AND ERIC HYMAN

New technology has stimulated rapid change in rural nonfarm activity across a broad range of developing country settings. In some cases, it opens up vast new vistas and powers rapid rural nonfarm growth (Box 14.1). In other instances, the new technology and quality standards brandished by expansionist large enterprises may enable them to outcompete legions of smaller, outmoded rural nonfarm firms (Box 14.2). Though clearly a two-edged sword, new technology frequently drives change in the rural nonfarm economy (RNFE) (Jeans, Hyman, and O'Donnell 1991).

Indeed technological change has accounted for over half of all income gains in China's RNFE in possibly the most dynamic cohort of rural nonfarm enterprises in the developing world over the past decade (Fan, Zhang, and Robinson 2003). New technology has likewise proven instrumental to the successful transition from Stage 1 rural industrialization (Z-goods[1]) to Stage 2 (modern Z-goods) in East Asia (Chapter 10). The ability of rural firms to maintain competitive quality and cost is crucial if they are to avoid the fate anticipated by Hymer and Resnick (1969), that of inexorable decline in rural manufacturing. In rural commerce as well, significant cost savings arise from adoption of modern organizational and supply chain management—40 percent cost reductions in some instances (Chapter 9). These substantial productivity gains pressure firms to adopt new technologies and the accompanying changes they imply for organizational management.

Poverty reduction, too, will require fundamental changes in both employment opportunities and labor productivity. Because of its prospects for raising worker productivity and improving product quality, new technology offers a potentially powerful means of expanding markets as well as worker earnings in nonfarm activities. Here, again, those wielding the two-edged sword of technology must keep it well balanced. Labor productivity needs to rise, but not at

---

1. Hymer and Resnick (1969) introduced the term *Z-goods* to describe the output produced by rural nonfarm businesses and to emphasize its highly heterogeneous composition.

the expense of unemploying vast cohorts of rural nonfarm workers. In order to raise the productivity and incomes of poor participants in the RNFE, "appropriate" technologies need to maintain a balance between accessibility and competitiveness, between technologies that poor entrepreneurs are capable of financing and managing and those that produce goods of appropriate quality for increasingly demanding markets, enabling them to successfully compete—and survive—in the newly globalized and increasingly competitive RNFEs of the developing world.

In spite of its importance, technology has remained underappreciated among many promoters of the RNFE. A group of devoted proponents has concentrated on the development and promotion of technology in the developing world, at least since the days of Gandhi and of Schumacher's (1965) *Buddhist Economics*. Likewise, many public efforts at rural nonfarm promotion in East Asia have emphasized technology development (see Chapters 10 and 13). However, the bulk of donor-financed efforts elsewhere in the developing world have focused instead on finance as the primary vehicle for promoting rural nonfarm enterprise (Chapter 12). Very fundamentally, raising the productivity of the poor will require improved human skills, more productive technologies, and better systems of organization. To stimulate sustained productivity gains in the RNFE, technology will require more attention than it has received in the past.

This chapter aims to redress this past imbalance by focusing specifically on technology and its potential for accelerating income growth and poverty reduction in the RNFE. In doing so, the chapter examines a series of analytical, empirical, and policy questions. The first concerns sources of innovation. Who and what determine the supply of new rural nonfarm technologies? Second, what determines adoption, particularly by the poor? And finally, where can public intervention play a useful role in pro-poor technology development and diffusion in the RNFE?

Determinants of Innovation

Key Innovators

It matters who supplies new technology to the RNFE. Suppliers' incentives and motives shape the cost, scale, and sophistication of the technology and hence influence adoption and distributional outcomes. The following discussion traces a progression of innovators, beginning with small private firms in a closed rural economy and then moving up to progressively larger and more distant innovators in the urban and international arena that nonetheless increasingly influence the technology available in the RNFE.

PRIVATE SECTOR INNOVATION.   Private individuals and firms dominate as innovators in the RNFE. The most pervasive examples come from the broad-based development of fermented food technologies throughout the developing world. By experimenting with varying starches and inoculants, rural women have over many centuries developed a broad range of indigenous fermented foods, such as *gari* (a precooked cassava-based porridge) in West Africa, sorghum beer and *mageu* (a fermented, nonalcoholic maize porridge) in Southern Africa, and *tapai* (a sweet, glutinous dessert made from fermented cassava and rice) in Malaysia (Steinkraus 1989). Likewise rural blacksmiths, tinsmiths, and metal-workers across the developing world design, manufacture, and modify an array of agricultural tools and consumer goods appropriate to the soils and consumer tastes of their localities. In rural Taiwan, for example, this local innovation in specific products led to the development of over nine kinds of harrows. One of these, the standard knife-tooth harrow, came in twelve regional variants, with its width, length, material, number of teeth, and shape of tooth blade varying according to regional topography and soil structure (Tomich, Kilby, and John-ston 1995).

Large firms likewise innovate, sometimes with a significant impact on smaller rural nonfarm enterprises. In the early 1900s, industrial research by the United Africa Company succeeded in developing the Pioneer palm oil press in Nigeria. In so doing, the company provided the mechanical technology neces-sary for the industrialization of palm oil extraction across West Africa (Purvis 1968). Jim Thompson, a former Office of Strategic Services operative during World War II, settled after the war in Thailand, where his work with local silk weavers led to the widespread introduction of improved looms, hybrid silk-worms, improved reeling equipment, and imposition of standardized quality, designs, and marketing that launched a sustained boom in the rural silk indus-try in Northeast Thailand (Chapter 15).

Urban-based private firms influence technologies in the RNFE. In many cases, inquisitive individuals seek out training and apprenticeship in urban areas and subsequently return to transform business opportunities in their home vil-lages. Kenneth King (1977) describes many intriguing case histories from Kenya, ranging from candlemakers to village mechanics to rural construction firms. In nonfarm activities, as in agriculture, urban suppliers frequently provide the improved inputs necessary for adopting new technologies. Across Southern Africa, for example, large maltsters proved instrumental in improving the prof-itability of home brewing by supplying improved "trade" malt that reduces grain input costs by as much as 40 percent and approximately doubles returns to la-bor (Table 14.1). Urban-to-rural subcontracting arrangements, likewise, pro-vide a common vehicle through which private firms introduce new technology to rural areas. Popular in weaving, garment- and jewelrymaking, and simple metal manufacturing, these modern putting-out systems have emerged promi-nently in heavily populated East and South Asia as well as in parts of Latin America (Mead 1992b; Hayami 1998a; Otsuka 1998).

International technology transfer to the RNFE has long proven a signifi-cant source of technical innovation. Probably most famous is the case of Ira

TABLE 14.1 Gains from new technology

Subsector	Location	Alternative technologies and efficiency			References
		Technology 1	Technology 2	Technology 3	
Banana wine	Rwanda	Home brewers: 29 to 54% extraction rate	Factory brewers: 73% extraction rate		Haggblade and Minot (1987)
Cassava	Ghana	Hand pressing: 100 kg in 8 hours	Machine pressing: 100 kg in 15 minutes		Carr (1996b)
Palm oil	West Africa	Traditional extraction: 6% / 340 person hours to process 3,000 kg of fruit	Manual Colin press: 10% / 150 person hours to process 3,000 kg of fruit	Motorized Colin press: 10% / 65.5 person hours to process 3,000 kg of fruit	Hyman (1990)
Silk	Thailand	Traditional home producers earn 4 baht/day; Native silkworms: 300 meter filaments	Specialized yellow yarn reelers earn 15 baht/day; Yellow hybrids: 600 meter filaments	Home-based subcontract weavers earn 120 baht/day; White hybrids: 1,300 meter filaments	Haggblade and Ritchie (1992)
Sorghum beer	Botswana	Home brewing with homemade malt: 25 kg grain/100 liters	Home brewing with factory malt: 15.7 kg grain/100 liters	Factory brewing: 15.2 kg grain/100 liters	Haggblade (1987)
Stoves	Senegal	All-metal charcoal stove: 3.4 kg charcoal per day	Ceramic-lined, metal-clad charcoal stove: 1.8 kg charcoal per day		Hyman et al. (1996)

NOTE: A blank cell indicates that data are not applicable.

Merritt Singer, whose development of the push-pedal treadle sewing machine during the mid-1800s revolutionized tailoring. His machine offered an increase of over 500 percent in labor productivity and permitted high-quality, mechanical stitching independent of a centralized power source, thus making it a technology immanently suitable across the developing world (Schmiechen 1984; Mokyr 1990). The Singer Sewing Machine Company's unparalleled marketing and distribution system led to rapid dominance, launching tailoring and garmentmaking as one of the major small-scale industries across the developing world.

Foreign firms that buy or manufacture in developing countries also introduce new technologies into rural areas. Nestlé-Brazil, for example, buys processed milk products in rural Brazil, while major U.S. grocery chains import processed food products from rural China. In these and similar cases, international firms impose quality standards that require the use of nontraditional rural nonfarm technologies. In some cases, these require significant investments, as in the case of cooling tanks for milk. This source of technological change has grown rapidly with the liberalization of regulations on foreign direct investment and with the rapid increase of trade in processed foods in Asia and Latin America (Chapter 9).

PUBLIC SECTOR INNOVATION. Public entities are also important innovators. A series of different groups have made important contributions to technology development for the RNFE:

- *Agricultural research organizations.* Public funding for rural technology development has historically focused on agriculture. But agricultural research institutes typically allocate only limited research funds for nonfarm production technologies in areas such as food processing and farm machinery manufacture. Prominent exceptions include the development of processors for roots and tubers by the Centro Internacional de Agricultura Tropical (CIAT) and the International Institute of Tropical Agriculture (Wheatley et al. 1995; Nweke et al. 2002), for cassava by the International Institute for Tropical Agriculture (Nweke et al. 2002), nontimber forest products by the Center for International Forestry Research (Ruiz-Perez and Arnold 1996), and threshing equipment by the International Rice Research Institute (IRRI). IRRI's coaxial paddy thresher subsequently spread to the Philippines and Thailand, where local metal shops manufactured and improved the design for local conditions (Duff 1987).

  Host country agricultural research institutes have often done better than international agricultural research centers in allocating research funds for agroprocessing and agricultural mechanization technologies. The Malaysian Agricultural Research and Development Institute has funded research on the processing of *tapai* in an effort to isolate microbiological processes that will enable the scaling up of this traditional rural household

FIGURE 14.1   The Thai silk subsector, 1991, simplified version

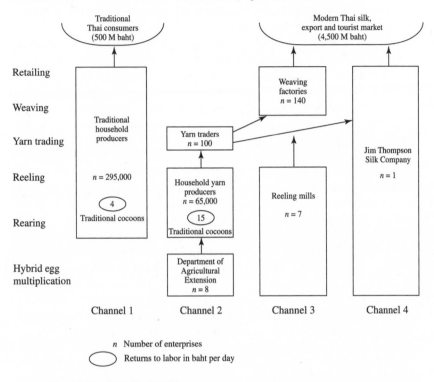

n   Number of enterprises

⟨ ⟩   Returns to labor in baht per day

SOURCE: Haggblade and Ritchie (1992).

industry and will improve keeping quality (Merican and Que-Lan 1989). Thailand's Department of Agricultural Extension conducts research on silkworms and has successfully crossed imported white silkworms with local yellow Thai silkworms, producing 100 percent increases in cocoon yields (Table 14.1). By producing and supplying hybrid yellow egg sheets, they have provided a crucial element necessary for village processors to improve their productivity and income while enabling their transition to rapidly growing market channels supplying weft yarn to the large weaving factories (Figure 14.1).

- *Industrial research institutes.* Often attached to technical universities and trade schools, industrial research institutes also operate in some countries. They typically receive funding allocations far more limited than those given to the public agricultural research establishment (Baron 1980; Henning and Mule 1998). Even so, some have made important contributions to rural nonfarm business development. Nigeria's Federal Institute of Industrial Research has conducted research on the processing of *gari* and *ogi* (a fermented starch cake made from maize, sorghum, or millet). Research at South Africa's Council for Scientific and Industrial Research has transformed the sorghum beer and *mageu* industries in Southern Africa by applying scientific techniques to microbiological research on local fermented foods (Novelli 1968; Haggblade and Holzapfel 1989).

Many developing countries have established government agencies or parastatals responsible for research on technologies for small-scale industries. The Rural Industries Innovation Center in Botswana successfully improved the design of an abrasive disk dehuller developed by the Prairie Regional Laboratory of Canada for use with coarse grains such as sorghum and millet (Bassey and Schmidt 1989). By no means have all efforts proven successful, however. Some have duplicated work done elsewhere, some have failed to lead to significant improvements in technologies, and some have not been sufficiently linked to commercialization (Segal et al. 1987).

- *Nonprofit and international research organizations.* Inspired by the early work of E. F. Schumacher (1976) on small-scale industries and by the work at the International Labor Organization (ILO) on employment creation in the informal sector (ILO 1979), many international agencies began to support technology research and information dissemination on behalf of rural nonfarm enterprises. Sponsors of this work have included the United Nations Industrial Development Organization, the Food and Agriculture Organization (FAO), the International Development Research Centre of Canada (IDRC), the International Labor Office (ILO), the Groupe de Recherche et d'Echanges Technologiques (GRET) of France, the Gesellschaft für Technische Zusammenarbeit (GTZ) of Germany, the United Nations Development Program, and the United Nations Fund for Women in Development. The FAO has published a wide range of materials on marketing, postharvest handling and processing of crops, fisheries, and forest products. The ILO likewise has produced many publications on technology for small-scale industry.[2] These agencies have produced or funded a variety of appropriate technology sourcebooks covering a multitude of rural technologies: oil extraction; the processing of fruits and vegetables, cereals, fish, rootcrops, and dairy products; drying, packaging, and storage; the manufacture of construction materials; rural transport; and marketing.[3]

Nongovernmental organizations (NGOs) work both nationally and internationally at technology development and transfer for rural nonfarm businesses. National NGOs such as the Ghana Regional Appropriate Technology and Industrial Service project, established at the University of Sci-

---

2. Bhalla (1975), Baron (1980), Van Ginneken and Baron (1984), Bhalla and James (1988).
3. Biggs and Grosvenor-Alsop (1984), Francis and Mansell (1988), Fellows and Hampton (1992), Darrow and Saxenian (1993), Creevey (1995).

ence and Technology at Kumasi, provide technical training, develop new technologies, and disseminate them in a range of specific nonfarm activities, including the processing of sheanut (*karité*) butter, groundnut oil, honey, and citronella oil; the manufacture of hand pumps; and small-scale gold mining (Baffour-Awuah 1998). Regional NGOs operating appropriate technology programs include Approtech Asia in the Philippines, the Asian Institute of Technology in Thailand, Environmental Development Action in Senegal and Zimbabwe, and the Tata Energy Research Institute in India.

The two largest international NGOs operating appropriate technology programs are the Intermediate Technology Development Group and EnterpriseWorks/VITA,[4] as well as IDRC, GRET, and GTZ. They aim to expand the use of new but appropriate technologies for small-scale producers throughout the developing world through technical research, prototype testing, demonstration, and transfer of production capacity to local firms.[5]

Motives

INDUCED LOCAL INNOVATION. Individuals and enterprises frequently innovate in response to economic incentives and pressures. Analytically, their motives fall into three categories: changing factor prices, pressure to economize on input use, and changes in output markets.

Changes in wage rates, interest rates, and costs of land and capital goods spur innovation and the development of technologies that economize on the use of increasingly scarce factors of production (Binswanger and Ruttan 1978). Increases in agricultural wages led to the development and adoption of a series of mechanical threshers in the Philippines and Thailand in order to reduce the already heavy labor demand at harvest time (Duff 1987). Similarly, in Taiwan rising labor demand in agriculture spurred a series of technical changes in farm equipment—the development of mechanical harrows, weeders, and harvesters —by a host of rural metalworkers (Tomich, Kilby, and Johnston 1995). Tax rates, interest rates, tariff rates, quotas, and exchange rates greatly influence the cost of equipment used in the RNFE. As the policies governing these change, they can induce dramatic shifts in rural nonfarm technology. For example, the suspension of import restrictions on diesel engines in Bangladesh led to a dramatic reduction in their cost and to the wholesale mechanization of two major rural nonfarm activities, small-scale rice milling and riverboat transport (Box 14.1).

Efficiency gains from new technology frequently aim to reduce raw material costs in production. Across a range of rural nonfarm activities, mechanical

---

4. EnterpriseWorks Worldwide was formerly Appropriate Technology International. VITA stands for Volunteers in Technical Assistance.

5. Carr (1988), Gamser et al. (1990), Hyman (1996, 1997b), EnterpriseWorks Worldwide (1997).

BOX 14.1   Unexpected new technology revolutionizes two major
rural nonfarm businesses: Bangladeshi river boats and rice mills

In the second half of the 1980s, Bangladesh liberalized the import of key agricultural inputs, including fertilizer, shallow tubewells, and the diesel engines required to power them. The resulting surge in agricultural input availability launched a wave of increased irrigated rice production on farms across Bangladesh (Ahmed, Haggblade, and Chowdhury 2000).

Simultaneously, but quite unexpectedly, the tens of thousands of newly available small diesel engines imported to power shallow tubewells launched a veritable revolution in two major rural nonfarm activities. Outside the dry season, when they were required on-farm to pump water for the irrigated rice crop, farmers quickly discovered multiple uses for these highly portable small diesel engines. After harvest, they transported the engines by wheelbarrow to nearby small local dehuller mills. This new source of plentiful, cheap power launched a revolution in rice milling as 30,000 seasonal hammer mills emerged within a decade, transforming the structure of rice milling and dramatically improving competition in rice markets (Figure 7.1).

Later in the cropping calendar, during the rainy season when no irrigation pumps were required and rice milling had subsided, Bangladesh's major rivers flooded vast sections of the countryside, making boat transport a preferred mode of transport. So farmers and millers again transported these highly mobile small engines to riverboat operators at the waters edge. With some adaptive engineering by local metalworkers and boatsmiths, these light engines motorized several thousand riverboats, converting the classic dhows from cheap-but-slow to cheap-and-rapid inland water transport (Jansen et al. 1989). In this instance, a policy change intended to stimulate agricultural growth quite unexpectedly opened up new technological opportunities that radically transformed both rice milling and river transport, spurring rapid growth in both.

---

expellers and improved microbiological and production processes routinely lead to input efficiencies in the range of 50 to 100 percent (Table 14.1).

Changes in output markets can likewise spur local technical innovation in rural nonfarm businesses. Growing urbanization and the consequent concentration of demand for food products lead to pressure for extended shelf life of perishable foodstuffs, along with improved packaging and distribution. As a result of this pressure, the large-scale private producers of *mageu* that emerged in South Africa during the 1960s introduced waxed paper carton packaging and ultimately low-heat pasteurization techniques to improve the shipping quality and shelf life of their product (Holzapfel 1989). Similarly, during the 1970s and 1980s, CIAT developed and introduced polyethylene bags for enhancing the storage of fresh cassava (Lozano et al. 1978). In these and many other cases, improved shelf life of processed foods has depended on microbiological research to isolate pure cultures of inoculants, pathogenic bacteria and optimal processing temperatures to ensure rapid fermentation and minimize the growth of pathogens and other spoilage-causing organisms (Steinkraus 1989).

ADAPTED OUTSIDE INNOVATIONS. Many entrepreneurial rural nonfarm business operators seek new technologies from urban areas, and even abroad, in order to upgrade their production technology. An enterprising metalworker in Burkina Faso sent his son to Europe to investigate and import machine tools that would enable him to extend his product lines in Burkina. Another, returned from many years working in Ivory Coast, built his own air compressor and established a small tire repair shop.

Many times, these imported technologies require adaptation to unique local conditions. In the 1920s, for example, West Indians brought a European dough brake to Lagos to reduce the labor required in kneading bread and to improve its texture. In 1954, a Nigerian entrepreneur adapted this design, using scrap metal, to produce a local dough brake at one-fifth the cost of the European model. This low-cost model allowed the number of bakery firms in Lagos to triple in just four years and subsequently spread to bakeries across Nigeria (Kilby 1962b). Similarly, artificial grain dryers from the United States initially proved too heavy and too costly for effective use in Taiwan. So local metalworking shops adapted them by introducing a kerosene burner and electric blower (Tomich, Kilby, and Johnston 1995).

INJECTED INNOVATIONS. Foreign direct investment by large agribusiness, retailing, or export firms can likewise shape output markets and the technology demanded of smaller rural suppliers. Both the growing scale of distribution channels and the importance of marketing image require uniformity of standards that large distributors must communicate to smaller rural suppliers. In order to survive, rural nonfarm firms must adapt to new standards or perish (Box 14.2).

Over time, the vector transmitting technological change to the RNFE has moved through a general progression: from local induction to adaptation of outside technology to large-scale injection from outside. This has resulted in an increasing extroversion of RNFEs. Economic incentives from an external environment increasingly determine the form of new production and distribution technology. Factor costs prevailing in the country of origin dictate the input intensity and scale of the technology adopted. Though profitable and appropriate in the United States, Europe, or Japan, these capital- and skill-intensive technologies may prove inappropriate or less cost effective when imported into a new developing country environment.

In many instances, only a subset of current rural nonfarm producers—those with sufficient human and financial capital—proves able to adopt the new technology. This leads to the exclusion of others and sometimes to their massive exit from the RNFE (Chapter 9). The source and form of the new technology

---

BOX 14.2   New technology challenges small firms:
Latin American dairies

In the 1990s, liberalization of foreign investment led to an influx of foreign direct investment in Brazil, Argentina, and Chile. In the dairy industry, global firms such as Parmalat, Royal Numico, MD Foods, and Nestlé all invested heavily. Dairy product price competition became heated, resulting in a 40 percent drop in real retail prices for milk between 1994 and 1997, while farmgate prices did not fall until 1997–98. As incomes rose, the dairy products market burgeoned.

Stiff price competition in dairy markets led to the adoption of new strategies of supply chain management. Leading processors such as Itambé (the largest Brazilian dairy co-op and second-largest dairy processor), Nestlé, and Parmalat imposed new private standards for milk producers to ensure quality and safety and to reduce losses in industrial processing. Among other specifications, these grades and standards require on-farm milk refrigeration together with volume and micro-biological requirements (Jank et al. 1999). Better raw material quality reduces losses in industrial processing, allowing large-scale transport and more efficient logistic strategies.

The private standards set by the large dairy companies have required producers to invest in costly refrigeration equipment at the farm level. In less than five years, the leading firms completed their "bulking" program, imposing these standards systemwide. Unable to finance these large refrigeration investments quickly enough, thousands of small dairies closed their operations or moved into the failing informal sector milk markets in Brazil, Argentina, and Chile (Jank, Farina, and Galan 1999; Dirven 2001; Gutman 2002).

---

adopted will influence its "appropriateness" in terms of both efficiency and equity.

Adoption of New Technology

Patterns of Technical Change

To gain some sense of the motivation for and the prevalence and impact of technological change in RNFEs, we have reviewed a broad range of case study literature. Using our own libraries and experiences as an indicative database, we have summarized instances in which technology change has been adopted by large numbers of rural nonfarm enterprises (Table 14A.1). Though not derived from any rigorously stratified sample, our material does cover a broad range of experience that seems to suggest several general tendencies.

RAPIDLY GROWING RURAL ECONOMIC REGIONS.   First of all, technological change in the RNFE occurs most frequently in rapidly growing rural regions (the two eastern quadrants in Table 14.2). Growing local demand in the rural economy seems to increase opportunities for market growth and attracts new entrepreneurial activity and investment as well as demand for higher-value goods and services. At the same time, shifting demand for labor in agriculture and other basic economic activities affects wage rates (Table 7.1) and hence encourages the introduction of new labor-saving technologies.

In these growing rural regions, private firms typically predominate as initiators of new nonfarm technology. At the small end of the enterprise spectrum, skilled workers are attracted back to their home regions as conditions and opportunities improve, bringing new technology and ideas with them. Likewise enticed by growing opportunities, large firms focus their attention on these prosperous zones. They introduce new, larger scales of operation and procurement, which normally dictate the simultaneous introduction of grades and standards and, in turn, require some form of capital- or skill-intensive investment. In many instances they introduce new technology from outside, often from abroad. This suggests that policies affecting foreign trade and foreign direct investment will be crucial determinants of the rate of technical change in the nonfarm economy.[6]

Public technology development has most frequently proven important in facilitating the modernization, scaling up, and quality improvement necessary to expand the production and distribution of locally specific indigenous agro-processing activities. South Africa's Sorghum Beer Institute, the Nigerian Federal Institute of Industrial Research, Malaysia's Agricultural and Rural Development Institute, and Thailand's Department of Agricultural Extension all fit into this mold. Because comparable products do not exist in Western countries, the food processing technology for these products has, of necessity, been developed locally.

SLOW-GROWING, LOW-POTENTIAL REGIONS. Our review documents far fewer instances of technical change in stagnant or low-potential rural zones (Table 14.2). It appears that resource-poor regions offer fewer economic incentives and attract less private sector interest than the prosperous zones. Where change occurs, it depends primarily on public and NGO efforts at technology development.

As a result, NGOs and government technology institutes rather than the private sector have proven to be major technical innovators in these zones. Though the potential is far lower here, their equity orientation leads them to explore ways of improving productivity in these resource-poor zones.

Consequences of Technological Change

EFFICIENCY. Technical changes that are widely adopted by rural non-farm enterprises typically improve economic efficiency. Improved processing

---

6. See Grossman and Helpman (1992), Coe et al. (1997), and Edwards (1998).

TABLE 14.2 A typology of factors affecting technical change

	Rural economic base		
	Sluggish		Dynamic
Source of new technology	1. Resource-poor	2. Unexploited potential	3. High-potential, fast-growing
Internal technology development			
Private			Cassava graters: Nigeria Farm implements: Taiwan Palm oil press: Nigeria Sorghum beer: Botswana, Zambia, Zimbabwe Ceramic-lined stoves: Ghana, Kenya, Mali, Senegal Treadle pumps: Bangladesh *Gari:* Nigeria *Mageu:* South Africa *Ogi:* Nigeria Paddy thresher: Philippines and Thailand Sorghum beer: South Africa *Tapai:* Malaysia
Nonprofit		Sheanut processing: West Africa	
Public		Hybrid silkworms: Thailand	
External technology sources			
Private		Internet marketing: Peru	Dairy: Brazil, Argentina, Chile Dough brake: Nigeria Rice milling: Bangladesh, Indonesia Riverboats: Bangladesh Rural mechanics: Kenya Small hammer mills: Zimbabwe Cell phones: Bangladesh
Nonprofit	Manual oil press: Tanzania, Uganda, Zimbabwe		
Public	Internet marketing: Guyana		

SOURCE: Table 14A.1.

NOTE: A blank cell indicates that data are not applicable.

technology routinely reduces input costs and improves the efficiency of material input use (Table 14.1). The considerable adaptive design modification of farm implements and processing equipment in response to rising rural wage rates offers classic examples of this endogenous technology change.

Policy-induced shifts in factor costs—primarily via changes in tariffs, exchange, and foreign exchange controls and policies on foreign direct investment as well as tax and fiscal policies and subsidization of petroleum product costs and regulation of formal and informal financial institutions—have proven to be powerful levers for rapidly altering economic incentives and inducing the introduction of new technologies in the RNFE. A famous example is that of the policy-induced change in rice-milling technology in Indonesia in the early 1970s (Timmer 1972). In some cases, as in that of the import liberalization that launched a surge of small diesel engine imports into Bangladesh (Box 14.1), the policy-induced change in factor costs has benefited tens of thousands of rural nonfarm enterprises, in this case small rice millers and riverboat transporters, as well as their customers. This change has proven both efficient and equitable. In other cases, such as that of the dairies in Brazil, Argentina, and Chile (Box 14.2), the liberalization of capital and foreign exchange markets has resulted in rapid technology change and rapid but highly inequitable growth.

CHANGING MARKET STRUCTURE. New technology frequently alters the structure of production and supply chains. Shifts in technology, from outmoded to more productive and profitable technologies, often require vertical deintegration and individual firm specialization (Mead 1984). To survive, small producers must shift to growing market channels and niches. Normally this requires tighter integration into distribution systems that rely on larger firms either for high-quality inputs or as purchasers of the small firms' new, higher-quality output.

In the example of the Thai silk subsector, vertically integrated traditional silk producers faced low-growth, low-return markets (Figure 14.1, Channel 1). To access the rapidly growing export markets for modern Thai silk they had to specialize as producers of higher-quality yellow weft yarn for the factory mills (Figure 14.1, Channel 2). In making this transition to a growing market niche, they became vertically linked to larger firms. But because village cocoon rearers cannot produce hybrid silkworm eggs themselves, they rely on the Department of Agricultural Extension (DOAE) for this crucial input. And in marketing their yarn to the weaving factories clustered around Pak Ton Chai they rely on a network of itinerant yarn merchants to purchase and assemble their product, then deliver it to the mills. New, higher-productivity technology leads to higher earnings for village producers, nearly quadrupling returns compared to the traditional technology in Channel 1. The same holds true for home brewers of sorghum beer, for whom procurement of factory-made inputs and specialization in home brewing (Channel 2) or retailing (Channel 3) leads to a doubling and quadrupling of returns (Figure 14.2). In these and most cases, access to improved technology leads simultaneously to tighter dependence on vertical supply channels and market relationships with larger firms.

EQUITY.   Nimbleness in making the transition to these new technologies and strategic niches becomes key to small firm survival. Thus, although new technology may offer opportunities for the poor, it also frequently poses new challenges and threats. Small and household producers must either adapt to new technology and market structure or be squeezed out of business by competitive forces.

Barriers to accessing new technology vary considerably across settings. In the case of Thai silk, a shift to the rearing of hybrid silkworms required no new equipment, only $1 in working capital each month to procure DOAE egg sheets. Where purchase of a diesel engine or other mechanical equipment is required, as in the Bangladeshi rice mills, capital requirements are much higher, limiting access by the very poor. In the Brazilian dairy industry, purchase of the cooling tanks required to meet the new quality standards of the multinational retailers required investments in the tens of thousands of dollars, steeply raising barriers to entry.

In the end, the equity impact of new technology will depend on capital costs, skill requirements, and on the organizational feasibility of poor participants shifting to more productive market niches. Current levels of income and poverty as well as their distribution clearly govern outcomes. Only by studying the dynamics of specific supply chains can policymakers and other interested agencies determine how the poor can most effectively participate in rapidly changing technological environments (see Chapter 15 for some examples).

Policy Issues

Market Failure

EFFICIENCY.   In spite of widespread private sector innovation and dissemination of new nonfarm technology, private firms normally underinvest in technology research for the RNFE. In many developing country settings, research on new nonfarm technology constitutes a classic public good—nonexcludable and nonrival in use. Because of an absence of effective patent law enforcement, rural nonfarm firms can—and routinely do—copy imported or urban designs with impunity. Imperfect information and high transaction costs make royalty payments and patent enforcement difficult and largely nonexistent. Persistent free rider problems arise when an innovator cannot prevent other similar firms from copying his or her new design. Because private firms cannot capture the entire gain from their new technology, they will generally underinvest in technical research for nonfarm activities.

Where significant nonmarket externalities exist, private firms will likewise underinvest in new technology development. Market prices for woodfuels

FIGURE 14.2 The Botswana sorghum beer sector, 1982

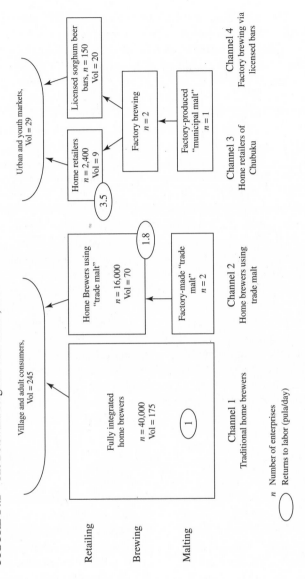

SOURCE: Boomgard et al. (1992).

normally fail to incorporate the full environmental cost of deforestation and erosion resulting from the firewood and charcoal industries. For this reason, improved stove designs that recognize and attempt to minimize these environmental costs remain largely limited to the confines of NGO and public sector research systems.

The small-scale and weak human capital endowments of many rural nonfarm enterprises compound these problems. In many rural nonfarm activities, large numbers of part-time household producers provide similar services or products to a large consumer market. Because they lack access to training and necessary resources, they are often unable to conduct the technical research required to upgrade their processes and improve their technical performance. For this reason, public research institutes have historically intervened in the application of scientific research to indigenous products (Table 14A.1). While no individual small producer enjoys the financial means or the technical capacity to conduct such research, it is in the public interest to do so. From the processing of sheanuts to the making of *tapai,* many thousands of rural processors stand to benefit from the increased extraction rates made possible by the adoption of new fermentation or mechanical technologies developed by publicly funded research.

EQUITY.   Where equity remains a policy objective, a pure laissez-faire attitude toward technology development becomes doubly doubtful. Much of the new technology introduced into the RNFE comes from external private firms that have developed the technology in response to factor pricing appropriate elsewhere. It often proves too expensive and too sophisticated for many rural entrepreneurs. Because they are unable to adapt quickly enough, many may go out of business (Box 14.2). This wholesale obliteration of firms operated by the rural poor clearly threatens regional income distribution and the livelihoods of low-income groups.

Policy Options

MAINTAINING INCENTIVES FOR PRIVATE INNOVATION.   Private innovation and technology transfer from outside has proven to be the dominant force driving technical change in rural nonfarm activities. Consequently, maintenance of incentives for private sector innovation and technology transfer remains crucial to fueling a steady stream of technical innovation. As one reviewer of technological change in the developing world concludes, "Government policies are critical to the success or failure of appropriate technology (AT). They are of far greater importance for AT than the specific micro-interventions which have been the main vehicle of those who support appropriate technology" (Stewart 1987, 297). Thus, as a first step, policymakers must create an environment that will foster private innovation and adoption of new technologies.

Policies governing foreign trade, investment, and travel will play a key role in influencing the availability of new technologies from outside. For this reason, the liberalization of trade and foreign direct investment regulations has routinely opened up key conduits of technology transfer from abroad.[7] Sudden changes in trade policy can induce rapid technical change by altering access and the cost of imported capital goods, literally overnight (Boxes 14.1 and 14.2). That can alter the relative factor prices in the recipient country, making some technologies "appropriate" (in the Hayami-Ruttan sense, where factor availability matches the factor bias of technologies). Enterprises can also borrow from other countries with relative factor scarcities similar to those of the recipient country. Policies that influence gains to innovation—such as intellectual property and patent laws—will likewise contribute to the long-term vitality of private sector research and development efforts.

FILLING KEY GAPS WITH PUBLIC AND NONPROFIT TECHNOLOGY RESEARCH. Externalities, lack of patent protection, and what are frequently very fragmented, dispersed legions of small-scale rural nonfarm producers all conspire to dampen private sector enthusiasm for technology research and development. In such cases, the public sector and private not-for-profits can justify intervention, as they have frequently in improving agroprocessing technologies for location-specific but widespread indigenous rural products such as *tapai, mageu, ogi,* and *gari.* Where externalities arise, the public sector and nonprofits have typically intervened. In the case of deforestation and inefficient charcoal stoves, they have labored to identify improved, ceramic-lined stoves. Public health concerns and the potential for generating significant additional income for rural households similarly drive much of the current interest in small-scale rural oil processing technologies (Hyman 1993b; Silva-Barbeau 1997).

Equity concerns likewise motivate public and nonprofit technology research. While private firms largely ignore resource-poor regions, the equity orientation of nonprofit and government agencies induce them to venture into this gap.

Critical questions about costs and returns to public nonfarm research too often remain unaddressed in the current evaluation literature. For this reason, a series of recent impact evaluations offers a welcome contribution to our understanding of where public monies can be effectively deployed in technology development.[8] The evidence they provide suggests that some significant successes have emerged, such as the IRRI coaxial thresher, the widely available ram press for oilseed extraction, the treadle pump that reduced the cost of pumping water to dry-season paddy fields, and the many improvements developed by the Sorghum Beer Institute of South Africa's Council for Scientific and Industrial Research (see Boxes 14.3 and 14.4). However, many failures dot the landscape as well (Segal et al. 1987). In general, experience suggests that cost-effective public technology development efforts must focus on a few key, widely produced products, on the commercial viability of new technologies, and on working with

---

7. In addition to this chapter, see the many examples from Chapters 9 and 15.

8. EnterpriseWorks Worldwide (1997), Hyman (1997a), Hyman, Njiku, and Herz (1997), Hyman et al. (1998).

BOX 14.3   Public research on rural nonfarm technology

IRRI's Axial Flow Thresher

The International Rice Research Institute (IRRI) began work on an axial flow thresher and winnower for rice in 1970. Convinced that growing labor demands in irrigated agriculture would require mechanized harvesting, IRRI further believed that private firms would not invest in the development of this technology because of their inability to capture patent fees to protect their intellectual property. In 1974, after four years of experimentation, IRRI provided several Philippine manufacturers with the design for a machine with capacity of 1 ton per hour and costing about $2,500. After field testing in the Philippines indicated a demand for a lighter, more mobile unit, IRRI designed a smaller model that cost about $1,000. The design underwent further refinement to facilitate its use with wheat and corn and make it more efficient and easier to clean.

IRRI provided design drawings and training for selected private manufacturers in the Philippines and Thailand. Ten years after the introduction of the threshers, some 79 assisted small workshops in the Philippines and 30 larger ones in Thailand had manufactured 55,000 of them. In addition, half as many additional firms spontaneously began production of the threshers in these two countries. The larger model proved more popular in Thailand, while the smaller one dominated in the Philippines. In 1985, over 200 manufacturers in 18 countries were producing these models. Once IRRI had underwritten the basic design work and absorbed the initial research and development risk, private manufacturers made numerous improvements and modifications to the basic IRRI design (Duff 1987).

South Africa's Sorghum Beer Institute

For millennia, rural farm households across Southern Africa have brewed sorghum and millet beer, traditionally in batches of about 40 liters. Specialized rural brewers, called *shebeens,* gradually developed a rural cottage industry with typical production of 200 liters per brewing cycle. Although factory brewing in South Africa began around 1910, production was hampered by technical problems.

Research by the South African Council for Scientific and Industrial Research (CISR) over a 30-year period played a critical role in allowing the growth of the large-scale sorghum beer factories from the mid-1950s onward. This research, funded by a levy on sales of factory beer in South Africa, identified the best cultivars and procedures for malting sorghum as well as optimal temperatures and procedures for brewing the traditional low-alcohol beer on an industrial scale.

As a result of this research, several scales of large-scale malting factories arose to supply both factory and home brewers. Modern factory breweries, producing

15,000–27,000 liters of sorghum beer per batch, began displacing home brewers in Botswana, South Africa, Zambia, and Zimbabwe. Growth of the large-scale producers coincided with an increase in the demand for beer arising from growing concentrations of mineworkers and increasingly affluent urban consumers. Confronted with stiff competition from these urban factories and their strong rural distribution systems, some rural brewers abandoned their business altogether, while some switched to retailing factory-brewed sorghum beer and others continued to compete by using improved industrial malts that reduced their grain inputs by as much as 40 percent (Haggblade and Holzapfel 1989, Figure 14.2).

local fabricators from the beginning to ensure profitable, ongoing production and repair services for new equipment.

PROTECTION. Because new technology available in the RNFE frequently comes from outside, it responds to factor prices and skill availabilities prevailing in other regions—unless it was specifically designed to be appropriate for small-scale rural producers. As a result, it may prove too expensive or too skill-intensive for current rural producers to convert and adopt. For this reason, many new technologies exclude existing small and household producers in favor of larger foreign or urban-based firms.

When confronted with this situation, policymakers sometimes respond by invoking protective measures such as tariffs, quotas, and even outright reservation of specific activities for rural and small-scale producers. The Indian and Sri Lankan governments have protected key rural cottage industries for decades. But then, when they ultimately liberalize, as both of them have, thousands of rural nonfarm producers have to find alternative livelihoods. Though politically popular, these broad-based protection schemes have normally proven fiscally costly and competitively unsustainable.

FACILITATING TRANSITIONS. An alternative response to protective legislation involves the provision of short-term assistance in facilitating the transition of small firms to new technologies in newly ascendant market channels. In Bangladesh, the Grameen Bank's Village Phone subsidiary has purchased the cell phone rights to a portion of the broadcast spectrum in order to ensure access for poor rural service providers to this lucrative and growing market (Burr 2000). Thailand's DOAE and the NGO CARE have both assisted Thai silk producers to shift from old technology in slow-growing markets to new, higher-return technology in fast-growing markets (Figure 14.1). These efforts offer examples of the kind of punctual assistance that may prove effective in enabling the rural poor to participate in growing, high-return segments of the RNFE.

In increasingly open rural economies, technical and structural change will continue to stimulate opportunities and challenges in the nonfarm economy. Left alone, these movements will sometimes benefit the rural poor and other

BOX 14.4   NGO-led appropriate technology development

The Ram Press

Small-scale oilseed processing in rural areas enables farmers and local entrepreneurs to add value locally and earn two to three times more gross income than they could by selling their harvest unprocessed. Manual equipment for processing of oilseeds leads to increased rural employment and provides more affordable cooking oil for low-income consumers, who often obtain inadequate calories and fat in their diets. Rural processing of oilseeds also yields seedcake for local use as a livestock feed.

In 1985, an EnterpriseWorks/VITA engineer, Carl Bielenberg, invented a hand-operated ram press for producing cooking oil from sunflower and sesame seeds. EnterpriseWorks/VITA began promoting commercial production of this technology in Tanzania in 1986. Subsequently, they and partner organizations have developed major ram press projects in the Gambia, Kenya, Mali, Mozambique, Uganda, Zambia, and Zimbabwe. Four sizes of ram press were eventually developed to fill different market niches. The smaller models can be easily operated by one woman and range in price from $80 to $300, depending on the size and country-specific costs.

Initially, EnterpriseWorks/VITA and partner organizations trained multiple small-scale manufacturers and repair artisans to produce the press in each country. The NGO designed jigs and fixtures to make production faster and more accurate and prepared a manual for manufacturers, along with technical drawings. Manufacturers had to repay the cost of jigs and fixtures and were responsible for procuring their own raw materials and working capital. Production costs were not subsidized, although project staff inspected the quality of the presses before they were sold. From the beginning, the price paid by press purchasers covered the full ex-factory price, including profit. In 1995, EnterpriseWorks/VITA moved toward a more commercial system for press distribution by increasing the margin on press sales to recover the full costs of distribution and creating a broader network of private sales agents.

After 12 years of operation, more than 6,800 ram presses had been sold in Africa. The value of the oil and seedcake produced exceeded $3.21 million in 1997, for a cumulative total of $13.79 million. A nutritional study in the Gambia found that women and children in villages with the ram presses had better diets due to the greater availability of edible oil for the household's own use as well as for sale to generate income for purchasing other food (Hyman 1993b; Hyman et al. 1998).

The Treadle Pump

High population density, extreme poverty, fertile soils, and a high water table converge along the heavily populated Gangetic floodplain of Bangladesh and northeastern India. In the late 1970s, a Norwegian engineer named Gunnar Barnes, working for the Lutheran World Federation in Bangladesh, invented an inexpensive treadle pump that radically reduced the cost of pumping water from these shallow water sources onto irrigated dry-season paddy fields. Subsequent development of high-yielding dwarf rice varieties by the Bangladesh Agricultural Rice Research Institute, together with the liberalization of fertilizer and input markets in the mid-1980s, propelled a surge in dry-season irrigated rice cultivation. Affordable pumping technology provided the key to small farmers' access to this new opportunity. The simplest bamboo treadle pump costs roughly $10 plus an additional $25 for the tubewell and pump frame, a total of less than 25 percent of the cost of comparable-capacity diesel pumps. While better-off small and larger farmers could afford small diesel pumps, poor households with extremely small landholdings could not.

In 1985, in order to facilitate poor households' access to the new, more productive rice production technology, an international NGO, International Development Enterprises (IDE), began to develop private manufacturing capacity and distribution networks in Bangladesh to ensure widespread access to these treadle pumps. IDE helped to train small metalworkers in pump manufacture and launched a major marketing campaign involving traveling troubadours and Bollywood-style movies about how treadle pumps had transformed the lives of nearly landless households. By 2000, some 84 private manufacturers in Bangladesh were selling treadle pumps through a network of private sector distributors. A variety of NGOs, such as Applied Technology International (now EnterpriseWorks/VITA) and ApproTech, have since disseminated these pumps across other parts of Asia and Africa as well. By 2000, these commercial distribution networks had sold 1 to 1.5 million treadle pumps in Bangladesh, with probably another 1 million distributed elsewhere in the developing world. Annual income gains lie in the range of $100 per household per year (Hyman, Lawrence, and Singh 1997; Shah et al. 2000; Armstrong and Karmali 2005).

times exclude them. Governments interested in equity as well as growth can frequently better these outcomes by maintaining an active interest in strategic nonfarm activities and facilitating the transition of poor households and small firms to more profitable market niches and technologies.

Appendix 14A: Supplementary Table

See table on pages 344–351.

TABLE 14A.1 Case studies of technical change in the rural nonfarm economy

Case study	Innovator	Motives				Impact	Reference
		Factor markets	Input economies	Product markets			
Cassava graters	Rural metalworkers NGOs	Locally developed machinery reduces labor requirements				Rising returns to labor	Carr (1996b)
Cell phones, Bangladesh	Grameen's Village Phone			Develop new businesses for rural poor		1,000 village phone providers in business 60,000 users Used by the poor mostly for economic purposes (obtaining prices for perishable products)	Burr (2000), Chowdhury (2000), Bayes et al. (1999)
Farm implements, Taiwan	Rural blacksmiths Importers	Rising rural wage rates induce development of labor-saving implements Region-specific adaptation for varying soils				Steady evolution of mechanization in agriculture across regions and over time	Tomich, Kilby, and Johnston (1995)

	Organizations	Technology	Objective	Results	References
Gari (fermented, toasted cassava flour), West Africa	Rural blacksmiths Federal Institute of Industrial Research Private-public corporation, Texagri		Scale up production Improve keeping quality	Mechanized cassava grating becomes a specialized business in rural villages Shelf life in factory production increases from 6 weeks to 2 years Range of processing scales remains competitive	Onyekwere et al. (1989)
Improved stoves, Senegal and Kenya	EnterpriseWorks/ VITA (Volunteers in Technical Assistance)	Ceramic-lined metal stoves reduce charcoal consumption by 40–50%		2 urban ceramics firms supply liners 35 artisans produce stoves 125 sales agents distribute stoves 24,000 stoves sold	Hyman (1987), Hyman, Singh, and Lawrence (1996), Jeans, Hyman, and O'Donnell (1991)
Internet marketing for rural weavers and artists, Peru	Private Web marketing company		Link artisans directly with customers via the World Wide Web	Price to artisan rises Price to consumer falls Sales rise	Dvorak (2000)

(continued)

TABLE 14A.1 *Continued*

| Case study | Innovator | Motives | | | Product markets | Impact | Reference |
| | | Factor markets | Input economies | | | | |

Case study	Innovator	Factor markets	Input economies	Product markets	Impact	Reference
Internet marketing for rural weavers, Guyana	Guyana Telephone and Telegraph			Link artisans directly with customers via the World Wide Web	Sales rise as marketing improves Price to artisan rises	Romero (2000)
Mageu (fermented, nonalcoholic maize gruel), South Africa	Mines and large agribusiness firm Council for Scientific and Industrial Research (CSIR)			Mineworkers and growing urban population demand larger-scale production Pure inocula permit scaled-up production Pasteurization ensures keeping quality	Rapid growth of factory production	Holzapfel (1989)
Maize milling, Zimbabwe	Small hammer mill operators			Market liberalization removes large millers' monopoly	Thousands of small hammer mills emerge within 5 years of liberalization Consumer price falls due to lower processing cost and increased competition	Jayne et al. (1996)

Mechanics, Kenya	Driver/mechanic who learns on large estates, returns to village to train sons and set up village mechanics school		New skills learned outside increase in relevance as car use increases in rural areas	9 paying trainees learn from one informal mechanic	King (1977)
Ogi (fermented, nonalcoholic grain porridge), Nigeria	Private firms Federal Institute of Industrial Research		Growing urbanization leads to needed increases in production scale and shelf life	Gradual growth in large-scale factory production	Onyekwere, Akinrele, and Koleoso (1989)
Paddy threshing, Philippines and Thailand	IRRI (publicly funded International Rice Research Institute)	Reduce labor requirements by one-third at harvest time		Rapid adoption in growing high-yielding variety zones 70 private manufacturers in Philippines; 20 in Thailand After experimentation, many modifications and patents issued to private firms	Duff (1987)

(continued)

TABLE 14A.1 *Continued*

Case study	Innovator	Motives				Impact	Reference
		Factor markets	Input economies	Product markets			
Palm oil extraction, the Pioneer Oil Mill, West Africa	United Africa Company		Newly developed machinery increases extraction rate from 50% to 85%			Rapid replacement of hand processing with mechanization	Abbott (1986)
Rice milling, Philippines	Government licensing and credit policy that promotes large-scale mechanical mills			Increase high-quality rice supplies for urban and export markets		Decentralized small-scale processors displaced by large mills	Ranis and Stewart (1987)
Rice milling, Indonesia	Government policy	Government loans for large mills				Tens of thousands of village women threatened by large-scale mills	Timmer (1973)
Rice milling, Bangladesh	Government liberalization of tubewell imports	Availability of small diesel engines increases (price falls), drastically decreasing cost of mechanized production				Thousands of small dehuller mills emerge	Chowdhury and Haggblade (2000)

Riverboat transport, Bangladesh	Government liberalization of tubewell imports	Cost of locomotion falls as diesel engines become widely available		50,000 to 100,000 riverboats converted from sail and paddle to diesel power	Jansen et al. (1989)
Sewing machines, worldwide	Singer Sewing Machine Company	Treadle action mechanical sewing machine developed and distributed worldwide		Makes tailoring the largest non-farm employer worldwide	Mokyr (1990)
Sheanut butter extraction, Ghana	Local metalworkers NGOs	Develop extraction machinery to reduce labor costs	Doubling of extraction rates		Carr (1996a)
Silk, Thailand	Jim Thompson Company Department of Agricultural Extension		Improved yields via hybrid silkworms	Quality improves via improved looms and designs	10% growth per year for modern Thai silk 65,000 home producers move from traditional cocoons and looms to specialized producers of hybrid silk yarn for modern weaving factories	Haggblade and Ritchie (1992)

(continued)

TABLE 14A.1 *Continued*

Case study	Innovator	Motives			Impact	Reference
		Factor markets	Input economies	Product markets		
Sorghum beer, Botswana	Chibuku Company, factory brewer Private maltsters		Improved malt raises consistency and reduces grain requirements	Imported brewing technology allows scaling up and packaging of traditional beer	56,000 home brewers threatened by competition from factory-brewed sorghum beer 16,000 home brewers switch from home-made to higher-quality factory-made malt	Haggblade (1987)
Sorghum beer, South Africa	Central government mandates municipal government monopoly on sorghum beer sales in all municipalities Government Research Institute, CSIR			Require consistent quality on a huge scale for mines and municipal beer halls	Municipal brewers given legal monopoly Home brewers and retailers (*shebeens*) operate underground	Haggblade and Holzapfel (1989)

Technology	Organization	Objective	Mechanism	Outcomes	References
Sunflower and sesame oil extraction via ram presses, Tanzania	EnterpriseWorks/VITA	Develop low-cost mechanical expeller to enable villagers to compete with factory mills		2,400 presses sold; 3 full-time manufacturers; 20 distributors; Technology disseminated in Zimbabwe, Mozambique, Zambia, Uganda, Senegal, Mali, and Gambia	Hyman et al. (1997), EnterpriseWorks Worldwide (1997)
Tapai, Malaysia	Technical research by the Malaysian Agricultural Research and Development Institute		Pure cultures of inocula improve shelf life, enable scaled-up production and long-distance distribution	Shelf life extended from two days to two weeks; industrial production made possible	Merican and Quee-Lan (1989)
Treadle pump, Bangladesh	Lutheran World Federation, International Development Enterprises		Rapid expansion of new irrigated rice varieties	Over 2 million sold worldwide at commercial price	Shah et al. (2000), Armstrong and Karmali (2005)

NOTE: A blank cell indicates that data are not applicable.

15 Subsector Supply Chains: Operational Diagnostics for a Complex Rural Economy

STEVEN HAGGBLADE

Most rural nonfarm enterprises operate in vertical supply chains. They procure inputs or market outputs through a network of related, often large-scale firms. Therefore, changes up- or downstream often govern prospects for growth in specific rural nonfarm activities. As a result, an understanding of these distribution circuits often proves essential to understanding both opportunities and constraints facing rural nonfarm firms. Because large firms often occupy strategic locations in these supply systems, as input suppliers or marketers of rural firm output, the tracing of alternate, competing supply channels quickly reveals complementarities and conflicts between large and small firms operating in the same vertical supply system. These diagnostics often yield important clues about system dynamics, opportunities for growth, and private sector partnerships required to link rural suppliers with dynamic markets.

Interest in rural supply chains has expanded rapidly over the past several decades (see Chapters 2 and 12). As a result, a set of closely related analytical tools has grown up to help organize understanding, diagnostics, and interventions in what are frequently complex rural nonfarm supply networks. These closely allied literatures refer to networks of functionally related firms as "supply chains," "value chains," "clusters," "networks," or "commodity subsectors." All begin by focusing on a specific nonfarm activity and the network of related vertical supply channels linking input suppliers, processors, and distributors together in systems that take products from raw materials through processing and distribution and on to final consumers. Diagnostic and prescriptive, these analytical frameworks offer a set of tools that aim to enhance understanding of the structure and dynamics of the rural nonfarm economy (RNFE), as well as opportunities for growth and key constraints. By slicing the RNFE into functionally meaningful yet manageable analytical units, these methods of analysis offer a way of unraveling the complex relationships that govern growth prospects for a given segment of the RNFE.

This chapter explores ways in which one particular variant of this systems analysis, subsector analysis, has been used in the past by a variety of operational organizations to identify and structure interventions on behalf of the RNFE.

This exposition concludes the policy and program discussions in Part III of this book by demonstrating how a range of organizations has applied these analytical techniques to identify opportunities for enhancing growth in rural nonfarm supply channels in which the poor can participate.

Subsector Fundamentals

Key Concepts

SUBSECTOR.   A subsector is a network of competing vertical supply channels through which related firms assemble raw materials, transform them, and distribute finished goods to a given final market. Figures 15.1–15.5 offer examples of common nonfarm subsectors from around the world. In contrast with *industries,* which cut a horizontal swath across a population of nonfarm firms, subsectors delve vertically into rural economic systems to identify functional linkages among firms in different industries. The silk subsector in Thailand, for example, includes the rearing, reeling, and weaving industries as well as related marketing and distribution activities. Altogether, it includes five alternative vertical supply channels through which firms distribute, process, and deliver final products to consumers (Figure 15.2).

Practitioners have used many different names to describe this same set of vertical networks. Agricultural marketing specialists, who originated many of the concepts and methods currently in use, call them "commodity subsectors" because most are based on a key agricultural input.[1] Business schools and large agribusiness firms call them variously "agribusiness commodity systems," "clusters," "supply chains," or, in French, *"filières."*[2] In Spanish, agribusiness practitioners refer to this same analysis as "commodity-chain analysis and action-oriented dialogue" (Bourgeois and Herrera 2000). Regional scientists, who borrowed the tools for study of rural-urban exchange and rural-urban linkages from agricultural marketing, refer to subsectors as "commodity flow studies" or "commodity systems."[3] Local economic development advocates promote the competitiveness of local economic "clusters" or "subsectors."[4] Some business development practitioners refer to these vertical networks as "value chains."[5]

---

1. Shaffer (1968, 1973), Marion (1976), Holtzman, Abbott, and Martin (1989), Wilcock (1991).

2. Goldberg (1968, 1974), Austin (1992), Montigard (1992), Lauret (1993), Porter (1998), Rosenfield (2001c), Van Roekel et al. (2002), Jaffee et al. (2003).

3. Bendavid-Val (1987, 1989), Karaska and Belsky (1987), Evans (1990, 2004), Belsky and Karaska (1993), Rondinelli (1993).

4. Dowds and Hinojosa (1999), Helmsing (2001), Meyer-Stamer (2002, 2003).

5. Likewise, starting from a vertical perspective, value chain analyses place particular emphasis on power relationships and governance within the supply systems, particularly in global value chains linking developing country producers with developed country markets and investors. See Kaplinsky (2000), Kaplinsky and Morris (2000, 2003), Gereffi and Kaplinsky (2001),

FIGURE 15.1   The Rwandan banana wine subsector, 1986

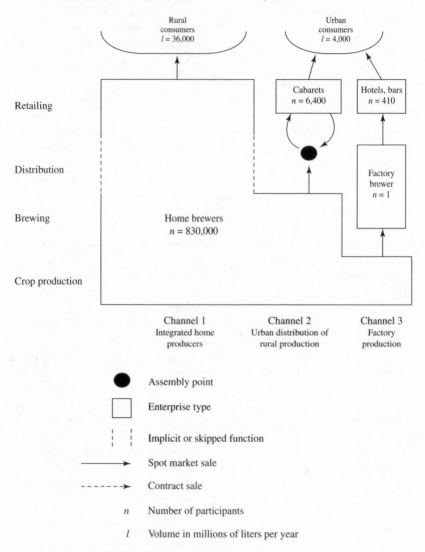

SOURCE: Haggblade and Minot (1987).

FIGURE 15.2 The Thai silk subsector, 1991

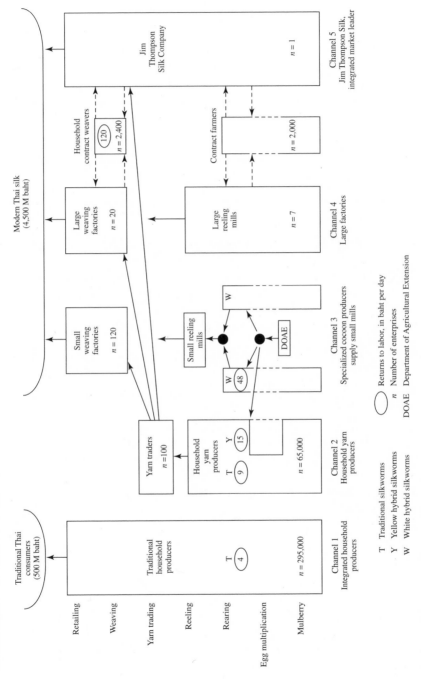

SOURCE: Haggblade and Ritchie (1992).

FIGURE 15.3　Water supply in Onitsha, Nigeria, 1990

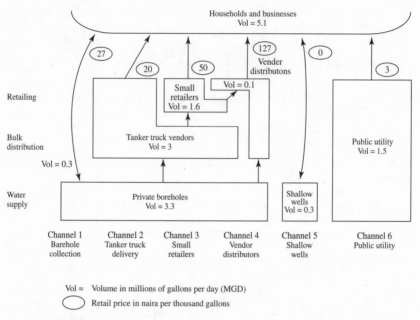

Vol = 　Volume in millions of gallons per day (MGD)

◯　Retail price in naira per thousand gallons

SOURCE: Whittington et al. (1991).

Others refer to them as "sector/systems," "subsector/trade groups," or simply "subsectors."[6]

VERTICAL SUPPLY CHANNELS.　Most rural nonfarm businesses operate in vertical "supply channels," also referred to as "supply chains" or "value chains."[7] They purchase inputs and market output through other firms, often much larger than themselves. In such cases, complementarities arise between large and small rural firms and between rural and urban-based nonfarm enterprises. In the case of rural banana wine producers in Rwanda, 6,400 urban

---

Sturgeon (2001), Vorley (2001), Humphrey and Schmitz (2002), and Giuliani, Pietrobelli, and Rabellotti (2005) for a good introduction to this literature.

6. Dichter (1988), Reiling (1990), Boomgard et al. (1992), Mead (1992a), Lusby (1995), Chen (1996), ATI (1997), Dawson and Jeans (1998), Hyman (1997b), Lusby and Panliburton (2002).

7. The use of the singular noun *supply chain* or *value chain* potentially leads to confusion, for some people take this to mean an entire network of competing supply channels, while others use it in referring to a single supply channel within a larger network. To avoid this potential confusion, discussion in this chapter refers to the larger network of competing channels as a "subsector," a "cluster," or a "network." It refers to competing vertical supply routes within this larger system as individual "supply channels" or "supply chains."

Value chains have been addressed by Kaplinsky and Morris (2000), Sturgeon (2001), Van Roekel et al. (2002), Jaffee et al. (2003).

FIGURE 15.4   Recycled fabric wastes in the Philippines, 1995

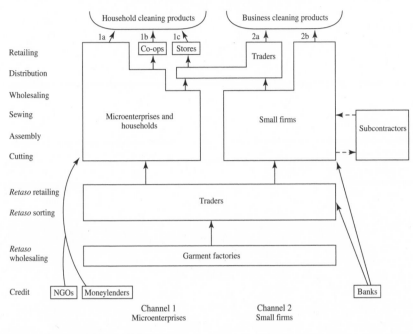

SOURCE: Overy and Giray (1996).

cabarets market output from over 800,000 home vintners (Figure 15.1). In the Philippine recycled fabric (*retaso*) subsector, a handful of large traders supply over 50,000 home producers with fabric wastes from major textile firms (Figure 15.3).

Most subsectors—or "clusters" or "networks"—encompass multiple supply channels, alternate routes through which raw materials travel en route to final consumers. Within these overall supply systems, rural nonfarm firms choose to operate in one of several alternative supply channels. Within channels, they may occupy a variety of different competitive niches. In the Thai silk subsector, for example, rural producers can choose to remain integrated traditional producers who grow their own mulberry trees, rear their own silkworms, reel the yarn, and weave it for final sale (Figure 15.2, Channel 1). Alternatively, they can specialize as yarn producers supplying the factory weavers via a network of itinerant yarn traders (Channel 2). Or, if they live within about a 15 kilometer radius of the large weaving factories, they can elect to become home-based contract weavers for these large firms (Channel 4).

Vertical relationships permit specialization, which often proves essential in improving productivity and income.[8] Many times, poor households can increase

---

8. See Mead (1984, 1992a), Hayami (1998a), and Chapter 10.

FIGURE 15.5a   The Gambian fertilizer subsector, prereform, circa 1980

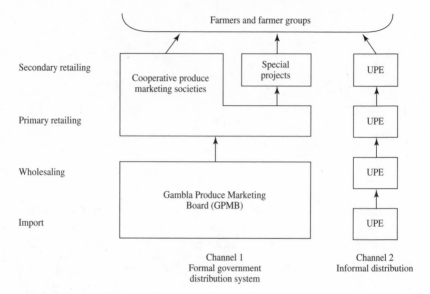

SOURCE: Nagarajan and Meyer (1995).
NOTE: UPE, unregistered private enterprise.

their earning power by moving from one low-productivity channel to a different, higher-productivity niche in an alternate channel. Continuing with the case of Thai silk, Figure 15.2 reveals that households can quadruple their hourly wage rate by moving from Channel 1 as traditional integrated suppliers to Channel 2 as more specialized suppliers of weft yarn to factory mills.

VERTICAL COORDINATION.   Yet specialization requires vertical coordination between the firms that supply inputs to or purchase output from the specialized rural nonfarm enterprises. Depending on their circumstances, firms adopt a variety of coordination mechanisms, including spot markets, subcontracts, and vertical integration (Figure 15.1). A growing literature on marketing, contracting, and supply chain management offers useful diagnostic tools for assessing which coordinating tools will prove most appropriate in different circumstances.[9] In contributing to these discussions, the value chain literature places particular emphasis on power relationships and alternative governance structures for coordinating these vertical relationships, often at a global level.[10]

COMPETITION ACROSS INDUSTRIES.   A horizontal slice across a subsector delineates an industry, that is, a group of firms competing to perform the same

---

9. Minot (1986), Jaffee (1992), Little and Watts (1994), Zylbersztajn (1996), Dorward, Kydd, and Poulton (1998), Jaffee et al. (2003), Goletti (2005).

10. See Kaplinsky and Morris (2000, 2003) for a good overview and Vorley (2001) for an instructive recent application.

FIGURE 15.5b   The Gambian fertilizer subsector, postreform, 1991

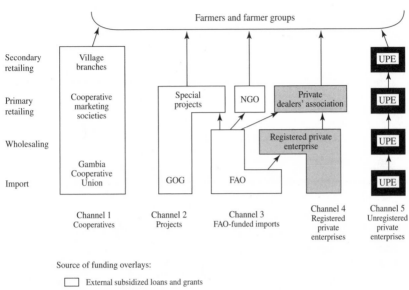

SOURCE: Nagarajan and Meyer (1995).
NOTE: FAO, Food and Agriculture Organization; GOG, government of Gambia; NGO, nongovernmental organization; UPE, unregistered private enterprise.

function. In the water supply subsector in Onitsha, Nigeria, private borehole owners successfully compete with the local public utility to pump water for use by households and businesses. Among distributors, large tanker trucks compete with smaller retailers and with integrated vendor distributors (Figure 15.3). Similarly, in Gambia's fertilizer subsector, cooperatives compete with large private firms as well as with smaller unregistered private distributors (Figure 15.5). Viewed in horizontal slices, a subsector map highlights competitive relationships that often emerge between large and small firms and between firms using alternative technologies.

DYNAMICS.   Using the snapshot provided by the subsector map as a point of departure, subsector studies attempt to identify broad changes under way. Often overall output will be growing, as with onion exports from Niger, furniture exports from Java, or green bean exports from Kenya.[11] In other cases, total production may be declining, such as with bamboo production and distribution in Bangladesh (Johnson and Ritchie 1993). At the same time, cost or quality advantages may drive growth in some channels while others atrophy or recede.

---

11. Boomgard (1988), Lev and Gadbois (1989), ECI (2001b).

As some channels grow at the expense of others, firms face incentives to switch from one niche to another. The combination of aggregate market growth and within-channel movements spells out where growth opportunities lie for rural nonfarm enterprises. Subsector participants and potential interveners use these dynamics to identify dying channels, growing channels, and within them the most profitable and promising niches for their client group.

LEVERAGED INTERVENTIONS.   An understanding of subsector dynamics frequently reveals opportunities for growth. Sometimes the key is to facilitate shifts out of dying channels and into more profitable channels and technologies. In these cases, interventions revolve around how to facilitate access to growing market channels. In other cases, the dynamics reveal system blockages—often in input supply or output marketing. In these cases, intervention will aim to remove these blockages and thereby unleash growth opportunities for many hundreds or even thousands of similar firms further up or down the supply chain.

Leveraged interventions are those that focus on key pressure points and in so doing unleash growth opportunities for large numbers of like firms at a single stroke. Policy change offers one of the most consistently powerful sources of leverage, for both good and ill. In practice, policy and regulatory changes frequently emerge as key sources of leverage in specific subsectors. Leverage can also arise from system nodes, points at which large volumes of product pass through small numbers of firms or confined geographic space. In many situations, exporters of agricultural or nonfarm products can generate opportunities for large numbers of rural suppliers operating upstream in specific channels. Suppliers of key inputs offer similar prospects for leverage, as the ensuing case studies will highlight. Geographic clustering, too, offers opportunities for leverage, because extension staff can reach large numbers of firms in a single visit and because of the demonstration effect that results when similar firms are clustered together.[12]

Objectives

Subsector analysis aims to identify cost-effective interventions that will expand the growth opportunities for large numbers of rural nonfarm firms simultaneously. It does so by systematically seeking out broad, systemic pressure points that, when actuated, will unleash growth opportunities for large numbers of like firms. Because rural nonfarm firms are often small and geographically dispersed, contact costs in working with individual enterprises prove expensive. So rather than working with individual firms across a broad range of sectoral activities, subsector interventions focus on specific trades and on the larger economic system within which rural firms operate. By focusing on groups of sim-

---

12. Schmitz and Nadvi (1999), Ceglie and Dini (2000), Clara, Russo, and Gulati (2000), Sandee and van Hulsen (2000).

ilar firms in a specific trade and on leveraged intervention points in the vertical supply systems in which rural nonfarm enterprises typically operate, subsector interventions seek cost-effectiveness by simultaneously minimizing per-firm contact costs and maximizing the number of beneficiaries and hence absolute gains.

Methods

Analysis centers around construction of a schematic subsector map (Figures 15.1–15.5). Using rapid appraisal techniques as well as secondary sources, investigators interview key informants in order to construct a basic picture that situates key actors, their interactions, and product flows. The map highlights vertical relationships among different categories of producers as well as competition between alternative supply channels. It serves as a vehicle for focusing discussion and for displaying key information.

Several guides have emerged outlining methods for conducting subsector analyses and the rapid appraisals on which they frequently depend.[13] In general, these efforts unfold in an iterative process that involves the following distinct stages: selection of a handful of promising subsectors, establishment of a basic understanding of each subsector structure, evaluation of dynamics and opportunities for leveraged interventions, and intervention.

In many instances, intervention itself further refines an agency's understanding of the subsector structure and dynamics. Conditions likewise change, sometimes rapidly, in the face of policy, weather, and other fluctuations. Constraints may change over time as interventions surmount one bottleneck and a second then becomes binding. Consequently, intervention strategies often evolve over time.[14]

Implementers

A variety of individuals, enterprises, associations, and organizations have conducted subsector analyses and interventions. Common interested parties include large agribusiness firms, management consultants, trade associations, business development service agencies and projects, government development agencies, nongovernmental organizations (NGOs), donors, regional planners, agricultural

---

13. Holtzman (1986), Haggblade and Gamser (1991), Miehlbradt, McVay, and Tanburn (2005).

See Bear et al. (1993), Lusby (1995), Chen (1996), Dowds and Hinojosa (1999), Bourgeois and Herrera (2000), Lusby and Panliburton (2001), Miles (2001), and IDE (2003, 2005) on subsector methods as well as related work by Porter (1985), Kaplinsky (2000), Kaplinsky and Morris (2000), Murphy (2001), Sturgeon (2001), Meyer-Stamer (2002), Jaffee et al. (2003), and Miehlbradt and McVay (2006) on clusters, supply chains, and value chains.

14. See, for example, Reiling (1990), Bear (1993), Malhotra and Santer (1994), Lusby (1995), Save the Children (2000), and Kapila and Mead (2002).

marketing specialists, and agricultural research organizations. Some, such as the National Agricultural Bank of India and the NGO International Development Enterprises, suggest conducting three to five subsector studies in a given region to gain a feel for the range of opportunities, constraints, and priorities for effective intervention (SGRNFS 1995; Magistro et al. 2004). Others, interested in general policy environments, suggest a similar number of subsector studies as "borehole" studies aimed at evaluating the policy environment across a diverse population of nonfarm firms (Snodgrass and Biggs 1996). Regional planners advocate review of a similar number of key subsectors in order to give planners a good feel for opportunities as well as infrastructural requirements in a given region.[15] Agricultural research institutions have adopted subsector analyses in order to help identify nonfarm constraints to agricultural growth.[16] Providers of business development services frequently apply subsector analyses in order to target their interventions most effectively.[17] A recent review of 82 business development service programs determined that over 40 percent began their operations with subsector market research studies (Loucks 1999). The following case studies illustrate the method and give a sense of the many different applications, motivations, and interveners.[18]

Illustrative Case Studies

Banana Wine in Rwanda

As one of a series of "policy borehole" studies, Rwanda's Ministry of Finance and Economy commissioned a review of the banana wine subsector in 1986.[19] Using rapid appraisal techniques supplemented by rich household survey data available at the Ministry of Finance, field work and analysis unfolded over a six-week period. Together with others in the series, these half dozen subsector studies aimed to explore the policy environment and constraints confronting small enterprises in a series of high-employment nonfarm activities.[20]

Involving over 800,000 rural households, banana wine production reaches consumers through three very simple supply channels (Figure 15.1). The first, involving home production for own use, ceremonies, and gifts, dominates the subsector, accounting for nearly 90 percent of total production. Commercial-

---

15. Bendavid-Val (1987, 1989), Belsky and Karaska (1993), Rondinelli (1993), Evans (2004).

16. Bernsten and Staatz (1992), Boughton et al. (1994, 1995).

17. Lusby (1995), EnterpriseWorks (1997), Hyman (1997b), Nelson (1997), Loucks (1999), Dawson (2002), Stosch and Hyman (2002).

18. For additional case studies, see the various reviews conducted by Boomgard et al. (1986), Grant et al. (1990, 1991), Grant (1992), Bear (1993), Malhotra and Santer (1994), Hussain, Syed, and Biswas (1995), SGRNFS (1995), Chen (1996), Dawson and Jeans (1997), and Loucks (1999).

19. This section summarizes information provided in Haggblade and Minot (1987).

20. See Haggblade and Minot (1987), Mead and Ngirabatware (1987), and Haggblade (1989).

ized production by rural home producers, in Channel 2, reaches urban cabarets via a dozen major distribution points throughout Rwanda. Every morning, from about 5:30 to 10:00, producers with banana wine for sale transport bulk containers to their nearest distribution point, where urban cabaret owners meet to sample the wine and purchase their daily supplies. To ensure the best quality and taste, cabaret managers insist on sampling available wines and then negotiating face to face with the producers. This system ensures heavy competition among buyers and sellers and permits variable pricing commensurate with quality. Because of the short distances involved, transport margins remain low. In much smaller volumes, one factory also produces bottled banana wine for sale through restaurants and hotels (Channel 3). Driven by growing urbanization, commercialized production in Channel 2 is growing most rapidly of all.

In examining potential interventions, the subsector assessment considered two potential arenas of action. In the policy sphere, which motivated the study, analysts concluded that the subsector operated efficiently and within a benign policy environment. Hence no policy adjustments were required. Exploring further sources of improved system performance, the study identified considerable variation in extraction rates across home producers, factories, and laboratories. Comparisons suggest that home brewers could increase their juice extraction rates by 50 to 100 percent by using enzymes such as those used by factory brewers (Table 14.1). Given the high population density and limited land for agricultural expansion, improved efficiency of extraction and the consequent reduction in banana volumes required would reduce land pressure appreciably. Moreover, the geographic nodes provided at the daily distribution points offer an important source of leverage; demonstrations or commercial distribution at those dozen points would reach tens of thousands of commercial brewers at very low cost.

Silk in Thailand

In 1991, CARE–Thailand commissioned a study of the Thai silk subsector in order to help focus their rural nonfarm promotion activities in Northeast Thailand.[21] Compared to the very simple structure of Rwanda's banana wine subsector, the Thai silk subsector proves far more complex, both technically and structurally. It also spans a far greater geographical space. The silk subsector includes not one but three closely related industries—the rearing, reeling, and weaving industries. A wealth of alternate contracting and delivery systems govern input supply and contracting relationships (Figure 15.2).

Within the resulting six supply channels, CARE's client group, low-income village women, can occupy four principal niches. They can operate, as they have

---

21. This section summarizes material detailed by Haggblade and Ritchie (1992) and Bear (1993).

for centuries, as integrated producers of mulberry trees, cocoons, yarn, and woven cloth (Channel 1). Or they can specialize as producers of yellow weft yarn (Channel 2), linked to the growing factory weavers by a network of about 100 itinerant yarn traders. Still others can specialize as suppliers of high-quality white cocoons to local reeling factories (Channel 3). Weavers who live near the cluster of large weaving factories that operate around the town of Pak Ton Chai can also elect to work as home-based subcontract weavers for the large factories (Channel 4).

The dynamics under way point to rapid growth in the modern segments of the silk subsector. Channels 2–5 have grown rapidly in recent years, driven by international export growth and the quality control efforts of the Jim Thompson Silk Company and the constellation of large factory spin-offs set up nearby, frequently by former factory employees. The integrated traditional producers in Channel 1 serve a shrinking market with low-productivity, low-returns technology, while the growing channels offer higher productivity (Table 14.1) in mulberry trees, cocoons, and weaving. These different technologies contribute to significantly higher returns to labor for rural women operating in Channels 2–4 (Figure 15.2).

Within these high-return niches, Channel 3 proves most risky. To protect the large-scale reeling industry, the Thai government has imposed import quotas on white warp yarn from Japan. In the face of fierce lobbying by the large weavers, these quotas were lifted, then reimposed, then lifted once again. In the face of these on-again, off-again quotas, prices for white cocoons fluctuated wildly, making Channel 3 the most risky of all for home producers.

The key strategic direction emerging from this review centered on how to help facilitate the transition by village silk producers from the slowly dying Channel 1 to higher-return and faster growing niches in Channels 2–4. Because its regional office operated outside the zone served by Channel 4 subcontract weavers, CARE concentrated on opportunities in Channels 2 and 3, where several prospects for leveraged interventions emerged from the subsector review. First, lobbying for a stable policy on yarn imports would remove the risk and uncertainty currently plaguing cocoon producers in Channel 3. Second, the extension of improved technology—high-yielding mulberry trees, high-yielding hybrid silkworms, and improved reeling equipment—via large farmers, egg sheet distribution points, and yarn merchants—offered prospects for improved productivity and income growth. In the end, CARE found policy lobbying difficult given its institutional contacts and expertise, so it elected to work on expanding hybrid silkworms and improved mulberry trees to village producers of yarn in Channel 2 (Bear 1993).

Water Supply in Onitsha, Nigeria

In order to examine the effectiveness of the existing water delivery system and to evaluate households' willingness to pay for water supplies, the Anhambra State Water Corporation commissioned a study of the water distribution system in Onitsha, Nigeria.[22] With donor support, they fielded a study team to conduct a rapid reconnaissance investigation over two months, June and July 1987.

The investigation discovered that four private supply channels provide the bulk of the water used in Onitsha. During the dry season, private suppliers deliver 70 percent by volume and 95 percent by value of all water consumed. During the rainy season, daily water usage increases by about 20 percent as households obtain roughly 40 percent of their water from rainwater capture. They purchase the remainder in equal quantities, 30 percent from private suppliers and 30 percent from the public utility. Rapid population growth coupled with inadequate and unreliable supplies available from the town's one public utility have underpinned the rapid ascent of the private supply channels.

Private firms charge considerably higher prices than the public utility because for-profit enterprises must fully cover their costs in order to survive. At the public utility, feeble efforts at public cost recovery result in an effective price of 3 naira per thousand gallons of water supplied. This price stands at a mere fraction of the private sector delivery prices, which range from 20 to 130 naira depending on the supply channel and the quantities procured (Figure 15.3). Ironically the poor, who cannot buy water in bulk, frequently pay the highest prices per gallon of any consumers in Onitsha. In the dry season, they spend up to 18 percent of their total income on water.

These observations, coupled with experimental assessments of households' willingness to pay, indicate that unserviced households stand ready to pay considerably more than the public utility currently charges for water. Given large economies of scale in water provision, expansion of the public utility would enable significant reduction in the consumer price.

Key interventions suggested by this review include an expansion of public water supply capacity coupled with an increase in public utility rates. Together, these changes would result in lower overall water costs for consumers and higher quality of service. They would likewise contribute to the financial viability of the expanded public utility investment and operations.

Fabric Waste Recycling in the Philippines

Save the Children, a U.S.-based NGO, began working with poor households in the Philippines in an effort to expand income-earning opportunities for microentrepreneurs there.[23] In 1993, as part of these efforts, the organization undertook a participatory subsector analysis of a major income-earning activity for poor women, the processing and recycling of fabric wastes called *retaso*. A

---

22. This case study summarizes a more detailed description provided by Whittington et al. (1991).

23. This section summarizes material produced by Overy and Giray (1996) and Save the Children (2000). In addition, we are grateful to Alexandra Miehlbradt for supplying supplemental details and clarification.

by-product of the growing Philippine garment factories, *retaso* is sorted, cut, and woven into a variety of shapes and products by about 50,000 poor Philippine households. Women dominate this business, accounting for 97 percent of all *retaso* workers. This activity remains concentrated in depressed and squatter communities where, in some cases, as many as 50 percent of all households participate in the *retaso* trade. Save the Children selected this subsector because of its economic importance to poor women, because of the huge scale of the market, and because the geographic clustering of activity enhanced the prospects for cost-effective organization and intervention.

From the textile factories, *retaso* moves through five different supply channels, three of them operated by poor households and microentrepreneurs to serve the large consumer market (Figure 15.4). Households use *retaso* products as cleaning rags for the bathroom, the kitchen, and other parts of the house. They likewise serve as doormats, bathmats, and even oven mitts. Among poor households, *retaso* products such as patchwork clothing, bed sheets, and mattresses prove popular as well.

Using the same raw materials, a growing number of small businesses process *retaso* wastes for use by business, primarily as cleaning rags. These prove popular with taxi drivers and bus owners for cleaning their vehicles and even for checking engine oil. Repair shops and factories of all kinds use *retaso* products for virtually every cleaning need—from machinery to shop floors. Large buyers, such as Philippine Airlines and major shipping companies, place orders for *retaso* products meeting standard size, shape, and weight specifications.

The business market has grown faster and proven more reliable than the consumer market served by the microenterprises. Only via a network of retail traders does a small portion of the poor households serve this fast-growing segment of the market. Moreover, they critically depend on another group of traders for supply of their key raw material, the *retaso* itself. Because Philippine law does not allow export firms to sell their goods locally, the government carefully restricts sales of these textile wastes. Consequently, a clandestine network of traders has emerged to buy *retaso* from the factories and sell it to household-based entrepreneurs. Given the dangers, payoffs, and high risks implicit in this sub rosa commerce, traders demand high margins. Their markups to households range from 200 to 500 percent. Because of the small volumes they procure and their lack of bargaining power, women working from the household pay margins up to 40 percent greater than those paid by small business owners.

Two of the three leveraged interventions identified by Save the Children and the producer associations they work with focus on improving supply of *retaso* inputs to poor household producers. First, Save the Children has lobbied the government to make fabric waste sales legal in order to reduce the kickbacks and high costs that, in part, drive markups higher. Though unable to fully legalize the trade, the NGO was able to negotiate permission for producer associations to take *retaso* out of the free trade zones. Second, it has worked with household producer associations and other intermediaries to negotiate direct bulk purchases of garment wastes from the textile factories. Both efforts aim at lowering costs for the thousands of poor households that participate in this subsector. A third effort aims to help boost market price and expand sales to the more lucrative business market. This work involves helping producer associations identify product specifications required by large firms, market samples, and organize to fill bulk orders for the large and growing business market.

Fertilizer Distribution in Gambia

Through the mid-1980s, the government of Gambia controlled fertilizer import and distribution through its parastatal, the Gambia Produce Marketing Board (GPMB).[24] Then in 1985, as part of a general structural adjustment program, the government initiated a gradual liberalization of both the import and the distribution of fertilizer. Six years into the liberalization period, a donor-funded study team reviewed changes in the subsector as part of government and donor efforts to monitor the consequences of the liberalization and its impact on fertilizer availability at the farm level. The study team conducted a rapid appraisal of the fertilizer subsector during a three-month period, from February to April 1992.

The study team discovered that the structure of the subsector had changed considerably in the six years following liberalization. In the prereform era, one public distribution channel dominated fertilizer import and distribution in Gambia. As the official government agency charged with this activity, the GPMB imported 2,850 tons of fertilizer per year. In a second, much smaller channel, informal private firms introduced supplementary quantities of fertilizer (Figure 15.5a). Given the subsidized prices of fertilizer sold via the GPMB, private traders' market share remained very small in the prereform era.

Following liberalization, a proliferation of cooperatives, donor projects, farmer associations, NGOs, and private traders emerged to import fertilizer, resulting in a rapid expansion in the number of delivery channels (Figure 15.5b). Highly concessional donor funding financed the great bulk of this new activity in the three largest channels, those run by the Gambia Cooperative Union, the FAO, and a series of government projects. Private firms distributed fertilizer via two much smaller channels, though their incentives improved due to the gradual withdrawal of subsidies. As a result of this increased activity, the total volumes of fertilizer sold increased slightly, to 3,200 tons per year by 1991.

The reviewers concluded that access to subsidized donor finance has driven growth in the first three channels in the postreform years. Meanwhile,

---

24. Nagarajan and Meyer (1995) provide the basis for the material summarized in this section.

the purely private sector response has proven sluggish both because of considerable uncertainty about government commitment to liberalization and because of problems in finding adequate commercial finance for private import and distribution. Local banks have largely refused to lend to private traders for fertilizer import and distribution because of their lack of familiarity with the trade and because of questions about government commitment to privatization. The substantial but often subsidized donor financing, though effective in initiating three new distribution networks (Channels 1–3), makes competition difficult for private traders. Their costs necessarily prove higher given their reliance on unsubsidized private and informal sources of finance. Given uncertainties about the continued availability of donor financing, the future growth and welfare of this subsector will hinge on the ability of the private sector to secure the necessary finance to sustain market supplies as grant funding recedes.

From this review, two interventions emerged as important. First, at a policy level, government needs to reassure the private trading and banking sectors that they are serious about privatization in order to remove the considerable uncertainty that surrounds private traders' willingness to engage in the emerging private sector supply channels. Second, private traders require better access to commercial financial markets if they are to effectively respond to the emerging opportunities in this subsector.

An Overview of Applications and Outcomes

A series of reviews has presented the results of over 100 specific subsector case studies.[25] Based on that extensive literature as well as the five case study summaries described earlier, the following discussion attempts to generalize and summarize some of the key outcomes emanating from this growing body of experience.

Differing Structures

Rural nonfarm enterprises operate in economic systems that range from the very simple to the very complex. Rwanda's banana wine producers operate in three very simply structured supply channels, with coordination between producers and retailers mediated through face-to-face bargaining at half a dozen daily national distribution points where home producers and cabaret owners meet to buy and sell wine in bulk (Figure 15.1). In contrast, silk producers in rural Thailand participate in any of a dozen different niches covering a much broader range of industries and supply channels linked over a much larger geographic space. The number of intermediaries and the variety of coordinating mechanisms increase

---

25. See Boomgard et al. (1986), Grant et al. (1990, 1991), Grant (1992b), Bear (1993), Malhotra and Santer (1994), SGRNFS (1995), Chen (1996), Dawson and Jeans (1997), and Loucks (1999).

considerably, including assembly point distribution, subcontracting, and vertical integration as well as emergence of specialized traders such as the 100 or so yarn merchants that link home reelers with the large textile mills around Pak ton Chai (Figure 15.2).

Complementarities and Competition between Large and Small Firms

Large and small firms' interests coincide in a great many cases (Table 15.1). As input suppliers, large firms sometimes sustain production for multitudes of rural operators. Steel importers supply blacksmiths in Burkina Faso, while large subcontractors supply yarn and cloth inputs to rural weavers and garment producers across much of rural Asia. In other instances, small firms supply inputs to large wholesalers or manufacturers. This commonly occurs in many agricultural and natural resource marketing chains where itinerant assemblers of bamboo, paddy, and wheat supply large wholesalers. Output marketing by large firms sustains large numbers of rural producers in many agricultural supply chains, among them rural weavers, garmentmakers, and furniture manufacturers.

But large firms likewise compete with smaller-scale producers across a range of specific industries (Table 15.1). Small hammer mills around the developing world vie for market share against larger, more modern continuous-flow milling establishments. Large dairies compete with small rural milk, yogurt, and cheese producers in many locations. Small tailors and distributors of used clothing compete with large garment factories. And small informal firms contest markets served by large fertilizer distributors.

In many cases, both competitive and complementary relationships exist within the same subsector (Table 15.1). For this reason, rural nonfarm and small enterprise development specialists have learned that they cannot evaluate growth prospects for small businesses by viewing small firms alone. As Humphrey and Schmitz (1996, 1873) conclude, "In many cases the growth prospects of small firms can neither be analyzed nor fostered by focusing on individual firms." Instead, policymakers must understand the broader economic supply network within which the small firms operate.

Dynamics

Some rural nonfarm systems face secular decline, either because of a dwindling raw material base, as with bamboo in Bangladesh, or because of changing policies and price structures, as with the rapidly declining rural hand looms in Sri Lanka (Osmani 1987; Johnson and Ritchie 1993). Other rural firms operate in rapidly growing markets, as do those engaged in fabric waste recycling in the Philippines, Thai silk production, water supply in Onitsha, and wheat and rice marketing in Bangladesh (Chowdhury and Haggblade 2000).

Within a given subsector, or cluster, some channels typically grow rapidly, while others stagnate or decline. In Onitsha, four private water supply channels have grown rapidly, spurred by population growth and stagnant capacity in the

TABLE 15.1 Relationships between small and large firms

Subsector	Location	Complementary relationships		Competitive relationships	Reference
		Input supplier	Output marketer		
Agricultural machinery	Burkina Faso	Steel importers supply blacksmiths		Blacksmiths vs. factories vs. imports	Grant et al. (1991)
Automobiles	Japan	Small rural contractors supply parts to Toyota			Wada (1998)
Bamboo products	Bangladesh		Large traders assemble and market output from small producers	Small producers vs. large factories	Begum et al. (1995)
Batik	Indonesia		Wholesalers market output of household producers	Household vs. medium-sized producers	Boomgard et al. (1986)
Bean marketing	Bolivia		Large exporter markets production from 2,500 rural producers		Loucks (1999)
Dairy products	India			Women producers vs. large co-ops	Sattar (1996)
Garments	Thailand	Large merchant manufacturers subcontract with home sewers	Then manufacturers sell output to exporters, who market it abroad	Modern factories vs. merchant manufacturers and home sewers	Ohno and Jirapatpimol (1998)

Activity	Country				Reference
Improved stoves	Kenya	Urban plant supplies ceramic liners to village producers			Jeans, Hyman, and O'Donnell (1991)
Maize marketing	Zimbabwe			Small hammer mills vs. large mills	Jayne et al. (1996)
Poultry	Bangladesh	Large hatchery supplies chicks to small farmers	Traders market eggs produced by many small farmers	Small producers vs. integrated large farms	Begum et al. (1995), Dawson and Jeans (1997)
Rice marketing	Japan	Small collectors supply large urban traders			Kawagoe (1998)
Rattan furniture	Indonesia	Factory producers market through itinerant retailers	Large exporters market village production	Small producers vs. large factories	Davies (1988)
Shrimp	Indonesia	Large hatcheries supply fry to small producers	Brokers buy from small producers	Small producers vs. large fishermen	Boomgard et al. (1986)
Vegetable marketing	India			Women small vendors vs. licensed retailers	Sattar (1996)
Wood	Rwanda	Large sawmills supply small woodworkers			Mead and Ngirabatware (1987)

NOTE: A blank cell indicates that data are not applicable.

one public water supply utility (Whittington et al. 1991). In Gambia's fertilizer distribution system, small and informal traders confront special hurdles because of an absence of bank lending for fertilizer trade; consequently, foreign or donor-backed traders have benefited from the lion's share of the rapid growth resulting from fertilizer liberalization there (Nagarajan and Meyer 1995). The profitability and growth potential of specific niches vary considerably across channels.

Interventions

Because opportunities and constraints vary dramatically across settings, prospects for intervention vary as well. In many instances, nonintervention may prove the most prudent course of action. CARE's subsector review of bamboo distribution in Bangladesh revealed no opportunities for leveraged intervention. Consequently, the CARE team recommended that no new bamboo-specific project be launched. Instead the team incorporated bamboo extension into its existing agricultural activities in an effort to restore the raw material base whose rapid decline had propelled the subsector downward (Johnson and Ritchie 1993). With promotional resources in chronically short supply, a recommendation for nonintervention can prove an important outcome for avoiding squandered resources and permitting their deployment to other, more attractive, arenas.

Policies frequently emerge from subsector reviews as presenting opportunities as well as constraints. Hence many of the most effective subsector interventions have revolved around policy advocacy or lobbying. Import controls emerged as important for Senegalese bakers and Gambian fertilizer distributors (Lusby 1995; Nagarajan and Meyer 1995). Prevention of police or large firm harassment proved crucial for vegetable vendors in India and home brewers in Botswana (Boomgard et al. 1992; Sattar 1996). Very specific regulations, such as government limits on the sale of fabric wastes, proved the focus of lobbying efforts in the Philippines (Overy and Giray 1996). Because they affect literally thousands of firms at a stroke, policy interventions consistently offer the greatest prospects for leverage and cost-effective intervention (see Snodgrass and Packard Winkler 2004).

Marketing or input supply constraints often limit growth in key subsectors, and for this reason many interventions have focused on relieving such constraints in order to permit growth up- or downstream. Work with model hatcheries, for poultry in Bangladesh and shrimp fry in Indonesia, unblocked key input supply constraints for literally thousands of rural producers (Boomgard 1988; Malhotra and Santer 1994). Work with a handful of urban ceramics firms in Kenya and Senegal permitted thousands of village stove manufacturers to obtain high-quality ceramic liners and expand their production of improved charcoal stoves (Jeans, Hyman, and O'Donnell 1991; Hyman, Singh, and Lawrence 1996; Dawson and Jeans 1997). Work with producers and distributors of simple foot-operated water pumps enabled private sector distribution of over one million treadle pumps to poor Bangladeshi farmers (Shah et al. 2000).

Output marketing offers similar prospects for leveraged impact. In Indonesia, work with two export firms opened up growth prospects for hundreds of rural rattan furniture manufacturers (Boomgard 1988; Davies 1988). Similarly, the Mennonite Economic Development Associates' work with an export marketing firm has expanded markets for 2,500 bean farmers in Bolivia (Loucks 1999). In Indonesian leather goods, a group of 14 traders markets output from several thousand rural producers in Yogyakarta, while the launching of one handicraft marketing firm in 1995 has expanded the export markets for over 5,000 rural producers operating in rural Java, Bali, and Lombok (Sandee and van Hulsen 2000).

Improved technology frequently offers prospects for raising technical efficiency, labor productivity, and income (see Table 14.1). Organizations such as the Intermediate Technology Development Group (ITDG), EnterpriseWorks Worldwide (formerly Appropriate Technology International), Volunteers in Technical Assistance (VITA), and Technoserve have developed a range of new technologies and assisted entrepreneurs across the Third World to improve extraction rates, processing speed, and product quality. In Tanzania, EnterpriseWorks' assistance to 15 commercial metalworking firms launched them into commercial production of an improved sunflower oil press, the ram press, allowing them to equip several thousand village processors (Hyman, Njiku, and Herz 1997). Because of what are frequently considerable efficiency gains, movement from one technology to another can yield significant income benefits to rural producers.

Though most credit programs offer loans to all sectors, subsector studies sometimes identify very specific financing needs that constrain growth in key rural activities. Assessments of the construction subsector in Burkina Faso, fertilizer distribution in Gambia, grain marketing in Ghana, and stone polishing in Andar Pradesh have all highlighted the need for financial interventions to unblock prospects for subsector growth.[26]

Infrastructure likewise matters. This article of faith permeates virtually all writing on the RNFE. Yet identification of specific priorities becomes difficult in practical settings. For this reason, regional planners have recommended selection of a few key commodity subsectors for initial study in a given region. Review of key regional subsectors offers local authorities an important window into regional planning and public infrastructure provision. In specific cases, the establishment of grading sheds and fiber collection points proved essential for wool producers in Bolivia and South Africa (ATI 1994; Hyman 1997a; Swart 2000). A major international supermarket chain collaborated with the Thai Central Retail Corporation to build a fresh fruit and vegetable distribution center together with standardized crates, pallets, and crate-washing facilities to enable

---

26. Grant et al. (1991), Nagarajan and Meyer (1995), SGRNFS (1995), Dawson (2002).

standardized packaging and grading in Thailand (Van Roekel et al. 2002). Abbott (1986) describes a similar series of investments in the construction and operation of rural assembly markets in Brazil and India as well as terminal markets in Manila and Dar Es Salaam.

Subsector studies of public services—such as water, education, and health —can also prove revealing. The assessment of water supply in Onitsha, Nigeria, concluded that expansion of the public segment of that system offered important opportunities for improved public hygiene and consumer welfare, particularly among poor households that spent as much as 18 percent of their total income on water during the dry season. Moreover, given economies of scale in water provision and the extremely high prices currently paid by poor households for their water, expansion of the public facility proves financially viable (Whittington et al. 1991).

Countervailing Analytical Power

Many potential interest groups have conducted subsector studies to design interventions, including rural nonfarm enterprises themselves, business associations, central government ministries, local governments, and donor-funded NGOs or project authorities. Large agribusiness firms conduct these strategic studies routinely as an aid to their own investment and operations. Yet their findings remain proprietary and focus on strategic objectives of the large firms. While the interests of large and small firms sometimes prove congruent, in other instances they directly conflict (Table 15.1). Frequently asymmetric political power and access to information favor large firms and place smaller counterparts at a clear competitive disadvantage.[27] Consequently, interest groups concerned with equity and income distribution have conducted similar analyses as a countervailing force for understanding how subsector dynamics and interventions could best serve their client group.

Operational Assessment

Strengths

Subsectors, supply chains, value chains, and related concepts provide a means of organizing thinking and interventions in a complex RNFE. Like the rural economy it serves, a subsector framework examines economics connections across sectors, firm sizes, and space. By taking a close look at a handful of key subsectors and intervening as appropriate to stimulate growth in them, it provides a good place to begin identifying and helping to stimulate key regional

---

27. See, for example, Reiling (1990), Bear (1993), Malhotra and Santer (1994), Lusby (1995), Kaplinsky (2000), Save the Children (2000), Vorley (2001), and Kaplinksy and Morris (2003).

growth linkages. Through a sequence of snapshots of key rural nonfarm activities, subsector analysis provides a practical means of assessing the rural business environment as well as a means of prioritizing public investments and policy interventions.

Through the participation of key interest groups, these analytical methods provide a flexible framework for building coalitions and bridging institutional gaps. Indeed, many practitioners urge the inclusion of key trade and interest groups at the analytical stage exactly because it improves the likelihood and facilitates the coordination of subsequent interventions.[28] In the institutional vacuum that pervades many rural settings, this offers considerable advantages.

Focus on a particular commodity subsector enables potential interveners to identify large groups of like firms facing similar opportunities and constraints. Because many rural nonfarm firms are small and geographically dispersed, firm-level contact costs are invariably high and net benefits to individual firms are frequently small in absolute value. By focusing on specific subsectors and supply chains within them that are accessible to the poor, this process aims to identify high payoff interventions that influence large numbers of similar firms simultaneously. Through policy leverage, large-firm input suppliers or output marketers operating at key system nodes, improved technologies that benefit numerous firms simultaneously, geographic clustering, and work with trade associations, subsector interventions seek out systemic interventions that improve the performance of many similar firms simultaneously. By influencing opportunities for large numbers of like firms at once, "successful enterprise development projects . . . achieve the greatest impact by improving dynamic growth within strategic sectors, value chains and industry clusters," according to a recent review of over 40 private enterprise promotion efforts (Snodgrass and Packard Winkler 2004, ix).

Subsector interventions tend to avoid the displacement problems that plague many assistance programs by viewing the entire economic system in which firms operate rather than individual firms one at a time.[29] In stagnant markets with low costs of entry, lending or other direct assistance to individual firms frequently results in simple redistribution of market share from unassisted to assisted firms. While the assisted firms may benefit, the net gains to the RNFE approach zero. By viewing competing channels and directly asking the question "How will this intervention increase aggregate income in the rural economy?" subsector analysis confronts the displacement problem head on.

---

28. See Shaffer et al. (1985), Mittendorf (1986), Lusby (1995), UNIDO (1995, 1996), Chen (1996), Bourgeois and Herrera (2000), Murphy (2001), and Snodgrass and Packard Winkler (2004).

29. The displacement problem arises when assistance to enterprises operating in stagnant markets merely redistributes market share away from unassisted firms to the assisted firms without increasing aggregate income. See Dawson and Jeans (1997) and Donor Committee (1997) for good discussions of this problem.

This focus likewise enables institutions to develop expertise, contacts, and credibility with key business groups. As Tendler (1989, 1034) notes, based on her review of six of the most successful small business promotion projects in the Ford Foundation portfolio, "The narrow sectoral focus of these organizations forced them to tailor their interventions to the needs of that particular sector or trade. This meant that they proceeded by doing careful studies of a sector, after which they would identify possible points of intervention. In this process, they gained a highly grounded understanding of one sector—production processes, sources of supply, product markets and industry structure."

Institutionally flexible, subsector analysis provides a framework for organizing diverse coalitions of interveners. Any interested party—an individual firm, a trade association, a government or project agency—can initiate a subsector investigation. In practice, a great variety of prime movers and participating members has emerged. Rather than creating new omnibus institutions, the subsector framework provides an organizing tool for focusing the input of a variety of existing interest groups. These, of course, will vary from setting to setting. Because of its adaptability across institutional landscapes and because it focuses on building coalitions among existing institutions rather than creating new ones, subsector interventions have been characterized as "institutionally light" (Boomgard et al. 1992). Given the institutional gaps among support institutions for the RNFE, this flexible framework for organizing coalitions represents a key advantage of this approach.

Practical Difficulties

Practitioners have identified three practical difficulties that need to be overcome in order to successfully apply subsector techniques. First, some practitioners suggest that subsector analysis and interventions require staff with a higher level of analytical and technical skills than do credit or other business development services.[30] Clearly, the approach requires staff who are capable of understanding both technical and strategic economic issues affecting business performance and prospects. In general, staff intending to intervene in a subsector need to understand the system they are endeavoring to change. Some agencies retain such staff routinely, while others do not. Where organizations do not have sufficient capacity in-house, they can seek out alternative intervention opportunities appropriate to their staffing skills. Or they can upgrade staff through new hires, provision of training, or the hiring of outside consultants to assist with initial assessments. Tendler (1989, 1034) suggests that in-house staff may rise to the occasion, noting that "the meticulous sectoral studies of these organizations, which informed so much of their thinking, were carried out by bright

---

30. Bowman and Reiling (1990), Bear (1993), Kilmer (1993), Lusby (1995).

young generalist staffs." Involvement of trade groups can bolster existing institutional resources by bringing an immediate understanding of the technologies and operational systems in place.

Second, the focus on indirect intervention troubles some agencies, particularly poverty-focused groups that need to ensure that their interventions improve the welfare of the very poor. If they work through a large export firm, for example, how can they ensure that benefits really reach their intended poor beneficiaries? Particularly when small numbers of large firms confront thousands of small ones, fears of abusive market power and oligopoly emerge. Most subsector practitioners have confronted this problem by instituting regular monitoring programs or by working with nonprofit or socially conscious intermediaries such as the Yayasan Dian Desa in Indonesia, the Body Shop in West Africa, or Oxfam marketing services. Alternatively, some have worked with producer groups to create countervailing bargaining power in the face of market asymmetries.[31]

Finally, the explicit search for policy leverage sometimes proves difficult for agencies unused to intervening at decisionmaking levels. CARE's work in Thailand identified clear trade policy issues—the on-again, off-again imposition of silk yarn import quotas that triggered wildly gyrating prices for white hybrid silk cocoons, making Channel 3 yarn production an unusually volatile and risky proposition for home producers. In spite of these important policy constraints, CARE staff note that policy intervention may prove difficult to effect in practice: "CARE's direct counterpart was the Provincial Governor's office and not the Ministry of Agriculture where these policies were debated and set. Also, silk is a multimillion dollar industry with powerful interests represented by powerful Thai companies. It was hard to see how CARE could parley its reputation as a competent field-based organization into a player at the policy level" (Bear 1993, 8). Indeed, influencing policy is often easier said than done (Salorio 1992). Even so, many agencies have successfully intervened in policy debates—the Self-Employed Women's Association in its work with Indian dairy cooperatives, Technoserve over the course of its long involvement with palm oil in Ghana, the Central Java Enteprise Development Project during its work with rattan makers in rural Indonesia, and the Bangladesh Rural Advancement Committee as a result of its involvement with sericulture producers in Bangladesh. Those who have succeeded contend that the leverage that emerges from policy influence proves well worth the effort.[32] Moreover, they point out that established expertise in a given subsector sometimes brings with it invitations to the policy table, where opportunities arise to influence policy in ways that benefit rural firms.

31. Malhotra and Santer (1994), Carr (1996a), Millard (1996), Magistro et al. (2004).
32. Boomgard (1988), Bowman and Reilling (1990), Chen (1996), Sattar (1996).

The Bottom Line

In practice, subsectors and related analytical frameworks have proven valuable to a broad array of firms, industry associations, government agencies, NGOs, and donors interested in developing programs of support for the RNFE. Growing interest in subsectors, supply chains, value chains, clusters, *filières,* and other closely related vertical system perspectives suggests a growing appeal among practitioners. By focusing on opportunities for cost-effective, systemic interventions that will trigger aggregate rural nonfarm growth, these perspectives provide a tractable entry point into the RNFE as well as a framework for building flexible coalitions of interested parties in what will likely remain an institutionally fractured promotional and regulatory environment.

PART IV

Synthesis

16 Research Perspectives and Prospectives on the Rural Nonfarm Economy

STEVEN HAGGBLADE, PETER B. R. HAZELL, AND THOMAS REARDON

In an effort to sum up, this chapter highlights the key themes emerging from the core chapters of this book. While Chapter 17 focuses on policy implications, this chapter summarizes the principal empirical and analytical findings of the past four decades of experience investigating the rural nonfarm economy (RNFE). Following a summary of past research findings, the chapter concludes by highlighting key gaps in our understanding as well as priority issues that merit further exploration.

Myths about the RNFE

The wide diversity of rural settings in the developing world, coupled with extreme heterogeneity within the RNFE, fosters confusion and conflicting perceptions of the RNFE. In the presence of substantial diversity, a welter of myths and half-truths abounds (Table 16.1). For simplicity, the following review examines nine common misconceptions about the RNFE.

Myth 1: The RNFE Is Small and Unimportant

The old view of rural economies as purely agricultural has given way to a growing recognition of the importance of nonfarm earnings in rural livelihoods. The standard two-sector models of the 1950s and 1960s instilled in the minds of policymakers the notion that rural economies were synonymous with agriculture. In the decades following the "discovery" of the RNFE in the mid-1970s, this oversimplification has gradually eroded away. Growing cohorts of investigators, armed with detailed household surveys and increasingly powerful microcomputers, have rendered rich and highly disaggregated portraits of rural economies across the developing world. Chapter 2 traced the evolution of these efforts in some detail, while subsequent chapters have described how the structure and composition of rural nonfarm activity varies across settings. Evidence from the 1990s and 2000s, presented in Chapter 6 and summarized in Chapter 1, suggests that nonfarm income accounts for 35 to 50 percent of rural household incomes across the developing world. Chapter 3 has described the functional

TABLE 16.1 Common myths about the rural nonfarm economy

Myth	Reality
1. The RNFE is small and unimportant economically.	Rural nonfarm income accounts for 35 to 50 percent of rural incomes.
2. Manufacturing dominates the rural nonfarm economy.	Rural services and commerce typically generate more employment and income than rural manufacturing. They consistently grow faster than manufacturing as well. Highly labor-intensive household manufacturing proves the most vulnerable segment of the RNFE.
3. Migrant remittances account for most rural nonfarm income.	Migration income typically accounts for less than 10 to 15 percent of total rural income, even in labor-exporting zones such as Northern Mexico and the West African Sahel. Local nonfarm earnings normally exceed remittances by a factor of 2 to 5.
4. Micro- and small enterprises dominate the rural nonfarm economy.	It is true that most RNF enterprises employ fewer than five workers. Yet larger firms often account for the majority of output and incomes. In many supply chains, large firms dominate growth prospects and key marketing functions.
5. The rural poor benefit most from the RNFE.	The equity impact of rural nonfarm activity is mixed.
6. Stagnant and tradition-bound, the RNFE changes little over time.	On the contrary, rapid change pervades many segments of the RNFE. Liberalization of the 1980s and 1990s has opened up the RNFE to both competition and opportunities as never before.
7. Poverty-oriented agencies should focus on the RNFE rather than on agriculture.	In sluggish rural regions, the key to improving welfare will be to find tradable engines of rural growth. Many times these will be in agriculture. In rapidly growing regions, many opportunities will open up in the RNFE, and agencies may help poor households take advantage of these opportunities.
8. Microcredit offers the most effective tool for promoting rural nonfarm activity.	In stagnant rural markets, injections of microcredit may merely redistribute poverty as new entrants divide a fixed-size pie into ever smaller increments. However, where new markets and more productive technologies open significant prospects for rural business growth, credit, rural roads, education, and improved communications infrastructure together enable business responses to these new opportunities.
9. Poverty-oriented agencies must work only with small and microenterprises in order to help the very poor.	Large firms frequently shape opportunities for smaller RNFEs by marketing output and supplying inputs or new technology to small firms. Because of these economic linkages, working with large firms may be key to unleashing growth opportunities for large groups of small firms.

composition of rural nonfarm earnings as well as their importance to both rich and poor households. Reviewing a wealth of household survey data, Chapter 6 has outlined a series of common household diversification strategies along with the importance of nonfarm earnings for even primarily agricultural households.

Routinely surprising policymakers, the current scale of the RNFE results from the cumulation of earnings in many diverse nonfarm activities. The spectrum of nonfarm pursuits ranges from homebound, female-dominated cottage industries to itinerant trading enterprises, agroprocessing establishments of various sizes, food kiosks, transport businesses, and rural manufacturing enterprises both large and small.

Because of their scale, nonfarm earnings can contribute significantly to aggregate economic growth. China's rapid economic transformation over the past several decades has demonstrated this most clearly. The highly dynamic RNFE has played a key role in China's structural transformation as well as in driving high overall rates of economic growth (see Chapter 13).

Myth 2: Manufacturing Dominates the RNFE

Despite widespread preoccupation with rural industries among both policymakers and researchers, the tertiary sector accounts for the bulk of rural nonfarm activity. Evidence from a wide range of settings suggests that commercial, trading, and service activities account for 50 to 75 percent of rural nonfarm employment in most rural regions (see Chapter 1).

Tertiary segments of the RNFE typically grow fastest as well. As consumers' incomes grow, their spending on processed foods, transport, health, education, housing, and other personal services rises rapidly (Chapter 4). While rural cottage industries and small manufacturing enterprises face stiff competition from urban manufactures, rural service providers remain more insulated from outside competition. As a result, in a majority of instances where time-series evidence is available, the service sector emerges as the most buoyant segment of the RNFE (Chapters 4 and 7). Evidence from the developing world's two largest economies, China and India, clearly illustrates the common disconnect between governments' policy preoccupation with rural manufacturing and the rapid growth of tertiary activity. In India rural commerce and services accounted for over 90 percent of rural nonfarm income and employment gains during the 1980s and 1990s, the latest decades for which full data are available. Similarly, in China commercial and service town and village enterprises (TVEs) generated employment gains double those in manufacturing through the late 1990s (see Chapter 13). Recent data from rural Bangladesh illustrate this common trend as well as the decline in household manufacturing that in part drives the slower growth in manufacturing (Table 16.2).

Over time, households' demand for personal and household services is supplemented by enterprises' demand for business services such as banking, finance, accounting, insurance, marketing, and communications. In rich countries these

TABLE 16.2 Dynamics of rural nonfarm employment in
Bangladesh, 1990–2003

| Sector | Rural nonfarm employment growth[a] by enterprise type | | |
	Permanent	Household	Total
Manufacturing	10.4	–0.9	0.6
Services	3.4	5.0	4.5
Total	4.5	2.9	3.3

SOURCE: World Bank (2004).

[a]Average annual growth rate from 1990 to 2003.

business services may account for as much as 25 to 35 percent of gross domestic product, further accelerating growth in tertiary sectors (Bear, Gibson, and Hitchins 2003). As Chapter 8 has emphasized, many of these business and personal services emerge in rural towns.

Myth 3: Migrant Remittances Account for a Majority of Nonfarm Rural Income

Migration is an important strategy for some households, particularly in resource-poor regions. In arid, sparsely populated zones such as Botswana, Namibia, and the former South African homelands, remittances from mine labor migration account for roughly half of rural incomes (Chapter 6).

Elsewhere, though, remittance earnings typically account for less than 10 to 15 percent of total rural incomes, even in labor-exporting regions such as Northern Mexico and the West African Sahel. Overall, the rural household income studies summarized in Chapter 6 suggest that local nonfarm earnings normally exceed remittances by a factor of 2 to 10.

Myth 4: Small and Microenterprises Dominate the Rural Nonfarm Economy

A majority of RNF enterprises employ fewer than five workers. Because of this, on equity grounds both policymakers and researchers have often focused on small rural nonfarm enterprises. Yet larger firms often account for the majority of output and incomes (Chapter 1).

Likewise, large firms—as input suppliers or wholesalers of final products —often govern prospects for growth in key supply channels where small firms participate. Chapter 15 has provided several examples of these vertical supply chain linkages. In many developing countries, large supermarkets and agricultural exporters drive growing concentration in rural supply chains and upstream processing (Chapter 9). In East Asia urban-based exporters increasingly subcontract production to lower-cost labor in rural areas, providing a key source of growth in rural nonfarm incomes (Chapter 10). Large firms supply key technologies to small rural enterprises engaged in milling, baking, transport, and communications (Chapter 14). As these examples suggest, large firms often govern change and opportunities facing their smaller rural counterparts.

Even among the smaller firms, considerable heterogeneity prevails. In the six countries described in Chapter 5, just 1 percent of firms accounted for 20 percent of employment growth. Lending programs similarly find that credit targeted at the upper end of the small enterprise spectrum yields a greater impact than that lending focused on the bottom end of the distribution (Chapter 12). Typically a handful of larger, more dynamic firms account for a disproportionate share of rural nonfarm growth.

Myth 5: The Rural Poor Benefit Most from Rural Nonfarm Activities

The equity impact of rural nonfarm activity is mixed. In some instances it contributes a greater income share to the poor than to the rich. But in other settings the rich earn a larger share of their income from nonfarm sources. Overall, no clear pattern emerges (see Chapter 3).

Some categories of nonfarm activity, however, consistently benefit the poor. Because of low barriers to entry and low skill requirements, nonfarm wage labor and labor-intensive cottage industries consistently target the rural poor. More educated and richer households dominate in management positions, in salaried administrative posts, and as owners and managers of capital-intensive mechanical processing, transport, and commercial enterprises as well as other high-return segments of the RNFE. The rural poor, on the other hand, typically remain confined to the low-productivity segments of the RNFE.

Myth 6: Stagnant and Tradition Bound, the RNFE Changes Little over Time

At the enterprise level, heavy turnover permeates the RNFE. According to evidence reported in Chapter 5, roughly 20 percent of nonfarm enterprises are newly created each year. Yet within three years up to 50 percent of all firms will die out.

At an aggregate level, too, rapid change pervades many segments of the RNFE. Improvements in rural infrastructure and communications open up the RNFE to new competition from urban manufactures. As a result, many categories of cottage industry face extinction as economic development proceeds (see Chapters 2, 4, and 8). These same forces open up new opportunities for accessing external markets. Indeed many examples of export-led rural nonfarm growth have emerged, from the TVEs of China to the urban-to-rural subcontracting systems in crowded parts of East Asia (see Chapters 10, 13, and 15).

Liberalization of trade and foreign exchange regulations in the early 1990s has opened up the rural economy to the forces of globalization. Consequently, agribusiness in particular has witnessed substantial concentration over the past decade and a half, leading to rapid consolidation in rural agroprocessing and related supply chains. Chapter 9 has described how this growing concentration in retailing and export led to subsequent consolidation among rural trading and wholesale markets, rural dairies, and retailers in secondary cities and rural towns.

Agricultural growth has similarly triggered rapid growth in pump manufacturing, fertilizer supply, farm equipment repair, and consumer goods and services, from the Indian subcontinent to Uganda to the plains of Central Chile (Chapter 7). New technology has revolutionized rural nonfarm businesses ranging from tailoring to grain milling to riverboat transport (Chapter 14). Change can occur rapidly in the RNFE, particularly in an era of increasing globalization and rapidly diminishing communication costs.

Myth 7: Poverty-Oriented Agencies Should Focus on the RNFE Rather than on Agriculture

The wisdom of this approach depends on the economic context. In sluggish rural regions, the key to improving welfare will be to find tradable engines of rural growth (see Chapter 4). These are necessary to generate overall income growth as well as rising labor productivity and wage rates.

Many times these engines will be found in agriculture, which will therefore need to remain the focus of poverty-reducing growth strategies. China and India, for example, have achieved rapid poverty reduction in recent decades following rapid productivity-led growth in agriculture (Ravallion and Datt 1996; Fan, Zhang, and Zhang 2004; Ravallion and Chen 2004; Chapter 13). A review of the evidence presented in Chapter 7 suggests that agricultural growth linkages generate between 30 and 80 cents in rural nonfarm income for each dollar of gain in direct farm earnings. Nonagricultural engines of growth also generate multipliers, but these are often smaller than those generated by agricultural growth (see Chapter 7).

Rapidly growing rural regions will typically generate growing market opportunities in the RNFE. In these instances, agencies may wish to consider helping poor households access the growing market channels. Thus the appropriate promotional strategy will depend on the dynamics under way in a particular regional setting.

Myth 8: Microcredit Offers the Most Effective Tool for Promoting Rural Nonfarm Activity

On the contrary, in stagnant rural markets injections of microcredit may merely redistribute poverty as new entrants displace existing suppliers. Studies of enterprise dynamics suggest that expanding markets constitute a prerequisite for stimulating aggregate RNFE growth (Chapter 5). In buoyant rural economies, however, where ongoing income growth drives demand for nonfarm goods and services, injections of credit can play a valuable role in enabling the poor to participate in these growing market niches (Chapters 11 and 12).

Like roads, telephones, and schools, rural credit provides an important lubricant enabling rural businesses to respond to existing economic opportunities. But evidence to date suggests that credit alone will be insufficient to drive broad-based poverty reduction. Quantum improvements in rural welfare will require new engines of economic growth, new technologies, and new ways of doing business. Although smoothly functioning financial markets play a key role in enabling these transitions, available evidence suggests that other forces are more likely to drive and accelerate change (Chapter 12).

Myth 9: Poverty-Oriented Agencies Must Work Only with Small and Microenterprises in Order to Help the Very Poor

Large firms frequently shape opportunities for smaller rural nonfarm enterprises. In some cases they support growth of small firms by marketing output or by supplying inputs or new technology to small firms. Large supermarkets may market cheese from small rural cooperatives (Chapter 9). Urban exporters supply fabric and fittings to rural garment producers in East Asia (Chapter 10). Large urban kilns supply ceramic liners for rural stoves in a number of African countries (Chapter 14).

In other instances, large firms compete directly with small rural nonfarm enterprises. Large dairies supplanted smaller rivals in Argentina, Chile, and Brazil during the 1990s. Large retailers drive many smaller rivals into bankruptcy (Chapter 9). In Thailand, automated yarn manufacturers compete with smaller village reelers (Chapter 15).

Because of these interdependencies, working with large firms may be key to identifying and unleashing growth opportunities for related clusters of small firms. For this reason, a growing array of rural development and business specialists has begun working in supply chains with key players up- and downstream from their rural nonfarm target groups. Chapters 9, 14, and 15 provide examples of these indirect intervention strategies.

Dynamics

Alternate Trajectories

Changes in the RNFE unfold across a wide variety of natural, policy, and institutional settings, as Parts II and III of this book have emphasized. Although growth trajectories differ as a result, several common patterns emerge. Returning to the typology introduced in Chapter 4, Table 16.3 helps to summarize the empirical evidence accumulated in subsequent chapters of the book.

Sources of growth clearly differ across settings. In sluggish or deteriorating regions, such as prewar Darfur, a lack of local opportunity pushes large numbers of unemployed into low-return self-employment or emigration (Chapter 6). In these settings, new one-person enterprise start-ups account for the bulk of rural nonfarm employment growth (Chapter 5).

Yet in dynamic rural regions, such as agriculturally prosperous Central Chile and green revolution Asia, rising agricultural productivity, wage rates,

TABLE 16.3 Patterns of rural nonfarm growth

	Regional economic base		
	Sluggish or deteriorating		Dynamic
	1. Resource-poor (low-potential, ecologically fragile, drought-prone)	2. Unexploited potential	3. High-potential, fast-growing
Sources of rural nonfarm growth	Push into low-return rural nonfarm activities (such as household manufacturing) New enterprise start-ups account for most growth in rural nonfarm employment		Pull into higher-return rural nonfarm activities (permanent wage employment, capital-intensive transport and other services, factory manufacturing) Expansion of existing enterprises accounts for a larger share of growth in rural nonfarm employment
Household opportunities in the RNFE			
Asset-poor households	Labor outmigration Unskilled wage labor Labor-intensive exports Household manufacturing		Local wage labor Labor-intensive services, commerce, or manufacturing for local markets
Asset-rich households	Skilled wage employment (government or private sector) Transport or commercial enterprises		Skilled wage employment (government or private sector) Skill- or capital-intensive rural nonfarm enterprises
Spatial patterns of rural nonfarm growth			
Inequitable distribution of assets and infrastructure	Survival activities in rural areas Migration to large urban centers		Rural areas and large urban centers attract most nonfarm growth
Equitable distribution of assets and infrastructure	Rural areas remain anemic		Rural towns grow rapidly

and consumer and business demand all pull labor into increasingly high-return nonfarm wage labor (Chapter 7). In these settings, growth of existing nonfarm firms becomes more important than new enterprise start-ups (Chapter 5). Primary motors of dynamism in these settings include new technology both on and off the farm (Chapters 7 and 14), access to new markets, external pressures and opportunities (Chapters 8 and 9), and an array of public investments and policy incentives (Chapters 11–13).

Household opportunities and responses likewise differ across these very different environments. Labor migration is more common in resource-poor zones, while local wage labor becomes more important in prosperous zones, as the many examples in Chapter 6 attest. Asset-poor households are most likely to engage in unskilled wage labor and household manufacturing, while wealthier households find skilled employment or establish more capital-intensive, higher-return transport, mechanical milling, or service enterprises.

Spatial patterns of rural nonfarm growth vary as well. In well-integrated, rapidly growing rural regions, growing rural towns become the locus for rural nonfarm services and trade (Chapter 8). This proves particularly true in regions with equitable distribution of land and economic resources. In sluggish and inequitable rural zones, such as much of rural Latin America, survival activities in rural areas coexist with a set of highly extroverted rural exchanges with large urban centers (see Chapter 7).

Outcomes likewise differ as a result of widely varying initial distribution of assets and political power. Social customs and mobility alter the opportunities open to key population groups (Chapter 3). The policy and institutional environment, state of rural infrastructure, and fluidity of rural financial markets all condition growth opportunities (Chapter 11). The influence of changing policy regimes is demonstrated most clearly in Chapter 13 in the detailed discussion of evolving rural nonfarm policies in India and China.

Stages of Rural Nonfarm Growth

In spite of widespread variations in resource endowments, policy environments, and rural nonfarm growth paths, evidence presented in previous sections of this book suggests that the RNFE passes through several distinct stages of development. Although various observers define these stages differently,[1] Chapter 10 has laid out what we believe are the two key distinctions. At an early stage in rural development, when communication and transport costs are high, outside influences are weak. During this period the RNFE is protected from urban competition and growth is driven primarily by economic forces internal to the rural sector. Among these, agriculture is typically most important.

---

1. See Saith (1992, 2001), Ranis and Stewart (1993), Start (2001), and Chapter 10 for good discussions of alternate categorizations of the various stages of rural nonfarm development.

TABLE 16.4 Stages of rural nonfarm growth

Stages of rural nonfarm growth	Rural-to-urban transport costs	Productivity	
		Agriculture	Surviving RNF activity
1. Rural-led RNF growth			
a. Low productivity	High	Low	Low (Z-goods)
b. Higher productivity	Moderate	Moderate	Moderate (modern Z-goods and services)
2. Urban- and export-led RNF growth	Low	High	High (modern Z-goods and services)

Later, as rural infrastructure improves, rural economies are opened up to outside influences. Urban manufactures penetrate the rural economy, as do modern inputs, technologies, and marketing methods. During this phase the RNFE faces increased competition and pressure to change. The key to survival in this stage lies in a firm's ability to access new markets and to adopt new technologies and new organizational arrangements. Urban-led subcontracting and export markets become increasingly important as sources of demand-led growth for rural nonfarm goods and services (Table 16.4).

Stage 1: Internal Engines of Rural Nonfarm Growth

Given agriculture's predominance in rural incomes and employment, it typically dominates incentives and opportunities for the RNFE in the early stages of economic growth, as Chapters 4 and 7 have emphasized. Most rural nonfarm goods and services are regional nontradables that are consumed within their producing regions. Thus their demand is constrained by local income, which increases with the production of tradables. These tradables, in turn, face elastic market demands outside the region or country. Therefore, technological change or some other source of growth translates directly into growing regional incomes. Agriculture has traditionally been the major source of tradable output for most rural regions. Hence agricultural growth has often proven to be an important requirement for RNFE growth.

Where agricultural productivity remains low (due to extensive cultivation, low use of modern inputs, and an absence of research and development systems that generate sustained genetic improvements), farm labor productivity and rural wage rates remain low, as do rural incomes (Table 16.4, Stage 1a). In the RNFE, market growth remains sluggish and technology and wage rates

↑ ng productivity can lead to a more "bouyant" RNFE.

remain low. Population growth and declining per capita incomes push labor into migration or self-employment in increasingly low-return rural nonfarm activities.

Improvements in agricultural productivity resulting from the availability of new technology, new inputs, or new high-value crops and livestock can alter these dynamics considerably (Table 16.4, Stage 1b). Higher on-farm labor productivity leads to rising farm incomes and wage rates. Growing demand for agricultural inputs and processing services and for household consumption goods and services entices nonfarm entrepreneurs and laborers into increasingly lucrative rural nonfarm activities. Where improved agricultural technology drives up labor productivity and demand, rural wage rates rise, inducing diversification into increasingly high-return rural nonfarm activities. Typically these rural-led growth dynamics rely on access to improved inputs (fertilizer, seed, chemicals, and mechanical pumps) produced in urban areas. Thus increased communication and diminishing transport costs to urban areas are often necessary enablers of these productivity gains in both agriculture and nonfarm activities.

In the early years of the twenty-first century, rural Africa as well as the more isolated rural regions of South Asia remain primarily at Stage 1. Elsewhere the East Asian tigers and coastal regions of China have moved into Phase 2, where urban- and export-led rural manufacturing growth probably predominates (see Chapters 10 and 13). In South Asia, extremely high population densities and rising incomes have made possible the beginnings of a shift to urban-led rural industrial growth in small zones clustered around major metropolitan centers and transport arteries. In highly urbanized and economically stratified Latin America, highly extroverted rural interactions with large cities leave much of this region open to urban and external influences.

Stage 2: Urban and Export-Led Rural Nonfarm Growth

As structural transformation proceeds and agriculture's share in rural employment and income declines, external forces from urban areas and even from abroad increase in importance. Improved roads and communications lower the transport costs of moving people and goods to and from urban areas. This opening up of rural areas brings both opportunities and challenges.

URBAN INFLUENCES. As a result of lower-cost access to urban areas, many rural regions enjoy greater opportunities today in locating additional drivers of local economic growth. The relevant "motor" no longer needs to be local. As long as the local economy is open, workers can commute and local firms can sell to areas where the economic base is growing rapidly. A mine or a big city in a coastal region, for example, may induce nonfarm employment growth in the nearby hinterlands. Of course the types of nonfarm labor and products demanded and the capital-labor ratio of the technology used in the economic base activities will condition the amount of nonfarm employment creation that is induced in the nearby hinterlands. A fancy tourist hotel may demand less local nonfarm labor per unit of output than does a roadside truck stop.

However, as urban and international incentives increasingly dominate the RNFE, change becomes more rapid, pressures become more acute, and many uncompetitive rural nonfarm firms succumb to external competition. Along with the demise of the so-called traditional Z-goods comes pressures to modernize and to adopt new technologies and new forms of organization. Nimble firms supplying modern Z-goods survive and thrive, although some may require help in making the transition to growing supply channels. The composition of rural nonfarm activity changes significantly during Stage 2, as low-productivity household manufacturing declines (Table 16.2) and higher-productivity, higher-capital mechanical milling, transport, health, education, and personal services grow. In Stage 2, surviving rural nonfarm activities must change and adapt to new opportunities and a new competitive environment. Much of their success depends on the speed of the transition, which is in turn affected by the forces of economic concentration and globalization.

GLOBALIZATION.   Since the 1990s, widespread liberalization of international trade and foreign investment has led to rapid globalization and consequently to concentration of market power, particularly in agribusiness supply chains (Chapter 9). Increasing firm sizes and the emergence of specialized wholesalers, large-volume contracts, and private standards tend to require new forms of organization and technology if rural enterprises are to meet growing quantity and quality requirements. This opening of the RNFE to outside forces exposes nonfarm businesses to new opportunities as well as to new competitive pressures, triggering accelerating growth as well as rapid transitions in specific supply channels.

The forces of trade and globalization often bring new competition to local markets—sometimes with breathtaking speed. Some categories of rural nonfarm activity have thrived in the past because of protection from outside competition by high transport costs, restrictive production (as in the case of reserved handicraft industries in India) and trade policies (for example, barriers to cheap imported consumer goods), subsidized inputs and credit, and preferential access to key markets (as was the case with many TVEs in China). Globalization and market liberalization remove many of these barriers, effectively "deprotecting" the RNFE. The transition may prove brutally abrupt for many traditional small-scale manufacturers whose products cannot compete with higher-quality, mass-produced goods. For this reason, the initial stages of deprotection can lead to massive job losses in the RNFE, even though many of these may later be recovered as new types of RNFE activity sprout up, as in India during the 1990s. Because poor households and women congregate disproportionately in the traditional low-investment, low-productivity rural nonfarm activities, they tend to suffer most during this transition.

These dynamics lead to a series of policy questions that are discussed further in Chapter 17.

Future Research Priorities

Over the past 40 years, four broad waves of investigation have illuminated wide swaths of the RNFE (Chapter 2). Yet the global economy has evolved rapidly during the past decade, as have the research technologies available to rural investigators. As these changes emerge, they raise new issues as well as new possibilities for exploration. While far from exhaustive, the following short list highlights a series of topics that appear particularly promising for investigation in the early decades of the twenty-first century.

Spatial Dimensions of the RNFE

New geographical information system (GIS) tools and satellite positioning systems have radically transformed opportunities for understanding the spatial dispersion of rural nonfarm activity. Beginning with simple mapping of population settlements, agricultural activities, nonfarm enterprises (by activity and firm size), and infrastructure, these baseline profiles open up rich possibilities for empirically exploring and refining the largely untested spatial hypotheses emerging from Chapter 8.

At a microeconomic level, spatial price and wage gradients will enable a more robust empirical investigation of the phenomena of labor migration and the geographic clustering of rural nonfarm activities. At a more aggregate subsectoral level, the new GIS tools permit examination of questions about the spatial dimension of prices and product flows, the effects of infrastructure placement, threshold effects, and spatial dynamics. Analysis of the trends and forces affecting rural-urban integration merits particular attention in these efforts.

Dynamic Trajectories

Time-series assessments of rural nonfarm development remain few in number. Yet with growing awareness of the importance of rural nonfarm activity, long-term data sets, including household and firm panels, are becoming increasingly available. These permit exploration of a series of unresolved dynamic questions. At a micro level, nonfarm enterprise and household resource allocation strategies promise a richer understanding of accumulation patterns, pathways out of poverty, and the role assets, nonfarm opportunities, and public policies play in successful—and unsuccessful—efforts at poverty reduction.

At a meso level, time-series portraits of specific subsectors and supply chains promise insights into the dynamic consequences of globalization, market integration, and concentration at various levels along the supply chain. These effects may well differ when international firms penetrate rural areas at Stage 1 (thus precipitously advancing them into Stage 2) as opposed to rural areas that have already advanced into Stage 2 of their transformation. In all settings, growing penetration by supermarkets and large-scale retailers supplying nonfarm goods and services merits increased attention in order to track potential effects on the RNFE as well as prospects for alternate interventions, including collective action, public infrastructure provision, and policies.

At a regional level, the dynamics of slow-growing regions remain largely uncharted. Paired comparisons of slow- and fast-growing regions, and of poor and non-poor households within each, offer prospects for revealing how aggregate trends in farm and nonfarm productivity, changing labor allocation and income composition, and the fluidity of rural-urban interactions drive dynamic transformations in a variety of rural settings.

Institutional Innovations

The RNFE remains an institutional orphan, as Chapter 11 has emphasized. In the public arena, responsibility for the RNFE cuts across line ministries, special agencies, and different levels of national, provincial, and local governments. One series of government-led efforts has focused on local governments as leaders of rural development. These initiatives fly under a variety of flags: local economic development, community-based development, and territorial development. Meanwhile, institutional innovations spearheaded by national governments, which proved popular during the 1970s, have atrophied in recent decades.

Outside of government, the private sector plays an increasingly prominent role in establishing market standards, contracting procedures, and marketing institutions. Recent efforts at "regoverning markets" aim to explore how equity-oriented groups can contribute to private sector–led growth and equity-enhancing supply chain development.

Further institutional experimentation, in both the private and the public arenas, could pay big dividends in helping to channel future promotional efforts more constructively. To be effective, this experimentation will require careful documentation of alternative models and their efficacy in accelerating rural nonfarm contributions to national economic growth and poverty reduction.

Labor Markets

Poor households' income and welfare depend primarily on the productivity of the one asset they possess in abundance—their largely unskilled labor. Thus fluid labor markets, human capital accumulation, and rising labor productivity and wages remain key ingredients of large-scale poverty reduction. The migration literature has made important contributions to our understanding of rural-urban labor flows. But few researchers have focused on the rural side of nonfarm and farm labor markets. Yet for rural households, most wage employment remains rural, in seasonal farm work or in local rural nonfarm businesses. Thus a more complete picture of the opportunities and constraints facing labor-selling households will require an expanded understanding of rural labor markets and how they interact spatially with regional and urban migration opportunities.

Private Services

Private commerce and services dominate the RNFE. Yet rural industries have received the lion's share of public policy and research resources. To rectify this disparity, researchers need to examine more systematically the structure and dynamics of key privately delivered rural services. Transport and commerce are typically integrated into supply chain studies of the type described in Chapter 15. Yet more sedentary services such as private schools, health clinics, communications, finance, construction, and personal services remain underexplored. Because rural consumers and businesses willingly spend growing income increments on these services, they continue to grow more rapidly than other segments of the RNFE. Given government budgetary pressure and the resulting shrinkage of public service delivery, these private enterprises not only play an important income-generating role in the RNFE; they also fill an important gap in the delivery of key social services. For these reasons, the tertiary segment of the RNFE merits more attention than it has received in the past.

Conclusions

Policymakers increasingly recognize the importance of the RNFE—to economic growth, as a counterweight to urban overcrowding, and potentially to poverty reduction. As in the past, the research community can contribute to improved public policy by focusing renewed attention on the RNFE. New analytical tools, the emergence of new issues, and elevated policy interest in the RNFE provide critical underpinnings for a fruitful new wave of exploration.

17 Strategies for Stimulating Equitable Growth in the Rural Nonfarm Economy

STEVEN HAGGBLADE, PETER B. R. HAZELL,
AND THOMAS REARDON

The rural nonfarm economy (RNFE) has grown too large to ignore. It provides 35 to 50 percent of rural incomes across the developing world. This diverse collection of household-based and large-scale agroprocessing, service, manufacturing, commercial, and seasonal trading activities plays a crucial role in sustaining rural populations, in servicing a growing and modern agriculture, and in supplying local consumer goods and services. In areas where landlessness prevails, rural nonfarm activity offers important economic alternatives for the rural poor.

Widespread economic liberalization during the 1990s has opened up rural nonfarm economies as never before—to new opportunities and to new threats. As governments have withdrawn from agricultural marketing, processing, and input supply, an array of private traders, processors, exporters, and supermarkets has begun filling this economic space. Foreign direct investment has risen sharply. As a result, rural areas have seen increasing concentration in private sector supply chains, as the many examples in Chapter 9 attest. In some instances, liberalization has benefited large numbers of small rural nonfarm enterprises by expanding their marketing and processing opportunities or by improving their input supply through private sector supply chains. In other cases, rapid exposure to sophisticated external competition has simply steamrollered the poor. Small, although beautiful on equity grounds, does not necessarily prove competitive in modern supply chains, which often require minimum investments and scales of operation to meet quality and delivery requirements. Given the growing scale of rural nonfarm activity, given its importance to the rural poor, and given the startlingly rapid new dynamics under way, policymakers can no longer ignore the RNFE as they have so often in the past.

In this diverse and rapidly changing environment, new institutions have assumed responsibility for support and promotion of the RNFE. Structural adjustment, liberalization, and budget reform programs have significantly reduced the scale of government businesses and business promotion activity. The shrinking government presence in input supply, marketing, credit, and other promotional activities has induced expansion into these arenas by the private sector, civil society, and nongovernmental organizations (NGOs). Even within government, the RNFE remains an institutional orphan, falling into the cracks between central and local governments and cutting across portfolio responsibilities in ministries of agriculture, commerce, industry, transport, communications, education, health, and trade. Given the economic and institutional transitions under way in the RNFE, the key challenge becomes how to expand opportunities for growth while at the same time enabling participation by the rural poor.

This chapter proposes a strategy for confronting these challenges. In doing so, it draws together many threads running through the previous sections of this book. It builds directly on the experience of legions of committed practitioners, described in Part III, who have experimented over many decades with a broad array of support efforts on behalf of the RNFE. In addition to that considerable body of experience, the discussion here draws inspiration from the reviews in Parts I and II of the evolving perceptions, structure, and dynamics under way in the RNFE. Several recurring themes come together here to suggest a possible way forward.

The Current Operational Context

Recurring themes from throughout this book suggest that any systematic strategy for rural nonfarm promotion must successfully grapple with the following key features of the RNFE:

- Diversity within the RNFE and across operating environments
- Spatial relationships between rural nonfarm firms and their final markets
- The small size of many pro-poor rural nonfarm enterprises
- Institutional overlaps and gaps

DIVERSITY. Rural regions differ dramatically in their resource endowments, economic structures, institutional histories, asset distribution, and economic performance. The contrasting experiences of India and China document these differences most clearly (see Chapter 13). Even within a given country—with homogenous macropolicies, demographic profiles, educational systems, and credit policies—situations can differ dramatically from one rural region to another. Northeast Brazil differs substantially from the southeastern part of the country (see Table 1.3). Southern Madagascar differs significantly from both the Central Highlands and the North Coast. Southwest Burkina Faso has a very different resource base and economic profile than does the eastern part of the country. As a result, the structure and composition of rural nonfarm activity routinely vary among rural regions, even within the same country. Differing resource bases and physical locations explain some of the difference. Variable asset distribution, coupled with historical accidents, first mover advantages, and the path dependence of business development, contributes to varying profiles of economic activity and poverty as well as differing distributions of large and small firms.

SPATIAL RELATIONSHIPS.   Intricate, often highly seasonal, networks link together itinerant and small-scale participants in complex and spatially far-flung supply chains with much larger firms that market inputs or outputs on which their economic survival depends. As a result, rural nonfarm supply chains cut across space and frequently across government jurisdictions, from rural authorities to local townships, urban municipalities, and national ministries and agencies, and even across international borders. Firms providing functional connections between agriculture and rural nonfarm enterprises, between small rural nonfarm enterprises and larger-scale input suppliers or marketing firms, provide the connective tissue linking raw materials, processing, trade, and final consumers together. Therefore, policymakers require some means of organizing thinking, operational diagnostics, and action that charts the economic pulsations of the RNFE across these spatial and functional landscapes.

SMALL FIRM SIZE.   The rural poor frequently depend on earnings from self-employment in small-scale, often one-person, rural nonfarm enterprises (see Chapter 5). The small size of many rural nonfarm enterprises, particularly those accessible to the poor, imposes large transaction costs on promotional agencies. Smallness raises individual firm contact costs while at the same time making per-firm benefits small in absolute size. Physical dispersion across rural landscapes, described in Chapter 8, further raises contact costs for would-be interveners and for larger firms that supply inputs or market outputs. In this common setting, aggregation becomes necessary for dealing with legions of small firms cost-effectively, as Chapter 12 has emphasized. At the same time, asymmetries in power and information between large and small firms raise the potential for oligopolistic abuse of market power.

THE FRACTURED INSTITUTIONAL ENVIRONMENT.   In spite of its size and economic importance, the RNFE remains an institutional orphan, unclaimed by any single government authority but influenced by many (see Chapter 11). Local governments regulate certain functions, such as registration, collection of market fees and local taxes, and maintenance of local infrastructure, while provincial and central governments manage trade policy, exchange rates, investment policies, major infrastructural investments, and education policy. Ministries of agriculture, commerce, trade, communications, transport, health, and education all affect different segments of the RNFE, though rarely in any coordinated fashion. In part because of the many gaps and inconsistencies in government coverage, a welter of private nonprofit agencies has emerged to promote business activity in rural areas. Equity-oriented, for the most part, they aim to reduce rural poverty by promoting rural nonfarm activities in which the poor can participate. Since the economic liberalization of the 1990s, large private firms have played an increasingly important role in input supply and output marketing for smaller rural firms. They have likewise assumed many formerly public functions, such as the provision of credit and technical assistance and the establishment of market grades and standards. Sometimes they even maintain assembly market infrastructure and rural roads or set the effective exchange rates at which they supply inputs and purchase outputs. These large modern corporations make strategic investments and operating decisions that increasingly govern opportunities for smaller rural nonfarm enterprises.

A Three-Pronged Strategy for Promoting Equitable Rural Nonfarm Growth

At this juncture, we three authors emerge from behind our cloak of editorial anonymity to propose a strategy for confronting these challenges. We recognize that, as in any such complex undertaking, other students of the RNFE may come away from the same evidence with different priorities and prescriptions. We welcome alternative solutions. We do not pretend to offer the only pathway through such complex and difficult terrain. Nor do we presume to address all facets of rural development writ large. We leave the social, political, and institutional dimensions of rural development largely to others. Instead we focus on developing feasible means of spurring more rapid, equitable growth in the RNFE. Given the common realities of diversity, spatial complexity, small firm sizes, and institutional fragmentation, this is a tall order in itself.

The Case for Intervention

Poverty reduction, which motivates much of the current interest in the RNFE, necessarily invokes an equity objective that efficient private market forces do not on their own address (Chapter 11). At the start of the twenty-first century, roughly 800 million people still go hungry. The majority lives in rural areas of the developing world. So governments and equity-minded groups that consider this an untenable state of affairs must intervene to help chart an economic course that will bring greater prosperity to vulnerable groups and reductions in the number of poor.

Even in purely efficiency-oriented regimes, public goods and collective action will prove necessary to stimulate rural economic growth. Many of the investments required to expand opportunities for rural nonfarm growth—investments in agricultural research, roads, and public health—are public goods that the private sector, left to pursue purely commercial incentives, will not supply in adequate amounts (Chapter 11). Likewise, given the small size of many rural nonfarm enterprises, integration into growing markets will increasingly require aggregation or some sort of collective action (Chapters 9 and 15). So public action will play a key role in stimulating rapid and equitable rural nonfarm growth.

Nonintervention may nonetheless prove the most prudent course of action in some rural nonfarm settings. In settings where the general enabling environment proves inimical to nonfarm business activity, that environment must change before effective promotion can take place. Where war, conflict, or political turmoil prevails, nonfarm businesses and promotional activity will likely prove of limited value. In transition economies where the basic property rights, contracts, legal systems, enforcement mechanisms, and labor laws remain highly fluid works in progress; where recently liberalized financial systems malfunction routinely or for the benefit of a favored few; and where uncertainties over state commitment to current policy regimes make business an intolerably risky proposition, rural nonfarm businesses face crippling policy constraints. Reform of that enabling environment will prove to be a necessary prior condition for efficient widespread rural nonfarm business activity.

Where the basic components of an incentive system favorable to rural business are in place, specific promotional activities can greatly accelerate rural growth as well as the participation of poor households in the RNFE. In such settings, the following three-step process offers practical guidelines for nurturing a dynamic RNFE:

1. Identify engines of regional growth.
2. Conduct supply chain diagnostics to identify strategic interventions.
3. Build flexible institutional coalitions for implementation.

As a point of departure, we assume that potential interveners, public or private, have targeted a specific rural region on the basis of economic, political, or philosophical criteria important to them. How, then, should they proceed to see how they can effectively help to stimulate equitable rural nonfarm growth?

Step 1: Identify Engines of Regional Growth

Rural regions differ substantially from one another in terms of natural resource endowments, economic structure, size, location, history, human capital, and institutional endowments. In the face of these widely diverging opportunities and constraints, effective interventions will necessarily vary across settings. Given our focus on both equity and growth, we find the two-dimensional typology from Chapter 4 useful in categorizing rural regions (see Table 4.5). Using that framework, the state of the region's economic base and the distribution of assets across household groups together govern prospects for growth as well as the potential for participation by the poor.

The economic base of a rural region encompasses those key productive activities that remain competitive in external markets. In most rural settings, agriculture forms the core of the economic base (Chapters 4 and 7). Many rural regions also contain natural resources—minerals, timber, or exotic natural settings—that, though less important in the aggregate, sustain the production of exportable raw materials, processed commodities, and tourism services. Administrative or entrepôt trading centers can also serve as economic bases along transport corridors that transit even remote rural locations. These core economic activities, in turn, generate local demand for schools, health clinics, restaurants, and commercial services in the region. The total economic activity in the region depends on the size of the economic base and the demand it generates for local goods and services. The regional science literature refers to these core activities as a region's "economic base." Economists typically refer to them as "tradables" and to the ancillary activities as "nontradables."

Over time, some nontradables may become competitive in external markets as productivity improves and production or transport costs fall. This happens routinely with livestock products, perishable agricultural products, and even medical and educational services. Increasing nontradable production—for example, in mechanical repair services or local seed supply—can likewise increase productivity in tradable agriculture and thus fuel second rounds of regional economic growth. Though the economic base sustains economic activity in the rural region, triggers of incremental growth can come from either tradables or nontradables, depending on specific circumstances. Strategically, the key is to find out where incremental output will generate the greatest aggregate regional growth. Typically the answer will depend on the existing economic base, untapped resource endowments, and market opportunities facing a particular region.

In resource-poor regions such as the horn of Africa, Northeast Brazil, and the Indian state of Bihar, rural populations struggle to subsist through nomadic herding, seasonal migration, and risky, low-productivity agriculture. In these types of rural regions, with scant potential in agriculture, tourism, or natural resource development, prospects for rural nonfarm activity are bleak. In the absence of standard motors of rural economic growth, efforts will need to focus on establishing markets outside the region. Labor migration, the export of services, offers one standard strategy in these settings. Export of local crafts or artwork may likewise prove feasible provided that marketing links can be established with outside buyers. In some situations, these regions can export low-cost labor without migration through assembly industries or even electronic offshore delivery of labor-intensive services such as drawing and drafting, though these activities require investment in the roads and communication infrastructure necessary to reduce transaction costs. Though daunting, promotional efforts in these regions can succeed by focusing on the development of external markets that match local resources with consumers outside the region (Box 17.1).

A second situation arises in slow-growing rural regions with unexploited potential. This may occur, for example, where fertile soils, a strategic location, or untapped natural resources exist, but exploitation of this economic potential requires some prior investment, technology, or policy reform. This situation prevailed in Bangladesh until about 1985, in Vietnam before the policy reforms

BOX 17.1   Intervening in resource-poor areas

Botswanacraft Exports: A Commercially Sustainable Model

During the 1960s and 1970s, before the discovery and development of large diamond deposits in the Kalahari, rural Botswana was sparsely inhabited and inhospitable. Several hundred thousand Bushmen, Herero, and Tswana cattle herders eked out a spartan existence on the fringes of the parched desert landscape where the gathering of wild desert products accounted for nearly 20 percent of rural incomes (Botswana 1976). From the hardy grasses and reeds that dotted the borders of the Okavango River, Botswana women produced tightly woven, utilitarian baskets with distinctive decorative patterns recorded using vegetable dyes. They limited production, however, to only as many as were required for their own household use.

In an effort to boost rural incomes, the Botswana Development Corporation established an export marketing company, Botswanacraft, to identify export markets for these distinctive, high-quality Tswana baskets. This business opportunity built on the abundant rural grasses and labor and on these preexisting skills and designs. Established in 1970, Botswanacraft has became a commercially viable concern by insisting on top quality and by marketing carefully to high-end markets in the United States and Europe. In 2001, Botswanacraft exported about $200,000 of baskets per year, supplying a significant income boost to its 2,000 rural suppliers (Haggblade, Hazell, and Reardon 2002).

Industrial Estates in Rural Kenya: Unsustainable White Elephants

In 1966, Kenya imported the Indian model of comprehensive enterprise support centered in nursery industrial estates. The second phase of the Rural Industrial Development Programme, in 1974, involved exporting this model from urban to rural areas via mini-industrial estates called Industrial Promotion Areas (IPAs). Established at Machakos, Kakamega, and Embu, the IPAs provided a broad array of subsidized assistance, including below-market rental of workshop facilities on the estate (at about 50 percent of the commercial rates), access to common facility workshops and equipment, bulk raw material purchasing schemes, new product development, and a broad range of technical assistance in managing production, bookkeeping, and marketing as well as access to subsidized loans.

Doubtful even in urban areas, these expensive, well-staffed facilities proved prohibitively expensive in rural zones. On average, each industrial estate staff member served only two enterprises. Though two-thirds attained financial viability in the highly subsidized estates, about one-third failed even in this cushioned artificial environment, and only two enterprises developed to the point of leaving the estates. Clearly not cost effective, the IPA estates provided "too much for too few" according to a major review (Kilby 1982).

of the 1990s, and in Botswana before the opening up of large-scale diamond mines in the 1980s. In these cases, some sort of investment or policy reform proved able to ignite impressive growth—led agriculturally in Bangladesh and Vietnam and via mineral development in Botswana. In these types of regions, where unexploited potential exists in the agricultural or natural resource base, promotion efforts should initially focus on sparking these latent motors to life (Box 17.2). These motors, in turn, will stimulate local demand for nontradable agricultural products, nonfarm goods and services, and rural labor. As in the well-documented cases of green revolution Asia, broad-based agricultural growth can prove a powerful motor of equitable growth and rural poverty reduction (Chapter 7).

In dynamic rural zones, growing agricultural incomes and tourist- or export-based trade fuel demand-led opportunities for growth in the RNFE. Agriculture-led booms in Taiwan during the 1950s and 1960s, in Southern Brazil during the 1970s and 1980s, and in Uganda during the 1990s all triggered significant growth in ancillary rural nonfarm activity. In these settings opportunities abound, particularly in nontraded segments of the nonfarm economy, such as commerce, transport, and services. Here the challenge becomes one of enabling the poor to participate in growing market segments. In some instances, this may require access to improved technology. In other cases, market linkages with large firms, establishment and understanding of grades and standards, or contract enforcement may be necessary. Supply-side promotional efforts on behalf of the RNFE become most effective in these situations (Box 17.3).

This typology, developed in Chapter 4 and amplified here, helps us to categorize situations and identify general strategies for locating promising sources of regional economic growth (Table 17.1). In the first two situations, in which the current economic base is stagnant, efforts must focus on identifying engines of regional economic growth. Opportunities may arise in agriculture, in natural resource-based industries, or even among rural manufacturing exports where transport corridors, rural wage rates, and location permit. In the third situation, where a region's economic base is already growing, efforts at stimulating rural nonfarm activity will focus not on the engine but rather on the caboose, on demand-led rural nonfarm activities likely to prosper given the preferences of increasingly affluent rural consumers and businesses. In each location, local knowledge will be necessary to identify a strategic portfolio of specific promising prospects. Selection criteria clearly depend on the values and priorities of the key instigators. In many actual settings, criteria include aggregate growth potential, prospects for direct participation by the rural poor, and the potential for raising unskilled labor demand and wage rates throughout the region.

Step 2: Conduct Supply Chain Diagnostics to Identify Strategic Interventions

To identify cost-effective means of unleashing this potential, prospective interveners will need to conduct diagnostic assessments of the current structure,

BOX 17.2   Activating unexploited rural potential

Rural Tourism in Chile

Through its Rural Tourism Program, the Chilean INDAP (Rural Development Institute) has promoted rural tourism for the past decade throughout most of the rural zones of Chile, including in hinterland areas. The program supports collective activities (such as a cooperative that runs a commercial campground), individual household activities undertaken in cooperatives (such as wine region tours with various participating households and small wineries), and, to a lesser degree, individual enterprises. The program trains participants, finances investments in equipment and buildings and other infrastructure, and advertises the tourism activities at national fairs and conventions. Many of the activities revolve around agrotourism in small farmer and ethnic areas such as the island of Chiloe and around eco- and wilderness area tourism. The program seeks to spur the development of areas with unexploited potential in terms of cultural or natural riches. The program also helps poor entrepreneurs in areas near developed tourist zones to tap into the tourism demand, attracting tourists who go to beaches or cultural sites in an effort to go to the "back country" and enjoy local traditional products and settings (Faiguenbaum 2001).

Resuscitating Agriculture in Hertzog, South Africa

In spite of rich agricultural potential, inhabitants along this stretch of the Kat River remained mired in poverty for over two decades. In the late 1970s, the government of South Africa expropriated white landholders in the region in order to constitute the "independent" homeland of Ciskei. The displaced white farmers abandoned their land and their irrigation infrastructure and left the region. The black former farm laborers remained behind but without clear title to the land. In spite of an 85 percent unemployment rate, the farmland remained fallow for 25 years, from 1979 to 1994, because the black farmers lacked tenure security.

With the advent of majority rule in South Africa, the ineffectual Ciskei regime disintegrated. Spurred by this opportunity, residents of the valley joined together to form the Hertzog agricultural cooperative. The key barrier to regional growth that they saw was their lack of secure legal access to the land. In response to their lobbying efforts, the new government proved far more obliging than the old regime, allowing people of the region to farm the land as individual units pending a final decision on access to state land. The cooperative accordingly allocated individual 1 hectare plots to members and pooled members' resources to operate an irrigation system. With secure access to the land they farmed, the members of the cooperative subsequently negotiated a commercial bank loan enabling them to bring still more land into irrigated cultivation. Income as much as tripled for many families as they grew staple foods for their own consumption as well as produce for sale to itinerant traders from major provincial centers. The key to regional development in this high-potential setting lay in revving up agriculture as the motor of regional growth (Nel 1996).

BOX 17.3   Intervention in dynamic rural zones

Chile's Dynamic Agriculture Zone

Rapid agricultural growth in Central Chile, particularly export-oriented horticulture, launched an agricultural boom in the 1980s and the early 1990s. A prosperous agriculture, in turn, stimulated a welter of opportunities in agroprocessing and trade as well as a marked increase in local consumer services (Berdegué et al. 2001). While the poor have benefited to some extent from this buoyant RNFE, a noticeable bimodality remains, with the poor relegated to poorly remunerated jobs that require little education or capital.

Thus interventions on behalf of the RNFE in these zones typically do not require jump-starting the RNFE, but rather facilitating the participation of poor households in growing market niches. As medium-sized and large firms increase the scale and sophistication of their operations in order to meet increasingly stringent quality and product safety standards, poor households face considerable challenges in meeting the new skill and educational standards required. Interventions in such regions need to focus on the specific private or collective assets that the poor lack but require for market entry in either wage or self-employment. Examples include the efforts of INDAP aimed at developing small and micro-enterprises for the processing of foods (cheese, yogurt, processed vegetables, and fruit juices) for marketing to the rural town and intermediate city markets, where Bennett's Law predicts that demand is growing for these processed nonstaples. INDAP also runs programs for manufacturers that use wood from local forests to make furniture for the growing markets in the rural towns and intermediate cities in dynamic zones.

Rural Traders: Handmaidens of Agricultural Growth in Uganda

In the early 1990s, a liberalized economy and key sectoral reforms ignited steady growth in Ugandan agriculture. Cotton, nontraditional horticultural crops, and livestock all grew steadily, raising farm income as well as demand for nonfarm goods and services. Pulled along by this growing demand, as many as one-third of rural households launched nonfarm businesses, mostly in trading.

Government investments in primary education, rural banking, and road infrastructure proved key determinants of nonfarm business start-up and performance. Given these basic public investments, nonfarm activity grew spontaneously in response to this prosperous agriculturally led economic advance (Reinikka and Collier 2001).

(*Continued on page 406*)

Timely Credit in Fada N'Gourma, Burkina Faso

In eastern Burkina Faso (then Upper Volta), an NGO lending scheme operated by the Partnership for Productivity (PfP) began operation in several locations throughout the region, beginning in the late 1970s. An evaluation of the impact of this lending revealed very different outcomes in the different rural zones. Shortly after the PfP program began, the Ministry of Roads completed the paving of the main road linking the regional headquarters at Fada N'Gourma with the capital city of Ouagadougou, launching a miniboom in this regional center. Sales, output, and the incomes of borrowers increased rapidly. In a booming economy such as this, credit can indeed lubricate business start-up and expansion and facilitate nonfarm supply response to growing opportunities and demand (Goldmark, Mooney, and Rosengard 1982; Kilby and D'Zmura 1985; Lassen et al. 1985).

---

growth, and constraints in each of the most promising identified subsectors. Because most rural enterprises operate in vertical supply systems, these opportunities and constraints often lie up- or downstream from the target firms. Agricultural marketing, processing, and export systems transit lengthy supply chains that link producers functionally and spatially across the rural landscape with input suppliers, distributors, and final markets. Home-based rural manufacturing, subcontracting, and local retail networks likewise depend on often surprisingly complex vertical supply chains.[1]

Even service activities—such as construction, energy, water, media, financial, health, education, laundry, and maid services—operate in vertical supply chains that, viewed in their entirety, offer valuable clues as to bottlenecks, system dynamics, current constraints, and future opportunities.[2] In service sector supply chains, such as maid or restaurant services, the vertical

---

1. In addition to the five case studies in Chapter 15, see the examples cited in Figures 1.2, 7.1, 9.1, 10.1, 14.1, and 14.2. The discussion in Chapter 2 describes how three of the four major strands of rural nonfarm investigation have gravitated toward the supply chain perspective as a means of improving understanding and operational diagnostics.

2. See Grant et al. (1990, 1991), Whittington et al. (1991), Taillefer et al. (2000), and Andriantsoa et al. (2005) for examples of service sector supply chains.

TABLE 17.1 Strategic priorities for promoting the rural nonfarm economy

	Rural economic base			
	Sluggish		Dynamic	
			3. High-potential, fast-growing	
	1. Resource-poor	2. Unexploited potential	a. Unequal	b. Equal
Does the region possess a dynamic economic base?	No	No	Yes	Yes
Does unexploited potential exist?	No	Yes	No	Yes
Are economic assets distributed equitably across household groups?			No	Yes
Strategic priority	RNF exports: people, goods, or services	Build up the rural economic base: agricultural growth or natural resource–based activity	Equity-enhancing RNF supply chains	Growth-enhancing RNF supply chains

NOTE: A blank cell indicates that data are not applicable.

supply chain perspective, in addition to highlighting alternative market outlets and market dynamics, focuses attention on key labor supply constraints and training institutions. Together, these opportunities and constraints frequently highlight the need for punctual training in specific skills areas—for instance, that provided through the housekeeping courses for maids at the Monterey Institute of Technology in Mexico, the chef training offered in advance of major hotel expansion at Victoria Falls in Zambia, and the new journalism courses at the University of Antananarivo in Madagascar following liberalization of the media laws. Even unskilled labor markets, such as the widespread systems of mine labor recruitment across Southern Africa, the network of labor recruiters and brokers who move surplus labor from Bangladesh and the Philippines to the Middle East, and the farm labor recruiters who move seasonal farm labor across regions within a given country, often operate in clearly structured vertical supply chains.

A supply chain focus offers a great many advantages for those conducting diagnostic assessments of opportunities and constraints in the identified priority segments of the rural economy. An equity orientation requires that potential interveners understand the supply chains in which the poor operate. In some supply channels, large firms serve as locomotives pulling large numbers of small firms and farms along as they expand markets and input availability. In other situations, as in the Chilean, Brazilian, and Argentinean dairy industries, growth of large retailers can obliterate armies of competitors or small suppliers that fail to adjust to new quality and quantity requirements.[3] In general, it is not possible to understand the competitive prospects for small players without understanding the larger supply chains in which they operate. The supply chains also offer opportunities for systemic interventions by identifying bottlenecks—in key input supply, transport arteries, or marketing infrastructure—where interventions can open up growth prospects for large numbers of small enterprises at once. Supply chains cut across space and across sectors, providing a tractable means of understanding and facilitating key spatial and intersectoral linkages. Finally, the supply chain approach affords a useful tool for assembling coalitions of interested parties whose collaboration will prove necessary in enabling the growth of the targeted subsectors.

An array of closely related methods exists for conducting these assessments. Agricultural marketing and small enterprise promotion specialists often refer to these diagnostic exercises as "subsector analyses," while the corporate and business school worlds generally refer to them as "supply chain," "value chain," or "cluster" analyses. Chapter 15 provides some examples of how different potential interveners have applied these diagnostic tools in a variety of

3. Dirven (2001), Jank et al. (1999), Gutman (2002).

practical situations, while a growing array of how-to manuals and training materials describes the methods in detail.[4]

These diagnostic assessments all aim to identify systemic interventions—what one of our colleagues refers to as "key logs in the jam"—that when unblocked open up growth opportunities for large numbers of players up- and downstream in the affected supply channels. System-level interventions—such as policy changes, public investments, introduction of new technology, and interventions via large-firm marketing or input supply intermediaries—generally prove most cost-effective (Chapter 12). In contrast, individual firm-level assistance typically proves very costly. For this reason, the diagnostic tools search systematically for these systemic, high-payoff, "leveraged" interventions first.

Ideally, coalitions of principal stakeholders should participate in the diagnostic supply chain reviews. These coalitions often include trade associations, key individual players in the relevant markets, NGOs involved in the subsector, and affiliated government agencies. Experience clearly indicates that effective interventions are most likely to take place, and most likely to be successful, when principal stakeholders participate in the diagnostics.[5]

Step 3: Build Flexible Institutional Coalitions for Implementation

Growing recognition of the economic importance of the RNFE suggests that it will increasingly need to become the focus of explicit government policy attention. By focusing on high-impact actions that influence opportunities for many similar firms at once—through policy reform, strategic public investment, new technology, or training—public intervention can prove cost-effective. By focusing on subsectors and supply channels accessible to the poor, these efforts can stimulate equity as well as aggregate nonfarm income growth. In an ideal world, concerned and well-funded governments would focus explicit attention on the needs of the RNFE.

But given the reality of tightly stretched government budgets, eroding civil service pay scales, scarce analytical skills, and consistently fragmented responsibility for the RNFE, even the best-intentioned governments cannot always easily take the lead. Recognizing this reality, the model proposed here urges other stakeholders to take the initiative as opportunities arise. Using the analytical tools described here, specific interest groups can initiate reviews and

---

4. See Porter (1980, 1998), Haggblade and Gamser (1991), Boomgard et al. (1992), Montigard (1992), Bear et al. (1993), Lauret (1993), Lusby (1995), Chen (1996), Dowds and Hinojosa (1999), Bourgeois and Herrera (2000), Kaplinsky and Morris (2000), Miles (2001), World Bank (2001), Lusby and Panliburton (2002), and Meyer-Stamer (2002).

5. Chen (1996), Dowds and Hinojosa (1999), Bourgeois and Herrera (2000), World Bank (2001), Meyer-Stamer (2002).

dialogues among key private and public stakeholders. An institutional audit, which emerges as part of any normal supply chain diagnostics, will quickly reveal which stakeholders have the capacity, interest, and willingness to intervene on behalf of specific groups in rural nonfarm supply channels benefiting the rural poor. From this audit, initiating entities can assemble working coalitions among the interested parties in each given subsector and location.

In this model, any interested party can initiate action. Indeed the diagnostic tools aim to empower and encourage interested stakeholders to seize the initiative. In the past, a growing cadre of business-oriented NGOs has effectively initiated supply chain reviews and interventions, as in the case of Philippine *retaso,* Thai silk, Ghanian palm oil, Zambian paprika, and Nepali vegetables, as well as Bangladeshi rural cell phone services and treadle pump distributorships.[6] In other instances, central government agencies have initiated reviews and responses, as in the case of Rwanda's banana wine assessment, the Botswanacraft and sorghum beer examples from Botswana, and a series of major subsector-specific reviews by India's National Bank for Agricultural and Rural Development.[7] Local governments have taken the lead in South Africa and throughout much of Latin America (Box 17.2). Private firms and industry groups have likewise initiated supply chain interventions. They have launched small farmer extension and input supply programs across Africa, business extension support for small retailers, handicraft export marketing services, and subcontracting arrangements involving input supply and technical support in a variety of developing country locations.[8] Even though they do not generally take the lead in most instances, large private firms have proven willing partners in promoting supply chain development, so long as their commercial interests and those of linked small firms coincide.

This flexible approach to coalition building offers a model that can work in a broad range of institutional and economic settings. Rather than relying on government initiative or the creation of new regional development authorities, this approach both encourages and facilitates collaboration among business groups, key NGOs, and a range of affected firms and agencies. Where opportunity arises, leadership from any available source can initiate action. In this way, coalitions emerge and coalesce as needs and opportunities arise.

Anticipated Outcomes

Reduction of rural poverty in the developing world will require more rapid economic growth than has occurred in the past. It will likewise require that growth

---

6. Bowman and Reiling (1990), Bear (1993), Budinich (1993), Malhotra and Santer (1994), Begum et al. (1995), Overy and Giray (1996), Burr (2000), Magistro et al. (2004).

7. See Mead and Ngirabatware (1987), Box 18.1; Haggblade (1989), Boomgard et al. (1992), and SGRNFS (1995).

8. Rodolo (1972), Mead (1984), Minot (1986), Jaffee and Gordon (1993), Little and Watts (1994), Millard (1996), Hayami (1998b).

occur in supply channels where the poor can participate. The strategy advocated here involves a systematic search for engines of rural economic growth and for supply channels within them where the poor can effectively compete. Through a sequential review of high-potential economic activities, this strategy seeks to identify priority interventions that will open up opportunities for multitudes of rural poor in specific subsectors and supply channels. As this happens, increased labor demand will lead to a tightening of rural labor markets and raise rural wage rates more broadly throughout the rural economy, leading to indirect benefits for the rural poor engaged in other farm and nonfarm activities.

Consider the rural economy as a fleet of different-sized vehicles—in varying states of design, repair, and disrepair—with a mandate to transport large numbers of rural poor to more prosperous economic niches in the rural economy. The strategy suggested here involves sequential tune-ups—and in some cases vehicle assembly—aimed at revving up a fleet of robust engines of rural economic growth. Through sequential tune-ups of the most potentially robust vehicles, this process aims to produce a well-oiled, revitalized fleet capable of moving large numbers of rural poor out of poverty.

Does this imply picking winners? No, it does not. Only one entrant can win any given contest. Rather than picking a solitary winner, this approach aims to create as many competitive participants as possible. As emphasized in the literature on competitive clusters, the more well-tuned engines the better (Porter 1998). Of course potential interveners must start somewhere. So yes, this approach requires picking as a starting point the most powerful potential poverty fighters and moving down the fleet maintenance list in the order of anticipated poverty-reducing potential. This iterative process aims to tune up a smoothly running, powerful rural economy with multiple economic opportunities for the rural poor.

This strategy represents an incrementalist approach to pro-poor regional development. It recognizes that no government starts, tabula rasa, to erect an ideal policy environment from the ground up. Even colonial authorities, who imported vast bodies of legislation wholesale at the stroke of a pen during the nineteenth century, imported them not into a void but rather into functioning institutional environments that they then modified. Still today, policymakers move incrementally from where they ended yesterday (Lindblom 1980). They modify and adjust policies and public investment programs as opportunities and pressures arise. They build policy environments incrementally, one brick at a time. As one recent review of the policy process in developing countries concluded, "The metaphors that have guided policy research over recent years suggest that it is actually rather messy, with outcomes occurring as a result of complicated political, social and institutional processes, which are best described as 'evolutionary'" (Juma and Clark 1995). The strategy we advocate recognizes this and proposes a sequential process aimed at expanding opportunities for the rural poor by whichever actors have the vision and the convening power to launch priority task force reviews.

Alternative Visions

Based on our quarter century of research and operational fieldwork on behalf the RNFE, we believe this three-pronged strategy represents a feasible, constructive path forward. Yet we readily admit that other strategies are also possible, many of them reviewed in prior chapters of this book. Indeed experienced colleagues have proposed a variety of alternative models that generally fall into the following categories.

Government-Centric

THE PRSP MODEL.　Because most developing country governments now prepare poverty reduction strategy papers (PRSPs) at the behest of the World Bank and the International Monetary Fund, some colleagues have suggested that this process provides a promising forum for coordinating interest and actions in support of equitable rural nonfarm growth. Certainly a well-organized central government could use the PRSP preparation and implementation process as a vehicle for orchestrating the high-level coordinating body model described in Chapter 11. We would welcome such an initiative, for indeed in some instances it might work well. But given the realities of PRSP execution in many countries, we are not optimistic that a majority of developing countries will continue this practice once donors absolve them of the obligation. Nor, having seen many PRSPs and central governments in action, are we optimistic that waiting for inspiration and coordination from the center will consistently provide the most rapid path to reinvigorating the RNFE. In some cases it may, and central government initiative would prove most welcome in those settings. But we see no reason to discourage other potential leaders, particularly given the growing role of the private sector in driving opportunities in key rural supply chains. The PRSP model, a special case of our more general strategy, offers an opportunity for central government leaders to take the initiative where they are so motivated. Elsewhere we urge the private sector, local governments, donors, and NGOs not to wait but rather to initiate supply chain task force reviews where they see opportunities.

DECENTRALIZATION.　Given the importance of local knowledge and support for basic market infrastructure, well-funded and well-staffed local governments can potentially play a pivotal role in identifying opportunities and bottlenecks and promoting effective solutions enabling rural nonfarm growth. Because most supply chains extend well beyond local jurisdictional boundaries and because many local governments are not well funded or well staffed, we cannot rely on local authorities to serve everywhere as effective champions of equitable rural nonfarm growth. As in the case of the central government–led PRSP model, where effective leadership and capacity exist within local governments, they can and should seize the initiative in launching supply chain reviews. In other instances, industry groups, central authorities, or NGOs should not hesitate to fill the breach and to involve local authorities as necessary. Though their capacities vary widely across settings, many local authorities are prepared to assist even when they lack the wherewithal to lead specific efforts.

NGO-Centric

Eroding civil service capacity, coupled with concerns about government corruption, has led donors in many locations to avoid government agencies and to channel resources to intended beneficiaries via NGOs or the private sector instead. For that reason, NGOs wield expanding resources in many developing country settings. In many of the instances described in Chapters 12, 14, and 15, they have provided innovative and effective promotional services on behalf of the RNFE. In the field, we have seen increasing numbers of nonprofit organizations focus on facilitating the development of commercially viable business development services that enable poor producers to aggregate production and attain quality standards sufficient to enable them to supply large intermediaries that, in turn, provide them with access to growing market channels. In many settings, particularly in resource-poor and highly inequitable rural environments, we see NGOs as potentially effective promoters of pro-poor rural nonfarm growth. Many, of course, focus on humanitarian relief and do not have the business or agricultural expertise necessary to play this role. Like the government-centered solutions, the NGO-centric approach can work in some instances but not all. The growing numbers of business-oriented NGOs, however, provide an important potential source of leadership, resources, and initiative for launching the supply chain reviews we see as necessary to rev up the RNFEs of the developing world.

Private Sector–Centric

INJECT CREDIT AS THE ALL-PURPOSE LUBRICANT.   The most prevalent intervention in nonfarm business promotion over the past two decades has involved delivering credit, and only credit, to poor entrepreneurs. The premise of the many thousands of no-frills microcredit programs is that poor households have ideas, income-earning opportunities, and the necessary management and technical skills, but they have no access to the financial resources necessary to bring these opportunities to fruition. In such situations, the argument goes, it is most effective to lend them the necessary financial resources, at cost-covering interest rates, and let them get on with the business of business. The poor have regularly proven reliable in repaying their loans. As discussed in greater detail in Chapters 11 and 12, we conclude from the available evidence that credit is indeed useful, even necessary in many cases, to stimulate rural nonfarm activity, in the same way that primary education, basic health, roads, and communications services are necessary to enable the rural poor to access productive business opportunities. Credit injections work most effectively in the Category 3 regions of our typology, where a prosperous agriculture or another component of the rural economic base is expanding, increasing rural incomes and along with them the demand for rural nonfarm goods and services, to which the availability of microcredit can help small producers respond. But not every rural person is a natural entrepreneur, and credit alone is not sufficient to stimulate broad-based rural nonfarm growth. We see credit as a necessary lubricant rather than as the primary engine of rural economic growth. It forms part of the solution to rural poverty alleviation, but only part.

SET THE ENABLING ENVIRONMENT AND STAND BACK. A more general statement of the basic microcredit proposition holds that governments should provide an enabling environment only. They should set favorable policies and build roads, schools, clinics, communication infrastructure, and banks, then let the private sector identify and exploit the resulting business opportunities.

While it is clear that governments must provide necessary public goods, because the private sector will not supply them in sufficient quantity, the common laissez-faire rendition of this proposition falls short in that it fails to offer useful operational guidelines. What roads should receive priority? Where should the bridges and power lines go? What kind of educational curriculum will prove most valuable? What policies require review? It likewise fails the equity test. While supermarket chains will undoubtedly respond to incentives in pro-business policy environments, the rural poor risk being left behind without assistance navigating the rapid rural transition currently under way in many rural regions of the developing world.

Even in generally favorable rural settings—where basic policies, infrastructure, and human resources exist—closer inspection frequently reveals deficiencies in the enabling environment for specific nonfarm businesses. In the highly pro-business environment of Botswana, misenforcement of arcane sorghum beer legislation threatened the income-earning opportunities of tens of thousands of rural home brewers, at the time the largest rural manufacturing employers in the country (Boomgard et al. 1992). Similarly, in the generally open business environment of rural Thailand, fluctuating quotas on silk yarn imports wreaked havoc on incentives and opportunities for tens of thousands of rural households rearing silkworms, reeling silk yarn, and weaving silk cloth (Chapter 15). Infrastructure requirements may likewise prove highly specific to given nonfarm activities. Inadequate provision of public water points proved a crucial constraint to small laundry services in Madagascar (Taillefer et al. 2000), while construction of a missing bridge provided an essential link for rural cheesemakers in Honduras (Zelaya and Reardon 2001).

We believe our three-pronged strategy represents a practical means of moving beyond the well-established platitudes that roads, electricity, education, credit, communication links, and policies all matter. This strategy helps interested parties to focus on the specific priority infrastructural investments, technical training, credit, public goods, and policies necessary to support growth in

key rural supply chains. Enabling environments are, in fact, everywhere contin-
uously evolving works in progress, built brick by brick as the cumulation of all
policies, infrastructure investments, and collective actions affecting a specific
economic activity. Clearly, enabling environments are important. Our strategy
involves systematic review to see how they can be incrementally improved to
enhance growth opportunities in a series of important segments of the rural
economy.

The Bottom Line

In the end, rapid pro-poor growth in the RNFE will occur where leadership and
opportunities coincide. Rather than depending on any one group to provide consistent leadership, we advocate harnessing initiative and vision wherever they
occur. We have witnessed impressive examples of rural business opportunities
transformed by leadership from farm groups, business associations, individual
private firms, NGO staff, local government leaders, and central government ministries and agencies. The supply chain task force method we suggest empowers
stakeholders from any of these constituencies to seize the initiative and attempt
to coordinate understanding and resources in ways that will stimulate rapid
growth and at the same time permit low-income groups to participate in growing supply channels.

Future Prospects

As structural transformation proceeds across rural regions of the developing
world, the RNFE is likely to grow. Commerce and services, normally the most
buoyant segments of the RNFE, promise expanded opportunities in personal,
educational, medical, and repair services as well as hostelry, prepared foods,
restaurants, trade, and transportation.

Translating rural nonfarm growth into significant poverty reduction will require that dynamic segments of the RNFE stimulate work opportunities for the
poor and that levels of labor productivity increase gradually over time. Yet direct
participation by the poor in the most rapidly growing and high-productivity
nonfarm activities is not guaranteed, as Chapter 3 has emphasized. This participation may require assets the poor do not possess—human skills, financial assets, and the organizational ability to supply sufficient quantities and quality to
satisfy key growing markets. In these instances, public involvement—or at least
some form of collective action—remains critical in ensuring adequate infrastructure, education, technical skills, and policies as well as in brokering the
organizational and legal frameworks that will enable the poor to participate
directly in growing market segments. Even where direct participation by the
poor proves difficult, indirect gains can accrue, via labor market links, as a
growing regional economic base stimulates aggregate rural wage rates as well

as employment opportunities for the poor. As the evidence from Chapters 3 and 7 suggests, these employment opportunities may arise in agriculture as well as off the farm.

In the liberalized rural economies of the developing world, large private firms increasingly govern prospects for growth in the most rapidly growing non-farm markets and supply channels (see Chapters 9, 14, and 15). In this environment, promotion of equitable growth in the RNFE will require collaboration with private firms in developing commercially viable organizational arrangements that will enable large numbers of small players to link up with growing market channels. Increasingly, advocates of the rural poor will have to work in concert with private firms to exploit these opportunities.

In coming decades, the RNFE can play an increasingly important role in economic growth and poverty alleviation efforts. We believe the flexible three-pronged strategy enunciated in this chapter offers a feasible pathway forward. Other strategies undoubtedly exist, and we welcome creative thinking and experimentation aimed at accelerating equitable growth of the RNFE across the developing world. Given its 35 to 50 percent contribution to rural incomes, rural nonfarm activity must increasingly contribute to poverty reduction efforts as a complement to necessary ongoing investments in broad-based agricultural growth. The RNFE has grown too large to ignore.

References

Abbott, J. C. 1986. *Marketing improvement in the developing world: What happens and what we have learned.* FAO Economic and Social Development Series 37. Rome: Food and Agriculture Organization.

Abdulai, A. 1994. The impacts of policy environment on rural-urban linkages: The case of Ghana. Ph.D. dissertation, Swiss Federal Institute of Technology, Zurich.

Abdulai, A., and A. Crole-Rees. 2001. Determinants of income diversification amongst rural households in Southern Mali. *Food Policy* 26: 437–452.

Abdulai, A., and C. Delgado. 1999. Determinants of nonfarm earnings of farm-based husbands and wives in Northern Ghana. *American Journal of Agricultural Economics* (February): 117–130.

Abe, M., and M. Kawakami. 1997. A distributive comparison of enterprise size in Korea and Taiwan. *Developing Economies* 35 (4): 382–400.

Abugre, A. 1994. When credit is not due: A critical evaluation of donor NGO experiences with credit. In *Financial landscapes reconstructed,* ed. F. J. A. Bouman and O. Hospes. Boulder, Colo.: Westview.

ACDI/VOCA. *See* Agricultural Cooperative Development International / Volunteers in Overseas Cooperative Assistance.

Action for Enterprise. 2001. Subsector analysis / BDS market assessment of the fresh vegetables for export subsector. Action for Enterprise, Washington, D.C.

Adams, D. W., and D. H. Graham. 1981. Critique of traditional agricultural credit projects and policies. *Journal of Development Economics* 8: 347–366.

Adams, D. W., and J. D. Von Pischke. 1992. Micro-enterprise credit programs: Déjà vu. *World Development* 20: 1463–1470.

Adams, D. W., D. H. Graham, and J. D. Von Pischke, eds. 1984. *Undermining rural development with cheap credit.* Boulder, Colo.: Westview.

Adams, R. H. 1998. Remittances, investment, and rural asset accumulation in Pakistan. *Economic Development and Cultural Change* 47 (1): 467–491.

———. 1999. Non-farm income, inequality and land in rural Egypt. Mimeo, World Bank, Washington, D.C.

———. 2000. Non-farm income and rural inequality in Egypt and Jordan. Mimeo, World Bank, Washington, D.C.

Adams, R., and J. He. 1995. Sources of income inequality and poverty in rural Pakistan. IFPRI Research Report 102. Washington, D.C.: International Food Policy Research Institute.

Adelman, I. 1984. Beyond export-led growth. *World Development* 12 (9): 937–949.

Adelman, I., J. E. Taylor, and S. Vogel. 1988. Life in a Mexican village: A SAM perspective. *Journal of Development Studies* 25 (1): 5–24.

Agarwal, B. 1990. Social security and the family: Coping with seasonality and calamity in rural India. *Journal of Peasant Studies* 17 (3): 341–412.

Agricultural Cooperative Development International / Volunteers in Overseas Cooperative Assistance (ACDI/VOCA). 2001. *ACDI/VOCA World Report.* Washington, D.C.: ACDI/VOCA.

Ahmed, C. S., and R. W. Herdt. 1984. Measuring the impact of consumption linkages on the employment effects of mechanisation in Philippine rice cultivation. *Journal of Development Studies* 20 (2): 242–255.

Ahmed, M. U. 1984. Financing rural industries in Bangladesh. *Bangladesh Development Studies* 12 (1–2): 55–68.

Ahmed, R. 2000. Liberalization of agricultural input markets in Bangladesh. In *Out of the shadow of famine: Evolving food markets and food policy in Bangladesh,* ed. R. Ahmed, S. Haggblade, and T. Chowdhury. Baltimore: The Johns Hopkins University Press.

Ahmed, R., and C. Donovan. 1992. *Issues of infrastructural development: A synthesis of the literature.* Washington, D.C.: International Food Policy Research Institute.

———. 1997. Issues of infrastructural development. In *Promoting third-world development and food security,* ed. L. G. Tweeten and D. G. McClelland. Westport, Conn.: Praeger, 89–117.

Ahmed, R., and M. Hossain. 1990. *Developmental impact of rural infrastructure in Bangladesh.* IFPRI Research Report 83. Washington, D.C.: International Food Policy Research Institute.

Ahmed, R., S. Haggblade, and T. Chowdhury. 2000. *Out of the shadow of famine: Evolving food markets and food policy in Bangladesh.* Baltimore: The Johns Hopkins University Press.

Alam, A., and S. Rajapatirana. 1993. Trade policy reforms in Latin America and the Caribbean during the 1980s. World Bank Working Paper. Washington, D.C.: World Bank.

Alderman, H., and C. H. Paxson. 1992. Do the poor insure? A synthesis of the literature on risk and consumption in developing countries. World Bank Policy Research Working Paper WPS 1008. Washington, D.C.: World Bank.

———. 1994. Do the poor insure? A synthesis of the literature on risk and consumption in developing countries. In *Economics in a changing world,* ed. D. Bacha, Vol. 4, *Development, trade, and the environment.* London: Macmillan.

Alexander-Tedeschi, G., and D. Karlan. 2006. Microfinance impact: Bias from dropouts. Department of Economics, Yale University, New Haven, Conn.

Alonso, W. 1964. *Location and land use.* Cambridge, Mass.: Harvard University Press.

Amane, E. 1989. Household consumption patterns and rural growth linkages in a developing country: The case of the commune of Timahdite in Morocco. Ph.D. dissertation, Institut Agronomique et Veterinaire Hassan II, Morocco.

Amsden, A. H. 1977. The division of labor is limited by the type of market: The case of the Taiwanese machine tool industry. *World Development* 5 (3): 217–233.

———. 1989. *Asia's next giant: South Korea and late industrialization.* New York: Oxford University Press.

———. 1991. Big business and urban congestion in Taiwan: The origins of small enterprise and regionally decentralized industry. *World Development* 19 (9): 1121–1135.

Ancey, G. 1974. Relations de voisinage ville campagne: Une analyse appliquée en Bouake; Sa couronne et sa région (Côte d'Ivoire). Mémoires ORSTOM 70. Paris: ORSTOM (Office de Recherche Scientifique et Technique d'Outre Mer).

Anderson, D. 1982. Small industry in developing countries: A discussion of issues. *World Development* 10 (11): 913–948.

Anderson, D., and F. Khambata. 1982. Small enterprise and development policy in the Philippines: A case study. World Bank Staff Working Paper 468. Washington, D.C.: World Bank.

Anderson, D., and M. Leiserson. 1978. Rural enterprise and nonfarm employment. World Bank Paper. Washington, D.C.: World Bank.

————. 1980. Rural non-farm employment in developing countries. *Economic Development and Cultural Change,* January: 227–248.

Anderson, J. R., P. G. Pardey, and J. Roseboom. 1994. Sustaining growth in agriculture: A quantitative review of agricultural research investments. *Agricultural Economics* 10 (1): 107–123.

Andriantsoa, P., N. Andriasendrarivony, V. Carbonneau, S. Haggblade, B. Minten, M. Rakotojaona, F. Rakotovoavy, and H. S. Razafinimanana. 2005. Media proliferation and democratic transition in Africa: The case of Madagascar. *World Development* 33 (11): 1939–1957.

Anthony, K. R. M., B. F. Johnston, W. O. Jones, and V. C. Uchendu. 1979. *Agricultural change in tropical Africa.* Ithaca, N.Y.: Cornell University Press.

Antipolo, S. B. 1989. Strengthening urban-rural linkages as an alternative strategy for regional development. INURD Working Paper 89. Washington, D.C.: World Bank.

Antle, J. M. 1983. Infrastructure and aggregate agricultural productivity: International evidence. *Economic Development and Cultural Change* 31 (April): 609–619.

Applegate, M. J., and D. D. Badger. 1979. Formulation of linkages in rural regions for purposes of regional development research. Mimeo, Oklahoma State University, Stillwater.

Appropriate Technology International (ATI). 1994. *ATI Bulletin 25.* Washington, D.C.: ATI.

————. 1997. *1997 Portfolio Report.* Washington, D.C.: ATI.

Armendáriz de Aghion, B., and J. Morduch. 2005. *The economics of microfinance.* Cambridge, Mass.: MIT Press.

Armstrong, D., and N. Karmali. 2005. Trickle-up economics: Farmers grow their way out of poverty. *Forbes* 175 (13): 55–56.

Asanuma, B. 1985. The organization of parts purchases in the Japanese automotive industry. *Japanese Economic Studies* 13 (4): 32–53.

ATI. *See* Appropriate Technology International.

Austin, J. E. 1992. *Agroindustrial project analysis: Critical design factors.* Baltimore: The Johns Hopkins University Press.

Awasthi, D. N., B. P. Murali, and B. N. Bhat. 1990. Entrepreneurship development and new enterprise creation: Experience of the Entrepreneurship Development Institute of India. Management Development Programme SED/17/E. Geneva: International Labor Office.

Bagachwa, M. S. D., and F. Stewart. 1992. Rural industries and rural linkages in Sub-Saharan Africa: A Survey. In *Alternative development strategies in SubSaharan Africa,* ed. F. Stewart, S. Lall, and S. Wangwe. New York: St. Martin's Press.

Bah, M., S. Cissé, B. Diyamett, G. Diallo, F. Lerise, D. Okali, E. Okpara, J. Olawoye, and C. Tacoli. 2003. Changing rural-urban linkages in Mali, Nigeria and Tanzania. *Environment and Urbanization* 15: 13–24.

Bahl, R. E., and J. F. Linn. 1992. *Urban public finance in developing countries.* New York: Oxford University Press.

Bahl, R. E., J. Miner, and L. Schroeder. 1984. Mobilizing local resources in developing countries. *Public Administration and Development* 4: 215–230.

Bairoch, P. 1988. *Cities and economic development: From the dawn of history to the present.* Chicago: University of Chicago Press.

Bala Subrahmanya, M. H. 2004. Small industry and globalisation: Implications, performance and prospects. *Economic and Political Weekly,* May 1: 1826–1834

Balihuta, A. M., and K. Sen. 2001. Macroeconomic policies and rural livelihood diversification: An Uganda case study. LADDER Working Paper 3. <www.uea.ac.uk/dev/odg/ladder> (accessed June 2006).

Balisacan, A. M. 1993. Agricultural growth, landlessness, off-farm employment and rural poverty in the Philippines. *Economic Development and Cultural Change* 41 (3): 533–562.

Balsevich, F., J. Berdegué, and T. Reardon. 2006. Supermarkets, new-generation wholesalers, tomato farmers, and NGOs in Nicaragua. Department of Agricultural Economics Staff Paper 2006-03. East Lansing: Michigan State University.

Balsevich, F., P. Schuetz, and E. Perez. 2006. Cattle producers' participation in market channels in Central America: Supermarkets, processors, and auctions. Department of Agricultural Economics Staff Paper 2006-01. East Lansing: Michigan State University.

Banco Central de Chile. 1986. *Indicadores economicos ye socials, 1960–1985.* Santiago: Banco Central de Chile, Direccion de Estudios.

———. 2002. *Chile social and economic indicators 1960–2000.* Santiago: Banco Central de Chile.

Bangladesh Bureau of Statistics. 1994. *Bangladesh population census, 1991: National series,* Vol. 1, *Analytical report.* Dhaka: Bureau of Statistics.

———. 2003. *Bangladesh population census, 2001: National report.* Dhaka: Bangladesh Bureau of Statistics.

Bardhan, P. 2003. Crouching tiger, lumbering elephant: A China-India comparison. In *Markets and governance,* ed. K. Basu, P. Nayak, and R. Ray. New Delhi: Oxford University Press.

Barnes, C. 1996. Assets and the impact of microenterprise finance programs. Working paper prepared for the Assessing the Impacts of Microenterprise Services (AIMS) project. Washington, D.C.: Management Systems International.

Barnes, D. F., and H. P. Binswanger. 1986. Impact of rural electrification and infrastructure on agricultural changes, 1966–80. *Economic and Political Weekly* 21 (1): 26–34.

Baron, C. 1980. *Technology, employment and basic needs in food processing in developing countries.* Oxford: Pergamon Press for the International Labour Office.

Barres, I. 2005. Bulletin highlights—Supply of funding. *MicroBanking Bulletin* 11, The scope of funding microfinance (August): 47–58.

Barrett, C. B. 1998. Immiserized growth in liberalized agriculture. *World Development* 26 (5): 743–753.

Barrett, C. B., T. Reardon, and P. Webb. 2001. Nonfarm income diversification and household livelihood strategies in rural Africa: Concepts, dynamics and policy implications. *Food Policy* 26: 315–331.

Barrett, C. B., M. Bezuneh, D. C. Clay, and T. Reardon. 2004. Heterogeneous constraints, incentives and income diversification strategies in rural Africa, revised version. Report to USAID/BASIS CRSP by Cornell and Michigan State Universities, August.

———. 2005. Heterogeneous constraints, incentives, and income diversification strategies in rural Africa. *Quarterly Journal of International Agriculture* 44 (1): 37–60.

Barton, C. 1997. Microenterprise business development services: Defining institutional options and indicators of performance. Microenterprise Best Practices Working Paper. Bethesda, Md.: Development Alternatives.

Bassey, M., and O. Schmidt. 1989. *Abrasive-disk dehullers in Africa from research to dissemination.* Ottawa: International Development Research Centre.

Bautista, R. M. 1990. Agricultural growth and food imports in developing countries: A reexamination. In *Economic development in East and Southeast Asia: Essays in honor of Professor Shinichi Ichimura,* ed. S. Naya and A. Takayam. Honolulu: Institute of Southeast Asian Studies.

———. 1995. Rapid agricultural growth is not enough: The Philippines, 1965–1980. In *Agriculture on the road to industrialization,* ed. J. W. Mellor. Baltimore: The Johns Hopkins University Press.

Baydas, M. M., D. H. Graham, and L. Valenzuela. 1997. Commercial banks in microfinance: New actors in the microfinance world. Economics and Sociology Occasional Paper 2372. Columbus, Ohio: Rural Finance Program, Department of Agricultural Economics, Ohio State University.

Bayes, A., J. V. Braun, and R. Akhter. 1999. The impact of village pay phones in Bangladesh. ZED Discussion Papers on Development Policy. Bonn: ZED.

Bear, M. 1993. Care and subsector analysis: A report on CARE's formative experience. GEMINI Working Paper 43. Bethesda, Md.: Development Alternatives.

Bear, M. A., C. Gibbon, S. Haggblade, and N. Ritchie. 1993. *Facilitator's guide for training in subsector analysis.* Includes a case study video. Atlanta, Ga.: CARE.

Bear, M., A. Gibson, and R. Hitchins. 2003. From principles to practice: Ten critical challenges for BDS market development. *Small Enterprise Development* 14 (4): 10–23.

Begum, G. A., M. K. Biswas, J. F. Burke, R. Dean, R. Hussain, Y. Lashker-Rashid, and A. A. Syed. 1995. Designing projects that have an impact: Five subsector studies in Bangladesh. GEMINI Technical Report 98. Bethesda, Md.: Development Alternatives.

Behrman, J. R., and A. B. Deolalikar. 1988. Health and Nutrition. In *Handbook of development economics,* ed. H. Chenery and T. N. Srinivasan, Vol. 1, Chap. 14. Amsterdam: North Holland.

Bell, C. L. G., and P. B. R. Hazell. 1980. Measuring the indirect effects of an agricultural investment project on its surrounding region. *American Journal of Agricultural Economics* 62 (1): 75–86.

Bell, C., P. B. R. Hazell, and R. Slade. 1982. *Project evaluation in regional perspective: A study of an irrigation project in Northwest Malaysia.* Baltimore: The Johns Hopkins University Press.

Belsky, E. S., and G. J. Karaska. 1990. Approaches to locating urban functions in developing rural areas. *International Regional Science Review* 13 (3): 225–240.

———. 1993. Toward effective regional and location planning for rural and urban linkages: The debate joined. *International Regional Science Review* 15 (3): 341–343.

Bendavid-Val, A. 1987. Means, motivators and markets in rural regional development. In *Patterns of change in developing rural regions,* ed. R. Bar-El, A. Bendavid-Val, and G. J. Karaska. Boulder, Colo.: Westview.

———. 1989. Rural-urban linkages: Farming and farm households in regional and town economies. *Review of Urban and Regional Development Studies* 2: 89–97.

Bendavid-Val, A., J. Downing, and G. Karaska. 1988a. Rural-urban dynamics: Synthesis report. Washington, D.C.: U.S. Agency for International Development.

———. 1988b. Rural-urban exchange in Kutus Town and its hinterland. International Development Programs, Clark University, Worcester, Mass.

Berdegué, J. A. 2001. Cooperating to compete: Associative peasant business firms in Chile. Ph.D. dissertation, Wageningen University and Research Center, Wageningen, The Netherlands.

Berdegué, J., E. Ramírez, T. Reardon, and G. Escobar. 2001. Rural nonfarm employment and incomes in Chile. *World Development* 29 (3): 411–425.

Berdegué, J. A., F. Balsevich, L. Flores, and T. Reardon. 2005. Central American supermarkets' private standards of quality and safety in procurement of fresh fruits and vegetables. *Food Policy* 30 (3): 254–269.

Berg, R. E. 1992. Social and spatial context in rural development strategies. *Regional Science Review* 15: 1–11.

Bernstein, H., B. Crow, and H. Johnson. 1992. *Rural livelihoods: Crises and responses.* London: Oxford University Press.

Bernsten, R. H., and J. Staatz. 1992. The role of subsector analysis in setting research priorities. Department of Agricultural Economics Staff Paper 92-104. East Lansing: Michigan State University.

Berry, B. J. L. 1967. *Geography of market centers and retail distribution.* Englewood Cliffs, N.J.: Prentice-Hall.

———. 1970. The geography of the United States in the year 2000. *Institute of British Geographers* 51: 21–53.

Berry, R. A. 1976. Non-agricultural activities in rural and small town areas of Latin America. Mimeo, World Bank, Washington, D.C.

———. 1987. The limited role of rural small-scale manufacturing for late-comers: Some hypotheses on the Colombian experience. *Journal of Latin American Studies* 19: 295–322.

———. 1995. The contribution of agriculture to growth: Colombia. In *Agriculture on the road to industrialization,* ed. John W. Mellor. Baltimore: The Johns Hopkins University Press.

Bhalla, A., and D. James. 1988. *New technologies and development: Experiences in technology blending.* Boulder, Colo.: Lynne Rienner.

Bhalla, A. S. 1975. *Technology and employment in industry.* Geneva: International Labour Office.

Bhalla, S. 1981. Islands of growth: A note on Haryana experience and some possible implications. *Economic and Political Weekly* (June 6): 1022–1030.

————. 1991. *Report of the study group on employment generation, National Commission on Rural Labor.* New Delhi: Government of India.

————. 1993. The dynamics of wage determination and employment generation in Indian agriculture. *Indian Journal of Agricultural Economics* 48 (3): 449–470.

————. 1994. *Rural industrialisation and nonfarm employment.* Delhi: International Labour Office.

————. 1997. The rise and fall of workforce diversification processes in rural India: A regional and sectoral analysis. Centre for Economic Studies and Planning, DSA Working Paper. New Delhi: Jawaharlal Nehru University.

Bhatt, V. V. 1998. On the relevance of East Asian experiences: A South Asian perspective. In *Toward the rural-based development of commerce and industry: Selected experiences from East Asia,* ed. Y. Hayami. Washington, D.C.: World Bank.

Biggs, S., and R. Grosvenor-Alsop. 1984. *Developing technologies for the rural poor.* London: Intermediate Technology Publications.

Bigsten, A. 1984. *Education and income determination in Kenya.* Aldershot, England: Gower.

Bigsten, A., and P. Collier. 1995. Linkages from agricultural growth in Kenya. In *Agriculture on the road to industrialization,* ed. J. W. Mellor. Baltimore: The Johns Hopkins University Press.

Binswanger, H. P. 1989. The policy response of agriculture. In *Proceedings of the World Bank Annual Conference on Development Economics: Supplement to the World Bank Economic Review and World Bank Research Observer,* ed. S. Fischer and D. de Tray. Washington, D.C.: World Bank.

Binswanger, H. P., and V. W. Ruttan. 1978. *Induced innovation.* Baltimore: The Johns Hopkins University Press.

Binswanger, H. P., S. R. Khandker, and M. R. Rosenzweig. 1989. How infrastructure and financial institutions affect agricultural output and investment in India. Working Paper Agriculture WPS 163. Washington, D.C.: World Bank.

Binswanger, H., M. C. Yang, A. Bowers, and Y. Mundlak. 1987. On the determinants of cross country aggregate agricultural supply. *Journal of Econometrics* 36: 111–131.

Bird, R. M., and F. Vaillancourt. 1998. *Fiscal decentralization in developing countries.* Cambridge: Cambridge University Press.

Birks, S., F. Fluitman, X. Oudin, and C. Sinclair. 1994. Skills acquisition in micro-enterprises: Evidence from West Africa. Report, Organization for Economic Cooperation and Development, Paris.

Blitzer, S., J. Davila, J. E. Hardoy, and D. Satterthwaite. 1988. *Outside the large cities: Annotated bibliography and guide to the literature on small and intermediate urban centres in the third world.* London: International Institute for Environment and Development.

Block, S. 1999. Agriculture and economic growth in Ethiopia: Growth multipliers from a four-sector simulation model. *Agricultural Economics* 20: 241–252.

Block, S., and C. P. Timmer. 1994. Agriculture and economic growth: Conceptual issues and the Kenyan experience. Mimeo, Consulting Assistance on Economic Reform Project, U.S. Agency for International Development, Washington, D.C.

————. 1997. Agriculture and economic growth in Africa: Progress and issues. U.S. Agency for International Development / Bureau for Africa, Washington, D.C.

Block, S., and P. Webb. 2001. The dynamics of livelihood diversification in post-famine Ethiopia. *Food Policy* 26 (4): 333–350.

Bolnick, B., and E. R. Nelson. 1990. Evaluating the economic impact of a special credit program: KIK/KMKP in Indonesia. *Journal of Development Studies* 26 (2): 299–312.

Boomgard, J. J. 1988. Developing small business in Central Java: Reflections on the CJEDP experiment. Development Alternatives, Washington, D.C.

———. 1989. AID microenterprise stock-taking: Synthesis report. AID Evaluation Special Study 65. Washington, D.C.: Agency for International Development.

Boomgard, J. J., and K. J. Angell. 1994. Bank Rakyat Indonesia's Unit Desa system: Achievements and replicability. In *The new world of microenterprise finance: Building healthy financial institutions for the poor,* ed. M. Otero and E. Rhyne. West Hartford, Conn.: Kumarian.

Boomgard, J. J., S. P. Davies, S. Haggblade, and D. C. Mead. 1986. Subsector analysis: Its nature, conduct and potential contribution to small enterprise development. MSU International Development Papers Working Paper 26. East Lansing: Michigan State University.

———. 1992. A subsector approach to small enterprise promotion and research. *World Development* 20 (2): 199–212.

Boselie, D. 2002. Business case description: TOPS supply chain project, Thailand. KLICT International Agri Supply Chain Development Program, Agrichain Competence Center, Den Bosch, The Netherlands.

Botswana, Government of. 1976. *The rural income distribution survey in Botswana 1974/75.* Gaborone, Botswana: Central Statistics Office, Ministry of Finance and Development Planning.

Boughton, D., J. Staatz, and J. Shaffer. 1994. From pilot study to commodity subsector economics program: Institutionalizing a market-oriented approach to agricultural research in Mali. Department of Agricultural Economics Staff Paper 94-74. East Lansing: Michigan State University.

Boughton, D., E. Crawford, J. Howard, J. Oehmke, J. Shaffer, and J. Staatz. 1995. A strategic approach to agricultural research program planning in Sub-Saharan Africa. MSU International Development Working Paper 49. East Lansing: Michigan State University.

Bourgeois, R., and D. Herrera. 2000. *Actor-led change for efficient agrifood systems: Handbook of the participatory actor-based CADIAC approach.* Bogor, Indonesia: CGRPT Centre (Regional Coordination Center for Research and Development of Coarse Grains, Pulses, Roots and Tuber Crops in the Humid Tropics of Asia and the Pacific).

Bowman, M., and P. Reiling. 1990. Expanding the benefits: A sector/systems approach. Technoserve, Norwalk, Conn.

Bravo-Ortega, C., and D. Lederman. 2005. Agriculture and national welfare around the world: Causality and heterogeneity since 1960. Policy Research Working Paper 3499. Washington, D.C.: World Bank.

Brom, F. 2002. Experiencia Argentina: Relación entre los proveedores y los Supermercados. Paper presented at the 7th Biennial Congress of the Costa Rican Food Industry Chamber of Commerce, San Jose, Costa Rica.

Bromley, R. J. 1983. The urban road to rural development: Reflections on USAID's urban functions approach. *Environment and Planning* 15: 429–432.

Brown, J. 1994. *Agroindustrial investment and operations.* Washington, D.C.: World Bank.

Bryceson, D. F. 1996. Deagrarianization and rural employment in sub-Saharan Africa: A sectoral perspective. *World Development* 24 (1): 97–111.

———. 1997. De-agrarianisation in Sub-Saharan Africa: Acknowledging the inevitable. In *Farewell to farms: De-agrarianisation and employment in Africa,* ed. D. F. Bryceson and V. Jamal. Aldershot, England: Ashgate.

———. 1999. African rural labour, income diversification and livelihood approaches: A long-term development perspective. *Review of African Political Economy* 26 (80): 171–189.

———. 2002. The scramble in Africa: Reorienting rural livelihoods. *World Development* 30 (5): 725–739.

Bryceson, D. F., and V. Jamal. 1997. *Farewell to farms: Deagrarianisation and employment in Africa.* Aldershot, England: Ashgate.

Buckley, Graeme. 1997. Microfinance in Africa: Is it either the problem or the solution? *World Development* 25 (7): 1081–1093.

Budinich, V. 1993. ATI's strategic subsector approach: Classes of small producers and the value added chain. AT International, Washington, D.C.

Burger, K., D. Kameo, and H. Sandee. 2001. Clustering of small agro-processing firms in Indonesia. *International Food and Agribusiness Management Review* 2 (3/4): 289–299.

Burr, C. 2000. Grameen Village phone: Its current status and future prospects. Paper presented at the International Conference on Business Services for Small Enterprises in Asia: Developing Markets and Measuring Performance, Hanoi, Vietnam, April 3–6. <www.ilo.org/public/english/employment/ent/papers/grameen.htm> (accessed May 2004).

Byerlee, D. 1973. Indirect employment and income distribution effects of agricultural development strategies: A simulation approach applied to Nigeria. African Rural Employment Paper 9. East Lansing: Department of Agricultural Economics, Michigan State University.

Byerlee, D., and C. K. Eicher. 1974. Rural employment, migration and economic development: Theoretical issues and empirical evidence from Africa. In *Agricultural policy in developing countries,* ed. N. Islam. New York: Macmillan.

———. 1997. *Africa's emerging maize revolution.* Boulder, Colo.: Lynn Reinner.

Bylerlee, D., C. Eicher, C. Liedholm, and D. Spencer. 1977. Rural employment in tropical Africa: Summary of findings. African Rural Economy Working Paper 20. East Lansing: Michigan State University.

Cabal, M. 1995. Growth, appearance, and disappearance of micro and small enterprises in the Dominican Republic. Ph.D. dissertation, Department of Agricultural Economics, Michigan State University, East Lansing.

Cameroun, République Unie. 1976. *Recensement général de la population et de l'habitat d'Avril,* Vol. 1. Yaounde: Bureau Central du Recensement.

Cameroun, République du. 1992. *Deuxième recensement général de la population et de l'habitat du Cameroun: Resultats bruts,* Tome 1. Yaoundé: Institut National de la Statistique.

Canagarajah, S., C. Newman, and R. Bhattamishra. 2001. Nonfarm income, gender and inequality: Evidence from rural Ghana and Uganda. *Food Policy* 26: 405–420.

Carney, D., ed. 1998. *Sustainable rural livelihoods: What contribution can we make?* London: Department for International Development.

Carr, M. 1982. Appropriate technology and rural industrialization. Occasional Paper 1. London: Intermediate Technology Development Group.

———, ed. 1984. *Blacksmith, baker, roofing-sheet maker: Employment for rural women in developing countries.* London: Intermediate Technology Publications.

———, ed. 1988. *Sustainable industrial development: Seven case studies.* London: Intermediate Technology Publications.

———. 1996a. Case VI: Shea nut processing in Northern Ghana. In *Beyond credit: A subsector approach to promoting women's enterprises,* ed. M. A. Chen. Ottawa: Aga Khan Foundation.

———. 1996b. Cassava processing in Nigeria and West Africa. In *Beyond credit: A subsector approach to promoting women's enterprises,* ed. M. A. Chen. Ottawa: Aga Khan Foundation.

Carter, M. R., and K. D. Wiebe. 1990. Access to capital and its impact on agrarian structure and productivity in Kenya. *American Journal of Agricultural Economics* (December): 1146–1150.

CDASED. *See* Committee of Donor Agencies for Small Enterprise Development.

Ceglie, G., and M. Dini. 2000. Clusters and network development in developing countries. In *Business development services: A review of international experience,* ed. Jacob Levitsky. London: Intermediate Technology Development Group.

CGAP. *See* Consultative Group to Assist the Poorest.

Chadha, G. K. 1985. Agricultural growth and rural nonfarm activities: An analysis of Indian experience. In *Rural industrialization and nonfarm activities of Asian farmers,* ed. Y.-B. Choe and F.-C. Lo. Seoul: Korea Rural Economics Institute.

———. 1986. The off-farm economic structure of agriculturally growing regions: A study of Indian Punjab. In *Off-farm employment in the development of rural Asia,* ed. R. T. Shand, Vol. 2. Canberra: Australian National University.

———. 1993. Nonfarm sector in India's rural economy: Policy, performance and growth prospects. Visiting Research Fellow Monograph Series 220. Tokyo: Institute of Developing Economies.

———. 1996. The industrialization strategy and growth of rural industry in India. SAAT Working Paper. New Delhi: International Labour Organization.

———. 2003. Rural nonfarm sector in the Indian economy: Growth, challenges and future direction. Mimeo, International Food Policy Research Institute, Washington D.C.

Chase, J. 1997. Managing urban settlements in Brazil's agro-industrial frontier. *Third World Planning Review* 19: 2.

Cheema, G. S., and D. A. Rondinelli. 1983. *Decentralization and development: Policy implementation in developing countries.* Beverly Hills, Calif.: Sage.

Chen, M. A. 1996. *Beyond credit: A subsector approach to promoting women's enterprises.* Ottawa: Aga Khan Foundation.

Chen, X., and W. L. Parish. 1996. Urbanization in China: Reassessing an evolving model. In *The urban transformation of the developing world,* ed. J. Gugler. Oxford: Oxford University Press.

Chenery, H., and M. Syrquin. 1975. *Patterns of development: 1950–70.* New York: Oxford University Press.

Child, F. C., and H. Kaneda. 1975. Links to the green revolution: A study of small-scale agriculturally related industry in the Pakistan Punjab. *Economic Development and Cultural Change* 23 (2): 249–275.

China Resource Enterprises. 2002. Retailing strategies and execution plan, July 2002. <www.cre.com.hk> (accessed May 4, 2003).

Chinn, D. 1979. Rural poverty and the structure of farm household income in developing countries: Evidence from Taiwan. *Economic Development and Cultural Change* 27 (2): 283–302.

Choe, Y.-B., and F.-C. Lo, eds. 1985. *Rural industrialization and nonfarm activities of Asian farmers.* Seoul: Korea Rural Economics Institute.

Chowdhury, N. 2000. Information and communications technologies and IFPRI's mandate: A conceptual framework. Mimeo, International Food Policy Research Institute, Washington, D.C.

Chowdhury, N., and S. Haggblade. 2000. Evolving rice and wheat markets. In *Out of the shadow of famine: Evolving food markets and food policy in Bangladesh,* ed. R. Ahmed, S. Haggblade, and T. Chowdhury. Baltimore: The Johns Hopkins University Press.

Christen, R. P., E. Rhyne, R. C. Vogel, and C. McKean. 1995. Maximizing the outreach of microfinance: An analysis of successful microfinance programs. USAID Program and Operations Assessment Report 10. Washington, D.C.: U.S. Agency for International Development.

Chuta, E. J. 1989. A Nigerian study of firm dynamics. Mimeo, U.S. Agency for International Development, Washington, D.C.

Chuta, E., and C. Liedholm. 1979. Rural non-farm employment: A review of the state of the art. MSU Rural Development Paper 4. East Lansing: Department of Agricultural Economics, Michigan State University.

———. 1982. Employment growth and change in Sierra Leone small-scale industry, 1974–80. *International Labour Review* 121 (1): 101–113.

———. 1985. *Employment and growth in small-scale industry: Empirical evidence and policy assessment from Sierra Leone.* London: St. Martin's Press.

Clara, M., F. Russo, and M. Gulati. 2000. Cluster development and BDS promotion: UNIDO's experience in Indonesia. Paper presented at the International Conference Business Services for Small Enterprises in Asia: Developing Markets and Measuring Performance, Hanoi, Vietnam, April 3–6.

Cleave, J. H. 1974. *African farmers: Labour use in the development of small-holder agriculture.* New York: Praeger.

Cleaver, H. M. 1972. The contradictions of the green revolution. *American Economic Review* 72: 177–188.

Coase, R. H. 1937. The nature of the firm. *Economica* 16 (16): 386–405.

Coe, D., E. Helpman, and A. Hoffmaister. 1997. North-south R&D spillovers. *Economic Journal* 107 (January): 134–149.

Coleman, B. E. 1999. The impact of group lending in Northeast Thailand. *Journal of Development Economics* 60: 105–141.

Collier, P., and D. Lal. 1986. *Labour and poverty in Kenya 1900–1980.* Oxford: Clarendon.

Collier, P., S. Radwan, S. Wangwe, and A. Wagner. 1990. *Labour and poverty in rural Tanzania: Ujamaa and rural development in the United Republic of Tanzania.* Oxford: Clarendon.

Committee of Donor Agencies for Small Enterprise Development (CDASED). 1995. Micro and small enterprise finance: Guiding principles for selecting and supporting intermediaries. <www.ilo.org/public/english/employment/ent/papers/financgd.htm#d_1a> (accessed August 2002).

———. 1997. *Business development services for SMEs: Preliminary guideline for donor-funded interventions.* <www.ilo.org/images/empent/static/seed/donor/besprelimgui-en.pdf> (accessed August 2002).

———. 2001. Business development services for small enteprises: Guiding principles for donor intervention. <www.ilo.org/public/english/employment/ent/papers/guide.htm> (accessed August 2002).

Consultative Group to Assist the Poorest (CGAP). 1995. A policy framework for the Consultative Group to Assist the Poorest (CGAP): A microfinance program. <www.worldbank.org/html/cgap/policy.htm> (accessed June 2006).

Consultative Group to Assist the Poorest (CGAP) / World Bank. 2004. Good Practice Guidelines for Funders of Microfinance: Microfinance Consensus Guidelines. <www.cgap.org/docs/donorguide.pdf> (accessed April 2007).

Corral, L., and T. Reardon. 2001. Rural nonfarm incomes in Nicaragua. *World Development* 29 (3): 427–442.

Cortes, M., A. Berry, and A. Ishaq. 1987. *Success in small and medium-scale enterprises: The evidence from Colombia.* New York: Oxford University Press.

Creevey, L., ed. 1995. *To build or to destroy dreams? Impacts of development projects on poor women.* New York: United Nations Development Fund for Women.

Crow, B. 2001. *Markets class and social change: Trading networks and poverty in rural South Asia.* New York: Palgrave.

Dabalen, A., S. Paternostro, and G. Pierre. 2004. The returns to participation in the nonfarm sector in rural Rwanda. World Bank Policy Research Working Paper 3462, December. Washington, D.C.: World Bank.

Daley-Harris, S. 2005. *State of the micro-credit summit campaign report 2005.* Washington, D.C.: Microcredit Summit Campaign.

Daniels, L., and Y. Fisseha. 1992. Micro- and small-scale enterprises in Botswana: Results of a nationwide survey. GEMINI Technical Report 46. Washington, D.C.: Development Alternatives.

Daniels, L., and D. C. Mead. 1998. The contribution of small enterprises to household and national income in Kenya. *Economic Development and Cultural Change* (October): 45–71.

Daniels, L., and A. Ngwira. 1993. Results of a nationwide survey on micro, small and medium enterprises in Malawi. GEMINI Technical Report 53, January. Washington, D.C.: Development Alternatives.

Daniels, L., D. C. Mead, and M. Musinga. 1995. Employment and income in micro and small scale enterprises in Kenya: Results from a 1995 survey. GEMINI Technical Report 92. Washington, D.C.: Development Alternatives.

Darrow, K., and M. Saxenian. 1993. *Appropriate technology sourcebook.* Stanford, Calif.: Volunteers in Asia.

Darwent, D. F. 1969. Growth poles and growth centres in regional planning: A review. *Environment and Planning* 1: 5–32.

Da Silva, J. G., and M. Del Grossi. 2001. Rural nonfarm employment in Brazil: Patterns and evolution. *World Development* 29 (3): 443–453.

Datt, G., and M. Ravallion. 1994. Transfer benefits from public works employment: Evidence for rural India. *Economic Journal* 104 (November): 1346–1369.

———. 1997. Why have some Indian states done better than others at reducing rural poverty? *Economica* 65: 17–38.

———. 2002. Is India's economic growth leaving the poor behind? *Journal of Economic Perspectives* 16 (3): 89–108.

David, C. C., and R. L. Meyer. 1980. Measuring the farm level impact of agricultural loans. In *Borrowers and lenders: Rural financial markets and institutions in developing countries,* ed. J. Howell. London: Overseas Development Institute.

David, C. C., and K. Otsuka. 1994. *Modern rice technology and income distribution in Asia.* Boulder, Colo.: Lynne Rienner.

David, P. A. 1975. *Technical choice, innovation, and economic growth.* Cambridge: Cambridge University Press.

Davies, S. P. 1988. A case study of the Central Java Enterprise Development Project (CJEDP) Rattan Furniture Subproject in Transgan, Central Java. Fort Collins: Colorado State University.

Davies, S. 1993. *Versatile livelihoods: Strategic adaptation to food insecurity in the Malian Sahel.* Brighton, England: Institute of Development Studies, Sussex University.

Davies, S., D. C. Mead, and J. L. Seale. 1992. Small manufacturing enterprises in Egypt. *Economic Development and Cultural Change* 40 (2): 381–412.

Davis, J., and D. Pearce. 2000. The non-agricultural rural sector in Central and Eastern Europe: Characteristics, importance and policies. Natural Resources Institute Paper 2631. Chatham Maritime, Kent: Natural Resources Institute.

Dawson, J. 1990. The wider context: The importance of the macroenvironment for small enterprise development. *Small Enterprise Development* 1 (3): 39–46.

———. 2002. Empowering Ghana's cereal producers in the marketplace. In *Building businesses with small producers: Successful business development services in Africa, Asia and Latin America,* ed. S. Kapila and D. Mead. Ottawa: International Development Research Center.

Dawson, J., with A. Jeans. 1997. *Looking beyond credit: Business development services and the promotion of innovation among small producers.* Rugby, England: Intermediated Technology Development Group.

Dawson, J., E. Hyman, S. Kapila, and D. Mead. 2000. Methodologies for the design and delivery of high impact business development services (BDS) for small producers. Ottawa: International Development Research Center.

De Alcantara, C. H. 1993. *Real markets: Social and political issues of food policy reform.* London: Frank Cass.

Deb, N., and M. Hossain. 1984. Demand for rural industries products in Bangladesh. *Bangladesh Development Studies* 12: 81–99.

De Brauw, A., J. Huang, S. Rozelle, L. Zhang, and Y. Zhang. 2002. The evolution of China's rural labor markets during the reform. *Journal of Comparative Economics* 30: 329–353.

De Crombrugghe, A., and J. C. Montes. 2000. Global experience in industrial subcontracting and partnerships. In *Business development services: A review of international experience,* ed. J. Levitsky. London: Intermediate Technology Publications.

De Ferranti, D., G. E. Perry, W. Foster, D. Lederman, and A. Valdes. 2005. *Beyond the city: The rural contribution to development.* Washington, D.C.: World Bank.

De Franco, M., and R. Godoy. 1993. Potato-led growth: The macroeconomic effects of technological innovations in Bolivian agriculture. *Journal of Development Studies* 29 (3): 561–587.

De Haan, A. 1999. Livelihoods and poverty: The role of migration; A critical review of the migration literature. *Journal of Development Studies* 36 (2): 1–47.

De Haan, A., and B. Rogaly. 2002. Labor mobility and rural society. *Journal of Development Studies* 38 (5): 1–14.

Deininger, K., and P. Olinto. 2001. Rural nonfarm employment and income diversification in Colombia. *World Development* 29 (3): 455–465.

Deininger, K., S. Jin, B. Adenew, G. Selassie, and B. Nega. 2003. *Tenure security and land-related investment: Evidence from Ethiopia.* World Bank Policy Research Working Paper 2991. Washington, D.C.: World Bank.

De Janvry, A. 1981. *The agrarian question and reformism in Latin America.* Baltimore: The Johns Hopkins University Press.

———. 1994. Farm-nonfarm synergies in Africa: discussion. *American Journal of Agricultural Economics* 76 (5): 1183–1185.

De Janvry, A., and E. Sadoulet. 1993. Rural development in Latin America: Relinking poverty reduction to growth. In *Including the poor,* ed. M. Lipton and J. van der Gaag. Washington, D.C.: World Bank.

———. 2001. Income strategies among rural households in Mexico: The role of off-farm activities. *World Development* 29 (3): 467–480.

———. 2002. World poverty and the role of agricultural technology: Direct and indirect effects. *Journal of Development Studies* 38 (4): 1–26.

De Janvry, A., E. Sadoulet, and L. Wilcox. 1986. Rural labour in Latin America. World Employment Programme Research Working Paper WEP 10-6/WP79. Geneva: World Employment Programme.

De Janvry, A., G. Gordillo, J. P. Platteau, and E. Sadoulet, eds. 2001. *Access to land, rural poverty, and public action.* Oxford: Oxford University Press.

Delgado, C. L., J. Hopkins, and V. Kelly. 1998. Agricultural growth linkages in Sub-Saharan Africa. IFPRI Research Report 107. Washington, D.C.: International Food Policy Research Institute.

Delgado, C., P. Hazell, J. Hopkins, and V. Kelly. 1994. Promoting intersectoral growth linkages in rural Africa through agricultural technology and policy reform. *American Journal of Agricultural Economics* 76 (5): 1166–1171.

Del Grossi, M. E., and J. G. Da Silva. 2001. Fabrica do agricultor, Paraná. Mimeo, Universidade de Campinas, Brazil.

Demombynes, G., C. Elbers, J. Lanjouw, P. Lanjouw, J. Mistiaen, and B. Ozler. 2004. Producing a better geographic profile of poverty: Methodology and evidence from three developing countries. In *Growth, inequality and poverty,* ed. A. Shorrocks and R. van der Hoeven. Oxford: Oxford University Press.

Dercon, S. 2002. Income risk, coping strategies, and safety nets. *World Bank Research Observer* 17 (2): 141–166

Dercon, S., and P. Krishnan. 1996. Income portfolios in rural Ethiopia and Tanzania: Choices and constraints. *Journal of Development Studies* 32 (6): 850–875.

Deshpande, S., and L. K. Deshpande. 1985. Census of 1981 and the structure of employment. *Economic and Political Weekly* (20): 969–973.

De Soto, H. 1989. *The other path: The invisible revolution in the third world.* New York: Harper and Row.

Dev, S. Mahendra. 2002. Pro-poor growth in India: What do we know about the employment effects of growth, 1980–2000? Overseas Development Institute (ODI) Discussion Paper 161. London: ODI.

Development Finance Forum. 2004. Capital plus: The challenge of development in development finance institutions: A practitioner perspective. Position paper, Development Finance Forum, Chicago.

D'Haese, M., and G. Van Huylenbroeck. 2005. The rise of supermarkets and changing expenditure patterns of poor rural households: Case study in the Transkei area, South Africa. *Food Policy* 30 (1): 97–113.

Dichter, T. W. 1986. Demystifying policy dialogue: How private voluntary organizations can have an impact on host country policies. Technoserve, Norwalk, Conn.

———. 1988. A commodity sector approach to small enterprise development: A paradoxical new synthesis. *VITA News,* January: 8–20.

———. 2006. Hope and hype: The worrisome state of the microcredit movement. In *eAfrica.* Bramfontein, South Africa: South African Institute of International Affairs. <www.siaa.org.za> (accessed May 2006).

Dickie, M., and S. Gerking. 1987. Interregional wage differentials: An equilibrium perspective. *Journal of Regional Science* 27 (4): 571–586.

Dione, J. 1989. Informing food security policy in Mali: Interactions between technology, institutions, and market reforms. Ph.D. dissertation, Michigan State University, East Lansing.

Dirven, M. 2001. Dairy sector clusters in Latin America. *International Food and Agribusiness Review* 2 (3): 301–313.

Dixit, A. 1993. In honor of Paul Krugman: Winner of the John Bates Clark Medal. *Journal of Economic Perspectives* 7 (2): 173–188.

Dixit, A. K., and J. E. Stiglitz. 1977. Monopolistic competition and optimum product diversity. *American Economic Review* 67 (3): 297–308.

Donaldson, G. 1993. Experience with World Bank funded rural development. *Review of Marketing and Agricultural Economics* 16 (2): 277–288.

Dorosh, P. A., and S. Haggblade. 1993. Agriculture-led growth: Foodgrains versus export crops in Madagascar. *Agricultural Economics* 9: 165–180.

———. 2003. Growth linkages, price effects and income distribution in Sub-Saharan Africa. *Journal of African Economies* 12 (2): 207–235.

Dorosh, P. A., M. K. Niazi, and H. Nazli. 2003. Distributional impacts of agricultural growth in Pakistan: A multiplier analysis. *Pakistan Development Review* 42 (3): 249–275.

Dorward, A., J. Kydd, and C. Poulton, eds. 1998. *Smallholder cash crop production under market liberalization: A new institutional economics perspective.* Wallingford, England: CAB International.

Dostie, B., J. Randriamamonjy, and L. Rabenasolo. 1999. La filière manioc: Amortisseur oublie des vulnerables. Antananarivo, Madagascar: Institut National de la Statistique.

Dowds, C. M., and J. Hinojosa. 1999. *An introductory guide to the subsector approach to community and economic development.* Washington, D.C.: National Council of La Raza.

Downing, J., and L. Daniels. 1992. The growth and dynamics of women entrepreneurs in Southern Africa. GEMINI Technical Report 47. Washington, D.C.: Development Alternatives.

Drèze, J. P. 1990. Famine prevention in India. In *The political economy of hunger,* ed. J. P. Drèze and A. K. Sen. 3 vols. Oxford, England: Clarendon.

Drèze, J. P., and A. K. Sen. 2002. *India: Development and participation.* Oxford: Oxford University Press.

Drèze, J. P., and P. V. Srinivasan. 1997. Widowhood and poverty in rural India: Some inferences from household survey data. *Journal of Development Economics* 54 (2): 217–234.

Dries, L., and T. Reardon. 2005. Central and Eastern Europe: Impact of food retail investments on the food chain. Report Series 6, February. London: Food and Agriculture Organization Investment Center–EBRD Cooperation Program.

Dries, L., T. Reardon, and J. Swinnen. 2004. The rapid rise of supermarkets in Central and Eastern Europe: Implications for the agrifood sector and rural development. *Development Policy Review* 22 (5): 525–556.

Dries, L., T. Reardon, and E. Van Kerckhove. 2004. The economic and transitional impact of food retail investments: Case-study of the Czech Republic and the Russian Federation. Report for EBRD/FAO, September.

Duff, B. 1987. Changes in small farm paddy threshing technology in Thailand and the Philippines. In *Macro-policies for appropriate technology in developing countries,* ed. F. Stewart. Boulder, Colo.: Westview.

Dunn, E. 2002. Research strategy for the AIMS core impact assessments. AIMS Project Report. Washington, D.C.: U.S. Agency for International Development.

Dvorak, J. C. 2000. Cutting out the middleman. *PC Magazine* (March 7): 99.

East Pakistan Small Industries Corporation. 1964. *Survey of small industries in East Pakistan.* Dacca: East Pakistan Small Industries Corporation.

Eaton, B. C., and R. G. Lipsey. 1976. The non-uniqueness of equilibrium in the Löschian location model. *American Economic Review* 66 (1): 77–93.

Ebony Consulting International (ECI). 2001a. The Kenyan dairy subsector: A study for DfID Kenya. Nairobi: Department for International Development.

———. 2001b. The Kenyan green bean subsector: A report of DfID Kenya. Nairobi: Department for International Development.

Echeverri, R. 1999. Empleo e ingreso rurales no agrícolas en Colombia. Paper presented at the Seminario Latinoamericano sobre Desarrollo del Empleo Rural No Agrícola, Santiago, Chile, September. Sponsored by IADB-FAO-ECLAC-RIMISP.

ECI. *See* Ebony Consulting International.

Economic and Political Weekly. 2004. Doubling rural credit, but how? Editorial, *Economic and Political Weekly,* June 12.

Economic and Social Commission for Asia and the Pacific (ESCAP) and the Asian Development Bank Institute (ADBI). 2004. *Building e-community centers for rural development: Report of a regional workshop* (Bali, Indonesia, 8–14 December). Bangkok: United Nations Publications.

Edesess, M., and P. Polak. 1993. *Market-driven product development as a model for AID-assisted international development.* Lakewood, Colo.: International Development Enterprises.

Edwards, S. 1998. Openness, productivity and growth: What do we really know? *Economic Journal* 108: 383–398.

Egypt, Arab Republic of. 1996. *Statistical yearbook 1952–1994.* Cairo: Central Agency for Public Mobilization and Statistics.

Elbers, C., and P. Lanjouw. 2001. Intersectoral transfer, growth and inequality in rural Ecuador. *World Development* 29 (3): 481–496.

Ellis, F. 1998. Household strategies and rural livelihood diversification. *Journal of Development Studies* 35 (1): 1–38.

———. 1999. Non-farm employment in Tanzania: A partial case study. Natural Resources Institute, Chatham, England.

———. 2000. *Rural livelihoods and diversity in developing countries.* Oxford: Oxford University Press.

———. 2005. Small-farms, livelihood diversification and rural-urban transitions: Strategic issues in Sub-Saharan Africa. Paper presented at the Research Workshop on the Future of Small Farms, organized by IFPRI, Imperial College, and ODI, Wye, England, June.

Ellis, F., and H. A. Freeman. 2004. Rural livelihoods and poverty reduction strategies in four African countries. *Journal of Development Studies* 40 (4): 1–30.

Enikolopov, R., and E. Zhuravskaya. 2003. Decentralization and political institutions. Research Discussion Paper 3857. London: Centre for Economic Policy Research.

Enke, S. 1962. Industrialization through greater productivity in agriculture. *Review of Economics and Statistics* 44: 88–91.

EnterpriseWorks Worldwide. 1997. *1997 Portfolio Review.* Washington, D.C.: EnterpriseWorks Worldwide.

ESCAP. *See* Economic and Social Commission for Asia and the Pacific.

Escobal, J. 2001. The determinants of nonfarm income distribution in rural Peru. *World Development* 29 (3): 497–508.

———. 2005. The role of public infrastructure in market development in rural Peru. Ph.D. dissertation, University of Wageningen, Wageningen, The Netherlands.

Escobal, J., V. Agreda, and T. Reardon. 2000. Institutional change and agroindustrialization on the Peruvian coast: Innovations, impacts, and implications. *Agricultural Economics* 23 (3): 267–278.

Escobar, G., T. Reardon, and J. A. Berdegué. 2001. Best practices and strategies for promoting non farm employment creation in rural development in Latin America: Synthesis of six case studies. RIMISP report to DFID, June.

Estache, A., and S. Sinha. 1995. Does decentralization increase spending on public infrastructure? Policy Research Working Paper 1457. Washington, D.C.: World Bank.

Estudillo, J. P., and K. Otsuka. 1999. Green revolution, human capital and off-farm employment: Changing sources of income among farm households in Central Luzon, 1966–1994. *Economic Development and Cultural Change* 47 (3): 497–523.

Estudillo, J. P, A. R. Quisumbing, and K. Otsuka. 2001. Income distribution in rice-growing villages during the post–green revolution periods: The Philippine Case, 1985 and 1998. *Agricultural Economics* 25: 71–84.

Ethiopia, Federal Democratic Republic of. 1998. *The 1994 population and housing census of Ethiopia: Results at country level.* Addis Ababa: Central Statistical Authority, Office of Population and Housing Census Commission.

Evans, H. E. 1986. Rural trade and production centres: Towards a strategy for implementation. Discussion Paper 6. Nairobi: Ministry of National Planning and Development.

———. 1990. Rural-urban linkages and structural transformation. Infrastructure and Urban Development Department Report INU 71. Washington, D.C.: World Bank.

———. 1992. A virtuous circle model of rural-urban development: Evidence from Kenya. *Journal of Development Studies* 28 (4): 640–667.

———. 2001. Regional development through rural-urban linkages: The PARUL program in Indonesia. In *New regional development paradigms,* ed. W. B. Stohr, J. S. Edralin, and D. Mani, Vol. 3, Chap. 6. Westport, Conn.: Greenwood.

———. 2004. Policy implications for RNFEs: Lessons from the PARUL project in Indonesia. In *The Indonesian rural economy: Mobility, work and enterprise,* ed. T. R. Leinbach, Chap. 11. Singapore: Institute of Southeast Asian Studies.

Evans, H., and P. Ngau. 1991. Rural-urban relations, household income diversification and agricultural productivity. *Development and Change* 22: 519–545.

Evans, H., M. Cullen, and P. Little. 1988. Rural-urban exchange in the Kismayo region of Somalia. International Development Programs, Clark University, Worcester, Mass.

Evenson, R. E. 1986. Infrastructure, output supply and input demand in the Philippines agriculture. *Journal of Philippine Development* 13 (23): 62–76.

Evenson, R. E., and D. Gollin. 2003. *Crop variety improvement and its effect on productivity.* Wallingford, England: CABI.

Evenson, R. E., and L. E. Westphal. 1995. Technological change and technological strategy. In *Handbook of development economics,* ed. J. Behrman and T. N. Srinivasan, Vol. IIIA. Amsterdam: Elsevier.

Fabella, R. V. 1985. Rural industry and modernization. In *Development and diversification of rural industries in Asia,* ed. S. Mukhopadhyay and C. P. Lim. Kuala Lumpur: Asian and Pacific Development Centre.

———. 1987. Rural manufacturing employment in the Philippines: Contributions and determinants. In *Rural industrialization and employment in Asia,* ed. R. Islam. New Delhi: International Labour Organisation Asian Employment Programme.

Fafchamps, M., and F. Shilpi. 2003. The spatial division of labor in Nepal. *Journal of Development Studies* 39 (6): 23–66.

Faiguenbaum, S. 2001. El programa de Turismo rural de INDAP: Santiago, Chile: RIMISP–Latin American Center for Rural Development.

Faiguenbaum, S., J. A. Berdegué, and T. Reardon. 2002. The rapid rise of supermarkets in Chile and its effects on the dairy, vegetable and beef chains. *Development Policy Review* 20 (4): 371–388.

Falcon, W. P. 1970. The green revolution: Generations of problems. *American Journal of Agricultural Economics* 52 (December): 698–710.

Fan, S., P. Hazell, and S. Thorat. 1999. Linkages between government spending, growth and poverty in rural India. Research Report 110. Washington, D.C.: International Food Policy Research Institute.

Fan, S., X. Zhang, and S. Robinson. 2003. Structural change and economic growth in China. *Review of Development Economics* 7 (3): 360–377.

Fan, S., L. Zhang, and X. Zhang. 2002. Growth, inequality and poverty in rural China: The role of public investments. Research Report 125. Washington, D.C.: International Food Policy Research Institute.

———. 2004. Reform, investment and poverty in rural China. *Economic Development and Cultural Change* 52 (2): 395–422.

FAO. *See* Food and Agriculture Organization.

Farina, E. M. M. Q., ed. 1997. *Estudos de Caso Em Agribusiness Focalizando As Seguintes Empresas: Moinho Pacifico, Illycaffe, Cocamar, Sadia, Iochpe-Maxion, Norpac.* São Paulo: Pioneira.

Farina, E., and T. Reardon. 2000. Agrifood grades and standards in the extended MERCOSUR: Conditioners and effects in the agrifood system. *American Journal of Agricultural Economics* 82 (5): 1170–1176.

Farina, E. M. M. Q., G. E. Gutman, P. J. Lavarello, R. Nunes, and T. Reardon. 2005. Private and public milk standards in Argentina and Brazil. *Food Policy* 30 (3): 302–315.

Farrell, G., and S. Thirion. 2001. Global competitiveness of rural areas: Creating a territorial development strategy in the light of the LEADER experience. Rural Innovation Dossier 6, Part 5. Brussels: LEADER European Observatory.

Fellows, P., and A. Hampton, eds. 1992. *Small-scale food processing: A guide to appropriate equipment.* London: Intermediate Technology Publications.

Fernandes, M., C. Gadi, A. Khanna, P. Mitra, and S. Narayanswamy. 2000. India's retailing comes of age. *McKinsey Quarterly* 4: 95–102.

Ferreira, F. H. G., and P. Lanjouw. 2001. Rural nonfarm activities and poverty in the Brazilian northeast. *World Development* 29 (3): 509–528.

Ferreira, F. G., P. Lanjouw, and M. Neri. 2003. A new poverty profile for Brazil using multiple data sources. *Revista Brasileira de Economia* 57 (1): 57–92.

Fields, G. S., and J. Leary. 1998. Economic and demographic aspects of Taiwan's rising family composition. In *The economics and political economy of comparative development into the 21st century,* ed. G. Ranis, S.-C. Hu, and Y.-P. Chu. London: Edward Elgar.

Fisher, T., and M. S. Sriram. 2002. *Beyond micro-credit: Putting development back into micro-finance.* New Delhi: Vistaar.

Fisher, T., V. Mahajan, and A. Singha. 1997. *The forgotten sector: Non-farm employment and enterprises in rural India.* London: Intermediate Technology Publications.

Fishlow, A. 1972. Brazilian size distribution of income. *American Economic Review* 62: 158–172.

Fisseha, Y. 1985. The contribution of small-scale forest-based processing enterprises to rural non-farm employment and income in selected developing countries. Michigan State University, East Lansing.

———. 1991. Small-scale enterprises in Lesotho: Summary of a country-wide survey. GEMINI Technical Report 14. Washington, D.C.: Development Alternatives.

Fisseha, Y., and M. A. McPherson. 1991. A countrywide study of small-scale enterprises in Swaziland. GEMINI Technical Report 24. Washington, D.C.: Development Alternatives.

Flores, L., and T. Reardon. 2006. Supermarkets, new-generation wholesalers, farmers organizations, contract farming, and lettuce in Guatemala: Participation by and effects on small farmers. Department of Agricultural Economics Staff Paper 2006–07. East Lansing: Michigan State University.

Fluitman, F. 1983. The socio-economic impact of rural electrification in developing countries: A review of evidence. World Employment Programme Working Paper WEP 2-22/WP 126. Geneva: International Labour Office.

Foeken, D. 1997. Urban trajectories in rural livelihood strategies: Household employment patterns in Kenya's Coast Province. In *Farewell to farms: De-agrarianisation and employment in Africa,* ed. D. F. Bryceson and V. Jamal. Aldershot, England: Ashgate.

Food and Agriculture Organization (FAO). 1998. *The state of food and agriculture,* Part 3, *Rural nonfarm income in developing countries.* Rome: FAO.

Foster, A. D., and M. R. Rosenzweig. 2004. Agricultural productivity growth, rural economic diversity and economic reforms: India, 1970–2000. *Economic Development and Cultural Change* 52 (3): 509–542.

Francis, A. J., and D. S. Mansell. 1988. *Appropriate engineering technology for developing countries*. Blackburn, Australia: Research Publications.

Francis, E., and J. Hoddinott. 1993. Migration and differentiation in Western Kenya: A tale of two sub-locations. *Journal of Development Studies* 30 (1): 115–145.

Freeman, D. B., and G. B. Norcliffe. 1985. Rural enterprise in Kenya: Development and spatial organization of the nonfarm sector. Research Paper 214. Chicago: Department of Geography, University of Chicago.

Friedmann, J. 1966. *Regional development policy: A case study of Venezuela*. Cambridge, Mass.: MIT Press.

———. 1973. *Urbanization, planning, and national development policy*. Beverly Hills, Calif.: Sage.

———. 1975. Regional development planning: The progress of a decade. In *Regional policy*, ed. J. Friedmann. Cambridge, Mass.: MIT Press.

Frischman, A. 1988. The survival and disappearance of small scale enterprises in urban Kano, 1973–1980. Draft paper, Hobart and William Smith Colleges, New York.

Fujita, M. 1988. A monopolistic competition model of spatial agglomeration: Differentiated product approach. *Regional Science and Urban Economics* 18 (1): 87–124.

———. 1993. Monopolistic competition and urban systems. *European Economic Review* 37 (2/3): 308–316.

Fujita, M., and P. Krugman. 1995. When is the economy monocentric? Von Thunen and Chamberlain unified. *Regional Science and Urban Economics* 25 (4): 505–528.

Fujita, M., and T. Mori. 1998. On the dynamics of frontier economies: Endogenous growth of the self-organization of a dissipative system? *Annals of Regional Science* 32 (1): 39–62.

Gabre-Madhin, E. Z., and T. Reardon. 1989. The importance and determinants of women's non-agricultural income strategies in rural Burkina Faso. Select Paper, 1989 AAEA Meetings. Abstract. *American Journal of Agricultural Economics* (December): 1343.

Gaile, G. L. 1992. Improving rural-urban linkages through small town market-based development. *Third World Planning Review* 14 (2): 131–148.

Gaile, G. L., and J. Foster. 1996. Review of methodological approaches to the study of the impact of microenterprise credit programs. Assessing the Impact of Microenterprise Services (AIMS) Working Paper. Washington, D.C.: Management Systems International.

Gamser, M., H. Appleton, and N. Carter. 1990. *Tinker, tiller, technical change*. London: Intermediate Technology Publications.

Gereffi, G., and R. Kaplinsky, eds. 2001. The value of value chains. *IDS Bulletin* 32 (3): 1–136.

Gibb, A. 1974. Agricultural modernization, non-farm employment and low level urbanization: A case study of a Central Luzon sub-region. Ph.D. dissertation, University of Michigan, Ann Arbor.

———. 1984. Tertiary urbanization: The agricultural market centre as a consumption-related phenomenon. *Regional Development Dialogue* 5 (1): 110–133.

Gilbert, A. 1992. Urban and regional systems: A suitable case for treatment? In *Cities, poverty and development*, 2nd ed., ed. A. Gilbert and J. Gugler. Oxford: Oxford University Press.

Giovannucci, D., ed. 2001. *World Bank guide to developing agricultural markets and agro-enterprises.* <www.worldbank.org/essd/essd/nsf/agroenterprise> (accessed December 2002).

Giovannucci, D., and T. Reardon. 2001. Understanding grades and standards and how to apply them. *World Bank guide to developing agricultural markets and agro-enterprises.* <www.worldbank.org/essd/essd/nsf/agroenterprise/grade_std> (accessed May 2002).

Giuliani, E., C. Pietrobelli, and R. Rabellotti. 2005. Upgrading in global value chains: Lessons from Latin American clusters. *World Development* 33 (4): 549–573.

Goldberg, N. 2005. *Measuring the impact of microfinance: Taking stock of what we know.* Washington, D.C.: Grameen Foundation USA.

Goldberg, R. A. 1968. *Agribusiness coordination: A systems approach to the wheat, soybean and Florida orange economies.* Boston: Harvard University Graduate School of Business Administration.

———. 1974. *Agribusiness management for developing countries: Latin America.* Cambridge, Mass.: Ballinger.

Goldmark, L., S. Berte, and S. Campos. 1997. Preliminary survey results and case studies on business development services for microenterprise. Washington, D.C.: Interamerican Development Bank.

Goldmark, S., and J. Rosengard. 1983. Credit to Indonesian entrepreneurs: An assessment of the Badan Kredit Kecamatan Program. Development Alternatives, Washington, D.C.

Goldmark, S., T. Mooney, and J. Rosengard. 1982. Aid to entrepreneurs: An evaluation of the Partnership for Productivity project in Upper Volta. Paper, Development Alternatives, Washington, D.C.

Goletti, F. 2005. Agricultural commercialization, value chains and poverty reduction. Making Markets Work Better for the Poor Discussion Paper 7. Hanoi: Asian Development Bank.

Gonzalez-Vega, C., G. Chalmers, R. Quiros, and J. Rodriquez-Meza. 2006. Hortifruti in Central America: A case study about the influences of supermarkets on the development and evolution of creditworthiness among small and medium agricultural producers. Working Paper. Department of Agricultural, Environmental and Development Economics, Ohio State University, Columbus.

Gordon, A., and C. Craig. 2001. Rural nonfarm activities and poverty alleviation in Sub-Saharan Africa. Policy Series 14. Natural Resources Institute, University of Greenwich, Greenwich, England.

Grabowski, R. 1979. The implications of an induced innovation model. *Economic Development and Cultural Change* 27: 723–734.

Grant, W. 1992a. The role of private sector advocacy groups in the Sahel. GEMINI Technical Report 32. Bethesda, Md.: Development Alternatives.

———. 1992b. Skins and hides in four countries in Africa: The potential role for micro- and small-scale enterprise development. GEMINI Technical Report 50. Bethesda, Md.: Development Alternatives.

———. 1993. A review of donor-funded projects in support of micro and small-scale enterprises in West Africa. GEMINI Technical Report 54. Bethesda, Md.: Development Alternatives.

Grant, W., K. Aldridge, J. Bell, M. Keita, A. Duval, and S. Haggblade. 1990. Mali micro-enterprise sector assessment and strategy. 2 vols. GEMINI Technical Report 20. Bethesda, Md.: Development Alternatives.

Grant, W., M. Gamser, J. Herne, K. McKay, A. Sow, and S. J.-M. Tapsoba. 1991. Burkina Faso microenterprise sector assessment and strategy. 2 vol. GEMINI Technical Report 18. Bethesda, Md.: Development Alternatives.

Grierson, J. P., D. C. Mead, and E. Kakore. 2000. Business linkages in Zimbabwe: The Manicaland project. In *Business development services: A review of international experience,* ed. J. Levitsky. London: Intermediate Technology Publications.

Grierson, J. P., D. C. Mead, and S. Moyo. 1997. Business linkages in Zimbabwe: Helping to shape win-win economic structure. *Development in Practice* 7 (3): 305–307.

Griffin, K. 1974. *The political economy of agrarian change: An essay on the green revolution.* Cambridge, Mass.: Harvard University Press.

Grosh, B., and G. Somolekae. 1996. Mighty oaks from little acorns: Can microenterprise serve as the seedbed of industrialization? *World Development* 24 (12): 1879–1890.

Grossman, G., and E. Helpman. 1992. *Innovation and growth in the global economy.* Cambridge, Mass.: MIT Press.

Grown, C., and J. Sebstad. 1989. Introduction: Toward a wider perspective on women's employment. *World Development* 17 (7): 937–952.

Guatemala. 1981. *Censos nacionales de 1981: IX censo de poblacion.* Guatemala City: Instituto Nacional de Estadistica.

Gutman, G. E. 1999. Desregulacion, apertura commercial y reestructuracion industrial: La industria lacteal en argentina en la decada de los noventa. In *La desregulación de los mercados: Paradigmas e inequidades de las politicas del neoliberalismo,* ed. D. Aspiazu, G. E. Gutman, and A. Vispo. Buenos Aires: Grupo Editorial Norma, S.A.

———. 2002. Impacts of the rapid rise of supermarkets on the dairy products supply chains in Argentina. *Development Policy Review* 4: 409–427.

Habtu, Y. 1997. Farmers without land: The return of landlessness to rural Ethiopia. In *Farewell to farms: Deagrarianisation and employment in Africa,* ed. D. F. Bryceson and V. Jamal. Aldershot, England: Ashgate.

Haggblade, S. 1982. *Rural industrial officer's handbook.* Gaborone: Ministry of Commerce and Industry.

———. 1987. Vertical considerations in choice-of-technique studies: Evidence from Africa's indigenous beer industry. *Economic Development and Cultural Change* 35 (4): 723–742.

———. 1989. A review of Rwanda's textile clothing subsector. Employment and Enterprise Policy Analysis Discussion Paper 24. Cambridge, Mass.: Harvard Institute for International Development.

———. 1992. The Shebeen queen and the evolution of Botswana's sorghum beer industry. In *Liquor and labor in southern Africa,* ed. J. Crush and C. Ambler. Athens: Ohio University Press.

———. 1995. Promoting rural industrial linkages within agrarian economies for rural poverty reduction. Vienna: United Nations Industrial Development Organization.

Haggblade, S., and M. S. Gamser. 1991. A field manual for subsector practitioners. GEMINI Tools for Microenterprise Programs: Nonfinancial Assistance Section. Washington, D.C.: Development Alternatives.

Haggblade, S., and P. Hazell. 1989. Agricultural technology and farm-nonfarm growth linkages. *Agricultural Economics* 3: 345–364.

Haggblade, S., and W. H. Holzapfel. 1989. Industrialization of Africa's indigenous beer brewing. In *Industrialization of indigenous fermented foods,* ed. K. H. Steinkraus. New York: Marcel Dekker.

Haggblade, S., and C. Liedholm. 1991. Agriculture, rural labor markets and the evolution of the rural nonfarm economy. In *Sustainable agricultural development: The role of international cooperation,* ed. G. H. Peters and B. S. Stanton. London: Dartmouth.

Haggblade, S., with N. Minot. 1987. Opportunities for enhancing performance in Rwanda's alcoholic beverage subsector. Kigali, Rwanda: Ministry of Finance and Economy and U.S. Agency for International Development.

Haggblade, S., and N. Ritchie. 1992. Opportunities for intervention in Thailand's silk subsector. GEMINI Working Paper 27. Bethesda, Md.: Development Alternatives.

Haggblade, S., J. Hammer, and P. Hazell. 1991. Modeling agricultural growth multipliers. *American Journal of Agricultural Economics* 73 (2): 361–374.

Haggblade, S., P. Hazell, and J. Brown. 1987. Farm-nonfarm linkages in rural Sub-Saharan Africa: Empirical evidence and policy implications. Agriculture and Rural Development Department Discussion Paper ARU 67. Washington, D.C.: World Bank.

———. 1989. Farm-nonfarm linkages in rural Sub-Saharan Africa. *World Development* 17 (8): 1173–1201.

Haggblade, S., P. Hazell, and T. Reardon. 2002. Strategies for stimulating poverty–alleviating growth in the rural nonfarm economy in developing countries. EPTD Discussion Paper 92. Washington D.C.: International Food Policy Research Institute.

Haggblade, S., C. Liedholm, and D. Mead. 1986. The effect of policy and policy reform on non-agricultural enterprises and employment in developing countries: A review of past experiences. MSU International Development Working Paper 27. East Lansing: Department of Agricultural Economics, Michigan State University.

Hallberg, K. 2001. A market-oriented strategy for small- and medium-scale enterprises. IFC Discussion Paper 40. Washington, D.C.: World Bank.

Hansen, N. M. 1967. Development pole theory in a regional context. *Kyklos* 20: 709–727.

———. 1981. Development from above: The center-down development paradigm. In *Development from above or below?* ed. W. B. Stohr and D. R. Fraser Taylor. Chichester, England: John Wiley and Sons.

———. 1992. The location-allocation versus functional integration debate: An assessment in terms of linkage effects. *International Regional Science Review* 14 (3): 299–305.

Hanson, G. H. 1998. Market potential, increasing returns and geographic concentration. Working Paper 6429. Cambridge, Mass.: National Bureau of Economic Research.

Hardoy, J. E., and D. Satterthwaite. 1986. *Small and intermediate urban centres: Their role in national and regional development in the third world.* Boulder, Colo.: Westview.

Harper, M. 1977. *Consultancy for small business.* London: Intermediate Technology Development Group.

———. 1979. The evaluation of extension for small-scale enterprises. Mimeo, Industrial Development and Finance Department, World Bank, Washington, D.C.

———. 1984. *Small business in the third world.* Chichester, England: John Wiley and Sons.

————. 1988. Training and technical assistance for microenterprises. Paper presented at the World Conference on Support for Microenterprises, Washington, D.C., June 6–9. Washington, D.C.: U.S. Agency for International Development, Inter-American Development Bank and World Bank.

Harper, M., and G. Finnegan. 1998. *Value for money? Impact of small enterprise development.* New Delhi: Oxford and IBH.

Harris, C. D. 1954. The market as a factor in the localization of industry in the United States. *Annals of the American Geographers* 44: 315–348.

Harrison, K., D. Henley, H. Riley, and J. Shaffer. 1975. Improving food marketing systems in developing countries: Experiences from Latin America. Latin American Studies Center Research Report 6. East Lansing: Michigan State University.

————. 1987. Improving food marketing systems in developing countries: Experiences from Latin America. MSU International Development Papers, Reprint 9. East Lansing: Department of Agricultural Economics, Michigan State University.

Harriss, B. 1987a. Regional growth linkages from agriculture. *Journal of Development Studies* 23 (2): 275–289.

————. 1987b. Regional growth linkages from agriculture and resource flows in the non-farm economy. *Economic and Political Weekly* 22: 31–46.

Harriss, J. 1977. The limitations of HYV technology in North Arcot district: The view from a billage. In *Green revolution,* ed. B. H. Farmer. Cambridge: Cambridge University Press.

Harriss, J., and B. Harriss. 1984. Generative or parasitic urbanism? Some observations from the recent history of a South Indian market town. *Journal of Development Studies* 20 (3): 82–101.

Hart, G. 1987. The mechanisation of Malaysian rice production: Will petty producers survive? World Employment Programme Research Working Paper. Geneva: International Labour Office.

————. 1989. The growth linkages controversy: Some lessons from the Muda case. *Journal of Development Studies* 25 (4): 571–575.

————. 1994. The dynamics of diversification in an Asian rice region. In *Development or deterioration? Work in rural Asia,* ed. B. Koppel, J. Hawkins, and W. James. Boulder, Colo.: Lynne Rienner.

Hatch, C. R. 2001. The limits of BDS market development; or, Why we need network strategies. *Developing Alternatives* 7 (1): 17–24.

Hattori, T. 1997. Chaebol-style enterprise development in Korea. *Developing Economies* 35 (4): 458–477.

Hattori, T., and Y. Sato. 1997. A comparative study of development mechanisms in Korea and Taiwan: An introductory analysis. *Developing Economies* 35 (4): 341–357.

Hayami, Y. 1998a. Toward an alternative paradigm of economic development: An introduction. In *Toward the rural-based development of commerce and industry: Selected experiences from East Asia,* ed. Y. Hayami. Washington, D.C.: World Bank Economic Development Institute.

Hayami, Y., ed. 1998b. *Toward the rural-based development of commerce and industry: Selected experiences from East Asia.* Washington, D.C.: World Bank.

Hayami, Y., and T. Kawagoe. 1993. *The agrarian origin of commerce and industry: A study of oeasant marketing in Indonesia.* London: Macmillan.

Hayami, Y., and K. Otsuka. 1993. *The economics of contract choice: An agrarian perspective.* Oxford: Clarendon.

Hayami, Y., M. Kikuchi, and E. B. Marciano. 1996. Structure of rural-based industrialization: Metal craft manufacturing in the Philippines. Social Sciences Division Discussion Paper 5/96. Manila, the Philippines: International Rice Research Institute (IRRI).

Hayami, Y., and S. Yamada. 1991. *The agricultural development of Japan.* Tokyo: University of Tokyo Press.

Hazell, P. B. R., and S. Haggblade. 1991. Rural-urban growth linkages in India. *Indian Journal of Agricultural Economics* 46 (4): 515–529.

———. 1993. Farm-nonfarm growth linkages and the welfare of the poor. In *Including the poor,* ed. M. Lipton and J. van der Gaag. Washington, D.C.: World Bank.

Hazell, P. B. R., and B. Hojjati. 1994. Farm/non-farm growth linkages in Zambia. *Journal of African Economies* 4 (3): 406–435.

Hazell, P., and C. Ramasamy. 1986. Household expenditure patterns and the growth of the nonfarm economy. Paper presented at the IFPRI/TNAU Workshop on Growth Linkages, Oatacamund, India, February 14–16.

———. 1991. *Green revolution reconsidered.* Baltimore: The Johns Hopkins University Press.

Hazell, P. B. R., and A. Roell. 1983. Rural growth linkages: Household expenditure patterns in Malaysia and Nigeria. Research Report 41. Washington, D.C.: International Food Policy Research Institute.

Hazell, P. B. R., and R. Slade. 1987. Regional growth linkages from agriculture: A reply. *Journal of Development Studies* 23 (2): 290–294.

Hazell, P. B. R., C. Ramasamy, and V. Rajagopalan. 1991. An analysis of the indirect effects of agricultural growth on the regional economy. In *Green revolution reconsidered,* ed. Peter B. R. Hazell and C. Ramasamy. Baltimore: The Johns Hopkins University Press.

Helmsing, A. H. J. 2001. *Partnerships, meso-institutions and learning: New local and regional economic development initiatives in Latin America.* The Hague: Institute of Social Studies.

Henderson, J. V. 1974. The sizes and types of cities. *American Economic Review* 64 (5): 640–656.

Henderson, J. V., T. Lee, and J. Y. Lee. 2001. Scale externalities in Korea. *Journal of Urban Economics* 49 (3): 479–504.

Henning, B., and H. Mule. 1998. Four strategies for protecting public research funding. In *Financing agricultural research: A sourcebook,* ed. S. Tabor, W. Janssen, and H. Bruneau. The Hague: International Service for National Agricultural Research.

Hernandez, R., T. Reardon, and J. Berdegué. 2006. Tomato farmer participation in supermarket market channels in Guatemala: Determinants and technology and income effects. Department of Agricultural Economics Staff Paper 2006-04. East Lansing: Michigan State University.

Hirschland, M. 2005. Savings products. In *Savings services for the poor: An operational guide,* ed. M. Hirshland. Bloomfield, Conn.: Kumarian.

Hirschman, A. O. 1958. *The strategy of economic development.* New Haven, Conn.: Yale University Press.

————. 1981a. A generalized linkage approach to development with special reference to staples. In *Essays in trespassing: Economics to politics and beyond.* Cambridge: Cambridge University Press.

————. 1981b. The rise and decline of development economics. In *Essays in trespassing: Economics to politics and beyond.* Cambridge: Cambridge University Press.

Hitchens, R., D. Elliot, and A. Gibson. 2004. Making business service markets work for the poor in rural Areas: A review of experience. Springfield Centre for Business in Development, Durham, England.

Ho, S. P. S. 1978. *Economic development of Taiwan, 1860–1970.* New Haven, Conn.: Yale University Press.

————. 1979. Decentralized industrialization and rural development: Evidence from Taiwan. *Economic Development and Cultural Change* 10: 77–96.

————. 1982. Economic development and rural industry in South Korea and Taiwan. *World Development* 10: 973–990.

————. 1986a. The Asian experience in rural non-agricultural development and its relevance for China. World Bank Staff Working Paper 757. Washington, D.C.: World Bank.

————. 1986b. Off-farm employment and farm households in Taiwan. In *Off-farm employment in the development of rural Asia,* ed. R. T. Shand, Vol. 1. Canberra: Australian National University.

Holdcroft, L. E. 1978. The rise and fall of community development in developing countries, 1950–1965: A critical analysis and an annotated bibliography. MSU Rural Development Paper 2. East Lansing: Department of Agricultural Economics, Michigan State University.

————. 1984. The rise and fall of community development, 1950–65: A critical assessment. In *Agricultural development in the third world,* ed. C. Eicher and J. Staatz. Baltimore: The Johns Hopkins University Press.

Holden, S., B. Shiferaw, and J. Pender. 2004. Non-farm income, household welfare, and sustainable land management in a less-favoured area in the Ethiopian highlands. *Food Policy* 29 (4): 369–392.

Holtzman, J. S. 1986. Rapid reconnaissance guidelines for agricultural marketing and food system research in developing countries. MSU International Development Papers, Working Paper 30. East Lansing: Department of Agricultural Economics, Michigan State University.

Holtzman, J. S., R. D. Abbott, and G. Martin. 1989. The Marketing Improvement Strategies project: Diagnosing marketing system constraints, identifying opportunities and prescribing policy changes and pilot innovations. *Journal of International Food and Agribusiness Marketing* 1 (1): 29–39.

Holzapfel, W. H. 1989. *Industrialization of mageu fermentation in South Africa.* New York: Marcel Dekker.

Honduras. 1976. *Marzo 1974 censo nacional de poblacion, resumen por departamento y municipio,* Tomo 1. Tegucigalpa: Direccion General de Estadistica y Censos.

Hoogeveen, J., and B. Özler. 2004. Not-separate, not-equal: Poverty and inequality in post-Apartheid South Africa. Mimeo, Development Economics Research Group, World Bank, Washington, D.C.

Hopkins, J., and T. Reardon. 1993. Agricultural price policy reform impacts and food aid targeting in Niger. Final report of the IFPRI/INRAN project. Mimeo, International Food Policy Research Institute, Washington D.C.

Hoselitz, B. F. 1957. Generative and parasitic cities. *Economic Development and Cultural Change* 3 (3): 278–294.

———. 1959. Small industry in underdeveloped areas. *Journal of Economic History* 19 (4): 600–618.

Hossain, M. 1984. Productivity and profitability in Bangladesh rural industries. In Special Issue on Rural Industrialization in Bangladesh, *Bangladesh Development Studies* 2 (March/June): 127–162.

———. 1988a. Credit for alleviation of rural poverty: The Grameen Bank in Bangladesh. Research Report 65. Washington, D.C.: International Food Policy Research Institute.

———. 1988b. Nature and impact of the green revolution in Bangladesh. Research Report 67. Washington, D.C.: International Food Policy Research Institute.

———. 1997. Rural nonfarm income in Bangladesh. Bangladesh Institute of Development Studies (BIDS) and International Rice Research Institute (IRRI) report. Dhaka.

———. 2004. Rural non-farm economy in Bangladesh: A view from household surveys. Center for Policy Dialogue (CPD) Occasional Paper Series 40. Dhaka: Center for Policy Dialogue.

Hu, D., T. Reardon, S. Rozelle, P. Timmer, and H. Wang. 2004. The emergence of supermarkets with Chinese characteristics: Challenges and opportunities for China's agricultural development. *Development Policy Review* 22 (4): 557–586.

Huang, J. 1999. Agricultural diversification and rural industrialization in China. Paper presented at the Symposium on Critical Food Policy Issues in Indochina in the Emerging Globalization Context, sponsored by IFPRI and the Ministry of Agriculture and Rural Development, Hanoi, March 1–2.

Huang, Y., and T. Khanna. 2003. Can India overtake China? *Foreign Policy* (July–August): 74–81.

Hulme, D. 2000. Impact assessment methodologies for microfinance: Theory, experience and better practice. *World Development* 28 (1): 79–98.

Hulme, D., and P. Mosely. 1996. *Finance against poverty.* London: Routledge.

Humphrey, J., and H. Schmitz. 1996. The triple C approach to local industrial policy. *World Development* 24 (12): 1859–1877.

———. 2002. How does insertion in global value chains affect upgrading in industrial clusters? *Regional Studies* 36 (9): 1017–1027.

Hussain, R., A. A. Syed, and M. Biswas. 1995. Designing projects that have impact: Five subsector studies in Bangladesh. GEMINI Technical Report 98. Bethesda, Md.: Development Alternatives.

Hyman, E. L. 1987. The strategy of production and distribution of improved charcoal stoves in Kenya. *World Development* 15 (3): 375–386.

———. 1990. An economic analysis of small-scale technologies for palm oil extraction in Central and West Africa. *World Development* 18 (3): 455–476.

———. 1993a. Making foreign aid more relevant and effective through a small-scale producers strategy. *Journal of Environment and Development* 2 (2): 79–95.

————. 1993b. Production of edible oils for the masses and by the masses: The impact of the ram press in Tanzania. *World Development* 21 (3): 429–444.

————. 1996. How NGOs can accelerate the commercialization of agricultural technology in Africa. Appropriate Technology International, Washington, D.C.

————. 1997a. Combining credit and technical assistance: Alpaca fiber production and processing in Bolivia. *Small Enterprise Development* 8 (3): 42–50.

————. 1997b. Subsector analysis: Theory into practice—Rattan in the Philippines. *Appropriate Technology* 24 (1): 9–11.

Hyman, E., and K. Dearden. 1996. A review of impact information systems of NGO microenterprise programs. Assessing the Impact of Microenterprise Services (AIMS) Working Paper. Washington, D.C.: Management Systems International.

Hyman, E., R. Chavez, and J. Skibiak. 1989. Reorienting export production to benefit rural producers: Annatto processing in Peru. *Journal of Rural Studies* 6: 85–101.

Hyman, E. L., E. T. Njiku, and J. Herz. 1997. Building the capacity of private sector in rural Tanzania through the promotion of rural, small scale oilseed processing: An evaluation of Phase I of the T-PRESS project. Appropriate Technology International, Washington, D.C.

Hyman, E. L., J. Singh, and E. G. Lawrence. 1996. Commercialisation of efficient household charcoal stoves in Senegal. *Science, Technology and Development* 14 (1): 1–20.

Hyman, E., L. Stosch, and P. Cunningham, eds. 1998. *1997 portfolio report.* Washington, D.C.: Appropriate Technology International.

Hymer, S., and S. Resnick. 1969. A model of an agrarian economy with nonagricultural activities. *American Economic Review* 59 (4): 493–506.

Ibrahim, H. el B. 1997. Coping with famine and poverty: The dynamics of nonagricultural rural employment in Darfur, Sudan. In *Farewell to farms: Deagrarianisation and employment in Africa,* ed. D. F. Bryceson and V. Jamil. Aldershot, England: Ashgate.

IDB. *See* Inter-American Development Bank.

IDE. *See* International Development Enterprises.

ILO. *See* International Labor Office.

ILO, UNOPS, EURADA, Italian Cooperation. 2000. *Local economic development agencies: International cooperation for human development.* Rome: United Nations Office for Project Services.

IMF. *See* International Monetary Fund.

India, Government of. Various years. *National sample survey (NSS).* New Delhi: Ministry of Statistics and Programme Implementation.

————. 1948. *Industrial policy resolution.* New Delhi.

————. 1968. *Small Scale Industries in India.* Delhi: Development Commissioner for Small Scale Industries.

————. 1971. *Census of India 1971,* Vol. 1, Part II-A (II), *General economic tables.* New Delhi: Census Commissioner.

Indonesia. 1974. *1971 population census.* Jakarta: Biro Pusat Statistik.

Indonesia Bureau of Statistics. 1998. Population of Indonesia: Results of the 1995 intercensal population survey, Series S2. Jakarta: Bureau of Statistics.

Inter-American Development Bank (IDB). 1997. Microenterprise development strategy. IDB, Washington, D.C.

International Development Enterprises (IDE). 2003. Poverty reduction through irrigation and smallholder markets (PRISM): A Manual. Paper, International Development Enterprise, Lakewood, Colo.

————. 2005. Guidelines for developing and implementing poverty reduction through irrigation and smallholder markets (PRISM) programs. Paper, International Development Enterprise, Lakewood, Colo.

International Herald Tribune. 1989. In India, hard times beset a charming Village. *International Herald Tribune,* December 28, 3.

International Labor Office (ILO). 1972. *Employment, incomes and equality: A strategy for increasing productive employment in Kenya.* Geneva: ILO.

————. 1974. World Employment Programme: Rural employment promotion through integrated rural development. Report of an ILO Advisory Working Group. Geneva: ILO.

————. 1979. Poverty and employment in rural areas of developing countries. Report presented to the ILO Advisory Committee on Rural Development, 9th Session, Geneva, November 27–December 6.

————. 1982. *Disparités de revenus entre les villes et les campagnes en Afrique noire francophone: Rapport de synthése.* Prepared by the Job and Skills Program for Africa (JASPA). Addis Ababa: ILO.

————. 1984. *Informal sector in Africa.* Addis Ababa: ILO.

————. 1986. *Bibliography of published research of the World Employment Programme,* 6th ed. Geneva: ILO.

————. 1992. Networking for entrepreneurship development: Selected entrepreneurship development programmes and guidelines for transfer. ILO, Geneva.

International Monetary Fund (IMF). 1986. *National census of population and housing.* Tehran: Statistical Centre of Iran.

Iran, Statistical Centre of. 1976. *National Census of population and housing, November 1976: Total Country.* Tehran: Plan and Budget Organization, Statistical Centre of Iran.

Isgut, A. E. 2004. Non-farm income and employment in rural Honduras: Assessing the role of locational factors. *Journal of Development Studies* 40 (3): 59–86.

Islam, N. 1997. The nonfarm sector and rural development. 2020 Discussion Paper 22. Washington, D.C.: International Food Policy Research Institute.

Islam, R. 1984. Nonfarm employment in rural Asia: Dynamic growth or proletarianisation? *Journal of Contemporary Asia* (UK) 14: 306–324.

————, ed. 1987a. *Rural industrialisation and employment in Asia.* New Delhi: International Labour Office.

————. 1987b. Rural industrialisation and employment in Asia: Issues and evidence. In *Rural industrialisation and employment in Asia,* ed. R. Islam. New Delhi: International Labour Office.

Itoh, M., and M. Tanimoto. 1998. Rural entrepreneurs in the cotton textile industry in Japan. In *Toward the rural-based development of commerce and industry: Selected experiences from East Asia,* ed. Y. Hayami. Washington, D.C.: World Bank.

Jacobs, J. 1984. *Cities and the wealth of nations.* New York: Random House.

Jaffee, S. M. 1992. How private enterprise organized agricultural markets in Kenya. Working Paper Series 823. Washington, D.C.: World Bank.

Jaffee, S., with P. Gordon. 1993. Exporting high-value food commodities: Success stories from developing countries. World Bank Technical Paper 424. Washington, D.C.: World Bank.

Jaffee, S., R. Kopicki, P. Labaste, and I. Christie. 2003. Modernizing Africa's agro-food systems: Analytical framework and implications for operations. Africa Region Working Paper 44. Washington, D.C.: World Bank.

Jank, M. S., E. M. M. Q. Farina, and V. B. Galan. 1999. *O agribusiness do leite no Brasil.* São Paulo: Editora Milkbizz.

Jansen, E. G., A. J. Dolman, A. M. Jerve, and N. Rahman. 1989. *The country boats of Bangladesh: Social and economic development and decision-making in inland water transport.* Dhaka: University Press.

Jayaraman, R., and P. Lanjouw. 1999. Poverty and inequality in Indian villages. *World Bank Research Observer* 14 (1): 1–30.

Jayaraman, R., Y. Kijima, and P. Lanjouw. 2003. Tamil Nadu poverty note: Poverty in the 1990s; A preliminary profile and emerging issues. Mimeo, World Bank, Washington, D.C.

Jayne, T. S., and S. Jones. 1997. Food marketing and pricing policy in Eastern and Southern Africa: A survey. *World Development* 25 (9): 1505–1527.

Jayne, T. S., L. Rubey, M. Chisvo, and M. T. Weber. 1996. Zimbabwe's food security success story: Maize market reforms improve access to food even while government eliminates food subsidies. Policy Synthesis 18. East Lansing: Michigan State University.

Jeans, A., E. Hyman, and M. O'Donnell. 1991. Technology: The key to increasing the productivity of micro-enterprises. *Small Enterprise Development* 2 (2): 14–23.

Johnson, E. A. J. 1970. *The organization of space in developing countries.* Cambridge: Cambridge University Press.

Johnson, K., and A. Ritchie. 1993. The bamboo subsector in Bangladesh. Technical Series Report 1. Dhaka, Bangladesh: CARE.

Johnson, S., and B. Rogaly. 1997. *Microfinance and poverty reduction.* London: Oxfam.

Johnston, B. F. 1970. Agriculture and structural transformation in developing countries: A survey of research. *Journal of Economic Literature* 3 (2): 369–404.

Johnston, B. F., and P. Kilby. 1975. *Agriculture and structural transformation: Economic strategies in late-developing countries.* London: Oxford University Press.

Johnston, B. F., and J. W. Mellor. 1961. The role of agriculture in economic development. *American Economic Review* 51 (4): 566–593.

Joliffe, D. 1998. Skills, schooling and household income in Ghana. *World Bank Economic Review* 12 (1): 81–104.

Jones, W. O. 1970. Measuring the effectiveness of agricultural marketing in contributing to economic development: Some African examples. *Food Research Institute Studies in Agricultural Economics, Trade and Development* 9: 175–196.

Jorgenson, D. W. 1961. The development of a dual economy. *Economic Journal* 71: 309–334.

Joumard, I., C. Liedholm, and D. C. Mead. 1992. *The impact of laws and regulations on micro and small enterprises in Niger and Swaziland.* OECD Development Centre Technical Paper 77. Paris: Organization for Economic Cooperation and Development. September.

Jovanovic, B. 1982. Selection and evolution of industry. *Econometrica* 50 (May): 649–670.

Juma, C., and N. Clark. 1995. Policy research in Sub-Saharan Africa: An exploration. *Public Administration and Development* 15: 121–137.

Kada, R. 1986. Off-farm employment and the rural-urban interface in Japanese economic development. In *Off-farm employment in the development of rural Asia,* ed. R. T. Shand, Vol. 1. Canberra: Australian National University.

Kamal, A. 1983. A cost-benefit analysis of rural telephone service in Egypt. *Case study no. 11 for ITU-OECD Communication Development Project.* Geneva: International Telecommunication Union.

Kamete, A. Y. 1998. Interlocking livelihoods: Farm and small town in Zimbabwe. *Environment and Urbanization* 10 (1): 23–34.

Kanbur, R., and X. Zhang. 2005. Fifty years of regional inequality in China: A journey through central planning, reform and openness. *Review of Development Economics* 9 (1): 87–106.

QA Kao, C. H. C., K. R. Anschel, and C. K. Eicher. 1964. Disguised unemployment in agriculture: A survey. In *Agriculture in economic development,* ed. C. K. Eicher and L. W. Witt. New York: McGraw-Hill.

Kapila, S., and D. Mead. 2002. *Building businesses with small producers: Successful business development services in Africa, Asia and Latin America.* Ottawa: ITDG Publishing.

Kaplinsky, R. 2000. Spreading the gains from globalization: What can be learned from value chain analysis? IDS Working Paper 110. Brighton, England: Institute of Development Studies, Sussex University.

Kaplinsky, R., and M. Morris. 2000. A handbook for value chain research. Ottawa: International Development Research Center.

———. 2003. Governance matters in value chains. *Developing Alternatives* 9 (1): 11–18.

Karaska, G. J., and E. S. Belsky. 1987. Rural/urban dynamics in regional planning: Examples from underdeveloped regions. In *Patterns of change in developing regions,* ed. R. Bar-El, A. Bendavid-Val, and G. J. Karaska. Boulder, Colo.: Westview.

Karlan, D. S. 2001. Microfinance impact assessments: The perils of using new members as a control group. *Journal of Microfinance* 3 (2): 75–85.

Kashyap, S. P. 1988. Growth of small-sized enterprises in India: Its nature and content. *World Development* 16 (6): 667–681.

Kasryno, F. 1986. Impact of off-farm employment on agricultural labor absorption and wages in Indonesia. In *Off-farm employment in the development in rural Asia,* ed. R. T. Shand. Canberra: Australian National University.

Kawagoe, T. 1998. Technical and institutional innovations in rice marketing in Japan. In *Toward the rural-based development of commerce and industry: Selected experiences from East Asia,* ed. Y. Hayami. Washington, D.C.: World Bank.

Keeble, D. E., P. L. Owens, and C. Thompson. 1982. Regional accessibility and economic potential in the European community. *Regional Studies* 16 (4): 419–432.

Kennedy, L. 1999. Cooperating for survival: Tannery pollution and joint action in the Palar Valley (India). *World Development* 27 (9): 1673–1692.

Key, N., and D. Runsten. 1999. Contract farming, smallholders, and rural development in Latin America: The organization of agroprocessing firms and the scale of outgrower production. *World Development* 27 (2): 381–402.

Keyler, S. K. 1996. Economics of the Namibian millet subsector. Ph.D. dissertation, Michigan State University, East Lansing.

Khandker, S. R. 1998. *Fighting poverty with microcredit: Experience in Bangladesh.* New York: Oxford University Press.

Khandker, S. 2003. Microfinance and poverty: Evidence using panel data from Bangladesh. World Bank Policy Research Working Paper 2945. Washington, D.C.: World Bank. January.

———. 2005. Microfinance and poverty: Evidence using panel data from Bangladesh. *World Bank Economic Review* 19 (2): 263–286.

Khandker, S. R., and H. P. Binswanger. 1989. The effect of formal credit on output and employment in rural India. Policy, Planning and Research Working Papers. Washington, D.C.: World Bank Population and Human Resources Department.

Kherallah, M., C. Delgado, E. Gabre-Madhin, N. Minot, and M. Johnson. 2002. *Reforming agricultural markets in Africa.* Baltimore: The Johns Hopkins University Press.

Kijima, Y., and P. Lanjouw. 2004. Agricultural wages, non-farm employment and poverty in rural India. Mimeo, Development Economics Research Group, World Bank, Washington, D.C.

———. 2005. Economic diversification and poverty in rural India. *Indian Journal of Labour Economics* 48 (2): 349–374.

Kikuchi, M. 1998. Export-oriented garment industries in the rural Philippines. In *Toward the rural-based development of commerce and industry,* ed. Y. Hayami. Washington, D.C.: World Bank.

Kikuchi, M., E. B. Marciano, M. Hossain, and Y. Hyami. 1997. A laguna rice village: Three decades of changes before and after green revolution. Social Sciences Division Discussion Paper 2/97. Manila: International Rice Research Institute.

Kilby, P. 1962. *The development of small industry in Eastern Nigeria.* Lagos: U.S. Agency for International Development.

———. 1971. *Entrepreneurship and economic development.* New York: Free Press.

———. 1979. Evaluating technical assistance. *World Development* 7 (3): 309–323.

———. 1982. Small scale industry in Kenya. MSU Rural Development Series Working Paper 20. East Lansing: Department of Agricultural Economics, Michigan State University.

———. 1988. Breaking the entrepreneurial bottleneck in late-developing countries: Is there a useful role for government? *Journal of Development Planning* 18: 221–249.

———. 2003. The heffalump revisited. *Journal of Entrepreneurship* 1 (1): 13–29.

Kilby, P., and P. Bangasser Jr. 1978. Assessing technical co-operation: The case of rural industry. *International Labour Review* 117 (3): 343–353.

Kilby, P., and D. D'Zmura. 1985. Searching for benefits. AID Special Study 28. Washington, D.C.: U.S. Agency for International Development.

Kilmer, G. D. 1993. Application of the GEMINI methodology for subsector analysis to MSE export activities: A case study in Ecuador. GEMINI Working Paper 39. Bethesda, Md.: Development Alternatives.

King, K. 1977. *The African artisan.* London: Heinemann.

King, R. P., and D. Byerlee. 1978. Factor intensities and locational linkages of rural consumption patterns in rural Sierra Leone. *American Journal of Agricultural Economics* (May): 197–206.

Kirkby, R., I. Bradbury, and G. Shen. 2000. *Small town China: Governance, economy, environment and lifestyle in Three Zhen.* Aldershot, England: Ashgate.

Klein, E., and V. Tokman. 2000. La estratifcacion social bajo tension en la era de la globalizacion. *Revista de la CEPAL* 72 (December): 7–30.

Knight, J., and L. Song. 2003. Chinese peasant choices: Migration, rural industry, or farming. *Oxford Development Studies* 31 (2): 123–147.

Kolshorn, R., and J. Tomecko. 1995. Understanding entrepreneurship and how to promote it. Bonn: GTZ.

Kolshorn, R., and U. Weihert. 2000. The case of CCEFE—A new look at entrepreneurship. In *Business development services: A review of international experience,* ed. J. Levitsky. London: Intermediate Technology Publications.

Koné, S., and E. Thorbecke. 1996. Sectoral investment priorities for renewed growth in Zaire. In *Economic reform and the poor in Africa,* ed. D. E. Sahn, Chap. 10. London: Oxford University Press.

Korea, Republic of. 1972. *1970 population and census housing report.* Seoul: Economic Planning Board.

Korean Rural Economics Institute (KREI). 2005. *Agro-industrial sector and agro-enterprise cluster development in selected transition economies.* Seoul: KREI. September.

KREI. *See* Korean Rural Economics Institute.

Krishna, R. 1975. Measurement of the direct and indirect employment effects of agricultural growth with technical change. In *Externalities in the transformation of agriculture: Distribution of benefits and costs from development,* ed. E. O. Heady and L. R. Whiting. Ames: Iowa State University Press.

Krugman, P. 1991. Increasing returns and economic geography. *Journal of Political Economy* 99 (3): 483–499.

———. 1993a. First nature, second nature, and metropolitan location. *Journal of Regional Science* 33 (2): 129–144.

———. 1993b. On the number and location of cities. *European Economic Review* 37 (2/3): 293–298.

———. 1995. *Development, geography, and economic theory.* Cambridge, Mass.: MIT Press.

———. 1996. *The self-organizing economy.* Cambridge, Mass.: Blackwell.

Krugman, P., and R. L. Elizondo. 1996. Trade policy and the Third World metropolis. *Journal of Development Economics* 49: 137–150.

Kung, J. K. S., and Y.-F. Lee. 2001. So what if there is income inequality? The distributional consequences of nonfarm income in rural China. *Economic Development and Cultural Change* 50: 19–46.

Kurosaki, T., and H. Khan. 2006. Human capital, productivity, and stratification in rural Pakistan. *Review of Development Economics* 10 (February): 116–134.

Kuyvenhoven, A. 1978. *Planning with the semi-input-output method.* Leiden: Martinus Nijhott.

Kuznets, P. W. 1988. An East Asian model of economic development: Japan, Taiwan, and South Korea. *Economic Development and Cultural Change* 36 (3): Supplement, S11–43.

LaFleur, J. 2000. Agriflora. *Developing alternatives.* Bethesda, Md.: DAI.

Lamb, J. E., and B. Brower. 2001. Agribusiness development centers. In *The Guide to Developing Agricultural Markets and Agro-Enterprises.* <www.worldbank.org/essd/essd/nsf/agroenterprise> (accessed June 2002).

Lane, D. W. 1998. Political bases of rural entrepreneurship: Korea and Taiwan, China. In *Toward the rural-based development of commerce and industry,* ed. Y. Hayami. Washington, D.C.: World Bank.

Lanjouw, J. O., and P. Lanjouw. 1995. Rural nonfarm employment: A survey. Policy Research Working Paper 1463. Washington, D.C.: World Bank.

Lanjouw, P. 1999. Rural nonagricultural employment and poverty in Ecuador. *Economic Development and Cultural Change* 48 (1): 91–122.

———. 2001. Nonfarm employment and poverty in rural El Salvador. *World Development* 29 (3): 529–547.

Lanjouw, P., and G. Feder. 2001. Rural non-farm activities and rural development: From experience towards strategy. Rural Strategy Background Paper 4. Washington, D.C.: World Bank.

———. 2001. The rural nonfarm sector: Issues and evidence from developing countries. *Agricultural Economics* 26: 1–23.

Lanjouw, P., and A. Shariff. 2002. Rural nonfarm employment in India: Access, income and poverty impacts. National Council of Applied Economics Research (NCAER) Working Paper 81. New Delhi: NCAER.

———. 2004. Rural non-farm employment in India: Access, incomes and poverty impact. *Economic and Political Weekly* 39 (40): 4429–4446.

Lanjouw, P., and N. H. Stern, eds. 1998. *Economic development in Palanpur over five decades.* New Delhi and Oxford: Oxford University Press.

Lanjouw, P., J. Quizon, and R. Sparrow. 2001. Nonagricultural earnings in peri-urban areas of Tanzania: Evidence from household survey data. *Food Policy* 26 (4): 385–403.

Lapenu, C., and M. Zeller. 2001. Distribution, growth and performance of microfinance institutions in Africa, Asia and Latin America. FCND Discussion Paper 114. Washington, D.C.: International Food Policy Research Institute.

Lassen, C., R. Traore, A. Brown, and J. Walton. 1985. Credit and enterprise development training that reach the small producer majority in Burkina Faso: Midterm evaluation of Association pour la Productivite / Burkina Faso. Washington, D.C.: Partnership for Productivity.

Lauret, F. 1993. Sur les études de Filières Agro-Alimentaires. *Economies et Sociétés* 17 (May): 175–192.

Layard, P. R. G., and A. A. Walters. 1978. *Micro-economic theory.* New York: McGraw-Hill.

Lee, J.-H., and C.-H. Suh. 1998. Rural entrepreneurship and industrial development in Korea. In *Toward the rural-based development of commerce and industry: Selected experiences from East Asia,* ed. Y. Hayami. Washington, D.C.: World Bank.

Lele, U. J. 1975. Marketing of agricultural output. In *The design of rural development: Lessons from Africa,* ed. U. J. Lele. Baltimore: The Johns Hopkins University Press.

Leones, J. P., and S. Feldman. 1998. Nonfarm activity and rural household income: Evidence from Philippine microdata. *Economic Development and Cultural Change* 46 (4): 789–806.

Lev, L. S., and M. A. Gadbois. 1989. Rapid reconnaissance study of the Nigerien onion subsector: A policy-oriented analysis of market performance. Moscow, Idaho: Postharvest Institute for Perishables.

Levitsky, J., ed. 2000. *Business development services: A review of international experience.* London: Intermediate Technology Publications.

Levy, B. 1991. Transaction costs, the size of firms and industrial policy: Lessons from a comparative case study of the footwear industry in Korea and Taiwan. *Journal of Development Economics* 34 (1/2): 151–178.

Levy, B., and W. J. Kuo. 1991. The strategic orientation of firms and the performance of Korea and Taiwan in frontier industries: Lessons from comparative studies of keyboard and personal computer assembly. *World Development* 19 (4): 363–374.

Lewis, A. 1954. Economic development with unlimited supplies of labour. *Manchester School of Economic and Social Studies* 22 (2): 139–191.

———. 1958. Unlimited labour: Further notes. *Manchester School of Economic and Social Studies* 26 (1): 1–32.

Lewis, B. D. 1988. Intersectoral and spatial linkages in regional economic development: A social accounting matrix approach applied to policy questions in Kutus region, Kenya. Ph.D. dissertation, Cornell University, Ithaca, N.Y.

Lewis, B, D., and E. Thorbecke. 1992. District-level economic linkages in Kenya: Evidence based on a small regional social accounting matrix. *World Development* 20 (6): 881–898.

Liedholm, C. 1973. Research on employment in the rural non-farm sector in Africa. African Rural Economy Paper 5. East Lansing: Michigan State University, Department of Agricultural Economics.

———. 1985. Small scale enterprise credit schemes, administrative costs and the role of inventory norms. MSU International Development Working Paper 25. East Lansing: Michigan State University, Department of Agricultural Economics.

———. 1992. Small-scale industry in Africa. In *Alternative development strategies in sub-Saharan Africa,* ed. F. Stewart. London: Macmillan.

Liedholm, C., and E. Chuta. 1976. The economics of rural and urban small-scale industries in Sierra Leone. African Rural Economy Paper 14. East Lansing: Michigan State University, Department of Agricultural Economics.

Liedholm, C., and M. McPherson. 1991. Small scale enterprises in Mamelodi and Kwazakhale Townships, South Africa: Survey findings. GEMINI Technical Report 16. Bethesda, Md.: Development Alternatives.

Liedholm, C., and D. C. Mead. 1986. Small-scale industry in Africa: An overview. In *Strategies for African development,* ed. R. J. Berg and J. S. Whitaker. Berkeley: University of California Press.

———. 1987. Small scale industries in developing countries: Empirical evidence and policy implications. MSU International Development Paper 9. East Lansing: Michigan State University, Department of Agricultural Economics.

———. 1991. Dynamics of microenterprises: Research issues and approaches. GEMINI Working Paper 12. Bethesda, Md.: Development Alternatives.

———. 1999. *Small enterprises and economic development: The Dynamics of micro enterprises.* London: Routledge.

Liedholm, C., M. McPherson, and E. Chuta. 1994. Small enterprise employment growth in rural Africa. *American Journal of Agricultural Economics* 76 (5): 1177–1182.

Lin, J. Y., and Y. Yao. 1999. Chinese rural industrialization in the context of the East Asian miracle. Working Paper E1999004. Beijing: Beijing University, China Center for Economic Research.

Lindblom, C. E. 1980. *The policy making process.* Englewood Cliffs, N.J.: Prentice-Hall.

Lipton, M. 1977. *Why poor people stay poor: Urban bias in world development.* London: Temple Smith.

Lipton, M., with R. Longhurst. 1989. *New seeds and poor people.* London: Unwin Hyman.

Lipton, M., and M. Ravallion. 1995. Poverty and policy. In *Handbook of development economics,* ed. J. Behrman and T. N. Srinivasan, Vol. 3B. Amsterdam: North Holland.

Little, I M. D., D. Mazumdar, and J. M. Page Jr. 1987. *Small manufacturing enterprises: A comparative analysis of India and other economies.* New York: Oxford University Press.

Little, P. D., and M. J. Watts. 1994. *Living under contract: Contract farming and agrarian transformation in Sub-Saharan Africa.* Madison: University of Wisconsin Press.

Little, P. D., K. Smith, B. A. Cellarius, D. L. Coppock, and C. B. Barrett. 2001. Avoiding disaster: Diversification and risk management among East African herders. *Development and Change* 32 (3): 401–433.

Litvack, J., J. Ahmad, and R. Bird. 1998. Rethinking decentralization in developing countries. Sector Studies Series. Washington, D.C.: World Bank.

Liu, D., and K. Otsuka. 1998. Township-village enterprises in the garment sector of China. In *Toward the rural-based development of commerce and industry: Selected experiences from East Asia,* ed. J. Hayami. Washington, D.C.: World Bank.

Livingstone, I. 1977. Rural industries for developing countries: An evaluation of Kenya's rural industrial development programme. *Journal of Modern African Studies* 15 (2): 495–504.

———. 1997. Rural industries in Africa: Hope and hype. In *Farewell to farms: Deagrarianisation and employment in Africa,* ed. D. F. Bryceson and V. Jamal. Aldershot, England: Ashgate.

Lo, F.-C., and K. Salih. 1978. *Growth pole strategy and regional development policy.* Oxford: Pergamon.

Lohmar, B., S. Rozelle, and C. Zhao. 2001. The rise of rural-to-rural labor markets in China. *Asian Geographer* 20 (1–2): 101–127.

Loucks, K. E. 1999. Designing and delivering high-impact, cost-effective business development services for small and medium-scale enterprises: An interim report on case study research. Paper presented at the International Conference on Developing a Modern and Effective Development Services Industry for Small Enterprises, sponsored by the Committee of Donor Agencies for Small Enterprise Development, Rio de Janeiro, March 2–5.

Loveridge, S. 1992. Les sources de revenu des ménages agricoles rwandais, les exportations et leur impact sur la disponibilité alimentaire en milieu rural. Mimeo, Division de Statistiques Agricoles, Ministry of Agriculture, Kigali, Rwanda.

Lozano, J. C., J. M. Cock, and J. Castano. 1978. New development in cassava storage. Paper presented at the Cassava protection workshop, CIAT, Cali, Colombia, November 7–12.

Lucas, R. E. B., and O. Stark. 1985. Motivations to remit: Evidence from Botswana. *Journal of Political Economy* 93 (5): 901–918.

Lusby, F. 1995. The subsector / trade group method: A demand-driven approach to non-financial assistance for micro and small enterprises. GEMINI Working Paper 55. Bethesda, Md.: Development Alternatives.

Lusby, F., and H. Panliburton. 2002. Subsector/business service approach to program design. Office of Microenterprise Development, U.S. Agency for International Development. Washington, D.C.

Magistro, J., M. Roberts, S. Haggblade, F. Kramer, P. Polak, E. Weight, and R. Yoder. 2004. PRISM: A model for smallholder wealth creation through integrated service provision, value chain market development and micro irrigation technology. Paper presented at the IWMI regional workshop and policy roundtable Pro-Poor Intervention Strategies in Irrigated Agriculture in Asia, Colombo, Sri Lanka, August 25–27.

Malawi Government. 1980. *Malawi population census, 1977: Final report,* Vol. 2. Zomba: National Statistical Office.

———. 2002. 1998 Malawi population and housing census: Analytical report. Zomba: National Statistical Office.

Malhotra, M., and J. Santer. 1994. Towards more cost-effective nonfinancial assistance: Case studies in subsector-based MSE development. GEMINI Working Paper 49. Bethesda, Md.: Development Alternatives.

Management Systems International (MSI). 1997. The entrepreneurship development program. Mimeo, MSI, Washington, D.C.

Mandal, M. A. S., and M. Asaduzzaman. 2002. Rural nonfarm economy in Bangladesh: Characteristics and issues for development. Dhaka: Bangladesh Institute of Development Studies.

Manor, J. 1999. *The political economy of democratic decentralization.* Washington, D.C.: World Bank.

Marenya, P. P., W. Oluoch-Kosura, F. Place, and C. B. Barrett. 2003. Education, nonfarm income and farm investment in land-scarce Western Kenya. Basis Brief 14. Madison: University of Wisconsin.

Marion, B. W. 1976. Vertical coordination and exchange arrangements: Concepts and hypotheses. In *Coordination and exchange in agricultural subsectors.* Monograph 2, North Central Regional Research Project 117. Madison: University of Wisconsin.

Maroc, R. du. 1995. *Recensement 1994: Les caractéristiques socio-economiques et démographiques de la population.* Rabat: Ministèrè Chargé de la Population, Direction de la Statistique.

Matlon, P. J. 1979. Income distribution among farmers in Northern Nigeria: Empirical results and policy implications. African Rural Economy Paper 18. East Lansing: Michigan State University, Department of Agricultural Economics.

Matshe, I., and T. Young. 2004. Off-farm labour allocation decisions in small-scale rural households in Zimbabwe. *Agricultural Economics* 30: 175–186.

Maxwell, J., and J. Holtzman. 1995. *Innovative approaches to agribusiness development in Sub-Saharan Africa,* Vol. 1, *Summary, conclusions, and cross-cutting findings.* Bethesda, Md.: Abt Associates.

Maxwell, S. 2003. Six characters (and a few more) in search of an author: How to rescue rural development before it's too late. Paper presented at the 25th International Conference of Agricultural Economists, Durban, South Africa, August 16–23.

McClelland, D. C. 1961. *The achieving society.* Princeton, N.J.: D. Van Nostrand.

McClelland, D. C., and D. G. Winter. 1969. *Motivating economic achievement.* New York: Free Press.

McNamara, R. S. 1973. Address to the Board of Governors, Nairobi, Kenya, September 24, 1972. World Bank, Washington, D.C.

McPherson, M. A. 1991. Micro and small-scale enterprises in Zimbabwe: Results of a country-wide survey. GEMINI Technical Report 25. Bethesda, Md.: Development Alternatives.

————. 1995. The hazards of small firms in Southern Africa. *Journal of Development Studies* 32 (1): 225–240.

————. 1996. Growth of micro and small enterprises in Southern Africa. *Journal of Development Economics* 48: 253–277.

McPherson, M., and C. Henry. 1994. Rural micro and small enterprises in Malawi: Effects of burley tobacco policy changes. GEMINI Technical Report. Bethesda, Md.: Development Alternatives.

McPherson, M., and C. Liedholm. 1996. Determinants of small and micro enterprise registration: Results from surveys in Niger and Swaziland. *World Development* 24 (3): 481–487.

McPherson, M., and J. Parker. 1993. A manual for conducting baseline surveys of micro and small-scale enterprises. GEMINI Field Research Paper 1. Bethesda, Md.: Development Alternatives.

McVay, M. 1999. Microenterprise marketing: Trends, lessons learned and challenges. A study by the Small Enterprise Education and Promotions (SEEP) Network funded by CARE International. Washington, D.C.: SEEP Network.

Mead, D. C. 1984. Of contracts and subcontracts: Small firms in vertically dis-integrated production/distribution systems in LDCs. *World Development* 12 (11/12): 1095–1106.

————. 1985. Subcontracting in rural areas of Thailand. MSU International Development Paper, Working Paper 4. East Lansing: Michigan State University.

————. 1991. Small enterprises and development. *Economic Development and Cultural Change* 39 (2): 409–420.

————. 1992a. Microenterprise development in a sub-sector context. *Small Enterprise Development* 3 (1): 35–42.

————. 1992b. Subcontracting systems and assistance programs: Opportunities for intervention. MSU International Working Paper 24. East Lansing: Michigan State University.

————. 1994a. The contribution of small enterprises to employment growth in Southern and Eastern Africa. *World Development* 22 (12): 1881–1894.

————. 1994b. Linkages within the private sector: A review of current thinking. FIT Working Paper 3. Geneva: International Labour Office.

Mead, D. C., and C. Liedholm. 1998. The dynamics of micro and small enterprises in developing countries. *World Development* 26 (1): 61–74.

Mead, D. C., and C. Morrisson. 1996. The informal sector elephant. *World Development* 24 (10): 1611–1619.

Mead, D., and A. Ngirabatware. 1987. Examen du sous-secteur bois au Rwanda. Document de Travail 2. Kigali, Rwanda: Ministère des Finances et de l'Economie.

Meagher, K., and A. R. Mustapha. 1997. Not by farming alone: The role of non-farm incomes in rural Hausaland. In *Farewell to farms: De-agrarianization and employment in Africa,* ed. D. Bryceson and V. Jamal. Aldershot, England: Ashgate.

Mellor, J. W. 1966. *The economics of agricultural development.* Ithaca, N.Y.: Cornell University Press.

———. 1976. *The new economics of growth.* Ithaca, N.Y.: Cornell University Press.

———. 1995. *Agriculture on the road to industrialization.* Baltimore: The Johns Hopkins University Press.

Mellor, J. W., and B. F. Johnston. 1984. The world food equation: Interrelations among development, employment and food consumption. *Journal of Economic Literature* 22 (June): 524–531.

Mellor, J. W., and U. J. Lele. 1971. A labor supply theory of economic development. Occasional Paper 42. Ithaca, N.Y.: Cornell University, Department of Agricultural Economics.

———. 1973. Growth linkages of the new food grain technologies. *Indian Journal of Agricultural Economics* 18 (1): 35–55.

Mellor, J. W., and M. S. Mudahar. 1974. Modeling agriculture, employment and economic growth: A simulation model. Occasional Paper 75, Employment and Income Distribution Project. Ithaca, N.Y.: Cornell University, Department of Agricultural Economics.

Merican, Z., and U. Quee-Lan. 1989. Tapai processing in Malaysia: A technology in transition. In *Industrialization of indigenous fermented foods,* ed. K. H. Steinkraus. New York: Marcel Dekker.

Meyanathan, S. D., ed. 1995. *Industrial structures and the development of small and medium enterprise linkages: Examples from East Asia.* Economic Development Institute Seminar Series. Washington, D.C.: World Bank.

Meyer, D. R. 1984. Intermediate cities in the system of cities in developing countries. Paper presented at the Conference on Urban Growth and Economic Development in the Pacific Region, Taipei, Institute of Economics, January 9–11.

Meyer, R. L. 2002. The demand for flexible microfinance products: Lessons from Bangladesh. *Journal of International Development* 14 (3): 351–368.

Meyer, R. L., and D. W. Larson. 1997. Issues in providing agricultural services in developing countries. In *Promoting Third-World development and food security,* ed. L. G. Tweeten and D. McClelland. Westport, Conn.: Praeger.

Meyer, R. L., and G. Nagarajan. 2000. *Rural financial markets in Asia: Policies, paradigms and performance.* Manila: Oxford University Press and Asian Development Bank.

Meyer-Stamer, J. 2002. *PACA: Participatory appraisal of competitive advantage.* <www.paca-online.de> (accessed May 2004).

———. 2003. Obstacles to cooperation in clusters and how to overcome them. *Developing Alternatives* 9 (1): 19–24.

Microcredit Summit. 1996. The Microcredit Summit Declaration and Plan of Action. *Journal of Developmental Entrepreneurship* 1 (2): 131–176.

Middleton, A. 1989. The changing pattern of petty production in Ecuador. *World Development* 17 (1): 139–155.

Miehlbradt, A. O., and M. McVay. 2006. *Implementing sustainable private sector development: Striving for tangible results for the poor: The 2006 reader.* Turin: International Labour Office.

Miehlbradt, A. O., M. McVay, and J. Tanburn. 2005. *From BDS to making markets work for the poor: The 2005 Reader.* Geneva: International Labour Office.

Miles, T. 2001. Agribusiness subsector assessments. In *World Bank guide to developing agricultural markets and agro-enterprises.* <www.worldbank.org/essd/essd/nsf/agroenterprise> (accessed May 2002).

Milimo, J. T., and Y. Fisseha. 1986. Rural small scale enterprises in Zambia: Results of a 1985 country-wide survey. MSU International Development Papers, Working Paper 28. East Lansing: Michigan State University, Department of Agricultural Economics.

Millard, E. 1996. *Export marketing for a small handicraft business.* Oxford: Oxfam/ITDG.

Mills, E. S. 1967. An aggregative model of resource allocation in a metropolitan area. *American Economic Review* 57 (1): 197–210.

———. 1972. *Urban economics.* Glenview, Ill.: Scott, Foresman.

Minot, N. 1986. Contract farming and its effect on small farmers in less developed countries. MSU International Development Working Paper 31. East Lansing: Michigan State University, Department of Agricultural Economics.

Minot, N., and M. Ngigi. 2003. Are horticultural exports a replicable success story? Evidence from Kenya and Côte d'Ivoire. Environment and Production Technology Division Working Paper. Washington, D.C.: International Food Policy Research Institute.

Minot, N., M. Epprecht, T. T. T. Anh, and L. Q. T. Trung. 2006. Income diversification and poverty in the Northern Uplands of Vietnam. Research Report 145. Washington, D.C.: International Food Policy Research Institute.

Mittendorf, H. J. 1986. Role of government in improving food market centres in less developed countries. Rome: Food and Agricultural Organization.

Mohan, R. 1984. The economic determinants of urbanisation: The regional pattern of urbanisation in India Explained. Discussion Paper DRD-78. Washington, D.C.: World Bank.

Mohapatra, S., S. Rozelle, and J. Huang. 2005. Climbing the development ladder: Economic development and the evolution of occupations in rural China. UC Davis Working Paper. Davis: University of California.

Mokyr, J. 1990. *The lever of riches: Technological creativity and economic progress.* New York: Oxford University Press.

Montigard, J. 1992. L'analyse des filières agro-alimentaires. *Economies et Sociétés, Cahiers de l'ISMEA* 26 (6): 59–70.

Moock, P., P. Musgrove, and M. Stelcner. 1990. Education and earnings in Peru's informal nonfarm family enterprises. Living Standards Measurement Study Working Paper 64. Washington, D.C.: World Bank.

Mooney, T., C. Stathacos, and C. Adoum. 1998. Promoting the development of private sector agribusiness: Lessons learned from the Agribusiness and Marketing Improvement Strategies (AMIS II) Project. Bethesda, Md.: Abt Associates.

Morduch, J. 1999a. The microfinance promise. *Journal of Economic Literature* 37: 1569–1614.

———. 1999b. The role of subsidies in microfinance: Evidence from the Grameen Bank. *Journal of Development Economics* 60: 220–248.

———. 2000. The microfinance schism. *World Development* 28 (4): 617–629.

Morduch, J., and B. Haley. 2002. Analysis of the effects of microfinance on poverty reduction. NYU Wagner Working Paper 1014. New York: New York University.

Morrisson, C., H.-B. S. Lecomte, and X. Oudin. 1994. *Micro-enterprises and the institutional framework in developing countries.* Paris: Organisation for Economic Cooperation and Development.

MSI. *See* Management Systems International.

Mukherjee, A. N., and Y. Kuroda. 2001. Effect of rural nonfarm employment and infrastructure on agricultural productivity: Evidence from India. Discussion Paper 938. Ibaraki, Japan: University of Tsukuba.

Mukhopadhyay, S. 1985. Rural non-farm sector in Asia: A characterization. *Economic and Political Weekly* (20): 966–968.

Mukhopadhyay, S., and C. P. Lim. 1985a. *Development and diversification of rural industries in Asia.* Kuala Lumpur: Asian and Pacific Development Centre.

———. 1985b. *The rural non-farm sector in Asia.* Kuala Lumpur: Asian and Pacific Development Centre.

Murphy, K. X. 2001. Agribusiness sector competitiveness: Implementing the right initiatives. In World Bank guide to developing agricultural markets and agro-enterprises. <www.worldbank.org/essd/essd/nsf/agroenterprise/ag-sector_comp> (accessed May 2002).

Mwanamwambwa-Wright, M. 2000. The private sector, agribusiness and rural development. Paper, Bimzi Ltd., Lusaka, Zambia.

Myrdal, G. 1957. *Economic theory and underdeveloped regions.* London: Methuen.

Nagarajan, G. 2001. Productivity drivers and trends. *MicroBanking Bulletin* 6 (April): 35–39.

Nagarajan, G., and R. L. Meyer. 1995. Incorporating finance into a modified subsector framework: The fertilizer subsector in Gambia. *World Development* 23 (7): 1115–1127.

———. 2005. Rural finance: Recent advances and emerging lessons, debates and opportunities. Working Paper AEDE-WP-0041-05. Columbus: Ohio State University.

Nattrass, N., and J. Nattrass. 1990. The homelands and rural development. *Development Southern Africa* 7 (October): 517–534.

Navajas, S., M. Schreiner, R. L. Meyer, C. Gonzalez-Vega, and J. Rodriguez-Meza. 2000. Microcredit and the poorest of the poor: Theory and evidence from Bolivia. *World Development* 28 (2): 333–346.

Nel, E. 1996. Local community economic development: Applied practice and current policy formation in small towns in South Africa. Paper presented at the twenty-eighth annual conference of the International Community Development Society, Melbourne, Victoria, Australia, July. <www.comm-dev.org/conf96/nel.htm> (accessed May 2002).

Nelson, C. 1997. Training goes to market: A comparative study of two Kenyan training programs. Microenterprise Best Practice Business Development Services Case Study. Bethesda, Md.: Development Alternatives.

Neven, D. 2004. Three essays on the rise of supermarkets and their impacts on fresh fruits and vegetables supply chains in Kenya. Ph.D. dissertation, Michigan State University, East Lansing.

Neven, D., and T. Reardon. 2004. The rise of Kenyan supermarkets and evolution of their horticulture product procurement systems: Implications for agricultural diversification and smallholder market access programs. *Development Policy Review* 22 (6): 669–699.

Nielsen, A. C. 2002. Modern trade (self-service)—Share of trade. PowerPoint presentation at the Food Marketing Institute Convention, May 6, Chicago.

Norman, D. W. 1972. An economic study of three villages in Zaria Province. Samaru Miscellaneous Paper 37. Zaria, Nigeria: Ahmadu Bello University.

————. 1973. Economic analysis of agricultural production and labor utilization among the Hausa in the North of Nigeria. African Rural Employment Paper 4. East Lansing: Michigan State University.

Novelli, L. 1968. Kaffir beer brewing: Ancient art and modern industry. *Wallerstein Laboratory Communications* 17: 354–361.

Nugent, J. B. 1996. What explains the trend reversal in the size distribution of Korean manufacturing establishments? *Journal of Development Economics* 48 (2): 225–251.

Nugent, J. B., and M. K. Nabli. 1992. An institutional analysis of the size distribution of manufacturing establishments: An international cross-country study. *World Development* 20 (10): 1489–1499.

Nweke, F., D. S. C. Spencer, and J. K. Lynam. 2002. *The cassava transformation: Africa's best-kept secret.* East Lansing: Michigan State University Press.

OECD. *See* Organisation for Economic Co-operation and Development (OECD).

Ohno, A., and B. Jirapatpimol. 1998. The rural garment and weaving industries in Northern Thailand. In *Toward the rural-based development of commerce and industry: Selected experiences from East Asia,* ed. Y. Hayami. Washington, D.C.: World Bank.

Ohno, A., and M. Kikuchi. 1998. Organizational characteristics of rural textile industries in East Asia. In *Toward the rural-based development of commerce and industry: Selected experiences from East Asia,* ed. Y. Hayami. Washington, D.C.: World Bank.

Okuda, S. 1997. Industrialization policies of Korean and Taiwan and their effects on manufacturing productivity. *Developing Economies* 35 (4): 358–381.

Onyekwere, O. O., I. A. Akinrele, and O. A. Koleoso. 1989. Industrialization of ogi fermentation. In *Industrialization of indigenous fermented foods,* ed. K. H. Steinkraus. New York: Marcel Dekker.

Onyekwere, O. O., I. A. Akinrele, O. A. Koleoso, and G. Heys. 1989. Industrialization of Gari fermentation. In *Industrialization of indigenous fermented foods,* ed. K. H. Steinkraus. New York: Marcel Dekker.

Organisation for Economic Co-operation and Development (OECD). 2003. *Investment policy review of China: Progress and reform challenges.* Paris: OECD.

Oshima, H. T. 1971. Labor force "explosion" and the labor-intensive sector in Asian growth. *Economic Development and Cultural Change* 19 (1): 161–183.

————. 1984. The significance of off-farm employment and incomes in post-war East Asian growth. Asian Development Bank Economic Staff Paper 21. Manila: Asian Development Bank.

————. 1986a. Off-farm employment and incomes in postwar East Asian growth. In *Off-farm employment in the development of rural Asia,* ed. R. T. Shand, Vol. 1. Canberra: Australian National University.

————. 1986b. The transition from an agricultural to an industrial economy in East Asia. *World Development* 34: 783–809.

————. 1993. *Strategic processes in monsoon Asia's economic development.* Baltimore: The Johns Hopkins University Press.

Osmani, S. R. 1987. The impact of economic liberalisation on the small-scale and rural industries of Sri Lanka. In *Rural industrialization and employment in Asia,* ed. R. Islam. New Delhi: International Labour Organisation.

———. 1989. Limits to the alleviation of poverty through nonfarm credit. *Bangladesh Development Studies* 17 (4): 1–19.

Otero, M., and E. Rhyne. 1994. *The new world of microenterprise finance: Building healthy financial institutions for the poor.* West Hartford, Conn.: Kumarian.

———. 1998. Rural industrialization in East Asia. In *The institutional foundation of East Asian economic development,* ed. Y. Hayami and M. Aoki. London: Macmillan.

Otsuka, K., G. Saxonhouse, and G. Ranis. 1988. *Comparative technology choice in development: The Indian and Japanese cotton textile industries.* London: Macmillan.

Overy, A., and V. Giray. 1996. Case VII: Fabric waste recycling in Manila, Philippines (Save the Children USA). In *Beyond credit: A subsector approach to promoting women's enterprises,* ed. M. A. Chen. Ottawa: Aga Khan Foundation.

Pack, H. 1987. *Productivity, technology and industrial development.* New York: Oxford University Press.

———. 1972. Employment and productivity in Kenyan manufacturing. *Eastern Africa Economic Review* 4: 29–52.

Page, J. M. Jr., and W. F. Steel. 1984. Small enterprise development: Economic issues from African experience. World Bank Technical Paper 26. Washington, D.C.: World Bank.

Painter, M. 1987a. Spatial analysis and regional inequality: Some suggestions for development planning. *Human Organization* 46 (4): 318–329.

———. 1987b. Spatial analysis of regional marketing systems in the Third World. In *Patterns of change in developing regions,* ed. R. Bar-El, A. Bendavid-Val, and G. J. Karaska. Boulder, Colo.: Westview.

Pakistan. 1985. *Pakistan statistical yearbook 1985.* Islamabad: Federal Bureau of Statistics, Statistics Division.

———. 2001. *1998 census report of Pakistan.* Islamabad: Population Census Organization, Statistics Division.

Papola, T. S. 1987. Rural industrialisation and agricultural growth: A case study on India. In *Off-farm employment in the development of rural Asia,* ed. R. T. Shand, Vol. 1. Canberra: Australian National University.

Parikh, A., and E. Thorbecke. 1996. Impact of rural industrialization on village life and economy: A SAM approach. *Economic Development and Cultural Change* 44 (2): 351–377.

Park, F. K. 1986. Off-farm employment in Korea: Current status and future prospects. In *Off-farm employment in the development of rural Asia,* ed. R. T. Shand, Vol. 1. Canberra: Australian National University.

Parker, J. 1995. Patterns of business growth: Micro and small enterprises in Kenya. Ph.D. dissertation, Department of Agricultural Economics, Michigan State University, East Lansing.

Parker, J., and C. A. Dondo. 1991. Kenya: Kibera's small enterprise sector: Baseline survey report. GEMINI Working Paper 17. Bethesda, Md.: Development Alternatives.

Parker, R. L., R. Riopelle, and W. F. Steel. 1995. Small enterprises adjusting to liberalization in five African countries. World Bank Discussion Paper, Africa Technical Department Series 271. Washington, D.C.: World Bank.

Perkins, D. 1977. *Rural small-scale industry in the People's Republic of China.* Report of the American Rural Small-Scale Industry Delegation. Berkeley: University of California Press.

Perkins, D., and S. Yusuf. 1985. *Rural development in China.* Baltimore: The Johns Hopkins University Press.

Perroux, F. 1950. Economic space, theory and applications. *Quarterly Journal of Economics* 64: 89–104.

———. 1955. Note sur la notion de pole de croissance. *Economie Appliquée* 8 (1–2): 307–320.

Peters, P. E. 1992. Monitoring the effects of grain market liberalization on the income, food security and nutrition of rural households in Zomba South, Malawi. Mimeo, Harvard Institute for International Development, Cambridge, Mass.

Peterson, G. E. 1997. *Decentralization in Latin America: Learning through experience.* World Bank Latin American and Caribbean Studies. Washington, D.C.: World Bank.

Phillips, R., ed. 1973. *Building viable food chains in developing countries.* Manhattan, Ks.: Kansas State University, Food and Feed Grain Institute.

Pinstrup-Andersen, P., and P. B. R. Hazell. 1985. The impact of the green revolution and prospects for the future. *Food Reviews International* 1 (1): 1–25.

Pitt, M. M., and S. R. Khandker. 1996. Household and intrahousehold impact of the Grameen Bank and similar targeted credit programs in Bangladesh. World Bank Discussion Papers 320. Washington, D.C.: World Bank.

———. 1998. The impact of group-based credit programs on the poor in Bangladesh: Does the gender of the participants matter? *Journal of Political Economy* 106 (5): 958–996.

Planning Commission. 2000. *Report of the Task Force on Employment Opportunities.* New Delhi: Government of India.

———. 2001. *Report of the Study Group on Development of Small Scale Enterprises.* New Delhi: Government of India.

Poapongsakorn, N. 1994. Transformations in the Thai rural labor market. In *Development or deterioration? Work in rural Asia,* ed. B. Koppel, J. Hawkins, and W. James. Boulder, Colo.: Lynne Rienner.

Porter, M. E. 1980. *Competitive strategy: Techniques for analyzing industries and competitors.* New York: Free Press.

———. 1985. *Competitive advantage: Creating and sustaining superior performance.* New York: Free Press.

———. 1998. Clusters and the new economics of competition. *Harvard Business Review* (November–December): 77–90.

Prebish, R. 1950. *The economic development of Latin America and its principal problems.* Lake Success, N.Y.: United Nations Department of Economic Affairs.

———. 1959. Commercial policy in the underdeveloped countries. *American Economic Review, Papers and Proceedings* 49 (May): 251–273.

Preston, D. 1978. Exploitation or symbiosis: The relationships between towns and countryside in Latin America. *Cahiers des Ameriques Latines* 17: 120–131.

Psacharopoulos, G. 1985. Returns to education: A further international update and implications. *Journal of Human Resources* 20 (4): 583–604.

Purvis, M. 1968. Report on a survey of the oil palm rehabilitation scheme in Eastern Nigeria. Consortium for the Study of the Nigerian Rural Economy, Michigan State University, East Lansing.

Qian, Y. 2003. How reform worked in China. In *In Search for prosperity: Analytic narratives on economic growth,* ed. D. Rodrik. Princeton, N.J.: Princeton University Press.

Radhakrishna, R., S. Sudhakar, and G. K. Mitra. 1988. *Determinants of labor force participation and living standards.* Hyderbad, India: Centre for Economic and Social Studies.

Rangarajan, C. 1982. Agricultural growth and industrial performance in India. Research Report 33. Washington, D.C.: International Food Policy Research Institute.

Ranis, G. 1989. Macro policies, the terms of trade and the spatial dimension of balanced growth. In *The balance between industry and agriculture in economic development,* ed. Nurul Islam, Vol. 5, *Factors influencing change.* London: Macmillan.

————. 1995. Another look at the East Asian miracle. *World Bank Economic Review* 9 (3): 509–534.

Ranis, G., and J. C. Fei. 1964. *Development of the labor surplus economy: Theory and policy.* Homewood, Ill.: Richard D. Irwin.

Ranis, G., and F. Stewart. 1987. Rural linkages in the Philippines and Taiwan. In *Macro policies for appropriate technology in developing countries,* ed. F. Stewart. Boulder, Colo.: Westview.

————. 1993. Rural nonagricultural activities in development: Theory and application. *Journal of Development Economics* 40: 75–101.

Ranis, G., F. Stewart, and E. Angeles-Reyes. 1990. *Linkages in developing economies: A Philippine study.* San Francisco: International Center for Economic Growth.

Ravallion, M. 1991. Reaching the rural poor through public employment: Arguments, evidence, and lessons from South Asia. *World Bank Research Observer* 6 (2): 153–175.

————. 1999. Appraising workfare. *World Bank Research Observer* 14 (1): 31–48.

Ravallion, M., and S. Chen. 2004. China's (uneven) progress against poverty. Mimeo, DECRG, World Bank, Washington, D.C.

Ravallion, M., and G. Datt. 1996. How important to India's poor is the sectoral composition of economic growth? *World Bank Economic Review* 10 (1): 1–25.

————. 1999. When is growth pro-poor? Evidence from the diverse experience of India's states. Policy Research Working Paper WPS 2263. Washington, D.C.: World Bank.

Rawlinson, H., and P. Fehr. 2002. Creating export markets for Bolivia's dried beans. In *Building business with small producers,* ed. S. Kapiola and D. Mead. Ottawa: International Development Research Center.

Reardon, T. 1997. Using evidence of household income diversification to inform study of the rural nonfarm labor market in Africa. *World Development* 25 (5): 735–747.

————. 1999. Diagnostico rápido del empleo rural (agrícola y no agrícola) en el Sur de Lempira, Honduras—Con implicaciones para el proyecto FAO PROLESUR. Mimeo, FAO Oficina Regional para America Latina y el Caribe, Santiago de Chile.

————. 2000. Interactions between the agricultural system and nonagricultural activities of farm households in developing countries. In *Research on agricultural systems:*

Accomplishments, perspectives and issues, ed. J.-P. Colin and E. W. Crawford. Huntington, N.Y.: Nova Science.

———. 2003. Desafios de la lucha contra la pobreza rural en la economía globalizada de América Latina: Instituciones, mercados y proyectos. In La pobreza rural en América Latina: Lecciones para una reorientación de la políticas, ed. Division Desarrollo Productivo y Empresarial, Unidad de Desarrollo Agricola, CEPAL. Series CEPAL—Seminarios y Conferencias 27, August. Proceedings of the International Conference Encuentro de altos directivos de la lucha contra la pobreza rural, organized by ECLAC, Rimisp, and FAO, in Valle Nevado, Chile, January 27–28, 2000.

———. 2004. The rise of supermarkets in Mexico: Implications for rural development strategy. Mimeo, U.S. Agency for International Development, Mexico City.

Reardon, T., and C. B. Barrett. 2000. Agroindustrialization, globalization, and international development: An overview of issues, patterns, and determinants. *Agricultural Economics* 23 (3): 195–205.

Reardon, T., and J. A. Berdegué. 2002. The rapid rise of supermarkets in Latin America: Challenges and opportunities for development. *Development Policy Review* 20 (4): 317–334.

Reardon, T., and L. Flores. 2006. Viewpoint: "Customized competitiveness" strategies for horticultural exporters: Central America focus with lessons from and for other regions. *Food Policy* 31 (6): 483–503.

Reardon, T., and J. E. Taylor. 1996. Agroclimatic shock, income inequality, and poverty: Evidence from Burkina Faso. *World Development* 24 (4): 901–914.

Reardon, T., and C. P. Timmer. 2007. Transformation of markets for agricultural output in developing countries since 1950: How has thinking changed? In *Handbook of agricultural economics,* ed. R. Evenson and P. Pingail, Vol. 3A. Amsterdam: North Holland.

Reardon, T., and S. A. Vosti. 1995. Links between rural poverty and environment in developing countries: Asset categories and investment poverty. *World Development* 23 (9): 1495–1506.

Reardon, T., J. Berdegué, and G. Escobar. 2001. Rural nonfarm employment and incomes in Latin America: Overview and policy implications. *World Development* 29 (3): 395–409.

Reardon, T., E. Crawford, and V. Kelly. 1994. Links between nonfarm income and farm investment in African households: Adding the capital market perspective. *American Journal of Agricultural Economics* 76 (5): 1172–1176.

Reardon, T., C. Delgado, and P. Matlon. 1992. Determinants and effects of income diversification amongst farm households in Burkina Faso. *Journal of Development Studies* 28 (January): 264–296.

Reardon, T., P. Matlon, and C. Delgado. 1988. Coping with household-level food insecurity in drought-affected areas of Burkina Faso. *World Development* 16 (9): 1065–1074.

Reardon, T., A. A. Fall, V. Kelly, C. Delgado, P. Matlon, J. Hopkins, and O. Badiane. 1993. Agriculture-led income diversification in the West African semi-arid tropics: Nature, distribution and importance of production-linkage activities. In *African economic issues,* ed. A. Atsain, S. Wangwe, and A. G. Drabek. Nairobi: African Economic Research Consortium.

Reardon, T., K. Stamolous, A. Balisacan, M. E. Cruz, J. Berdegué, and B. Banks. 1998. Rural nonfarm income in developing countries. In *The state of food and agriculture 1998,* Special Chapter. Rome: Food and Agricultural Organization of the United Nations.

Reardon, T., J. E. Taylor, K. Stamoulis, P. Lanjouw, and A. Balisacan. 2000. Effects of nonfarm employment on rural income inequality in developing countries: An investment perspective. *Journal of Agricultural Economics* 51 (2): 266–288.

Reardon, T., J.-M. Codron, L. Busch, J. Bingen, and C. Harris. 2001. Global change in agrifood grades and standards: Agribusiness strategic responses in developing countries. *International Food and Agribusiness Management Review* 2 (3): 195–205.

Reardon, T., C. P. Timmer, C. Barrett, and J. Berdegué. 2003. The rise of supermarkets in Africa, Asia and Latin America. *American Journal of Agricultural Economics* 85 (5): 1140–1146.

Regmi, A., and M. Gehlar. 2005. Processed food trade pressured by evolving global supply chains. *Amberwaves* (USDA magazine), February, 12–19.

Reiling, P. A. 1990. The sector approach to enterprise analysis and development. Norwalk, Conn.: Technoserve.

Reinhart, N. 1987. Modernizing peasant agriculture: Lessons from El Palmar, Colombia. *World Development* 15: 221–247.

Reinikka, R., and P. Collier. 2001. *Uganda's recovery: The role of farms, firms and government.* Washington, D.C.: World Bank.

Rello F. 1997. Ciudades intermedias y desarrollo rural: El caso de Zamora, Michoacán (México). Informe de la Oficina Regional para América Latina y el Caribe de la Organización de las Naciones Unidas para la Agricultura y la Alimentación (FAO), Santiago de Chile.

Reserve Bank of India. Various years. *RBI annual reports.* New Delhi: Reserve Bank of India.

Resnick, S. 1970. The decline of rural industry under export expansion: A comparison among Burma, Philippines and Thailand, 1870–1938. *Journal of Economic History* 30 (1–2): 51–73.

Richardson, H. W. 1976. Growth pole spillovers: Dynamics of backwash and spread. *Regional Studies* 10: 1–9.

———. 1978a. Growth centres, rural development and national urban policy: A defense. *International Regional Science Review* 3 (2): 133–152.

———. 1978b. *Urban economics.* Hinsdale, Ill.: Dryden.

———. 1985. Input-output and economic base multipliers: Looking backward and looking forward. *Journal of Regional Science* 25: 607–661.

Rietveld, P. 1993. Methods for planning urban facilities in rural areas of developing countries: Comparison of approaches. *International Regional Science Review* 15 (3): 345–356.

Riley, H. M., and M. T. Weber. 1983. Marketing in developing countries. In *Future frontiers in agricultural marketing research,* ed. P. L. Farris. Ames: Iowa State University Press.

Riley, T. A., and W. F. Steel. 2000. Kenya voucher programme for training and BDS. In *Business development services: A review of international experience,* ed. J. Levitsky. London: Intermediate Technology Development Services.

Riskin, C. 1971. Small industry and the Chinese model of development. *China Quarterly* (April/June): 245–273.

Roach, S. 2004. The challenge of China and India. *Financial Times,* September 1. <http://search.ft.com/ftArticle?queryText=Stephen+Roach&aje=true&id=040901000911&page=14> (accessed April 2007).

Robinson, M. S. 2002. *Microfinance revolution,* Vol. 2, *Lessons from Indonesia.* Washington, D.C.: World Bank.

Rodolo, T. 1972. *A business guide for African shopkeepers.* Durban, South Africa: Intermint Proprietary Ltd. for Unilever South Africa.

Rogaly, B. 1996. Micro-finance evangelism, destitute women and the hard selling of a new anti-poverty formula. *Development in Practice* 6: 100–112.

Rogers, G. R. 1986. The theory of output-income multipliers with consumption linkages: An application to Mauritania. Ph.D. dissertation, University of Wisconsin, Madison.

Romjin, H. A. 1987. Employment generation through cottage industries in rural Thailand: Potentials and constraints. In *Rural industrialization and employment in Asia,* ed. R. Islam. New Delhi: International Labour Office.

Rondinelli, D. 1981. Government decentralization in comparative perspective: Theory and practice in developing countries. *International Review of Administrative Science* 47 (2): 133–145.

———. 1985. *Applied methods of regional analysis: The spatial dimensions of development policy.* Boulder, Colo.: Westview.

———. 1986. The urban transition and agricultural development: Implications for international assistance policy. *Development and Change* 17 (2): 231–263.

———. 1987a. Cities as agricultural markets. *Geographical Review* 77 (4): 408–420.

———. 1987b. Roles of towns and cities in the development of rural regions. In *Patterns of change in developing rural regions,* ed. R. Bar-El, A. Bendavid-Val, and G. J. Karaska. Boulder, Colo.: Westview.

———. 1988. Market towns and agriculture in Africa: The role of small urban centres in economic development. *African Urban Quarterly* 3 (1): 3–12.

———. 1993. Location analysis and regional development: Summing up and moving on. *International Regional Science Review* 15 (3): 325–340.

Rondinelli, D. A., and H. Evans. 1983. Integrated regional development planning: Linking urban centres and rural areas in Bolivia. *World Development* 11 (1): 31–54.

Rondinelli, D. A., and K. Ruddle. 1978. *Urbanization and rural development: A spatial policy for equitable growth.* New York: Praeger.

Rosegrant, M. W., and P. B. R. Hazell. 2000. *Transforming the rural Asian economy: The unfinished revolution.* Hong Kong: Oxford University Press.

Rosenfield, S. A. 2001a. Advancing the understanding of clusters and their opportunities for less favored regions, less advantaged populations and small and mid-sized enterprises. Regional Technology Strategies. <www.trsinc.org> (accessed May 2002).

———. 2001b. Backing into clusters: Retrofitting public policies. Paper presented to the symposium on integration pressures, Lessons from Around the World. The John F. Kennedy School Symposium, Harvard University, March 29–30.

———. 2001c. Networks and clusters: The yin and yang of rural development. Regional Technology Strategies. <www.trsinc.org> (accessed May 2002).

Rosenstein-Rodan, P. N. 1943. Problems of industrialization of Eastern and Southeastern Europe. *Economic Journal* 53 (June): 202–211.

Rosenzweig, M. R. 1988. Labor markets in low-income countries. In *Handbook of development economics,* ed. H. Chenery and T. N. Srinivasan, Vol. 1. Amsterdam: North Holland.

Rosenzweig, M. R., and O. Stark. 1989. Consumption smoothing, migration and marriage: Evidence from rural India. *Journal of Political Economy* 97: 905–926.

Ruben, R., and M. Van Den Berg. 2001. Nonfarm employment and poverty alleviation of rural farm households in Honduras. *World Development* 29 (3): 549–560.

Rubey, L. 1995. The impact of policy reform on small-scale agribusiness: A case study of maize processing in Zimbabwe. *African Rural and Urban Studies* 2 (2–3): 93–119.

Ruiz-Perez, M., and J. E. M. Arnold. 1996. *Current issues in non-timber forest products research.* Bogor, Indonesia: Center for International Forestry Research.

Rushton, G. 1988. Location theory, location-allocation models, and service development planning in the Third World. *Economic Geography* 64 (2): 97–120.

———. 1993. Lessons from the debate on location analysis in rural economic development. *International Regional Science Review* 15 (3): 317–324.

Ruttan, V. W. 1975. Integrated rural development programs: A skeptical perspective. *International Development Review* 2: 129–151.

———. 1977. The green revolution: Several generalizations. *International Development Review* 4: 16–23.

———. 1984. Integrated rural development programmes: A historical perspective. *World Development* 12 (4): 393–401.

Sadoulet, E., and A. de Janvry. 1995. *Quantitative development policy analysis.* Baltimore: The Johns Hopkins University Press.

Saith, A. 1987. Contrasting experiences in rural industrialisation: Are the East Asian successes transferable? In *Rural industrialisation and employment in Asia,* ed. R. Islam. New Delhi: International Labour Office.

———. 1992. *The rural non-farm economy: Processes and policies.* Geneva: International Labour Organisation.

———. 2001. From village artisans to industrial clusters: Agendas and policy gaps in Indian rural industry. *Journal of Agrarian Change* 1 (1): 81–123.

Salorio, E. M. 1992. Commodity system politics and U.S. agricultural policy: A model of agribusiness interests and the government decision-making process. *Research in Domestic and International Agribusiness Management* 10: 181–218.

Samuelson, P. 1997. *The start and improve your business programme: Achievement and experiences worldwide.* Small Enterprise Development Working Paper SED 23/E. Geneva: International Labour Office.

Sanchez, P., and M. S. Swaminathan. 2005. Cutting world hunger in half. *Science* 307 (5708): 357–359.

Sandee, H., and S. C. van Hulsen. 2000. Business development services for small and cottage industry clusters in Indonesia: A review of case studies from Central Java. Paper presented at an international conference, Business Services for Small Enterprises in Asia: Developing Markets and Measuring Performance, Hanoi, International Labour Office, April 3–6.

Sander, W. 1983. Irrigation development and nonfarm employment changes in two communities in the Philippines. *Indian Journal of Agricultural Economics* 38 (1): 1–14.

Sandesara, J. C. 1980. Small industries in India: Evidence and interpretation. Presidential address, Gujarat Economic Association, Ahmedabad.

Sanghvi, R. L. 1975. *Role of industrial estates in a developing economy.* Bombay: Multi-Tech.

Sato, Y. 1997. Diverging development paths of the electronics industry in Korea and Taiwan. *Developing Economies* 35 (4): 401–421.

Sattar, A. 1996. Case I. SEWA's dairy cooperatives and case II. SEWA's vegetable vendors' cooperatives. In *Beyond credit: A subsector approach to promoting women's enterprises,* ed. M. A. Chen. Ottawa: Aga Khan Foundation.

Satterthwaite, D. 2000. Seeking an understanding of poverty that recognizes rural-urban differences and rural-urban linkages. Paper presented at the World Bank Urban Forum on Urban Poverty Reduction in the 21st Century. Washington, D.C., April.

Saunders, R. J., J. J. Warford, and B. Wellenius. 1983. *Telecommunications and economic development.* Baltimore: The Johns Hopkins University Press.

Save the Children. 2000. From the margins to the mainstream: A documentation of the Women's Microenterprise Networks (WMEN) Program Implementation in the Retaso Subsector. Manila: Save the Children.

Schatzberg, M. 1979. Islands of privilege: Small cities in Africa and the dynamics of class formation. *Urban Anthropology* 8 (2): 173–190.

Schejtman, A. 1998. Agroindustria y pequeña agricultura: experiencias y opciones de transformación. In *Agroindustria y pequeña agricultura: vínculos, potencialidades y oportunidades comerciales.* Serie Libros de la CEPAL 46 (LC/G.2007-P). Publicación de las Naciones Unidas, N° de venta: S.98.II.G.4.Santiago de Chile: Comisión Económica para América Latina y el Caribe (CEPAL).

Schmiechen, J. 1984. *Sweated industries and sweated labor.* Champaign: University of Illinois Press.

Schmitz, H. 1982. Growth constraints on small-scale manufacturing in developing countries: A critical review. *World Development* 10 (6): 429–450.

———. 1999. Global competition and local cooperation: Success and failure in the Sinos Valley, Brazil. *World Development* 27 (2): 1627–1650.

Schmitz, H., and K. Nadvi. 1999. Industrial clusters in developing countries. *World Development* 27 (9): 1503–1514.

Schreiner, M. 2003. A cost-effectiveness analysis of the Grameen Bank. *Development Policy Review* 21 (3): 357–382.

Schreiner, M., and Y. Yaron. 2001. *Development finance institutions: Measuring their subsidy.* Washington, D.C.: World Bank.

Schubert, B. 1983. Market information services. FAO Agricultural Services Bulletin 57. Rome: Food and Agriculture Organization.

Schultz, P. 1996. Reproducible human capital and wages in two West African economies. Mimeo, Yale University Growth Center, Yale University, New Haven, Conn.

Schultz, T. P. 1998. Income inequality in Taiwan, 1976–1993: Aging, fertility, and family composition. In *The economics and political economy of comparative development into the 21st century,* ed. G. Ranis, S.-C. Hu, and Y.-P. Chu. London: Edward Elgar.

Schultz, T. W. 1964. *Transforming traditional agriculture.* New Haven, Conn.: Yale University Press.

Schumacher, E. F. 1965. *Buddhist economics*. London: Christian Frontier Council.

———. 1976. *Small is beautiful: A study of economics as if people mattered*. New York: Harper and Row.

Scitovsky, T. 1954. Two concepts of external economies. *Journal of Political Economy* 62 (2): 143–151.

Sebstad, J., and G. Chen. 1996. Overview of studies on the impact of microenterprise credit. Assessing the Impact of Microenterprise Services (AIMS) Working Paper. Washington, D.C.: Management Systems International.

Segal, A., W. Koehler Jr., W. Ting, R. Suttmeir, W. Moorhouse, and B. Bupta. 1987. *Learning by doing: Science and technology in the developing world*. Boulder, Colo.: Westview.

Sellers, C. 1991. *The market revolution: Jacksonian America, 1815–1846*. New York: Oxford University Press.

Sen, A. K. 1968. *Choice of technique*. Oxford: Basil Blackwell.

———. 1999. *Development as freedom*. New Delhi: Oxford University Press.

SGRNFS. *See* Study Group on the Rural Non-Farm Sector.

Shaffer, J. 1968. Changing orientation of marketing research. *American Journal of Agricultural Economics* 50 (5): 1437–1449.

———. 1973. On the concept of subsector studies. *American Journal of Agricultural Economics* 55 (2): 333–336.

———. 1980. Food systems organization and performance: Toward a conceptual framework. *American Journal of Agricultural Economics* 62 (2): 248–267.

Shaffer, J. D., M. T. Weber, H. M. Riley, and J. Staatz. 1985. Designing marketing systems to promote development in the Third World. Proceedings of the International Workshop Agricultural Markets in the Semi-Arid Tropics, October 24–28, 1983. Patancheru, India: International Crops Research Institute for the Semi-Arid Tropics (ICRISAT).

Shah, T., M. Alam, M. D. Kumar, R. I. Nagar, and M. Singh. 2000. Pedaling out of poverty: Social impact of a manual irrigation technology in South Asia. IWMI Research Report 45. Colombo, Sri Lanka: International Water Management Institute.

Shand, R. T. 1986a. *Off-farm employment in the development in rural Asia*. Canberra: Australian National University.

———. 1986b. Off-farm employment in the development of rural Asia: Issues. In *Off-farm employment in the development of rural Asia*, ed. R. T. Shand. Canberra: Australian National University.

Shand, R. T., and T. A. Chew. 1986. Off-farm employment in the Kemubu Project in Kelantan, Malaysia. In *Off-farm employment in the development of rural Asia*, ed. R. T. Shand. Canberra: Australian National University.

Sharma, H. R. 2001. Employment and wage earnings of agricultural labourers: A statewise analysis. *Indian Journal of Labour Economics* 44 (1): 27–38.

Shih, J. T. 1983. Decentralized industrialization and rural nonfarm employment in Taiwan. *Industry of Free China* 60 (2): 1–20.

Siamwalla, A. 1995. Land-abundant agricultural growth and some of its consequences: The case of Thailand. In *Agriculture on the road to industrialization*, ed. J. W. Mellor. Baltimore: The Johns Hopkins University Press.

Sigurdson, J. 1977. *Rural industrialization in China.* Cambridge, Mass.: Harvard University, Council on East Asian Studies.

Silva-Barbeau, I., M. S. Prehm, K. Samba-Ndure, K. Jorne, A. Jawneh, and S. G. Hull. 1997. The direct and indirect benefits of sesame oil production on the nutritional security of women and children. Paper presented at the 16th annual Congress of Nutrition, Montreal, July 27–August 1.

Simler, K. 1994a. Agricultural policy and technology options in Malawi: Modelling smallholder responses and outcomes. Working Paper 49. Ithaca, N.Y.: Cornell University Food and Nutrition Policy Program.

———. 1994b. Rural poverty and income sources of smallholder farmers: A household economics analysis with panel data from Northern Malawi. Ph.D. dissertation, Cornell University, Ithaca, N.Y.

Simmons, E. B. 1976. Economic research on women in rural development in Northern Nigeria. OLC Paper 10. Washington, D.C.: Overseas Liaison Committee.

Singer, H. 1950. The distribution of gains between investing and borrowing countries. *American Economic Review, Papers and Proceedings* 40 (May): 473–485.

Singh, I., L. Squire, and J. Strauss, eds. 1986. *Agricultural household models.* Baltimore: The Johns Hopkins University Press.

Smith, C. A. 1976. Regional economic systems, linking geographical models and socioeconomic problems. In *Regional analysis,* ed. C. A. Smith, Vol. 1, *Economic systems.* New York: Academic Press.

———. 1977. How marketing systems affect economic opportunity in agrarian societies. In *Peasant livelihood,* ed. R. Halperin and J. Dow. New York: St. Martin's Press.

———. 1984. Survival strategies among rural smallholders and petty commodity procedures: A case study of Western Guatemala. World Employment Programme Research Working Paper WEP 10-6/WP77. Geneva: International Labour Office.

Smith, D. R., A. Gordon, K. Meadows, and K. Zwick. 2001. Livelihood diversification in Uganda: Patterns and determinants of change across two rural districts. *Food Policy* 26: 421–435.

Snodgrass, D. R., and T. Biggs. 1996. *Industrialization and the small firm: Patterns and policies.* San Francisco: International Center for Economic Growth.

Snodgrass, D. R., and J. Packard Winkler. 2004. *Enterprise growth initiatives: Strategic directions and options.* Bethesda, Md.: Development Alternatives.

Somasekhara, N. 1975. *The efficacy of industrial estates in India with particular reference to Mysore.* Delhi: Vikas.

Sonobe, T., and K. Otsuka. 1999. Changing industrial structure and economic development: Prewar Japan revisited. In *The economics and political economy of comparative development into the twenty-first century,* ed. G. Ranis, S.-C. Hu, and Y.-P. Chu. London: Edward Elgar.

———. 2006a. *Cluster-based industrial development: An East Asian model.* Basingstoke, England: Palgrave Macmillan.

———. 2006b. The division of labor and the formation of industrial clusters in Taiwan. *Review of Development Economics* 10 (1): 71–86.

Sonobe, T., M. Kawakami, and K. Otsuka. 2003. Changing role of innovation and imitation in development: The case of the machine tool industry in Taiwan. *Economic Development and Cultural Change* 52 (1): 103–128.

Southall, A., ed. 1979. *Small urban centres in rural development in Africa.* Madison: University of Wisconsin.

———. 1982. What causes overconcentration or decentralization in the urbanization process? *Urban Anthropology* 8 (2): 173–190.

———. 1988. Small towns in Africa revisited. *African Studies Review* 31 (3).

Spodek, H. 1975. From "parasitic" to "generative": The transformation of post-colonial cities in India. *Journal of Interdisciplinary History* 5: 413–443.

———. 1986. The urban history of India: An update. *Journal of Urban History* 12 (May): 293–308.

Staley, E., and R. Morse. 1965. *Modern small industry of developing countries.* New York: McGraw-Hill.

Start, D. 2001. The rise and fall of the rural non-farm economy: Poverty impacts and policy options. *Development Policy Review* 19 (4): 491–505.

Statistics South Africa. 1996. *South Africa population census, 1996.* Pretoria: Statistics South Africa.

Steel, W. F. 1977. *Small-scale employment in production in developing countries: Evidence from Ghana.* New York: Praeger.

Steel, W. F., and L. M. Webster. 1990. Small enterprises in Ghana: Responses to adjustment. Industry and Energy Department Working Paper, Industry Series Paper 33. Washington, D.C.: World Bank.

Steel, W. F., J. Tanburn, and K. Hallberg. 2000. The emerging strategy for building BDS markets. In *Business development services: A review of international experience,* ed. J. Levitsky. London: Intermediate Technology Development Group.

Steinkraus, K., ed. 1989. *Industrialization of indigenous fermented foods.* New York: Marcel Dekker.

Stepanek, J. 1960. *Small industry advisory services: An international study.* Glencoe, Ill.: Free Press.

Stewart, F. 1977. *Technology and underdevelopment.* Boulder, Colo.: Westview.

———, ed. 1987. *Macro-policies for appropriate technology in developing countries.* Boulder, Colo.: Westview.

Stigler, G. J. 1951. The division of labor is limited by the extent of the market. *Journal of Political Economy* 59 (3): 185–193.

Stohr, W. B. 2001. Subsidiarity: A key concept for regional development policy. In *New regional development paradigms,* ed. W. B. Stosh, J. S. Edralin, and D. Mani, Vol. 3, *Decentralization, governance and the new planning for local-level development.* Westport, Conn.: Greenwood.

Stohr, W. B., and D. R. Taylor. 1981. *Development from above or below?* Chichester, England: John Wiley and Sons.

Stosch, L., and E. L. Hyman. 2002. El Salvador: Coffee production and processing. In *Building businesses with small producers: Successful business development services in Africa, Asia and Latin America,* ed. S. Kapila and D. Mead. London: Intermediate Technology Publications.

Strauss, J., and D. Thomas. 2000. Nutrition and economic development. *Journal of Economic Literature* 36 (2): 766–817.

Study Group on the Rural Non-Farm Sector (SGRNFS). 1995. *The rural non-farm sector in India: Executive summary.* Bern, Switzerland: Münstergasse Bookshop.

Sturgeon, T. J. 2001. How do we define value chains and production networks? *IDS Bulletin* 32 (3): 9–18.

Subbarao, K., A. Bonerjee, J. Braithwaite, S. Carvalho, K. Ezemaneri, C. Graham, and A. Thompson. 1997. Safety net programs and poverty reduction: Lessons from cross-country experience. World Bank, Washington, D.C.

Subramanian, S., and E. Sadoulet. 1990. The transmission of production fluctuations and technical change in a village economy: A SAM approach. *Economic Development and Cultural Change* 39 (1): 131–173.

Tacoli, C. 1998. Rural-urban interactions: A guide to the literature. *Environment and Urbanization* 10 (1): 147–166.

———. 2003. The links between urban and rural development. *Environment and Urbanization* 15 (1): 3–12.

Tacoli, C., and D. Satterthwaite. 2003. The urban part of rural development: The role of small and intermediate urban centres in rural and regional development and poverty reduction. Rural-Urban Interactions and Livelihood Strategies Working Paper 9. London: International Institute for Environment and Development.

Taillefer, C., R. Rakotosolofo Soloarijaona, G. Ralaimidona, F. Rasoloharinjatovo, G. Zafimanjaka, and S. Rasolofomanana. 2000. Evaluation de l'outil analyse de filière: Strategie potentielle pour le developpement d'un service AGR. Mimeo, CARE, Antananarivo, Madagascar.

Tannuri-Pianto, M., D. Pianto, O. Arias, and M. Beneke de Sanfeliu. 2005. Determinants and returns to productive diversification in rural El Salvador. Background paper for *Beyond the city: The rural contribution to development.* Washington, D.C.: World Bank.

Taylor, J. E., and A. Yúnez-Naude. 2000. The returns from schooling in a diversified rural economy. *American Journal of Agricultural Economics* 82 (May): 287–297.

Taylor, J. E., S. Rozelle, and A. de Brauw. 2003. Migration and incomes in source communities: A new economics of migration perspective from China. *Economic Development and Cultural Change* 52 (1): 75–101.

Technoserve. 2004. Partnerships for agribusiness development, agricultural trade and market access: A concept note for NEPAD. Johannesburg: Technoserve.

Tendler, J. 1989. What ever happened to poverty alleviation? *World Development* 17 (7): 1033–1044.

———. 1993. *New lessons from old projects: The workings of rural development in Northeast Brazil.* Washington, D.C.: World Bank, Operations Evaluation Department.

Tendler, J., and V. Amorim. 1996. Small firms and their helpers: Lessons on demand. *World Development* 24 (3): 407–426.

Tewari, V. K. 1992. Improving access to services and facilities in developing countries. *International Regional Science Review* 15 (1): 25–37.

Thailand. 1996. Report of the labor force survey: Whole kingdom, February 1996 (Round 1). Bangkok: National Statistical Office.

Thanh, H. X. 2002. Rural-urban linkages in Vietnam: Background paper on rural employment patterns and market mechanisms in Ha Nam Province. London: International Institute for Environment and Development.

Thiele, G. 1984. Location and enterprise choice: A Tanzanian case study. *Journal of Agricultural Economics* 35 (1): 257–264.

Thomi, W. H., and P. W. K. Yankson. 1985. Small scale industries and decentralization in Ghana: A preliminary report on small scale industries in small and medium sized towns in Ghana. Frankfurt: Institut für Wirtschaft und Sozialgeographie.

Thorbecke, E. 1985. The social accounting matrix and consistency-type planning models. In *Social accounting matrices: A basis for planning*, ed. G. Pyatt and J. I. Round. Washington, D.C.: World Bank.

———. 1994. *Intersectoral linkages and their impact on rural poverty alleviation: A social accounting matrix approach.* Vienna: United Nations Industrial Development Organization.

Timberg, T. 1978. Report on the survey of small scale industry units in Bombay. Washington D.C.: World Bank.

Timmer, C. P. 1972. Employment aspects of investment in rice marketing in Indonesia. *Food Research Institute Studies* 11: 59–88.

———. 1973. Choice of technique in rice milling on Java. *Bulletin of Indonesian Economic Studies* (Canberra) 9 (2): 57–76.

———. 1988. The agricultural transformation. In *Handbook of development economics*, ed. H. Chenery and T. N. Srinivasan, Vol. 1. Amsterdam: North Holland.

———. 1997. Building efficiency in agricultural marketing: The long-run role of BULOG in the Indonesian food economy. *Journal of International Development* 9 (January–February): 133–145.

Tinbergen, J. 1966. Some refinements of the semi-input-output Method. *Pakistan Development Review* 6: 243–247.

Tomich, T. P., P. Kilby, and B. F. Johnston. 1995. *Transforming agrarian economies: Opportunities seized, opportunities missed.* Ithaca, N.Y.: Cornell University Press.

Townsend, R., and J. Yaron. 2001. The credit risk contingency system of an Asian Development Bank. *Economic Perspectives* Q3: 31–48.

Trung, T. Q. 2000. Determinants of income from rural non-farm business activities in Vietnam. M.Sc. thesis, National Economics University, Hanoi.

Tschirley, D. L., and M. T. Weber. 1994. Food security strategies under extremely adverse conditions: The determinants of household income and consumption in rural Mozambique. *World Development* 22 (2): 159–173.

Tseng, W., and H. Zebregs. 2002. Foreign direct investment in China: Some lessons for other countries. IMF Policy Discussion Paper 02/3. Washington D.C.: International Monetary Fund.

Turkey, Republic of. 1972. *Census of population, 1970.* Ankara: Devlet Istatistik Enstitüsü.

———. 1995. *1990 census of population: Social and economic characteristics of population.* Istanbul: Prime Ministry, State Institute of Statistics.

Tyagi, D. S. 1990. *Managing India's food economy.* New Delhi: Sage.

UNDP/UNCHS. *See* United Nations Development Programme / U.N. Centre for Human Settlements.

UN-Habitat. *See* United Nations Human Settlements Programme.

UNIDO. *See* United Nations Industrial Development Organization.

United Nations Department for Economic and Social Information and Policy Analysis. 1996. *1994 demographic yearbook,* 46th issue. New York: United Nations.

United Nations Department of International Economic and Social Affairs. 1986. *Demographic yearbook 1984,* 36th issue. New York: United Nations.

————. 1990. *Demographic yearbook 1988,* 40th issue. New York: United Nations.

United Nations Development Programme / U.N. Centre for Human Settlements (UNDP/ UNCHS). 1995. Rural-urban linkages: Policy guidelines for rural development. Paper prepared for the 23rd meeting of the ACC Sub-committee on Rural Development, UNESCO Headquarters, Paris, May 31–June 2.

United Nations Human Settlements Programme (UN-Habitat). 2005. *Promoting local economic development through strategic planning.* Local Economic Development (LED) series, 4 vols. Nairobi: UN-Habitat.

United Nations Industrial Development Organization (UNIDO). 1978. *Guidelines for the establishment of industrial estates in developing countries.* New York: United Nations.

————. 1995. Présentation de l'approche de Gestion Strategique du Développement Industriel. Antananarivo, Madagascar: UNIDO.

————. 1996. Technical report: Long-term strategies and impact of the hides and skins improvement component of the Regional Africa Leather and Leather Products Programme, Phase I and Phase II. ISED/R.66. Vienna: UNIDO.

United States Agency for International Development (USAID). 1987. AID's experience with integrated rural development projects. AID Program Evaluation Report 19. Washington, D.C.: U.S. Agency for International Development.

————. 1995. *Microenterprise development policy paper.* Washington, D.C.: USAID.

United States Bureau of the Census. 2000. *International database.* Washington, D.C.: U.S. Bureau of the Census, International Program Center.

Unni, J. 1990. Inter-regional variations in non-agricultural employment in rural India: An exploratory analysis. Working Paper 30. Ahmedabad: Gujarat Institute of Area Planning.

Unwin, T. 1989. Urban-rural interaction in developing countries: A theoretical perspective. In *The geography of urban-rural interaction in developing countries,* ed. R. B. Potter and T. Unwin. London: Routledge.

Uruguay, Republica Oriental del. 1989. *Censo de población y de viviendas.* Montevideo: Direccion General de Estadistica Y Censo.

USAID. *See* United States Agency for International Development.

Vaidyanathan, A. 1986. Labour use in rural India: A study of spatial and temporal variations. *Economic and Political Weekly* 21 (52): A130–A146.

Valenzuela, L. 2002. Getting the recipe right: The experience and challenges of commercial bank downscalers. In *The commercialization of microfinance: Balancing business and development,* ed. D. Drake and E. Rhyne. Bloomfield, Conn.: Kumarian.

Van de Walle, D., and D. Cratty. 2003. Is the emerging nonfarm market economy the route out of poverty in Vietnam? Policy Research Working Paper 2950. Washington, D.C.: World Bank, January.

Van de Walle, D., and D. Gunewardena. 2001. Sources of ethnic inequality in Vietnam. *Journal of Development Economics* 65 (1): 177–207.

Van Ginneken, W., and C. Baron. 1984. *Appropriate products, employment, and technology: Case studies on consumer choice and basic needs in developing countries.* New York: St. Martin's Press.

Van Roekel, J., R. Kopicki, C. J. E. Broekmans, and D. M. Boselie. 2002. Building agrisupply chains: Issues and guidelines. World Bank, Washington, D.C.

Van Zyl, J., C. Machethe, H. Sartorius von Bach, and R. Singini, 1991. The effects of increased earnings from traditional agriculture in Lebowa. *Agrekon* 30 (4): 276–278.

Venezuela, Republica de. 1985. *Xi censo general de poblacion y vivienda, 20 de Octubre de 1981, total nacional.* Caracas: Oficina Central de Estadistica e Informatica.

———. 1993. *El censo 1990 en Venezuela.* Caracas: Oficina Central de Estadistica e Informatica.

Vijverberg, W. 1988. Profits from self-employment: A case-study of Cote d'Ivoire. Living Standards Measurement Study Working Paper 43. Washington, D.C.: World Bank.

———. 2002a. Adding rural specificity to investment climate survey. Paper prepared for the Rural Development Department. Mimeo, World Bank, Washington, D.C.

———. 2002b. Nonagricultural family enterprises in Cote d'Ivoire: A descriptive analysis. Living Standards Measurement Study Working Paper 46. Washington, D.C.: World Bank.

Visaria, P., and R. Basant. 1993. *Non-agricultural employment in India: Trends and prospects.* New Delhi: Sage.

VITA. *See* Volunteers in Technical Assistance.

Vogel, R. C., and D. W. Adams. 1997. Old and new paradigms in development finance. *Savings and Development* 22 (4): 361–382.

Vogel, S. J. 1994. Structural change in agriculture: Production linkages and agricultural demand-led industrialization. *Oxford Economic Papers* 46 (1): 136–156.

Volunteers in Technical Assistance (VITA). 1988. *Village technology handbook.* Arlington, Va.: Volunteers in Technical Assistance.

Von Braun, J., and U. Grote. 2002. Does decentralization serve the poor? In *Managing fiscal decentralization,* ed. E. Ahmad and V. Tanzi. New York: Routledge.

Von Braun, J., and R. Pandya-Lorch, 1991. Income sources of malnourished people in rural areas: Microlevel information and policy implications. Working Papers on Commercialization of Agriculture and Nutrition 5. Washington, D.C.: International Food Policy Research Institute.

Von Braun, J., D. Puetz, and P. Webb. 1989. Irrigation technology and commercialization of rice in the Gambia: Effects on income and nutrition. Research Report 75. Washington, D.C.: International Food Policy Research Institute.

Von Pischke, J. D. 1991. *Finance at the frontier.* Washington, D.C.: World Bank Economic Development Institute.

———. 2002. Current foundations of microfinance best practices in developing countries. In *Replicating microfinance in the United States,* ed. J. H. Carr and Z. Y. Tong. Baltimore: The Johns Hopkins Woodrow Wilson Center Press.

Vorley, B. 2001. The chains of agriculture: Sustainability and the restructuring of agrifood markets. In *Opinion: World Summit on Sustainable Development.* London: International Institute for Environment and Development.

———. 2004. Regoverning markets electronic conference: Final summary. London: International Institute for Environment and Development.

Vyas, V. S., and G. Mathai. 1978. Farm and nonfarm employment in rural areas. *Economic and Political Weekly* 13 (6–7): 333–347.

Wada, K. 1998. The formation of Toyota's relationships with suppliers: A modern application of the community mechanism. In *Toward the rural-based development of commerce and industry: Selected experiences from East Asia,* ed. Y. Hayami. Washington, D.C.: World Bank.

Wade, R. 1990. *Governing the market: Economic theory and the role of government in East Asian industrialization.* Princeton, N.J.: Princeton University Press.

Wakefield, C., and A. Duval. 1996. *CARE savings and credit sourcebook.* Atlanta: CARE International.

Wanmali, S. 1983. *Service centres in rural India: Policy, theory and practice.* Delhi: B. R. Publishing.

———. 1985. Rural household use of services: A study of Mronalguda Taluka, India. Research Report 48. Washington D.C.: International Food Policy Research Institute.

———. 1988a. Dilemma of absorbing the poor in the urban economy: Looking beyond the cities in India. *Regional Development Dialogue* 9 (4): 61–74.

———. 1988b. Provision and use of rural infrastructure in the growth of the regional economy. Washington, D.C.: International Food Policy Research Institute.

———. 1992. Rural infrastructure, the settlement system, and development of the regional economy in Southern India. IFPRI Research Report 91. Washington, D.C.: International Food Policy Research Institute.

Wanmali, S., and J. He. 1991. Determinants of service use among rural households in Eastern Province. In *Adopting improved technology: A study of smallholder farmers in Eastern Province, Zambia,* ed. R. Celis, J. T. Milimo, and S. Wanmali. Washington, D.C.: International Food Policy Research Institute.

Watanabe, S. 1970. Entrepreneurship in small enterprises in Japanese manufacturing. *International Labor Review* 102 (6): 531–576.

———. 1971. Subcontracting, industrialization and employment creation. *International Labor Review* 20 (2): 157–179.

Weatherspoon, D. D., and T. Mumbreño. 2004. PFID-F&V: Facilitating market linkages for small-scale farmers in Nicaragua. PFID Project Brief presented at the conference Supermarkets and Agricultural Development, Washington, D.C., April 28.

Weatherspoon, D. D., and T. Reardon. 2003. The rise of supermarkets in Africa: Implications for agrifood systems and the rural poor. *Development Policy Review* 21 (3): 333–355.

Webb, P., and J. von Braun. 1994. *Famine and food security in Ethiopia: Lessons for Africa.* Chichester, England: John Wiley and Sons.

Webster, L. 1989. World Bank lending for small and medium enterprises: Fifteen years of experience. Industry and Energy Department Working Paper 20. Washington, D.C.: World Bank.

Webster, L., and P. Fidler. 1996. *The informal sector and microfinance institutions in West Africa.* Washington, D.C.: World Bank.

Webster, L. M., R. Riopelle, and A. M. Chidzero. 1996. World Bank lending for small enterprises 1989–1993. World Bank Technical Paper 311. Washington, D.C.: World Bank.

Weijland, H. 1999. Microenterprise clusters in rural Indonesia: Industrial seedbed and policy target. *World Development* 27 (9): 1515–1530.

Wheatley, C., G. J. Scott, R. Best, and S. Wiersema. 1995. *Adding value to root and tuber crops: A manual on product development.* Cali, Colombia: Centro Internacional de Agricultura Tropical.

White, L. J. 1978. The evidence on appropriate factor proportions for manufacturing in less developed countries: A survey. *Economic Development and Cultural Change* 27: 27–59.

Whittington, D., D. T. Lauria, and X. Mu. 1991. A study of water vending and willingness to pay for water in Onitsha, Nigeria. *World Development* 19 (2/3): 179–198.

Wiens, T., and C. Sobrado. 1998. *Haiti: The challenges of poverty reduction,* Vol. 2, *Technical papers.* Washington, D.C.: World Bank.

Wilcock, D. 1981. Rural small scale enterprises in Eastern Upper Volta: Survey results. African Rural Economy Working Paper 38. East Lansing: Michigan State University.

———. 1991. The subsector approach to agribusiness projects. *Developing Alternatives* 1 (2): 1–7.

Winters, P., B. Davis, and L. Corral. 2002. Assets, activities, and income generation in rural Mexico: Factoring in social and public capital. *Agricultural Economics* 27: 139–156.

Winters, P., G. Carletto, B. Davis, K. Stamoulis, and A. Zezza. 2006. Rural income-generating activities in developing countries: A multi-country analysis. Paper presented at the FAO conference Beyond Agriculture? The Promise of the Rural Non-Farm Economy for Growth and Poverty Reduction, Rome, January 16–18.

Woller, G. 2000. Reassessing the financial viability of village banking: Past performance and future prospects. *MicroBanking Bulletin* 5: 308.

Women's World Banking. 1994. Achieving policy ompact. *What Worked: A Women's World Banking Newsletter* 4 (5): 2–3.

World Bank. 1983. *Thailand: Rural growth and employment.* Washington, D.C.: World Bank.

———. 1987. *Rural development: World Bank experience, 1965–86.* Washington, D.C.: World Bank, Operations Evaluation Department.

———. 1990. *The Aga Khan rural support program in Pakistan.* Washington, D.C.: World Bank, Operations Evaluation Department.

———. 1993a. *The East Asian miracle: Economic growth and public policy.* New York: Oxford University Press.

———. 1993b. *World development report 1993.* Washington, D.C.: World Bank.

———. 1994. *World development report 1994: Infrastructure for development.* Washington, D.C.: World Bank.

———. 1996. Poverty profile for Zimbabwe. Mimeo, World Bank, Washington, D.C.

———. 2001. Local economic development. <www.worldbank.org/urban/led> (accessed May 2002).

———. 2003. *World Bank development indicators.* Washington, D.C.: World Bank.

———. 2004. Promoting the rural nonfarm sector in Bangladesh, 2 vols. Washington, D.C.: World Bank, Rural Development Unit, South Asia Region, team led by Forhad Shilpi, August.

———. 2005a. Investment climate survey online. <http://iresearch.worldbank.org/ics/jsp/index.jsp> (accessed June 2005).

———. 2005b. *World development indicators.* Washington, D.C.: World Bank.

World Development. 1977. The choice of technology in developing countries. Special issue. *World Development* 5 (September–October).

Wright, G. A. 2000. *Microfinance systems: Designing quality financial services for the poor.* London: Zed.

Yamamura, E., T. Sonobe, and K. Otsuka. 2003. Human capital, cluster formation, and international relocation: The case study of the garment industry in Japan, 1968–98. *Journal of Economic Geography* 3 (1): 37–56.

Yaron, J., M. P. Benjamin Jr., and G. L. Piprek. 1997. Rural finance: Issues, design and best practices. Environmentally and Socially Sustainable Development Studies and Monographs Series 14. Washington, D.C.: World Bank.

Yúnez-Naude, A., and J. E. Taylor. 2001. The determinants of nonfarm activities and incomes in rural households in Mexico, with emphasis on education. *World Development* 29 (3): 561–572.

Yúnez-Naude, A., J. E. Taylor, and G. A. Dyer. 1998. Farm-nonfarm linkages and agricultural supply response in Mexico: A villagewide modeling perspective. Paper prepared for the IFPRI Workshop on Strategies for Stimulating Growth of the Rural Farm-Nonfarm Economy in Developing Countries, Airlie Conference Center, Va., May 17–21.

Zambia, Republic of. 2003. Zambia 2000 census of population and housing: Main census report. Lusaka: Central Statistics Office.

Zelaya, C. A., and T. Reardon. 2001. La incorporación del fomento del empleo rural no agrícola en los proyectos de desarrollo: El caso del proyecto Lempira Sur (FAO) en Honduras. Tegucigalpa, Honduras: FAO Honduras and Michigan State University.

Zeller, M., and R. L. Meyer, eds. 2002. *The triangle of microfinance: Financial sustainability, outreach and impact*. Baltimore: The Johns Hopkins University Press.

Zhang, X., and S. Fan. 2004. Public investment and regional inequality in rural China. *Agricultural Economics* 30: 89–100.

Zhang, X., and R. Kanbur. 2005. Spatial inequality in education and health care in China. *China Economic Review* 16: 189–204.

Zhang, X., and G. Li. 2003. Does guanxi matter to nonfarm employment? *Journal of Comparative Economics* 31 (2): 315–331.

Zhang, X., and K. Tan. 2004. Blunt to sharpened razor: Incremental reform and distortions in the product and capital markets in China. Development Strategy and Governance Division Discussion Paper 13. Washington, D.C.: International Food Policy Research Institute.

Zylbersztajn, D. 1996. Governance structures and agribusiness coordination: A transaction cost economics based approach. *Research in Domestic and International Agribusiness Management* 12: 245–310.

Zylbersztajn, D., and E. M. M. Q. Farina. 1999. Strictly coordinated food systems: Exploring the limits of the coasian firm. *International Food and Agribusiness Management Review* 2 (2): 249–265.

Contributors

Raisuddin Ahmed (r.ahmed@cgiar.org) is research fellow emeritus at the International Food Policy Research Institute, Washington, D.C.

Christopher B. Barrett (cbb2@cornell.edu) is international professor of applied economics and co-director of the African Food Security and Natural Resources Management Program at Cornell University, Ithaca, New York.

Julio Berdegué (jberdegue@rimisp.org) is the executive director of Rimisp-Latin American Center for Rural Development, Santiago, Chile.

Paul A. Dorosh (p.dorosh@worldbank.org) is a senior economist with the Spatial and Local Development Group, Sustainable Development Division, World Bank, Washington, D.C. At the time he contributed to this work, he was a senior research fellow with the Markets and Structural Studies Division of the International Food Policy Research Institute.

Steven Haggblade (blade@msu.edu) is a professor of international development in the Department of Agricultural Economics, Michigan State University, East Lansing.

Peter B. R. Hazell (p.hazell@cgiar.org) is a visiting professor at Imperial College, London. At the time he contributed to this work he was director of the Development Strategy and Governance Division of the International Food Policy Research Institute.

Eric Hyman (ehyman@usadf.gov) is a senior economist and environmental officer at the U.S. African Development Foundation, Washington, D.C.

Peter Lanjouw (planjouw@worldbank.org) is lead economist in the Development Research Group at the World Bank, Washington, D.C.

Carl Liedholm (liedhol1@msu.edu) is a professor of economics at Michigan State University, East Lansing.

Donald C. Mead (mead@msu.edu) is professor emeritus of agricultural economics at Michigan State University, East Lansing.

Richard L. Meyer (meyer.19@osu.edu) is professor emeritus and senior research specialist in the Department of Agricultural, Environmental, and Development Economics, Ohio State University, Columbus.

Anit Mukherjee (anit@nipfp.org.in) is a consultant at the National Institute of Public Finance and Policy in New Delhi.

Keijiro Otsuka (otsuka@grips.ac.jp) is a professorial fellow at the Foundation for Advanced Studies on International Development and a professor of development economics at the National Graduate Institute for Policy Studies, Tokyo.

Thomas Reardon (reardon@msu.edu) is professor of agricultural economics at Michigan State University, East Lansing.

Mitch Renkow (renkow@ncsu.edu) is professor of agricultural and resource economics at North Carolina State University, Raleigh.

Kostas Stamoulis (Kostas.Stamoulis@fao.org) is chief of the Agricultural Sector in Economic Development Service at the Food and Agriculture Organization headquarters in Rome.

Xiaobo Zhang (x.zhang@cgiar.org) is senior research fellow in the Development Strategy and Governance Division of the International Food Policy Research Institute, Washington, D.C.

Index

Page numbers for entries occurring in boxes are followed by a *b;* those for entries in figures, by an *f;* those for entries in notes, by an *n;* and those for entries in tables, by a *t.*